JUNOS Cookbook™

Other resources from O'Reilly

Related titles
IPv6 Network Administration Cisco IOS in a Nutshell
IPv6 Essentials TCP/IP Network
Cisco Cookbook Administration
DNS and BIND

oreilly.com
oreilly.com is more than a complete catalog of O'Reilly books. You'll also find links to news, events, articles, weblogs, sample chapters, and code examples.

oreillynet.com is the essential portal for developers interested in open and emerging technologies, including new platforms, programming languages, and operating systems.

Conferences
O'Reilly brings diverse innovators together to nurture the ideas that spark revolutionary industries. We specialize in documenting the latest tools and systems, translating the innovator's knowledge into useful skills for those in the trenches. Visit *conferences.oreilly.com* for our upcoming events.

Safari Bookshelf (*safari.oreilly.com*) is the premier online reference library for programmers and IT professionals. Conduct searches across more than 1,000 books. Subscribers can zero in on answers to time-critical questions in a matter of seconds. Read the books on your Bookshelf from cover to cover or simply flip to the page you need. Try it today for free.

JUNOS Cookbook™

Aviva Garrett

O'REILLY®

Beijing · Cambridge · Farnham · Köln · Paris · Sebastopol · Taipei · Tokyo

JUNOS Cookbook™
by Aviva Garrett

Copyright © 2006 O'Reilly Media, Inc. All rights reserved.
Printed in the United States of America.

Published by O'Reilly Media, Inc., 1005 Gravenstein Highway North, Sebastopol, CA 95472.

O'Reilly books may be purchased for educational, business, or sales promotional use. Online editions are also available for most titles (*safari.oreilly.com*). For more information, contact our corporate/institutional sales department: (800) 998-9938 or *corporate@oreilly.com*.

Editor: Mike Loukides	**Cover Designer:** Karen Montgomery
Production Editor: Laurel R.T. Ruma	**Interior Designer:** David Futato
Copyeditor: Laurel R.T. Ruma	**Cover Illustrator:** Riverside Natural History
Proofreader: Matt Hutchinson	**Illustrators:** Robert Romano, Jessamyn Read,
Indexer: Lucie Haskins	and Lesley Borash

Printing History:

April 2006:   First Edition.

 This book uses RepKover™, a durable and flexible lay-flat binding.

ISBN-10: 0-596-10014-0
ISBN-13: 978-0-596-10014-8
[M]   [7/07]

Table of Contents

Foreword

The early days at Juniper Networks were not for the faint of heart. Joining during the hiring rush of early 1997, I found that the cubes and offices of the small office in Santa Clara, California were already packed with experienced old hands—people whom I knew had been around the block once before and would not be shy of expressing themselves. Everyone had strong views on nearly every aspect of building a router from scratch. If you had the misfortune to sit next to a busy conference room, a good pair of headphones and large CD collection were required to drown out the arguments. Design meetings often became heated, and egos were occasionally bruised. Our friends from previous employers taunted us with predictions of doom.

Despite the arguments, we were all united and driven by one solitary goal: to win the competition to build the best Internet core router available. This was a serious challenge, considering the primary competition was a 300-pound gorilla in the form of Cisco Systems. Beating Cisco would require us to produce a router that tackled the perceived weaknesses in its core router platform. A Juniper Networks core router would have to provide line-rate performance (which, for the M40 router meant forwarding around 40 million packets per second), robust core routing protocols, and stable control software. In short, it had to make customers really want to use it.

The performance requirements meant that the network traffic had to be forwarded entirely in hardware. This was something that had never before been attempted for a core network router. As a result, the hardware design of the M40 looked like science fiction to Juniper recruits who had worked on other networking products. The entire forwarding path of the router was constructed from four Application Specific Integrated Circuits (ASICs), designed entirely by Juniper. These four ASICs (called A, B, C, and D to prevent loose lips from revealing their function) were huge, intricate, and enormously ambitious. A large design team of experienced engineers was assembled to implement the ASICs and partnered with another large verification team to check that the designs were functionally correct. Since Silicon Valley was littered with networking startups that had failed because of silicon design problems, there was enormous pressure on the ASIC teams to get it right first time. We all knew that a failed ASIC would probably sink the company.

Not that there was any less pressure on the software teams. Convincing customers to deploy a brand new—and essentially untried—core router into the very heart of their networks is an enormous task. A new router that crashes, forwards packets erratically, or just basically behaves weirdly won't make any friends in the network operations team and will find itself unceremoniously removed from the network. The problem is that designing and implementing a core router that works completely reliably is a feat that has defeated many companies. And those were "simple" routers where the packets had been forwarded by software. In contrast, not only did the Juniper router require robust routing protocols that could scale to the largest networks, but it also had to have a robust software infrastructure on the CPU-based control boards that managed the fiendishly complicated packet-forwarding ASICs. Just like the ASIC team, the software team had to get it right the first time.

The JUNOS team started from a basic FreeBSD software base and reworked much of the network software in the kernel. New user daemons were written, and a carrier-grade routing protocol suite was implemented. The routing protocols had to be designed to scale to the largest networks and be robust enough to withstand wild fluctuations in the networks around them, something that the competing routers often struggled with. Thankfully, Juniper had a deep well of routing protocol talent available that could pool its cumulative knowledge to design high-quality routing protocol implementations. Potential customers still had to be convinced that the new protocol implementations would interoperate safely within their existing networks. To allow early evaluation, a fledgling JUNOS system appeared in the form of Olive, which was a standard rackmount PC pretending to be a JUNOS routing engine board. This prototype system was delivered to potential customers to give them a feel for the current state of the system and to allow the routing protocols to be debugged.

Juniper had outgrown the offices it occupied in Santa Clara and moved to Mountain View, just off of Highway 237. We didn't trust the movers to shift the servers between sites and decided to move all the systems ourselves. At one point, we realized that all of Juniper's primary software servers were loaded into just one car; paranoia dictated that we split them between two cars just in case something happened on the short drive to the new office. We drove gingerly to the new site once the rush hour had finished and breathed a huge sigh of relief when all the servers powered up again. We also got a surprise bonus when we arrived at the new site. The previous occupants of our new office block had left a huge rat's nest of network cables in their old data center; they'd obviously decided that it was just too much work to untangle it. However, since money was tight, we refused to throw the huge bundle of cables out and spent the next couple of weeks teasing CAT5 cables out of the jumble during quiet moments. There were enough cables from the bundle to let us completely rewire the first software engineering lab for free.

Throughout 1997 and early 1998, all the Juniper engineering teams worked pretty much flat-out to finish the M40. The engineering labs were seldom quiet, and it was hard to tell the weekends from the weekdays by counting cars in the parking lot. The software teams designed and implemented a truly astonishing amount of code in a very short period of time. FreeBSD kernel extensions were added to provide support for chassis management and new Juniper network interfaces. A clean user interface was designed and implemented to provide a seamless interface to the system and prevent users from having to edit raw configuration files by hand. An entire embedded microkernel was written to manage the packet-forwarding engine boards in the system (a fully-loaded M40 would have nine PFE-related boards), which would allow users to exchange configuration and status messages with the routing engine and each other. Drivers for the embedded microkernel were written to manage the ASICs and to allow the route engine to configure the PFE. The size and complexity of the software required to manage just the various control boards eventually grew to rival the route engine itself.

The real headache for the software team was that the hardware wasn't available to test with. It can take many months after a system is assembled in the engineering lab to get it to a usable state as a complete system. But Juniper couldn't afford for us to spend six months in the lab; there just wasn't enough money or time. The solution was to get extremely creative with test equipment, evaluation boards, and generic PCs before the final hardware was available. All sorts of emulation environments were developed to allow the new routing engine and embedded software to be debugged ahead of the actual hardware. For months, we used a motley collection of machines cobbled together from parts and equipment that emulated the final hardware. We didn't really have to disguise the lab for external visitors—they wouldn't have been able to guess that each ratty bundle of machines was a virtual M40.

The payback from this approach was enormous. When the hardware finally arrived, it took just one week in the engineering lab for the first network packets to be forwarded successfully! Considering the complexity of the routing engine and PFE interaction, this was a monumental achievement and meant that we could quickly verify that the hardware worked before shipping the systems to our early test customers in September of 1998.

Designing and implementing the first release of the JUNOS software was an unforgettable time. Although the reader may think I've concentrated way too much on the hardware, the JUNOS software is intrinsically the way it is because of the hardware. That it has gone through so many iterations since then, and continues to evolve with the advancement of Juniper routers, is the first item you should learn in this book.

The second thing that you should know is that although creating the JUNOS software really was a team effort, Aviva Garrett had the dubious task of documenting our efforts. In fact, she wrote the first manual. And then, as the manager of Juniper Networks technical publications, she led the effort from Version 1.0 until very recently, somewhere after 7.x. Now she has come back and worked on this marvelous book for an entire year, revisiting everything we once did and everything that has evolved since those early days. *JUNOS Cookbook* represents a full circle for the JUNOS software suite somehow, looping from those early, midday conference room marathons to today's ability to route a large portion of the world's network traffic. Aviva and her team of reviewers and technical experts have broken it all down into bite-size recipes and discussions that make today's complex array of features seem like that simple, erudite version we created back in 1998. Enjoy it, and cheers.

—Scott Mackie
Former Distinguished Engineer, Juniper Networks
February 2006

Preface

Over the past decade, network service providers have been adding high-performance Juniper Networks routers to their networks to run their IP backbones. With the recent introduction of smaller routers with the same basic functionality as the larger core routers, more people will be using Juniper Networks routers in their business networks and will need to learn how to configure and run the JUNOS software that runs on their routers. *JUNOS Cookbook* explains the design of the JUNOS software and provides recipes and guidelines for setting up common features that you need to configure and secure your Juniper Networks router.

For those of you who are familiar with Cisco IOS or other routers, you will find the JUNOS software and the design of the router hardware similar to the other routers in some ways, but very different in many ways. The initial design of the JUNOS software began in 1996, when the TCP/IP protocol suite was already mature and it was clear that this protocol suite was the only one needed for network devices to run on the Internet. Those involved in developing the original JUNOS software and router hardware all had previous experience designing similar products and were intent on building something better. Some of the JUNOS features that improve the router operation include:

Software modularity
> The JUNOS software comprises several dozen processes, or daemons, rather than a single process, so you can stop a single process and restart it without having to reboot the entire router.

Separation of forwarding and routing
> The actual forwarding of packets is performed by custom high-speed Application-Specific Integrated Circuits (ASICs), while routing is performed by a CPU in a small PC that is built into the router. This separation of the routing and forwarding functions improves router performance.

Powerful configuration editor and batch configuration activation

The JUNOS configuration editor supports command completion and text files and allows you to return to previous configurations. Activating JUNOS configurations is a batch process, and interdependent configuration segments take effect at the same time.

Hard disk in the router

Having a built-in hard disk provides storage on the router for software images needed for software upgrades, core dumps, and JUNOS documentation, which is accessed with online help.

The first version of JUNOS software, released in 1998 with the first router, the M40 router, focused on features for large-capacity Internet service provider (ISP) and telephone company (telco) networks. Like any network operating system, additions are regularly being made to the software to incorporate new technologies, protocols, and feature sets. The JUNOS software is updated four times per year. *JUNOS Cookbook* was written for Release 7.4, which shipped at the end of 2005. You will find, however, that most of the recipes in this book also work on earlier software releases, and they should continue to work on future releases. All recipes in this book were developed on M7i or J2300 routers. And, except where noted, they should run on any Juniper Networks J-series, M-series, and T-series routing platform. I have indicated when I use features that are available only with certain software releases or hardware.

Given the diversity and complexity of the JUNOS software, this book cannot cover the entire operating system. Instead, *JUNOS Cookbook* consists of a collection of sample router configurations for the proper installation, configuration, and optimization of your Juniper Networks routers and is focused on helping you set up the common components of your router: the network interfaces and the routing protocols themselves.

JUNOS Cookbook is not intended to replace the detailed feature information available on the Juniper Networks web site (*http://www.juniper.net*). This book doesn't have the space to provide details about how particular protocols actually work, and you can find this information in the Internet Engineering Task Force (IETF) Request for Comment (RFC) and Internet draft documents (*http://www.ietf.org*), as well as in a wide variety of books.

I welcome feedback from readers. If you have comments, suggestions, or ideas for other recipes, please let me know. If there are future editions of the *JUNOS Cookbook*, I will include any suggestions that I think are especially useful. You can reach me at *aviva@juniper.net*.

Organization

As the name suggests, *JUNOS Cookbook* is organized as a series of recipes. Each recipe begins with a problem statement that describes a common situation you might face. After each problem statement is a brief solution that shows a sample router configuration or script that you can use to resolve that particular problem. A discussion section then describes the solution, how it works, and when you should or should not use it.

I have tried to construct the recipes so that you can turn directly to the one that addresses your specific problem and find a useful solution without needing to read the entire book. If the solution includes terms or concepts you are not familiar with, the chapter introductions should help bridge the gap. Many recipes refer to other recipes or chapters that discuss related topics. I have also included a variety of references to other sources in case you need more background information on a particular subject.

The chapters are organized by the feature or protocol discussed. If you are looking for information on a particular feature such as BGP, MPLS, or SNMP, you can turn to that chapter and find a variety of related recipes. Most chapters list basic problems first and any unusual or complicated situations last. But there are some exceptions to this, such as where I have instead grouped related recipes together.

What's in This Book

The first chapters cover essential system administration functions of the router:

Chapter 1, Router Configuration and File Management
   Covers router configuration and file management issues

Chapter 2, Basic Router Security and Access Control
   Focuses on router security, describing user access and privileges on the router and how to protect your router from undesired access

Chapter 3, IPSec
   Describes how to use IPSec to encrypt and secure traffic

The next three chapters focus on managing the router:

Chapter 4, SNMP
   Discusses how to use the Internet standard SNMP protocol to remotely manage your router

Chapter 5, Logging
   Explains how to log events that occur on the router so you can trace the causes of router and network malfunctions

Chapter 6, NTP
> Explains how to properly set the time on your router, both manually and using NTP, to synchronize time across all network devices

Chapter 7, Router Interfaces
> Discusses router interfaces and how to configure interface properties, including the physical device itself as well as all network addresses associated with an interface, including IPv4, IPv6, and ISO addresses

The next six chapters cover various aspects of IP routing:

Chapter 8, IP Routing
> Looks at IP routing in general, including routing tables, route preferences, and selecting active routes

Chapter 9, Routing Policy and Firewall Filters
> Discusses routing policy, which control the routes that are stored in and advertised from the routing tables. This chapter also covers firewall filters, which are applied to traffic entering and exiting router interfaces

Chapter 10, RIP
> Looks at RIP, including both Versions 1 and 2 and RIPng

Chapter 11, IS-IS
> Looks at IS-IS

Chapter 12, OSPF
> Discusses OSPF

Chapter 13, BGP
> Discusses the BGP protocol, which controls all IP routing through the backbone of the Internet

The remaining chapters all cover separate topics:

Chapter 14, MPLS
> Discusses MPLS, which is commonly used along with RSVP for traffic engineering

Chapter 15, VPNs
> Covers BGP-MPLS (Layer 3) VPNs, which are an application of BGP and MPLS that provides private virtual networks

Chapter 16, IP Multicast
> Covers the IP multicast protocols

Conventions

The following formatting conventions are used throughout this book:

Italic
> Used for commands, filenames, directories, script variables, keywords, emphasis, technical terms, and Internet domain names

Constant width
    Used for code sections, interface names, and IP addresses
Constant width italic
    Used for replaceable text
Constant width bold
    Used for user input and emphasis within code
Constant width bold italic
    Used to highlight replaceable items within code

Comments and Questions

Please address comments and questions about this book to the publisher:

O'Reilly Media, Inc.
1005 Gravenstein Highway North
Sebastopol, CA 95472
(800) 998-9938 (in the United States or Canada)
(707) 829-0515 (international/local)
(707) 829-0104 (fax)

There is a web page for this book, which lists errata, examples, or any additional information. You can access this page at:

http://www.oreilly.com/catalog/junosckbk

To comment or ask technical questions about this book, send email to:

bookquestions@oreilly.com

For more information about books, conferences, Resource Centers, and the O'Reilly Network, see the O'Reilly web site at:

http://www.oreilly.com

Safari® Enabled

 When you see a Safari® Enabled icon on the cover of your favorite technology book, that means the book is available online through the O'Reilly Network Safari Bookshelf.

Safari offers a solution that's better than e-books. It's a virtual library that lets you easily search thousands of top tech books, cut and paste code samples, download chapters, and find quick answers when you need the most accurate, current information. Try it for free at *http://safari.oreilly.com*.

Acknowledgments

I have been a professional technical writer for 25 years, and I never imagined how huge an undertaking it would be to write a book on JUNOS software as the sole responsible author. Writing any technical book, especially one like this, is never a project that a single person does by herself. There are always many people involved to review the topics included in the book, answer questions, review drafts, and set up and maintain lab equipment. Many people helped me in all these areas, providing me both with general help and with comments in their particular area or areas of JUNOS and networking expertise. Without their time and patience, this book would not have been possible. These people include Zaid Albanna, Arthi Ayyangar, Serpil Bayraktar, Ron Bonica, Avram Dorfman, Jeff Doyle, Simon Gerraty, Steve Gill, Lenny Giuliano, Walter Goralski, Hannes Gredler, Steve Holman, Ian Jarrett, Dave Katz, Steven Lin, Julian Lucek, Ivan Lum, Umesh Mangla, Pedro Marques, Brian Matheson, Scott McIntyre, Ina Minei, Andrew Partan, Prakesh Patil, David Ranch, Yakov Rehkter, Rich Salaiz, Phil Shafer, Nischal Sheth, Gary Tate, Paras Trivedi, Quaizar Vohra, Jim Washburn, Chris White, and Kiho Yum. Vijay Gill, John Heasley, and Scott McIntyre helped by providing JUNOS output used to explain a few of the recipes.

Mike Bushong was a great help in setting up and maintaining the router labs used to develop this book. Richard Hendricks, Brian Matheson, and Michael Estrada also helped with the lab. Sonia Saruba considerably improved on my writing by editing the entire manuscript.

I would also like to thank a few key people who encouraged me to undertake and continue this project, especially Patrick Ames, who kept me focused, and also Michael Taillon, Scott Kriens, and Allen Lo.

Everybody at O'Reilly was great to work with. I particularly appreciate the input from my editors, David Brickner and Mike Loukides. They helped to create a book of which we can all be proud.

Finally, I must thank my husband David and my daughter Sage for helping me through this project.

—Aviva Garrett
Saratoga, California

## CHAPTER 1

Router Configuration and File Management

1.0   Introduction

Juniper Networks routers are specialized network devices that run network operating system software, which is called JUNOS software. In this book, we talk about JUNOS features that run on the J-series, M-series, and T-series router platforms. The M-series and T-series platforms are larger routers typically used by network service providers, telephone companies, large enterprise companies, and universities. The J-series routers are smaller routers designed for use by businesses and other organizations to connect multiple sites or to connect to the Internet. The JUNOS software is pre-installed on a new Juniper Networks routers: when you turn the router on, the software automatically starts running. The first task you have to perform is configuring the router.

JUNOS software is distributed as a set of modular software packages that contain the various components of the software. A given JUNOS software release runs on all J-series, M-series, and T-series routers. The examples in this book are based on the JUNOS 7.4 release of the software on either M20 routers or J2300 routers, but all are applicable for the most recent JUNOS releases and for future releases on the M-, T-, and J-series families of routers.

This chapter discusses basic router configuration, including how to configure the router for the first time, configuring from the command-line interface (CLI), loading and saving configuration files, and working with the filesystems and files used by the JUNOS software. It also discusses how to upgrade the JUNOS software and how to gather hardware and software inventory information.

When you first start a router, you must configure basic network information, such as the router name, IP address, and domain name, so that the router is reachable on the network. You then configure the desired software features. To configure the router, you generally log in to the router and use the JUNOS CLI. Some routers, including the J-series, also have a web-based interface called J-Web. From the CLI, you specify the configuration in a plain-text (ASCII) configuration file, which you can read from the CLI (on the router) or by using any ASCII text editor (on a server). From J-Web, the configuration is saved in an ASCII file that you can read using J-Web, the CLI, or an ASCII text editor.

JUNOS CLI Modes

Throughout this book, we'll show you how to use the JUNOS CLI to configure and monitor the router. While it is beyond the scope of this book to describe the design of the CLI and all its capabilities, this section gives an overview of the CLI modes and describes a few of the basic features. Throughout the rest of this chapter, we'll give more examples of CLI features. For complete information about the JUNOS CLI, refer to the JUNOS product documentation on the Juniper Networks web site, *http://www.juniper.net/techpubs*.

The underlying operating system for the JUNOS software is FreeBSD. As we talk about the various CLI commands, if a command is derived from FreeBSD or a standard Unix utility, or is simply the FreeBSD or Unix command packaged with a JUNOS name, we will mention the command it is based on. If you are already familiar with the FreeBSD or Unix equivalent, this will help you understand the JUNOS command.

The CLI has two modes: operational mode and configuration mode. Both modes have distinct commands. In *operational mode*, you monitor everything about the router's hardware and software and check on network operation. In *configuration mode*, the commands let you define the behavior of the router, such as indicating what network addresses to use and protocols to run. It is important for you to understand the differences between these two modes, what types of actions you can take in which mode, and how to keep track of which mode you are working in. Throughout the rest of this book, we'll show you how to work in both modes as you configure the router and verify its operation.

On the router, you can identify which mode you are in by looking at the CLI prompt. The base prompt has the format *username@router-name*. When you are in operational mode, the prompt ends with a >; when you are in configuration mode, the prompt ends with a #. We follow this same convention throughout this book, so by paying attention to the prompt that precedes each command, you can determine whether you issue the command in operational or configuration mode.

When you first log in to a JUNOS router, you are in operational mode. The commands available in operational mode let you monitor router and network operations. For example, you can get information about the router's hardware and software, the network traffic that is coming to the router, and configured routing protocols. Throughout this book, we'll show you how to use operational mode commands to check what is happening on the router.

You can use a number of operational mode commands, grouped together into related commands, to monitor your router and network. On the router, you can find out what the commands are by typing a question mark (**?**) to activate the online help. If you type a **?** at the top level of operational mode, you see the broad types of commands you can use to monitor the router and perform operations not related to configuring the router:

```
aviva@router1> ?
Possible completions:
  clear              Clear information in the system
  configure          Manipulate software configuration information
  file               Perform file operations
  help               Provide help information
  monitor            Show real-time debugging information
  mtrace             Trace multicast path from source to receiver
  ping               Ping remote target
  quit               Exit the management session
  request            Make system-level requests
  restart            Restart software process
  set                Set CLI properties, date/time, craft interface message
  show               Show system information
  ssh                Start secure shell on another host
  start              Start shell
  telnet             Telnet to another host
  test               Perform diagnostic debugging
  traceroute         Trace route to remote host
```

For example, you use the various show commands to display information about the router, router interfaces, and protocol software, and you use the various request commands to perform operations on the router, such as rebooting and downloading and installing software upgrades.

Two commands in operational mode are not designed to monitor the router or the network:

quit

Use to log out of the CLI and the router

configure

Use to enter configuration mode so you can configure the router

When you enter configuration mode, the prompt changes from *username@router-name>* to *username@router-name#*, and a line before the prompt, [edit], indicates that you are in configuration mode. Specifically, [edit] indicates that you are at the top of the configuration hierarchy, which is similar to being at the top of a Unix filesystem (/). A synonym for the configure command is edit. (edit is a hidden command, so you won't see it in the list of possible completions.)

Configuration mode has two basic components:

commands
    Use to perform actions within the router's configuration

statements
    The actual keywords that define the configuration

To create or modify the router's configuration, use the commands that are available in configuration mode to add statements to the configuration that define the behavior of the router. If you type a **?** at the top level of configuration mode, you see the broad types of commands you can use while configuring the router:

```
[edit]
aviva@router1# ?
Possible completions:
  <[Enter]>          Execute this command
  activate           Remove the inactive tag from a statement
  annotate           Annotate the statement with a comment
  commit             Commit current set of changes
  copy               Copy a statement
  deactivate         Add the inactive tag to a statement
  delete             Delete a data element
  edit               Edit a sub-element
  exit               Exit from this level
  help               Provide help information
  insert             Insert a new ordered data element
  load               Load configuration from ASCII file
  quit               Quit from this level
  rename             Rename a statement
  rollback           Roll back to previous committed configuration
  run                Run an operational-mode command
  save               Save configuration to ASCII file
  set                Set a parameter
  show               Show a parameter
  status             Show users currently editing configuration
  top                Exit to top level of configuration
  up                 Exit one level of configuration
  wildcard           Wildcard operations
```

When creating or modifying a configuration, you primarily use the edit and set commands to control which configuration statement to include. Use the edit command to move to the portion of the configuration you want to modify (this is similar to using the Unix cd command to move to a different directory) and use the set command to configure a specific item. The up command moves up one hierarchy level, and the top command returns to the top of the hierarchy, [edit] (this command is similar to the Unix cd / command). At the top level, use the exit or quit command to return to operational mode.

The show command displays the items in the configuration, starting at the current hierarchy level. If you start at the [edit] level, you see the entire configuration:

```
[edit]
aviva@router1# show
version "7.4R1.7";
groups {
    re0 {
        system {
            host-name router1;
        }
        interfaces {
            fxp0 {
                unit 0 {
                    family inet {
...
```

If you are at a lower level, you see just that portion of the configuration. The following example starts in the OSPF portion of the configuration:

```
[edit protocols ospf]
aviva@router1# show
export export-statics;
area 0.0.0.0 {
    interface fe-0/0/1.0;
    interface fe-1/0/1.0;
}
```

Why are there curly braces here? The JUNOS software uses curly braces to represent the structure of the configuration file, delineating related sections of configuration parameters. If you are a C-language programmer, you will be very familiar with them.

The opposite of the set command is delete, which removes an item from the configuration. You can delete an individual item from the configuration (such as delete interface *fe-1/0/1.0* from the OSPF configuration above), or you can delete an entire section—here the area 0.0.0.0 section from the OSPF configuration:

```
[edit protocols ospf]
aviva@router1# delete area 0.0.0.0
aviva@router1# show
export export-statics;
```

Another time-saving command is run, which allows you to issue an operational command from within configuration mode. For example, the run show route command from configuration mode is the same as the show route command from operational mode:

```
[edit]
aviva@router1# run show route    <-- # in prompt indicates configuration mode
inet.0: 20 destinations, 20 routes (19 active, 0 holddown, 1 hidden)
+ = Active Route, - = Last Active, * = Both
```

```
0.0.0.0/0            *[Static/5] 07:36:18
                        Discard
...
aviva@router> show route  <-- > in prompt indicates operational mode
inet.0: 20 destinations, 20 routes (19 active, 0 holddown, 1 hidden)
+ = Active Route, - = Last Active, * = Both

0.0.0.0/0            *[Static/5] 07:36:18
                        Discard
...
```

What does it mean to move to a portion of the configuration? You can think of the JUNOS configuration as a hierarchy of configuration statements and containers, delimited by braces ({ }) that define the scope in which those statements apply. This hierarchy provides a way to organize the large number of features and functions that you can configure on the router, grouping related functions together so that you can locate them when configuring the router and when reviewing the configuration. When you first enter configuration mode, you are at the top of the hierarchy. You see your location in the hierarchy in the line that precedes the configuration mode prompt. The line [edit] indicates that you are at the top of the hierarchy. The edit command allows you to move within the configuration hierarchy so that all configuration commands take place within the current container. As you move through the hierarchy, the text in square brackets changes to indicate your location in the hierarchy.

The configuration statements that you use to set the router's behavior are also arranged in a hierarchical fashion. If you type **edit ?** at the top level of the configuration hierarchy, you see the broad functional JUNOS software areas that you can control through the configuration:

```
[edit]
aviva@router1# edit ?
Possible completions:
> access               Network access configuration
> accounting-options   Accounting data configuration
> applications         Define applications by protocol characteristics
> chassis              Chassis configuration
> class-of-service     Class-of-service configuration
> firewall             Define a firewall configuration
> forwarding-options   Configure options to control packet sampling
> groups               Configuration groups
> interfaces           Interface configuration
> logical-routers      Logical routers
> policy-options       Routing policy option configuration
> protocols            Routing protocol configuration
> routing-instances    Routing instance configuration
> routing-options      Protocol-independent routing option configuration
> security             Security configuration
> services             Service PIC applications settings
> snmp                 Simple Network Management Protocol configuration
> system               System parameters
```

Each listed completion is the configuration statement at the top of a particular configuration hierarchy. For example, the statement protocols is at the top of the hierarchy in which you configure all JUNOS routing protocols:

```
[edit]
aviva@router1# edit protocols ?
Possible completions:
  <[Enter]>                Execute this command
> bfd                      Bidirectional Forwarding Detection (BFD) options
> bgp                      BGP options
> connections             Circuit cross-connect configuration
> dvmrp                    DVMRP options
> igmp                     IGMP options
> isis                     IS-IS options
> l2circuit                Configuration for Layer 2 circuits over MPLS
> ldp                      LDP options
> link-management          LMP options
> mld                      MLD options
> mpls                     Multiprotocol Label Switching options
> msdp                     MSDP configuration
> ospf                     OSPF configuration
> ospf3                    OSPFv3 configuration
> pgm                      PGM options
> pim                      PIM configuration
> rip                      RIP options
> ripng                    RIPng options
> router-advertisement IPv6 router advertisement options
> router-discovery        ICMP router discovery options
> rsvp                     RSVP options
> sap                      Session Advertisement Protocol options
> vrrp                     VRRP options
  |                        Pipe through a command
```

If you move down through the hierarchy—for example, into the protocols portion—the prompt changes to [edit protocols] to show you where you are:

```
[edit]
aviva@router1# edit protocols
[edit protocols]
aviva@router1#
```

Learning About the CLI While on the Router

In some of the command lines in the previous section, we showed how to use the ? to get context-sensitive help about the CLI and the software. This feature is part of the CLI's built-in help, and you will find yourself using it regularly. When you type a ? at a prompt, the CLI shows a list of commands or statements you can use, along with a short description of the command or statement. If you partially type a command or configuration statement name and then type a ?, you see a subset of the available commands or statements.

For example, in operational mode, you can find a subset of the show commands:

```
aviva@router1> show r?
Possible completions:
  rip                 Show Routing Information Protocol information
  ripng               Show Routing Information Protocol for IPv6 information
  route               Show routing table information
  rsvp                Show Resource Reservation Protocol information
aviva@router1> show r
```

The CLI displays the list of available commands and then redisplays the portion of the command you already typed so you do not have to retype it. For example, to show the contents of the routing table, you would now just type **oute**:

```
aviva@router1> show r?
Possible completions:
  rip                 Show Routing Information Protocol information
  ripng               Show Routing Information Protocol for IPv6 information
  route               Show routing table information
  rsvp                Show Resource Reservation Protocol information
aviva@router1> show r
aviva@router1> show route
```

In configuration mode, you can list the subset of available configuration statements:

```
[edit system]
aviva@router1# set s?
Possible completions:
  saved-core-context  Save context information for core files
  saved-core-files    Number of saved core files per executable (1..64)
> services            System services
> static-host-mapping Static hostname database mapping
> syslog              System logging facility
aviva@router1# set s^
```

To minimize the amount of typing you have to do, press the spacebar or Tab key to have the CLI complete a nonambiguous command or statement name. This is similar to how some Unix shells operate.

```
aviva@router1# commit a<space>
Possible completions:
  and-quit            Quit configuration mode if commit succeeds
  at                  Time at which to activate configuration changes
aviva@router1# commit an<space>
aviva@router1# command and-quit
```

The first command above is ambiguous because there are two possible completions. The second command is unique, so when you press the spacebar key (or Tab key), the CLI automatically completes the command. Press the Enter key to execute the command.

After you have typed a complete command (but before pressing Enter), another set of commands becomes available to allow you to control the format of the output. To access these commands, you first type a | (pipe), which directs the output from the

---

command on the left side of the pipe into the command on the right side of the pipe, in exactly the same way that a Unix pipe works. The following commands are available:

```
aviva@router1> show route | ?
Possible completions:
  count               Count occurrences
  display             Show additional kinds of information
  except              Show only text that does not match a pattern
  find                Search for first occurrence of pattern
  hold                Hold text without exiting the --More-- prompt
  last                Display end of output only
  match               Show only text that matches a pattern
  no-more             Don't paginate output
  request             Make system-level requests
  resolve             Resolve IP addresses
  save                Save output text to file
  trim                Trim specified number of columns from start of line
```

Another way to minimize typing is to use keyboard sequences. The simplest are the up and down arrows, which scroll through the most recent commands you typed. (The JUNOS software maintains a command history similar to Unix shell history.) If you want to modify rather than retype a command, you can use the left and right arrows and the Backspace and Delete keys. There are also a number of keyboard sequences that are similar or identical to Emacs commands that you can use to move around on a command line and edit it. Table 1-1 lists some common keystrokes.

Table 1-1. Keystroke sequences

Keystroke sequence	Action
Ctrl-p	Display previous command history line
Ctrl-n	Display next command history line
Ctrl-a	Move to beginning of line
Ctrl-e	Move to end of line
Ctrl-b	Move back one character
Ctrl-f	Move forward one character
Esc-b	Move back one word
Esc-f	Move forward one word
Ctrl-k	Delete everything from cursor to end of line
Esc-d	Delete one word forward (the word after the cursor)
Esc-Backspace	Delete one word backward (the word before the cursor)
Ctrl-y	Paste the deleted word or text at the cursor

Another aspect of the CLI help is online documentation, which is installed on the router's hard disk. This documentation is taken from the JUNOS product configuration guides. You can use the online documentation to get information about configuration statements while you are logged in to the router. To get high-level information about a configuration statement, you can use the help topic command. The following example shows how to get high-level help about configuring the domain name on the router:

```
aviva@router1> help topic system domain-name
Configuring the Router's Domain Name
    For each router, you should configure the name of the domain in which the
    router is located. This is the default domain name that is appended to
    hostnames that are not fully qualified. To configure the domain name,
    include the domain-name statement at the [edit system] hierarchy level:
    [edit system]
    domain-name domain-name;
  Example: Configuring the Router's Domain Name
  Configure the router's domain name:
    [edit]
    user@host# set system domain-name company.net
    [edit]
    user@host# show
    system {
        domain-name company.net;
    }
```

Use the help reference command to get help about the syntax and options of a configuration statement, similar to Unix manpages. The following shows the reference help that is displayed for the domain-name configuration statement:

```
aviva@router1> help reference system domain-name
domain-name
 Syntax
  domain-name domain-name;
 Hierarchy Level
  [edit system]
 Description
  Configure the name of the domain in which the router is located. This is
  the default domain name that is appended to hostnames that are not fully
  qualified.
 Options
  domain-name--Name of the domain.
 Usage Guidelines
  See "Configuring the Router's Domain Name".
 Required Privilege Level
  system--To view this statement in the configuration.
  system-control--To add this statement to the configuration.
```

How We Show Commands and Configurations in This Book

In the explanation of the JUNOS CLI so far, we have described the different types of commands and illustrated what they look like when you type them on the router. Because it can be a bit confusing for newcomers, this section summarizes how we show the commands in this book.

Here is an operational mode command:

```
aviva@router1> show route table inet.0
```

The > tells you that you are in operational mode, and the bold font shows what you type. The command is show route. The word table is an option for this command, and *inet.0* is a variable (the name of a specific routing table) that is required to complete the table option. The table name is italicized because you can substitute the desired routing-table name.

Here are two configuration mode commands:

```
[edit]
aviva@router1# edit system
[edit system]
aviva@router1# set login user aviva class operator
```

You know you are in configuration mode because of the # after the prompt and because the CLI shows your location in the hierarchy of configuration statements by displaying the [edit] and [edit system] lines. edit and set are configuration mode commands. system, login, user, and class are configuration statements. *aviva* is a variable required for the user statement, and *operator* is an option required for the class statement. Again, what you type is shown in bold. The commands and statements, which you have to type exactly as shown, are in bold, and the variables, which you substitute with the proper values for your network, are italicized.

In this book, when we show how to configure the router, we generally show just the commands that you type and the configuration hierarchy level at which you type them, as shown above. Sometimes, however, if you have to type several commands to configure a feature or if you type a command that results in a multilevel hierarchy, we'll show you what the resulting configuration looks like. The configuration commands that we typed above result in the following configuration:

```
[edit system]
aviva@router1# show
login {
    user aviva {
        class operator;
    }
}
```

When viewed from the top level of the statement hierarchy, it looks like this:

```
[edit]
aviva@router1# show
system {
    login {
        user aviva {
            class operator;
        }
    }
}
```

We show this format for a couple of reasons. When you are on the router and configuring it, you might get lost or forget what you have already configured. The text in square brackets above the prompt (here, [edit]) is your road map to your location in the configuration statement hierarchy, and the show command displays what's already in the configuration. Another reason is that a JUNOS configuration is, in reality, just a text file. The format of the file is the same as what you see when you type the show command. The indentions indicate the configuration hierarchy levels, the curly braces ({ and }) indicate related groups of configuration statements, and a semicolon marks the end of an individual statement. In the book, we'll sometimes use this format as a way to summarize all the statements you need to include to configure a particular feature. You can compare what's in the book with what you have configured on the router to make sure that you have included everything.

1.1   Configuring the Router for the First Time

Problem

You have just installed and turned on a router and are configuring the JUNOS software for the first time.

Solution

Use the following commands to configure the router:

```
root# cli
root@>
cli> configure
[edit]
root@# set system host-name router1
root@# set system domain-name mynetwork.com
root@# set interfaces fxp0 unit 0 family inet address 192.168.15.1/24
root@# set system backup-router 192.168.15.2
root@# set system name-server 192.168.15.3
root@# set system root-authentication plain-text-password
New password:
Retype password:
root@ show
system {
    host-name router1;
    domain-name mynetwork.com;
    backup-router 192.168.15.2;
    root-authentication {
        encrypted-password "$1$ZUlES4dp$OUwWo1g7cLoV/aMWpHUnC/"; ## SECRET-DATA;
    }
    name-server {
        192.168.15.3;
    }
}
interfaces {
    fxp0 {
        unit 0 {
            family inet {
                address 192.168.15.1/24;
            }
```

```
            }
        }
    }
root@# commit
root@router1# exit
root@router1>
```

Discussion

On most JUNOS routers, the JUNOS software is installed in two places: the flash drive and the hard disk. When you first turn on the router, it runs the version of the software that is installed on the flash drive. The copy on the hard disk is a backup. Another backup copy of the software is provided on removable media, typically a PC card or a compact Flash card.

When you turn on your router for the first time, the JUNOS software automatically boots and starts. On some routers, a script prompts you for basic information about the router. On other routers, you use the J-Web browser to perform the initial configuration. At this point, you need to enter enough basic configuration information so that the router can be on the network and others can log in over the network. To work on the router to perform the initial configuration, you need to connect a terminal or laptop computer to the router through the console port, which is a serial port on the front of the router.

When you first connect to the router's console, you must log in as the user root. The root user is similar to the Unix superuser and has complete access to all functions on the router. Initially, the root account has no password. You can see that you are root because the prompt on the router shows the username root#. Start the JUNOS CLI using the command cli. The prompt root@> shows that you are the user root and that you are in operational mode. Once you have started the CLI, type the command configure to enter configuration mode. The prompt root@# indicates that you are now in configuration mode. If you look at the end of the previous example, you see that after you have activated the configuration with the commit command, the hostname that you configured is added to the end of the prompt, so the prompts become root@router1# in configuration mode and root@router1> in operational mode.

When you first configure the router, you set a number of basic properties for the router:

- Name of the router (the router's hostname), with the set system host-name command.
- Your domain name, with the set system domain command.
- IP address of the router's fxp0 interface, with the set interfaces fxp0 command. fxp0 is an Ethernet management interface that provides a separate out-of-band management network on the router. (The J-series routers do not have a dedicated management interface. You use one of the built-in Fast Ethernet interfaces, fe-0/0/0 or fe-0/0/1, instead.) Juniper Networks recommends that you

manage all M-series and T-series routers using the fxp0 interface, which is reserved for managing the router, so no traffic is forwarded through it. As part of the physical setup for the router, you should connect fxp0 to an Ethernet network over which you can perform management tasks. Optimally, the router should also be able to reach its DNS and NTP servers through this network. If you prefer, you can use any other interface router as a management interface. For the remainder of this book, we assume that fxp0 (or fe-0/0/0 on J-series routers) is configured as the management interface.

- IP address of a backup router, with the set system backup-router command. Choose a router that is directly connected to the local router. Your router uses this backup router only when it is booting and only if the JUNOS routing software (called the *routing protocol process*, or RPD) does not start. If RPD does not start, the router will have no static or default routes, so you will not be able to access it directly but will have to go through the backup router. When the router is booting, it creates a static route to the backup router. This route is removed from the routing table as soon as the routing software starts.

  For routers with two Routing Engines, the backup Routing Engine, RE1, still uses the backup router as a default gateway after the router has booted, so you can use the backup router to log in to RE1. (RE0 is the primary, or master, Routing Engine. See Recipe 1.30.)

- IP address of one or more DNS name servers on your network, with the set system name-server command. The router uses the DNS name server to translate hostnames into IP addresses.

- Password for the root account. When you initially start a new router, the root account has no password. To protect the security of the router and your network, it is critical that you configure a root password. The easiest way to configure this is by entering a plain-text (ASCII) password using the plain-text-password statement to configure a password. After you press Enter, the CLI prompts you for the password and then asks you to retype it but does not display what you type. The password you use cannot be all lowercase letters, all uppercase letters, or all numbers. There must be a mixture of cases, letters, digits, and punctuation. If you choose a password that doesn't meet these criteria, you see an error message:

      error: require change of case, digits or punctuation

  When you display the password with the show command, the CLI never shows the actual text that you type. It immediately encrypts the password string using MD5 and displays the encrypted version in the show command output. The section "Strategies for Choosing Passwords" in the Introduction to Chapter 2 discusses ways to choose secure passwords. Recipe 2.2 explains how to use SSH authentication for the root user.

For the initial router configuration to take effect—and in fact for any router configuration or configuration changes to take effect—you use the commit command. This command verifies that there are no syntax errors in the configuration and then activates it.

```
root@# commit
root@router1#
```

It's worthwhile to take a moment to comment on the style you use to type configuration statements on JUNOS routers. In this recipe, you are at the [edit] configuration hierarchy level, which is the very top level of the hierarchy, so you have to type the full hierarchy to the statement as well as the statement itself. This hierarchy is fairly shallow, so there is not too much extra typing. When you are working in deeper hierarchies, you may find it easier to move to that hierarchy level, both so you have less typing to do and have a better sense of where you are in the configuration. For this recipe, you could type most of the configuration commands from the [edit system] hierarchy level:

```
root# cli
root@>
cli> configure
[edit]
root@# edit system
[edit system]
root@# set host-name router1
root@# set domain-name mynetwork.com
root@# set backup-router 192.168.15.2
root@# set name-server 192.168.15.3
root@# set root-authentication plain-text-password
New password: $123poppI
Retype password: $123poppI
```

Then when you use the show command, you see only the statements at the [edit system] level:

```
[edit system]
root@#show
host-name router1;
domain-name mynetwork.com;
backup-router 192.168.15.2;
root-authentication {
    encrypted-password "$1$ZUlES4dp$OUwWo1g7cLoV/aMWpHUnC/"; ## SECRET-DATA;
}
name-server {
    192.168.15.3;
}
```

In portions of the configuration where you are using the same configuration command repeatedly with only minor variations, it is handy to use the keystroke sequences listed in Table 1-1.

While the configuration shown in this recipe provides the minimum needed to access the router from another system on the network, you should add a few other settings to the configuration to provide a more robust level of basic network connectivity:

```
[edit]
root@router1# set system ntp server 192.168.2.100
root@router1# set system time-zone America/Los_Angeles
root@router1# set system services ssh
root@router1# set interfaces lo0 unit 0 family inet address 207.17.139.42/32
root@router1# set system login user aviva class superuser
root@router1# set system log user aviva authentication plain-text-password
New password:
Retype new password:
root@router1# commit
```

The first command, set system ntp server, configures the IP address of an NTP server so that the router can set its time properly. Because we have already configured DNS on the router, you could specify the name of the time server instead of an IP address and it will be translated to an IP address. To have the router obtain accurate time from the servers, it is good practice to configure a minimum of four NTP servers. You can also optionally configure the time zone in which the router is located (see Recipe 6.2); by default, the time zone is UTC.

To be able to log in to the router over the network using SSH, enable SSH services on the router with the set system services ssh command. For this to work, SSH must also be configured on the network servers. SSH is also used to copy files to and from the router. (The JUNOS SSH uses the Unix scp command.) Note that you can also copy files with FTP or HTTP (see Recipe 2.1), but these are less secure than SSH. On routers with two Routing Engines, you can copy files between the two (see Recipe 1.30).

The set interfaces command sets the router's IP address by configuring an address on the loopback interface (see Recipe 7.3). The last two commands set up a non-root user account so an individual user can log in to the router (see Recipe 2.5).

If your router has two Routing Engines, you also need to configure a hostname and IP address for the second Routing Engine (see Recipe 1.30).

Again, issue the commit command for the configuration changes to take effect:

```
root@router1# commit
```

Recipes 1.7, 1.15, and 1.16 explain how the commit operation works, including how to provisionally commit configuration changes.

At this point, you are logged in to the router as the user root, so you have complete control over the router. As root, you can perform operational actions that shut down the router or make it inaccessible to the network. While there are times when you want to legitimately perform these types of operations, you generally want to make sure that the router continues to operate normally, and you want to minimize the chance of accidentally interfering with the router's operation.

At this point in configuring the router, you should either load an existing router configuration file, as described in Recipe 1.12, or add user accounts to the configuration (see Recipe 2.5), including one for yourself, and then log out and log back in to the router using your user ID.

See Also

Recipes 1.7, 1.12, 1.15, 1.16, 1.17, 1.30, 2.1, 2.2, 2.5, 6.2, and 7.3

1.2   Configuring the Router from the CLI

Problem

You need to modify the router's configuration using the JUNOS CLI.

Solution

You need to be in configuration mode to configure the router:

```
aviva@router1> configure
Entering configuration mode
[edit]
aviva@router1#
```

Discussion

When you want to modify the router's configuration, log in to the router, enter configuration mode as shown in this example, and then create a hierarchy of configuration statements that define the desired router operation. There are other ways to configure the router, which are discussed later in the chapter, including loading a configuration file from a remote server or from the local router and loading a previous router configuration.

When you want the configuration to take effect, you must activate, or *commit,* it.

See Also

Recipe 1.7

1.3   Getting Exclusive Access to Configure the Router

Problem

More than one person can log in to the router and modify the configuration at one time; you want to prevent someone from overwriting your configuration changes.

Solution

Use the following version of the configure command to enter configuration mode:

```
aviva@router1> configure exclusive
warning: uncommitted changes will be discarded on exit
Entering configuration mode
[edit]
aviva@router1#
```

Discussion

Because more than one person can log in to the router at the same time, several people may be modifying the configuration simultaneously. You will know that another person is editing the configuration when you enter configuration mode:

```
aviva@router1> configure
Entering configuration mode
Users currently editing the configuration:
    mike terminal p3 (pid 1088) on since 2005-02-30 19:47:58 PST, idle 00:00:44
[edit]
aviva@router1#
```

Here you can see that mike is also logged in, is working in configuration mode, and has not typed anything for 44 seconds. However, if someone enters configuration mode after you do, the CLI does not display any message, so you will not be notified. Instead, you need to check:

```
[edit]
aviva@router1# status
Users currently editing the configuration:
  aviva terminal p0 (pid 3358) on since 2005-06-09 11:22:18 PDT
      [edit]
  mike terminal p1 (pid 3768) on since 2005-06-09 11:48:31 PDT
      [edit]
```

If you need to ensure that no one else can change the configuration while you are modifying it, use the configure exclusive command to enter configuration mode. With this option, no other users can change the configuration as long as you are in configuration mode. If you do not commit the changes you make, they are lost when you exit from configuration mode.

If another user has locked the configuration, you can forcibly log him out:

```
aviva@router1> request system logout user mike
```

You get the username from the message displayed when you enter configuration mode or from the status command.

1.4 Displaying the Commands to Recreate a Configuration

Problem

You have a copy of a JUNOS router configuration or you need to duplicate a router configuration on another router and you want to know the commands to use to create the configuration.

Solution

Use the following command to list the commands for creating a configuration:

```
[edit]
aviva@RouterA# show | display set
```

Discussion

The show | display set command is a handy way to reverse-engineer a router configuration when you are trying to duplicate portions of a configuration on many routers or when you need to write up configuration, monitoring, or troubleshooting procedures for your network operations staff. This command is especially useful if the configuration is complex and when setting it up involves many long commands and lots of typing.

When you pipe the output of the configuration mode show command into the display set command, the JUNOS CLI prints a list of the commands you need to issue from that hierarchy level to create the existing configuration. When you use the command at the top level of the configuration (at the [edit] level), the CLI shows all the commands necessary to configure the router, which for most routers is a lot of commands. By way of illustration, here's a sample of the output for four interfaces on the router from the [edit interfaces] level:

```
[edit interfaces]
aviva@RouterA# show | display set
set interfaces fe-0/0/1 unit 0 family inet address 10.0.15.2/24
set interfaces se-0/0/2 unit 0 family inet address 10.0.21.1/24
set interfaces se-0/0/3 serial-options clocking-mode dce
set interfaces se-0/0/3 unit 0 family inet address 10.0.16.1/24
set interfaces lo0 unit 0 family inet address 192.168.13.1/32
```

You can cut and paste these commands individually or all at once. They produce the following configuration:

```
[edit interfaces]
aviva@RouterA# show
fe-0/0/1 {
    unit 0 {
        family inet {
            address 10.0.15.2/24;
```

```
                }
            }
        }
        se-0/0/2 {
            unit 0 {
                family inet {
                    address 10.0.21.1/24;
                }
            }
        }
        se-0/0/3 {
            serial-options {
                clocking-mode dce;
            }
            unit 0 {
                family inet {
                    address 10.0.16.1/24;
                }
            }
        }
        lo0 {
            unit 0 {
                family inet {
                    address 192.168.13.1/32;
                }
            }
        }
```

See Also

Recipe 1.13

1.5   Including Comments in the Configuration

Problem

You want to add comments to the router configuration file to help other people reading the file understand how the router is configured.

Solution

Use the annotate command to add a comment:

```
[edit protocols ospf]
aviva@router1# set area 0.0.0.0 interface fe-0/0/0
aviva@router1# annotate area 0.0.0.0 "backbone routers"
aviva@router1# show
/* backbone routers */
area 0.0.0.0 {
    interface fe-0/0/0.0;
}
```

Discussion

It is generally good practice to include comments in the configuration to clarify what is included for others who read the configuration. You can add comments for statements at the current hierarchy level in the configuration. In this recipe, we add a comment for the area statement at the [edit protocols ospf] level. The comment appears immediately before the statement.

To delete a comment, use the annotate command with an empty string:

```
[edit protocols ospf]
aviva@router1# annotate area 0.0.0.0 ""
```

1.6   Checking the Syntax of the Configuration

Problem

You want to check the syntax of your configuration to make sure there are no errors or missing statements.

Solution

Check the syntax of the configuration:

```
[edit]
aviva@router1# commit check
configuration check succeeds
[edit]
aviva@router1#
```

Discussion

As you are configuring the router, if you mistype a JUNOS configuration statement or command, the CLI gives you immediate feedback and pesters you until you type it correctly. However, this does not guarantee that you have spelled all variable names correctly or that you haven't omitted any required statements. Use the commit check command from time to time to check the syntax of the configuration. This command only checks the syntax; it does not activate the configuration.

If the syntax has no errors, you see the message configuration check succeeds.

If you have made any mistakes in the configuration, a message reports where in the configuration hierarchy the mistake is and describes the problem. The following example shows that a RIP neighbor router has been incorrectly configured in two RIP groups:

```
[edit]
aviva@router1# commit check
[edit protocols rip group alpha-rip-group]
  'neighbor fe-0/0/0.0'
     Failed to configure neighbor fe-0/0/0.0: already in group alpha-rip-group
error: configuration check-out failed
```

This is a mistake because a RIP neighbor can be in only one group. You can see from the output that the mistake is at the [edit protocols rip group alpha-rip-group] hierarchy level of the configuration.

Even if the syntax of the configuration is correct, that is no guarantee that the configuration will work as expected.

1.7   Activating the Router Configuration

Problem

You have created or modified the router's configuration using the CLI and you want to put the configuration into effect.

Solution

Use the following command to activate a router configuration:

```
[edit]
aviva@router1# commit
commit complete
[edit]
aviva@router1#
```

Discussion

When you modify the configuration on the router, you are editing a copy of the router's configuration. This copy is called the *candidate* configuration. Any modifications that you make to the configuration are recorded only in the copy of the configuration and have no impact on the operation of the router. When you want the configuration to take effect, you must activate, or *commit*, it. When you do this, your configuration file is checked to make sure the syntax is correct. It is then activated, becoming the *running* configuration.

The commit process is a batch mode operation. While you are in configuration mode, you can make any number of changes, but these appear only in the candidate configuration and have no effect on the running configuration. You can even verify the syntax without activating the changes (with the commit check command; see Recipe 1.6). The commit command batches up all your changes (as well as changes made by anyone else who is also in configuration mode) and activates them all at once. This means that interdependent configuration segments take effect at the same time, so you don't have to worry about the order in which you add statements to the configuration.

When you activate a configuration, the JUNOS software saves a copy of it on the router. This is discussed further in Recipe 1.14.

It bears repeating that you must activate a configuration using the commit command for it to take effect. It is a common mistake to forget to commit your changes, so this is often the first thing to check when debugging an operational problem on the router. It's very easy to see how this might happen. You might make a change in the configuration and then immediately use the run command to issue an operational mode command to verify that the router behavior matches the changed configuration, or you might get interrupted or distracted while configuring and issue a run command without committing.

If you have not committed your changes, you are warned when you try to exit configuration mode and return to operational mode:

```
aviva@router1# exit
The configuration has been changed but not committed
Exit with uncommitted changes? [yes,no] (yes)
```

If you choose to exit without committing the changes by pressing Enter or typing yes, the changes are retained in the candidate configuration but are not activated. When you again enter configuration mode, you are reminded of the uncommitted changes:

```
aviva@router1> configure
Entering configuration mode
The configuration has been changed but not committed
[edit]
aviva@router1#
```

If you decide not to exit configuration mode just yet, you can find out what changes you (and anyone else in configuration mode) made by comparing the candidate configuration to the one that is active and running:

```
[edit]
aviva@router1# exit
The configuration has been changed but not committed
Exit with uncommitted changes? [yes,no] (yes) no
Exit aborted
[edit]
aviva@router1# show | compare
[edit system services]
+    telnet;
```

Use the following command if you are not at the top of the configuration:

```
[edit system services]
aviva@router1# top show | compare
[edit system services]
+    telnet;
```

For routers with two Routing Engines, use the commit synchronize command to commit the configuration simultaneously on both Routing Engines (see Recipe 1.30).

See Also

Recipes 1.6, 1.11, 1.14, 1.15, 1.17, and 1.30

1.8 Debugging a Failed Commit

Problem

You are trying to activate a configuration and the commit command continues to fail.

Solution

Watch each step of the commit operation:

```
[edit]
aviva@router1# commit | display detail
2005-02-24 11:49:49 PST: exporting juniper.conf
2005-02-24 11:49:49 PST: expanding groups
2005-02-24 11:49:49 PST: finished expanding groups
2005-02-24 11:49:49 PST: setup foreign files
2005-02-24 11:49:49 PST: propagating foreign files
2005-02-24 11:49:49 PST: complete foreign files
2005-02-24 11:49:50 PST: dropping unchanged foreign files
2005-02-24 11:49:50 PST: daemons checking new configuration
2005-02-24 11:49:50 PST: commit wrapup...
2005-02-24 11:49:50 PST: updating '/var/etc/filters/filter-define.conf'
2005-02-24 11:49:50 PST: activating '/var/etc/keyadmin.conf'
2005-02-24 11:49:50 PST: activating '/var/etc/gtpcd.conf'
2005-02-24 11:49:50 PST: activating '/var/etc/certs'
2005-02-24 11:49:50 PST: executing foreign_commands
2005-02-24 11:49:50 PST: /bin/sh /etc/rc.ui ui_setup_users (sh)
2005-02-24 11:49:50 PST: executing ui_commit in rc.ui
2005-02-24 11:49:51 PST: copying configuration to juniper.save
2005-02-24 11:49:51 PST: activating '/var/run/db/juniper.data'
2005-02-24 11:49:51 PST: notifying daemons of new configuration
2005-02-24 11:49:51 PST: signaling 'Routing protocol daemon', pid 2884, signal 1,
status 0 with notification errors enabled
commit complete
```

Discussion

The previous output shows the results of a successful commit operation. If the configuration contains a mistake, the output indicates where the mistake is:

```
[edit]
aviva@router1# commit | display detail
2005-02-24 13:46:03 PST: exporting juniper.conf
2005-02-24 13:46:03 PST: expanding groups
2005-02-24 13:46:03 PST: finished expanding groups
2005-02-24 13:46:03 PST: setup foreign files
2005-02-24 13:46:03 PST: propagating foreign files
2005-02-24 13:46:03 PST: complete foreign files
2005-02-24 13:46:03 PST: dropping unchanged foreign files
2005-02-24 13:46:03 PST: daemons checking new configuration
[edit protocols rip group alpha-rip-group]
  'neighbor fe-0/0/0.0'
    Failed to configure neighbor fe-0/0/0.0: already in group alpha-rip-group
error: configuration check-out failed
```

In this example, the error is in the RIP routing protocol, and this error is flagged by the software process (the JUNOS term for a Unix daemon) that checks the configuration.

1.9   Exiting Configuration Mode

Problem

After you have completed making changes to the configuration, you want to activate the configuration and return to operational mode.

Solution

From the top hierarchy level, activate the configuration and exit configuration mode:

```
[edit]
aviva@router1# commit
aviva@router1# quit
aviva@router1>
```

From a lower level in the hierarchy, commit and exit configuration mode:

```
[edit system]
aviva@router1# commit
aviva@router1# top
[edit]
aviva@router1# quit
aviva@router1>
```

The following command is a quicker variation:

```
[edit system]
aviva@router1# commit
aviva@router1# exit configuration-mode
aviva@router1>
```

From any hierarchy level, activate the configuration and exit configuration mode with a single command:

```
[edit system]
aviva@router1# commit and-quit
aviva@router1>
```

Discussion

The commands in this recipe show several variations of quitting configuration mode after you have committed a configuration. If you issue separate commit and quit (or exit) commands, you must be at the top level of the hierarchy (at the [edit] level) for the exit command to quit configuration mode. From a lower level, use the top command to return quickly to the [edit] level. If you use the exit command at a lower level, it returns you to the highest hierarchy from which you previously issued an edit command.

Here's an example sequence of edit and exit commands to illustrate this:

```
[edit]
aviva@router1# edit protocols
[edit protocols]
aviva@router1# edit ospf
[edit protocols ospf]
aviva@router1# edit area 0.0.0.1
[edit protocols ospf area 0.0.0.1]
aviva@router1# exit
[edit protocols ospf]
aviva@router1# exit
[edit protocols]
aviva@router1# exit
[edit]
aviva@router1# exit
Exiting configuration mode
aviva@router1>
```

A quicker way to commit and then exit configuration mode from a lower level in the hierarchy is to use the commit command followed by the exit configuration-mode command.

Perhaps the quickest way to commit and get back to operational mode is to use the commit and-quit command. You can use this command at any hierarchy level. One caveat is that this command succeeds only if there are no mistakes or syntax errors in the configuration. If the commit fails, the CLI shows an error message, and you remain in configuration mode.

See Also

Recipe 1.7

1.10   Keeping a Record of Configuration Changes

Problem

When you activate a configuration, you want to include a short message that describes the changes you made.

Solution

Include a comment when you activate the configuration:

```
aviva@router1# commit comment "turned on telnet"
```

Discussion

It's good practice to include a short description of the changes you made to each version of a configuration file so you can keep a history of configuration changes. You do this by using the comment option with the commit command.

To track down what changed in the configuration and when, you can review the comments:

```
aviva@router1> show system commit
0    2005-03-31 20:26:16 UTC by aviva via cli
     turned on telnet
1    2005-03-31 11:12:28 UTC by aviva via cli
     set host gildor facility-override local4
```

See Also

Recipe 1.17

1.11 Determining What Changes You Have Made to the Configuration

Problem

You want to check what changes you have already made when editing a configuration.

Solution

To find out what changes were made during the current configuration session, use the following command:

```
[edit]
aviva@RouterG# show | compare
[edit interfaces]
-    fe-1/0/1 {
-        unit 0 {
-            family inet {
-                address 10.0.1.2/24;
-            }
-        }
-    }
```

To compare the current configuration to the previous one, use the following command:

```
[edit]
aviva@RouterG# show | compare rollback 1
[edit protocols ospf]
-    export send-direct;
```

Discussion

When you are working in a small portion or hierarchy of the configuration, you can issue the show command from time to time to see the configuration statements that were added or deleted so you can confirm the configuration. However, when making changes throughout the configuration hierarchy, you generally just want a summary of all the changes so you don't have to dig through the entire router configuration. The easiest way to see all the changes is to move to the top of the configuration hierarchy with the top command and then use the show | compare command, which is equivalent to the show | compare rollback 0 command. This is actually two commands: the show command displays the entire configuration, and the output is piped to the compare command, which lists only the differences between the two commands (just like the Unix diff command).

The output shown in the "Solution" indicates that you have deleted the fe-1/0/1 interface from the [edit interfaces] configuration hierarchy. The first line of the output shows the hierarchy level, and the minus signs indicate the deletions. Plus signs are used when you have added statements, as in this example:

```
[edit]
aviva@RouterG# show | compare
[edit interfaces lo0 unit 0 family inet]
        address 192.168.19.1/32 { ... }
+       address 127.0.0.1/32;
```

You can also compare the current configuration with a previously committed one. The second command shows how to do this. rollback 1 is the version of the configuration you committed immediately before committing the current one. The output shown above indicates that the export send-direct statement was present at the [edit protocols ospf] hierarchy in the previous configuration but has been removed.

You can also use a filename with the compare command to compare the candidate configuration to a saved file. This supports URLs and scp-style filenames, so you can use commands such as the following:

```
[edit]
aviva@RouterG# show | compare aviva@archives:nightly/my-rtr/2005-12-01.conf
[edit system login user testuser]
-       class operator;
+       class read-only;
```

See Also

Recipe 1.17

1.12   Configuring the Router by Copying a File from a Server

Problem

You have a router configuration file on a server and you want to copy it to the router and activate it.

Solution

Use the following command to copy the configuration to the router:

```
aviva@router1> file copy server1:router-base-configuration .
aviva@router1's password:
router-base-configuration                100%   10KB  10.0KB/s   00:00
```

Verify that the file has been copied to the router:

```
aviva@router1> file list
/var/home/aviva/:
.ssh/
router-base-configuration
```

Then load the file into the JUNOS CLI:

```
[edit]
aviva@router1# load override router-base-configuration
load complete
```

You should use the show command to review the loaded configuration and make sure it's what you expect:

```
aviva@router1# show
```

Then activate the configuration:

```
[edit]
aviva@router1# commit
commit complete
```

Discussion

JUNOS configuration files are simply formatted text files, so you can create a configuration file on a server and then load it onto the router. Use the file copy command on the router to copy the file from the server to the router. This command is similar to the Unix scp command. In this example, the file is copied from the user's home directory on the server to her home directory on the router. The home directory is effectively the current directory, so you can type a dot (.) for the directory name, just as in Unix. The explicit path is */var/home/aviva*. No text is shown here for the password because the CLI does not echo what you type when you enter the password.

Because the file copy command uses SSH, the server must also be running SSH. (You can use the file copy command because you enabled SSH when you initially configured the router [see Recipe 1.1].)

If the file on the server is not in your home directory, you can specify the full path to the directory. In this example, the file you want to copy is in the */tmp/config* directory:

```
aviva@router1> file copy server1:/tmp/config/router-base-configuration .
```

Including the override option with the load command replaces the entire candidate configuration with the contents of the file you are loading.

If you are just adding a new section to the configuration, use the load merge command instead. For instance, if you are setting up router access for a new user, you can create a file that contains the configuration information. For example, if you create the file router-config-new-user that contains the following:

```
system {
    login {
        user mike {
            class superuser;
        }
    }
}
```

after you copy this file to the router, use the load merge command to incorporate only this section of the configuration into the candidate configuration:

```
[edit]
aviva@router1# show system
host-name router1;
domain-name mynetwork.com;
backup-router 192.168.600.1;
time-zone America/Los_Angeles
root-authentication {
    encrypted-password "$1$ZUlES4dp$OUwWo1g7cLoV/aMWpHUnC/"; ## SECRET-DATA;
}
name-server {
    192.168.400.1;
}
login {
    class superuser-local {
        permissions all;
    }
    user aviva {
        class superuser;
    }
}
aviva@router1# load merge router-config-new-user
aviva@router1# show system
host-name router1;
domain-name mynetwork.com;
backup-router 192.168.600.1;
time-zone America/Los_Angeles;
root-authentication {
    encrypted-password "$1$ZUlES4dp$OUwWo1g7cLoV/aMWpHUnC/"; ## SECRET-DATA;
}
name-server {
    192.168.400.1;
}
```

```
login {
    class superuser-local {
        permissions all;
    }
    user aviva {
        class superuser;
    }
    user mike {
        class superuser;
    }
}
```

You can see from this output that the user mike is now in the [edit system] section of the candidate configuration. Again, remember to use the commit command to activate these changes.

If the file containing the configuration for the new users is on a server, you can load and merge it directly into the configuration:

```
[edit]
aviva@router1# show system login
class superuser-local {
    permissions all;
}
user aviva {
    class superuser;
}
aviva@router1# load merge relative server1:/tmp/router-config-new-user
aviva@server1's password:
router-config-new-users                    100%   54      0.1KB/s   00:00
load complete
[edit]
aviva@router1# show system login
class superuser-local {
    permissions all;
}
user aviva {
    class superuser;
}
user mike {
    class superuser;
}
```

The relative option in the load merge command performs the operation without needing the full hierarchy level. To use this option, the hierarchy level in the file must be clear and unambiguous.

If the file containing the configuration of the new users is on another router, you can use the same command to copy it to your router. Specify the router name instead of the server name.

1.13 Configuring the Router by Copying Text from a Terminal Window

Problem

You have a portion of a router configuration displayed in another window on your terminal or computer and you want to copy it to another router and activate it.

Solution

Use the load merge terminal command:

```
aviva@router1> configure
Entering configuration mode
[edit]
aviva@router1# load merge terminal
[Type ^D at a new line to end input]
```

Then, cut the configuration snippet and paste it here. When you are done, type Ctrl-d.

Discussion

A time-saver when configuring the router is to cut the configuration text from one window on your computer and paste it into the router's terminal window with the load merge terminal command. This is a great technique when you are copying configuration text from a browser or email window or when you are propagating identical or similar configurations from one router to another. To illustrate with a simple example, suppose you are configuring PIM-SM on all routers and are copying the configuration from a browser window. Here's the configuration in the browser:

```
protocols {
    pim {
        interface all {
            mode sparse;
            version 2;
        }
        interface fxp0.0 {
            disable;
        }
    }
}
```

Copy the text from the browser window; then, in the router's configuration window, go into configuration mode, move to the correct configuration hierarchy level, and paste the text.

If PIM is not yet configured, merge it into the existing configuration:

```
aviva@router1> configure
Entering configuration mode
[edit]
aviva@router1# load merge terminal
[Type ^D at a new line to end input]
cut and paste here to add the lines shown below
protocols {
    pim {
        interface all {
            mode sparse;
            version 2;
        }
        interface fxp0.0 {
            disable;
        }
    }
}
^D
load complete
```

First type the load merge terminal command and press Enter. Then paste the copied text and press Ctrl-d when done. This snippet starts at the top level of the configuration, [edit protocol], so you can drop it in with no typing. If the snippet is at a lower level, you either need to move down to that hierarchy level in the configuration (using the edit configuration mode command) or type in the opening hierarchy statements and closing braces yourself. If the PIM configuration you have is just the two interface commands and you are at the [edit] level, you need to type opening lines for protocols { and pim { and two lines of closing braces:

```
[edit]
aviva@router1# load merge terminal
[Type ^D at a new line to end input]
protocols {
pim {
type your paste command here to paste the lines shown below
interface all {
    mode sparse;
    version 2;
}
interface fxp0.0 {
    disable;
}
}
}
}
^D
load complete
```

If you forget to include the proper number of closing braces, the CLI displays an error.

Here, the first line of the error shows that one closing brace was omitted, and the second line indicates the hierarchy level:

```
terminal:9:(0) syntax error: }
  [edit protocols pim]
    ''
       syntax error
load complete (1 errors)
```

However, for a simple syntactical error like this, the CLI adds the remaining closing brace. You can verify this by checking the configuration:

```
[edit]
aviva@router1# show protocols
pim {
    interface all {
        mode sparse;
        version 2;
    }
    interface fxp0.0 {
        disable;
    }
} <-- CLI added this last brace

[edit]
aviva@router1# commit check
configuration check succeeds
```

You see that the CLI added the final brace. The commit check command confirms this correction, indicating that there are no syntax errors in the configuration file.

1.14   Backing Up the Router's Configuration

Problem

You want to back up the router's configuration to a remote server.

Solution

You can use the following command to copy the active configuration file to a server:

```
aviva@router1> file copy /config/juniper.conf.gz server1:/homes/aviva/tmp
aviva@server1's password:
juniper.conf.gz                           100% 2127     2.1KB/s   00:00
```

From configuration mode, use the save command to copy the candidate configuration to your home directory on a server:

```
[edit]
aviva@router1# save server1:configuration-march02
aviva@server1's password:
tempfile                                  100%   11KB  11.2KB/s   00:00
Wrote 433 lines of configuration to 'server1:configuration-march02'
```

You can also save it to a file in your home directory on the router:

```
[edit]
aviva@router1# save configuration-march02
Wrote 433 lines of configuration to 'configuration-march02'
aviva@router1# run file list
/var/home/aviva:
.ssh/
configuration-march02
```

Another way to back up configuration files is to automatically transfer the file each time you commit the configuration:

```
[edit system]
aviva@router1# set archival configuration transfer-on-commit
aviva@router1# set archival configuration archive-sites ftp://aviva:password@server1.
mynetwork.com:/m20-config-archives
```

Discussion

This recipe shows several ways to save a backup copy of the router's configuration. Use the first command from operational mode to copy the currently running version of the configuration to a server. The next two commands are configuration mode commands that save the candidate configuration either to a server or to your home directory on the router. If you use the save command after committing the configuration, you are effectively backing up the running configuration. The save command saves the configuration starting at your current hierarchy level. In this recipe, the commands are issued from the top hierarchy level (the [edit] level), so the entire configuration is saved. If you issue the command from a lower level, only that portion of the configuration is saved. The following command saves only the BGP configuration:

```
[edit protocols bgp]
aviva@router1# save configuration-bgp-march02
Wrote 15 lines of configuration to 'configuration-bgp-march02'
```

Use the file show command to verify the contents:

```
[edit protocols bgp]
aviva@router1# run file show configuration-bgp-march02
protocols {
replace:
    bgp {
        export send-statics;
        group internal {
            type internal;
            local-address 10.0.0.1;
            neighbor 10.0.0.2;
            neighbor 10.0.0.3;
            neighbor 10.0.0.5;
            neighbor 10.0.0.4;
            neighbor 10.0.0.6;
        }
    }
}
```

Notice that the CLI inserts the replace: tag into the file. If you later load this file into the configuration with the load replace configuration-bgp-march02 command, the CLI replaces the entire [edit protocols bgp] portion of the configuration with the contents of the file you are loading.

The last command in this recipe automatically transfers the configuration file each time you commit the configuration, in this case saving all files in the server's directory *m20-config-archives*. The file is saved in a compressed (*.gz*) format with a name that includes the router name and the date and time of the commit operation, as in this example:

```
router1_juniper.conf.gz_20050627_190538
```

The numbers at the end of the filename are the date (27 June 2005) and the time (1905 hours, or 7:05 p.m., and 38 seconds). One thing to pay attention to is that the time is always in UTC, even if your router is set to run local time. A variation is to use the set archival command to save the configuration at specific time intervals—here, every 1,440 minutes (24 hours):

```
[edit system]
aviva@router1# set archival configuration transfer-interval 1440
aviva@router1# set archival configuration archive-sites ftp://aviva:password@server1.
mynetwork.com:/m20-config-archives
```

You can specify any interval from 15 minutes up to 2,880 minutes (48 hours).

One disadvantage of the set archival command is that the password is not encrypted in the configuration file but is shown in ASCII (clear text).

The JUNOS software also saves a copy of a configuration each time you activate it with any version of the commit command. The JUNOS software saves the last 50 versions of the configuration: the currently active configuration and the last 49 committed ones. The active (currently running) configuration (*juniper.conf.gz*) and the three most recent previous configurations (*juniper.conf.1.gz, juniper.conf.2.gz,* and *juniper.conf.3.gz*) are in the */config* directory, which is on the router's flash disk. Because space is limited on the flash disk, the files are stored in a compressed format (*.gz*).

```
aviva@router1> file list /config
/config:
juniper.conf.1.gz
juniper.conf.2.gz
juniper.conf.3.gz
juniper.conf.gz
license/
rescue.conf.gz
```

The remaining configurations—named *juniper.conf.4.gz* through *juniper.conf.49.gz*—are in the */var/db/config* directory on the router's hard disk.

These files are also compressed.

```
aviva@router1> file list /var/db/config
/var/db/config:
juniper.conf++
juniper.conf.10.gz
juniper.conf.11.gz
juniper.conf.12.gz
juniper.conf.13.gz
juniper.conf.14.gz
juniper.conf.15.gz
...
juniper.conf.49.gz
juniper.conf.5.gz
juniper.conf.6.gz
juniper.conf.7.gz
juniper.conf.8.gz
juniper.conf.9.gz
```

Each time you commit a configuration, that configuration is named *juniper.conf.gz*, the existing *juniper.conf.gz* file is renamed *juniper.conf.1.gz*, and all the remaining numbered configurations from before are renumbered. This means that the JUNOS backup configuration files are continually renamed. This behavior points out one advantage of using the save command: it allows you to store the configuration in a file with a fixed name.

A publicly available software tool for archiving and monitoring router hardware and software configuration is RANCID (*http://www.shurbbery.net/rancid*). You can also use this tool to track configuration changes.

See Also

Recipe 1.18

1.15   Scheduling the Activation of a Configuration

Problem

You want to activate a new or modified router configuration at a later time.

Solution

You schedule when the software should activate a configuration:

```
[edit]
aviva@router1# commit at 10:45
configuration check succeeds
commit at will be executed at 2005-02-25 10:45:00 PST
Exiting configuration mode
```

The time is in 24-hour (military) format, so to specify a time after 12 p.m., use the following command:

```
[edit]
aviva@router1# commit at 22:45
configuration check succeeds
commit at will be executed at 2005-02-25 22:45:00 PST
Exiting configuration mode
```

To schedule the activation of a configuration to occur on another day, use the full date and time:

```
[edit]
aviva@router1# commit at "2005-02-26 10:45"
configuration check succeeds
commit at will be executed at 2005-02-26 10:45:00 PST
Exiting configuration mode
```

To cancel a commit operation scheduled with the commit at command, use the following command:

```
aviva@router1> clear system commit
Pending commit cleared
```

Discussion

Sometimes you want to delay the activation of a configuration, scheduling it to occur at some later time. For example, if you are a network provider and have a service window in which network changes are made, you want the new configuration to take effect during that window. Or, if you are making changes on a number of routers, you might want the changes to take effect on all the routers at the same time or within the same time window, especially if you are making changes to routing protocols that might affect routing and route convergence across the network.

One way to schedule the activation of a configuration is to use the commit at command. The first two commands in this recipe commit the configuration at a specific time on the current day, one at 10:45 a.m. and the second at 10:45 p.m. The third command schedules the commit at 10:45 a.m. on another day.

Verify that the commit command has actually executed by looking at the timestamp on the currently running configuration file:

```
aviva@router1> file list detail /config

/config:
total 34
-rw-r-----  1 root  wheel       2127 Feb 25 03:10 juniper.conf.1.gz
-rw-r-----  1 root  wheel       2127 Feb 25 03:00 juniper.conf.2.gz
-rw-r-----  1 root  wheel       2127 Feb 24 12:56 juniper.conf.3.gz
-rw-r-----  1 root  wheel       2127 Feb 25 10:45 juniper.conf.gz
drwxr-xr-x  2 root  wheel        512 Jan 18  2004 license/
```

You see that the running configuration file, *juniper.conf.gz,* was activated February 25 at 10:45 a.m.

When you use the commit at command, you must be at the [edit] hierarchy level in the configuration. The time and date that you specify are interpreted based on the router's time clock. Use the show system uptime command to determine the current date and time as set on the router:

```
aviva@router1> show system uptime
Current time: 2005-02-25 10:59:09 PST
System booted: 2005-02-25 03:07:42 PST (07:51:27 ago)
Protocols started: 2005-02-25 03:10:07 PST (07:49:02 ago)
Last configured: 2005-02-25 10:45:12 PST (00:13:57 ago) by aviva
10:59AM PST up 7:51, 1 user, load averages: 0.01, 0.02, 0.00
```

To determine whether and when a configuration activation has been scheduled, use the show system commit command:

```
aviva@router1> show system commit
commit requested by aviva via cli at 2005-02-26 10:00:00 PST
0   2005-02-25 10:45:12 PST by aviva via cli commit at
1   2005-02-25 03:10:21 PST by aviva via cli
2   2005-02-25 03:01:01 PST by aviva via cli
```

The first line shows that a configuration activation has been requested, who requested it, and when it will occur. This command also lists the history of all the commit operations that have occurred on the router and who activated them, and provides you with a history of configuration changes.

Another way you know that a configuration activation has been scheduled is that you see a message when you enter configuration mode:

```
aviva@router1> configure
Entering configuration mode
Users currently editing the configuration:
   aviva terminal p0 (pid 6231) on since 2005-02-25 11:55:07 PST, idle 00:15:54
      commit-at
```

Note that when a delayed configuration activation is scheduled, you cannot commit any changes to the configuration:

```
[edit]
aviva@router1# commit
error: Another commit is pending
```

To cancel a scheduled commit, use the clear system commit command.

1.16 Provisionally Activating a Configuration

Problem

You want to activate a new or modified router configuration but you are not sure whether the configuration will somehow disable the router.

Solution

Use the following command to commit the configuration changes provisionally:

```
[edit]
aviva@router1# commit confirmed
commit confirmed will be automatically rolled back in 10 minutes unless confirmed
commit complete
```

To make the provisional activation permanent, issue the following command:

```
[edit]
aviva@router1# commit
commit complete
```

Discussion

When you need to verify that a new or modified configuration is working properly—and especially if the changes might lock you out of the router—you can provisionally commit it using the commit confirmed command.

By default, the commit confirmed command activates the configuration for 10 minutes. Within this time, you must explicitly confirm that the configuration is acceptable—either by issuing another commit command or by entering the commit check command—to make the provisional activation permanent. If you do not, the router loads and activates the previous configuration when 10 minutes have passed. You have to keep track of the time yourself, because the CLI doesn't warn you when it is expiring. The CLI displays a message if you do not confirm the commit when returning to the previous configuration:

```
Broadcast Message from root@router1
        (no tty) at 15:05 PDT...
Commit was not confirmed; automatic rollback complete.
```

When working on a production router, if you are concerned that the change you are making might not go as expected, specify an interval of less than 10 minutes. If you are quite worried, one minute might be as long as you want to wait:

```
[edit]
aviva@router1# commit confirmed 1
commit confirmed will be automatically rolled back in 1 minutes unless confirmed
commit complete
```

1.17   Loading a Previous Router Configuration

Problem

You need to undo the active router configuration and return to a previous configuration.

Solution

The rollback configuration mode command loads a previous router configuration as the candidate configuration:

```
[edit]
aviva@router1# rollback 1
load complete
[edit]
aviva@router1# show
[edit]
aviva@router1# commit
commit complete
```

Discussion

You can reload any of the previously committed versions of the configuration file. You identify the version by the number, which is the number in the filename. In this example, we reload the last saved configuration file, */config/juniper.conf.1.gz*. The rollback command only loads the configuration, making it the candidate configuration, but does not activate it. The commit command activates the retrieved configuration. While using the show command here is optional, it's good practice to verify that the configuration you loaded is what you expect.

To figure out which previous configuration you want to retrieve, you can use a few commands that we have already discussed, including show system commit and file list detail /config. You can use the file list detail /var/db/config command to find out when the older configuration files were activated and by whom. You can also see this information when you issue the rollback command by using the router's built-in help:

```
[edit]
aviva@router1# rollback ?
Possible completions:
  <[Enter]>              Execute this command
  0                      2005-02-25 12:31:52 PST by aviva via cli
  1                      2005-02-25 10:45:12 PST by aviva via cli commit at
  2                      2005-02-25 03:10:21 PST by root via cli
...
  48                     2005-02-19 03:01:04 PST by root via cli
  49                     2005-02-18 18:24:21 PST by aviva via cli
  |                      Pipe through a command
```

See Also

Recipes 1.10, 1.14, and 1.18

1.18 Creating an Emergency Rescue Configuration

Problem

You want to store a copy of a known good and working configuration that you can load in case of an emergency without having to remember which rollback number to use.

Solution

When a known stable and working configuration is loaded and running on the router, save it as the *rescue* configuration:

```
aviva@router1> request system configuration rescue save
```

You can also save it directly from configuration mode:

```
aviva@router1# run request system configuration rescue save
```

Discussion

You create a rescue configuration to define a known working configuration or a configuration with a known state that you can roll back to at any time. This alleviates having to know the rollback number when you use the rollback command. You use the rescue configuration when you need to roll back to a known configuration or as a last resort if your router configuration and the backup configuration files become damaged beyond repair. The JUNOS software does not provide a default rescue configuration.

To return to the rescue configuration, load it with the following command:

```
[edit]
aviva@router1# rollback rescue
[edit]
aviva@router1# commit
commit complete
```

The JUNOS software stores the rescue configuration in the */config* directory:

```
aviva@router1> file list /config
/config:
juniper.conf.1.gz
juniper.conf.2.gz
juniper.conf.3.gz
juniper.conf.gz
rescue.conf.gz
```

To save a different configuration as the rescue configuration, just use the request system configuration rescue save command to overwrite the existing file. If you discover that the existing rescue configuration is not correct, but you don't have something to replace it with, delete the rescue configuration so no one accidentally uses it:

```
aviva@router1> request system configuration rescue delete
```

See Also

Recipe 1.17

1.19 Backing Up Filesystems on M-Series and T-Series Routers

Problem

You are preparing to load a different release of the JUNOS software or reload the current release and you want to save the files that are already on the router.

Solution

On M-series and T-series routers, use the following command to back up the files in the router's filesystems:

```
aviva@router1> request system snapshot
```

Discussion

Before you install any JUNOS software, either upgrading, downgrading, or reinstalling the current software version, you should always back up the files in the router's filesystem. This operation is sometimes called *taking a snapshot* of the software. The request system snapshot command copies the files and filesystems from the current running active partitions to standby partitions. Specifically, it copies the / (root) filesystem to */altroot*, and the */config* filesystem to */altconfig*. You see information about the copying as the command is running:

```
aviva@router1> request system snapshot
Copying '/' to '/altroot' .. (this may take a few minutes)
Copying '/config' to '/altconfig' .. (this may take a few minutes)
The following filesystems were archived: / /config
```

You can take a snapshot of the software at any time, but you should always do so before installing a new JUNOS software version so that you can recover to a known, stable environment in case something goes wrong when you load the software. You should also always run it after you have successfully loaded a new version of the software.

Why do you need to back up the JUNOS filesystems? One seasoned administrator has said that the less you know about the JUNOS filesystems, the more sane you will be—but still, you have to know at least a little bit. Routers have two internal storage areas, the flash drive (by default, the primary boot device) and the hard disk (the secondary boot device). A copy of the JUNOS software is stored in both. The flash drive has two filesystems (or partitions): */config*, which contains the active and most recent backup configurations, the rescue configuration, and software licenses, and /, which contains the JUNOS software (everything installed by the jinstall or jbundle command), the router's SSH keys, and a few other files generated from the configuration. The hard disk has one filesystem, /var, which is a large partition that contains system logfiles, diagnostic dump files, archived configuration files, and user home directories. (Also on the hard disk are the /altroot and /altconfig partitions, which contain a copy of the JUNOS software and related files and a swap partition.) When booting from the flash drive, the router uses the software and files on the flash drive. If the boot fails, it automatically tries the software and files on the hard disk. For the boot failover process to work, you must have already created a snapshot from a working version of the software.

There is one additional filesystem on the router, /tmp, which is a RAM disk (a memory filesystem).

To verify that the snapshot was successful, you might want to list the contents of the filesystems (with the file list command). However, the /altroot and /altconfig filesystems are not mounted, so they are not visible even though the underlying directories are still present:

```
aviva@router1> show system storage
Filesystem      Size     Used    Avail  Capacity   Mounted on
/dev/ad0s1a     77M      39M      32M        55%    /devfs
                16K      16K       0B       100%    /dev/
/dev/vn0        13M      13M       0B       100%    /packages/mnt/jbase
/dev/vn1        37M      37M       0B       100%    /packages/mnt/jkernel-7.4R1.7
/dev/vn2        12M      12M       0B       100%    /packages/mnt/jpfe-M40-7.4R1.7
/dev/vn3        2.3M     2.3M      0B       100%    /packages/mnt/jdocs-7.4R1.7
/dev/vn4        14M      14M       0B       100%    /packages/mnt/jroute-7.4R1.7
/dev/vn5        5.1M     5.1M      0B       100%    /packages/mnt/jcrypto-7.4R1.7
/dev/ad0s1e     12M      16K      11M         0%    /config
procfs          4.0K     4.0K      0B       100%    /proc
/dev/ad1s1f     9.4G     1.2G     7.4G       14%    /var
```

How do you know from the output of this command which partition is where? /dev/ad0s1a refers to a portion of a disk. It is drive ad0 (the storage device) slice 1 (the first "slice," and there's generally just one slice), partition a (which is the first partition on a disk and always refers to the root partition). Similarly, /dev/ad1s1f refers to drive ad1, slice 1, partition f.

On most M- and T-series routers, ad0 is the flash disk. In the case of router1, an M20 router that has an RE-2.0, ad0 is the flash disk and ad1 is the hard disk:

```
aviva@router1> show chassis hardware detail
Hardware inventory:
Item             Version  Part number  Serial number   Description
Chassis                                25708           M20
Backplane        REV 03   710-002334   BB9738          M20 Backplane
Power Supply A   REV 06   740-001465   005234          AC Power Supply
Display          REV 04   710-001519   BA4681          M20 FPM Board
Routing Engine 0 REV 06   740-003239   1000224893      RE-2.0
Routing Engine 0                       58000007348d9a01 RE-2.0
  ad0      91 MB SanDisk SDCFB-96      i3238140903     Compact Flash
```

```
  ad1    11513 MB  IBM-DARA-212000        AHOAHGN1017        Hard Disk
Routing Engine 1 REV 06    740-003239     9000022146         RE-2.0
Routing Engine 1                          d800000734745701   RE-2.0
  ad0       91 MB  SanDisk SDCFB-96       ggbsc410020        Compact Flash
  ad1     8063 MB  TOSHIBA MK2016GAP      Y0T39909T          Hard Disk
...
```

The output of this command also shows the manufacturer of the disks.

Use the show system storage command to find out the drive names:

```
aviva@router1> show system storage
Filesystem          Size     Used     Avail  Capacity   Mounted on
/dev/ad0s1a          77M      40M       31M       56%   /
devfs                16K      16K        0B      100%   /dev/
/dev/vn0             13M      13M        0B      100%   /packages/mnt/jbase
/dev/vn1             37M      37M        0B      100%   /packages/mnt/jkernel-
7.3-20050504.0
/dev/vn2             12M      12M        0B      100%   /packages/mnt/jpfe-M40-
7.3-20050504.0
/dev/vn3            2.3M     2.3M        0B      100%   /packages/mnt/jdocs-7.
3-20050504.0
/dev/vn4             14M      14M        0B      100%   /packages/mnt/jroute-7.
3-20050504.0
/dev/vn5            5.1M     5.1M        0B      100%   /packages/mnt/jcrypto-
7.3-20050504.0
mfs:102             1.5G      12K      1.4G        0%   /tmp
/dev/ad0s1e          12M      24K       11M        0%   /config
procfs              4.0K     4.0K        0B      100%   /proc
/dev/ad1s1f         9.4G     2.4G      6.2G       28%   /var
```

You see that */dev/ad0s1a* is mounted at /, and you know that's the flash disk. */config* is also on ad0 (the flash disk again) but on a different partition, and */var* is on ad1 (the hard disk). The */dev/vn0* devices refer to the software installed on the router. All these partitions are stored on / (and */altroot*).

The show system storage command output is cluttered and contains more information than you normally care about. You can shorten by filtering out the installed software devices:

```
aviva@router1> show system storage | except /dev/vn
Filesystem          Size     Used     Avail  Capacity   Mounted on
/dev/ad0s1a          77M      39M       32M       55%   /
devfs                16K      16K        0B      100%   /dev/
mfs:102             1.5G     8.0K      1.4G        0%   /tmp
/dev/ad0s1e          12M      16K       11M        0%   /config
procfs              4.0K     4.0K        0B      100%   /proc
/dev/ad1s1f         9.4G    1013M      7.6G       11%   /var
```

or even more:

```
aviva@router1> show system storage | match ad
/dev/ad0s1a          77M      39M       32M       55%   /
/dev/ad0s1e          12M      16K       11M        0%   /config
/dev/ad1s1f         9.4G    1013M      7.6G       11%   /var
```

If the router boots from the hard disk or if you manually reboot from the hard disk (take a fresh snapshot first, though), you'll notice that ad0 is still the flash disk and ad1 is still the hard disk, but the root filesystem is now on the hard disk because you're running on alternate media:

```
aviva@router1> request system reboot media disk
aviva@router1> show system storage
Filesystem            Size     Used    Avail  Capacity  Mounted on
/dev/ad1s1a           107M      37M      61M       38%  /
.
.
.
mfs:172               1.9G     4.0K     1.8G        0%  /tmp
/dev/ad1s1e            12M      21K      11M        0%  /config
procfs               4.0K     4.0K       0B      100%  /proc
/dev/ad1s1f            25G     3.5G      19G       15%  /var
```

The request system reboot media disk command takes a fairly long time to complete, and you need to log back in to the router when it completes.

See Also

Recipe 1.20

1.20   Backing Up Filesystems on J-Series Routers

Problem

You are preparing to load a different release of the JUNOS software or reload the current release on a J-series router and you want to save the files that are already on the router.

Solution

On any J-series router, back up the filesystem to a device that is connected to the router's USB port:

```
aviva@RouterA> request system snapshot media usb
```

On J4300 and J6300 routers, you can also back up the files in the router's filesystem to a removable compact flash disk:

```
aviva@RouterA> request system snapshot media removable-compact-flash
```

Before installing the software upgrade, delete old log- and crashfiles:

```
aviva@RouterA> request system storage cleanup
```

Discussion

The snapshot process on J-series routers differs from the process for M-series and T-series routers because of hardware differences. You can place a snapshot of the

J-series filesystems on a device connected to the router's USB port or, for J4300 and J6300 routers, on a removable compact flash disk.

You can take a snapshot of the software at any time, but you should always do so before installing a new JUNOS software version so that you can recover to a known, stable environment in case something goes wrong when you load the software. You should also always take a snapshot after you have successfully loaded a new version of the software.

Before installing a new software package, you can use the request system storage cleanup command to remove older files to free up space in the filesystem. This command deletes any rotating logfiles in */cf/var/log* that are not current files in */cf/var/tmp* that have not been modified in the last two days and all crashfiles in */cf/var/crash*. Before you delete files in the directories, you can use the file list command to check what they contain:

```
aviva@RouterA> file list detail /cf/var/tmp
/cf/var/tmp:
total 28
-rw-r--r--  1 root  wheel        6379 Nov 3  00:10 cleanup-pkgs.log
drwxrwxrwx  2 root  wheel         512 Apr 15  2005 install/
-rw-r-----  1 root  wheel        2492 Nov 3  00:10 sampled.pkts

aviva@RouterA> file list detail /cf/var/log/messages*
-rw-rw-r--  1 root  wheel          65 Nov 3  00:06 /cf/var/log/messages
-rw-rw----  1 root  wheel        2587 Nov 3  00:06 /cf/var/log/messages.0.gz
-rw-rw-r--  1 root  wheel       21746 Apr 16  2005 /cf/var/log/messages.1.gz
-rw-rw----  1 root  wheel       12381 Dec 9  2004 /cf/var/log/messages.10.gz
-rw-rw-r--  1 root  wheel       11066 Apr 9  2005 /cf/var/log/messages.2.gz
-rw-rw-r--  1 root  wheel       12844 Feb 24  2005 /cf/var/log/messages.3.gz
-rw-rw-r--  1 root  wheel        8751 Feb 18  2005 /cf/var/log/messages.4.gz
-rw-rw----  1 root  wheel       12280 Feb 17  2005 /cf/var/log/messages.5.gz
-rw-rw----  1 root  wheel       11486 Feb 10  2005 /cf/var/log/messages.6.gz
-rw-rw----  1 root  wheel       44407 Feb 8  2005 /cf/var/log/messages.7.gz
-rw-rw----  1 root  wheel       22260 Dec 10  2004 /cf/var/log/messages.8.gz
-rw-rw----  1 root  wheel       18618 Dec 9  2004 /cf/var/log/messages.9.gz
total 12
```

The show log command is another way to find out when logfiles were last modified:

```
aiva@RouterA> show log
  messages          Size: 65, Last changed: Nov 03 00:06:10
  messages.0.gz     Size: 2587, Last changed: Nov 03 00:06:10
  messages.1.gz     Size: 21746, Last changed: Apr 16 2005
  messages.10.gz    Size: 12381, Last changed: Dec 09 2004
  messages.2.gz     Size: 11066, Last changed: Apr 09 2005
  messages.3.gz     Size: 12844, Last changed: Feb 24 2005
  messages.4.gz     Size: 8751, Last changed: Feb 18 2005
  messages.5.gz     Size: 12280, Last changed: Feb 17 2005
  messages.6.gz     Size: 11486, Last changed: Feb 10 2005
  messages.7.gz     Size: 44407, Last changed: Feb 08 2005
  messages.8.gz     Size: 22260, Last changed: Dec 10 2004
  messages.9.gz     Size: 18618, Last changed: Dec 09 2004
```

See Also

Recipe 1.19

1.21 Restoring a Backed-Up Filesystem

Problem

You want to restore a filesystem that you backed up by taking a snapshot.

Solution

First, reboot the router from the alternate boot media to which you saved the snapshot. On M-series and T-series routers, this is the hard disk:

```
aviva@RouterA> request system software reboot media disk
```

On J-series routers, this is either a removable compact flash card or a device connected to the router's USB port:

```
aviva@RouterA> request system software reboot media removable-compact-flash
or
aviva@RouterA> request system software reboot media usb
```

Then, retake the snapshot to copy the filesystem to the media from which you didn't boot:

```
aviva@router1> request system snapshot
```

or

```
aviva@RouterA> request system snapshot media removable-compact-flash
```

Discussion

The procedure for returning to a snapshot filesystem backup is very straightforward. You boot the router from the alternate media and then run the snapshot command again, which copies the filesystem from the alternate media to the media from which you didn't boot. M-series and T-series routers normally boot from the internal flash drive, and the hard disk is the alternate boot media. J-series routers also normally boot from an internal flash drive, and the alternate boot media is a compact flash card that is either installed in the router's compact flash drive or in a USB device connected to the router.

See Also

Recipes 1.19 and 1.20

1.22 Installing a Different Software Release on M-Series and T-Series Routers

Problem

You want to install a different release of JUNOS software on an M-series or T-series router.

Solution

First, retrieve the JUNOS install package, `jinstall`, from the Juniper Networks web site (*http://www.juniper.net/support*) and place it on a local server. You can install the software directly from the server:

```
aviva@router1> request system software add validate server1:jinstall-7.4R1.7-domestic-signed.tgz
```

If you want to have a copy of the software on the router, copy it to the router. You can use SSH:

```
aviva@router1> file copy server1:jinstall-7.4R1.7-domestic-signed.tgz /var/tmp
aviva@server1's password:
jinstall-7.4R1.7-domestic-signed.tgz          100%   64MB 774.5KB/s   01:24
aviva@router1> file list /var/tmp
/var/tmp:
cores/
install/
jbundle-7.4jbundle-7.4R1.7-domestic-signed.tgz
```

You can also use FTP to install the software directly from a server:

```
aviva@router1> request system software add validate ftp://aviva:prompt@server1.mynetwork.com/jinstall-7.4R1.7-domestic-signed.tgz
```

If you are using anonymous FTP, just specify the name of the server:

```
aviva@router1> request system software add validate ftp://server1.mynetwork.com/jinstall-7.4R1.7-domestic-signed.tgz
```

If you want a copy of the software on the router, you can also copy it over with FTP:

```
avive@router1> file copy ftp://aviva:prompt@server1.mynetwork.com/jinstall-7.4R1.7-domestic-signed.tgz /var/tmp/jinstall-7.4R1.7-domestic-signed
Password for aviva@server1.mynetwork.com:
/var/home/aviva/...transferring.file.........YoE4Qe/jinstall-7.4R1.7-domestic-signed.tgz100% of   63 MB   794 kBps 00m00s
```

After copying the software to the router, install it:

```
aviva@router1> request system software add validate /var/tmp/jinstall-7.4R1.7-domestic-signed.tgz
```

Once you have installed the new software version, reboot the router to activate it:

```
aviva@router1> request system reboot
```

You can reboot directly as part of the software download process:

```
aviva@router1> request system software add validate /var/tmp/jinstall-7.4R1.7-
domestic-signed.tgz reboot
```

Discussion

JUNOS software is distributed as a set of modular software packages that contain the various components of the software. The packages include the base JUNOS operating system software, the routing software, and the forwarding software. These packages are bundled together in the jinstall package, which you use to install the software when you are upgrading. There is a domestic version for use in the United States and Canada (domestic) and a worldwide version (export) of each package. A given JUNOS software release runs on all J-series, M-series, and T-series routers, and you use the same jinstall package to upgrade the software on M-series and T-series router products.

Upgrade to a newer software release or downgrade to an older one by loading a different version of JUNOS software. You generally never downgrade except when you receive a new router that is running a more recent version than those of your other routers. Retrieve the JUNOS install package, jinstall, from the Juniper Networks web site (*http://www.juniper.net/support*) and copy it to a local server. The install package is a large file, so you can either install it directly from the server or, if you copy it to the router, put it on the hard disk, which has a large filesystem. A good place is */var/tmp*.

When copying files to the router, you normally use SSH because SSH connections are encrypted, so your password and files are secure. FTP connections are not encrypted and hence are not secure. However, you can use FTP if you want, because all JUNOS software packages are signed and the JUNOS software validates the signature to ensure that the package has not been altered in any way. To use the router as an FTP server to transfer the files to the router when you are logged in to the server, enable FTP on the router:

```
[edit]
aviva@router1# set system services ftp
aviva@router1# commit
```

You need to enable FTP only if you want to FTP something to the router—that is, when the router is the FTP server. If the router is the FTP client and you are copying a file from an FTP server, you do not need to enable FTP on the router. The FTP client on the router is always present and running.

If you enable the FTP server, disable it after you have copied the file to the router:

```
[edit]
aviva@router1# delete system services ftp
aviva@router1# commit
```

Use the request system software add command to install the new software. During the installation, the filesystem on the router's flash disk is rebuilt and all components of the JUNOS software are completely reinstalled. Configuration information from the previous software installation is retained, but the contents of logfiles might be erased. This is why you take a snapshot of the software using the request system snapshot command before you load a new version of the software (see Recipe 1.19).

In the request system software add command, include the validate option to check that the new software is compatible with your current router configuration file. When you are updating to a different release of the JUNOS software, the validation check is performed automatically.

In all these commands, the password is not displayed when you type it.

After you have installed the new software version and rebooted the router, verify that the software is operating properly. Then take another snapshot of the software.

If you don't want to rebuild the entire filesystem each time you upgrade software, you can install the software using the jbundle package:

```
aviva@router1> request system software add validate /var/tmp/jbundle-7.4R1.7-
domestic-signed.tgz
```

jbundle installs the new software components and modifies the smallest number of files needed to move the new software version.

See Also

Juniper Networks web site (*http://www.juniper.net/support*); Recipes 1.19, 1.23, and 1.31

1.23   Installing a Different Software Release on J-Series Routers

Problem

You want to install a different release of JUNOS software on a J-series router.

Solution

First, retrieve the JUNOS install package, junos-jseries, from the Juniper Networks web site (*http://www.juniper.net/support*) and copy it to a local server. You can install the software directly from the server:

```
aviva@RouterA> request system software add validate unlink reboot server1:junos-
jseries-7.4R1.7-export-cf256.gz
```

You can also copy the software to the router and then install that copy:

```
aviva@RouterA> file copy server1:junos-jseries-7.4R1.7-export-cf256.gz /cf/var/tmp
aviva@server1's password:
junos-jseries-7.4R1.7-export-cf256.gz          100%   64MB 774.5KB/s   01:24
aviva@RouterA> request system software add validate unlink reboot /cf/var/tmp/junos-
jseries-7.4R1.7-export-cf256.gz
```

Discussion

To upgrade to a newer software release, first download the J-series install package, junos-jseries, from the Juniper Networks web site (*http://www.juniper.net/support*) and copy it to a local server and then to the router. When moving the package to the router, a good place to put it is */cf/var/tmp*.

The request system software command includes a few options. The validate option checks that the new software is compatible with your current router configuration file. When you are updating to a different release of the JUNOS software, the validation check is performed automatically. The unlink option removes the software package from the router as soon as possible to make more room on the hard disk for the installation to complete. The final option reboots the router after the validation and the installation complete and if the upgrade is successful. When the reboot is complete, you see the login prompt.

Use the request system software add command to install the new software. During the installation, the filesystem on the router's flash disk is rebuilt and all components of the JUNOS software are completely reinstalled. Configuration information from the previous software installation is retained, but the contents of logfiles might be erased. This is why you take a snapshot of the software using the request system snapshot command before you load a new version of the software (see Recipe 1.19).

See Also

Juniper Networks web site (*http://www.juniper.net/support*); Recipes 1.19, 1.20, and 1.22

1.24   Creating an Emergency Boot Disk

Problem

You want to create a boot disk to use in an emergency if the software and filesystems on the router become so damaged that you just want to reconfigure the router from scratch.

Solution

Create a PCMCIA boot flash card that contains the JUNOS install media. First, copy the install media from the JUNOS software download page on the Juniper Networks support site (*http://www.juniper.net/support*). On M-series and T-series routers, copy this file to the router's */var/tmp* directory. Then, insert a PC card into the router's drive and copy the install media to the PC card:

```
aviva@router1> start shell
aviva@router1% cd /var/tmp
aviva@router1% su
root@router1% dd if=/dev/zero of=/dev/rad3 count=20
root@router1% dd if=install-media-7.4R1.7-domestic of=/dev/rad3 bs=64k
```

To create a boot flash card for a J-series router, copy the install media to a Windows or Unix PC and uncompress it with *gzip* or WinZip. Connect a PCMCIA adapter or USB card reader to the PC and insert a compact flash card into the device. On a Unix PC, use the following commands to copy the image to the compact flash:

```
root@RouterJ# dd if=junos-jseries-7.4R1.7-export-cf256. of=/dev/hde
250368+0 records in
250368+0 records out
```

On a Windows XP or Windows 2000 PC, use either the Norton Ghost utility or the dd command shown previously.

Discussion

One of the tasks you can do to prepare for router disaster recovery is to create an emergency PCMCIA boot media. This is a bootable media that contains an image of a specific JUNOS software release. When you boot the router from this media, it installs the complete router from scratch, first doing a full reformat of the hard disk and flash, then completing a full new install of all the JUNOS software.

Use the PCMCIA boot media in disaster recovery when a router is hosed and you need to execute a complete reinstall from scratch. To boot from this media, the PCMCIA must first be inserted into the slot on the Routing Engine. When the router boots, the first thing it looks for is a PCMCIA in the slot. If it's not there, it moves on to the flash drive. If the PCMCIA is there, the router stops and waits for a user with console access to the router to press Enter to continue. The router does not automatically execute the reformat and reinstallation; you must tell it to do so. That way, if someone inserts the PCMCIA in the slot by mistake, the router doesn't format and reinstall when you didn't plan for it to do so.

The J-series router follows the same procedure but uses a compact flash card instead of a PCMCIA card. This recipe shows the commands to use for a 256-MB compact flash. J-series install media are also available for other sizes, including 128, 512, and 1,024 MB.

See Also

Juniper Networks web site (*http://www.juniper.net/support*)

1.25   Gathering Software Version Information

Problem

You want to determine which software version is running on the router.

Solution

The following command shows the software version and lists all the software components that are running on the router:

```
aviva@router1> show version
Hostname: router1
Model: m20
JUNOS Base OS boot [7.4-20051024.0]
JUNOS Base OS Software Suite [7.4-20051024.0]
JUNOS Kernel Software Suite [7.4R1.7]
JUNOS Packet Forwarding Engine Support (M20/M40) [7.4R1.7]
JUNOS Routing Software Suite [7.4R1.7]
JUNOS Online Documentation [7.4R1.7]
JUNOS Crypto Software Suite [7.4R1.7]
```

On the J-series routers, the software ships as a single package:

```
aviva@RouterA> show version
Hostname: RouterA
Model: j2300
JUNOS Software Release [7.4R1.7] (Export edition)
```

Discussion

The show version command tells you which software version is running on the router. The first two lines show the name of the router and its type. This is followed by a list of the software packages that are running. The text in square brackets is the software version. Here, the complete software version number is 7.4R1.7. The software release number is 7.4. When the release-naming scheme was devised, the first number was supposed to indicate the major release and the second number the minor release, but, in practice, this never came to be. The JUNOS software releases do not distinguish between major and minor releases. Each release of software, be it 7.4, 7.5, or whatever, is considered an equivalent collection of new software and hardware features.

From a historical point of view, the initial JUNOS release was 3.0. The first digit in the release number increments from time to time, typically as a consequence of a new ASIC family, a new hardware platform family, or an upgrade to the underlying FreeBSD software. The second digit in the release number starts at 0 and increments with each software release. A new version of JUNOS software is released quarterly. So, for example, JUNOS releases 6.0 through 6.4 were released quarterly, from July 2003 through July 2004 (third quarter 2003 through third quarter 2004), and

JUNOS 7.0 was released in the fourth quarter of 2004. In this case, the first digit in the release changed from 6 to 7 to correspond with the introduction of a new platform family, the TX Matrix.

The letter in the version number indicates the type of release. As a customer, you generally see R, for released software. If you are a beta customer, you receive B (beta) versions during the beta test period—for example, 7.4B1 and 7.4B2. If you are working with customer support to resolve a problem, you may also see I (internal) versions of the software or daily builds, which are named with the software version and a numeric string that includes the build date and time.

The digits following the letter are the maintenance release number and the build, or spin, of that maintenance. The first maintenance release number is always 1, and the first spin that is released is generally a number greater than 1. In the case of the show version command output in this recipe, the spin number is 7. The names of the JUNOS Base OS Software Suite and the Support Tools Package include the date that they were created rather than a maintenance release number, because these packages do not change as often as the others.

When checking the software version, make sure the versions of all the packages are the same. In this example, the packages are all 7.4. If they are not the same, the router will likely have operational issues.

The previous output shows all the standard JUNOS packages, which consist of five basic components:

Operating system
> The JUNOS Base OS Software Suite, the JUNOS Kernel Software Suite, and the JUNOS Support Tools Package comprise the JUNOS operating system. The base OS is the underlying operating system software, which is based on FreeBSD, and the kernel is the software that runs on the various hardware boards, including the networking cards (the Flexible PIC Concentrators, or FPCs, and the Physical Interface Cards, or PICs).

Forwarding software
> The JUNOS Packet Forwarding Engine Support package is the forwarding software, which runs on the forwarding board and is responsible for receiving and forwarding network traffic.

Routing software
> The JUNOS Routing Software Suite is the routing software. It runs on the Routing Engine, which you can think of as a separate computer within the router dedicated to handling all routing functions, such as calculating the best routes to network destinations and managing the routing tables.

Security software
> The crypto (security) software is provided only with JUNOS software shipped within the United States and Canada.

Online documenation

Online documentation is installed on the hard disk and is available while you are logged in to the router.

If you are debugging a problem with the JUNOS software and suspect that one of the software components is not running, use the show version detail command to list all the software processes that are installed:

```
aviva@router1> show version detail
...
KERNEL 7.4R1.7 #0 built by builder on 2005-10-24 02:03:37 UTC
MGD release 7.4R1.7 built by builder on 2005-10-24 02:03:58 UTC
CLI release 7.4R1.7 built by builder on 2005-10-24 02:03:44 UTC
CHASSISD release 7.4R1.7 built by builder on 2005-10-24 01:50:01 UTC
DFWD release 7.4R1.7 built by builder on 2005-10-24 01:52:13 UTC
DCD release 7.4R1.7 built by builder on 2005-10-24 01:48:04 UTC
RPD release 7.4R1.7 built by builder on 2005-10-24 02:04:09 UTC
SNMPD release 7.4R1.7 built by builder on 2005-10-24 01:56:24 UTC
MIB2D release 7.4R1.7 built by builder on 2005-10-24 01:54:12 UTC
APSD release 7.4R1.7 built by builder on 2005-10-24 01:49:52 UTC
VRRPD release 7.4R1.7 built by builder on 2005-10-24 01:57:05 UTC
ALARMD release 7.4R1.7 built by builder on 2005-10-24 01:49:44 UTC
PFED release 7.4R1.7 built by builder on 2005-10-24 01:55:25 UTC
CRAFTD release 7.4R1.7 built by builder on 2005-10-24 01:52:01 UTC
SAMPLED release 7.4R1.7 built by builder on 2005-10-24 01:56:04 UTC
ILMID release 7.4R1.7 built by builder on 2005-10-24 01:53:34 UTC
RMOPD release 7.4R1.7 built by builder on 2005-10-24 01:55:47 UTC
COSD release 7.4R1.7 built by builder on 2005-10-24 01:51:46 UTC
KMD release 7.4R1.7 built by builder on 2005-10-24 01:45:24 UTC
FSAD release 7.4R1.7 built by builder on 2005-10-24 01:52:24 UTC
SERVICED release 7.4R1.7 built by builder on 2005-10-24 01:56:16 UTC
IRSD release 7.4R1.7 built by builder on 2005-10-24 01:53:39 UTC
NASD release 7.4R1.7 built by builder on 2005-10-24 01:55:20 UTC
FUD release 7.4R1.7 built by builder on 2005-10-24 01:52:27 UTC
PPMD release 7.4R1.7 built by builder on 2005-10-24 02:04:06 UTC
LMPD release 7.4R1.7 built by builder on 2005-10-24 02:03:51 UTC
RTSPD release 7.4R1.7 built by builder on 2005-10-24 01:56:01 UTC
SMARTD release 7.4R1.7 built by builder on 2005-10-24 01:47:34 UTC
KSYNCD release 7.4R1.7 built by builder on 2005-10-24 01:53:50 UTC
LRMUXD release 7.4R1.7 built by builder on 2005-10-24 02:03:54 UTC
SPD release 7.4R1.7 built by builder on 2005-10-24 01:56:46 UTC
ECCD release 7.4R1.7 built by builder on 2005-10-24 01:52:23 UTC
PGMD release 7.4R1.7 built by builder on 2005-10-24 02:04:03 UTC
BFDD release 7.4R1.7 built by builder on 2005-10-24 02:03:42 UTC
L2TPD release 7.4R1.7 built by builder on 2005-10-24 01:57:17 UTC
SDXD release 7.4R1.7 built by builder on 2005-10-24 02:08:36 UTC
PPPOED release 7.4R1.7 built by builder on 2005-10-24 01:55:39 UTC
GCDRD release 7.4R1.7 built by builder on 2005-10-24 01:52:33 UTC
RDD release 7.4R1.7 built by builder on 2005-10-24 01:55:44 UTC
jkernel-dd release 7.4R1.7 built by builder on 2005-10-24 01:42:10 UTC
jroute-dd release 7.4R1.7 built by builder on 2005-10-24 01:42:36 UTC
jcrypto-dd release 7.4R1.7 built by builder on 2005-10-24 01:42:50 UTC
```

Some of the main processes are MGD, the management process, which communicates between the CLI and all the other processes; RPD, the routing protocol process; SNMPD, the SNMP process; MIB2D, the SNMP MIB II process; and PFED, the packet-forwarding software process. The JUNOS processes are the equivalent of Unix daemons, which is why their names end with the letter d. It is worth pointing out that all the software processes running on the router are separate and modular, so if one of them fails, the other processes that make up the router software continue to run.

The show system processes command, which is a repackaged version of the Unix ps command, also lists the running processes:

```
aviva@router1> show system processes
PID  TT  STAT     TIME COMMAND
...
2630  ??  I     0:00.07 /usr/sbin/tnetd -N
2632  ??  S     5:27.60 /usr/sbin/chassisd -N
2633  ??  S     0:06.00 /usr/sbin/alarmd -N
2634  ??  I     0:00.16 /usr/sbin/craftd -N
2635  ??  I     0:00.32 /usr/sbin/mgd -N
2636  ??  I     0:00.14 /usr/sbin/inetd -N
2637  ??  S     0:00.29 /usr/sbin/tnp.sntpd -N
2641  ??  I     0:00.05 /usr/sbin/smartd -N
2645  ??  S     0:00.09 /usr/sbin/eccd -N
2727  ??  S     0:03.54 /usr/sbin/xntpd -j -N (ntpd)
2728  ??  S     0:07.88 /usr/sbin/snmpd -N
2729  ??  I     0:10.81 /usr/sbin/mib2d -N
2730  ??  S     0:03.87 /usr/sbin/rpd -N
2731  ??  I<    0:00.39 /usr/sbin/apsd -N
2732  ??  I     0:00.41 /usr/sbin/vrrpd -N
2733  ??  IN    0:00.51 /usr/sbin/sampled -N
2734  ??  I     0:00.22 /usr/sbin/ilmid -N
2735  ??  I     0:00.46 /usr/sbin/rmopd -N
2736  ??  I     0:00.55 /usr/sbin/cosd
2737  ??  I     0:00.29 /usr/sbin/nasd -N
2738  ??  I     0:00.17 /usr/sbin/fud -N
2739  ??  S     0:01.39 /usr/sbin/ppmd -N
2740  ??  I     0:00.25 /usr/sbin/lmpd
2741  ??  I     0:00.22 /usr/sbin/rtspd -N
2742  ??  S     0:00.76 /usr/sbin/fsad -N
2743  ??  I     0:00.40 /usr/sbin/spd -N
2744  ??  I     0:00.14 /usr/sbin/pgmd -N
2745  ??  I     0:00.86 /usr/sbin/bfdd -N
2746  ??  I     0:00.14 /usr/sbin/sdxd -N
2747  ??  I     0:00.20 /usr/sbin/rdd -N
2749  ??  S     0:00.47 /usr/sbin/dfwd -N
2751  ??  I     0:01.00 /usr/sbin/kmd -N
2752  ??  S     0:08.86 /sbin/dcd -N
2753  ??  I     0:01.03 /usr/sbin/pfed -N
2754  ??  S     0:06.14 /usr/sbin/irsd -N
...
```

If you suspect that an installed software process is not running, you can check the process. Here, we check for RPD, the routing-protocol process:

```
aviva@router1> show system processes | match /rpd
```

We see that RPD is not running. Because the Routing Engine and the forwarding plane in JUNOS routers are separate processes, even when RPD is not up, the router continues to operate and forward traffic. However, it cannot perform any routing operations, such as sending routing-protocol updates and maintaining the routing table.

See Also

Recipe 4.7

1.26 Gathering Hardware Inventory Information

Problem

You are taking a hardware inventory to track which hardware components are installed in which router, along with serial numbers.

Solution

The following command lists all the hardware components installed in the router:

```
aviva@router1> show chassis hardware
Hardware inventory:
Item               Version  Part number  Serial number   Description
Chassis                                  25688           M20
Backplane          REV 03   710-002334   BB9683          M20 Backplane
Power Supply A     REV 06   740-001465   005169          AC Power Supply
Display            REV 04   710-001519   BA4667          M20 FPM Board
Routing Engine 0   REV 06   740-003239   9000016755      RE-2.0
Routing Engine 1   REV 06   740-003239   9001018324      RE-2.0
SSB slot 0         REV 02   710-001951   AZ8025          Internet Processor IIv1
SSB slot 1         N/A      N/A          N/A             Backup
FPC 0              REV 03   710-003308   BB5185          E-FPC
  PIC 0            REV 08   750-002303   BB5887          4x F/E, 100 BASE-TX
  PIC 1            REV 07   750-004745   BC9318          2x CT3-NxDS0
  PIC 2
FPC 1              REV 03   710-003308   BF7478          E-FPC
  PIC 0            REV 03   750-002914   BC0119          2x OC-3 ATM, MM
```

Discussion

When you need to find out what hardware is installed in the router, use the show chassis hardware command. The first column of the output lists each hardware component installed in the router, starting with the chassis, which is the router itself. This router, an M20 system, has one power supply, two Routing Engines, one switching board (the SSB), and two FPCs with a total of four PICs. PICs are the network interface cards in the router. All these items are field-replaceable units (FRUs), so you or a service technician can replace them in the field.

The next three columns list the revision number, the Juniper Networks manufacturing part number, and the serial number. This information is very useful if you are tracking what router hardware you have and if you need to replace or return a defective piece of hardware.

The last column has a brief description of each hardware component. This is especially useful for finding out which PICs are installed on which FPC and in which location on the FPC. You need this information when you are configuring the router's interfaces because you must specify the FPC number and the PIC location to identify the interface (see Chapter 7). Most M-series and T-series routers have either four or eight slots for FPCs, and each FPC typically has four locations for PICs. The FPCs are numbered 0 through 7 (or 0 through 3), and the PICs are numbered 0 through 3. The numbering is always indicated on the router chassis itself, but if your routers are in a secured room, you likely don't have physical access to them.

The J-series router is a smaller router and has fewer hardware components:

```
aviva@RouterA> show chassis hardware
Hardware inventory:
Item            Version  Part number  Serial number  Description
Chassis                               JN002648AA     J2300
Routing Engine  REV 07   750-009992   AA04451163     RE-J.1
FPC 0           REV 04   750-010739   AC04430335     FPC
  PIC 0                                              2x FE, 2x Serial
```

You can also get information about the memory storage areas on the router:

```
aviva@router1> show chassis hardware detail
Hardware inventory:
Item            Version  Part number  Serial number     Description
Chassis                               25708             M20
Backplane       REV 03   710-002334   BB9738            M20 Backplane
Power Supply A  REV 06   740-001465   005234            AC Power Supply
Display         REV 04   710-001519   BA4681            M20 FPM Board
Routing Engine 0 REV 06  740-003239   1000224893        RE-2.0
Routing Engine 0                      58000007348d9a01  RE-2.0
  ad0      91 MB  SanDisk SDCFB-96    i3238140903       Compact Flash
  ad1   11513 MB  IBM-DARA-212000     AH0AHGN1017       Hard Disk
Routing Engine 1 REV 06  740-003239   9000022146        RE-2.0
Routing Engine 1                      d800000734745701  RE-2.0
  ad0      91 MB  SanDisk SDCFB-96    ggbsc410020       Compact Flash
  ad1    8063 MB  TOSHIBA MK2016GAP   Y0T39909T         Hard Disk
SSB slot 0      REV 02   710-001951   AZ8112            Internet Processor IIv1
  SSRAM bank 0  REV 02   710-001385   242525            2 Mbytes
  SSRAM bank 1  REV 02   710-001385   242741            2 Mbytes
  SSRAM bank 2  REV 02   710-001385   242886            2 Mbytes
  SSRAM bank 3  REV 02   710-001385   242482            2 Mbytes
SSB slot 1      N/A      N/A          N/A               Backup
```

```
FPC 0            REV 03   710-003308   BD8455        E-FPC
  SSRAM          REV 02   710-001385   241669        2 Mbytes
  SDRAM bank 0   REV 01   710-000099   0003409       64 Mbytes
  SDRAM bank 1   REV 01   710-000099   0003408       64 Mbytes
  PIC 0          REV 08   750-002303   AZ5310        4x F/E, 100 BASE-TX
  PIC 1          REV 07   750-004745   BC9368        2x CT3-NxDS0
  PIC 2          REV 03   750-002965   HC9279        4x CT3
FPC 1            REV 03   710-003308   BB9032        E-FPC
  SSRAM          REV 01   710-001385   V00818        2 Mbytes
  SDRAM bank 0   REV 01   710-000099   0003803       64 Mbytes
  SDRAM bank 1   REV 01   710-000099   0003847       64 Mbytes
  PIC 0          REV 03   750-002914   BC0131        2x OC-3 ATM, MM
```

See Also

Recipe 4.8

1.27   Finding Out How Long the Router Has Been Up

Problem

You want to know how long the router has been up and running.

Solution

Use the following command to find out how long the router has been up:

```
aviva@router1> show system uptime
Current time: 2005-03-15 19:05:08 UTC
System booted: 2005-03-15 11:09:57 UTC (07:55:11 ago)
Protocols started: 2005-03-15 11:11:31 UTC (07:53:37 ago)
Last configured: 2005-03-15 19:05:04 UTC (00:00:04 ago) by aviva
 7:05PM  up 7:55, 1 user, load averages: 0.07, 0.02, 0.01
```

Discussion

The show system uptime command is similar to the Unix uptime utility. The first line of output shows the current time on the router. The second line shows when the router was last booted and how long it has been up (here, 7 hours, 55 minutes, 11 seconds). The last line also shows how long the router has been up. The third line shows when the protocol software started, and the last line tells when the configuration was last changed and by whom.

See Also

Recipe 6.1

1.28   Gathering Information Before Contacting Support

Problem

A problem has occurred on the router and you need to gather basic information before contacting support.

Solution

Use the following command to gather information about the router:

```
aviva@router1> request support information | save support-file
```

Discussion

The request support information command actually runs a number of JUNOS commands that provide detailed information and status about the running hardware and software, boot and log messages, the configuration itself, and the router's interfaces. The output of this command is quite extensive, so you should always save it to a file. Then copy the file to a server for further analysis or to send to technical support.

If a problem is occurring on your router, you should check for core dumps, which are files that contain information about the start of the router or of particular processes just before they crashed. Core dumps are placed in the */var/tmp* directory, and the software also saves a compressed version of the file that you can provide to support:

```
aviva@router1> file list detail /var/tmp
/var/tmp:
total 505330
-rw-------  1 root  field     185309 Apr 26 00:32 snmpd.core-tarball.0.tgz
-rw-rw----  1 root  field    1314816 Apr 26 00:32 snmpd.core.0
```

If you suspect that faulty hardware is causing or contributing to a problem, use the show chassis hardware command, or its detail version, to get the serial number, version, and part number for that component.

See Also

Recipe 1.26

1.29   Managing Routers with Similar Configurations

Problem

Some of the configuration sections for many of the routers in your network are identical, and you want to propagate the common information to all routers so your network operations center (NOC) staff never has to set it.

Solution

Define the common information in a configuration group:

```
[edit]
aviva@router1# edit groups global
[edit groups global]
aviva@router1# set system domain-name mynetwork.com
aviva@router1# set system backup-router 192.168.15.2
aviva@router1# set system name-server 192.168.15.3
aviva@router1# set system root-authentication encrypted-password $123poppI
aviva@router1# set system ntp server 192.168.2.100
aviva@router1# set system services ssh
aviva@router1# set snmp location "JUNOS cookbook lab"
aviva@router1# set snmp contact cookbook-lab-admin
aviva@router1# set snmp interface fxp0.0
aviva@router1# set snmp community public authorization read-only
```

Then apply the group to the configuration:

```
[edit]
aviva@router1# set apply-groups global
```

Discussion

JUNOS *configuration groups* define common configuration snippets in one part of the router configuration, which you then import, or apply, in other parts of the configuration. This allows you to define common portions of the configuration once and have them apply in many places in the configuration, thus minimizing or eliminating the risk of configuration inconsistencies or errors. If you are a network designer who develops router configurations that are then distributed to a number of routers in a point of presence (POP) or NOC, configuration groups are a good tool for propagating common configuration snippets across a number of routers. Having this information in a separate part of the configuration also lessens the possibility that others might inadvertently modify it. Use configuration groups for network-wide information, such as the domain name, addresses of name and authentication servers, router login accounts, and static routes (as we have done in this recipe) and to make it easier to configure items that have multiple instances, such as all channels on channelized interfaces.

Create the configuration groups under the [edit groups] hierarchy. The structure of the statements in the configuration group mirrors that of the complete JUNOS configuration.

In this recipe, we create one configuration group named global that defines the basic router information discussed in Recipe 1.1, along with pointers to our SNMP NMS system. You can create any number of group configurations, each with a distinct name.

The apply-groups statement causes the statements in a group be inherited by the proper location in the configuration. This recipe applies the global group at the top level ([edit] level) of the configuration because the group includes statements that affect a number of different top-level hierarchies ([edit system], [edit snmp], and [edit routing-options]).

You can include the configuration group statements in the configuration file of each router or in a template file that you use when configuring new routers. An easy way to add the information to existing configurations is to copy the configuration snippet using the load merge terminal command (see Recipe 1.13).

When you issue a plain show command in configuration mode, you see the statements only where you actually typed them. This means that you see the configuration group statements in the [edit groups] portion, not in the hierarchies where they are applied. If you pipe the show output to the display inheritance command, you see the statements in the hierarchy that inherited them:

```
[edit system]
aviva@router1# show | display inheritance
host-name router1;
domain-name mynetwork.com;
##
## 'backup-router' was inherited from group 'global'
## '192.168.71.254' was inherited from group 'global'
##
backup-router 192.168.15.2;
##
## 'root-authentication' was inherited from group 'global'
##
root-authentication {
    ##
    ## '$1$ZUlES4dp$OUwWo1g7cLoV/aMWpHUnC/' was inherited from group 'global'
    ##
    encrypted-password "$1$ZUlES4dp$OUwWo1g7cLoV/aMWpHUnC/"; ## SECRET-DATA
}
name-server {
    ##
    ## '192.168.15.3' was inherited from group 'global'
    ##
    192.168.15.3;
}
services {
    ##
    ## 'ssh' was inherited from group 'global'
    ##
    ssh;
    ##
}
##
```

```
## 'ntp' was inherited from group 'global'
##
ntp {
    ##
    ## '192.168.2.100' was inherited from group 'global'
    ##
    server 192.168.2.100;
    ##
}
```

Although this recipe shows how to apply a group at the top level of the configuration, you can apply a group anywhere in the configuration. For example, if all the serial interfaces on your router act as data terminal equipment (DCE), you can use groups to configure the common serial options:

```
[edit groups serial-dte-options]
aviva@RouterA# set interfaces <se-*> serial-options clocking-mode dce
aviva@RouterA# set interfaces <se-*> serial-options clock-rate 125.0khz
```

Here, the group is called serial-dte-options. The angle brackets enclose the wildcard se-* to apply the statements to all serial interfaces. You can then apply the group in the interfaces portion of the configuration:

```
[edit interfaces}
aviva@routerA# set apply-groups serial-dte-options
```

Look at the group configuration to verify it:

```
[edit groups]
aviva@RouterA# show
serial-dte-options {
    interfaces {
        <se-*> {
            serial-options {
                clocking-mode dce;
                clock-rate 125.0khz;
            }
        }
    }
}
```

In the interfaces section, set up the basic configuration of the serial interfaces and verify it:

```
[edit interfaces]
aviva@RouterA# show
se-0/0/2 {
    unit 0 {
        family inet {
            address 10.0.21.1/24;
        }
    }
}
se-0/0/3 {
    unit 0 {
        family inet {
```

```
                address 10.0.16.1/24;
        }
    }
}
```

Finally, check that the DCE configuration is inherited:

```
[edit interfaces]
aviva@RouterA# show | display inheritance
se-0/0/2 {
    ##
    ## 'serial-options' was inherited from group 'serial-dte-options'
    ##
    serial-options {
        ##
        ## 'dce' was inherited from group 'serial-dte-options'
        ##
        clocking-mode dce;
        ##
        ## '125.0khz' was inherited from group 'serial-dte-options'
        ##
        clock-rate 125.0khz;
    }
    unit 0 {
        family inet {
            address 10.0.21.1/24;
        }
    }
}
se-0/0/3 {
    ##
    ## 'serial-options' was inherited from group 'serial-dte-options'
    ##
    serial-options {
        ##
        ## 'dce' was inherited from group 'serial-dte-options'
        ##
        clocking-mode dce;
        ##
        ## '125.0khz' was inherited from group 'serial-dte-options'
        ##
        clock-rate 125.0khz;
    }
    unit 0 {
        family inet {
            address 10.0.16.1/24;
        }
    }
}
```

The output confirms that both serial interfaces inherited the serial-options statement into the configurations.

See Also

Recipe 1.13

1.30   Managing Redundant Routing Engines

Problem

Your router has two Routing Engines, and you want them both to have the same configuration.

Solution

Configure a hostname for each Routing Engine and an IP address for each fxp0 interface:

```
[edit groups]
aviva@router1# set re0 system host-name router1
aviva@router1# set re0 interfaces fxp0 unit 0 family inet address 192.168.15.1/24
aviva@router1# set re1 system host-name router1-a
aviva@router1# set re1 interfaces fxp0 unit 0 family inet address 192.168.15.2/24
[edit]
aviva@router1# set apply-groups [re0 re1]
```

Commit the same configuration on both Routing Engines:

```
aviva@router1# commit synchronize
re0:
configuration check succeeds
re1:
configuration check succeeds
```

Discussion

Most routers, especially those used by network providers, have redundant hardware components, such as fans, power supplies, and Routing Engines, so that if one of them fails, a backup component takes over immediately and router operation continues. You can replace most redundant components without having to power down the router; this is called *hot swapping*. For most hardware components, no software configuration is required. They are simply present in the router, which you can verify with the show chassis hardware command, and if any problems occur, a message or alarm is logged by the system logging facility (described in Chapter 5). Redundant Routing Engines, however, require some configuration.

By default, the Routing Engine in slot 0 is the master (RE0) and is used when the router boots. The one Routing Engine in slot 1 (RE1) is the backup. You configure hostnames and addresses for the two Routing Engines using configuration groups (in the [edit groups] hierarchy level). Specifically, you must use the special configuration group re0 (for the Routing Engine in slot 0) and re1 (for the Routing Engine in slot 1) to define properties specific to the individual Routing Engines. Configuring the re0 and re1 groups lets both Routing Engines use the same configuration file. Then use the apply-groups statement to propagate the configuration group information to the main part of the configuration.

The commit synchronize command commits the same configuration on both Routing Engines. This command makes the active or applied configuration for both Routing Engines the same with the exception of the groups, re0 being applied only to RE0 and re1 being applied only to RE1. If you don't synchronize the configurations between the two Routing Engines and one of them fails, the router may end up in a very crippled state if the backup Routing Engine has a different configuration.

If the configuration on the other Routing Engine has been modified but not committed, the commit synchronize operation fails:

```
[edit]
aviva@router1# commit synchronize
re0:
error: configuration database modified
re1:
error: remote lock-configuration failed on re1
```

If you use the show | display inheritance command to see the statements that are inherited from the re0 and re1 groups, you see only what is inherited from the master Routing Engine, re0; you won't see anything inherited from the backup:

```
[edit]
aviva@router1# show | display inheritance | match re0
    ## 'router1' was inherited from group 're0'
    ## 'fxp0' was inherited from group 're0'
        ## '0' was inherited from group 're0'
            ## 'inet' was inherited from group 're0'
                ## '192.168.15.1/24' was inherited from group 're0'
[edit system]
aviva@router1# show | display inheritance | match re1
[edit system]
aviva@router1#
```

Use the following command to see which Routing Engine is the master and which is the backup:

```
aviva@router1> show chassis routing-engine
Routing Engine status:
  Slot 0:
    Current state                  Master
    Election priority              Backup
    Temperature                    33 degrees C / 91 degrees F
    CPU temperature                38 degrees C / 100 degrees F
    DRAM                          768 MB
    Memory utilization             20 percent
    CPU utilization:
      User                         11 percent
      Background                     0 percent
      Kernel                        19 percent
      Interrupt                      1 percent
      Idle                          69 percent
    Model                          RE-2.0
    Serial ID                      58000007348d9a01
```

```
Start time                2005-04-26 22:31:45 UTC
Uptime                    3 minutes, 13 seconds
Load averages:            1 minute   5 minute  15 minute
                             0.86       0.65      0.28
Routing Engine status:
 Slot 1:
   Current state          Backup
   Election priority      Backup (default)
   Temperature            30 degrees C / 86 degrees F
   CPU temperature        30 degrees C / 86 degrees F
   DRAM                   768 MB
   Memory utilization     15 percent
   CPU utilization:
     User                   0 percent
     Background             0 percent
     Kernel                 0 percent
     Interrupt             0 percent
     Idle                 100 percent
   Model                  RE-2.0
   Serial ID              d800000734745701
   Start time             2005-02-18 07:48:14 UTC
   Uptime                 67 days, 14 hours, 46 minutes, 37 seconds
```

The highlighted lines show the master and backup information, and the remainder of
the output shows Routing Engine status information.

To find out which software version is running on the backup Routing Engine or to
edit its configuration file, log in to that Routing Engine:

```
aviva@router1> request routing-engine login re1
--- JUNOS 7.4-R1.7
aviva@router1a>
```

The prompt shows the hostname you configured for RE1.

Both Routing Engines have an identical filesystem layout, and the filesystems are distinguished by the identifiers re0 and re1. When you list files, you see the ones on the
Routing Engine you are logged in to. To list files on the other Routing Engine,
include the identifier:

```
aviva@router1> file list re1:/
re1:
/:
COPYRIGHT
altconfig/
altroot/
bin/
boot/
config/
data/
dev/
etc/
kernel@ -> /packages/jkernel
mnt/
```

```
modules/
packages/
proc/
root/
sbin/
tmp/
usr/
var/
```

The master and backup Routing Engines exchange keepalive messages to detect that each is alive and well. You can protect the operation of the router by automatically switching from the master to the backup Routing Engine if the backup has not received keepalives from the master for five minutes:

```
[edit chassis redundancy]
aviva@router1# set failover on-loss-of-keepalives
```

The problem with this type of failover—and with manually resetting the mastership—is that the router stops forwarding packets during the time it takes to start the routing protocol software on the other Routing Engine. A way to automate the failure without packet loss is to use graceful switchover:

```
[edit chassis redundancy]
aviva@router1# set graceful-switchover enable
```

The CLI prompt then changes to indicate which Routing Engine you are using:

```
{master}[edit]
aviva@router1a#
{backup}
aviva@router1>
```

With graceful switchover, the backup Routing Engine regularly synchronizes its configuration and state with the master Routing Engine. The master Routing Engine sends keepalives to the backup every two seconds by default. (You can change this value with the set chassis redundancy keepalive-time command.) If the backup Routing Engine stops receiving these messages, it assumes mastership and the router's Packet Forwarding Engine (PFE) breaks its connection with the routing tables on the old master and connects to the new master. From the point of view of packet forwarding, the switching of the PFE connection from one router to the next happens immediately, so no packet loss occurs. One caveat about graceful switchover is that both Routing Engines must be running the same version of the JUNOS software. If you are using the backup Routing Engine to upgrade to a different software release, you need to disable graceful switchover.

If you are using graceful switchover, you can automatically switch to the backup Routing Engine if it receives a hard disk failure error from the master:

```
[edit chassis redundancy]
aviva@router1# set failover on-disk-failure
```

By default, when you reboot the router, RE0 is the master. Use the following commands to have RE1 permanently be the master even after a reboot:

```
[edit chassis]
aviva@router1# set redundancy routing-engine 0 backup
aviva@router1# set redundancy routing-engine 1 master
aviva@router1# commit synchronize
```

See Also

Recipe 8.12

1.31 Using the Second Routing Engine to Upgrade to a New Software Version

Problem

You want to upgrade the JUNOS software version on the router incrementally to protect against something going wrong during the upgrade.

Solution

If your M-series or T-series router has two Routing Engines and you have configured Routing Engine redundancy (see Recipe 1.30), place the new software version on the second Routing Engine while keeping the currently running version on the first Routing Engine.

First, log in to RE0 and enter configuration mode:

```
{master}
aviva@router1> configure
```

Disable Routing Engine redundancy:

```
{master} [edit]
aviva@router1> delete chassis redundancy
```

Save the configuration changes on both Routing Engines:

```
{master} [edit]
aviva@router1> commit synchronize and-quit
```

Upgrade the JUNOS software version on the backup Routing Engine:

```
{master}
aviva@router1> request routing-engine login other-routing-engine
aviva@router1-backup> request system software add validate /var/tmp/jinstall-7.4R1.7-
domestic-signed.tgz reboot
```

When the reboot of the backup Routing Engine begins, you are logged out of this Routing Engine and return to the master Routing Engine. Wait a few minutes for the backup Routing Engine to reboot. Then log back in to RE1 and verify that the software is running properly.

At this point, you can also upgrade the JUNOS software version on the master Routing Engine:

```
{master}
aviva@router1> request system software add validate /var/tmp/jinstall-7.4R1.7-
domestic-signed.tgz reboot
```

This time, you are logged out of the router. Log back in a few minutes after the reboot and reconfigure redundancy:

```
{master}
aviva@router1> configure
[edit]
aviva@router1# set chassis redundancy routing-engine 0 master
aviva@router1# set chassis redundancy routing-engine 1 backup
aviva@router1# set chassis redundancy routing-engine graceful-switchover enable
aviva@router1# set chassis redundancy routing-engine 0 master
aviva@router1# commit synchronize and-quit
```

Then verify that the router is running properly and that RE0 is again the master.

Discussion

In the upgrade procedure described in Recipe 1.22, you overwrite the existing version of JUNOS software with the newer version. If something goes wrong during the upgrade process or if the image you load is damaged in some way, you might not be able to access the router, so you might not be able to reload the previous working version of the software.

Most M-series or T-series routers have two Routing Engines, and you can take advantage of this when you are upgrading software releases. You can install the new software release on the backup Routing Engine while keeping the currently running version on the master Routing Engine. Then make sure that the new software version is running correctly on the backup Routing Engine before upgrading the software on the master Routing Engine.

See Also

Recipes 1.22 and 1.30

CHAPTER 2
Basic Router Security and Access Control

2.0   Introduction

In the last few years, routers have increasingly become targets of malicious hackers attempting to launch distributed denial-of-service (DDoS) and other attacks across the Internet. Having control of a router, especially one with high-speed links, provides an even greater opportunity for mischief than just controlling PCs. A hacker in control of your router can reconfigure the system and take over your entire autonomous system (AS). Hackers are often able to log in to and take over routers simply because of negligence on the part of a router administrator who doesn't implement basic security precautions, such as setting a password for the root account, or who uses a password that can easily be discovered, such as juniper, cisco, root, or admin. Given the increasing number of malicious attacks occurring on the Internet, it is vital for you to secure your router.

This chapter talks about how to configure router access, including setting up login accounts, and other basic security measures you should take to control access to the router and to protect your router from undesired access.

There is nothing complicated about what you need to do to protect your router. Basic router security consists of three components. Two of these—limiting physical access to your router and configuring the JUNOS software to minimize the vulnerability of your router—are under your control. Properly configuring the router to be as secure as possible, while at the same time ensuring that you don't misconfigure the router to increase its vulnerability to attack, is often called *hardening* the configuration. The third component of security is some of the default behaviors of the JUNOS software that help protect the router.

To limit physical access to your router, we strongly recommend keeping your router in an area that has restricted access, such as a room that is locked or has badge access, and then limiting the number of people who have access to that area. Anyone who can physically get to a router can do a lot of damage, from removing hardware or cables from the router to connecting a PC to the router's console port, which lets them gain access to the router as root and gives full access to and control of the router's configuration and files. You should also never leave a modem connected to the router's console port to ensure that no one can gain access this way.

In the basic router configuration that you set up (described in Recipe 1.1), the following default software behaviors are in place to protect the security of your router:

- Only console access to the router is enabled by default. Remote management access to the router and all management access protocols, including Telnet, FTP, and SSH (secure shell), are disabled. When you initially configure the router, you connect a terminal to the router's console port. After this, you want to keep the router in an area that has limited physical access, so you need to enable a way to remotely log in to the router. For the best security, you should enable only SSH access.

- The JUNOS software does not support the SNMP Set capability for editing configuration data, although it does support this capability for monitoring and troubleshooting the network. There are no known security issues associated with this. (You can configure the software to disable the SNMP Set capability.)

- The JUNOS software does not forward directed broadcast messages. (Directed broadcasts are datagrams with a destination address of an IP subnetwork broadcast address.) Directed broadcasts are open to spoofing, which is used in DoS attacks.

- The JUNOS software ignores martian addresses that contain the following prefixes: 0.0.0.0/8, 127.0.0.0/8, 128.0.0.0/16, 191.255.0.0/16, 192.0.0.0/24, 223.255.55.0/24, and 240.0.0.0/4. (Martian addresses are reserved host or network addresses about which all routing information should be ignored.) You may want to add other prefixes to the martian list, such as RFC 1918 address space and bogon prefixes (see Recipe 9.5).

A key to router security is controlling who can log in to the router and what they can do once they are logged in. For each user who is allowed to work on the router, you should create a login account that defines the user's login name and password and the class of operations that they can perform on the router.

Strategies for Choosing Passwords

Passwords for the root account and for user accounts are often the weakest links in router security. For root and for any user who can log in to the router, you should always set a password, and the password you choose should be a strong password, one that is hard to crack, not a weak one. You want to make it impossible for a person with malicious intentions to gain login access to your router, especially as root or any user who has root permission or who has permission to modify the router's configuration or any files on the router, or to shut down or reboot the router.

All JUNOS passwords are encrypted, but this means only that the password stored on the router or in a configuration file is stored in an encrypted form. Someone reading the configuration on the router won't be able to see the plain-text password, and if you copy the file over the network and someone sniffs the session, they won't see the passwords in the file. Even though the passwords are encrypted in the configuration, you should take care not to let them circulate. It's still possible to use programs such as crack to guess clear-text passwords, encrypt them, and compare them to a list of encrypted strings (although this is not the case with, for example, SSH public keys). For this reason, you always need to use strong passwords and prevent even encrypted versions of your passwords from falling into the wrong hands.

To understand what a strong password is, we should look first at what constitutes a weak password. It should go without saying, but bears repeating anyway, that the weakest password is no password at all. A number of groups that monitor network security still find routers that have no passwords set on them. Other weak passwords are those that are easy to guess and include common words such as the name of your router vendor (such as juniper), the string admin, using the username as the password (for example, username root, password root, or admin/admin), and using the string password or Password. Other guessable passwords are words or strings like your birthday, spouse's name, or the name of any person. Weak passwords are also those that are vulnerable to brute-force attacks, in which an automated program tries a large number of possible passwords, and to dictionary attacks, which are automated programs that try all words in a dictionary in an attempt to crack an account's password. Keep in mind that dictionaries for all languages are now available on the Internet, as are dictionaries specific to technical and other fields, so all words that might be present in them are weak passwords, even derivations that substitute numbers for letters.

A strong password is everything a weak password is not, and then some. It should include numbers, symbols, and a mix of uppercase and lowercase characters. Other suggestions are to pick a couple of letters from a phrase you know well or to pick some unrelated words and connect them into a single string with punctuation marks or other symbols. Remember that a strong password is a good password only if you can remember it without writing it down.

User Authentication

Each user must have a login account and password to be able to log in to the router. The JUNOS software supports three methods of user authentication: local password authentication, Remote Authentication Dial-In User Service (RADIUS), and Terminal Access Controller Access Control System Plus (TACACS+). With local password authentication, you set a password for each user in the router's configuration file. RADIUS and TACACS+ are centralized authentication databases for validating users who attempt to access the router using any access method. They are both distributed client/server systems—the RADIUS and TACACS+ clients run on the router, and the server runs on a remote network system.

You can configure the router to be both a RADIUS and TACACS+ client and can also configure authentication passwords in the JUNOS configuration file. If you use multiple authentication methods, you can set the order in which the router tries the different authentication methods when verifying user access. If you do not set the order, the router uses the local password first.

Password Encryption

All passwords that you enter in a JUNOS configuration are encrypted. The JUNOS software supports several methods for securing passwords using encryption and hashing algorithms (encryption is a one-to-one mapping, so it's possible to decrypt, while hashing is a many-to-many mapping, so it's impossible to unhash):

SHA1

> Secure Hash Algorithm 1 is the newest algorithm, developed in 1995. It is a secure hashing algorithm that produces a 160-bit message digest that is used as a signature for a message and that must be verified by the recipient. SHA1 is considered secure because it is computationally infeasible to find a message that corresponds to a given message digest or to find two different messages that produce the same message digest. Any change to a message in transit results in a different message digest, so the signature fails to verify. However, SHA1 has recently been proven not to be as strong as originally thought.

MD5

> Message Digest 5, developed in 1991, is a message-hashing algorithm that takes a message of arbitrary length and produces a 128-bit hash function. When developed, it was thought to be computationally infeasible to produce two messages with the same message digest. The use of MD5 has recently been deprecated by the U.S. Department of Defense.

DES

> Data Encryption Standard, an encryption algorithm developed in 1976, uses a 56-bit key. Many people never thought DES was very strong in the first place.

SSH

> Secure shell, Version 1 (RSA) and Version 2 (DSA), is a security protocol that was originally developed with the Unix BSD software.

Even when you configure a plain-text password, the JUNOS software encrypts it immediately after you type it. Also, the software forces you to use a somewhat strong password, because the password must be at least six characters long and must include either a change of case or a special character.

2.1   Allowing Access to the Router

Problem

You just installed your router and can log in to it only through the console port. You want to allow administrators to securely log in to it over the network.

Solution

You should use SSH to provide secure encrypted sessions to the router:

```
aviva@router1# set system services ssh
```

Discussion

With SSH, both the password you type and the connection itself are encrypted using a well-tested industry-standard protocol, so both are protected. The systems that you use to connect to the router must have SSH client software. For greater security, you should use SSH keys on the client. You can find information about obtaining SSH software at *http://www.ssh.com* and *http://www.openssh.com*.

When you log in to the router with SSH, you are prompted for your password:

```
aviva-server1% 122: ssh router1
The authenticity of host 'router1-mycompany.com (192.168.71.246)' can't be
established.
DSA key fingerprint is 2c:a9:35:c5:2a:db:12:5b:b6:6e:0b:17:ae:ec:d4:55.
Are you sure you want to continue connecting (yes/no)? yes
Warning: Permanently added 'router1-mycompany.com' (DSA) to the list of known hosts.
aviva@router1-mycompany.com's password:
--- JUNOS 7.4R1.7 built 2005-10-24 08:10:28 UTC
aviva@router1>
```

You can also allow users to connect to the router with Telnet, but if security is your highest priority, you should not use Telnet. Telnet connections and passwords are not encrypted so they can be intercepted. However, if your network itself is well protected with firewalls, you can enable Telnet to let users access the router:

```
aviva@router1# set system services telnet
```

The only user who can never log in using Telnet is root. To log in as root, you must use SSH or the console.

SSH and Telnet provide terminal sessions to the router so you can log in to the router. The commands in the JUNOS software that copy files to and from the router use SSH, but they can also use FTP. Because FTP is not secure in and of itself, if you want to use it to copy files, the best thing to do is to enable FTP just before you need to copy the files:

```
aviva@router1# set system services ftp
aviva@router1# commit
```

You need to enable FTP only if you want to FTP something to the router—that is, when the router is the FTP server. If the router is the FTP client and you are fetching a file from an FTP server, you do not need to enable FTP on the router. The FTP client on the router is always present and running.

Then disable FTP after you have copied the files:

```
aviva@router1# delete system services ftp
aviva@router1# commit
```

One way to secure FTP is to create a firewall filter that uses source address filters to limit access to the FTP port, particularly if the source addresses are forced to come through an encrypted tunnel. Recipe 9.8 discusses how to create firewall filters.

If you are using a router that supports the J-Web browser for configuring and monitoring the router, you can enable secure HTTP on the router:

```
[edit system]
aviva@router1# set services web-mangement https
```

See Also

Recipes 2.14 and 9.8

2.2   Controlling Root Authentication

Problem

When you first installed your router, you created a password for the root user (see Recipe 1.1). With this initial configuration, anyone who knows the root password can log in to the router using Telnet. You want to make the root login more secure.

Solution

There are two solutions, depending on the desired level of security. One solution is to use SSH for the root password. You can specify the root password in plain text as you are configuring the router:

```
[edit]
root@router1# set system root-authentication ssh $1991poppI
```

You can also load an SSH key file from a server:

```
[edit]
aviva@router1# set system root-authentication load-key-file server1:/homes/aviva
/.ssh/id_dsa.pub
.file.19692                    |        0 KB |   0.3 kB/s | ETA: 00:00:00 | 100%
aviva@router1# show
system {
    root-authentication {
```

```
        ssh-rsa "1024 35
972763820408425105546822675724986424163032220740496252839038203869014158453496417001 9
610608358722961563475784918273603361276441874265946893207739108344810126831259577226 2
546166799927831612350043866091586628382248974673260566119218148953981396556156378621 1
940327687806538169602027491641637359132693963440084 43 root@mynetwork.com"; # SECRET-
DATA
        }
    }
```

The second solution for providing root authentication forces the root user to log in using the router's console port:

```
[edit system]
aviva@router1# set services ssh root-login deny
```

Discussion

There are two schools of thought about root access to the router. One suggests using SSH for the root password because SSH is more secure than using just the password you initially configured on the router. SSH provides inband access to the router, meaning that the root user can log in from anywhere in the network, especially if the router is part of a service provider network. A second school of thought suggests disabling SSH access for root altogether, forcing the root user to log in on the router's console port. Access using the console port is assumed to be secure in that you must be on the company's internal network to even have access to the console port.

Generally, there's very little reason to provide access to the root login inband, so unless you really need this on your network, for strict security you should not provide root SSH access.

If you use SSH to authenticate the root password, you need to first enable SSH services on the router and be running SSH on your server.

This first command in this recipe sets the root's SSH password by entering it directly in plain text in the router's configuration file. When you use the show command to view the configuration, you see only an encrypted version of the password. The second command copies an SSH key file from a server. After you type the command, the contents of the key file are immediately copied into the configuration file.

Any SSH password you set is in addition to the plain-text password. You should leave a local root password on the router so you can log in using the console port.

The second command in this recipe disables SSH for the root user altogether. Anyone needing to log in to the router as root must log in through the router's console. The reason for doing this is not so much that you want the root user to come in to the router through the console, but rather that you want him to log in using an individual account and then exit to the shell and use the su command to become root only if he needs to. There are two reasons for this. First, you want to avoid habitual use of the root account. Logging in with root is like running with scissors: there are lots of ways to hurt yourself. It's much better to get in the habit of using a nonroot account and su only when required. Second, and more importantly, you want to maintain accountability. If you log in to a router, su to root, and then do something horrible, there will be an audit trail to trace the source of the problem. However, if you had logged in as root in the first place, the action wouldn't be traceable to an individual router user.

See Also

Recipe 2.3

2.3 Logging In to the Router's Console

Problem

You have lost access to the router through other means and you need a way to log in.

Solution

Log in to the router using the console port:

```
aviva@server1% telnet router1-con
Trying 172.19.121.19...
Connected to router1-con.mycompany.com.
Escape character is '^]'.
router1 (ttyd0)
login:
```

Discussion

The console port on JUNOS routers is enabled by default. If you ever lose access to the router through normal login means, you can log in using the console port. While it is possible to disable the console port, it is really not recommended.

Use of the console port is not really required other than when you are initially installing the router. However, many people use the console port as the access of last resort. You can set up a terminal server with console connections to a number of devices in the event that the network fails. Also, if someone accidentally misconfigures the router and locks themselves out, or if routing has failed, you can still get into the router remotely using the console port.

Access over the console port is the only method that allows you to remain connected to the router during a reboot. A reboot logs you out of the session on the router, but you will still be connected and will be able to halt the reboot or watch the messages as the router reboots.

2.4 Setting the Login Authentication Methods

Problem

You want to use a RADIUS or TACACS+ server to authenticate user logins to the router, and you want to specify a backup login authentication method in case the primary method is unavailable.

Solution

Use the following command to set RADIUS as the primary authentication method and to set as the backup method the user accounts configured on the local router:

```
[edit]
aviva@router1> set system authentication-order [ radius password ]
```

If you are using TACACS+, you can set up something similar:

```
[edit]
aviva@router1# set system authentication-order [ tacacs password ]
```

Discussion

When users log in to the router, the JUNOS software can authenticate the username and password against an account that is configured locally in the router configuration file or against an account that is configured on a remote RADIUS or TACACS+ server.

There are a number of methods to authenticate users attempting to log in to the router. The default method is to use the username and password configured on the router and to try no other method if the authentication fails. This method is the equivalent of using the set system authentication-order password command with no options. You should always configure passwords in the configuration file for at least a few users so someone can always log in to the router (see Recipe 2.8).

To have the router use a RADIUS or TACACS+ server as the primary user authentication method, you must change the order in which the JUNOS software tries different authentication methods. The first command in the recipe configures RADIUS to be the primary user authentication method, and the second command configures TACACS+ as the primary method. Both commands set the user account configured on the router (password) as the backup authentication method. Providing a backup method means that users will always be able to log in to the router if there are problems with the RADIUS or TACACS+ server. (Recipes 2.12 and 2.13 describe how to configure RADIUS and TACACS+ user authentication.)

With the configuration in this recipe, when a user tries to log in to the router, the router first checks the username and password against the RADIUS or TACACS+ server. If they match, the user is authenticated and the router logs her in. If the remote authentication fails, the router checks its local configuration. If the user has a local account and the password matches, the user is logged in. If there is no match in either place, the user is denied access to the router.

A slight twist to this recipe is to use only a single authentication, specifying a remote method. The following command uses only RADIUS authentication:

```
[edit]
aviva@router1> set system authentication-order radius
```

This configuration allows users to log in to the router only if the RADIUS server has an account for them and only if the RADIUS server is up. This means that as long as the RADIUS server is up, users not listed in the RADIUS database won't be able to log in to the router even if there is a configured account for them on the router. However, if the RADIUS server fails or becomes unreachable, the JUNOS software authenticates the users locally. If you configure multiple RADIUS servers, the software checks for locally configured user accounts only after all the servers fail.

Make sure you configure user accounts and assign passwords in the JUNOS configuration for some users (see Recipe 2.5) so that login access to the router will be possible if the RADIUS or TACACS+ servers fail.

See Also

Recipes 2.5, 2.8, 2.12, and 2.13

2.5   Setting Up Login Accounts on the Router

Problem

You want a number of people to be able to work on the router to monitor and configure it.

Solution

Set up a login account for each person who is allowed to log in to the router:

```
[edit system login]
aviva@router1# set user sage class operator
aviva@router1# set user sage full-name "sage david"
aviva@router1# set user sage uid 1991
aviva@router1# set user sage authentication plain-text-password
New password:
Retype new password:
```

Discussion

For each user who you want to log in to the router, create a login account, providing information about the user that is similar to what you set for Unix accounts. The JUNOS software uses this account to locally authenticate the user.

Each account requires two pieces of information: a login name (configured with the user statement) and a login class (configured with the class statement), which associates a set of privileges with the user, defining the scope of operations that can be performed on the router. As with Unix account names, the username must be unique on the network and cannot contain spaces, colons, or commas.

This recipe configures an account for the username sage, who has a privilege level operator, which allows her to perform most operational commands but not enter configuration mode. operator is one of the predefined privilege classes. Recipe 2.10 explains the other predefined classes and how to create custom privilege classes.

The set user sage full-name command configures the user's complete name. Setting this is optional, but you may find it convenient or easier to read the person's given name rather than her account name when checking the configuration to see who has access to a router. Enclose the full name in quotation marks if it contains spaces.

The third command, set user sage uid, assigns a user ID (UID) of 1991. The UID is basically the same as the Unix UID. It's included in the JUNOS configuration primarily because UIDs are integral to Unix systems and the JUNOS software runs on FreeBSD. As with Unix, the JUNOS software uses the UID when establishing and enforcing file permissions and file access. Configuring the UID is optional. If you do not configure it, the JUNOS software assigns one, generally using the lowest available UID number, starting at 2000. Here's an example of automatic assignment:

```
[edit system login]
aviva@router1# set user sage class operator
aviva@router1# commit check
configuration check succeeds
aviva@router1# show
user sage {
    uid 2006;
    class operator;
}
```

You see that UID 2006 has been assigned to the user sage. You might want to explicitly configure the UID if users will be transferring files to Unix systems to ensure that users have the same UID on both JUNOS and Unix systems so that there are no file ownership issues.

The last command in this recipe establishes a plain-text password for the login account. You are prompted for the password, and nothing is displayed when you type and retype it.

To set up a user account, only the username and privilege class are required, but the password and other information are optional. If you omit the class, the CLI displays a warning:

```
[edit system login]
aviva@router1# set user sage full-name "sage david"
aviva@router1# show
user sage {
    full-name "sage david";
    ## Warning: missing mandatory statement(s): 'class'
}
```

Also, you will not be able to commit a configuration if you forget to assign a class:

```
[edit system login]
aviva@router1# commit check
[edit system login]
  'user sage'
    Missing mandatory statement: 'class'
error: configuration check-out failed: daemon file propagation failed
```

If you configure a password with a user's login account the software authenticates the user against this password during the login process. This is the default authentication method. You should always configure passwords in the configuration file for at least a few users so there is always someone who can log in to the router.

If you configure a password with the user's login account but want the router to have a RADIUS or TACACS+ database authenticate the user before checking against the password configured on the router, you must change the authentication order so that the RADIUS or TACACS+ server is checked before the local user account (see Recipe 2.4). You must also configure RADIUS or TACACS+ user authentication (see Recipes 2.12 and 2.13). In this situation, users will be able to log in to the router if the remote authentication server fails.

If you do not configure a password with the user's login account, authentication is done only remotely, using a centralized RADIUS or TACACS+ authentication database, instead of locally based on the router configuration file. This type of account is analogous to a Unix account that has a * in the password field, which does not allow logins based on the password file but can allow logins based on other valid means of authentication, such as RADIUS. For this to work, you must change the authentication order so that RADIUS or TACACS+ is checked first (see Recipe 2.4), and you must configure the RADIUS or TACACS+ user authentication (see Recipes 2.12 and 2.13). Users with this type of account will not be able to log in to the router if the authentication server is down or if network problems occur when accessing the server.

You can also create a generic login account (see Recipe 2.8) or a group login account (see Recipe 2.9) instead of configuring individual accounts for each user. These types of accounts authenticate against the RADIUS or TACACS+ database. Here, too, you must change the authentication order so that RADIUS or TACACS+ is checked first (see Recipe 2.4), and you must configure the RADIUS or TACACS+ user authentication (see Recipes 2.12 and 2.13). Users with this type of account will not be able to log in to the router if the authentication server is not available.

This recipe configures a plain-text password for the user's authentication. The password must be at least six characters long and must contain at least one case or one letter-to-number change. (Recipe 2.6 explains how to modify the default password format.) Here, you type the plain-text-password keyword slightly differently than for some other JUNOS configuration statements. After you type plain-text-password, press Enter. The software then prompts you to type and then retype the password. Type the password in plain text, and the JUNOS management process, MGD, immediately encrypts it using SHA1 encryption by default. (To change the default encryption, see Recipe 2.7.) You then see only the encrypted version of the password. Notice that the keyword plain-text-password has changed to reflect the fact that the password is now encrypted:

```
encrypted-password "$1$bO1I/WUw$bfaYFOLHxHxVCm7XyS7eG."; ## SECRET-DATA
```

To insert a previously encrypted DES, MD5, SHA1, SSH Version 1 (RSA), or SSH Version 2 (DSA) password, cut and paste (or type) the encrypted password into the configuration statement, enclosing it in quotation marks. Here is an example of an encrypted MD5 password:

```
aviva@router1# set user sage authentication encrypted-password
"$1$EpZ4gDEb$52KHLKA2QuqfJ83tFUvWd1"
```

You can define both encrypted and SSH passwords for a single user:

```
aviva@router1# show
user sage {
    authentication {
        encrypted-password "$1$kfpFHEom$wrWWtk69gvdbWInzsoIob."; ## SECRET-DATA
        ssh-rsa "1024 35 146330645491100487853835020619342411984360224858469539555321060688875175310154483709227844608606382760951789174798485714598660044125244467118449773046093423978096647125609338481821966335068887626379011183227170529556264636153739986671412936949237931460389138872790447839157168037660941582648407663918539435503 sage@red.juniper.net"; ## SECRET-DATA
    }
}
```

For basic router security considerations, you should limit access to the router to only those people who really need access, and you should carefully consider which privileges each person is given, so that a person can perform his job function and responsibilities, and nothing more.

See Also

Recipes 2.4, 2.6, 2.7, 2.8, 2.9, 2.10, 2.12, and 2.13

2.6   Changing the Format of Plain-Text Passwords

Problem

You want to require the passwords for user accounts to be longer than six characters and to have more than one case change.

Solution

Set all plain-text passwords to be from 8 to 20 characters long and to contain at least two case changes:

```
[edit system login]
aviva@router1# set password maximum-length 20
aviva@router1# set password minimum-length 8
aviva@router1# set password minimum-changes 2
```

Discussion

By default, plain-text passwords must be at least six characters long and must contain one change from either letters to numbers (or vice versa) or from lowercase to uppercase (or vice versa). You can harden the router's security even more by increasing the minimum password length and the minimum number of case and letter-to-number changes.

The commands in this recipe require that all plain-text passwords be from 8 to 20 characters long and contain at least 2 case changes. The changes take effect when you next configure a plain-text password for a user:

```
[edit system login]
aviva@router1# set user sage authentication plain-text-password
New password:T91912
error: minimum password length is 8
error: require 2 changes of case, digits or punctuation
```

This password is not acceptable because it is shorter than eight characters and has only one change from a letter to a number. An example of a valid password with these conditions is $1991poppI.

When you change the requirements for plain-text passwords, the new parameters affect only newly created passwords, so already existing passwords may not be as secure as your new password policy.

See Also

Recipe 2.5

2.7 Changing the Plain-Text Password Encryption Method

Problem

When setting up passwords for login accounts on the router, if you assigned plain-text passwords, the default encryption is SHA1. You want to change this to either DES or MD5.

Solution

Use the following command to change the encryption used for plain-text passwords to DES:

```
[edit]
aviva@router1# set system login password format des
```

For MD5 encryption, use the following command:

```
[edit]
aviva@router1# set system login password format md5
```

Discussion

All passwords that you enter in a JUNOS configuration are encrypted. For plain-text passwords, you can use one of three types of encryption: SHA1 (the default and the strongest), MD5, or DES. The encryption type that you configure is used for all plain-text passwords. You cannot specify different encryption types for different users.

See Also

Recipe 2.5

2.8   Creating a Login Account for Remote Authentication

Problem

You want to use a RADIUS or TACACS+ database to authenticate users instead of setting up individual login accounts for them on the router.

Solution

Create a login account that has the username remote:

```
[edit system]
aviva@router1# set login user remote class operator
aviva@router1# set login user remote full-name "remote account"
aviva@router1# set login user remote uid 9999
```

Then set the authentication order so that the remote authentication server is checked before the router's configuration file. The following command uses a RADIUS server:

```
[edit system]
aviva@router1# set authentication-order [ radius password ]
```

Use the following command for TACACS+:

```
[edit system]
aviva@router1# set authentication-order [ tacacs password ]
```

Discussion

When you want users to be able to log in to and work on the router but always want to use a central authentication server, you can set up a placeholder account named remote instead of creating login accounts on the router for these users. When a user with no account in the local configuration files tries to log in to the router using her regular username, the authentication is handled by the remote account, which queries the RADIUS or TACACS+ server to authenticate the user. If the user's name and password match what is on the server, the user is authenticated and the router logs her in. (Recipes 2.12 and 2.13 explain how to configure the RADIUS and TACACS+ server information.)

As with an individual user account (see Recipe 2.5), you configure a privilege level with the set user remote class command and a user ID with the set user remote uid command. This recipe sets the privilege level to operator, which allows these users to perform most operational commands but not enter configuration mode. (Recipe 2.10 discusses privilege classes.)

This recipe includes the set user remote full-name command to provide a description of this account. This command is not required.

Users who are authenticated only by the remote account will not be able to log in to the router if the authentication server is down. You should always configure some individual user accounts with passwords on the router so someone can always log in to the router (see Recipe 2.5).

You can create only one remote account on the router. This means that all users who don't have an individual user account on the router and who are authenticated by RADIUS or TACACS+ share the same privilege level, which is configured in the set user remote class command. Recipe 2.9 describes how to set up remote accounts that have different privilege levels.

See Also

Recipes 2.5, 2.9, 2.10, 2.12, and 2.13

2.9   Creating a Group Login Account

Problem

You want to use a RADIUS or TACACS+ database to authenticate a group of users who perform similar job functions and tasks on the router, instead of setting up individual login accounts for them on the router.

Solution

Create a group account on the router to allow multiple users to be authenticated by the same RADIUS or TACACS+ server account:

```
[edit system login]
aviva@router1# set user noc class operator
aviva@router1# set user noc full-name "NOC team"
```

Then set the authentication order so that the remote server is checked before the router's configuration file. The following command uses TACACS+:

```
[edit system]
aviva@router1# set authentication-order [ tacacs password ]
```

Finally, map the users on the server to the account name configured on the router. The following is the map on a TACACS+ server:

```
user = mike {
    service = junos-exec {
        local-user-name = noc
    }
}
user = sage {
    service = junos-exec {
        local-user-name = noc
    }
}
```

Discussion

When you want a group of users to be able to log in to and work on the router but always want to use a central authentication server, you can set up a common account instead of creating login accounts on the router for these users. Then in the RADIUS or TACACS+ database, you map the username to the common account name.

The first command in this recipe creates the group account noc that has operator privileges and can perform most operational commands but cannot enter configuration mode. This second command, set user remote full-name, provides a description of the account. This command is optional but is suggested so that the meaning of the account is clear. The third command sets TACACS+ as the primary authentication method.

The TACACS+ database in this recipe has two usernames, mike and sage. When these two users try to log in to the router using their regular login names mike and sage, the login request is authenticated by the TACACS+ server, which sees that their local username (their login account name on the router) is noc. The server returns this information to the router, which logs them in using the noc account and gives them operator privileges.

Users who are authenticated only by a group account will not be able to log in to the router if the authentication server is down. You should always configure some individual user accounts with passwords on the router so someone can always log in to the router (see Recipe 2.5).

See Also

Recipes 2.4, 2.5, 2.10, and 2.13

2.10 Customizing Account Privileges

Problem

You want to create a custom privilege class to define the operations and actions a user can perform while logged in to the router.

Solution

Create a privilege class that allows users to read but not modify the configuration and then let them perform all operational mode commands:

```
[edit system login]
aviva@router1# set class operator-plus-read-config permissions [ admin clear
configure floppy interface network reset routing shell snmp system trace view
maintenance firewall rollback security ]
```

Discussion

When you set up login accounts on the router (see Recipe 2.5), each account must have a privilege level, or class, which defines the operations and actions the user can and cannot perform on the router. Each privilege level consists of a collection of *permission bits* that specifies what a user is allowed to do. Table 2-1 lists all the permission bits.

Table 2-1. Login class permissions

Permission	Bit name
All (superuser)	all (can perform all actions)
Delete data from system log, tracing, and other files	clear (using the clear commands)
All control-level operations (bits ending in -control)	control (can view and change all portions of the configuration)
Configure the router	configure (using the configure and commit commands)
Access removable media	floppy
Halt and reboot the router; start a shell and become superuser	maintenance (using the request system commands, and using the CLI start shell command and the su root command)
Access the network	network (using the ping, ssh, telnet, and traceroute commands)
Start and stop software processes	reset (using the restart command, and configure at [edit system processes])

Table 2-1. Login class permissions (continued)

Permission	Bit name
Return to previous configuration	rollback (using the rollback command)
Start a local shell	shell (using the start shell command)
Display router, routing table, and protocol values	view (using the show commands)
User account information (login classes, user IDs)	admin (read-only, using the show configuration command) admin-control (read, and configure at [edit system login])
Firewall filters	firewall (read-only, using the show configuration command) firewall-control (read, and configure at [edit firewall])
Interfaces, chassis, class of service, forwarding options	interface (read-only, using the show configuration command) interface-control (read, and configure at [edit interfaces], [edit chassis], [edit class-of-service], [edit forwarding-options])
Routing, routing protocols, routing policy	routing (read-only, using the show configuration command) routing-control (read, and configure at [edit routing], [edit routing-options], [edit policy-options])
Passwords and authentication keys	secret (read-only, using the show configuration command) secret-control (read and configure)
IPSec security	security (read-only, using the show configuration command) security-control (read, and configure at [edit security])
SNMP	snmp (read-only, using the show configuration command) snmp-control (read, and configure at [edit snmp])
Router name, RADIUS, TACACS+, NTP, and other system-wide information	system (read-only, using the show configuration command) system-control (read, and configure at [edit system])
Tracing and trace files	trace (read tracing files and configuration using the show configuration command) trace-control (read and configure)

Notice that some bits have two forms, a "simple" form, which gives read-only permission, and a -control form, which gives read and write permission. Except for the all bit (which grants all permissions) and the control bit (which grants read/write permission to the entire configuration), the permission bits are not cumulative, so when you create a custom privilege class, you must list all the bits that apply. Always include the view bit so users can use the show commands in operational mode. If you want users to be able to modify the configuration, include the configure bit.

The JUNOS software has four built-in privilege levels:

superuser or super-user
> Can perform any operations on the router (equivalent to the all permission bit). This is similar to the Unix superuser.

operator
> Can perform all actions in operational mode available with the clear, network, reset, trace, and view permission bits. Cannot display or alter the configuration and cannot shut down or reboot the router.

read-only

> Can perform all actions in operational mode available with the view permission bit to show information about the router or network. Cannot perform any operations that delete or change files or file contents, clear statistics, or change the information on the router.

unauthorized

> Can log in to the router but cannot perform any operations on the router except to log out.

The default privilege levels are not explicitly defined in the configuration, but if you did configure them, the first three would look like this:

```
[edit system login]
aviva@router1# set class superuser permissions all
aviva@router1# set class read-only permissions view
aviva@router1# set class operator permissions [clear network reset trace view]
```

There is no way to explicitly configure the unauthorized level.

The command in this recipe defines a custom privilege class that allows users to perform all operational mode commands and to read but not modify the configuration. The clear, network, reset, trace, and view permission bits allow this class to use all operational mode commands. The configure bit allows this class to issue the configure command to enter configuration. The remaining bits are all the read-only bits that allow this class to use the show command in configuration mode. Users in this class can view all the contents of the configuration file except for passwords and keys (we have omitted the secret bit). Because this class has no -control bits, users can't change the configuration, even though the configure bit allows them to issue the commit command:

```
[edit]
aviva@router1# set
unknown command
```

To find out what privileges you have, use the show cli authorization command. Here is a user with superuser privileges:

```
aviva@router1> show cli authorization
Current user: 'aviva' class 'superuser'
Permissions:
    admin          -- Can view user accounts
    admin-control-- Can modify user accounts
    clear          -- Can clear learned network information
    configure      -- Can enter configuration mode
    control        -- Can modify any configuration
    edit           -- Can edit full files
    field          -- Special for field (debug) support
    floppy         -- Can read and write from the floppy
    interface      -- Can view interface configuration
    interface-control-- Can modify interface configuration
    network        -- Can access the network
```

```
    reset       -- Can reset/restart interfaces and daemons
    routing     -- Can view routing configuration
    routing-control-- Can modify routing configuration
    shell       -- Can start a local shell
    snmp        -- Can view SNMP configuration
    snmp-control-- Can modify SNMP configuration
    system      -- Can view system configuration
    system-control-- Can modify system configuration
    trace       -- Can view trace file settings
    trace-control-- Can modify trace file settings
    view        -- Can view current values and statistics
    maintenance -- Can become the super-user
    firewall    -- Can view firewall configuration
    firewall-control-- Can modify firewall configuration
    secret      -- Can view secret configuration
    secret-control-- Can modify secret configuration
    rollback    -- Can rollback to previous configurations
    security    -- Can view security configuration
    security-control-- Can modify security configuration
    access      -- Can view access configuration
    access-control-- Can modify access configuration
    view-configuration-- Can view all configuration (not including secrets)
Individual command authorization:
    Allow regular expression: none
    Deny regular expression: none
    Allow configuration regular expression: none
    Deny configuration regular expression: none
```

Here is a user with operator privileges:

```
mike@router1> show cli authorization
Current user: 'mike' class 'operator'
Permissions:
    clear       -- Can clear learned network information
    network     -- Can access the network
    reset       -- Can reset/restart interfaces and daemons
    trace       -- Can view trace file settings
    view        -- Can view current values and statistics
Individual command authorization:
    Allow regular expression: none
    Deny regular expression: none
    Allow configuration regular expression: none
    Deny configuration regular expression: none
```

If you do not have permission to perform an operation, you are either "blind" to that operation or you see some type of indication that you cannot perform it. If you try to view the configuration without permission, you see the following warnings:

```
aviva@router1> show configuration
version /* ACCESS-DENIED */;
system { /* ACCESS-DENIED */ };
interfaces { /* ACCESS-DENIED */ };
routing-options { /* ACCESS-DENIED */ };
protocols { /* ACCESS-DENIED */ };
policy-options { /* ACCESS-DENIED */ };
```

If you try to enter a command that you don't have permission to use, the CLI acts as if that command doesn't exist:

```
aviva@router1> clear
unknown command.
```

You should keep these permission levels in mind when trying to use the commands discussed in this book. If you cannot enter the command or do not see it with the CLI help, review your authorization level and check with your system administrator if you need additional permission.

If a user who has a login account but no login class tries to log in, she can get as far as the operational mode prompt but she can't do anything except log out:

```
warning: user "aviva" does not have a valid login class
aviva@router1> exit
```

How do you find out which permissions are associated with each command and statement? On the router, you can use the help reference command to see the permissions for the configuration statements:

```
aviva@router1> help reference interface address
...
Required Privilege Level
interface--To view this statement in the configuration.
interface-control--To add this statement to the configuration.
```

For a configuration that already exists on the router, you can see the permissions for the statements in the configuration. Use this command from operational mode:

```
aviva@router1> show configuration system | display detail
```

and use this command in configuration mode:

```
[edit system]
aviva@router1# show | display detail
```

Both show the same output:

```
##
## system: System parameters
## require: admin system
## domain-name: Domain name for this router
## match (regex): ^[[:alnum:]._-]+$
## require: system
##
domain-name mynetwork.com;
##
## name-server: DNS name servers
## require: system
##
name-server {
    ##
    ## DNS name server address
    ##
```

```
    192.168.15.2;
}
##
## login: Names, login classes, and passwords for users
## require: admin
##
login {
    ##
    ## Login class name
    ## match (regex): ^[[:alnum:]_-]+$
    ##
```

The only way to find out the permissions for operational mode commands is to look in the JUNOS product documentation.

Login classes have one more feature to help with basic router security. You can set a time after which all users in that class are automatically logged out if they have not typed anything at the keyboard. (By default, a user can remain logged in indefinitely.) Here, the users in the class we created will be automatically logged out if the keyboard is idle for five minutes:

```
[edit system login]
aviva@router1# set class operator-plus-read-config permissions idle-timeout 5
```

Warning messages are displayed beforehand:

```
aviva@router1> show system users
 9:56PM  up 18:48, 2 users, load averages: 0.16, 0.09, 0.04
USER     TTY     FROM                          LOGIN@  IDLE WHAT
aviva    p0      server.juniper.net            9:42PM    4 cli

aviva@router1> Warning: session will be closed in 1 minute if there is no acti
vity
Warning: session will be closed in 10 seconds if there is no activity
Idle timeout exceeded: closing session
Connection closed by foreign host.
```

As if all this control weren't enough, you can also control, down to the specific command and configuration hierarchy level, what commands users in a particular login class can and cannot issue and what portions of the configuration they can view and modify. For example, you can create a class that has the standard operator permissions but also can issue the request system support command to collect information to send when reporting a problem with the router:

```
[edit system login]
aviva@router1# set class operator-plus-support permissions [ clear network reset
trace view ]
aviva@router1# set class operator-plus-support allow-commands "request support
information"
```

Or you can take the basic operator class and modify it so users can issue all clear commands except clear system commit (which clears pending configuration commit operations) and clear system reboot (which clears pending router reboots):

```
[edit system login]
```

```
aviva@router1# set class operator-plus-support permissions [ clear network reset
trace view ]
aviva@router1# set class operator-plus-support deny-commands "clear system"
```

Parallel statements allow you to fine-tune what portions of the configuration can be
edited or viewed in configuration mode. This is a way to lock portions of the configuration. The following command does not allow users to modify the protocols portion of the configuration:

```
[edit system login]
aviva@router1# set class all-but-protocols permissions [ all ]
aviva@router1# set class all-but-protocols deny-configuration "protocols"
```

A user in this permission class can edit all portions of the configuration except for
the [edit protocols] section:

```
[edit]
aviva2@router1# edit protocols
                       ^
syntax error, expecting <statement> or <identifier>.
```

2.11 Creating a Privilege Class that Hides Encrypted Passwords

Problem

You need to have all permissions on the router but you don't want to have all of the
encrypted passwords displayed.

Solution

Create a new class that explicitly includes all the permission bits except for control
and secret:

```
[edit system login]
aviva@router1# set class power-user permissions [ admin admin-control clear configure
field floppy interface interface-control network reset routing routing-control shell
snmp snmp-control system system-control trace trace-control view maintenance firewall
firewall-control secret-control rollback security security-control access access-
control view-configuration ]
```

Discussion

Many network operators like to trim shared secrets and other encrypted data out of
their configurations before sharing the configurations with others. The JUNOS software uses the secret permission bit to control viewing access to the passwords and
the secret-control permission bit to control setting them. This recipe still allows
shared secrets and passwords to be set on the router, but the values are not shown,
copied, or saved (using the configuration mode save command) by the user during
normal operations.

Password and secret settings are, of course, still preserved with the commit operation, however, and the full configuration with secret data included is still accessible to the user by virtue of the maintenance permissions.

2.12 Setting Up RADIUS User Authentication

Problem

You use RADIUS for user authentication in your network and you want to set up the router to authenticate against the RADIUS server.

Solution

Configure information about your RADIUS server:

```
[edit system]
aviva@router1# set radius-server 192.168.63.10 secret $1991poppI
aviva@router1# show
radius-server {
    192.168.63.10 secret "$9$90m6AO1EcyKWLhcYgaZji"; ## SECRET-DATA
}
```

Discussion

The Remote Authentication Dial-In User Service (RADIUS) provides a centralized method for authenticating users on the router. RADIUS uses a client/server model. A RADIUS server receives user connection requests, authenticates the user, and returns all configuration information necessary for the client—in this case, the router—to deliver service to the user. All transactions between the server and the client are authenticated by a password called a *shared secret*.

To configure the router as a RADIUS client, you set the IP address of your RADIUS server and the password (secret) that the router should use to access the server. The secret on the router and the RADIUS server must be the same. After you type the secret, the CLI never displays it but shows it in a pseudoencrypted format. The show output is a simple obfuscation to prevent someone from reading the password over your shoulder.

By default, the JUNOS software sends authentication requests to UDP port 1812 on the RADIUS server, as defined in RFC 2865. Also by default, the router waits three seconds to receive a response from the RADIUS server and, if it doesn't hear from the server, tries three more times to connect. You can modify these values if necessary. Here, we allow just 1 retry and wait 10 seconds to receive a response from the server:

```
[edit system]
aviva@router1# set radius-server 192.168.63.10 retry 1
aviva@router1# set radius-server 192.168.63.10 timeout 10
```

If you use a centralized server, it represents a single point of failure if it should go down. To provide redundancy, you can configure several servers:

```
[edit system]
aviva@router1# set radius-server 192.168.0.23 secret 2lip123
aviva@router1# set radius-server 10.0.16.1 secret 883roZe
```

When you configure more than one server, initially the primary server is the one you configured first. After that, the primary server is the one that last responded. If the router cannot reach this server, it tries the remaining ones in the order configured. Use the show command to see the order in which the router tries the servers:

```
[edit system]
aviva@router1# show
radius-server {
    192.168.63.10 secret "$9$vsOW7-oJGiqm24fzF3AtKvWL7V"; ## SECRET-DATA
    10.0.16.1 secret "$9$4DojHQFnCpoTzIcrKXxbs2"; ## SECRET-DATA
    192.168.0.23 secret "$9$7edYgq.5QF/iktuB1hcwY2"; ## SECRET-DATA
}
```

Notice that this example specifies different secrets for each server to improve network security. If you suspect that the password of the primary server has been compromised, you can switch to one of the secondary servers.

The JUNOS software defines vendor-specific RADIUS attributes, which are included in packets sent to the RADIUS server. You can configure your server to interpret the Juniper-specific information (see Table 2-2). The Juniper Networks vendor ID is 2636. All the Juniper attributes are used only in RADIUS Access-Accept packets.

Table 2-2. Juniper-specific RADIUS attributes

Attribute name	Description	Type field value	Length field value	String
Juniper-Local-User-Name	Name of user template.	1	3 or more	One or more ASCII octets
Juniper-Allow-Commands	Allows user to run operational mode commands in addition to those authorized by the user's login class. Same action as the allow-command statement.	2	3 or more	One or more ASCII octets written as an extended regular expression
Juniper-Deny-Commands	Disallows user to run operational mode commands authorized by the user's login class. Same action as the deny-command statement.	3	3 or more	One or more ASCII octets written as an extended regular expression
Juniper-Allow-Configuration	Allows the user to modify portions of the configuration in addition to those authorized by the user's login class. Same action as the allow-statement statement.	4	3 or more	One or more ASCII octets written as an extended regular expression
Juniper-Deny-Configuration	Disallows user to modify portions of the configuration in addition to those authorized by the user's login class. Same action as the deny-statement statement.	5	3 or more	One or more ASCII octets written as an extended regular expression

See Also

RFC 2865, *Remote Authentication Dial In User Service (RADIUS)*

2.13 Setting Up TACACS+ User Authentication

Problem

You want to use a TACACS+ server to authenticate people who log in to the router.

Solution

Configure information about your TACACS+ server:

```
[edit system]
aviva@router1# set tacacs-server 192.168.62.10 secret $1991poppI
aviva@router1# show
tacacs-server {
    192.168.62.10 secret "$9$90m6A01EcyKWLhcYgaZji"; ## SECRET-DATA
}
```

Discussion

TACACS+ is a newer version of the older TACACS authentication software. Like RADIUS, TACACS+ uses a client/server model, with the router being the client. All transactions between the server and the client are authenticated by a shared secret.

The JUNOS configuration for TACACS+ is almost identical to that for RADIUS. You set the IP address of your TACACS+ server and the password (secret) that the router should use to access the server. The secrets on the router and the server must match. For redundancy, you can configure multiple servers.

There are also JUNOS-specific TACACS+ attributes that you can configure on the TACACS+ server. These attributes are named local-user-name, allow-commands, deny-commands, allow-configuration, and deny-configuration and have the same description, length, and string as the parallel RADIUS attributes (see Table 2-2).

2.14 Restricting Inbound SSH and Telnet Access

Problem

You want to allow SSH and Telnet access to the router but you want to restrict the access to make the router more secure.

Solution

Add a term to an existing firewall filter that restricts SSH and Telnet access:

```
[edit firewall filter protect-RE]
```

```
aviva@RouterF# set term ssh-telnet from source-address 10.0.8.0/24
aviva@routerF# set term ssh-telnet from destination-port [ ssh telnet ]
aviva@RouterF# set then accept
```

Also include a term at the end of the filter to reject access attempts from any other subnets:

```
[edit firewall filter protect-RE]
aviva@RouterF# set term allow-nothing-else then count reject-counter
aviva@RouterF# set term allow-nothing-else then log
aviva@RouterF# set term allow-nothing-else then syslog
aviva@RouterF# set term allow-nothing-else then reject
```

For the filter to affect incoming traffic, apply it to the desired interfaces:

```
[edit interfaces]
aviva@RouterF# set lo0 unit 0 family inet filter input protect-RE
```

Discussion

SSH and Telnet are two very common ways to access the router. However, SSH brute-force attempts to guess passwords are a very common way to try to compromise routers, and Telnet connections are not very secure. To protect the router, you should restrict the systems from which people can use SSH and Telnet to the router. Even though Telnet is not a secure access method, you may want to allow it because your network management tools use Telnet to access routers, and it is more of a hassle to change the access method than to just allow restricted access. As much as possible, you should lock down access to all management services on the routers and on any other systems in your network to maintain tight security. You can never be sure that people are not using passwords that are easy to guess, and Telnet sends passwords over the network in clear text, so they could easily be sniffed. Restricting inbound access to the router also protects against potentially unknown vulnerabilities with SSH and Telnet.

You restrict Telnet access using a firewall filter. This recipe shows a single term in a firewall filter that acts on all TCP traffic whose destination port is the Telnet port (port 23), and it accepts Telnet connections only from the 10.0.0.0/8 subnet and rejects all other connection attempts. Each interface can have one inbound firewall filter, so you include the term shown in this recipe in the complete firewall filter that you apply on an incoming interface.

It's important to note that if you use the term in the recipe as the only filter on an interface, it will block all traffic to the Routing Engine except for Telnet from subnet 10.0.0.0/8. This means that SNMP, OSPF, IS-IS, PIM, and BGP will all be blocked. Make sure you include this term as part of a longer firewall filter.

You have to decide where in the filter to place the term. Because the terms in the firewall filter are evaluated in the order in which they appear, the placement affects the efficiency of the filter. Generally, terms for operations that need to be performed quickly, such as BGP peering and IGP and DNS traffic, are at the beginning of the filter. For operations that are less time-critical, including processing Telnet connections, place the term toward the end of the filter.

Then apply the filter to the desired interfaces. Here, we apply the filter to the lo0 interface because we want it to apply to all traffic destined to the router's management addresses, even traffic that is coming to the address of one of the network (PIC) interfaces.

The term in this recipe is just one of several terms in a single firewall filter. As a general point, you rarely just reject a firewall term without also either logging, syslogging, or running a counter on the rejections (which gives you data that you can graph). Tracking the rejections is useful for showing abuse of your router, attacks on the router, or even misconfigurations. For example, if you forget about an automated process that uses Telnet to read configuration information on your router that comes from 192.168.0.0/16 and you only permit 10.0.0.0/8, then the then syslog action (and appropriate syslog configuration statements) can be very handy for resolving issues.

See Also

Recipes 9.8, 9.11, 9.12, and 9.13

2.15 Setting the Source Address for Telnet Connections

Problem

You want to force Telnet to use a specific IP address when connecting from the router to another system.

Solution

Include the source address in the Telnet command:

```
aviva@RouterA> telnet source 172.19.121.15 server1
Trying 172.19.121.246...
Connected to server1.mycompany.com.
Escape character is '^]'.
server1 (ttyp0)
login:
```

Discussion

By default, the source address included in locally generated Telnet and other TCP/IP packets is the address of the interface on which the Telnet request is sent. This means the source address may change from connection to connection. If multiple equal-cost next hops are present for a destination, the lo0 loopback interface address is used as the source address. If you configure the system default-address-selection statement in the configuration, which uses the lo0 interface address as the router's system address, this address is used as the source for most Telnet connections (see Recipe 7.4).

The result of this behavior is that the default Telnet source address is not always the same and not always deterministic. If the source address matters when using Telnet to access another system, include it in the telnet command. One instance when you should do so is when filtering the source address on incoming connections, which may block packets coming to the default source address. Another instance is when you use Telnet as a generic way to check and troubleshoot other TCP ports (such as connecting to a server on port 25 to see if it is listening for SNMP mail connections). The source address that you specify must be an address that's configured on the router.

See Also

Recipes 7.4 and 7.12

2.16 Creating a Login Banner

Problem

You want to display a banner during login that indicates that the router is for authorized users only.

Solution

You define a login banner:

```
[edit system login]
aviva@router1# set message "\n\
n==============================================================\n\nAccess to this device
is limited to authorized users only.\n\n    WARNING: All unauthorized access is
prohibited.\n\n==================================================
=========\n\n"
```

Discussion

A login banner is displayed each time anyone logs in to the router, before the login prompt:

```
aviva-server% telnet router1
===========================================================
Access to this device is limited to authorized users only.
    WARNING: All unauthorized access is prohibited.
===========================================================
router1 (ttyp0)
login:
```

It may seem rather trivial to set a login banner, and you may wonder what this has to do with router security because it doesn't do anything to restrict access to the router. Although this is true, having a login banner is good practice for legally protect your router. From a legal point of view, you want to warn unauthorized users that they are not permitted to use the router and you want to do so with a strongly worded message, as we've shown here. While you might think that you want to welcome users to the router, you should not use the word "welcome" or any similar words in the login banner.

You can also have a login message that is displayed after users log in to the router:

```
[edit system]
aviva@router1# set announcement "Reminder: maintenance window schedule at 0200 UTC"
```

These messages are a way to remind authorized users of network or router issues:

```
aviva-server1% telnet router1
router1 (ttyp0)
login: aviva
password: ********
--- JUNOS 7.4R1.7 built by builder on 2005-10-23 02:03:58 UTC
Reminder: maintenance window schedule at 0200 UTC
aviva@router1>
```

2.17   Finding Out Who Is Logged In to the Router

Problem

You are logged in to the router and you want to see who else is logged in.

Solution

Use the show system users command to see who is logged in to the router:

```
aviva@router1> show system users
 9:10PM  up 11 hrs, 2 users, load averages: 0.00, 0.00, 0.00
 USER     TTY     FROM                              LOGIN@  IDLE WHAT
 mike     p0      server1.juniper.net               9:09PM     - -tcsh (csh)
 aviva    p1      server1.juniper.net               8:42PM     - cli
```

Discussion

More than one person can log in to the router at one time. Each person can perform various operations, from viewing router statistics to rebooting the router and changing the router's configuration. Once you access the router, you might also want to see who else is working on the router. You display who is logged in using the show system users command, which is basically the same as the Unix w command. This command shows the username, the terminal number through which they are connected, the server they have logged in from, when they logged in, how long they have been idle, and what they are doing. The output in this recipe shows that the user mike is working in the Unix shell on the router and the user aviva is working in the CLI.

As you are logging in to the router, if others are logged in, the CLI does not display any messages. However, when you enter configuration mode, the CLI indicates that another user is also configuring the router:

```
aviva@router1> configure
Entering configuration mode
Users currently editing the configuration:
  mike terminal p2 (pid 5465) on since 2005-04-06 21:30:42 UTC
      [edit class-of-service scheduler-maps]
The configuration has been changed but not committed
```

Here, you see that the user mike is also working in configuration mode and has made changes to the class-of-service portion of the configuration.

See Also

Recipe 2.19

2.18   Logging Out of the Router

Problem

You are done using the router and want to log out so that no one can sit down at your terminal and access the router.

Solution

Log out of the router:

```
aviva@router1> exit
[server1.mycompany.com] aviva@server%
```

Discussion

One of the simplest and most obvious ways to protect the security of the router is to log out when you have no reason to be logged in or when you have to step away from your terminal for a few minutes. You must be in operational mode to log out. If you are in configuration mode, exit from it first:

```
[edit]
aviva@router1# exit
aviva@router1> exit
aviva@server1%
```

When you are not at the top level of configuration mode, you can go there before exiting:

```
[edit snmp v3 vacm]
aviva@router1# top
[edit]
```

```
aviva@router1# exit
aviva@router1> exit
aviva@server1%
```

You can also exit directly from a lower level in the hierarchy:

```
[edit snmp v3 vacm]
aviva@router1# exit configuration-mode
aviva@router1> exit
aviva@server1%
```

By default, a user can remain logged in to the router for an unlimited amount of time when your login session is idle. You can limit the time by setting an idle timeout value for each login privilege class (see Recipe 2.10).

2.19   Forcibly Logging a User Out

Problem

Someone is logged in to the router who shouldn't be and you need to log them out.

Solution

Forcibly log the user out:

```
aviva@router1> request system logout user mike
```

Discussion

There are a number of situations when someone is logged in to the router who shouldn't be. A user may have walked away from the terminal or may be in configuration mode when you must change the configuration to deal with a problem situation.

Use the show system users command to list who is logged in to the router:

```
aviva@router1> show system users
 5:20AM  up 81 days,  6:41, 1 user, load averages: 0.00, 0.00, 0.00
 USER    TTY     FROM                           LOGIN@  IDLE WHAT
 mike    p0      172.10.28.108                  5:20AM  4:07 -cli (cli)
 aviva   p1      172.10.28.107                  2:06AM    - -cli (cli)
```

If another user is in configuration mode, you see his username in the message displayed when you enter configuration mode.

If you are logged in as root or have root privileges, you can forcibly log a user out of the router:

```
aviva@router1> request system logout user mike
```

Mike would be logged out:

```
mike@router1> Connection closed by foreign host.
[server1.mycompany.com] mike@server%
```

You can send the user a message beforehand using a command similar to the Unix write utility:

```
aviva@router1> request message user mike message "log out immediately"
```

You can send the message to a particular user, as we've done here, or to all logged-in users (similar to the Unix wall utility):

```
aviva@router1> request message all message "log out immediately"
```

You can also specify the terminal (TTY) to forcibly log out a user:

```
aviva@router1> request system logout terminal p0
```

CHAPTER 3

IPSec

3.0   Introduction

IP Security (IPSec) is a protocol suite developed in the late 1990s that provides security services for Layer 3 IP datagrams, which otherwise have no inherent security. It is defined in RFCs 2401 through 2412. IPSec is optional for IPv4 and mandatory for IPv6. Because it operates at Layer 3, IPSec provides security for higher-level traffic, including TCP and UDP.

The IPSec suite defines the security protocols, the algorithms used to provide security, and the cryptographic keys required to provide the services.

Traffic protection is provided by two security protocols, Authentication Header (AH) and Encapsulation Security Payload (ESP). AH provides connectionless integrity and data origin authentication for IP packets, authenticating the complete packet, including the IP header, except for IP header fields that change in transit. It also provides protection against replay attacks, a type of network attack in which valid data is maliciously transmitted repeatedly. ESP offers encryption to provide data confidentiality, and it authenticates the packet payload and the ESP header itself, but not the outer IP header. In the JUNOS software, you can configure either AH or ESP, or a combination of the two.

IPSec authentication algorithms use a *shared key* to verify the identity of the sending IPSec device. The protocol suite defines two algorithms, MD5 and SHA1. MD5 uses a one-way hash function to convert messages to a 128-bit digest. The calculated digest is compared with one that has been decrypted with a shared key, and if the two match, the IPSec device is authenticated. SHA1 is a stronger algorithm, producing a 160-bit digest. The JUNOS software implements the HMAC version of both these algorithms, and they are available for the AH and ESP protocols and for the Internet Key Exchange (IKE) protocol, which establishes and maintains SAs and exchanges the authentication and encryption keys between IPSec devices.

Encryption, which is the encoding of packet data, is also done with algorithms that create and verify shared keys. The JUNOS software implements DES and Triple-DES for encryption, both with cipher block chaining (CBC). DES-CBC uses a 64-bit key for encryption (56 bits for encryption and 8 bits for error checking), and the stronger 3DES-CBC uses three times the number of bits (168 bits) for encryption.

To identify the traffic to protect, IPSec creates *security associations* (SAs) to negotiate the desired security services. Each SA, which is identified by a *security parameter index* (SPI), defines preferences for authentication, encryption, and security protocol. SAs can be either unidirectional or bidirectional and are created either manually or dynamically. For manual SAs, you configure matching preset shared keys for authentication and encryption, security protocols, and fixed SPI values on both ends of the IPSec connection. Dynamic SAs are negotiated by IKE, but you can configure recommended suggestions for all IPSec parameters. As a result of the negotiation with the peer, an SA pair is set up, one inbound and one outbound. The inbound half of the SA pair de-encrypts and authenticates the incoming traffic from the IPSec peer, and the outbound half encrypts and authenticates the outbound traffic going to the peer.

IPSec SAs operate in one of two modes, tunnel mode or transport mode. A tunnel mode SA is essentially an IP tunnel between two security gateways, which are routers or other devices protecting the networks behind them. One common way to use tunnel mode is to send secure traffic between two sites on an intranet (that is, within a corporate network). The router at each end of the tunnel acts as a security gateway. Any data transferred between the two sites is protected as it traverses the tunnel between the security gateways. Transport mode provides security between two hosts, protecting traffic (such as OSPF and BGP traffic) that is destined for the router itself.

For a tunnel mode SA, an IP header specifies the IPsec processing destination and an inner IP header specifies the packet's ultimate destination. The security protocol header is placed between the outer and inner headers. If the protocol is AH, portions of the outer IP header and the entire tunneled IP packet (the inner IP header and the higher-layer protocols) are protected. With ESP, only the tunneled packet is protected, not the outer header.

To use IPSec with M-series and T-series routers, the router must have either an ES PIC or an Adaptive Services (AS) PIC. The configuration for these two PICs differs slightly. The J-series routers also run IPSec but require no additional hardware because they have built-in AS functionality. In this chapter, we show how to configure IPSec with both PICs.

3.1   Configuring IPSec

Problem

You need a secure method of sending information between sites.

Solution

Start by defining the IPSec SA between your two intranet sites. On each security router, define identical SAs:

```
[edit security ipsec]
aviva@router1# edit security-association site1-site2
[edit security ipsec security-association site1-site2]
aviva@router1# set description "SA from site1 to site2"
aviva@router1# set mode tunnel
aviva@router1# set manual direction bidirectional protocol bundle
aviva@router1# set manual direction bidirectional spi 400
aviva@router1# set manual direction bidirectional auxiliary-spi 400
aviva@router1# set manual direction bidirectional authentication algorithm hmac-sha1-
96
aviva@router1# set manual direction bidirectional authentication key ascii-text
$1991poPPi
aviva@router1# set manual direction bidirectional encryption algorithm des-cbc
aviva@router1# set manual direction bidirectional encryption key ascii-text
$1991poPPi
```

Configuring a firewall filter accepts all traffic returning from the remote site:

```
[edit firewall filter traffic-out-of-ipsec-tunnel]
aviva@router1# set term out-of-ipsec-tunnel from source-address 10.0.97.0/24
aviva@router1# set term out-of-ipsec-tunnel from destination-address 10.0.12.0/24
aviva@router1# set term out-of-ipsec-tunnel then accept
```

Finally, apply the second filter on the ES interface that goes from the local security gateway to the remote security gateway:

```
[edit interfaces es-3/0/0]
aviva@router1# set unit 0 tunnel source 10.0.12.33
aviva@router1# set unit 0 tunnel destination 10.0.97.62
aviva@router1# set unit 0 family inet ipsec-sa site1-site2
aviva@router1# set unit 0 family inet filter input traffic-out-of-ipsec-tunnel
```

Discussion

This recipe shows how to set up IPSec for M-series and T-series routers that have ES PICs. The setup process is fairly involved. There are three basic components to the configuration: defining the SA and the tunnel to carry the secured traffic, creating firewall filters to place traffic going from one site to the other into the tunnel, and configuring the interfaces to apply the filters and create the tunnel on the ES PIC. This recipe shows how to set up a manual SA, in which you specify all SA parameters in the configuration. While setting up SAs manually can be manageable in small networks, it does not scale well. As the network size increases, having IPSec dynamically configure SAs is a better option (see Recipe 3.2).

The SA is bidirectional, so the same encryption and authentication keys are used on incoming and outgoing traffic through the IPSec tunnel. To use different keys in each direction, use the set direction inbound and set direction outbound commands.

To start, define the SA. Because you have two routers acting as the security gateways between your two sites, you use tunnel mode. For the other SA parameters, this example chooses to use both the AH and ESP protocols (specified with the protocol bundle statement), HMAC-SHA1-96 authentication, DES-CBC encryption, and a SPI value of 400. The auxiliary SPI is needed because we are using both AH and ESP. Both security gateway routers must have the same SA configuration.

Next, you create a firewall filter to accept traffic returning from the remote site and you apply it to the ES interface. You need to set up similar firewall filters on the remote security gateway router.

Finally, you configure the router interfaces. On the ES interface facing the remote security gateway router, configure the tunnel on the logical unit, and for the IPv4 protocol family, associate the SA and apply the traffic-out-of-ipsec-tunnel filter. Set up the remote router in a similar fashion.

Use the following command to verify that the SA is active:

```
aviva@router1> show ipsec security-associations detail
Security association: site1-site2, Interface family: Up

  Local gateway: 10.0.12.33, Remote gateway: 10.0.97.62
  Local identity: ipv4_subnet(any:0,[0..7]=0.0.0.0/0)
  Remote identity: ipv4_subnet(any:0,[0..7]=0.0.0.0/0)

    Direction: inbound, SPI: 400, AUX-SPI: 400
    Mode: tunnel, Type: manual, State: Installed
    Protocol: BUNDLE, Authentication: hmac-sha1-96, Encryption: des-cbc
    Anti-replay service: Disabled

    Direction: outbound, SPI: 400, AUX-SPI: 400
    Mode: tunnel, Type: manual, State: Installed
    Protocol: BUNDLE, Authentication: hmac-sha1-96, Encryption: des-cbc
    Anti-replay service: Disabled
```

The first line shows that the SA is active (Up), and you see that the inbound and outbound SAs are installed. This command also shows the configured SA parameters.

You can check the status of the IPSec tunnel with the ping and traceroute commands. You should be able to ping a system at the remote site:

```
aviva@router1> ping 10.0.97.2
PING 10.0.97.2 (10.0.97.2): 56 data bytes
64 bytes from 10.0.97.2: icmp_seq=0 ttl=253 time=0.939 ms
64 bytes from 10.0.97.2: icmp_seq=1 ttl=253 time=0.886 ms
```

```
64 bytes from 10.0.97.2: icmp_seq=2 ttl=253 time=0.826 ms
^C
--- 10.0.97.2 ping statistics ---
3 packets transmitted, 3 packets received, 0% packet loss
round-trip min/avg/max/stddev = 0.826/0.884/0.939/0.046 ms
```

Use the traceroute command to verify that the traffic travels over the tunnel:

```
aviva@router1> traceroute 10.0.97.2
traceroute to 10.0.97.2 (10.0.97.2), 30 hops max, 40 byte packets
 1  10.0.12.2 (10.0.12.2)  0.655 ms  0.549 ms  0.508 ms
 2  10.0.0.3 (10.0.0.3)  0.833 ms  0.786 ms  0.757 ms
 3  10.0.97.2 (10.0.97.2)  0.808 ms  0.741 ms  0.716 ms
```

In the second line of the traceroute output, you don't see 10.0.97.62, which is the IP address of the remote side of the tunnel, but rather 10.0.0.3, which is the loopback address of the remote security gateway router.

The configuration is a bit complex, so it's worth looking at the structure of the relevant portions of the configuration file rather than all the commands that you use to configure it. Some comments have been added.

```
[edit security ipsec]
security-association site1-site2 { # <-- define the SA
     description "tunnel from site1 to site2";
     mode tunnel; # <-- use tunnel mode
     manual { # <-- negotiate SA parameters up front
          direction bidirectional {
               protocol bundle;
               spi 400;
               auxiliary-spi 400;
               authentication {
                    algorithm hmac-sha1-96;
                    key ascii-text "$9$..."; ## SECRET-DATA
               }
               encryption {
                    algorithm des-cbc;
                    key ascii-text "$9$b..."; ## SECRET-DATA
               }
          }
     }
}

[edit firewall]
filter traffic-out-of-ipsec-tunnel { # <-- receive remote traffic
     term out-of-ipsec-tunnel {
          from {
               source-address { # <-- remote subnet
                    10.0.97.0/24;
               }
               destination-address { # <-- local subnet
                    10.0.12.0/24;
               }
          then accept;
```

```
        }
    }

[edit interfaces]
es-3/0/0 { # <-- interface facing remote security gateway router
    unit 0 {
        tunnel {
            source 10.0.12.33;
            destination 10.0.97.62;
        }
        family inet {
            ipsec-sa site1-site2;
            filter {
                input traffic-out-of-ipsec-tunnel;
            }
        }
    }
}
```

3.2   Configuring IPSec Dynamic SAs

Problem

You want IPSec to automatically generate keys and negotiate the SA parameters.

Solution

Use dynamic IPSec to automatically generate keys and negotiate SAs. First, create an
IKE SA proposal and policy:

```
[edit security ike proposal site1-site2-ike-proposal]
aviva@router1# set authentication-method pre-shared-keys
aviva@router1# set dh-group group1
aviva@router1# set authentication-algorithm sha1
aviva@router1# set encryption-algorithm 3des-cbc
aviva@router1# up
[edit security ike]
aviva@router1# edit policy 10.0.97.62
[edit security ike policy 10.0.97.62]
aviva@router1# set proposals site1-site2-ike-proposal
aviva@router1# set pre-shared-key ascii-text $1991poPPix
```

Next, create an IPSec SA negotiation proposal and policy:

```
[edit security ipsec proposal site1-site2-ipsec-proposal]
aviva@router1# set protocol bundle
aviva@router1# set authentication-algorithm hmac-sha1-96
aviva@router1# set encryption-algorithm 3des-cbc
aviva@router1# up
[edit security ipsec]
aviva@router1# edit policy site1-site2-ipsec-policy
[edit security ipsec policy site1-site2-ipsec-policy]
aviva@router1# set perfect-forward-secrecy keys group1
aviva@router1# set proposals site1-site2-ipsec-proposal
```

Then, associate the policy with the dynamic SA:

```
[edit security ipsec]
aviva@router1# set security-association site1-site2-dynamic mode tunnel
aviva@router1# set security-association site1-site2-dynamic dynamic replay-window-
size 64
aviva@router1# set security-association site1-site2-dynamic ipsec-policy site1-site2-
policy
```

Configure two firewall filters. These are the same as those for the manual SA. The first directs all traffic from the local site into the IPSec tunnel:

```
[edit firewall filter traffic-into-ipsec-tunnel]
aviva@router1# set term into-ipsec-tunnel from source-address 10.0.12.0/24
aviva@router1# set term into-ipsec-tunnel from destination-address 10.0.97.0/24
aviva@router1# set term into-ipsec-tunnel then count ipsec-tunnel
aviva@router1# set term into-ipsec-tunnel then ipsec-sa site1-site2
aviva@router1# set term last-term then accept
```

The second firewall filter accepts all traffic returning from the remote site:

```
[edit firewall filter traffic-out-of-ipsec-tunnel]
aviva@router1# set term out-of-ipsec-tunnel from source-address 10.0.97.0/24
aviva@router1# set term out-of-ipsec-tunnel from destination-address 10.0.12.0/24
aviva@router1# set term out-of-ipsec-tunnel then accept
```

Finally, apply the firewall filters as we did with the manual SA. Apply the first one, directing traffic into the tunnel, on the interface that comes from the local site into the security gateway:

```
[edit interfaces fe-0/0/0]
aviva@router1# set unit 0 family inet address 10.0.12.2/24
aviva@router1# set unit 0 family inet filter input traffic-into-ipsec-tunnel
```

Apply the second filter on the ES interface that goes from the local security gateway to the remote security gateway:

```
[edit interfaces es-3/0/0]
aviva@router1# set unit 0 tunnel source 10.0.12.33
aviva@router1# set unit 0 tunnel destination 10.0.97.62
aviva@router1# set unit 0 family inet ipsec-sa site1-site2-dynamic
aviva@router1# set unit 0 family inet filter input traffic-out-of-ipsec-tunnel
```

Configure the router at the remote site in the same way, substituting the correct address and interface names.

Discussion

In the IPSec manual SA setup, you predefine all SA parameters. It is generally a bother to manually coordinate keys with the administrator in charge of the remote site, so it is more common and practical to use dynamic SAs so that key negotiation and authentication are automated. For a dynamic SA, you define your preferences and IPSec negotiates the SA parameters, using IKE to establish and exchange keys. So you still define an IPSec SA and associate the SA with the ES interface. You also have to set up an IKE SA and a firewall filter to direct traffic into the tunnel. Again, this recipe is for M-series and T-series routers with ES PICs.

The IKE negotiation happens in two phases, Phase 1 and Phase 2. In Phase 1, the IKE SA is negotiated based on the IKE policy and IKE proposal, and the result is the creation of an IKE SA. This negotiated IKE SA is then used to secure the Phase 2 exchange, which uses the IPSec proposal and IPSec policy to create an IPSec SA pair (one SA for inbound and a second for outbound traffic). The IKE policy is used for the negotiation during Phase 1, and IPSec policy is used for the negotiation in Phase 2. This means that the IKE and IPSec proposals can use different algorithms.

For IKE, this recipe defines a negotiation proposal, here called site1-site2-ike-proposal, that creates an IKE SA based on the stated authentication and encryption algorithms. The set dh-group command configures this proposal to use 768-bit Diffie-Hellman prime modulus group when establishing the IKE session keys. By default, the IKE SA is valid for 3,600 seconds (1 hour). When it expires, a new one is negotiated. The IKE SA references an IKE policy (here, policy 10.0.97.62) that defines the preshared key to use for negotiation. The policy is identified by the IP address of the security gateway at the remote end of the tunnel, which is the tunnel destination addresses configured on ES interface es-3/0/0.

For IPSec, also define a proposal (here, site1-site2-ipsec-proposal) and a policy (site1-site2-ipsec-policy). The proposal uses the same parameters as in the manual SA in Recipe 3.1. By default, the negotiated SA is valid for 28,800 seconds (8 hours). When it expires, a new one is negotiated. On the ES PIC, anti-replay is disabled by default. (On the AS PIC, it is enabled by default with a default window size of 64 bits.) This recipe enables anti-replay with a window size of 64 bits.

The lifetime of both the IKE and IPSec proposals is configurable by using the set lifetime-seconds command. Here, you change the IKE proposal lifetime to 2 hours and the IPSec proposal lifetime to 10 hours:

```
[edit security ike]
aviva@router1# set proposal site1-site2-ike-proposal lifetime-seconds 7200
[edit security ipsec]
aviva@router1# set proposal site1-site2-ipsec-proposal lifetime-seconds 36000
```

The IPSec policy, site1-site2-ipsec-policy, defines which proposals IKE should consider and in which order (if you configure more than one). This recipe also enables perfect forward secrecy (PFS) security for keys, which means that the shared key material can be used to drive the IPSec SA keys only once. With PFS, if an IKE SA is present (Phase 1 of the negotiation), then during the IPSec SA negotiation (Phase 2 of the negotiation), a Diffie-Hellman exchange is required for every rekeying to generate the shared key material. Without PFS, a Diffie-Hellman exchange is done only during the initial keying but is not done again during the rekeying operation. PFS is considered to be more secure because it gets fresh keying material every time an IPsec SA is renegotiated.

As the last step, associate the dynamic SA with the tunnel on the ES interface.

You create firewall filters to direct traffic into and out of the tunnel and you have to configure the interface on the security gateway router that faces the local site. These configurations are the same as those shown in Recipe 3.1.

Configure the security gateway router at the remote site in the same way, using the appropriate address and interface names.

Verification of the dynamic IPSec SA is similar to that for the manual IPSec SA. You can use ping and traceroute to check the reachability of a host at the remote site and can look at the IPSec SA to verify that it is active and to see the SA parameters:

```
aviva@router1> show ipsec security-associations detail
Security association: site1-site2-dynamic, Interface family: Up

  Local gateway: 10.0.12.33, Remote gateway: 10.0.97.62
  Local identity: ipv4_subnet(any:0,[0..7]=10.1.12.0/24)
  Remote identity: ipv4_subnet(any:0,[0..7]=10.1.56.0/24)

    Direction: inbound, SPI: 2133029543, AUX-SPI: 0
    Mode: tunnel, Type: dynamic, State: Installed
    Protocol: BUNDLE, Authentication: hmac-sha1-96, Encryption: des-cbc
    Soft lifetime: Expires in 26212 seconds
    Hard lifetime: Expires in 26347 seconds
    Anti-replay service: Enabled

    Direction: outbound, SPI: 1759450863, AUX-SPI: 0
    Mode: tunnel, Type: dynamic, State: Installed
    Protocol: BUNDLE, Authentication: hmac-sha1-96, Encryption: des-cbc
    Soft lifetime: Expires in 26212 seconds
    Hard lifetime: Expires in 26347 seconds
    Anti-replay service: Enabled
```

The last thing to check is the IKE SA:

```
aviva@router1> show ike security-associations detail
IKE peer 10.0.97.62
  Role: Initiator, State: Matured
  Initiator cookie: b5dbdfe2f9000000, Responder cookie: a24c868410000041
  Exchange type: Main, Authentication method: Pre-shared-keys
  Local: 10.0.12.33:500, Remote: 10.0.97.62:500
  Lifetime: Expires in 401 seconds
  Algorithms:
   Authentication        : sha1
   Encryption            : des-cbc
   Pseudo random function: hmac-sha1
  Traffic statistics:
   Input  bytes  :                  1736
   Output bytes  :                  2652
   Input  packets:                     9
   Output packets:                    15
  Flags: Caller notification sent
  IPSec security associations: 3 created, 0 deleted
  Phase 2 negotiations in progress: 0
```

Here's what the relevant portions of the dynamic SA configuration look like, with comments added:

```
[edit security ike]
proposal site1-site2-ike-proposal { # <-- IKE proposal
    authentication-method pre-shared-keys;
    dh-group group1;
    authentication-algorithm sha1;
    encryption-algorithm 3des-cbc;
}
policy 10.0.97.62 { # <-- IKE policy to peer security gateway router
    proposals site1-site2-ike-proposal; # <-- pointer to IKE proposal
    pre-shared-key ascii-text "$9$6..."; ## SECRET-DATA
}

[edit security ipsec]
proposal site1-site2-ipsec-proposal { # <-- IPSec proposal
    protocol bundle;
    authentication-algorithm hmac-sha1-96;
    encryption-algorithm 3des-cbc;
}
policy site1-site2-ipsec-policy { # <-- IPSec policy
    perfect-forward-secrecy {
        keys group1;
    }
    proposals site1-site2-ipsec-proposal; # <-- pointer to IPSec proposal
}
security-association site1-site2-dynamic { # <-- dynamic IPSec SA
    mode tunnel;
    dynamic {
        replay-window-size 64;
        ipsec-policy site1-site2-ipsec-policy;
    }
}

[edit interfaces]
fe-0/0/0 { # <-- interface facing local site
    unit 0 {
        family inet {
            filter {
                input traffic-into-ipsec-tunnel;
            }
            address 10.0.12.2/24;
        }
    }
}
es-3/0/0 { # <-- interface facing remote security gateway router
    unit 0 {
        tunnel {
            source 10.0.12.33;
            destination 10.0.97.62;
        }
        family inet { # <-- associate IPSec SA with interface
            ipsec-sa site1-site2-dynamic;
```

```
        filter {
            input traffic-out-of-ipsec-tunnel;
        }
    }
}
}
```

3.3   Creating IPSec Dynamic SAs on J-Series Routers or Routers with AS PICs

Problem

You want to configure basic IPSec on an M-series or T-series router that has an AS PIC, or on a J-series router, which has built-in software emulation of the AS PIC functionality.

Solution

Use dynamic IPSec to automatically generate keys and negotiate SAs. First, create an IKE policy:

```
[edit services ipsec-vpn]
aviva@RouterA# set ike policy ike-dynamic-policy pre-shared-key ascii-text $1991poPPi
```

Then, create a rule for a bidirectional dynamic IKE SA that references the IKE policy:

```
[edit services ipsec-vpn rule ike-rule]
aviva@RouterA# set term ike then remote-gateway 10.0.15.2
aviva@RouterA# set term ike then dynamic ike-policy ike-dynamic-policy
aviva@RouterA# set match-direction input
```

To configure IPSec, define a service set:

```
[edit services service-set ipsec-dynamic]
aviva@RouterA# set ipsec-vpn-rules ike-rule
aviva@RouterA# set ipsec-vpn-options local-gateway 10.1.15.1
aviva@RouterA# set next-hop-service inside-service-interface sp-1/2/0.1
aviva@RouterA# set next-hop-service outside-service-interface sp-1/2/0.2
```

Next, configure the router interfaces. First, set up the service interfaces to use for IPSec:

```
[edit interfaces]
aviva@RouterA# set sp-1/2/0 unit 0 family inet
aviva@RouterA# set sp-1/2/0 unit 1 family inet
aviva@RouterA# set sp-1/2/0 unit 1 service-domain inside
aviva@RouterA# set sp-1/2/0 unit 2 family inet
aviva@RouterA# set sp-1/2/0 unit 2 service-domain outside
```

Then, configure the physical interface to be used for the IPSec tunnel:

```
[edit interfaces]
aviva@RouterA# set so-0/0/1 unit 0 family inet address 10.1.15.1/30
```

Finally, configure the domain's IGP traffic to use the IPSec tunnel:

```
[edit protocols ospf area 0.0.0.0]
aviva@RouterA# set interface so-0/0/0
aviva@RouterA# set interface lo0.0 passive
aviva@RouterA# set interface sp-1/2/1
```

Discussion

The JUNOS IPSec configuration for routers with AS PICs is quite a bit different than that for the ES PIC, because the PIC uses a different ASIC that has its own architecture. Instead of configuring at the [edit security] hierarchy, you configure IPSec at the [edit services] hierarchy, creating what the JUNOS software calls *service sets*, which define *IPSec VPN rules* for setting up the IPSec and IKE SAs. You also create service sets and rules for other services that require the AS PIC, such as Network Address Translation (NAT) and stateful firewalls. The M-series and T-series routers have built-in AS PICs. You use the same configuration on J-series routers, which don't use an AS PIC but instead have built-in software emulation of the AS PIC functionality.

The basic requirements for configuring IPSec on an interface with an AS PIC are the same as for the ES PIC. You define an IKE policy and negotiation proposal and create an IPSec policy and proposal. This recipe uses the default IKE and IPSec policy and proposal settings (see Table 3-1), so no configuration commands are necessary.

Table 3-1. IPSec and IKE defaults with AS PIC

Value	IKE default	IPSec default
Proposal values		
Authentication algorithm	SHA-1	HMAC SHA-1-96
Authentication method	Preshared keys	Not applicable
Diffie-Hellman keys	group2 (1,024-bit Diffie-Hellman scheme)	Not applicable
Encryption algorithm	Triple DES CBC	Triple DES CBC
Protocol	Not applicable	ESP
SA lifetime	3,600 seconds	28,800 seconds
Policy values		
Proposal name to reference	Default	Default
PFS Diffie-Hellman keys	Not applicable	group2 (1,024-bit Diffie-Hellman scheme)
Policy mode	main	Not applicable

The first part of this recipe configures IKE. The set ike policy command defines an IKE policy. This recipe use the default policy settings. Because preshared keys is the default authentication method for IKE, you have to configure the key itself.

Next, define a rule for the IKE SA. This recipe creates the rule named ike-rule. The rule in this recipe has two set term commands that are similar in syntax to a policy or firewall then statement. The first command sends matching packets to the remote end point of the IPSec tunnel (here, 10.0.15.2), and the second command associates the IKE policy with the SA so that matching packets can be sent across the IPSec tunnel. The final command in the IKE SA rule, set match-direction, specifies a match direction for marking which traffic to encrypt or decrypt. This statement is a bit confusing in the IPSec configuration because all IKE-enabled IPSec VPNs are bidirectional by default. However, you need to issue either this command or the set match-direction command. The IKE SA rule is effectively a firewall filter, directing traffic into and out of the IPSec tunnel, so you don't need to configure a separate firewall filter as you do when configuring the ES PIC.

Next, configure IPSec. You do this by creating a *service set* that defines IPSec-specific information. (You can configure multiple services on a single AS PIC, each in its own service set.) The service set in this recipe is called ipsec-dynamic. The first command associates the IKE SA rule with IPSec, and the second command defines the address of the local end of the IPSec security tunnel. The last two commands configure the logical interfaces that participate in the IPSec services. The set next-hop-service inside-service-interface command configures the inward-facing interfaces, and the set next-hop-service outside-service-interface command configures the interface that faces the remote IPSec site. You configure these interfaces at the [edit interfaces] level. The final part of the IPSec configuration is to define an IPSec proposal and policy. This recipe uses the default values (see Table 3-1), so no configuration commands are required.

For IPSec to work, you need to configure the interfaces on the AS PIC, which are services (sp-) interfaces. For J-series routers, configure the sp-0/0/0 interface. You also configure the physical interface that carries the IPSec tunnel.

For the services interface, you configure logical interfaces. Each service interface has three logical interfaces. The first, unit 0, has no special configuration. You just set it to support IPv4 traffic (family inet). The other two logical interfaces handle the IPSec traffic. The first one, unit 1 in this recipe, is for inward-facing traffic (service-domain inside); it is the logical interface you include in the set next-hop-service inside-service-interface command. The second logical interface, unit 2, is for outward-facing traffic; it is the one you include in the service outside-service-interface command.

This recipe uses the so-0/0/1 interface to carry the IPSec tunnel.

To direct traffic from the local domain into the IPSec tunnel, include the services interface when configuring the IGP. This recipe uses OSPF and adds the services interface with the set interface sp-1/2/1 command.

Configure the security gateway router at the remote site in the same way, using the appropriate address and interface names.

You can check that the IKE SA negotiation is successful:

```
aviva@RouterA> show services ipsec-vpn ike security-associations
Remote Address  State       Initiator cookie  Responder cookie  Exchange type
10.0.15.2       Matured     03075bd3a0000003  4bff26a5c7000003  Main
```

Use the following command to check that the IPSec SA is active:

```
aviva@RouterA> show services ipsec-vpn ipsec security-associations detail
Service set: ipsec-dynamic-service-set

  Rule: ike-rule, Term: term-ike, Tunnel index: 1
  Local gateway: 10.0.15.1, Remote gateway: 10.0.15.2
  Local identity: ipv4_subnet(any:0,[0..7]=10.0.15.30/24)
  Remote identity: ipv4_subnet(any:0,[0..7]=10.0.15.20/24)

    Direction: inbound, SPI: 2666326758, AUX-SPI: 0
    Mode: tunnel, Type: dynamic, State: Installed
    Protocol: ESP, Authentication: hmac-sha1-96, Encryption: 3des-cbc
    Soft lifetime: Expires in 26863 seconds
    Hard lifetime: Expires in 26998 seconds
    Anti-replay service: Enabled, Replay window size: 64

    Direction: outbound, SPI: 684772754, AUX-SPI: 0
    Mode: tunnel, Type: dynamic, State: Installed
    Protocol: ESP, Authentication: hmac-sha1-96, Encryption: 3des-cbc
    Soft lifetime: Expires in 26863 seconds
    Hard lifetime: Expires in 26998 seconds
    Anti-replay service: Enabled, Replay window size: 64
```

The output shows that the SA is using the default settings, including ESP for the protocol and HMAC-SHA1-96 for the authentication algorithm.

To check that traffic is traveling over the IPSec tunnel, use the following command:

```
aviva@RouterA> show services ipsec-vpn ipsec statistics
PIC: sp-1/2/0, Service set: ipsec-dynamic

ESP Statistics:
  Encrypted bytes:            2248
  Decrypted bytes:            2120
  Encrypted packets:            27
  Decrypted packets:            25
AH Statistics:
  Input bytes:                   0
  Output bytes:                  0
  Input packets:                 0
  Output packets:                0
Errors:
  AH authentication failures: 0, Replay errors: 0
  ESP authentication failures: 0, ESP decryption failures: 0
  Bad headers: 0, Bad trailers: 0
```

Again, it's worthwhile showing all sections of the configuration together, with added comments:

```
[edit services]
service-set ipsec-dynamic {
    next-hop-service {
        inside-service-interface sp-1/2/0.1; # <--bind IPSec to sp-1/2/0.1 interface
        outside-service-interface sp-1/2/0.2; # <--bind IPSec to sp-1/2/0.2
interface
    }
    ipsec-vpn-options {
        local-gateway 10.1.15.1: # <-- define local side of IPSec tunnel
    }
    ipsec-vpn-rules ike-rule; # <-- bind IKE rule to service set
}
ipsec-vpn {
    rule ike-rule { # <-- policy to allow traffic into IPSec tunnel
        term ike {
            then {
                remote-gateway 10.0.15.2:
                dynamic {
                    ike-policy ike-dynamic-policy; # <-- bind IKE policy to IPSec
                }
            }
        }
        match-direction input;
    }
    ike { # <-- define IKE policy
        policy ike-dynamic-policy {
            pre-shared-key ascii-text $1991poPPi;
        }
    }
}

[edit interfaces]
so-0/0/1 { # <-- physical interface for IPSec tunnel
    unit 0 {
        family inet {
            address 10.1.15.2/30;
        }
    }
}
sp-1/2/0 { # <-- services interface to IPSec
    unit 0 {
        family inet {
    unit 1 { # <-- logical interface for IPSec inward-facing traffic
        family inet;
        service-domain inside;
    }
    unit 2 { # <-- logical interface for IPSec outward-facing traffic
        family inet;
    }
}
```

```
[edit protocols ospf area 0.0.0.0]
ospf {
    area 0.0.0.0 {
        interface so-0/0/0;
        interface lo0.0 passive;
        interface sp-1/2/1.0; # <-- direct OSPF traffic into IPSec tunnel
    }
}
```

3.4 Using Digital Certificates to Create Dynamic IPSec SAs

Problem

You want an outside certificate authority (CA) to provide a digital certificate that sets the shared keys instead of using internal preshared keys.

Solution

Before you can configure IPSec, you must request a digital certificate from a trusted CA and put a copy of it on your router. First, configure a CA profile:

```
[edit security]
aviva@RouterA# set pki ca-profile entrust ca-identity entrust
aviva@RouterA# set pki ca-profile entrust enrollment url http://server.ca.com/
cgi-bin/pkiclient.exe
aviva@RouterA# commit and-quit
```

Then, use the CA profile to request a CA certificate from the CA and load it onto the router:

```
aviva@RouterA> request security pki ca-certificate enroll ca-profile entrust
Received following certificates:
  Certificate: C=us, O=mycompany
    Fingerprint: 00:8e:6f:58:dd:68:bf:25:0a:e3:f9:17:70:d6:61:f3:53:a7:79:10
  Certificate: C=us, O=mycompany, CN=First Officer
    Fingerprint: bc:78:87:9b:a7:91:13:20:71:db:ac:b5:56:71:42:ad:1a:b6:46:17
  Certificate: C=us, O=mycompany, CN=First Officer
    Fingerprint: 46:71:15:34:f0:a6:41:76:65:81:33:4f:68:47:c4:df:78:b8:e3:3f
Do you want to load the above CA certificate ? [yes,no] (no) yes
```

Next, generate a public/private key pair, which is required to submit a request for a local certificate:

```
aviva@RouterA> request security pki generate-key-pair certificate-id local-entrust
Generated key pair local-entrust, key size 1024 bits
```

Then, send a request for a local certificate to the CA:

```
aviva@RouterA> request security pki generate-certificate-request certificate-id
local-entrust domain-name RouterA.mycompany.com filename entrust-request-RouterA
subject cn=RouterA.mycompany.com
```

```
Generated certificate request
-----BEGIN CERTIFICATE REQUEST-----
MIIBoTCCAQoCAQAwGjEYMBYGA1UEAxMPdHAxLmp1bmlwZXIubmVVOMIGfMA0GCSqG
SIb3DQEBAQUAA4GNADCBiQKBgQCiUFklQws1Ud+AqN5DDxRs2kVyKEhh9qoVFnz+
Hz4c9vsy3B8ElwTJlkmIt2cB3yifB6zePd+6WYpf57Crwre7YqPkiXM31F6z3YjX
H+1BPNbCxNWYvyrnSyVYDbFj8ooXyqog8ACDfVL2JBWrPNBYy7imq/K9soDBbAs6
5hZqqwIDAQABoEcwRQYJKoZIhvcNAQkOMTgwNjAOBgNVHQ8BAf8EBAMCB4AwJAYD
VR0RAQH/BBowGIIWdHAxLmVuZ2xhbmQuanVuaXBlci5jb20wDANBgkqhkiG9w0BAQQF
AAOBgQBc2rq1v5SOQXH7LCb/FdqAL8ZM6GoaN5d6cGwq4bB6a7UQFgtoH406gQ3G
3iH0Zfz4xMIBpJYuGd1dkqgvcDoH3AgTsLkfn7Wi3x5H2qeQVs9bvL4P5nvEZLND
EIMUHwteolZCiZ70fO9Fer9cXWHSQs1UtXtgPqQJy2xIeImLgw==
-----END CERTIFICATE REQUEST-----
Fingerprint:
0d:90:b8:d2:56:74:fc:84:59:62:b9:78:71:9c:e4:9c:54:ba:16:97 (sha1)
1b:08:d4:f7:90:f1:c4:39:08:c9:de:76:00:86:62:b8 (md5)
```

After the CA digitally signs the local certificate and returns it to you, copy it to the router and load it:

```
aviva@RouterA> request security pki local-certificate load filename /tmp/RouterA-cert
certificate-id local-entrust
Local certificate local-entrust loaded successfully
```

Repeat this procedure to obtain and configure the digital certificate on the remote IPSec peer router.

Now you can configure IKE and IPSec to use the digital certificate. First, configure IKE to use the digital certificate for authentication:

```
[edit services ipsec-vpn]
aviva@RouterA# set ike proposal ike-proposal authentication-method rsa-signatures
```

Create an IKE policy:

```
[edit services ipsec-vpn ike policy digital-cert-policy]
aviva@RouterA# set proposals ike-proposal
aviva@RouterA# set local-id fqdn RouterA.mycompany.com
aviva@RouterA# set remote-id fqdn RouterB.mycompany.com
aviva@RouterA# set local-certificate local-entrust
```

Then, create a rule for a bidirectional dynamic IKE SA that references the IKE policy:

```
[edit services ipsec-vpn rule digital-cert-rule]
aviva@RouterA# set term ike then remote-gateway 10.0.15.2
aviva@RouterA# set term ike then dynamic ike-policy digital-cert-policy
aviva@RouterA# set match-direction input
```

Define a service set for IPSec:

```
[edit services service-set digital-cert-service]
aviva@RouterA# set ipsec-vpn-rules digital-cert-rule
aviva@RouterA# set ipsec-vpn-options local-gateway 10.1.15.1
aviva@RouterA# set ipsec-vpn-options trusted-ca entrust
aviva@RouterA# set next-hop-service inside-service-interface sp-1/2/0.1
aviva@RouterA# set next-hop-service outside-service-interface sp-1/2/0.2
```

Then, configure the IPSec tunnel to be established immediately:

```
[edit services ipsec-vpn]
aviva@RouterA# establish-tunnels immediately
```

Next, configure the router interfaces. First, set up the service interfaces to use for IPSec:

```
[edit interfaces]
aviva@RouterA# set sp-1/2/0 unit 0 family inet
aviva@RouterA# set sp-1/2/0 unit 1 family inet
aviva@RouterA# set sp-1/2/0 unit 1 service-domain inside
aviva@RouterA# set sp-1/2/0 unit 2 family inet
aviva@RouterA# set sp-1/2/0 unit 2 service-domain outside
```

Then, configure the physical interface to be used for the IPSec tunnel:

```
[edit interfaces]
aviva@RouterA# set so-0/0/1 unit 0 family inet address 10.1.15.1/30
```

Finally, configure the IGP traffic to use the IPSec tunnel:

```
[edit protocols ospf area 0.0.0.0]
aviva@RouterA# set interface so-0/0/0
aviva@RouterA# set interface lo0.0 passive
aviva@RouterA# set interface sp-1/2/1
```

Configure the other IPSec peers in a similar fashion.

Discussion

Digital certificates provide an additional level of security for connections between IPSec peers. They use a *public-key infrastructure* (PKI) to provide public-key encryption and digital-signature services for managing keys and certificates. A trusted third party, called a *certificate authority* (CA), registers the identity of PKI users, storing the identities in a digital format called a public-key certificate, also called a CA certificate. The CA creates a CA certificate that includes your public key and its public key and signs it with its own private key. You then install the CA certificate, along with a local certificate that you generate, on your routers. When routers are setting up an IPSec tunnel between each other, each router receives a copy of its peer's local certificate, which has been signed by the CA's private key. The router uses the CA's public key to de-encrypt the local certificate and to learn its peer's public key, which it then uses to encrypt the data it sends. In networks that do not use digital certificates, IPSec encrypts data with the private key and its peers de-encrypt the data with the public key. This recipe works only on routers running JUNOS 7.5 and later.

Before you can configure IPSec to use digital certificates, you must request a certificate from the CA. The first commands in this recipe show how to make the request from the router. First, you configure a CA profile. This recipe creates a profile named entrust for the CA Entrust. The second command provides the URL of the CA.

After you have committed the CA profile, use the request security pki ca-certificate enroll command to request a certificate from the CA and load it onto the router. If you instead obtain the certificate from the CA in an email or by downloading it from its web site, use the following command instead to load the certificate onto the router:

```
aviva@RouterA> request security pki ca-certificate load filename server1://tmp/
RouterA-cert certificate-id entrust
```

To request a local certificate from the CA, you need to first generate a private-/public- key pair with the request security pki generate-key-pair command. In the certificate-id option, specify the name you want to use for the local certificate (here, local-entrust). Once IPSec is operational, the public key will be included in the local digital certificate and the private key will be used to de-encrypt data received from peers.

The request security pki generate-certificate-request sends a request for a local certificate to the CA. When the CA returns the digitally signed local certificate, use the request security pki local-certificate load command to copy the certificate to the router. You can check the digital certificate with the following command:

```
aviva@RouterA> show security pki ca-certificate detail
Certificate identifier: entrust
  Certificate version: 3
  Serial number: 4355 9235
  Issuer:
    Organization: mycompany, Country: us
  Subject:
    Organization: mycompany, Country: us
  Validity:
    Not before: 2005 Oct 18th, 23:54:22 GMT
    Not after: 2025 Oct 19th, 00:24:22 GMT
  Public key algorithm: rsaEncryption(1024 bits)
    cb:9e:2d:c0:70:f8:ea:3c:f2:b5:f0:02:48:87:dc:68:99:a3:57:4f
    0e:b9:98:0b:95:47:0d:1f:97:7c:53:17:dd:1a:f8:da:e5:08:d1:1c
    78:68:1f:2f:72:9f:a2:cf:81:e3:ce:c5:56:89:ce:f0:97:93:fa:36
    19:3e:18:7d:8c:9d:21:fe:1f:c3:87:8d:b3:5d:f3:03:66:9d:16:a7
    bf:18:3f:f0:7a:80:f0:62:50:43:83:4f:0e:d7:c6:42:48:c0:8a:b2
    c7:46:30:38:df:9b:dc:bc:b5:08:7a:f3:cd:64:db:2b:71:67:fe:d8
    04:47:08:07:de:17:23:13
  Signature algorithm: sha1WithRSAEncryption
  Fingerprint:
    00:8e:6f:58:dd:68:bf:25:0a:e3:f9:17:70:d6:61:f3:53:a7:79:10 (sha1)
    71:6f:6a:76:17:9b:d6:2a:e7:5a:72:97:82:6d:26:86 (md5)
  Distribution CRL:
    C=us, O=mycompany, CN=CRL1
    http://CA-1/CRL/mycompany.crl
  Use for key: CRL signing, Certificate signing

Certificate identifier: entrust
  Certificate version: 3
  Serial number: 4355 925c
```

```
Issuer:
  Organization: mycompany, Country: us
Subject:
  Organization: mycompany, Country: us, Common name: First Officer
Validity:
  Not before: 2005 Oct 18th, 23:55:59 GMT
  Not after: 2008 Oct 19th, 00:25:59 GMT
Public key algorithm: rsaEncryption(1024 bits)
  c0:a4:21:32:95:0a:cd:ec:12:03:d1:a2:89:71:8e:ce:4e:a6:f9:2f
  1a:9a:13:8c:f6:a0:3d:c9:bd:9d:c2:a0:41:77:99:1b:1e:ed:5b:80
  34:46:f8:5b:28:34:38:2e:91:7d:4e:ad:14:86:78:67:e7:02:1d:2e
  19:11:b7:fa:0d:ba:64:20:e1:28:4e:3e:bb:6e:64:dc:cd:b1:b4:7a
  ca:8f:47:dd:40:69:c2:35:95:ce:b8:85:56:d7:0f:2d:04:4d:5d:d8
  42:e1:4f:6b:bf:38:c0:45:1e:9e:f0:b4:7f:74:6f:e9:70:fd:4a:78
  da:eb:10:27:bd:46:34:33
Signature algorithm: sha1WithRSAEncryption
Fingerprint:
  bc:78:87:9b:a7:91:13:20:71:db:ac:b5:56:71:42:ad:1a:b6:46:17 (sha1)
  23:79:40:c9:6d:a6:f0:ca:e0:13:30:d4:29:6f:86:79 (md5)
Distribution CRL:
  C=us, O=mycompany, CN=CRL1
  http://CA-1/CRL/mycompany.crl
Use for key: Key encipherment

Certificate identifier: entrust
  Certificate version: 3
  Serial number: 4355 925b
  Issuer:
    Organization: mycompany, Country: us
  Subject:
    Organization: mycompany, Country: us, Common name: First Officer
  Validity:
    Not before: 2005 Oct 18th, 23:55:59 GMT
    Not after: 2008 Oct 19th, 00:25:59 GMT
  Public key algorithm: rsaEncryption(1024 bits)
    ea:75:c4:f3:58:08:ea:65:5c:7e:b3:de:63:0a:cf:cf:ec:9a:82:e2
    d7:e8:b9:2f:bd:4b:cd:86:2f:f1:dd:d8:a2:95:af:ab:51:a5:49:4e
    00:10:c6:25:ff:b5:49:6a:99:64:74:69:e5:8c:23:5b:b4:70:62:8e
    e4:f9:a2:28:d4:54:e2:0b:1f:50:a2:92:cf:6c:8f:ae:10:d4:69:3c
    90:e2:1f:04:ea:ac:05:9b:3a:93:74:d0:59:24:e9:d2:9d:c2:ef:22
    b9:32:c7:2c:29:4f:91:cb:5a:26:fe:1d:c0:36:dc:f4:9c:8b:f5:26
    af:44:bf:53:aa:d4:5f:67
  Signature algorithm: sha1WithRSAEncryption
  Fingerprint:
    46:71:15:34:f0:a6:41:76:65:81:33:4f:68:47:c4:df:78:b8:e3:3f (sha1)
    ee:cc:c7:f4:5d:ac:65:33:0a:55:db:59:72:2c:dd:16 (md5)
  Distribution CRL:
    C=us, O=mycompany, CN=CRL1
    http://CA-1/CRL/mycompany.crl
  Use for key: Digital signature
```

The output shows three certificates. The first one is used to sign the certificate, the second is for encrypting the key, and the last is the CA's digital signature.

Use the following command to display information about the local certificate:

```
aviva@RouterA> show security pki local-certificate
Certificate identifier: local-entrust
  Issued to: RouterA.mycompany.com, Issued by: mycompany
  Validity:
    Not before: 2005 Nov 21st, 23:28:22 GMT
    Not after: 2008 Nov 21st, 23:58:22 GMT
  Public key algorithm: rsaEncryption(1024 bits)
  Public key verification status: Passed
```

The first line of the output shows the name of the certificate—here, local-entrust. The second line shows the router and company to whom the certificate has been issued. The certificate is valid for three years from the date of issue.

When you have the signed local certificate, configure IKE and IPSec to use it. The configuration is more involved than that shown in Recipe 3.3 because this recipe uses fewer of the default values.

In configuring IKE, the set ike proposal command has IKE use the digital certificate for authentication (with the option authentication-method rsa-signatures) instead of the default preshared keys. In the IKE policy, the set proposals command references the IKE proposal. The second and third commands give the fully qualified domain names of the local and remote routers that are the IPSec tunnel peers. The last command configures the name of the local router's digital certificate. Finally, define a rule for the IKE SA. This recipe creates a rule named digital-cert-rule. The first set term command defines the IP address of the remote end of the IPSec tunnel, and the second associates the IKE policy with the SA so that matching packets can be sent across the tunnel.

Next, configure IPSec. The service set is the same as that shown in Recipe 3.3, with the addition of the set ipsec-vpn-options trusted-ca command, which points to the CA you defined with the set security pki ca-profile command. Finally, use the set ipsec-vpn establish-tunnels immediately command to create the IPSec tunnel immediately after the configuration is activated rather than wait for traffic before setting it up.

In this recipe, the configuration for the services interface, the physical interface, and the IGP is the same as in Recipe 3.3. And again, configure the remote security router in the same way.

To check the operation of IKE and IPSec, use the commands shown in Recipe 3.3. Use the show services ipsec-vpn certificates command to check that the correct digital certificates are being used to establish the IPSec tunnel:

```
aviva@RouterA> show services ipsec-vpn certificates
Service set: ipsec-domain, Total entries: 3
  Certificate cache entry: 3
    Flags: Non-root Trusted
    Issued to: RouterB.mycompany.com, Issued by: mycompany
```

```
      Alternate subject: RouterB.mycompany.com
      Validity:
        Not before: 2005 Nov 21st, 23:33:58 GMT
        Not after: 2008 Nov 22nd, 00:03:58 GMT

   Certificate cache entry: 2
     Flags: Non-root Trusted
     Issued to: RouterA.mycompany.com, Issued by: mycompany
     Alternate subject: RouterA.mycompany.com
     Validity:
        Not before: 2005 Nov 21st, 23:28:22 GMT
        Not after: 2008 Nov 21st, 23:58:22 GMT

   Certificate cache entry: 1
     Flags: Root Trusted
     Issued to: mycompany, Issued by: mycompany
     Validity:
        Not before: 2005 Oct 18th, 23:54:22 GMT
        Not after: 2025 Oct 19th, 00:24:22 GMT
```

The three certificates shown in this output map to the three you see with the show
security pki ca-certificate detail command.

Again, this is a fairly complex configuration, so here are all the sections of the configuration in one place, with added comments:

```
[edit security]
pki { # <-- how to reach certificate authority
    ca-profile entrust {
        ca-identity entrust;
        enrollment {
            url http://server.ca.com/cgi-bin/pkiclient.exe;
        }
    }
}

[edit services]
service-set digital-cert-service {
    next-hop-service {
        inside-service-interface sp-1/2/0.1; # <-- bind IPSec to sp-1/2/0.1
interface
        outside-service-interface sp-1/2/0.2; # <--bind IPSec to sp-1/2/0.2
interface
    }
    ipsec-vpn-options {
        trusted-ca entrust; # <-- bind service set to CA defined in ca-profile
        local-gateway 10.1.15.1; # <-- local side of IPSec tunnel
    }
    ipsec-vpn-rules digital-cert-rule;
}
ipsec-vpn {
    rule digital-cert-rule { # <-- policy to allow traffic into IPSec tunnel
        term ike {
            then {
```

```
                    remote-gateway 10.1.15.2; # <-- remote side of IPSec tunnel
                    dynamic {
                        ike-policy digital-cert-policy; # <-- bind IKE policy to IPSec
                    }
                }
            }
            match-direction input;
        }
        ike {
            proposal ike-proposal {
                authentication-method rsa-signatures; # <-- use digital certificates
            }
            policy digital-cert-policy { #<-- define IKE policy
                proposals ike-proposal;
                local-id fqdn RouterA.mycompany.com;
                local-certificate local-entrust;
                remote-id fqdn RouberB.mycompany.com;
            }
        }
        establish-tunnels immediately;
    }

    [edit interfaces]
    so-0/0/0 { #<-- physical interface for IPSec tunnel
        unit 0 {
            family inet {
                address 10.1.15.1/30;
            }
        }
    }
    sp-1/2/0 { # <-- services interface to IPSec
        unit 0 {
            family inet;
        }
        unit 1 { # <-- logical interface for IPSec inward-facing traffic
            family inet;
            service-domain inside;
        }
        unit 2 { # <-- logical interface for IPSec outward-facing traffic
            family inet;
            service-domain outside;
        }
    }

    [edit protocols ospf area 0.0.0.0]
    interface so-0/0/0.0;
    interface sp-1/2/0.1; # <-- direct OSPF traffic into IPSec tunnel
    interface lo0.0;
```

## CHAPTER 4

SNMP

4.0 Introduction

The Simple Network Management Protocol (SNMP) is an Internet standard protocol for remotely managing routers, switches, servers, workstations, and other devices on an IP network. SNMP was first introduced in the late 1980s and is now widely supported. The first version of SNMP, Version 1 (SNMPv1; RFC 1157), defines the architecture and framework for SNMP.

SNMP Version 2 (SNMPv2) was proposed in 1993 to improve performance, manager-to-manager communications, and security. It was defined in RFCs 1155 and 1213. However, SNMPv2 was not widely accepted because the IETF did not reach consensus on the security features. A revised version, referred to as Community SNMPv2, or SNMPv2c, was later approved by the IETF (RFCs 1902 and 3416). This version contains all the proposed SNMPv2 enhancements except for the security features, including more detailed error codes, addition of the GetBulk operation for more efficient retrieval of large amounts of data, and support for 64-bit counters. For security, this version supports community strings, which act as text-based passwords for determining how SNMP managers can access the data on SNMP agents. SNMPv2 is currently the most commonly deployed version of SNMP.

The newest version, SNMP Version 3 (SNMPv3), introduced in 1999 (RFCs 3410 through 3418), defines stronger security features, including authentication for accessing network devices and encryption of SNMP packets. SNMPv3 uses a user-based security model (USM) for authentication, data integrity, message replay protection, and protection of the message payload, and a view-based access control model (VACM) to define access to the management information. SNMPv3 is currently not used much because it is fairly new and only a few network device manufacturers and network management system (NMS) vendors support it.

SNMP uses UDP port 161, and SNMP traps use UDP port 162.

The JUNOS software supports SNMP Versions 1, 2c, and 3.

This chapter discusses how to configure the SNMP agent on the router with SNMPv2 and SNMPv3 and illustrates some basic techniques for using SNMP to query the router to collect information. Much of the information gathering done by SNMP is done from the NMS system, either with GUI or CLI tools. Discussion of the workings of the NMS systems is beyond the scope of this book; you should refer to your NMS documentation. For more information about SNMP see *SNMP, SNMPv2, SNMPv3, and RMON 1 and 2* (Addison-Wesley).

SNMP Management Model

SNMP uses a client–server model. The SNMP client is called a *manager*, and the server is called an *agent*. The managers are centralized systems on the network that actively monitor the agents, which are the actual network devices, by querying and collecting status and statistics information from them. Managers can run on PCs or workstations but more often run on dedicated devices called NMS systems that are developed and sold by third-party companies. An example is the HP OpenView Network Node Manager product.

Agents are individual processes running on the network devices that are being managed. These processes gather and store the status and statistics about their host platform and send them to the managers primarily in one or two ways. When the agent receives an SNMP Get request from the manager, as a Get, GetBulk, or GetNext request, it responds with the requested information. The second way is that the agent sends to the manager unsolicited notifications, called traps, that are triggered by events on the agent. The SNMP manager can also modify information on the agent by sending SNMP Set requests. A JUNOS router running SNMP is simply an SNMP agent. There are two JUNOS SNMP processes (daemons in Unix terminology): SNMPD, the SNMP process, and MIB2D, the MIB-II process. snmpd is the main entry point, or master agent, for dealing with SNMP, and it communicates with mib2d, which is a subagent.

MIBs and OIDs

SNMP agents store information in a *Structure of Management Information* (SMI), which is a hierarchical database that is similar to the directory structure in a filesystem. The individual files that store the information are called *Management Information Bases* (MIBs). Each MIB contains nodes of information that are stored in a tree structure. The tree contains branches, which move down from a root node. The branches are similar to the directory names in a directory path. Each branch eventually ends in a leaf, similar to a filename in a filesystem, that contains a specific piece of information about the SNMP agent. Each branching point in the tree corresponds to a MIB object and is identified by a number and a text string. The series of numbers that uniquely identifies a node or a leaf is called the *Object Identifier* (OID). As examples, OID .1.3.6.1.2.1.1.4 corresponds to sysContact (system contact information) in the standard MIB-II MIB, and OID .1.3.1.4.1.2636 corresponds to juniperMIB, which is the top node of the Juniper enterprise-specific portion of the MIB tree. Both these OIDs are absolute references because they start at the root node, which is indicated by the dot (.) before the first number (.1.3.1.4.1.2636 rather than 1.3.1.4.1.2636). In NMS and JUNOS software, you can refer to the OIDs by absolute OID or by name; the names are generally easier to remember and type. Figure 4-1 illustrates a portion of the MIB tree that leads to these OIDs and shows that each node has both text and a number to identify it.

```
+-iso(1)
    +--org(3)
        +--dod(6)
            +--internet(1)
            |        +--directory(1)
            |        +--mgmt(2)
            |            +--mib-2(1)
            |                +--system(1)
            |                        sysDescr(1)
            |                        sysObjectID(2)
            |                        sysUpTime(3)
            |                        sysContact(4)
            |                        sysName(5)
            |                        sysLocation(6)
            |                        sysServices(7)
...         |
            +-private(4)
                +-enterprises(1)
                    +-juniperMIB(2636)
                        +-jnxProducts(1)
                        +-jnxServices(2)
                        +-jnxMIBs(3)
                            +-jnxBoxAnatomy(1)
                            +-mpls(2)
                            +-ifJnx(32)
                            +-jnxAlarms(4)
                            +-jnxFirewalls(5)
                            +-mpls(2)
...
```

Figure 4-1. MIB tree with OIDs

The SNMP manager targets specific nodes in the MIB tree when gathering status and statistics about the agent systems.

While the OID relates to the location in the MIB tree, it is the instance that relates to the data object or value at that location. For example, the OID .1.3.6.1.2.1.1.4 corresponds to sysContact, and .1.3.6.1.2.1.1.4.0 corresponds to the value in that field, such as "Fred Flintstone."

MIB objects can be defined as being read-only, meaning that the SNMP manager can retrieve its information only with an SNMP Get command (or with Get derivatives such as GetNext and GetBulk), or as being read-write, meaning that the manager can change the object's information with an SNMP Set command.

MIBs are defined using a language called *Abstract Syntax Notation 1 (ASN.1)*. The IETF has defined a number of MIBs in various RFCs that contain objects common across all network devices. Some of these MIBs are mandatory, while others are optional. On NMS systems, most of the mandatory MIBs are typically compiled into the SNMP manager software. If you need standard MIBs that are not provided with your NMS, you can find them in the IETF RFCs and at other web sites, including *http://www.net-snmp.org*, *http://www.rfc-editor.org*, and *http://net-snmp.sourceforge. net*. There is a list of SMI numbers on the IANA web site (*http://www.iana.org*).

For objects specific to a device, the manufacturer of the device provides enterprise-specific MIBs. They must have the same structure as standard MIBs. The following example of the beginning Juniper chassis MIB illustrates the ASN.1 language:

```
-- Juniper Enterprise Specific MIB: Chassis MIB
JUNIPER-MIB DEFINITIONS ::= BEGIN

...
-- Juniper Box Anatomy MIB
-- Top level objects
jnxBoxClass OBJECT-TYPE
    SYNTAX    OBJECT IDENTIFIER
    MAX-ACCESSread-only
    STATUS    current
    DESCRIPTION
        "The class of the box, indicating which product line
        the box is about, for example, 'Internet Router'."
    ::= { jnxBoxAnatomy 1 }

jnxBoxDescr OBJECT-TYPE
    SYNTAX    DisplayString (SIZE (0..255))
    MAX-ACCESSread-only
    STATUS    current
    DESCRIPTION
        "The name, model, or detailed description of the box,
        indicating which product the box is about, for example
        'M40'."
    ::= { jnxBoxAnatomy 2 }

jnxBoxSerialNo OBJECT-TYPE
    SYNTAX    DisplayString (SIZE (0..255))
    MAX-ACCESSread-only
    STATUS    current
    DESCRIPTION
        "The serial number of this subject, blank if unknown
        or unavailable."
    ::= { jnxBoxAnatomy 3 }
```

These three objects provide information about the physical Juniper Networks router, specifically the family, model name, and serial number.

Juniper Networks provides several dozen enterprise MIBs for the JUNOS software. For a complete list, see *http://www.juniper.net/techpubs/software/junos/mibs.html*. From this page, you can download the individual MIB files or a complete MIB package that contains the relevant standard MIBs and all the enterprise MIBs. For JUNOS 7.4, this file is called *juniper-mibs-7.4R1.tgz* (there is a separate file for each JUNOS release). You can load this complete MIB package or the individual MIB files onto your NMS system or MIB browser. MIBs often have dependencies because they reference other MIBs, so when you load them onto the NMS, you need to load them in the correct sequence. The complete JUNOS MIB package places all objects into an SMI, which is loaded first. All the other information in the MIB files reference the SMI, so the files load correctly.

SNMP Security

SNMPv2 uses a simple security scheme to control the access between managers and servers. Security is controlled by a *community string*, which is a password that the NMS system uses to access the agent's MIBs. The community string is a very weak password because it is not encrypted but rather is sent as clear text across the network. All SNMP requests from the manager to the agent must be configured with the same community name for the manager to be able to collect information from the agent. Because the password is not encrypted, the JUNOS SNMP implementation does not support most SNMP Set operations and read-write MIB objects, even those specified as read-write in the MIB RFCs. The exceptions are the ping and the traceroute MIBs, for which JUNOS supports Set operations. Some additional security is provided by the fact that you can limit the MIBs and specific objects that the NMS systems can access on the agent by configuring SNMP views on the router and granting access to specific views by community (see RFC 3415).

SNMPv3 defines a USM to provide authentication and data encryption. It uses the HMAC with either MD5 or SHA1 to authenticate users, and CBC-DES to encrypt the message payload.

4.1   Configuring SNMP

Problem

You want to set the router up to be an SNMP agent so your network SNMPv2 NMS system can monitor the router.

Solution

Use the following commands to configure the router to be an SNMP agent:

```
[edit]
aviva@router1# set snmp community public authorization read-only
aviva@router1# show
```

```
snmp {
    community public {
        authorization read-only;
    }
}
```

Discussion

To make the router an SNMP agent, configure one or more communities to autho-
rize the NMS to access your router. Each community has a name, which must be the
same name used by the NMS, and an authorization level (read-only or read-write).
Here, we have configured one community called public with read-only access, which
means that the router responds only to Get requests from the NMS system.

Use the following command to check that SNMP is up and running, that requests are
being properly transmitted, and that the number of requests is incrementing over time:

```
aviva@router1> show snmp statistics
SNMP statistics:
  Input:
    Packets: 24044, Bad versions: 0, Bad community names: 0,
    Bad community uses: 0, ASN parse errors: 0,
    Too bigs: 0, No such names: 0, Bad values: 0,
    Read onlys: 0, General errors: 0,
    Total request varbinds: 24041, Total set varbinds: 0,
    Get requests: 3, Get nexts: 24041, Set requests: 0,
    Get responses: 0, Traps: 0,
    Silent drops: 0, Proxy drops: 0, Commit pending drops: 0,
    Throttle drops: 0, Duplicate request drops: 0
  V3 Input:
    Unknown security models: 0, Invalid messages: 0
    Unknown pdu handlers: 0, Unavailable contexts: 0
    Unknown contexts: 0, Unsupported security levels: 0
    Not in time windows: 0, Unknown user names: 0
    Unknown engine ids: 0, Wrong digests: 0, Decryption errors: 0
  Output:
    Packets: 24044, Too bigs: 0, No such names: 3,
    Bad values: 0, General errors: 0,
    Get requests: 0, Get nexts: 0, Set requests: 0,
    Get responses: 24044, Traps: 0
```

The output shows the number and types of packets the router has received from and
sent to the NMS. If you see any bad (invalid) community names, or if the number of
names increases, this can indicate that one or more community names are configured incorrectly, or that an unauthorized manager, possibly a malicious user, is trying to access the agent.

4.2 Setting Router Information for the MIB-II System Group

Problem

You need to define specific information about the router, such as its name and location, to pass to the SNMP manager.

Solution

Set description, location, and contact information about the router:

```
[edit snmp]
aviva@router1# set description "JUNOS cookbook M20, aka router1"
aviva@router1# set location "JUNOS cookbook kitchen"
aviva@router1# set contact "aviva at extension 12345"
```

Discussion

These commands provide general information, which is placed into objects in the MIB-II system group, about the router to the SNMP manager. The description string identifies the router and is placed into the sysDescription object. The location describes the router's physical location and is placed into the sysLocation object. The contact identifies how to contact the router's administrator and goes into the sysContact object. The name of the router you configured when you installed the router (the name in the set system host-name command) is placed into the sysName object. You can set a different router name to be used just for SNMP:

```
[edit snmp]
aviva@router1# set name junos-cookbook-router
```

You can use a utility like snmpwalk from a Unix workstation to retrieve the agent's information. (snmpwalk uses SNMP GetNext requests to query a network entity for a tree of information.) The following command uses the hostname of the agent (router1), but you can also use the IP address:

```
aviva-server> snmpwalk -c public router1 system.sysDescr
system.sysDescr.0 = JUNOS cookbook M20, aka router1
aviva-server> snmpwalk -c public router1 system.sysContact
system.sysContact.0 = aviva at extension 12345
```

You can also get this information on the router itself. The following command shows all the settings in the system MIB:

```
aviva@router1> show snmp mib walk system
sysDescr.0     = JUNOS cookbook M20, aka router1
sysObjectID.0 = jnxProductNameM20
sysUpTime.0    = 2888368
sysContact.0   = aviva at extension 12345
sysName.0      = junos-cookbook-router
```

```
sysLocation.0 = JUNOS cookbook kitchen
sysServices.0 = 4
```

You can also look at a single MIB object:

```
aviva@router1> show snmp mib get sysDescr.0
sysDescr.0    = JUNOS cookbook M20, aka router1
```

In this command, specify both the name of the object and the instance, which is 0.
Similarly, you can look at more than one object:

```
aviva@router1> show snmp mib get "sysUpTime.0 sysName.0"
sysUpTime.0  = 2865092
sysName.0    = router1
```

For this command to work, make sure to enclose the list of objects in quotation
marks.

See Also

Recipe 1.1

4.3 Setting Up SNMP Traps

Problem

You want to create triggers on the router to send unsolicited notifications to the
NMS system when a router event occurs.

Solution

Configure traps by setting up SNMP trap groups:

```
[edit snmp]
aviva@router1# set trap-group authentication-traps targets 10.0.10.1
aviva@router1# set trap-group authentication-traps targets 192.168.15.27
aviva@router1# set trap-group authentication-traps categories authentication
```

Discussion

SNMP traps report significant events that occur on the router, commonly errors or
failures. You always want the SNMP agent to send traps to the manager so that the
manager receives current information without always having to poll for it. To have
the router send traps to the SNMP manager, create one or more trap groups. For
each group, set two things: the IP address of the NMS server (or servers) to receive
the trap and the events that trigger the traps. The targets statement identifies the
receiving NMS systems, and the categories statement specifies the triggering event
or events (see Table 4-1). The JUNOS software supports standard trap categories
and provides several that are enterprise-specific. This recipe sends a trap to two NMS
systems (our primary system and a backup one for redundancy) whenever an SNMP
manager uses the incorrect community to access data held by the agent.

Table 4-1. SNMP trap categories

Keyword	Type	Category description
authentication	Standard	Agent (router) authentication failures
chassis	Enterprise	Chassis and router environment notifications
configuration	Enterprise	Configuration mode notifications
link	Enterprise	Link-related transitions, such as when hardware transitions from up to down, or vice versa
rmon-alarm	Enterprise	RMON event alarms
routing	Enterprise	Routing protocol notifications
sonet-alarms *alarm-name*	Enterprise	SONET alarm notifications
startup	Standard	Router warm and full reboots
vrrp-events	Enterprise	VRRP events

SNMP traps are defined in the MIBs themselves. The IETF defines the standard traps in various RFCs, and they are normally compiled into the SNMP manager software that runs on the NMS system. Juniper Networks defines enterprise-specific traps for SNMPv1 and SNMPv2 and sends both versions of the traps to the NMS. To find a list and an explanation of the JUNOS traps, look in the enterprise MIBs, searching for the string NOTIFICATION-TYPE in the MIB. For example, in the Juniper Networks chassis MIB, the OID for the trap that reports the failure of a power supply, jnxPowerSupplyFailure, is jnxChassisTraps 1:

```
-- definition of chassis related traps
Traps for chassis alarm conditions
jnxPowerSupplyFailure NOTIFICATION-TYP
    OBJECTS ...
    STATUS current
    DESCRIPTION
"A jnxPowerSupplyFailure trap signifies that the SNMP entity, acting in an agent
role, has detected that the specified power supply in the chassis has been in the
failure (bad DC output) condition."
::= { jnxChassisTraps 1 }
```

4.4   Controlling SNMP Access to the Router

Problem

You need to improve upon the security offered by the SNMPv2 community password.

Solution

There are two straightforward solutions. One is to identify which NMS systems are allowed to use the SNMP community:

```
[edit snmp]
aviva@router1# set community public clients 10.0.0.1/32
```

The second is to limit the router interfaces that can communicate with the NMS system:

```
[edit snmp]
aviva@router1# set interface [fe-0/0/0]
```

Discussion

SNMPv2 is inherently insecure because the community string, which acts as the password between the manager and agent, is sent as clear text across the network. You can improve the security a bit by limiting SNMP manager access to the router and to the MIB on the router. Perhaps the simplest way to improve security is to define which NMS systems can or cannot use a particular community string. The first command in this recipe allows only a single system, 10.0.10.1/32, to access the router using the community string public. While this example and the examples throughout this chapter use a community named public, this name is very well known, so for security reasons, it is recommended that you use a different name, preferably one that's difficult to guess (for example, mYsnmPcommunitYversioNonE).

You can also disallow access for specific NMS systems. One plausible use of this is to allow access by all the NMS systems on a subnet and then deny access to just a few:

```
[edit snmp]
aviva@router1# set community public clients 10.0.0.0/8
aviva@router1# set community public clients 10.0.0.1/32 restrict
```

This configuration allows all NMS systems on the 10.0.0.0/8 subnet to access the router, with the exception of 10.0.0.1/32.

Another way to restrict access is to define which router interfaces can receive requests from NMS systems. The second command in this recipe does this by specifying a physical interface, or you can name individual logical interfaces to be more specific:

```
[edit snmp]
aviva@router1# set interface [fe-0/0/0.0 fe-0/0/0.1]
```

See Also

The introduction to Chapter 7

4.5   Using a Firewall Filter to Protect SNMP Access

Problem

You have a firewall filter on your interfaces and want to add a term to restrict NMS system access to the router.

Solution

You can add a term to the existing firewall filter that allows access to the desired NMS systems:

Add a term to an existing firewall filter that restricts SSH and Telnet access:

```
[edit firewall filter protect-RE term allow-snmp-from-nms-systems]
aviva@router1# set from source-address 10.0.0.1/32
aviva@router1# set from source-address 10.0.5.1/32
aviva@router1# set from source-address 10.0.6.1/32
aviva@router1# set from source-address 10.10.1.50/32
aviva@router1# set from protocol udp
aviva@router1# set from destination-port snmp
aviva@router1# set then accept
```

For the filter to affect incoming traffic, apply it to the desired interfaces:

```
[edit interfaces]
aviva@router1# set fe-0/0/0 unit 0 family inet filter input protect-RE
```

Discussion

An interface can have one inbound and one outbound firewall filter, so if you already have filters in place that control the incoming and outgoing interface traffic, you can add a term that applies to NMS access. To filter polling requests from NMS systems, add the term to the inbound filter; to filter the router's responses, add it to the outbound filter. This term allows four NMS systems, all identified by IP address, to send SNMP requests to the router. The destination-port option matches the SNMP port number in the IP packet's destination field, and you include the udp option because SNMP exchanges use UDP, not TCP.

You then have to decide where in the filter to place the term. Because the terms in the firewall filter are evaluated in the order in which they appear, the placement affects the efficiency of the filter. Generally, terms for operations that need to be performed quickly, such as BGP peering and IGP and DNS traffic, are at the beginning of the filter. For operations that are less time-critical, including processing SNMP traffic, place the term towards the end of the filter.

For the filter to do anything, you apply it to the desired interface with the set filter input command.

To create a parallel filter for outbound SNMP traffic, you can incorporate the same term into the interface's outbound firewall filter and then apply it on the ongoing side:

```
[edit interfaces]
aviva@router1# set fe-0/0/0 unit 0 family inet filter output outgoing-from-me
```

Fashion the firewall filter for outgoing SNMP a bit differently to allow the router to send SNMP traps. Specify a source port of snmp (port 161) and a destination port of snmptrap (port 162):

```
[edit firewall filter outgoing-from-me]
aviva@router1# set term allow-snmp-to-nms-systems source-port snmp
aviva@router1# set term allow-snmp-to-nms-systems destination-port snmptrap
```

Instead of listing addresses individually in the from source-address portion of the configuration, a shortcut creates a prefix list and then just references the list. A prefix list is simply a named list of IP prefixes created in the [edit policy-options] portion of the configuration and then referred to in firewall filters and in routing policies.

See Also

Recipes 9.3, 9.15, and 9.16

4.6   Controlling Access to Router MIBs

Problem

You want to limit the access of a group of NMS systems so they can gather only basic system and chassis information from the router.

Solution

Use the following commands to define the MIB branches that a community can access:

```
[edit snmp]
aviva@router1# set view chassis-info-only oid jnxBoxAnatomy include
aviva@router1# set view chassis-info-only oid snmpMIBObjects include
aviva@router1# set view chassis-info-only oid system include
```

Then associate the MIB view with the community:

```
[edit snmp]
aviva@router1# set community chassis-access-only view chassis-info-only
```

Discussion

By default, an SNMP community can access the whole MIB installed on the router. You can limit the MIB access that a community has by creating partial *views* of the MIB. This recipe creates a community that can view information only about objects in the Juniper Networks chassis MIB and in the standard MIB-II MIB. Controlling access consists of two steps: create the view itself using the set view commands and then associate the view with the community using the set community command.

If you want a community to be able to read most but not all of the MIB, you can restrict access to just a few MIB branches.

You might want to give access to all MIB branches except the two in which the
JUNOS software allows SNMP Set operations, the ping and traceroute MIB
branches:

```
[edit snmp]
aviva@router1# set view ping-traceroute-exclude oid jnxPingMIB exclude
aviva@router1# set view ping-traceroute-exclude oid jnxTraceRouteMIB exclude
aviva@router1# set community public view ping-traceroute-exclude
```

4.7   Extracting Software Inventory Information with SNMP

Problem

You want to use SNMP to retrieve software version information from the router.

Solution

From an NMS system, use the snmpwalk command:

```
aviva-server1% snmpwalk 192.168.15.1 public .1.3.6.1.2.1.25.6.3
...
host.hrSWInstalled.hrSWInstalledTable.hrSWInstalledEntry.hrSWInstalledName.2 = "JUNOS
Base OS Software Suite [7.4R1.7.0]"
host.hrSWInstalled.hrSWInstalledTable.hrSWInstalledEntry.hrSWInstalledName.3 = "JUNOS
Kernel Software Suite [7.4R1.7.0]"
host.hrSWInstalled.hrSWInstalledTable.hrSWInstalledEntry.hrSWInstalledName.4 = "JUNOS
Packet Forwarding Engine Support (M20/M40) [7.4R1.7.0]"
host.hrSWInstalled.hrSWInstalledTable.hrSWInstalledEntry.hrSWInstalledName.5 = "JUNOS
Routing Software Suite [7.4R1.7.0]"
host.hrSWInstalled.hrSWInstalledTable.hrSWInstalledEntry.hrSWInstalledName.6 = "JUNOS
Online Documentation [7.4R1.7.0]"
host.hrSWInstalled.hrSWInstalledTable.hrSWInstalledEntry.hrSWInstalledName.7 = "JUNOS
Crypto Software Suite [7.4R1.7.0]"
host.hrSWInstalled.hrSWInstalledTable.hrSWInstalledEntry.hrSWInstalledName.9 = "JUNOS
Support Tools Package [7.4R1.7.0]"
```

From the router, use the following equivalent command:

```
aviva@router1> show snmp mib walk .1.3.6.1.2.1.25.6.3
hrSWInstalledName.2 = JUNOS Base OS Software Suite [7.4R1.7.0]
hrSWInstalledName.3 = JUNOS Kernel Software Suite [7.4R1.7.0]
hrSWInstalledName.4 = JUNOS Packet Forwarding Engine Support (M20/M40) [7.4R1.7.0]
hrSWInstalledName.5 = JUNOS Routing Software Suite [7.4R1.7.0]
hrSWInstalledName.6 = JUNOS Online Documentation [7.4R1.7.0]
hrSWInstalledName.7 = JUNOS Crypto Software Suite [7.4R1.7.0]
hrSWInstalledName.9 = JUNOS Support Tools Package [7.4R1.7.0]
```

Discussion

The SNMP standard Host Resources MIB, specified in RFC 2790, contains objects that allow you to retrieve the versions of the software running on the router. The absolute path to the OID for installed software is .1.3.6.1.2.1.25.6.3. From the CLI, you get this same information with the show version command (see Recipe 1.25):

```
aviva@router1> show version
Hostname: router1
Model: m20
JUNOS Base OS boot [7.4-20051024.0]
JUNOS Base OS Software Suite [7.4-20051024.0]
JUNOS Kernel Software Suite [7.4R1.7]
JUNOS Packet Forwarding Engine Support (M20/M40) [7.4R1.7]
JUNOS Routing Software Suite [7.4R1.7]
JUNOS Online Documentation [7.4R1.7]
JUNOS Crypto Software Suite [7.4R1.7]
```

In the SNMP output, the software version is shown as 7.42R1.7.0, which includes the instance (.0) of the software package.

See Also

Recipe 1.25

4.8 Extracting Hardware Inventory Information with SNMP

Problem

You want to use SNMP to find out router hardware information and which field-replaceable units (FRUs) are present in the router.

Solution

If you are logged in to the router, you can get information using the show snmp mib commands. To get information about a single router component:

```
aviva@router1> show snmp mib get sysObjectID.0
sysObjectID.0 = jnxProductNameJ230M20
```

To get information about the next router component in the MIB:

```
aviva@router1> show snmp mib get jnxBoxClass.0
jnxBoxClass.0 = jnxProductLineM20.0
aviva@router1> show snmp mib get-next jnxBoxClass.0
jnxBoxDescr.0 = Juniper m20 Internet Backbone Router
```

For information about a number of router components, list each one separately:

```
aviva@router1> show snmp mib get "jnxBoxClass.0 jnxBoxClass.0"
jnxBoxClass.0 = jnxProductLineM20.0
jnxBoxClass.0 = jnxProductLineM20.0
```

To get information about all the router components:

```
aviva@router1> show snmp mib walk jnxBoxAnatomy
jnxBoxClass.0 = jnxProductLineM20.0
jnxBoxDescr.0 = Juniper m20 Internet Backbone Router
jnxBoxSerialNo.0 = 25708
...
jnxContainersType.1 = jnxChassisM20.0
jnxContainersType.2 = jnxM20SlotPower.0
jnxContainersType.4 = jnxM20SlotFan.0
jnxContainersType.6 = jnxM20SlotSSB.0
jnxContainersType.7 = jnxM20SlotFPC.0
jnxContainersType.8 = jnxM20MediaCardSpacePIC.0
jnxContainersType.9 = jnxM20SlotRE.0
jnxContainersType.10 = jnxM20SlotFrontPanel.0
jnxContainersDescr.1 = chassis frame
jnxContainersDescr.2 = Power Supply slot
jnxContainersDescr.4 = Fan slot
jnxContainersDescr.6 = SSB slot
jnxContainersDescr.7 = FPC slot
jnxContainersDescr.8 = PIC slot
jnxContainersDescr.9 = Routing Engine slot
jnxContainersDescr.10 = Front Panel Display slot
...
```

To get information about the FRUs, walk through the jnxContentsTable object:

```
aviva@router1> show snmp mib walk jnxContentsTable
...
jnxContentsType.1.1.0.0 = jnxBackplaneM20.0
jnxContentsType.2.1.0.0 = jnxM20Power.0
jnxContentsType.4.1.0.0 = jnxM20Fan.0
jnxContentsType.4.2.0.0 = jnxM20Fan.0
jnxContentsType.4.3.0.0 = jnxM20Fan.0
jnxContentsType.4.4.0.0 = jnxM20Fan.0
jnxContentsType.6.1.0.0 = jnxM20SSB.0
jnxContentsType.6.2.0.0 = jnxM20SSB.0
jnxContentsType.7.1.0.0 = jnxM20FPC.0
jnxContentsType.7.2.0.0 = jnxM20FPC.0
jnxContentsType.8.1.1.0 = jnxM20QuadEther.0
jnxContentsType.8.1.2.0 = jnxM20DualChDs3toDs0.0
jnxContentsType.8.1.3.0 = jnxM20QuadChT3.0
jnxContentsType.8.2.1.0 = jnxM20DualAtmOc3.0
jnxContentsType.9.1.0.0 = jnxM20RE.0
jnxContentsType.9.1.1.0 = jnxPCMCIACard.0
jnxContentsType.9.2.0.0 = jnxM20RE.0
jnxContentsType.9.2.1.0 = jnxPCMCIACard.0
jnxContentsType.10.1.0.0 = jnxM20FrontPanel.0
```

Discussion

In the Juniper Networks chassis MIB, router family information is in the jnxBoxAnatomy object and FRU information is in the jnxContentsTable object. On the router, you use the show snmp mib commands to collect data from these objects.

The three variations, show snmp mib get, show snmp mib get-next, and show snmp mib walk, are identical to the snmpget, snmpgetnext, and snmpwalk commands, respectively.

For the NMS system to extract this data, it needs to access the Juniper Networks chassis MIB to parse the MIB objects in the jnxBoxAnatomy and jnxContentsTable objects.

You can collect a range of information for each FRU. Here, we show data about the Routing Engine in slot 0:

```
aviva@router1> show snmp mib get jnxContentsType.9.1.0.0
jnxContentsType.9.1.0.0 = jnxM20RE.0
aviva@router1> show snmp mib get jnxContentsDescr.9.1.0.0
jnxContentsDescr.9.1.0.0 = Routing Engine 0
aviva@router1> show snmp mib get jnxContentsSerialNo.9.1.0.0
jnxContentsSerialNo.9.1.0.0 = 58000007348d9a01
aviva@router1> show snmp mib get jnxContentsRevision.9.1.0.0
jnxContentsRevision.9.1.0.0 = REV 06
```

If you are gathering hardware inventory information on the router, you use the show chassis hardware command (see Recipe 1.26):

```
aviva@router1> show chassis hardware
Hardware inventory:
Item             Version  Part number  Serial number   Description
Chassis                                25708           M20
Backplane        REV 03   710-002334   BB9738          M20 Backplane
Power Supply A   REV 06   740-001465   005234          AC Power Supply
Display          REV 04   710-001519   BA4681          M20 FPM Board
Routing Engine 0 REV 06   740-003239   1000224893      RE-2.0
Routing Engine 1 REV 06   740-003239   9000022146      RE-2.0
SSB slot 0       REV 02   710-001951   AZ8112          Internet Processor IIv1
SSB slot 1       N/A      N/A          N/A             Backup
FPC 0            REV 03   710-003308   BD8455          E-FPC
  PIC 0          REV 08   750-002303   AZ5310          4x F/E, 100 BASE-TX
  PIC 1          REV 07   750-004745   BC9368          2x CT3-NxDS0
  PIC 2          REV 03   750-002965   HC9279          4x CT3
FPC 1            REV 03   710-003308   BB9032          E-FPC
  PIC 0          REV 03   750-002914   BC0131          2x OC-3 ATM, MM
```

4.9 Collecting Router Operational Information with SNMP

Problem

You want the NMS server to check and record operational information about the router.

Solution

Look at the contents of the jnxOperatingTable table in the chassis MIB:

```
aviva@router1> show snmp mib walk jnxOperatingTable
...
jnxOperatingDescr.1.1.0.0 = backplane
jnxOperatingDescr.2.1.0.0 = Power Supply A
jnxOperatingDescr.4.1.0.0 = Front Upper Fan
jnxOperatingDescr.4.2.0.0 = Front Middle Fan
jnxOperatingDescr.4.3.0.0 = Front Bottom Fan
jnxOperatingDescr.4.4.0.0 = Rear Fan
jnxOperatingDescr.6.1.0.0 = SSB 0 Internet Processor IIv1
jnxOperatingDescr.6.2.0.0 = SSB 1
jnxOperatingDescr.7.1.0.0 = FPC: E-FPC @ 0/*/*
jnxOperatingDescr.7.2.0.0 = FPC: E-FPC @ 1/*/*
jnxOperatingDescr.8.1.1.0 = PIC: 4x F/E, 100 BASE-TX @ 0/0/*
jnxOperatingDescr.8.1.2.0 = PIC: 2x CT3-NxDS0 @ 0/1/*
jnxOperatingDescr.8.1.3.0 = PIC: 4x CT3 @ 0/2/*
jnxOperatingDescr.8.2.1.0 = PIC: 2x OC-3 ATM, MM @ 1/0/*
jnxOperatingDescr.9.1.0.0 = Routing Engine 0
jnxOperatingDescr.9.2.0.0 = Routing Engine 1
jnxOperatingDescr.10.1.0.0 = Front Panel Display
jnxOperatingTemp.1.1.0.0 = 22
jnxOperatingTemp.2.1.0.0 = 22
jnxOperatingTemp.4.1.0.0 = 0
jnxOperatingTemp.4.2.0.0 = 0
jnxOperatingTemp.4.3.0.0 = 0
jnxOperatingTemp.4.4.0.0 = 0
jnxOperatingTemp.6.1.0.0 = 30
jnxOperatingTemp.6.2.0.0 = 0
jnxOperatingTemp.7.1.0.0 = 28
jnxOperatingTemp.7.2.0.0 = 27
jnxOperatingTemp.8.1.1.0 = 0
jnxOperatingTemp.8.1.2.0 = 0
jnxOperatingTemp.8.1.3.0 = 0
jnxOperatingTemp.8.2.1.0 = 0
jnxOperatingTemp.9.1.0.0 = 29
jnxOperatingTemp.9.2.0.0 = 31
jnxOperatingTemp.10.1.0.0 = 0
...
```

Discussion

The jnxOperatingTable table in the chassis MIB lists all the components installed in the chassis along with information about their operation state. This table has an absolute OID of .1.3.6.1.4.1.2636.3.1.13.

The abridged output in the recipe shows the router hardware components and the current temperature (in degrees Celsius) for each component. This table contains much more information about the hardware, such as DRAM size (in bytes) for components that have memory:

```
jnxOperatingDRAMSize.6.1.0.0 = 67108864
jnxOperatingDRAMSize.7.1.0.0 = 33554432
jnxOperatingDRAMSize.7.2.0.0 = 33554432
jnxOperatingDRAMSize.9.1.0.0 = 805306368
jnxOperatingDRAMSize.9.2.0.0 = 805306368
```

Referring back to the list of hardware components, jnxOperatingDRAMSize.6.1.0.0 is the router's System and Switch Board (SSB), which handles forwarding for M20 routers. The other items are the FPC0 and FPC1 boards and the two Routing Engines. The output also shows how long a component has been up:

```
jnxOperatingUpTime.1.1.0.0 = 35718300
jnxOperatingUpTime.2.1.0.0 = 35719533
jnxOperatingUpTime.4.1.0.0 = 35719534
jnxOperatingUpTime.4.2.0.0 = 35719535
jnxOperatingUpTime.4.3.0.0 = 35719536
jnxOperatingUpTime.4.4.0.0 = 35719537
jnxOperatingUpTime.6.1.0.0 = 6515160
jnxOperatingUpTime.6.2.0.0 = 0
jnxOperatingUpTime.7.1.0.0 = 6511883
jnxOperatingUpTime.7.2.0.0 = 6511798
jnxOperatingUpTime.8.1.1.0 = 6509154
jnxOperatingUpTime.8.1.2.0 = 6509150
jnxOperatingUpTime.8.1.3.0 = 6509100
jnxOperatingUpTime.8.2.1.0 = 6508973
jnxOperatingUpTime.9.1.0.0 = 35718300
jnxOperatingUpTime.9.2.0.0 = 1978055600
jnxOperatingUpTime.10.1.0.0 = 35719549
```

The output shows that RE0 has been up for 35,718,300 10-second intervals, which is about 99 hours, or just over 4 days. You can confirm the Routing Engine information shown in the MIB objects with the following CLI command:

```
aviva@router1> show chassis routing-engine
Routing Engine status:
  Slot 0:
    Current state            Master
    Election priority        Master (default)
    Temperature              29 degrees C / 84 degrees F
    CPU temperature          30 degrees C / 86 degrees F
    DRAM                     768 MB
    Memory utilization       36 percent
```

```
CPU utilization:
    User                           0 percent
    Background                     0 percent
    Kernel                         1 percent
    Interrupt                      0 percent
    Idle                          99 percent
Model                             RE-2.0
Serial ID                         58000007348d9a01
Start time                        2005-12-07 13:28:55 PST
Uptime                            4 days, 3 hours, 57 minutes, 35 seconds
Load averages:                    1 minute   5 minute  15 minute
                                      0.07       0.05       0.02
```

4.10 Logging SNMP Access to the Router

Problem

You want to keep a log of SNMP operations that occur on the router and of the NMS systems that connect to the router to gather status and statistics.

Solution

Use the following command to log SNMP operations and NMS connections:

```
[edit snmp]
aviva@router1# set traceoptions flag pdu
```

Discussion

You log SNMP access and operations by using SNMP trace logging. By default, the log messages are saved to a number of tracing files in the */var/log* directory, including *snmpd*.

To see which NMS systems have connected to the router, this recipe sets the PDU tracing flag, which logs all NMS system request and responses to them, as well as any traps that get generated. To see the PDU traces, look in the */var/log/snmpd* file:

```
Apr 27 12:04:34 snmpd[1370dced] >>>>>>>>>>>>>>>>>>>>>>>>>>>>>>>>>>>>>>>>>>>>>>
Apr 27 12:04:34 snmpd[1370dced] >>> Get-Request
Apr 27 12:04:34 snmpd[1370dced] >>> Source:      172.16.20.182
Apr 27 12:04:34 snmpd[1370dced] >>> Destination: 192.168.15.1
Apr 27 12:04:34 snmpd[1370dced] >>> Version:     SNMPv2
Apr 27 12:04:34 snmpd[1370dced] >>> Request_id:  0x1370dced
Apr 27 12:04:34 snmpd[1370dced] >>> Community:   public
Apr 27 12:04:34 snmpd[1370dced] >>> Error:       status=0 / vb_index=0
Apr 27 12:04:34 snmpd[1370dced] >>>   OID  : sysName.0
Apr 27 12:04:34 snmpd[1370dced] >>>>>>>>>>>>>>>>>>>>>>>>>>>>>>>>>>>>>>>>>>>>>>
Apr 27 12:04:34 snmpd[1370dced] <<<<<<<<<<<<<<<<<<<<<<<<<<<<<<<<<<<<<<<<<<<<<<
Apr 27 12:04:34 snmpd[1370dced] <<< Get-Response
Apr 27 12:04:34 snmpd[1370dced] <<< Source:      192.168.15.1
Apr 27 12:04:34 snmpd[1370dced] <<< Destination: 172.16.20.182
Apr 27 12:04:34 snmpd[1370dced] <<< Version:     SNMPv2
```

```
Apr 27 12:04:34 snmpd[1370dced]  <<<  Request_id:  0x1370dced
Apr 27 12:04:34 snmpd[1370dced]  <<<  Community:   public
Apr 27 12:04:34 snmpd[1370dced]  <<<  Error:         status=0 / vb_index=0
Apr 27 12:04:34 snmpd[1370dced]  <<<   OID  : sysName.0
Apr 27 12:04:34 snmpd[1370dced]  <<<   type : OctetString
Apr 27 12:04:34 snmpd[1370dced]  <<<   value: "router1"
Apr 27 12:04:34 snmpd[1370dced]  <<<   HEX  : 74 61 6e 71  75 65 72 61
Apr 27 12:04:34 snmpd[1370dced]  <<<          79
Apr 27 12:04:34 snmpd[1370dced]  <<<<<<<<<<<<<<<<<<<<<<<<<<<<<<<<<<<<<<<<<<<<<<<
```

This output shows a Get request from the NMS system 172.16.20.182 for the OID sysName. The router returned the value of router1 in its Get-Response message.

See Also

Recipe 5.1

4.11 Logging Enterprise-Specific Traps

Problem

You want to collect Juniper Networks enterprise-specific traps in the router's system logging files.

Solution

Use the following commands to save all log messages to a file called *snmp-critical-traps*:

```
[edit]
user@router1# edit system syslog file snmp-critical-traps
[edit system syslog file snmp-critical-traps]
user@router1# set daemon critical
```

Discussion

The traps from the Juniper Networks chassis MIB all have a system logging severity level associated with them. You can take advantage of this to collect these traps in a system logfile. The chassis traps record chassis component information that is critical to the operation of the router, such as power supply and fan failures. In this recipe, we collect all critical and alert logging messages generated by all JUNOS processes, including SNMPD and MIB2D, which captures most of the SNMP chassis traps.

Table 4-2 shows all the chassis traps and their corresponding severity level. In the system logging file, these messages are prefixed with the identifier CHASSISD_SNMP_TRAP.

Table 4-2. System logging severity levels for Juniper Networks chassis SNMPv2 traps

Severity level	Chassis SNMPv2 trap

Notice	jnxFruInsertion
	  Insertion of a replaceable chassis component
	jnxFruPowerOff
	  Powering down of a replaceable chassis component
	jnxFruPowerOn
	  Powering up of a replaceable chassis component
	jnxFruRemoval
	  Removal of a replaceable chassis component

Critical	jnxFanFailure
	  Chassis fan or impeller failure
	jnxFanOK
	  Chassis fan or impeller recovery
	jnxOverTemperature
	  Overheating of a hardware component
	jnxPowerSupplyOK
	  Power supply recovery
	jnxRedundancySwitchOver
	  Chassis component has switched from master to backup, or vice versa

Alert	jnxPowerSupplyFailure
	  Power supply failure
	jnxTemperatureOK
	  Overheating recovery by a hardware component

The Juniper Networks chassis MIB traps are the only enterprise-specific traps that are associated with a system logging severity level, so they are the only ones that you can specifically log.

See Also

Recipe 5.1

4.12 Using RMON Traps to Monitor the Router's Temperature

Problem

You want to use remote monitoring (RMON) to have the router monitor and proactively report on overtemperature conditions in the router.

Solution

Create an RMON trap that watches the internal temperature of the router by tracking the backplane temperature:

```
[edit snmp]
aviva@router1# set trap-group overtemperature
aviva@router1# set trap-group overtemperature categories rmon-alarm
aviva@router1# set trap-group overtemperature targets 10.0.10.1
aviva@router1# edit rmon
[edit snmp rmon]
aviva@router1# set alarm 1 description "overtemperature for M20 backplane"
aviva@router1# set alarm 1 interval 300
aviva@router1# set alarm 1 variable jnxOperatingTemp.1.1.0.0
aviva@router1# set alarm 1 sample-type absolute-value
aviva@router1# set alarm 1 rising-threshold 40
aviva@router1# set alarm 1 startup-alarm rising-alarm
aviva@router1# set alarm 1 rising-event-index 1
aviva@router1# set event 1 description Heap-Events
aviva@router1# set event 1 type log-and-trap
aviva@router1# set event 1 community heap-traps
```

This is an involved configuration, so here's what it looks like when viewed all together:

```
[edit snmp]
aviva@router1# show
trap-group overtemperature {
    categories {
        rmon-alarm;
    }
    targets {
        10.0.10.1;
    }
}
rmon {
    alarm 1 {
        description "overtemperature for M20 backplane";
        interval 300;
        variable jnxOperatingTemp.1.1.0.0;
        sample-type absolute-value;
        rising-threshold 40;
        rising-event-index 1;
    }
    event 1 {
        description Overtemperature-Events;
        type log-and-trap;
        community overtemperature;
    }
}
```

Discussion

RMON is an SNMP specification that allows an SNMP agent (your router) to proactively monitor its system health and performance and then send traps to an SNMP manager. The local SNMP agent compares MIB values against predefined thresholds and generates exception alarms without the need for polling by a central SNMP management platform. This is an effective mechanism for proactive management, provided that you have baselined and set the thresholds correctly. RMON also decreases the amount of traffic between the manager and the router because the SNMP manager does not always have to poll for information and it allows the manager to get more timely status reports because the router reports events as they occur.

You can monitor many things. This recipe monitors the router's backplane temperature. The backplane is in the center of the router, so the temperature gives you an idea of whether the router might be overheating. This recipe sets the threshold at 40 degrees Celsius. When this value is exceeded, an RMON event is triggered, a trap is sent, and the event is logged.

To set up RMON, configure the OID and the threshold values that trigger the alarm (with the set alarm commands), the router's response to the alarm (with the set event commands), and the NMS systems to receive the trap (with the set trap-group commands).

The alarm's threshold value can be an actual value, as in these two alarms (set with the sample-type statement and absolute-value option), or the difference between the current value and the last value (set with the delta-value option).

Finally, choose a number to identify the alarm and to link the alarm with the event. Specify the number in the rising-alarm-index statement when monitoring a rising threshold or in the falling-alarm-index statement when monitoring a falling threshold. For alarm 1, rising-alarm-index 1 associates event 1 with this alarm.

The event statement hierarchy defines the router's response to the alarm. In this recipe, the type log-and-trap statement logs both sets of traps. The community statement associates the events with the trap group overtemperature, which sends the traps to the NMS system defined in the targets statement.

When you configure the trap group to handle the RMON event, the category must be rmon-alarm. The targets are all the NMS systems to receive the trap.

Events are generated only when the threshold is first crossed in any one direction, not after each sample period. Once the threshold is crossed, no more events are generated until after the value crosses back into the normal range and again crosses the threshold. This mechanism considerably reduces the quantity of alarms produced by the router, making it easier for you to react when alarms do occur. Keep in mind that because SNMP uses UDP, there is no guarantee of the delivery of the alarm to the SNMP manager.

To verify that the RMON alarm is set, use the following command on the router:

```
aviva@router1> show snmp rmon alarms
Alarm
Index  Variable description                          Value State
     1 monitor: overtemperature for M20 backplane
       jnxOperatingTemp.1.1.0.0                         22 falling threshold
```

The Value column in the output shows the current value of the object, which here is 22 degrees. You can verify the temperature by looking at the object's value directly:

```
aviva@router1> show snmp mib get jnxOperatingTemp.1.1.0.0
jnxOperatingTemp.1.1.0.0 = 22
```

You can also see it with the show chassis environment command:

```
aviva@router1> show chassis environment
Class Item               Status    Measurement
Power Power Supply A      OK
      Power Supply B      Absent
Temp  FPC 0               OK        28 degrees C / 82 degrees F
      FPC 1               OK        27 degrees C / 80 degrees F
      Power Supply A      OK        22 degrees C / 71 degrees F
      Power Supply B      Absent
      SSB 0               OK        30 degrees C / 86 degrees F
      Backplane           OK        22 degrees C / 71 degrees F
      Routing Engine 0    OK        30 degrees C / 86 degrees F
      Routing Engine 1    OK        31 degrees C / 87 degrees F
Fans  Rear Fan            OK        Spinning at normal speed
      Front Upper Fan     OK        Spinning at normal speed
      Front Middle Fan    OK        Spinning at normal speed
      Front Bottom Fan    OK        Spinning at normal speed
Misc  Craft Interface     OK
```

To see the events that are set, use this command:

```
aviva@router1> show snmp rmon events
Event
Index  Type                    Last Event
     1 log and trap
```

When the backplane temperature crosses the rising threshold, you can see the log using the show snmp rmon logs command.

From the NMS system and from the router, you can retrieve RMON data from the alarmTable, eventTable, and logTable MIB objects. Here's what you would see when looking at the alarm table from the router:

```
aviva@router1> show snmp mib walk eventTable
eventIndex.1   = 1
eventDescription.1 = Overtemperature-Events
eventType.1    = 4
eventCommunity.1 = overtemperature
eventLastTimeSent.1 = 0
eventOwner.1
eventStatus.1 = 1
```

See Also

RFC 2819, *Remote Network Monitoring MIB*

4.13 Configuring SNMPv3

Problem

You want to set up the router to be an SNMP agent so your network SNMPv3 NMS system can monitor it.

Solution

First, define the NMS systems that can access the router and their passwords:

```
[edit snmp v3]
aviva@router1# set usm local-engine user nms1 authentication-sha authentication-
password $1991poppI
aviva@router1# set usm local-engine user nms1 privacy-des privacy-password $1991poppI
```

Then, define the MIBs to which the users have access:

```
[edit snmp]
aviva@router1# set view chassis-info-only oid jnxBoxAnatomy include
aviva@router1# set view chassis-info-only oid snmpMIBObjects include
aviva@router1# set view chassis-info-only oid system include
```

You create groups and assign users to them and then define access privileges for each group:

```
[edit snmp v3]
aviva@router1# set vacm security-to-group security-model usm security-name nms1 group
chassis-only
aviva@router1# set vacm access group chassis-only default-context-prefix security-
model usm security-level privacy read-view chassis-info-only
aviva@router1# set vacm access group chassis-only default-context-prefix security-
model usm security-level privacy notify-view chassis-info-only
```

Discussion

The basic SNMPv3 setup is similar to the SNMPv2 configuration. You define the NMS systems that can make SNMP requests to the router and which MIBs they can access. In the recipe shown here, we give access only to the objects related to the hardware chassis components.

SNMPv3 uses a USM for security, which you configure in the usm statement hierarchy. Each NMS system is a user. For each user, configure an authentication type and password to ensure that the SNMP messages come from a trusted source. Here we have configured SHA1 authentication. USM also supports MD5 authentication, which you configure with the authentication-md5 keyword.

To protect the SNMP message payload, you encrypt it, here with DES. The CLI converts both passwords into keys:

```
[edit snmp v3 usm local-engine]
aviva@router1# show
user nms1 {
    authentication-sha {
        authentication-key "$9$5Qz6uOIrlMOOLxN-2gUjH.mTFn/CAOaZFnCtOBNdVbgoGDiPfzGU.
5TzCAM8LXbs24aZGiM8ZUjHmPRhcyM8-ds2aZVb.
Pf5F3SrlKLxdVYaJDKMjHqmTQreKMNds24Djq8XGDjkPfylevxN4aZqP5LxDiHqQz369CtOhclKWLz3cyrK8L
JGUDqm"; ## SECRET-DATA
    }
    privacy-des {
        privacy-key "$9$bcsYoji.zF/iHApoOcSM8XN-w24aZGilK24ZUHkoB1ISrvWLdVYvMNbwYZG/
CAtIEcylKvL/CKM8X-dmf5Q/COBEclK1INdVb2gTzFnApB1hleWn/8X7-wsz3n/
OBEcyW87CtvW8xdVQF36pOylK7dbApWLX7sYgoJZUHf5Fn9AYg5QznCAevMW7-"; ## SECRET-DATA
    }
}
```

As with SNMPv2, you create views to define which MIB branches the NMS systems can access (use the `view` statement at the [edit snmp] level, not at the [edit snmp v3] level). The view we configure, `chassis-info-only`, allows access to the Juniper Networks enterprise chassis MIB and to portions of other MIBs that retrieve chassis-related information. Because we use the notify view for the `chassis-only` group, we need to allow the `sysUpTime` object, which is part of the `system` OID. The notify view is used when the router sends SNMPv3 notifications (informational messages and traps) to the NMS system. We show how to configure notifications in Recipe 4.15.

Next, define the NMS system's access to the router (in the `vacm` statement hierarchy). SNMPv3 uses a VACM to grant access privileges to groups. You create groups that are identified by a name, then assign the desired access. A group is simply a collection of NMS systems (users) that are defined in the USM and that share the same access privileges (set in the `access` statement hierarchy). Here, we have a group called `chassis-only` that includes our NMS system `nms1`.

In the `access` commands, set the security and access privileges for the group. In our recipe, the security model is USM and the security level is `privacy`, which authenticates all messages and encrypts the message payload. You can also choose `authentication`, which provides only authentication, and `none`, which provides neither. The `read-view` and `notify-view` statements set the access privileges for incoming NMS requests and outgoing notifications, respectively.

To see the SNMPv3 configuration settings, use the following command:

```
aviva@router1> show snmp v3
Local engine ID: 80 00 0a 4c 01 c0 a8 47 f6
Engine boots:         123
Engine time:     24951 seconds
Max msg size:     2048 bytes
Engine ID: local
    User                          Auth/Priv   Storage     Status
```

```
    nms1                                      sha/3des   nonvolatile  active
Group name              Security  Security                  Storage      Status
                        model     name                      type
chassis-only            usm       nms1                      nonvolatile  active
Access control:
Group                   Context   Security     Read      Write     Notify
                        prefix    model/level  view      view      view
chassis-only                      usm/privacy  chassis-in
```

The JUNOS structure for configuring SNMPv3 follows the structure of the protocol specification itself. Because it is a bit complex, it's worthwhile to look at the SNMPv3 portion of the configuration file that is created by the commands in this recipe, along with some added comments.

```
aviva@router1# show | except SECRET-DATA
v3 {
    usm { # <-- which NMS systems can access the router
        local-engine {
            user nms1 {
                authentication-sha {
                privacy-des {
                }
            }
        }
    }
    vacm { # <-- what the NMS systems can access on the router
        security-to-group { # <-- which access group each NMS is in
            security-model usm {
                security-name nms1 {
                    group chassis-only;
                }
            }
        }
        access { # <-- which MIB views the NMS systems can access
            group chassis-only {
                default-context-prefix {
                    security-model usm {
                        security-level privacy {
                            read-view chassis-info-only;
                            notify-view chassis-info-only;
                        }
                    }
                }
            }
        }
    }
}
view chassis-info-only { # <-- define a view that allows all chassis objects
    oid jnxBoxAnatomy include;
    oid snmpMIBObjects include;
    oid system include;
}
```

4.14 Tracking Router Configuration Changes

Problem

You want an NMS system to track when the router's configuration has been changed.

Solution

First, define the NMS system and its password:

```
[edit snmp v3]
aviva@router1# set usm local-engine user nms2 authentication-sha authentication-
password $0212roZH
aviva@router1# set usm local-engine user nms2 privacy-des privacy-password 0212roZH
```

Then, define two views that allow the NMS access to the configuration information. The first view defines what the NMS can read from the MIB:

```
[edit snmp v3]
aviva@router1# set view config-info-read oid jnxCfgMgmt include
```

The second view sets what the router includes in notifications sent to the NMS:

```
[edit snmp v3]
aviva@router1# set view config-info-notify oid jnxCfgMgmt include
aviva@router1# set view config-info-notify oid jnxCmNotifications include
aviva@router1# set view config-info-notify oid snmpMIBObjects include
aviva@router1# set view config-info-notify oid system include
```

Finally, create groups and their users and assign access privileges for the groups:

```
[edit snmp v3]
aviva@router1# set vacm security-to-group security-model usm security-name nms2 group
config-only
aviva@router1# set vacm access group config-only default-context-prefix security-
model usm security-level privacy read-view config-info-read
aviva@router1# set vacm access group config-only default-context-prefix security-
model usm security-level privacy notify-view config-info-notify
```

Discussion

To use SNMP to extract the router configuration, use the Juniper Networks configuration management MIB extension, which tracks who made changes to the configuration and when. This recipe gives the NMS system called nms2 access to configuration information.

The first commands in this recipe configure USM for security, with SHA1 authentication and DES message payload encryption. You then create two views, one that defines what nms2 can read from the MIB and a second that sets what the router can include in notifications. The final commands configure the VACM to provide access to desired groups.

Again, this recipe is somewhat involved, so here's what the resulting configuration looks like after you issue the commands in this recipe, with some added comments:

```
aviva@router1# show | except SECRET-DATA
v3 {
    usm { # <-- which NMS systems can access the router
        local-engine {
            user nms2 {
                authentication-sha {
                privacy-des {
                }
            }
        }
    }
    vacm { # <-- what the NMS systems can access on the router
        security-to-group { # <-- which access group each NMS is in
            security-model usm {
                security-name nms2 {
                    group config-only;
                }
            }
        }
        access { # <-- which MIB views the NMS systems can access
            group config-only {
                default-context-prefix {
                    security-model usm {
                        security-level privacy {
                            read-view config-info-read;
                            notify-view config-info-notify;
                        }
                    }
                }
            }
        }
    }
}
view config-info-read { # <-- view of enterprise configuration management objects
    oid jnxCfgMgmt include;
}
view config-info-notify { # <-- view for objects used by SNMPv3 traps
    oid jnxCfgMgmt include;
    oid jnxCmNotifications include;
    oid snmpMIBObjects include;
    oid system include;
}
```

4.15 Setting Up SNMPv3 Traps

Problem

You want SNMPv3 to generate traps about chassis and configuration events and send the traps to the NMS system.

Solution

For the chassis events, first configure the trap notification:

```
[edit snmp v3]
aviva@router1# set notify chassis-notification-list type trap
aviva@router1# set notify chassis-notification-list tag chassis-trap-receivers
```

Next, define the traps to send:

```
[edit snmp v3]
aviva@router1# set notify-filter chassis-traps oid jnxChassisTraps include
aviva@router1# set notify-filter chassis-traps oid jnxChassisOKTraps include
```

Identify the NMS systems (the targets) to receive the traps:

```
[edit snmp v3]
aviva@router1# edit target-address nms1
[edit snmp v3 target-address nms1]
aviva@router1# set address 10.0.10.1
aviva@router1# set tag-list chassis-trap-receivers
aviva@router1# set target-parameters nms1-parameters
```

Finally, configure which traps the NMS systems receive and the security used when sending the traps:

```
[edit snmp v3]
aviva@router1# edit target-parameters nms1-parameters
[edit snmp v3 target-parameters nms1-parameters]
aviva@router1# set parameters message-processing-model v3
aviva@router1# set parameters security-model usm
aviva@router1# set parameters security-level privacy
aviva@router1# set parameters security-name nms1
aviva@router1# set notify-filter chassis-traps
```

To set up traps that correspond to the JUNOS configuration management MIB extension we showed in Recipe 4.14, configure them in a similar way. First, set up the trap notification:

```
[edit snmp v3]
aviva@router1# set notify config-notification-list type trap
aviva@router1# set notify config-notification-list tag config-trap-receivers
```

Next, define the trap to send:

```
[edit snmp v3]
aviva@router1# set notify-filter config-traps oid jnxCmNotifications include
```

Specify the NMS systems to receives the traps:

```
[edit snmp v3]
aviva@router1# set target-address nms2 address 192.168.15.27
aviva@router1# set target-address nms2 tag-list config-trap-receivers
aviva@router1# set target-address nms2 target-parameters nms2-parameters
```

Finally, configure which traps the NMS systems receive and the security used when sending the traps:

```
[edit snmp v3]
aviva@router1# set target-parameters nms2-parameters notify-filter config-traps
aviva@router1# set target-parameters nms2-parameters parameters message-processing-
model v3
aviva@router1# set target-parameters nms2-parameters parameters security-model usm
aviva@router1# set target-parameters nms2-parameters parameters security-level
privacy
aviva@router1# set target-parameters nms2-parameters parameters security-name nms2
```

Discussion

The configuration of SNMPv3 traps is much more involved than for SNMPv2, so let's look at each step of the process. The first part of this recipe sets up traps for the objects related to the hardware chassis components.

First, configure a notification. SNMPv3 defines two types of notifications: informational and trap. You want to set type trap. You'll also want to name the notification with the tag statement (here, chassis-trap-receivers) so that later in the configuration, you can associate the trap type with the NMS system that will be receiving the traps.

Second, create a filter that identifies which traps are sent to the NMS. Here, the filter named chassis-traps sends all traps from the Juniper chassis MIB.

Next, define the NMS systems to receive the trap notifications in the target-address statement hierarchy. Each target has a name, here nms1, which is the username of the NMS (also referred to as the security name). Then set the NMS system's address and associate a tag list and security parameters with it. Here, we associate the chassis-trap-receivers tag and the nms1-parameters security parameters, which we define next.

Finally, associate a trap notification filter with the target NMS system (here, the chassis-traps filter) and define the security to use in all trap message exchanges. SNMPv3 security has three components: the message-processing model, the security model, and the security level. The processing model is SNMPv1, SNMPv2, or SNMPv3, which corresponds to the v1, v2, and v3 options of the message-processing-model statement. The security model is SNMPv1, SNMPv2, or USM, corresponding to the v1, v2c, and usm options of the security-model statement. Finally, the security level can be noAuthnoPriv, authNoPriv, or authPriv, which match the none, authentication, and privacy options of the security-level statement. Bundled in with defining the security parameters is the username (security name) of the receiving NMS system. Here, the security-name nms1 statement associates the security parameters with the system we defined in the target-address nms1 statement hierarchy.

Check the configuration using the show snmp v3 command. The following output shows only the portion related to the trap notifications:

```
aviva@router1> show snmp v3
SNMP Target:
Address         Address         Port   Parameters    Storage      Status
name                                   name          type
nms1            10.0.10.1       162    nms1-parame   nonvolatile  active
Parameters      Security        Security      Notify  Storage      Status
name            name            model/level   filter  type
nms1-parameter  nms1            usm/privacy chassis nonvolatile  active
SNMP Notify:
Notify                     Tag                  Type     Storage      Status
name                                                     type
trap-notification-li NMS-trap-receiver   trap     nonvolatile  active
Filter                     Subtree              Filter   Storage      Status
name                                            type     type
chassis-traps         1.3.6.1.4.1.2636.  include  nonvolatile  active
```

The Target and Parameters portions of the output list the NMS systems configured to receive traps and lists the security parameters. The Notify and Filter portions give information about the traps that will be sent.

Here's the traps portion of the SNMPv3 configuration file; you can see how all the pieces fit together:

```
[edit snmp v3]
target-address nms1 {
    address 10.0.10.1;
    tag-list NMS-trap-receivers;
    target-parameters nms1-parameters;
}
target-address nms2 {
    address 10.0.0.1;
    tag-list config-trap-receivers;
    target-parameters nms2-parameters;
}
target-parameters nms1-parameters {
    parameters {
        message-processing-model v3;
        security-model usm;
        security-level privacy;
        security-name nms1;
    }
    notify-filter chassis-traps;
}
target-parameters nms2-parameters {
    parameters {
        message-processing-model v3;
        security-model usm;
        security-level privacy;
        security-name nms2;
    }
    notify-filter config-traps;
```

```
}
notify chassis-notification-list {
    type trap;
    tag chassis-trap-receivers;
}
notify config-notification-list {
    type trap;
    tag config-trap-receivers;
}
notify-filter chassis-traps {
    oid jnxChassisTraps include;
    oid jnxChassisOKTraps include;
}
notify-filter config-traps {
    oid jnxCmNotifications include;
}
```

CHAPTER 5

Logging

5.0   Introduction

Logging events that occur on the router is an important tool available to router and network administrators. Logging provides real-time and historical information about router operations, which you can use to help trace and analyze the sequences of events leading to a problem on the router or network, or both. The JUNOS software provides two mechanisms for logging events: system logging (sometimes called syslog) and tracing. With *system logging*, the JUNOS software generates system log messages (also called syslog messages) that record events that occur systemwide on the router, such as a user logging in to the router or an interface starting up; failure and error conditions, such as a login failure or the unexpected closure of a peer process; and emergency or critical conditions, such as a router shutting down due to excessive heat. JUNOS system logging is very similar to the Unix syslog function. *Tracing* (sometimes also called trace logging) is specific to routing protocols and records information about protocol operation, such as the exchange of protocol packets when a protocol is starting or sending regularly scheduled updates.

Both system logging and tracing save log messages to files. These files are stored in the */var/log* directory on the router's hard disk for M-series and T-series routers and in the */cf/var/log* directory on J-series routers. You can redirect system log messages to a remote server that is running a standard syslogd utility, to the terminal of a user who is logged in to the router, or to the console.

The JUNOS software can generate thousands of different system log messages, from all parts of the system, including hardware, routing software processes, and forwarding software. The messages are categorized by source and severity. Because you are almost never interested in saving and reviewing all system log messages generated by the router, use the source and severity as log message filters.

Each system logging message is identified with a *priority*, consisting of a facility and a severity level. The *facility* is the source of the message, which is the router process or event that generated the message. Table 5-1 lists all the JUNOS system log facilities.

Some are the same as those used by the Unix syslog utility, and some are specific to the JUNOS software.

Table 5-1. JUNOS system log facilities

Facility name	Facility code	Message source
any	—	Any facility
authorization	AUTH, AUTHPRIV	Authentication and authorization attempts
change-log	CHANGE	Router configuration changes
conflict-log	CONFLICT	Router configuration changes that are inconsistent with the router hardware
	CONSOLE	Kernel messages to the console (/dev/console)
	CRON	Scheduled processes
daemon	DAEMON	JUNOS software processes
firewall	FIREWALL	Packet filtering done by firewall filters
ftp	FTP	FTP
interactive-commands	INTERACT	Commands issued at the JUNOS CLI or by a JUNOScript client application
kernel	KERNEL	JUNOS kernel
	NTP	NTP
pfe	PFE	Packet forwarding software
	SYSLOG	System logging
user	USER	User processes

Each system log message has a *severity level* (see Table 5-2) that reflects the seriousness of the event that generates the message. Each severity level has a name and number, which are the same as those used by the Unix syslog utility. The lower the number, the more critical the event.

Table 5-2. JUNOS system log severity levels

Severity name	Severity number	Description
any	—	All severity levels
none	—	No severity levels
debug	7	Information normally used in debugging
info	6	Informational events about normal router operations
notice	5	Conditions that are not errors but are of more interest than normal router events
warning	4	General warnings for events you might want to keep an eye on
error	3	General error conditions
critical	2	Critical errors, such as hard drive failures
alert	1	Errors that require immediate correction, such as corrupted system files
emergency	0	Conditions that cause the router to stop functioning

Depending on how you configure system logging, the JUNOS system log messages have one of the following formats. The first format is the default.

```
Mar 17 11:12:29  router1 mib2d[2885]: SNMP_TRAP_LINK_DOWN: ifIndex 2,
   ifAdminStatus up(1), ifOperStatus down(2), ifName t1-0/0/0:1

Mar 17 11:12:29  router1 mib2d[2885]: %DAEMON-4-SNMP_TRAP_LINK_DOWN: ifIndex 2,
   ifAdminStatus up(1), ifOperStatus down(2), ifName t1-0/0/0:1
```

The system log message includes a timestamp, the router's name, and the message itself. The timestamp indicates the date and time when the message was logged. Missing from the timestamp is any indication of the time zone. If all your routers are located in a small geographic area, this is not much of a problem. However, if your operations are more global, you should make sure that you either configure all routers to use the same time zone (UTC is a good choice) or, less optimally, that you know which routers are using which time zone. Knowing the time accurately on your network's routers is critical when you are searching through logfiles to debug a problem between two routers and are trying determine what happened when. Setting time zones is discussed in Recipe 6.2.

The second part of the log message is the actual log message itself, which shows the source of the message and the message code and description. The message in the previous example was generated by the MIB-II process, and the specific process number is 2885. (If the process is still running, you can see it with the show system processes command.) The message code consists of a prefix, in this case SNMP_, which is the process that generated the message, and a unique message identifier (TRAP_LINK_DOWN). The text string at the end describes the message. The second message format above shows two other pieces of information, the facility code name (here, DAEMON, indicating that the message source is a JUNOS software process) and the numeric severity level (4, which is a warning message).

A quick way to find out what a system log message means is to use the help syslog command. You can just cut and paste the message code into the command:

```
aviva@router1> help syslog SNMP_TRAP_LINK_DOWN
Name:          SNMP_TRAP_LINK_DOWN
Message:       ifIndex <if-index>, ifAdminStatus <admin-status>, ifOperStatus
               <oper-status>, ifName <interface-name>
Help:          linkDown trap was sent
Description:   The SNMP agent process (snmpd) generated a linkDown trap because
               the indicated interface changed state to 'down'.
Type:          Event: This message reports an event, not an error
Severity:      warning
```

5.1 Turning On Logging

Problem

You want to monitor all systemwide operations by saving all log messages to a file on the router.

Solution

Use the following commands to save all log messages to a file called messages:

```
[edit]
aviva@router1# set system syslog file messages any info
```

Discussion

The most common place to save system logging messages is on the router. If you do not configure logging, it is turned on by default and sends messages to the file messages (located in /var/log on M-series and T-series routers and in /cf/var/log on J-series routers). The messages logged are those from all facilities that have a severity notice and all authorization messages. If you were to configure the default settings, the configuration file would look like this:

```
[edit system syslog]
file messages {
    any notice;
    authorization info;
}
```

This recipe modifies the default so messages from all facilities (any) and all severities (info) are logged. Keep in mind that for a given severity level, the software logs all messages at that level and at all more serious levels, so when you specify the lowest severity level, info, you are in effect recording all system log messages except for debug messages. You could also specify any instead of info here.

When you want to review the system log messages, use the show log command. In all system log message files, the messages are listed in order, from oldest to newest. As the file gets large, you have to scroll through a lot of lines to get to the most recent messages. You can shorten the output by using some of the CLI command filters. For example, you can specify today's date and time to list only the most recent messages (match is simply the Unix grep utility):

```
aviva@router1> show log messages | match "Mar  9 11:5"
Mar  9 11:54:31  router1 login: LOGIN_INFORMATION: User aviva logged in from host
172.17.28.19 on device ttyp1
Mar  9 11:54:34  router1 mgd[29108]: UI_DBASE_LOGIN_EVENT: User 'aviva' entering
configuration mode
Mar  9 11:56:13  router1 mgd[29108]: UI_DBASE_LOGOUT_EVENT: User 'aviva' exiting
configuration mode
Mar  9 11:57:52  router1 mgd[28332]: UI_DBASE_LOGOUT_EVENT: User 'aviva' exiting
configuration mode
```

If you want to find out who has logged in to the router today, you can set up a chain of filters:

```
aviva@router1> show log messages | match LOGIN | match "Mar 16"
Mar 16 11:00:53  router1 login: LOGIN_INVALID_LOCAL_USER: No entry in local password
file for user pwd
```

```
Mar 16 11:00:54  router1 login: LOGIN_PAM_AUTHENTICATION_ERROR: PAM auhentication
error for user pwd
Mar 16 11:00:54  router1 login: LOGIN_FAILED: Login failed for user pwd from host
Mar 16 11:00:55  router1 login: LOGIN_INFORMATION: User root logged in from host
[unknown] on device ttyd0
Mar 16 21:57:59  router1 login: LOGIN_INFORMATION: User aviva logged in from host
172.17.28.108 on device ttyp0
Mar 16 21:58:04  router1 mgd[4102]: UI_DBASE_LOGIN_EVENT: User 'aviva' entering
configuration mode
```

You can create multiple system logging files to track messages from different sources and of different severities. Instead of sifting through the messages file to find out what users and processes have been logging in to the router, you can configure a system logging file for only those activities.

```
[edit system syslog]
aviva@router1# set file security authorization info
```

The following are examples of some of the logging messages that are saved as a result of this configuration:

```
aviva@router1> show log security
Mar 18 01:53:41  router1 init: ntp (PID 4194) exit on SIGHUP, will be restarted to
get the new config
Mar 18 01:53:41  router1 init: ntp (PID 4644) started
Mar 18 01:54:16  router1 login: LOGIN_INFORMATION: User aviva logged in from host
172.17.28.108 on device ttyp0
Mar 18 01:55:41  router1 init: ntp (PID 4644) exit on SIGHUP, will be restarted to
get the new config
Mar 18 01:55:41  router1 init: ntp (PID 5006) started
```

By default, only the root user and users with the JUNOS maintenance permission can read the contents of logfiles (see Recipe 2.10). If a number of people need to be able to read a system logfile, you should change the permission on the file. This is similar to the Unix chmod utility.

```
[edit system syslog]
aviva@router1# set file messages archive world-readable
aviva@router1# set file security archive world-readable
```

To verify that the file permissions have changed, use the file list detail command. The files are still owned by root, but they are readable by anyone.

```
aviva@router1> file list detail /var/log
-rw-rw-r--  1 root  wheel       5883 Mar 18 02:00 messages
-rw-rw-r--  1 root  wheel      17638 Mar 18 02:01 security
```

See Also

Recipe 2.10

5.2   Limiting the Messages Collected

Problem

You have turned on system logging and are collecting messages from all facilities in your logging files. You are not interested in the messages from one or two of the facilities and would like to stop messages from these facilities without configuring each priority.

Solution

Disable the facilities that you don't want showing up in your logfile:

```
[edit system syslog file messages]
aviva@router1# set any notice
aviva@router1# set interactive none
```

Discussion

When you want to capture logging messages from all sources on the router, you can configure this easily with a single command that specifies the facility as any. When you want to capture all facilities but one or two, the quickest way is to disable the facilities that you are not interested in. In this case, you are not interested in collecting any of the commands that users type at the CLI, but you do want any other commands. These two commands are a shortcut that saves you from having to type 10 commands, one for each facility you want to enable.

5.3   Including the Facility and Severity in Messages

Problem

Your system logfiles contain lots of messages, and you want to use the severity levels to distinguish the important ones from the informational ones.

Solution

Include the severity level in each logging message:

```
[edit system syslog file messages]
aviva@router1# set explicit-priority
```

Discussion

When you configure each system logfile and include the explicitly-priority statement, all system log messages contain the priority, which is a combination of the facility and severity level. The following example highlights the priority for messages in the logfile.

```
aviva@router1> show log messages | match "Mar  9 11:5"
Mar  9 11:54:31  router1 login: %AUTH-6-LOGIN_INFORMATION: User aviva logged in from
host 172.17.28.19 on device ttyp1
Mar  9 11:54:34  router1 mgd[29108]: %INTERACT-5-UI_DBASE_LOGIN_EVENT: User 'aviva'
entering configuration mode
Mar  9 11:56:13  router1 mgd[29108]: %INTERACT-5-UI_DBASE_LOGOUT_EVENT: User 'aviva'
exiting configuration mode
Mar  9 11:57:52  router1 mgd[28332]: %INTERACT-5-UI_DBASE_LOGOUT_EVENT: User 'aviva'
exiting configuration mode
```

In the first message the priority is %AUTH-6, which indicates that this message was generated by the authorization facility. The severity is 6, so you know that it's an informational message. The remaining three messages have a priority of %INTERACT-5, so they come from the interactive commands facility and have a severity of 5, or notice.

You could also match on a specific priority of interest. Here we show only critical messages (severity of 2):

```
aviva@router1> show log messages | match -2-
Jun 10 03:06:51  router1 /kernel: %KERN-2-CPU: Pentium II/Pentium II Xeon/Celer
on (331.71-MHz 686-class CPU)
Jun 10 03:06:51  router1 /kernel: %KERN-2-DEVFS: ready for devices
Jun 10 03:06:51  router1 /kernel: %KERN-2-DEVFS: ready to run
Jun 10 03:07:10  router1 snmpd[2722]: %DAEMON-2-SNMPD_TRAP_COLD_START: trap_gen
erate_cold: SNMP trap: cold start
```

The message string always reports the original, local facility. If a message belongs to a JUNOS-specific facility, the JUNOS system logging utility still uses an alternate facility for the message itself when directing messages to a remote machine.

5.4   Changing the Size of a Logging File

Problem

You need to change the size of your logfiles.

Solution

You can change the default size of all logfiles with the following command:

```
[edit system]
aviva@router1# set syslog archive size 256k
```

You can also change the size of an individual logfile:

```
[edit system]
aviva@router1# set syslog log file messages archive size 512k
```

Discussion

The default maximum size of logging files is 128 KB. You might want to increase the maximum if the files are filling up too quickly, and you might want to make the files smaller if you are running out of hard disk space on the router. All JUNOS logging files are the same size. The first command in this recipe shows how to change the default file size for all syslog files, here changing it to 256 KB. The second command changes the file size just for the *messages* logging file.

Depending on how much system logging information you are collecting and what errors and problems might be occurring on the router, a logging file can reach its maximum size quickly, in just a few hours, or over the course of several days or weeks. Instead of discarding the oldest information, the JUNOS software renames the full file and compresses it, and continues collecting new logging information in the original, now empty file. For the *messages* file we created, when it fills up, it is renamed to *messages.0.gz*. When the messages file fills up a second time, *messages.0.gz* is renamed to *messages.1.gz* and the new file is compressed and renamed to *messages.0.gz*. This continues until there are 10 files (the default value):

```
aviva@router1> show log messages?
Possible completions:
  <filename>          Name of log file
  messages            Size: 59682, Last changed: Mar 09 15:13:53
  messages.0.gz       Size: 8886, Last changed: Mar 03 04:00:00
  messages.1.gz       Size: 7820, Last changed: Feb 22 12:00:00
  messages.10.gz      Size: 7834, Last changed: Feb 10 04:00:00
  messages.2.gz       Size: 9189, Last changed: Feb 18 04:00:00
  messages.3.gz       Size: 7115, Last changed: Feb 17 21:00:01
  messages.4.gz       Size: 7191, Last changed: Feb 17 09:00:00
  messages.5.gz       Size: 7579, Last changed: Feb 16 22:00:00
  messages.6.gz       Size: 7241, Last changed: Feb 16 10:00:01
  messages.7.gz       Size: 9059, Last changed: Feb 15 23:00:01
  messages.8.gz       Size: 17682, Last changed: Feb 15 11:00:01
  messages.9.gz       Size: 14807, Last changed: Feb 15 04:00:01
```

After the tenth file, the file contents are overwritten. If you want to save the older contents of the logging message files, you can increase the number of files that the software saves. When you change the number of logging files, it affects all the logging files maintained by the router. You can't change this value for an individual logging file.

```
[edit system]
aviva@router1# set syslog archive file 20
```

Keep an eye on hard disk usage to make sure there is enough storage for all logfiles. The logfiles are in the */var/log* directory, which is mounted on the */var* partition:

```
aviva@router1> show system storage | match ad
Filesystem            Size     Used     Avail  Capacity   Mounted on
```

/dev/ad0s1a	77M	39M	32M	55% /
/dev/ad0s1e	12M	16K	11M	0% /config
/dev/ad1s1f	9.4G	1.2G	7.4G	14% /var

When space gets low, clear or delete any old or unnecessary logfiles or move them to a file server.

If you are logging to a remote server and are running out of disk space on the server, either change how many messages you log to the remote server by changing the facilities or levels you log to the remote server, or reconfigure the remote server to roll over its logfiles faster.

5.5 Clearing the Router's Logfiles

Problem

You want to delete the contents of the router's logfiles.

Solution

Use the clear log command to delete the contents of a logging file:

```
aviva@router1> clear log messages
```

Discussion

Logging files fill up with messages very quickly, and if you are trying to debug a recent problem, you may be overwhelmed with the number of older messages. This command removes the messages from a file:

```
aviva@router1> clear log messages
aviva@router1> show log mes?
Possible completions:
  <filename>            Name of log file
  messages              Size: 59, Last changed: Mar 09 15:24:43
  messages.0.gz         Size: 8886, Last changed: Mar 03 04:00:00
  messages.1.gz         Size: 7820, Last changed: Feb 22 12:00:00
  messages.10.gz        Size: 7834, Last changed: Feb 10 04:00:00
  messages.2.gz         Size: 9189, Last changed: Feb 18 04:00:00
  messages.3.gz         Size: 7115, Last changed: Feb 17 21:00:01
  messages.4.gz         Size: 7191, Last changed: Feb 17 09:00:00
  messages.5.gz         Size: 7579, Last changed: Feb 16 22:00:00
  messages.6.gz         Size: 7241, Last changed: Feb 16 10:00:01
  messages.7.gz         Size: 9059, Last changed: Feb 15 23:00:01
  messages.8.gz         Size: 17682, Last changed: Feb 15 11:00:01
  messages.9.gz         Size: 14807, Last changed: Feb 15 04:00:01
aviva@router1> show log messages
Mar 9 15:24:43 router1 clear-log[29140]: logfile cleared
```

To free up disk space, you can also delete logfiles that you are no longer using (for example, if files are left over from a previous debugging operation) or files that you no longer need. Here, we logged RIP protocols operations a while ago to debug a problem and now want to delete those logfiles:

```
aviva@router1> file list detail /var/log/rip*
-rw-r-----  1 root                1689 Feb 28 10:05 /var/log/rip-update-log
-rw-r-----  1 root                7610 Feb 28 10:05 /var/log/rip-update-log.0.gz
-rw-r-----  1 root                7286 Feb 28 09:39 /var/log/rip-update-log.1.gz
-rw-r-----  1 root                7427 Feb 28 09:15 /var/log/rip-update-log.2.gz
-rw-r-----  1 root                7334 Feb 28 08:49 /var/log/rip-update-log.3.gz
-rw-r-----  1 root                7316 Feb 28 08:25 /var/log/rip-update-log.4.gz
-rw-r-----  1 root                7382 Feb 28 08:01 /var/log/rip-update-log.5.gz
-rw-r-----  1 root                7380 Feb 28 07:37 /var/log/rip-update-log.6.gz
-rw-r-----  1 root                7243 Feb 28 07:12 /var/log/rip-update-log.7.gz
-rw-r-----  1 root                7346 Feb 28 06:48 /var/log/rip-update-log.8.gz
total 10
aviva@router1> file delete /var/log/rip*
aviva@router1> file list /var/log/rip*
/var/log/rip*: No such file or directory
```

5.6 Sending Log Messages to Your Screen

Problem

You log in to the router to try to track a serious problem that is currently happening, and you want to see logging messages as they are being generated.

Solution

You can use the monitor command to temporarily see logging messages as they are occurring:

```
aviva@router1> monitor start messages
aviva@router1>
*** messages ***
Apr  4 22:00:00  router1 syslogd: %SYSLOG-6: restart
*** 'messages' has been deleted ***
*** 'messages' has been created ***
*** messages ***
Apr  4 22:00:00 router1 newsyslog[4939]: logfile turned over
```

To see the messages for a longer period of time, you can configure the router to display them on your screen:

```
[edit]
aviva@router1# edit system syslog user aviva
[edit system syslog user aviva]
aviva@router1# set any critical
```

Discussion

An easy way to see logging messages as they are occurring without modifying the router's configuration is to use the monitor start command. Include the name of one of the system logging files that you have already configured. This operation is similar to the Unix tail -f command.

When you are done, turn off the display:

```
aviva@router1> monitor stop
```

If you want to see the logging messages over a longer period of time, or always want a particular person to watch logging messages when they are logged in to the router, add that information to the router's configuration. With the configuration shown above, if the user aviva is logged in to the router, she will see any critical and more serious messages on her terminal screen as soon as the router generates them:

```
aviva@router1> Mar 18 11:12:30  router1 chassisd[2800]: %DAEMON-2-CHASSISD_SNMP_
TRAP10: SNMP trap generated: redundancy switchover (jnxRedundancyContentsIndex 6,
jnxRedundancyL1Index 2, jnxRedundancyL2Index 0, jnxRedundancyL3Index 0,
jnxRedundancyDescr SSB 1, jnxRedundancyConfig 3, jnxRedundancyState 2,
jnxRedundancySwitchoverCount 2, jnxRedundancySwitchoverTime 5611,
jnxRedundancySwitchoverReason 4)
```

If a number of people are trying to track down a problem on the router, you can have them all receive logging messages on their screens:

```
[edit system syslog]
aviva@router1# set system syslog user * any critical
```

Or, if you are logged in through the console, you can see the logging messages on the console:

```
[edit system syslog]
aviva@router1# set system syslog console any critical
```

To turn off this logging, you need to remove or deactivate the statements in the configuration:

```
[edit]
aviva@router1# deactivate system syslog user aviva
```

5.7   Sending Logging Messages to a Log Server

Problem

You want to collect and save system logging messages over long periods of time, but you don't want to constantly manage the disk space availability on your routers.

Solution

You can set up a log server on your network that has many gigabytes of storage space and then redirect the router's logging messages to that server.

```
[edit system syslog]
aviva@router1# set host 172.17.12.30 any info
aviva@router1# set host 172.17.12.30 explicit-priority
```

Discussion

This configuration redirects all logging messages to the file server 172.17.12.30. You can also specify the hostname instead of the IP address. The file server must be running a standard syslogd utility. You find the system logging messages in the */var/log/ messages* file on the server, unless the server has been configured to save them someplace else:

```
aviva-server1%: tail /var/log/messages
Mar 23 09:27:29 server1 /kernel: linux: syscall mmap2 is obsoleted or not implemented
(pid=12624)
%INTERACT-5-UI_DBASE_LOGIN_EVENT: User 'aviva' entering configuration mode
Mar 23 17:48:40 router1-fxp0.mycompany mgd[4098]: %INTERACT-5-UI_COMMIT: User 'aviva'
performed commit: no comment
Mar 23 17:48:44 router1-fxp0.mycompany xntpd[4860]: %NTP-5: ntpd 4.0.99b Sat Mar 12
07:43:39 GMT 2005 (1)
Mar 23 17:48:44 router1-fxp0.mycompany xntpd[4860]: %NTP-5: using kernel phase-lock
loop 2001
Mar 23 17:48:44 router1-fxp0.mycompany xntpd[4860]: %NTP-5: using kernel phase-lock
loop 2041
Mar 23 17:48:45 router1-fxp0.mycompany mgd[4098]: %INTERACT-5-UI_DBASE_LOGOUT_EVENT:
User 'aviva' exiting configuration mode
```

The output shows both the server's and the router's logging messages intermixed in the logging file. You can identify the messages from the router because the field after the timestamp identifies the router by IP address and router port or, if the server can resolve the IP address, by its DNS name. The router messages in this output show router1-fxp0.mycompany. The router name is router1, and the messages were sent to the log server over port (or interface) fxp0, which is the router's out-of-band management interface. The JUNOS software has a tendency to send logging messages out the interface with the shortest path to the syslog server. This can cause all sorts of problems, depending on how your log server and firewall filters are set up. To circumvent these problems, specifically include the interface from which to send the messages:

```
[edit system syslog]
aviva@router1# set source-address 192.168.15.42/32
```

This command sets the messages to go out 192.168.15.42, which is the router's loopback address. You normally use the router's loopback address when sending system logging messages, but you can use any interface dedicated to management. With this configuration, logging messages from the router will include the resolved hostname of the IP address for lo0 (for example, lo.router1.mycompany.com) rather than showing router1-fxp0.mycompany.

Sometimes you want to have more information to identify the source of the message than just the router name. You can specify a text string that is also included in the logging message:

```
[edit system syslog]
```

```
aviva@router1# set host 172.17.12.30 log-prefix M20-JUNOS-cookbook
```

The messages from your router now contain this string:

```
Mar 23 12:01:57 server1 named[45618]: zoneref: Masters for slave zone "mycompany.com"
REFUSED transfer
Mar 23 20:15:46 router1-fxp0.mycompany M20-JUNOS-cookbook: xntpd[5633]: %NTP-5: ntpd
4.0.99b Sat Mar 12 07:43:39 GMT 2005 (1)
```

How you specify the router identifier string is a little bit different from how you specify other strings in JUNOS statements. You can use all alphanumeric and special characters except equals signs and colons, but you cannot include spaces, even if you enclose them in quotation marks.

The syslog utility running on your server understands just the standard syslog message facilities. Many of the JUNOS system logging facilities map to the standard syslog ones, but some are JUNOS specific. For example, the JUNOS ftp facility maps to LOG_FTP and kernel maps to LOG_KERNEL, but INTERACT and PFE don't map to anything in syslog. By default, the JUNOS software maps the facilities to a syslog alternate facility. Just as in the Unix syslog utility, the JUNOS software has eight alternate facilities, local0 through local7. Table 5-3 shows the default mappings of the JUNOS-specific facilities to alternate facilities.

Table 5-3. Mappings for JUNOS-specific system logging facilities

JUNOS facility	syslogd alternate facility
change-log	local6
conflict-log	local5
firewall	local3
interactive-commands	local7
pfe	local4

To have the server process messages from the JUNOS-specific logging facility, you direct messages having these alternate facilities to a file on the server. On a FreeBSD system, you define this mapping in the */etc/syslog.conf* file. To place the interactive messages in a logging file, you could include the following line in the */etc/syslog.conf* file:

```
local7.*                /var/log/router-command-messages
```

When you are collecting logs from a number of routers on the same server, the server cannot distinguish among the different routers and places all messages that have the same facility in the same file. This can get rather messy when you are trying to sort out which messages came from which routers, so you should send each router's messages to its own file. To set this up on the router, choose an alternate facility:

```
[edit system syslog]
aviva@router1# set host 172.17.12.30 facility-override local0
```

This command causes all messages sent to the remote host to be flagged with the standard local0 facility. On the server, you map to a file in the */etc/syslog.conf* file:

```
local0.*                        /var/log/M20-JUNOS-cookbook-messages
```

A check of the file shows the system log messages from the router:

```
aviva-server1%: tail -4 M20-JUNOS-cookbook-messages
Mar 24 00:45:40 <local0.info> router1-fxp0.mycompany M20-JUNOS-cookbook: mgd[5257]:
%INTERACT-6-UI_CMDLINE_READ_LINE: User 'aviva', command 'edit system syslog '
Mar 24 01:00:00 <local0.info> router1-fxp0.mycompany M20-JUNOS-cookbook: CRON[8784]:
%CRON-6: (root) CMD (newsyslog)
Mar 24 01:01:00 <local0.info> router1-fxp0.mycompany M20-JUNOS-cookbook: CRON[8787]:
%CRON-6: (root) CMD (adjkerntz -a)
Mar 24 01:08:04 <local0.info> router1-fxp0.mycompany M20-JUNOS-cookbook: mgd[5257]:
%INTERACT-6-UI_CMDLINE_READ_LINE: User 'aviva', command 'edit host server1 '
```

You can run system logging management software on the central log server to help analyze the collected log messages. One widely used product is syslog-ng (*http://www.balabit.com/products/syslog_ng*), which filters logging messages based on source IP address and separates messages from different sources into different files instead of placing them into one file. This is particularly useful for network operators who aggregate messages from several devices. Another widely used tool is swatch (simple watcher; *http://swatch.sourceforge.net*), which actively scans logfiles entries as soon as syslogd receives them and reports what is happening in real time. swatch can also take action when it encounters certain log messages.

5.8   Saving Logging Messages to the Other Routing Engine

Problem

Your router has a second Routing Engine for redundancy, but the router runs fine off the primary Routing Engine and never fails over to the second one. You want to take advantage of the storage space available on the second Routing Engine's hard disk to save some of your logging messages.

Solution

Redirect the logging messages to the other Routing Engine:

```
[edit system syslog]
aviva@router1# set host other-routing-engine authorization notice
```

Discussion

If you always run your router off the primary Routing Engine (RE0), there is likely a lot of available hard disk space on the second Routing Engine's hard disk that you can use to store system logfiles. Here we can see that there's almost nothing on RE1's hard disk (*/dev/ad1s1f*, mounted on */var*):

```
aviva@router1a> show system storage | except /dev/vn
Filesystem              Size     Used    Avail  Capacity   Mounted on
/dev/ad0s1a             77M      37M      35M     51%   /
devfs                   16K      16K       0B    100%   /dev/
mfs:172                 1.5G     4.0K     1.3G      0%   /tmp
/dev/ad0s1e             12M      9.0K      11M      0%   /config
procfs                  4.0K     4.0K       0B    100%   /proc
/dev/ad1s1f             17G      622M      15G      4%   /var
```

The messages you save to RE1 are placed in the file */var/log/messages* and include the string re0 after the timestamp and router name to distinguish those messages that originated from RE0 from the messages from RE1:

```
Apr 29 21:39:09  router1a rshd[3811]: root@re0 as root: cmd='mv /var/db/dcd.snmp_ix+
/var/db/dcd.snmp_ix'
Apr 29 22:30:14  router1a login: LOGIN_INFORMATION: User aviva logged in from host
re0 on device ttyp0
Apr 29 22:38:08  router1a login: LOGIN_INFORMATION: User aviva logged in from host
re0 on device ttyp0
Apr 29 22:51:51 router1a re0 init: ntp (PID 4752) exit on SIGHUP, will be restarted
to get the new config
Apr 29 22:51:51 router1a re0 init: ntp (PID 4977) started
Apr 29 22:51:51 router1a re0 xntpd[4977]: ntpd 4.1.0-a Wed Apr 27 07:11:10 GMT 2005
(1)
Apr 29 22:51:51 router1a re0 xntpd[4977]: kernel time discipline status 2040
Apr 29 22:52:13 router1a rshd[3829]: root@re0 as root: cmd='rcp -T -t /var/db/dcd.
snmp_ix+'
Apr 29 22:51:51 router1a re0 mgd[4791]: UI_DBASE_LOGOUT_EVENT: User 'aviva' exiting
configuration mode
Apr 29 22:52:14 router1 rshd[3832]: root@re0 as root: cmd='mv /var/db/dcd.snmp_ix+ /
var/db/dcd.snmp_ix'
Apr 29 22:52:22 router1a login: LOGIN_INFORMATION: User aviva logged in from host re0
on device ttyp0
```

To have RE1 send its log messages to files on RE0, you configure this in the configuration file on RE1:

```
aviva@router1> request routing-engine login re1
aviva@router1a> configure
[edit]
aviva@router1a# set system syslog host other-routing-engine authorization notice
aviva@router1a# commit and-quit
```

Because this is the same configuration as on RE0, you can also configure both Routing Engines from RE0:

```
[edit system syslog]
aviva@router1# set host other-routing-engine authorization notice
aviva@router1# commit synchronize
```

Then check for the messages on RE0:

```
aviva@router1a> exit
aviva@router1> show log messages | last
```

```
Apr 29 22:55:16  router xntpd[4977]: kernel time discipline status change 2041
Apr 29 22:56:47 router re1 mgd[3841]: UI_DBASE_LOGOUT_EVENT: User 'aviva' exiting
configuration mode
```

See Also

Recipe 1.30

5.9   Turning Off Logging

Problem

You no longer want to record system log messages in a file.

Solution

To stop recording system log messages, mark the configuration statements so that
they do not take effect:

```
[edit system syslog]
aviva@router1# deactivate system syslog file messages
aviva@router1# commit
```

Discussion

The best way to stop recording system log messages to a particular logging file is to
deactivate that portion of the configuration. Doing this leaves the configuration
statements in the configuration but marks them as inactive:

```
[edit system syslog]
aviva@router1# show
inactive: file messages {
    any notice;
    archive world-readable;
    explicit-priority;
}
```

If you type the show command one level lower in the configuration hierarchy, you see
an even longer reminder that this portion of the configuration has been deactivated:

```
[edit system syslog file messages]
aviva@router1# show
##
## inactive: file messages
##
```

Another way to turn off logging is to delete the configuration statements from the
configuration:

```
[edit system syslog]
aviva@router1# delete system syslog file messages
aviva@router1# commit
```

The advantage of deactivating rather than deleting is that you can still see the configuration statements. If the problem you were investigating recurs later, you can remove the inactive: tag to start collecting those system log messages again:

```
[edit system syslog]
aviva@router1# activate system syslog file messages
aviva@router1# commit
```

5.10   Turning On Basic Tracing

Problem

The system logging messages give you high-level information about the processes and events that are occurring on the router, but you need specific information about the operation of a routing protocol.

Solution

Use tracing to get more details about the operations of your routing protocols. You can start by collecting global information about all the routing operations occurring on your router:

```
[edit routing-options]
aviva@router1# set traceoptions file traceoptions-routing-all world-readable
aviva@router1# set traceoptions flag all
```

Discussion

Basic tracing lets you collect information about all the routing protocols that are actively running on your router. Configuring tracing is almost the same as configuring system logging. You specify the file to which you want to direct information, and you decide whether only the root user or all users can read the file. Here, the filename is traceoptions-routing-all and it is readable by everyone.

This recipe uses the default trace file size of 1 MB and the default of 10 trace files. The JUNOS software handles the tracing files the same way as logging files. When the file reaches its maximum size, it is renamed with a *.0* extension. When the file again fills up, the *.0* file is renamed with a *.1* extension, the newly filled file is renamed with a *.0* extension, and so on. Where there are 10 files, the files start getting overwritten.

Use the following commands to change the default file size and number of files:

```
[edit routing-options]
aviva@router1# set traceoptions file size 10M
aviva@router1# set traceoptions file files 5
```

The traceoption flags indicate the information to monitor. This recipe traces all routing protocol traffic.

For a router running RIP, IS-IS, and MPLS, you would see messages like this in the tracing file:

```
Apr  5 16:09:43 mpls LSP update start
Apr  5 16:09:43 mpls LSP update complete
Apr  5 16:12:23 task_timer_dispatch: returned from IS-IS I/0./var/run/ppmd_control_
PPM Keepalive, rescheduled in 40
Apr  5 16:12:27 task_receive_packet: task RIPv2 I/0.0.0.0.0+520 from 192.168.220
.18+520 to 224.0.0.9 if t1-0/1/0:0.0 (ix 70) msgix 70 socket 14 length 164
```

All the messages are timestamped and indicate the protocol or tasks that generated them.

When debugging global routing operations, one or more of the following can be traced:

```
[edit routing-options]
aviva@router1# show traceoptions flag ?
Possible completions:
  all                  Trace everything
  config-internal      Trace configuration internals
  general              Trace general events
  normal               Trace normal events
  parse                Trace configuration parsing
  policy               Trace policy processing
  regex-parse          Trace regular-expression parsing
  route                Trace routing information
  state                Trace state transitions
  task                 Trace routing protocol task processing
  timer                Trace routing protocol timer processing
```

Generally, when you are trying to debug a problem with a routing protocol, you turn on tracing for that protocol only. You can do this for BGP, DVMRP, IGMP, IS-IS, LDP, MPLS, MSDP, OSPF, PGM, PIM, RIP, RIPng, RSVP, SNMP, and VPLS. Throughout this book, in the appropriate protocol chapters, we show how to use tracing to debug problems. You can also use traceoptions to debug interface problems. Tracing all routing operations is not recommended on a busy router because the tracing and routing protocol operations use the same CPU and the processing time required for tracing can slow down the protocol processing. In this case, you should consider tracing a smaller scope of operations, or even not using tracing at all.

5.11 Monitoring Interface Traffic

Problem

You want to look at the headers of packets transiting an interface to debug protocol operation.

Solution

Use the monitor traffic command:

```
aviva@RouterG> monitor traffic interface fe-1/0/1 size 1492 detail
```

Discussion

The monitor traffic command is equivalent to the Unix tcpdump command and is useful for watching protocol traffic on an interface when attempting to debug a problem. This recipe watches all traffic on interface fe-1/0/1, which is an interface in an OSPF backbone area (area 0.0.0.0). The default packet size for the monitor traffic command is 68 bytes, which captures the beginning of packet headers, but not much more. We specify a packet size of 1,492 bytes, which is the maximum OSPF packet size. Here's what the output looks like:

```
Listening on fe-1/0/1, capture size 1492 bytes

05:14:46.915999  In IP (tos 0xc0, ttl   1, id 2843, offset 0, flags [none], prot
o: OSPF (89), length: 68) 10.0.0.2 > OSPF-ALL.MCAST.NET: OSPFv2, Hello (1), leng
th: 48
        Router-ID: 192.168.17.1, Backbone Area, Authentication Type: none (0)
        Options: [External]
          Hello Timer: 10s, Dead Timer 40s, Mask: 255.255.255.0, Priority: 128
          Designated Router 10.0.0.2, Backup Designated Router 10.0.0.1
          Neighbor List:
            192.168.19.1
05:14:50.715849 Out IP (tos 0xc0, ttl   1, id 63978, offset 0, flags [none], pro
to: OSPF (89), length: 68) 10.0.0.1 > OSPF-ALL.MCAST.NET: OSPFv2, Hello (1), len
gth: 48
        Router-ID: 192.168.19.1, Backbone Area, Authentication Type: none (0)
        Options: [External]
          Hello Timer: 10s, Dead Timer 40s, Mask: 255.255.255.0, Priority: 128
          Designated Router 10.0.0.2, Backup Designated Router 10.0.0.1
          Neighbor List:
            192.168.17.1
...
^C
6 packets received by filter
0 packets dropped by kernel
```

Type Ctrl-c to end the monitoring.

One disadvantage of monitoring interface traffic is that it uses a lot of the Routing Engine's CPU and can degrade performance on the router.

## CHAPTER 6

NTP

6.0 Introduction

Having the correct time and time zone on your routers and having the time be synchronized across your network is useful to accurately track events that occur on the router and network and to correlate events that occur on different routers. The time and date are used to mark when the files stored on the router, including the active and previous configuration files, the system logging files, and the tracing files, were created or last updated. The messages in JUNOS logging and tracing files are timestamped to mark when events, errors, and problems occurred. All these dates and times are based on the router's time. A number of JUNOS commands, including the ones you use to check the status and uptime of the router, report the current time and the time at which events occurred.

On JUNOS routers, you can configure the time manually by simply setting it. This is generally sufficient for smaller or less complex networks. However, for larger or more global networks, you should use Network Time Protocol (NTP) to set the time for you. NTP is an IETF standard described in RFC 1305 that synchronizes time across computers and routers on the Internet. The router synchronizes the system time with an NTP server and periodically accesses the server to maintain the correct time. NTP uses a hierarchical system of clock strata to derive time. The top-level stratum 1 clock, also called the primary NTP server, is a computer that is connected to a high-precision accurate clock, such as an atomic clock, or to a radio clock, such as a GPS, Loran, or WWVB, which is the NIST time signal radio station. NTP stratum 2 systems derive their time from a stratum 1 system and are one hop away from a stratum 1 system; NTP stratum 3 systems derive their time from a stratum 2 clock, and are one hop from the stratum 2 machine and two hops from the stratum 1 machine. Note that these hops are *NTP hops*, not network hops. The systems can be any number of network hops apart. NTP can have up to 16 strata.

You should not confuse the NTP stratum with the telco concept of clocking stratum, which describes frequency accuracy.

The JUNOS implementation of NTP is based on the FreeBSD ntpd utility.

For more information about NTP, see *http://www.ntp.org*, the web site of the NTP research and development project, as well as the documentation page of the NTP Public Services Project (*http://ntp.isc.org/bin/view/Main/DocumentationIndex*).

6.1   Setting the Date and Time on the Router Manually

Problem

You want to manually set the date and the local time on the router.

Solution

You set the date and time from operational mode:

```
aviva@router1> set date 200503171626
Thu Mar 17 16:26:00 UTC 2005
```

Discussion

On a relatively simple network, you can manually set the date and the local time on the routers in your network so you can keep an accurate record of all events that occur on the routers.

To set the local time, use the set date command, which is an operational mode command. This example sets the year, month, date, hour, and minute. For more accuracy, you can include the seconds:

```
aviva@router1> set date 200503151049.30
```

After you have set the date and time, the router uses these values in any commands that include the date, in log and tracing files, and in the filesystems when marking files with the date and time. Use the show system uptime command to find out the current time. This command is similar to the Unix uptime utility.

```
aviva@router1> show system uptime
Current time: 2005-03-15 19:05:08 UTC
System booted: 2005-03-15 11:09:57 UTC (07:55:11 ago)
Protocols started: 2005-03-15 11:11:31 UTC (07:53:37 ago)
Last configured: 2005-03-15 19:05:04 UTC (00:00:04 ago) by aviva
 7:05PM  up 7:55, 1 user, load averages: 0.07, 0.02, 0.01
```

This command also shows other information about the router, including when it was last booted (the first line) and how long it has been up (the last line), when the protocol software started, and when the configuration was last changed.

6.2   Setting the Time Zone

Problem

You want to set the time zone.

Solution

Configure the local time zone. You can do this in a number of different styles:

```
[edit system]
aviva@router1# set time-zone UTC-8

[edit system]
aviva@router1# set time-zone PST8PDT

[edit system]
aviva@router1# set time-zone America/Los_Angeles
```

Discussion

When you set the time on the router, the default time zone is UTC (Coordinated Universal Time). You might be more familiar with UTC's old name, GMT, or Greenwich Mean Time, or with the term *zulu*, which is the U.S. military term for the time at the prime meridian, which runs through Greenwich, England. If you have a global organization and want to run all the routers on your time in a common global time zone, just leave the default time zone unchanged. You don't have to configure anything to make this happen.

If you want to change the time zone, use the time-zone statement in configuration mode. You can't set the local router time and the time zone at the same time because you set the time with an operational mode command, and you set the time zone in configuration mode.

The JUNOS time-zone statement is based on the FreeBSD time zone function, which is controlled with the FreeBSD tzsetup utility. The JUNOS time zone list is the same as the FreeBSD list, which you can find in the file */usr/share/zoneinfo/zone.tab*.

You can specify the time zone by hour-offset from UTC, by common time zone three-letter abbreviation, or by continent/city pairings. There are several dozen different zone names; type set time-zone ? to get the entire list. This recipe shows three ways to set the local time in California.

To verify that the time zone change has taken effect, use the show system uptime command:

```
aviva@router1> show system uptime
Current time: 2005-03-15 11:10:22 PST
System booted: 2005-03-15 03:09:57 PST (08:00:25 ago)
Protocols started: 2005-03-15 03:11:31 PST (07:58:51 ago)
Last configured: 2005-03-15 11:10:19 PST (00:00:03 ago) by aviva
11:10AM  up 8 hrs, 1 user, load averages: 0.07, 0.02, 0.01
```

You can see that the time zone has changed to PST, and the current hour has changed from 19:00 UTC to 11:00 Pacific Time.

While consistent time zones aren't really necessary, you will find it helpful if all the routers on your network use the same time zone, whether it's UTC or the local time zone. All events recorded in system logging and tracing files that you keep on the router all have a timestamp associated with them that consists of the date and the time but gives no indication of the time zone. If you are trying correlate events on different routers, it will be much easier if the routers are in the same time zone.

6.3   Synchronizing Time When the Router Boots

Problem

You want the router to synchronize its time when it boots.

Solution

Have the router get the time when it boots:

```
[edit system]
aviva@router1# set ntp boot-server 172.10.23.196
```

Discussion

The easiest way to have NTP set the time on your router is to get the time when the router boots. You include the ntp boot-server statement, and you set the address of an NTP server. Typically, you want to have at least one time server on the local network—either another router or a server of some kind—and you want all the other routers to get their time from this router. If the boot server is another router, you need to make sure that NTP is running on that router and that it is set up as an NTP peer so it can send its time to other routers.

A good practice is to configure a boot server on any router that is running NTP in case the time is wildly off when the router starts or has drifted beyond the point where it can be periodically sychnronized by a boot server (see Recipe 6.4); otherwise, the time is never set. The time might be off by a lot with a new router or Routing Engine. Once the time is set, the Routing Engine's battery-powered time-of-day clock keeps running even with the power off, so it seeds the time to within a few seconds when the router boots. Another common reason for the time to be wildly off is if you manually set the time without setting the time zone first, so the clock might be off by some number of hours.

The NTP boot server must be reachable when the router boots, without any routing protocols running and with any of the interfaces being up. This means it must be directly reachable from the management Ethernet interface, fxp0. When the Routing

Engine boots, the ntpdate utility runs early in the boot process, before chassisd and rpd are up. The only thing that is up and configured at that point is fxp0.

With this method of setting up NTP, the router gets the time once, when it boots, and sets its clock based on the time it receives from the server. While you could choose this as the only method for getting accurate time on the router, the clock time can drift over long periods, so it is a better idea to get the time when the router boots and to also synchronize the time periodically with time servers to slowly correct any drifting.

If the NTP boot server is another router, you cannot boot both routers at once, for instance, if you are power-cycling all the routers in your POP. You must start the boot server first.

See Also

Recipe 6.4

6.4 Synchronizing Time Periodically

Problem

You want to periodically resynchronize the time on the router to limit the effects of clock drift.

Solution

Configure the router to periodically get time updates from an NTP server:

```
[edit system]
aviva@router1# set ntp server 192.168.27.46
aviva@router1# show
system {
    ntp {
        server 192.168.27.46;
    }
}
```

Discussion

Setting the router's time by configuring a boot server provides a one-time method for the router to get time when it boots. However, once a router is up and stable, you will almost never have to reboot it, so if its time starts to drift from the time on your other network devices, you have to go into the router and manually reconfigure the time. To automatically keep the router in sync with the rest of the network, you can have it periodically get time updates from an NTP server. To do this, place the JUNOS NTP software into NTP server mode with the set ntp server command, specifying the IP address of the NTP server. The NTP server will then periodically send the correct time to the router, which then adjusts its system clock.

From a network-wide perspective, you generally want to have a local NTP server that is your main time server and that stays synchronized with a stratum 1 clock. You then have a number of redundant NTP peers that keep their time synchronized with this local NTP server. The remainder of the local routers on your network poll the NTP peers to get accurate time. The local routers that receive time from an NTP peer run in what is called NTP server mode. This terminology is a bit confusing, because the local router is passively accepting time from the remote NTP server. The term *server mode* applies to the NTP protocol software, which is running in server mode, not to the router, which is actually running as an NTP client. When the NTP software is in server mode, the clock on the router can be synchronized to a remote NTP server, but a remote server can never be synchronized to the local clock. Thus the time sharing is an asymmetric relationship; server mode is also called *asymmetric mode*.

For the routers on your network that are the NTP time servers, you configure them to run in NTP peer mode so that they actively keep their clocks synchronized. Peer mode is also called active symmetric mode, because the local and remote routers are willing to synchronize time with each other. If there is any time drift, the NTP synchronization process slowly corrects the routers' clocks so that they match up. To configure a router to run NTP peer mode, specify the address of the NTP peer:

```
[edit system]
aviva@router1# set ntp peer 192.168.1.16
```

If your network has multiple NTP peers, include additional addresses. You need to configure all the peer routers to operate in NTP peer mode.

In larger networks, you might have multiple NTP servers for redundancy to ensure that time in properly synchronized across the network even when a server or a part of the network goes down. To set up a backup NTP server for a router operating in NTP server mode, configure the address of the second server. To bias the selection toward a particular server, mark it as preferred:

```
[edit system]
aviva@router1# set ntp server 192.168.27.46 prefer
aviva@router1# set ntp server 172.10.23.196
```

If you have multiple NTP servers, configure them in the same way:

```
[edit system]
aviva@router1# set ntp peer 192.168.1.16 prefer
aviva@router1# set ntp peer 172.10.23.196
```

When you configure multiple servers and peers, an NTP relationship is established with all of them. The candidates are sorted by NTP stratum (the smallest stratum is always selected). If multiple candidates are at the smallest stratum, NTP chooses based on perceived accuracy, round-trip time, and jitter. The prefer keyword weights the selection, but does not guarantee that the said system will be selected. It is even possible for multiple systems to be selected and an integration of their times to be performed.

You can also have all the routers synchronize time (chime) with each other. This is only practical for relatively small networks of, say, less than 50 routers. (For larger networks, you may want to have all the routers in a region or POP chime with each other.) You still want to have some stratum 1 clocks someplace in the mix. This arrangement allows the entire network to keep reasonable time even if some or all of the stratum 1 clocks go down for a while.

Note that you can configure both server and peer statements on the same router.

NTP automatic time synchronization works only if the times on the two systems are very close. Very close means between 128 milliseconds and 128 seconds apart. Time differences less than 128 milliseconds are dealt with by slowly slewing the time (speeding up or slowing down the clock), which means that the time is always monotonically increasing. Between 128 milliseconds and 128 seconds, the time is stepped, which means that it may go backward. Above this, the time is not changed at all. If the time is more than 1,000 seconds off, NTP records a system log message:

```
Mar 16 16:41:41 5htp-fxp0 xntpd[28243]: time error 4217 over 1000 seconds; set
clock manually
```

If the time is this far off, you need to reset the clock manually:

```
aviva@router1# set date ntp
```

This command uses the NTP servers that you have configured. You do not have to reboot the router for the new time to take effect.

On an operational note, one system will not synchronize to another that is not itself synchronized. Because the synchronization process is recursive, there must be an authoritative time source as the stratum 1 clock or all systems will be free running. An NTP purist will ensure that there are at least three or, better yet, four, independent sources of time available (traceable to three different stratum 1 servers) because this allows "false tickers" to be detected and discarded. At least two independent sources are needed for robustness, because if that one stratum 1 server goes down, the entire synchronization tree will basically come apart and all systems will free run in the mean time. Normally this isn't too serious, but if the stratum 1 server never comes back, there will be no time synchronization whatsoever.

6.5   Authenticating NTP

Problem

You want to make sure that the router gets time updates only from known and trusted NTP servers.

Solution

Set up NTP authentication:

```
[edit system ntp]
aviva@router1# set authentication-key 12 type md5 value $1991poppI
aviva@router1# set server 172.10.23.196 key 12
aviva@router1# set trusted-key 12
aviva@router1# show
authentication-key 12 type md5 value "$9$G4UjHqmfT365TIEhcMW4aZGHmP5Fn/A"; ## SECRET-
DATA
server 172.10.23.196 key 12; ## SECRET-DATA
trusted-key 12;
```

Discussion

By default, your router queries time to whichever NTP servers appear to be most accurate. To ensure that routers receive time only from known and trusted sources, enable NTP authentication. The JUNOS implementation of NTP uses MD5 for authentication. You set up one or more trusted keys. Each key is identified by a number, here 12, and you establish a password for each key in the value option of the authentication-key statement. We are using a password of $1991poppI. When you configure the NTP server's address, you also set which NTP key the local router will send in all NTP updates. Finally, you configure in the trusted-key statement which NTP keys the router accepts so that when it receives NTP updates, it can authenticate and accept them. You have to configure the same trusted keys and passwords on all the NTP server and peer routers on your network. Based on the example here, you need to configure the router 172.10.23.196 to accept trusted key 12 and you need to configure the same MD5 password ($1991poppI) so that it can exchange NTP updates with your local router.

After you type the plain-text version MD5 password, when you display the configuration, you see the encrypted version of the password. You can use the encrypted version (the string that starts with 9G) when you configure the same password on other routers, or you can also use the plain-text password. In the configuration, the JUNOS software marks all encrypted information with the string ## SECRET-DATA. You can use this additional text as a way to hide these portions of the configuration when you have to share the configuration file with an insecure source or when you want to locate and remove this information before archiving the configuration in a location that might not be secure.

```
aviva@router1> show configuration system ntp | except SECRET-DATA
server 172.10.23.196;
trusted-key 123456;
```

Notice that while the authentication-key statement is not shown at all, the server statement is shown, but you see only the server's address. The password information is removed.

6.6 Checking NTP Status

Problem

You want to check that NTP is working properly on your network, and you want to check which NTP peers your router is getting time information from.

Solution

Use the show ntp associations command to verify that NTP is operating correctly:

```
aviva@router1> show ntp associations
     remote           refid      st t when poll reach   delay   offset  jitter
==============================================================================
*ntpserver.mynet .GPS.            1 u  108  256  377   6.915    3.977   0.078
```

Discussion

You can verify that NTP operation and status from any router on the network. The show ntp associations command output is the same as that of the FreeBSD ntpq -p utility. The first column in the output, remote, shows the servers and peers that you have configured on the router, either by name or IP address. The asterisk (*) before the server name indicates that this is the NTP server that is being used for time synchronization. If you had multiple NTP servers configured, a plus sign (+) would indicate alternate NTP servers that the router could use for time synchronization.

The second, third, and fourth columns—the reference ID, stratum, and type—show that the current source of the time synchronization is a GPS and that the remote server is a stratum 1 time source sending in unicast. (The remote server is a directly tied to a GPS receiver, which is an authoritative source of time. The GPS is effectively a stratum 0 device.) The next fields tell you when the router last received an NTP message (in seconds), how often the local router polls the NTP server (in seconds), the status of the NTP reachability register (in octal). The last three fields show specific information pertaining to the accuracy of clocks (the latest time delay, offset, and jitter), which NTP peers use to correct their clocks as they attempt to synchronize time.

You can also check the NTP operation and the clock on the local router:

```
aviva@router1> show ntp status
status=0664 leap_none, sync_ntp, 6 events, event_peer/strat_chg,
processor="i386", system="JUNOS7.2-20050317.0", leap=00, stratum=2,
precision=-28, rootdelay=7.058, rootdispersion=11.410, peer=27124,
refid=ntpserver.mynetwork.com,
reftime=c5e45c16.17eb399f  Thu, Mar 17 2005 19:42:14.093, poll=7,
clock=c5e45c74.a72fba01  Thu, Mar 17 2005 19:43:48.653, state=4,
phase=1.340, frequency=75.783, jitter=0.411, stability=0.004
```

A detailed explanation of all these fields is beyond the scope of this discussion. Most of the variables are defined in RFC 1305. However, there are a few fields are of general interest. The value sync_ntp in the first line tells you that this router has synchronized its time with an NTP server. If the output shows sync_alarm or sync_unspec, it means that the router is not synched. This could mean that it was more than 128 seconds off and never synched, but assuming that it was synched at least once since it was manufactured, it more likely means that none of its NTP servers are themselves synched or they are unreachable. Having multiple stratum 1 servers minimizes the chances of this latter case happening. If the router's time has drifted more than 128 seconds from the time on the NTP server, manually reset the time on the router with the set date ntp command.

Another field of interest is stratum. This output shows that the NTP server is a stratum 2 time source, so it is one hop from a stratum 1 server. The refid field lists the stratum 1 server. If the value in this field shows 0.0.0.0, it provides another indication that the router's clock is not synchronized with the NTP server.

## CHAPTER 7

Router Interfaces

7.0 Introduction

JUNOS routers have three types of interfaces: network, services, and special interfaces. As you might expect, network interfaces physically connect to the network and carry network traffic. Services interfaces manipulate the traffic before transmitting or receiving it, for example, to perform Network Address Translation (NAT), IPSec functions, or monitoring traffic flows. Special interfaces include two internal Ethernet management interfaces and the loopback interface, which is not used for performance monitoring but as a place to define an IP address for the router as a whole. The naming conventions for the three types of interfaces are the same, and you configure them the same way.

For interfaces to work, you must configure them. Simply installing the hardware in the router is not sufficient. The router detects that network hardware is present and you can list the hardware and interfaces with the show chassis hardware and show interfaces terse commands, but they will not carry traffic. You can also configure interfaces that are not present in the router, which is a handy feature when you are preparing to receive new hardware or to move a Flexible PIC Concentrator (FPC) or a Physical Interface Card (PIC) to another slot. When checking the configuration during a commit operation, MGD, the management process (daemon), checks whether the hardware corresponding to the configuration is present in the router. If it is, MGD hands that portion of the configuration over to the proper processes for activation. If the hardware is not present, MGD ignores that portion of the configuration.

When configuring interfaces on the router, you identify the interface by media type and location in the router. The media type is a string, typically two letters, that identifies the network device. Table 7-1 lists some of the common interface media names.

Table 7-1. Some interface media names

Interface type	Identifier	Name
Network	at	ATM over SONET/SDH
	fe	Fast Ethernet
	ge	Gigabit Ethernet
	se	Serial
	so	SONET/SDH
	t1	T1
Services	es	Encryption Services
	gr	Generic Route Encapsulation tunnel interface
	mo	Monitoring Services
	mt	Multicast tunnel interface
	sp	Services (for ES and AS PICs)
Special	lo0	Loopback
	fxp0	Out-of-band management
	fxp1	Internal management

The location portion of the interface name identifies which slot the FPC is in, which PIC slot on the FPC the media is installed on, and the specific port on the PIC. Most M-series and T-series routers have either four or eight FPC slots, and each slot has either two or four PIC locations. On J-series routers, there can be up to six FPC slots.

To illustrate interface naming, the interface name for the first port of a Fast Ethernet PIC installed on the FPC in slot 2, in the first PIC position, would be:

```
fe-2/0/0
```

For channelized interfaces, such as T1, the interface name includes the channel number. The name for the first channel on a T1 interface would be:

```
t1-1/1/0:0
```

When numbering the slots, ports, and channels in an interface name, the first item is 0, not 1. For routers that have eight FPC slots, the slots are numbered from 0 through 7. Most PICs have four locations, numbered 0 through 3, and port and channel numbering starts at 0. You can find the FPC and PIC slot numbers on the router chassis, and the port numbers on the PIC faceplate.

JUNOS interfaces consist of a number of layers that affect how you configure them. Like an onion with an outer skin and inner layers, the outer skin of the interface is the *physical interface*, which generally encompasses the entire physical device. On the physical interface, you set properties that control the behavior of the device itself. These properties typically correspond to OSI Reference Model Layer 1 and Layer 2 properties. As examples, Ethernet physical interface properties include the speed (10 Mbps or 100 Mbps) and half-duplex or full-duplex operation; T1 interface properties include framing, encoding, loopback, and setting up a Bit Error Rate Test (BERT); and for SONET, Automatic Protection Switching (APS) is a physical property. You configure the physical properties of an interface in two places: directly under the name of the interface and in an interface-specific -options section directly under the name of the interface. So for a Fast Ethernet interface to run at 100 Mbps, use the set fe-2/0/0 speed 100m command, which in the configuration looks like this:

```
[edit]
aviva@router1# show
interfaces {
    fe-2/0/0 {
        speed 100m; # <--physical property of the interface
    }
}
```

You see that the speed statement is directly under the name of the interface. An example of including the statement in an -options grouping is when setting a SONET interface to run APS. In this case, you use commands that place statements under the sonet-options hierarchy, as in this example configuration:

```
[edit]
aviva@t320# show
interfaces {
    so-3/1/0 {
        sonet-options { # <-- options group of physical interface properties
            aps {
                working-circuit APS-at-my-colo;
                authentication key $1991poPPi;
            }
        }
    }
}
```

The next layer of our interface onion is the logical interface (sometimes also referred to as a subinterface), which is the mechanism that divides a single interface into one or more virtual devices. Logical interfaces take all the traffic traversing the physical interface and create separate streams or flows that can have different properties. Virtual device properties include Frame Relay DLCIs and ATM virtual paths (VPs) and virtual circuits (VCs). For a physical interface to function, you must create at least one logical interface on it. Each logical interface is identified by a unit statement under each physical interface and a number that identifies the specific instance. The first logical interface is 0. So, to configure a Frame Relay DLCI, use the set t1-0/0/3 unit 0 dlci 100 command, which results in the following configuration:

```
[edit]
aviva@router1# show
interfaces {
    t1-0/0/3 {
        encapsulation frame-relay; # <-- physical interface property
        unit 0 { # <-- logical interface opener
            dlci 100; # <-- logical interface property
        }
    }
}
```

When you configure an IGP to run over an interface, the JUNOS software forms IGP adjacencies over the logical interface.

The third layer of the interface onion is the *protocol family*, which is where you start tying together the routing protocols on the routers and the interfaces on which they can run. For IPv4 protocols to run on an interface, an inet family must be present on the logical interface. Other common families are inet6, for IPv6 protocols, iso for IS-IS, mpls for MPLS, and vpls for VPLS. Multiple protocol families can run on a single logical interface. If you do not configure the appropriate family on the logical interface, the router will not recognize any packets in that protocol family and will discard them even though you have configured the interface in the routing protocol's configuration.

The final layer is the *address*, which associates the network address with the protocol family and controls other address properties. For any protocol family to operate, an address must be configured. For example, for an IPv4 protocol such as BGP or RIP to work on an interface, you must assign an IPv4 address for the logical interface's inet family with a command such as set interfaces fe-0/0/0 unit 0 family inet address 10.0.16.1/32. For IS-IS to also run on this logical interface, add the family iso:

```
[edit]
aviva@router1# show
interfaces {
    fe-0/0/0 {
        unit 0 {
            family inet { # <-- set the IPv4 protocol family
                address 10.0.16.1/32; # <-- set an IPv4 address
            }
            family iso; # <-- set for IS-IS
        }
    }
}
```

This chapter is organized into three groups of recipes. The first group shows how to view interface status. This is something you do regularly to check on the operation of the router and to troubleshoot problems with the interfaces themselves or with the protocol software. The second group of recipes shows how to set various addresses and families on logical interfaces. The final group shows how to configure and troubleshoot specific network and special interfaces.

7.1 Viewing Interface Status

Problem

You want to check the status of an interface.

Solution

Use the show interfaces command to see the status of the interfaces on the router. With no options, this command shows the status of all interfaces on the router:

```
aviva@router1> show interfaces
```

You can also look at the status for a particular interface:

```
aviva@router1> show interfaces fe-0/0/0
```

If you want shorter summaries of the status, use one of these command versions:

```
aviva@router1> show interfaces brief
aviva@router1> show interfaces terse
```

For maximum information for debugging purposes, use one of these commands:

```
aviva@router1> show interfaces detail
aviva@router1> show interfaces extensive
```

Discussion

Because the operation of the router revolves around the network interfaces, you often need to get information about the interfaces to check status or to troubleshoot a router or network problem. The basic commands for doing this are variations of the show interfaces command. To just find out what PICs are installed and which interfaces are configured, use the show interfaces terse command (see Recipe 7.12). For basic information about the physical and logical interface settings, use the show interfaces command, or for an abridged view, use the show interfaces brief command. The show interfaces detail command adds traffic statistics and queue counters, and the show interfaces extensive command adds alarms, error statistics, and additional counters.

The output of these commands varies depending on the type of interface. However, the general format of the information is the same for all interfaces, so it's worth examining the output of one so you can become familiar with what to expect in the output. Here's the information displayed by the show interfaces command for a Fast Ethernet interface:

```
aviva@router1> show interfaces fe-0/0/0
Physical interface: fe-0/0/0, Enabled, Physical link is Up
  Interface index: 128, SNMP ifIndex: 79
  Description: to nutmeg fe-000
  Link-level type: Ethernet, MTU: 1514, Speed: 100mbps, Loopback: Disabled,
  Source filtering: Disabled, Flow control: Enabled
  Device flags   : Present Running
  Interface flags: SNMP-Traps 16384
  Link flags     : 4
  CoS queues     : 4 supported
  Current address: 00:05:85:02:a4:00, Hardware address: 00:05:85:02:a4:00
  Last flapped   : 2005-05-12 14:58:08 PDT (05:04:29 ago)
  Input rate     : 0 bps (0 pps)
```

```
Output rate     : 0 bps (0 pps)
Active alarms   : None
Active defects  : None

Logical interface fe-0/0/0.0 (Index 66) (SNMP ifIndex 84)
  Flags: SNMP-Traps Encapsulation: ENET2
  Protocol inet, MTU: 1500
    Flags: None
    Addresses, Flags: Is-Preferred Is-Primary
      Destination: 192.168.220.0/30, Local: 192.168.220.1,
      Broadcast: 192.168.220.3
  Protocol iso, MTU: 1497
    Flags: Is-Primary
```

Here's the same interface with the show interfaces brief command:

```
aviva@router1> show interfaces brief fe-0/0/0
Physical interface: fe-0/0/0, Enabled, Physical link is Up
  Description: to nutmeg fe-000
  Link-level type: Ethernet, MTU: 1514, Speed: 100mbps, Loopback: Disabled,
  Source filtering: Disabled, Flow control: Enabled
  Device flags   : Present Running
  Interface flags: SNMP-Traps 16384
  Link flags     : 4

  Logical interface fe-0/0/0.0
    Flags: SNMP-Traps Encapsulation: ENET2
    inet  192.168.220.1/30
    iso
```

The output has two parts. The top part shows information about the physical interface, and the bottom shows information about the logical interface, including the protocol family and the interface addresses.

The first line of the output shows the most important information when you are checking interface status:

```
Physical interface: fe-0/0/0, Enabled, Physical link is Up
```

This line tells whether the interface is operational. Enabled means that the interface has been configured and is administratively up. The output shows Disabled if it's not. The physical link (connection) is up, which means that the interface is receiving the correct Layer 1 physical signaling from the other side of the link, indicating that the interface at the other end of the link is configured and operational. This line of the output is one of the first things to check when you are troubleshooting routing or connectivity problems.

The next line gives indexing information about the physical interface:

```
Interface index: 137, SNMP ifIndex: 29
```

The interface index is the physical interface's index number, which is based on the order in which it was initialized. The SNMP ifIndex is the SNMP index number of the physical interface. It allows you to correlate the values in the interface MIB OIDs with actual interfaces. You can also see this information on the router:

```
aviva@router1> show snmp mib walk ifTable
ifDescr.29    = fe-0/0/0
```

The next line gives more information about the physical properties of the interface:

```
Link-level type: Ethernet, MTU: 1514, Speed: 100mbps, Loopback: Disabled,
```

This shows the Layer 2 (link-level) encapsulation type and Maximum Transmission Unit (MTU) of the interface. Both are using the default encapsulations for their interface types. For the IPv4 address family, Ethernet is the only allowed link-level type. If you look in the logical interface section of the output, you see the encapsulation that is being used on the logical interface. The physical encapsulation applies to all protocols running on the interface, and logical interface encapsulation applies only to that address family. You can use the encapsulation statement in both portions of the configuration to modify the defaults:

```
[edit interfaces fe-0/0/0]
aviva@router1# set encapsulation vlan-ccc

[edit interfaces fe-0/0/0 unit 0]
aviva@router1# set encapsulation ppp-over-ether
```

The MTU is 1,514 bytes. This is the default media (Layer 2) MTU size, which is the size of the largest packet that the router can transmit through this interface. It applies to all protocols that use this interface. The protocol MTU size is in the logical interfaces portion of the output. Both logical interfaces are running IPv4 (Protocol inet), and the IPv4 MTU size is the standard 1,500 bytes for both interfaces. The media MTU is the sum of the IP MTU and the encapsulation overhead, which is 14 bytes for Ethernet interfaces. All devices on the Ethernet LAN must support the same MTU size. If you notice that a device is dropping traffic, check its MTU.

The speed for the Ethernet shows that this is Fast Ethernet, running at 100 Mbps.

The next line of output shows whether source filter and flow control are configured on the interface:

```
Source filtering: Disabled, Flow control: Enabled
```

Source address filtering blocks traffic from specific Ethernet MAC addresses. This is off by default. Flow control, which is on by default on Fast Ethernet interfaces, regulates the amount of traffic sent out on a full-duplex interface. (Flow control, also called pause frames, is an optional clause on the specification for full-duplex Ethernet, defined by the IEEE 802.3x Task Force in Annex 31B.) Source filtering and flow control are explained more in Recipe 7.13.

The device flags list information about the physical device. You see this line for all router interfaces:

```
Device flags   : Present Running
```

The output shows that the PIC has been recognized by the router software and is operating normally. If the output shows Down instead of Running, check that the interface is configured. If the Present flag is missing, it might indicate that the PIC is not installed properly or is broken.

The next several lines show that SNMP trap notifications are enabled, the number of link flags set on the interface, the number of class-of-service (CoS) queues supported by the PIC, and the PIC's MAC address. The first address is the one currently being used and the second is the one hard-coded on the PIC.

```
Interface flags: SNMP-Traps 16384
Link flags    : 4
CoS queues    : 8 supported
Current address: 00:05:85:ca:ca:70, Hardware address: 00:05:85:ca:ca:70
```

The last lines about the physical interface show how long it has been up, the traffic rates in and out the interface, and whether any interface alarms are active:

```
Last flapped    : 2005-04-23 05:16:57 UTC (1w4d 00:49 ago)
Input rate      : 0 bps (0 pps)
Output rate     : 0 bps (0 pps)
Active alarms   : None
Active defects  : None
```

The logical interfaces portion of the output starts with the logical interface name and indexing information. The second line shows that SNMP trap notifications are also enabled on the logical interface, and the encapsulation is Ethernet II (RFC 894):

```
Logical interface fe-0/0/0.0 (Index 66) (SNMP ifIndex 39)
    Flags: SNMP-Traps Encapsulation: ENET2
```

The final portion shows the protocol families configured on the interface. Here, IPv4 (inet) and ISO are configured. For IPv4, the MTU size is 1,500 bytes (for Ethernet, this is the default), and no logical interface flags are set. You then see the IPv4 address flags, here showing that this is default local address for packets originating from the local router and sent to destinations on the subnet (Is-Preferred) and the default address for broadcast and multicast packets (Is-Primary). For ISO, the MTU size is 1,497 bytes (the default), and this is the default local address for broadcast addresses.

See Also

Recipes 7.12 and 7.13

7.2 Viewing Traffic Statistics on an Interface

Problem

You want to check how much traffic is passing through an interface.

Solution

The show interfaces extensive command shows detailed statistics about the traffic on an interface:

```
aviva@router1# show interfaces extensive fe-0/0/0
```

Discussion

When you need to get traffic statistics about an interface, use either the show interfaces extensive command for maximal information or the show interfaces detail for a slightly abridged view. The extensive version displays quite a bit of information. Again, the specifics of the output vary depending on the interface type. Here is the relevant output for a Fast Ethernet interface:

```
aviva@router1> show interfaces extensive fe-0/0/0
...
Traffic statistics:
   Input  bytes  :              302512              672 bps
   Output bytes  :                   0                0 bps
   Input  packets:                2081                0 pps
   Output packets:                   0                0 pps
  Input errors:
    Errors: 0, Drops: 0, Framing errors: 0, Runts: 0, Policed discards: 0,
    L3 incompletes: 1682, L2 channel errors: 0, L2 mismatch timeouts: 0,
    FIFO errors: 0, Resource errors: 0
  Output errors:
    Carrier transitions: 1, Errors: 0, Drops: 0, Collisions: 0, Aged packets: 0,
    FIFO errors: 0, HS link CRC errors: 0, MTU errors: 0, Resource errors: 0
  Queue counters:        Queued packets  Transmitted packets     Dropped packets
    0 best-effort                     0                    0                   0
    1 expedited-fo                    0                    0                   0
    2 assured-forw                    0                    0                   0
    3 network-cont                    0                    0                   0
  Active alarms  : None
  Active defects : None
  MAC statistics:                     Receive              Transmit
    Total octets                      466604                    0
    Total packets                       3763                    0
    Unicast packets                        0                    0
    Broadcast packets                   1686                    0
    Multicast packets                   2077                    0
    CRC/Align errors                       0                    0
    FIFO errors                            0                    0
    MAC control frames                     0                    0
    MAC pause frames                       0                    0
    Oversized frames                       0
    Jabber frames                          0
    Fragment frames                        0
    VLAN tagged frames                     0
    Code violations                        0
  Filter statistics:
```

```
Input packet count               3763
Input packet rejects                0
Input DA rejects                 1682
Input SA rejects                    0
Output packet count                        0
Output packet pad count                    0
Output packet error count                  0
CAM destination filters: 5, CAM source filters: 0
```

The traffic statistics show input and output counters in both bytes and packets. You then see errors and counters specific for this Fast Ethernet interface.

The show interfaces extensive command takes a snapshot in time of the traffic statistics. To watch the traffic in real time, use the monitor interface command. This can be very useful when you are watching traffic flow through the interfaces or are tracking down a traffic flow issue. This command is just the FreeBSD iftop utility. Again, what you see depends on the type of interface. Here's the sample for the same Fast Ethernet interface:

```
aviva@router1> monitor interface fe-0/0/0
router1                        Seconds: 134           Time: 16:35:302
                                                      Delay: 2/0/9

Interface: fe-0/0/0, Enabled, Link is Up
Encapsulation: Ethernet, Speed: 100mbps
Traffic statistics:                                 Current delta
  Input bytes:           304124 (672 bps)              [892]
  Output bytes:               0 (0 bps)                  [0]
  Input packets:           2092 (0 pps)                  [6]
  Output packets:             0 (0 pps)                  [0]
Error statistics:
  Input errors:               0                          [0]
  Input drops:                0                          [0]
  Input framing errors:       0                          [0]
  Policed discards:           0                          [0]
  L3 incompletes:          1691                          [5]
  L2 channel errors:          0                          [0]
  L2 mismatch timeouts:       0                          [0]
  Carrier transitions:        1                          [0]
  Output errors:              0                          [0]
  Output drops:               0                          [0]
  Aged packets:               0                          [0]
Active alarms : None
Active defects: None
Input MAC/Filter statistics:
  Unicast packets             0                          [0]
  Broadcast packets        1695                          [5]
  Multicast packets        2088                          [6]
  Oversized frames            0                          [0]
  Packet reject count         0                          [0]
  DA rejects               1691                          [5]
  SA rejects                  0                          [0]
Output MAC/Filter Statistics:
  Unicast packets             0                          [0]
```

```
Broadcast packets                0                      [0]
Multicast packets                0                      [0]
Packet pad count                 0                      [0]
Packet error count               0                      [0]

Next='n', Quit='q' or ESC, Freeze='f', Thaw='t', Clear='c', Interface='i'
```

The output updates every second, so you can see we've been watching for 134 seconds and the current time is 16:35. The second line shows the delay, which is how many milliseconds it took to display the statistics. The first number, here 2, is the time difference for the currently displayed statistics. The second number, here 0, is the shortest time difference since the monitoring started, and the third number, here 9, is the longest time difference since monitoring started.

The next two lines briefly describe the interface. The traffic and error statistics and the active alarm and defects sections parallel the fields in the show interfaces extensive command output. The input and output MAC/filter statistics show some of the information that's in the MAC and filter statistics sections of the show command output.

The bottom line contains commands you can issue. You can scroll through all the router's interfaces (Next='n')—they appear in the same order as in the show interfaces terse command—or you can name a specific interface to display (Interface='i'):

```
New interface:
Next='n', Quit='q' or ESC, Freeze='f', Thaw='t', Clear='c', Interface='i'
```

The remaining commands freeze (f) and unfreeze (t) the display, zero the statistics (c), and return to the CLI (q).

See Also

FreeBSD, *http://www.freebsd.org/ports/net-mgmt.html*

7.3   Setting an IP Address for the Router

Problem

You want to assign an address to the router itself so that you can reach it at all times, even when a particular interface is not available and so that applications such as SNMP can always reach the router.

Solution

Use the following command to configure a permanent address for the router:

```
[edit]
aviva@RouterA# set interfaces lo0 unit 0 family inet address 192.168.16.1/32
```

Discussion

Most of the IP addresses you configure on a router are for physical network interfaces, such as an Ethernet or T1 interface. While these interfaces are generally present and operating in the router, you don't want to use them to find out the status of the router, because someone might remove the PIC from the router or because the physical interface may not be up or may not be configured properly even though the router is up and running fine. The solution is to configure an IP address that uniquely identifies your router. You do this by configuring the lo0, or loopback, address.

In the JUNOS software, the loopback address is named lo0. This name doesn't follow the standard JUNOS interface naming conventions. It is just the same name as the Unix loopback interface. You don't need to specify a PIC, FPC, or slot number because the loopback address is not associated with hardware, but is just an internal address on the router. You configure the loopback address on logical unit 0, and the address is an IPv4 address (set with the keyword inet). In this recipe, we set the loopback address to 192.168.16.1/32.

The loopback address on a JUNOS router is used as the IP address of the router itself and is similar to the Unix localhost, which is the address of the local system. The JUNOS software uses this address when it needs to talk to itself using IP.

To see that the loopback address has been configured, you can look at its status:

```
aviva@RouterA> show interfaces lo0
Physical interface: lo0, Enabled, Physical link is Up
  Interface index: 6, SNMP ifIndex: 6
  Type: Loopback, MTU: Unlimited
  Device flags   : Present Running Loopback
  Interface flags: SNMP-Traps
  Link flags     : None
  Last flapped   : Never
  Input packets : 19
  Output packets: 19

  Logical interface lo0.0 (Index 69) (SNMP ifIndex 16)
    Flags: SNMP-Traps Encapsulation: Unspecified
  Input packets : 0
  Output packets: 0
    Protocol inet, MTU: Unlimited
      Flags: None
      Addresses, Flags: Is-Default Is-Primary
        Local: 192.168.16.1

  Logical interface lo0.16385 (Index 64) (SNMP ifIndex 21)
    Flags: SNMP-Traps Encapsulation: Unspecified
```

```
    Input packets : 5
   Output packets: 5
     Protocol inet, MTU: Unlimited
       Flags: None
       Addresses, Flags: Is-Default Is-Primary
         Local: 10.0.0.1
       Addresses
         Local: 10.0.0.16
```

You see the loopback interface address in the logical interface portion of the output. You can see that the lo0 interface is operational (from the Present and Running device flags) and that it is a loopback interface (from the Loopback device flag) with an unlimited MTU size. SNMP traps are enabled on the router, no link flags are set (these flags are only for network interfaces, which lo0 is not), and the interface has never gone down and come back up (flapped). The input and output fields show the number of packets that have passed through the interface. One interesting thing to notice is the existence of logical interface lo0.16385. This is a nonconfigurable interface created by the JUNOS software for routing platform control traffic. The two addresses shown for this logical interface are used internally.

Because the address is just an address for the router and is not used for a software loopback mechanism, it can be any /32 address. You are not limited to using the standard loopback address of 127.0.0.1. Some JUNOS applications, including NTP, RADIUS, TACACS+, and SSL for the JUNOScript API, require a loopback address of 127.0.0.1. You either can set this as your primary loopback address or can configure multiple loopback addresses:

```
[edit]
aviva@RouterA# set interfaces lo0 unit 0 family inet address 192.168.16.1/32
aviva@RouterA# set interfaces lo0 unit 0 family inet address 127.0.0.1/32
```

You see that this address is configured, but is not the default or primary address:

```
aviva@RouterA# run show interfaces lo0.0
  Logical interface lo0.0 (Index 69) (SNMP ifIndex 16)
    Flags: SNMP-Traps Encapsulation: Unspecified
  Input packets : 0
  Output packets: 0
    Protocol inet, MTU: Unlimited
      Flags: None
      Addresses
        Local: 127.0.0.1
      Addresses, Flags: Is-Default Is-Primary
        Local: 192.168.42.1
```

See Also

Recipes 7.1 and 7.10

7.4   Setting the Router's Source Address

Problem

All IP traffic that is sourced from the router includes a source address in the IP header. The address chosen for packets depends on the interface that is used to reach the destination when the connection is established. You want to configure the router to used a fixed address.

Solution

Use the following command to always uses lo0 loopback address as the source address in IP packets:

```
[edit]
aviva@router1# set system default-address-selection
```

Discussion

When selecting an address to include in the source address field of IP packets, the JUNOS software chooses from among the addresses configured on the router. The first candidate to use is the first non-127.0.0.1 address configured on the lo0 interface. However, this means that the software usually, but not always, chooses the loopback address. To ensure that the software always uses the router's IP address, use the set system default-address-selection command. Including this command is considered good practice so that when other systems on the network receive traffic from the local router, the packets always have the same address in the IP packet's source address field. This command forces the router to use one specific address, the lo0 address, for most of the traffic that originates from the router. The source address never affects traffic that is forwarded by the router, only packets that are sourced from the router. If multiple addresses are configured for lo0, the software chooses the one with the lowest address. However, if you assign the parameter primary or preferred to a higher IP address, the software uses the higher IP address. The following command makes one of the loopback addresses the primary one:

```
[edit]
aviva@RouterA# set interfaces lo0 unit 0 family inet address 192.168.16.1/32 primary
```

Figure 7-1 illustrates why you should set the router's source address. In this topology, if you ping 1.0.2.1 from Mars, Mars normally sends the packet out the so-0/0/0 interface and uses 1.0.2.2 as the source address for that ping packet. Venus receives the ping and sends a response back to 1.0.2.2 (the source address).

If Mars, Venus, and Earth have lo0 addresses 1.1.0.1/32, 1.1.0.2/32, and 1.1.0.3/32, and you have the default address selection configured on Mars, what happens is different. If you ping 1.0.2.1 from Mars, Mars uses 1.1.0.1 (its lo0 address) as the source address. It still sends the packet out so-0/0/0, and Venus still receives it and sends a response back to the source address of the ping, 1.1.0.1.

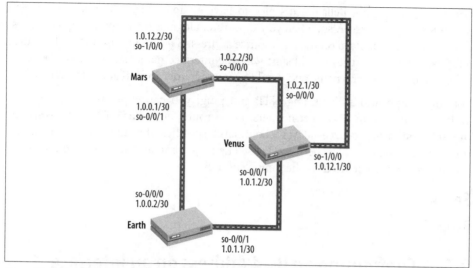

Figure 7-1. Topology for setting the router's source address

Venus needs to know how to get back to 1.1.0.1. Venus knows how to get to 1.0.2.2, because it's a connected network. It's going to need a route back to 1.1.0.1, however. You can set this up by distributing lo0 addresses with an IGP, such as OSPF. Let's say that all three routers are distributing their loopback addresses using OSPF on all the interfaces in the figure so that all three know how to reach all the loopback addresses of each other. Venus is still trying to send its echo response back to Mars and might send it out either so-0/0/0 or so-1/0/0. Either way, it gets to Mars, and the ping application sees the response.

Now, if you ping 1.1.0.2 (venus-lo0) from Mars, Mars sends it out either so-0/0/0 or so-1/0/0. Venus receives the ping and replies back, again over either link. If so-0/0/0 goes down for some unknown reason, the ping still works because there's still a path using so-1/0/0. However, pinging 1.0.2.1 does not work because that interface is down.

If both so-0/0/0 and so-1/0/0 go down, the ping still works, because Mars sends the packet to Earth, Earth forwards it to Venus, and Venus sees it and replies back, going through Earth. In other words, you can still get to Venus with the same IP address even if all your direct links to Venus are down.

In a large network with hundreds of routers and dozens of links per router (any number of which might be down or congested), figuring out which address to ping is a hassle you can avoid by setting the router's source address. One disadvantage of doing this, however, is that it tends to hide network outages.

There are some other side benefits to using the lo0 address as the router's source address. When you are stringing together IP addresses to use for DNS, it's often convenient to use some hostname–interface name combination for it, such as Bellagio-ge-1-1-0-Gash2-link.jnpr.net or 0.so-1-0-0.XL2.SJC2.ALTER.NET. But if you just want to ping Bellagio, it's nice to have an lo0 address around to which to assign the ping request. Also, when you save system logfiles on a remote log server, syslog does a reverse lookup on the log's source address. If you don't use lo0 as the source address, the logfile entries would start with the interface name, such as venus-fe-0-0-0, instead of the router's name and would be much harder to read and interpret.

For some applications, including NTP and ping, you can explicitly set the source address to include in IP packet headers. For a router acting as an NTP time server, the set system ntp source-address command specifies the address to use in the router's responses to NTP client requests. The ping command source option includes a source address to be used by the ping responses.

See Also

Recipe 7.3

7.5 Configuring an IPv4 Address on an Interface

Problem

You want to configure an interface to work on an IPv4 network.

Solution

Use the following command to configure an IPv4 address on an interface:

```
[edit]
aviva@router1# set interfaces fe-0/0/0 unit 0 family inet address 192.168.220.1/24
```

Discussion

For any IPv4 routing protocol such as BGP, OSPF, RIP, and ICMP to work, not only do you have to configure the protocol, but you also have to configure the interfaces on which the protocol can run. You configure the address under the logical interfaces portion. For IPv4 addresses, the address family is inet.

To see that the IPv4 address has been set, you can look at the logical interface:

```
aviva@router1> show interfaces fe-0/0/0.0 brief
Logical interface fe-0/0/0.0
  Flags: SNMP-Traps Encapsulation: ENET2
    inet  192.168.220.1/24
```

The JUNOS software allows more than one address on a logical interface. Issuing a second set command does not overwrite an existing address, but simply adds the second address. To correct an IP address, use the rename command:

```
[edit interfaces fe-0/0/0]
aviva@router1# rename unit 0 family inet address 192.168.220.1/24 to address 192.168.220.2/24
```

To remove an extra IP address, use the delete command:

```
[edit interfaces fe-0/0/0]
aviva@router1# delete unit 0 family inet address 192.168.220.1/24
```

If you have many interfaces to configure and need to conserve IP addresses, you do not have to assign an address to the logical interface:

```
[edit interfaces]
aviva@router1# set fe-1/0/0 unit 0 family inet
```

This command creates what is called an unnumbered interface. When packets are sent out this interface, their source address contains the router's default address, which is the address you set on the loopback (lo0) interface. If you have not set an address on lo0, make sure that you have configured an address on another interface on the router.

See Also

Recipes 7.3, 7.4, and 7.12

7.6   Configuring an IPv6 Address on an Interface

Problem

You want to configure an interface to work on an IPv6 network.

Solution

The IPv6 address configuration is very similar to that for IPv4:

```
[edit]
aviva@router1# set interfaces fe-0/0/3 unit 0 family inet6 address fec0:1:1:1::2/64
```

Discussion

For an interface to operate on an IPv6 network, it needs an IPv6 address in the inet6 address family. To see that the IPv6 address has been set, look at the logical interface:

```
aviva@router1> show interfaces fe-0/0/3.0 brief
  Logical interface fe-0/0/3.0
    Flags: SNMP-Traps Encapsulation: ENET2
    inet6 fe80::205:85ff:fe02:a403/64
          fec0:1:1:1::2/64
```

See Also

Recipe 7.12

7.7   Configuring an ISO Address on an Interface

Problem

You want to configure an interface to support IS-IS.

Solution

Configure the ISO protocol family on the interface running IS-IS:

```
[edit]
aviva@RouterA# set interfaces fe-0/0/0 unit 0 family iso
```

Discussion

IS-IS is an OSI protocol, so you need to create an OSI family on the interface for IS-IS to work. You also need to configure one or more addresses for the loopback interface, which IS-IS uses for its interface addresses (see Recipe 7.3). Here's how to check the configuration:

```
aviva@router1# show interfaces fe-0/0/0.0 brief
  Logical interface fe-0/0/0.0
    Flags: SNMP-Traps Encapsulation: ENET2
    inet  192.168.220.1/30
      iso
```

See Also

Recipes 7.3, 7.12, and 11.1

7.8   Creating an MPLS Protocol Family on a Logical Interface

Problem

You want to configure an interface to support Multiprotocol Label Switching (MPLS).

Solution

Set up the MPLS protocol family on the interface running MPLS:

```
[edit]
aviva@RouterA# set interfaces fe-0/0/0 unit 0 family mpls
```

Discussion

For MPLS traffic to transit an interface, you must create an MPLS protocol family on the logical interface. You don't need to configure an address. Here's how to check the configuration:

```
aviva@router1# show interfaces fe-0/0/0.0 brief
  Logical interface fe-0/0/0.0
    Flags: SNMP-Traps Encapsulation: ENET2
    inet  192.168.220.1/30
      mpls
```

See Also

Recipes 7.12, 14.1, 14.6

7.9   Configuring an Interface Description

Problem

You want to include a description of an interface in the configuration.

Solution

Use the following command to configure a description of the interface:

```
[edit interfaces fe-0/0/0]
aviva@router1# set interfaces fe-0/0/0 description "to router2 fe-0/0/0"
```

Discussion

It's often convenient to include a short description of the interface to make a note of any administrative information that is useful to you or your staff, such as the remote interface. This recipe sets a description of the interface that describes the remote router and interface that is at the other end of this link.

The configured interface description script shows up in the show interfaces command output:

```
aviva@router1> show interfaces fe-0/0/0
Physical interface: fe-0/0/0, Enabled, Physical link is Up
  Interface index: 128, SNMP ifIndex: 79
  Description: to router2 fe-0/0/0
  Link-level type: Ethernet, MTU: 1514, Speed: 100mbps, Loopback: Disabled,
  Source filtering: Disabled, Flow control: Enabled
  Device flags   : Present Running
  Interface flags: SNMP-Traps 16384
  ...
```

You can use the show interfaces descriptions command to list the descriptions for all interfaces:

```
aviva@router1> show interfaces descriptions
Interface        Admin Link  Description
fe-0/0/0         up    up    to router2 fe-0/0/0
fe-0/0/1         up    up    to router2 fe-0/0/1
fe-0/0/2         up    up    to router2 fe-0/0/2
```

7.10 Choosing Primary and Preferred Interface Addresses

Problem

You have an Ethernet or other point-to-multipoint interface and have to set up multiple addresses on the interface—for example, so you can treat class of service for each flow differently—but you need to always use one of the addresses first.

Solution

Use the following commands to pick one address to always be the source address for traffic on the same subnet:

```
[edit interfaces fe-0/0/0]
aviva@router1# set unit 0 family inet address 192.168.220.1/24
aviva@router1# set unit 0 family inet address 192.168.220.2/24 preferred
```

Use the following commands to choose one address that is used as the source address in broadcast and unnumbered traffic sent out an interface:

```
[edit interfaces fe-0/0/1]
aviva@router1# set unit 0 family inet address 192.168.220.1/24
aviva@router1# set unit 0 family inet address 192.168.220.2/24 primary
```

Discussion

Each JUNOS interface has a *preferred* address, which is the default local address used when there is more than one address in the same subnet on the same interface. Each JUNOS interface also has a *primary* address, which is used by default as the source address when you originate packets out the interface where the destination gives no hint about the subnet. By default, the software chooses the numerically lowest address as the preferred and primary address. The show interfaces command output indicates which addresses are the preferred and primary:

```
aviva@router1> show interfaces fe-0/0/0.0
  Logical interface fe-0/0/0.0 (Index 66) (SNMP ifIndex 84)
    Flags: SNMP-Traps Encapsulation: ENET2
    Protocol inet, MTU: 1500
```

```
    Flags: None
    Addresses, Flags: Is-Preferred Is-Primary
        Destination: 192.168.220.0/24, Local: 192.168.220.1,
        Broadcast: 192.168.220.3
```

Here we see that the address configured on the Fast Ethernet logical interface, 192.168.220.1/30, is both the preferred and primary address for the interface.

For some point-to-multipoint and other applications, you configure multiple address on a single logical interface:

```
[edit interfaces fe-0/0/0]
aviva@router1# set unit 0 family inet address 192.168.220.2/24
aviva@router1# show
unit 0 {
    family inet {
        address 192.168.220.1/24;
        address 192.168.220.2/24;
    }
}
```

With this configuration, the first address continues to be the preferred and primary address because, numerically, it is the lower of the two:

```
aviva@router1> show interfaces fe-0/0/0.0
    Logical interface fe-0/0/0.0 (Index 66) (SNMP ifIndex 84)
    Flags: SNMP-Traps Encapsulation: ENET2
    Protocol inet, MTU: 1500
        Flags: None
        Addresses, Flags: Is-Preferred Is-Primary
            Destination: 192.168.220.0/24, Local: 192.168.220.1,
            Broadcast: 192.168.220.3
        Addresses
            Destination: 192.168.220.0/24, Local: 192.168.220.2,
            Broadcast: 192.168.220.3
```

To have the higher address be the primary or preferred address, use the commands shown in the recipe:

```
aviva@router1# show
unit 0 {
    family inet {
        address 192.168.220.1/24;
        address 192.168.220.2/24 {
            primary;
            preferred;
        }
    }
}
aviva@router1> show interfaces fe-0/0/0.0
    Logical interface fe-0/0/0.0 (Index 66) (SNMP ifIndex 84)
    Flags: SNMP-Traps Encapsulation: ENET2
    Protocol inet, MTU: 1500
        Flags: None
        Addresses
```

```
Destination: 192.168.220.0/24, Local: 192.168.220.1,
Broadcast: 192.168.220.3
Addresses, Flags: Primary Preferred Is-Preferred Is-Primary
Destination: 192.168.220.0/24, Local: 192.168.220.2,
Broadcast: 192.168.220.3
```

It's helpful to expand the configuration a bit to illustrate how the source addresses are used. Let's say we have:

```
[edit interfaces fe-0/0/0 unit 0 family inet]
address 192.168.220.1/24;
address 192.168.220.2/24 {
    primary;
    preferred;
}
address 192.168.222.1/24;
address 192.168.222.2/24 {
    preferred;
}
```

IP traffic bound for 192.168.220.10 uses 192.168.220.2 as the source address because this is the preferred address. Traffic for, say, 100.0.0.1 also uses 192.168.220.2 (if there is a route to that network pointing out fe-0/0/0) because this is the interface's primary address. Traffic for 192.168.222.10 uses 192.168.222.2 as the source address, again because this is the interface's preferred address.

Another situation is to have multiple addresses on the loopback interface, which you might want for any number of reasons. You might want a public address for the router's IP address, a private one for management access, and 127.0.0.1 as the traditional loopback address.

Yet another reason to have multiple address on an interface is to increase the number of IP addresses on an Ethernet network without renumbering devices that are already there. While this is often not considered good practice, sometimes it's the easiest way to deal with the growing number of addresses. Say you have interface fe-0/0/0 with IP address 205.134.233.254/24. When you've used all the addresses in that /24 address space, you can either renumber all 250 or so devices on that network, grow that network (which requires planning ahead; in this case you could just make the network a /23 if you're not using 205.134.232.0/24 for anything else), or just add another network. As an interim measure, you can just add the second address for the new network address space to the interface and set the desired one to be the primary and preferred address.

7.11   Using the Management Interface

Problem

You want to enable out-of-band management access to the router.

Solution

Configure the router's management interface:

```
[edit interfaces]
aviva@router1# set fxp0 unit 0 family inet address 192.168.70.246/24
```

Use the following command to configure the J-series management interface:

```
[edit interfaces]
aviva@RouterA> set fe-0/0/0 unit 0 family inet address 10.0.15.1/24
```

Discussion

JUNOS routers provide a separate out-of-band management interface for monitoring the router independently of the network links. This interface is named fxp0 and is an internal Ethernet interface that is permanently installed in the router. The router does not route traffic from network and services interfaces over fxp0, and traffic arriving on this interface is never directed to network interfaces, so you cannot use it to route traffic.

You can connect to the management interface over the network using SSH and Telnet, and SNMP NMS systems can connect to the router using this interface to query for router status and statistics.

This recipe shows how to configure an address for the fxp0 interface. Because it is an Ethernet interface, you can configure a subnet address. You cannot configure a host (/32) address.

Use the show interfaces command to get status about the management interface:

```
aviva@router1> show interfaces fxp0
Physical interface: fxp0, Enabled, Physical link is Up
  Interface index: 1, SNMP ifIndex: 1
  Type: Ethernet, Link-level type: Ethernet, MTU: 1514, Speed: 100mbps
  Device flags   : Present Running
  Interface flags: SNMP-Traps
  Link type      : Half-Duplex
  Link flags     : 4
  Current address: 00:a0:a5:12:2f:04, Hardware address: 00:a0:a5:12:2f:04
  Last flapped   : Never
  Input packets : 217004
  Output packets: 2808

  Logical interface fxp0.0 (Index 2) (SNMP ifIndex 13)
    Flags: SNMP-Traps Encapsulation: ENET2
    Protocol inet, MTU: 1500
      Flags: Is-Primary
      Addresses, Flags: Is-Default Is-Preferred Is-Primary
        Destination: 192.168.64/21, Local: 192.168.71.246,
        Broadcast: 192.168.71.255
```

The output shows that this is a 100-Mbps Ethernet interface running in half-duplex mode.

The hardware architecture of the J-series routers differs from the M-series and T-series routers, so instead of fxp0 being the management interface, it is one of the nonremovable Fast Ethernet interfaces, fe-0/0/0. The interface status shows the same basic information as on the M- and T-series routers:

```
aviva@RouterA> show interfaces fe-0/0/0
Physical interface: fe-0/0/0, Enabled, Physical link is Up
  Interface index: 137, SNMP ifIndex: 29
  Link-level type: Ethernet, MTU: 1514, Speed: 100mbps, Loopback: Disabled,
  Source filtering: Disabled, Flow control: Enabled
  Device flags   : Present Running
  Interface flags: SNMP-Traps 16384
  Link flags     : 4
  CoS queues     : 8 supported
  Current address: 00:05:85:ca:ca:70, Hardware address: 00:05:85:ca:ca:70
  Last flapped   : 2005-05-04 23:37:59 PDT (1w0d 18:17 ago)
  Input rate     : 0 bps (0 pps)
  Output rate    : 304 bps (0 pps)
  Active alarms  : None
  Active defects : None

  Logical interface fe-0/0/0.0 (Index 66) (SNMP ifIndex 39)
    Flags: SNMP-Traps Encapsulation: ENET2
    Protocol inet, MTU: 1500
      Flags: Is-Primary
      Addresses, Flags: Is-Preferred Is-Primary
        Destination: 10.0.16/24, Local: 10.0.15.1, Broadcast: 10.0.15.255
```

While you can actually configure the fxp0 interface on a J-series router, the values are applied to the fe-0/0/0 interface and show up under fe-0/0/0 in the show interfaces output. The recommended procedure is to place all management interface configuration at the [edit interfaces fe-0/0/0] hierarchy level.

The process for configuring many of the JUNOS protocols is to associate one or more interfaces with the protocol to make the interfaces aware that they will be receiving packets for that protocol, and vice versa. You can do this by calling out specific interfaces in the configuration, such as here:

```
[edit protocols]
aviva@RouterA# set pim interface fe-0/0/1
```

It's often faster and easier just to configure all the interfaces at once:

```
[edit protocols]
aviva@RouterA# set pim interface all
```

When you do this, you end up configuring the protocol on the out-of-band interface also. It's not considered good practice to do this, so in these cases, you should turn off the protocol on that interface with a disable command.

On an M-series or a T-series router, the command looks like this:

```
[edit protocols]
aviva@router1# set pim interface fxp0 disable
```

On a J-series router, use a command like this:

```
[edit protocols]
aviva@RouterA# set pim interface fe-0/0/0 disable
```

The primary reason you want to turn off the protocol is because this is the management interface, and you most likely are not using any routing protocols on it. Disabling the protocol leaves you with a "clean" configuration, because you are configuring only the functionality that you actually want the router to use. If you choose not to disable the protocol on the management interface, routing protocols may establish adjacencies to the fxp0 or fe-0/0/0 interface, but there is no negative impact on the performance of the Routing Engine.

7.12 Finding Out What IP Addresses Are Used on the Router

Problem

You want to find out the IP addresses assigned to router interfaces.

Solution

Use the following command to find out what IP addresses have been assigned on the router:

```
aviva@RouterB> show interfaces terse
Interface           Admin Link Proto Local              Remote
fe-0/0/0            up    up
fe-0/0/0.0          up    up   inet  10.0.24.2/24
gr-0/0/0            up    up
ip-0/0/0            up    up
ls-0/0/0            up    up
lt-0/0/0            up    up
mt-0/0/0            up    up
pd-0/0/0            up    up
pe-0/0/0            up    up
sp-0/0/0            up    up
sp-0/0/0.16383      up    up   inet
fe-0/0/1            up    up
fe-0/0/1.0          up    up   inet  10.0.29.2/24
t1-0/0/2            up    up
t1-0/0/2.0          up    down inet  10.0.31.1/24
t1-0/0/3            up    down
dsc                 up    up
gre                 up    up
ipip                up    up
```

```
loo                    up    up
loo.0                  up    up    inet   192.168.14.1        --> 0/0
loo.16385              up    up    inet   10.0.0.1            --> 0/0
                                          10.0.0.16           --> 0/0

lsi                    up    up
mtun                   up    up
pimd                   up    up
pime                   up    up
ppo                    up    up
tap                    up    up
```

Another way to display IP addresses quickly is to always include the interface's IP address when configuring the interfaces:

```
[edit interfaces]
aviva@RouterD# set fe-0/0/0 description "10.0.24.2/24; to RouterH's fe-1/0/1"
```

Then use the following command to list the addresses:

```
aviva@RouterD> show interfaces descriptions
Interface    Admin Link Description
fe-0/0/0     up    up   10.0.24.2/24; to RouterH's fe-1/0/1
fe-0/0/1     up    up   10.0.29.2/24; to RouterC's fe-0/0/1
t1-0/0/2     up    up   10.0.31.1/24; to RouterF's t1-0/0/2
loo          up    up   192.168.14.1/32; local loopback
```

Discussion

When you are modifying a router configuration or trying to debug a problem, sometimes you need a quick way to find out what IP addresses are configured on the router. You can read through the interfaces portion of the configuration file, which is where all IP addresses are configured, but if you have a number of PICs and ports or if you have many logical interfaces, the information will likely be spread out over many screens. A simple way to get a list of configured IP addresses is to use the show interfaces terse command. The IP address is shown in the Local column. The output in this recipe shows IP addresses for three network interfaces, fe-0/0/0, fe-0/0/1, and t1-0/0/2, and for the loo interface.

Another strategy for displaying IP addresses quickly is to always include the interface's IP address in the description statement when configuring the interfaces. Then use the show interfaces descriptions command to list all interface IP addresses.

The output of the show interfaces terse command also provides a quick view of which slot each of the PICs is installed in. When PICs are installed in the router, the JUNOS software detects their presence and displays them in the output of the show interfaces command. In this example, the router (a J-series box) has two Fast Ethernet PICs in slot 0 (interfaces fe-0/0/0 and fe-0/0/1) and two serial cards in slot 0 (interfaces se-0/0/2 and se-0/0/3).

You can confirm the presence of these PICs with the show chassis hardware command, but this command does not tell you which slot the PICs are in:

```
aviva@RouterB> show chassis hardware
Hardware inventory:
Item              Version  Part number  Serial number    Description
Chassis                                 JN002447AA       J2300
Routing Engine    REV 07   750-009992   AA04350171       RE-J.1
FPC 0             REV 04   750-010739   AC04430288       FPC
  PIC 0                                                  2x FE, 2x Serial
```

Some of the interfaces (gr-0/0/0, ip-0/0/0, ls-0/0/0, lt-0/0/0, mt-0/0/0, pd-0/0/0, and pe-0/0/0) are virtual interfaces that are used for tunneling. They are virtual in that they are not necessarily tied to a specific network card. gr-0/0/0 and ip-0/0/0 are for unicast tunnels with GRE or IP-IP encapsulation, ls-0/0/0 is a link services interface, lt-0/0/0 is a logical tunnel interface, mt-0/0/0 is a multicast tunnel, and pd-0/0/0 and pe-0/0/0 are PIM tunnels. lo is the loopback interface (see Recipe 7.3), and the remaining are nonconfigurable interfaces used internally by the JUNOS software (see Recipe 7.23).

See Also

Recipes 7.3 and 7.23

7.13   Configuring Ethernet Interfaces

Problem

Your router has an Ethernet interface and you want to configure it.

Solution

Use the following command to activate a Fast Ethernet interface:

```
[edit interfaces]
aviva@router1# set fe-0/0/3 unit 0 family inet address 192.168.220.13/24
```

Use the following commands to activate a Gigabit Ethernet interface:

```
[edit interfaces]
aviva@M5# set ge-0/2/0 unit 0 family inet6 address 3010::2/64
aviva@M5# set ge-0/2/0 unit 0 family iso
```

Discussion

The basic configuration for Ethernet interfaces is very straightforward. Just assign the desired addresses, and the interface is up and running. Here, for the Fast Ethernet interface, we configure an IPv4 address, and for the Gigabit Ethernet interface, we configure an IPv6 address and the iso family (for IS-IS). You can also configure other address families depending on the protocols that the interface needs to support.

With this configuration, the show interfaces output displays the default JUNOS settings for Ethernet interfaces. The Fast Ethernet defaults are highlighted:

```
aviva@router1> show interfaces fe-0/0/3
Physical interface: fe-0/0/3, Enabled, Physical link is Up
  Interface index: 131, SNMP ifIndex: 82
  Link-level type: Ethernet, MTU: 1514, Speed: 100mbps, Loopback: Disabled,
  Source filtering: Disabled, Flow control: Enabled
  Device flags   : Present Running
  Interface flags: SNMP-Traps 16384
  Link flags     : 4
  CoS queues     : 4 supported
  Current address: 00:05:85:02:a4:03, Hardware address: 00:05:85:02:a4:03
  Last flapped   : 2005-05-12 14:58:08 PDT (04:58:52 ago)
  Input rate     : 0 bps (0 pps)
  Output rate    : 0 bps (0 pps)
  Active alarms  : None
  Active defects : None

  Logical interface fe-0/0/3.0 (Index 69) (SNMP ifIndex 87)
    Flags: SNMP-Traps Encapsulation: ENET2
    Protocol inet, MTU: 1500
      Flags: None
      Addresses, Flags: Is-Preferred Is-Primary
        Destination: 192.168.220.12/24, Local: 192.168.220.13,
        Broadcast: 192.168.220.255
    Protocol iso, MTU: 1497
      Flags: None
```

The Gigabit Ethernet defaults are the same except for the link speed:

```
aviva@M5> show interfaces ge-0/2/0
Physical interface: ge-0/2/0, Enabled, Physical link is Up
  Interface index: 134, SNMP ifIndex: 29
  Link-level type: Ethernet, MTU: 1514, Speed: 1000mbps, Loopback: Disabled,
  Source filtering: Disabled, Flow control: Enabled
  Device flags   : Present Running
  Interface flags: SNMP-Traps 16384
  Link flags     : None
  CoS queues     : 4 supported
  Current address: 00:90:69:69:6c:3e, Hardware address: 00:90:69:69:6c:3e
  Last flapped   : 2005-05-16 16:11:53 PDT (3d 01:07 ago)
  Input rate     : 456 bps (0 pps)
  Output rate    : 0 bps (0 pps)
  Active alarms  : None
  Active defects : None

  Logical interface ge-0/2/0.0 (Index 66) (SNMP ifIndex 22)
    Flags: SNMP-Traps Encapsulation: ENET2
    Protocol iso, MTU: 1497
      Flags: Is-Primary
```

```
    Protocol inet6, MTU: 1500
      Flags: Is-Primary
      Addresses, Flags: Is-Preferred Is-Primary
        Destination: 3010::/64, Local: 3010::2
      Addresses, Flags: Is-Preferred
        Destination: fe80::/64, Local: fe80::290:69ff:fe69:6c3e
```

For both types of interfaces, the family MTU size is the default for that family (1,500 bytes for IPv4 and IPv6, and 1,497 bytes for ISO).

Source filtering, off by default, is a security feature for accepting traffic only from a specific MAC interface and rejecting all other traffic. If you want to enable it, set in on the physical interface:

```
[edit interfaces fe-0/0/2 fastether-options]
aviva@router1# set source-filtering
aviva@router1# set source-address-filter 00:05:85:02:38:02
```

Flow control, which is enabled by default, allows the receiving devices on the link to detect when they are experiencing congestion and notify their neighboring devices of this. The neighboring devices can moderate the flow of traffic to reduce or eliminate the congestion.

One interface default not shown in the output is whether the interface operates full duplex or half duplex. By default, Fast Ethernet interfaces run in full-duplex mode. You can configure half-duplex mode with the following command:

```
[edit interfaces fe-0/0/3]
aviva@router1# set link-mode half-duplex
```

Gigabit Ethernet interfaces operate only full duplex. For interoperability the remote end of the link must also be full duplex.

Each Ethernet interface has a Layer 2 MAC address that is hard-coded on the hardware, and this is the default MAC address used for the interface:

```
Current address: 00:05:85:02:a4:03, Hardware address: 00:05:85:02:a4:03
```

There may be security or other reasons to change this hard-coded address, which you can do with following command

```
[edit interfaces fe-0/0/3]
aviva@router1# set mac 00.11.22.33.44.55.66
```

Checking in the show interfaces command output again, you see that the interface's MAC address is now different from its hardware address:

```
Current address: aa:bb:cc:dd:ee:ff, Hardware address: 00:05:85:02:a4:03
```

The show interfaces command output displays the IPv4 broadcast address, here 192. 168.220.255. This is the default broadcast address, in which the host portion of the subnet (which is 192.168.220.12/24) is set to all ones (for a /24 network, the last 8 bits of the address are ones, which is 255 in decimal).

Both the physical and logical interfaces have encapsulations. The default for both is Ethernet II (RFC 894).

The physical interface shows the encapsulation in the Link-level type field, and the logical interface shows it in the Encapsulation field:

```
Physical interface: fe-0/0/3, Enabled, Physical link is Up
  Interface index: 131, SNMP ifIndex: 82
  Link-level type: Ethernet, MTU: 1514, Speed: 100mbps, Loopback: Disabled,

  Logical interface fe-0/0/3.0 (Index 69) (SNMP ifIndex 87)
    Flags: SNMP-Traps Encapsulation: ENET2
```

The JUNOS software supports IEEE 802.1Q VLAN tagging on Ethernet interfaces, which channelizes an Ethernet interface, allowing it to carry traffic from different Ethernet segments over the same physical link but keeping the traffic on separate logical interfaces. VLAN tagging works on an entire physical Ethernet interface, and you configure each logical interface to carry traffic from different Ethernet segments, as shown in this example:

```
[edit interfaces fe-2/1/2]
aviva@router1# set vlan-tagging
aviva@router1# set unit 0 vlan-id 0
aviva@router1# set unit 0 family inet address 10.10.1.0/24
aviva@router1# set unit 1 vlan-id 1
aviva@router1# set unit 1 family inet address 10.10.1.1/24
aviva@router1# set unit 2 vlan-id 0
aviva@router1# set unit 2 family inet address 10.10.1.2/24
```

You see the VLAN configuration parameters in the logical portion of the show interfaces command output:

```
aviva@router1# show interfaces fe-2/1/2.2
  Logical interface fe-2/1/2.2 (Index 75) (SNMP ifIndex 214)
    Flags: SNMP-Traps 16384 VLAN-Tag [ 0x8100.2 ]  Encapsulation: ENET2
  Input packets : 0
  Output packets: 1
    Protocol inet, MTU: 1500
      Flags: None
      Addresses, Flags: Is-Preferred Is-Primary
        Destination: 10.10.1/24, Local: 10.10.1.2, Broadcast: 10.10.1.255
```

7.14 Using VRRP on Ethernet Interfaces

Problem

You want to set up a router to be a backup default gateway to provide redundancy in case the primary default gateway router goes down.

Solution

Use the Virtual Router Redundancy Protocol (VRRP) to set up a master and a backup gateway. First set up the master gateway on one router:

```
[edit interfaces fe-1/0/0 unit 0 family inet address 10.0.2.2/24]
aviva@RouterJ# set vrrp-group 1 virtual-address 10.0.2.100
aviva@RouterJ# set vrrp-group 1 priority 254
aviva@RouterJ# set vrrp-group 1 authentication-type md5
aviva@RouterJ# set vrrp-group 1 authentication-key $1991poPPi
```

Then set up the backup gateway on a second router:

```
[edit interfaces fe-1/0/0 unit 1 family inet address 10.0.2.1/24]
aviva@RouterH# set vrrp-group 1 virtual-address 10.0.2.100
aviva@RouterH# set vrrp-group 1 authentication-type md5
aviva@RouterH# set vrrp-group 1 authentication-key $1991poPPi
```

Discussion

With VRRP, you create a master default gateway router, which is active, on the LAN and one or more backup gateways that can take over automatically if the master goes down. The master and backup gateways share the same virtual IP address, which is the address that is advertised to the hosts on the LAN. If one of the backups takes over, the hosts on the LAN can still reach the default gateway without needing to be reconfigured.

This recipe sets up VRRP group 1 that has one backup gateway. The shared virtual address is 10.0.2.100. The priority value (a value from 1 to 255, with a default of 100) determines which router is the master and the order in which the backups take over. The router with the highest priority becomes the master. Notice that the backups must be on different routers than the master and than each other.

To check the configuration, use the show vrrp detail command. The following output shows that RouterJ is the master:

```
aviva@RouterJ> show vrrp
Interface   Unit  Group  Type  Address      Int state   VR state   Timer
fe-1/0/0    0     1      lcl   10.0.2.2     up          master     A 0.736
                         vip   10.0.2.100
```

RouterH is the backup:

```
aviva@RouterH> show vrrp
Interface   Unit  Group  Type  Address      Int state   VR state   Timer
fe-1/0/0    0     1      lcl   10.0.2.1     up          backup     D 3.443
                         vip   10.0.2.100
                         mas   10.0.2.2
```

The output on both routers shows the real (local) IP address and the virtual address (VIP). The backup's output also shows the real IP address of the master.

The show vrrp extensive command displays the protocol exchanges and master-backup transitions among the VRRP group. Here's the output on the current master:

```
aviva@RouterJ> show vrrp extensive
Interface: fe-1/0/0.0, Interface index: 68, Groups: 1, Active : 1
  Interface VRRP PDU statistics
    Advertisement sent                      :              392
    Advertisement received                  :                0
    Packets received                        :                0
    No group match received                 :                0
  Interface VRRP PDU error statistics
    Invalid IPAH next type received         :                0
    Invalid VRRP TTL value received         :                0
    Invalid VRRP version received           :                0
    Invalid VRRP PDU type received          :                0
    Invalid VRRP authentication type received:               0
    Invalid VRRP IP count received          :                0
    Invalid VRRP checksum received          :                0

  Physical interface: fe-1/0/0, Unit: 0, Address: 10.0.2.2/24
    Index: 68, SNMP ifIndex: 42, VRRP-Traps: disabled
    Interface state: up, Group: 1, State: master
    Priority: 254, Advertisement interval: 1, Authentication type: md5
    Preempt: yes, Accept-data mode: no, VIP count: 1, VIP: 10.0.2.100
    Advertisement timer: 0.658s, Master router: 10.0.2.2
    Virtual router uptime: 00:08:22, Master router uptime: 00:08:19
    Virtual MAC: 00:00:5e:00:01:01
    Tracking: disabled
    Group VRRP PDU statistics
      Advertisement sent            :         392
      Advertisement received        :           0
    Group VRRP PDU error statistics
      Bad authentication type received:         0
      Bad password received         :           0
      Bad MD5 digest received       :           0
      Bad advertisement timer received:         0
      Bad VIP count received        :           0
      Bad VIPADDR received          :           0
    Group state transition statistics
      Idle to master transitions    :           0
      Idle to backup transitions    :           1
      Backup to master transitions  :           1
      Master to backup transitions  :           0
```

7.15 Connecting to an Ethernet Switch

Problem

The router connects to an Ethernet switch, and you want to aggregate a number of the switch's Ethernet interfaces onto a single JUNOS Ethernet interface.

Solution

There are three steps to setting up an aggregated Ethernet interface. First, enable Ethernet aggregation on the router:

```
[edit chassis]
aviva@router1# set aggregated-devices ethernet device-count 24
```

Second, enable aggregation on the Ethernet interface:

```
[edit interfaces fe-0/0/3]
aviva@router1# set fastether-options 802.3ad ae0
```

Finally, configure the aggregated Ethernet interface:

```
[edit interfaces ae0]
aviva@router1# set vlan-tagging
aviva@router1# set unit 0 vlan-id 1
aviva@router1# set unit 0 family inet address 10.10.10.1/24
```

Discussion

Link aggregation of Ethernet interfaces, defined in the IEEE 802.3ad standard, is a way to aggregate multiple connections from a switch into a single logical interface on a Fast Ethernet or Gigabit Ethernet interface on an M-series or T-series router. (J-series boxes do not support Ethernet aggregation). The JUNOS software balances traffic across all member links within an aggregated Ethernet bundle.

This recipe configures a bundle of 24 aggregated logical interfaces. The set aggregated-devices ethernet command tells the router chassis process to treat the Ethernet logical interfaces configured for aggregation as separate virtual devices. On the Fast Ethernet interface, the set fastether-options 802.3ad ae0 command turns on aggregation on the interface and associates the interface with aggregated Ethernet interface 0. Because the aggregation creates virtual links on the interface, do not configure a logical interface on the Fast Ethernet interface.

To set up the aggregated Ethernet interface itself, configure VLAN tagging and a logical interface with an IP address on interface ae0.

Verify the configuration by looking at the Fast Ethernet and aggregated Ethernet interfaces. On the Fast Ethernet interface, you see the logical interface points to the aggregated Ethernet bundle:

```
aviva@router1> show interfaces fe-0/0/3
Physical interface: fe-0/0/3, Enabled, Physical link is Up
  Interface index: 131, SNMP ifIndex: 82
  Description: to nutmeg fe-003
  Link-level type: Ethernet, MTU: 1518, Speed: 100mbps, Loopback: Disabled,
  Source filtering: Disabled, Flow control: Enabled
  Device flags   : Present Running
  Interface flags: SNMP-Traps 16384
  Link flags     : 4
  CoS queues     : 4 supported
```

```
Current address: 00:05:85:02:a7:f0, Hardware address: 00:05:85:02:a4:03
Last flapped    : 2005-05-26 03:10:25 PDT (05:39:39 ago)
Input rate      : 0 bps (0 pps)
Output rate     : 0 bps (0 pps)
Active alarms   : None
Active defects  : None

Logical interface fe-0/0/3.0 (Index 72) (SNMP ifIndex 87)
  Flags: SNMP-Traps 16384 VLAN-Tag [ 0x8100.1 ]  Encapsulation: ENET2
Input packets : 0
Output packets: 0
  Protocol aenet, AE bundle: ae0.0

Logical interface fe-0/0/3.32767 (Index 73) (SNMP ifIndex 88)
  Flags: SNMP-Traps 16384 VLAN-Tag [ 0x0000.0 ]  Encapsulation: ENET2
Input packets : 0
Output packets: 0
```

The first logical interface points to the ae0.0 aggregated Ethernet bundle. The JUNOS software creates a second logical interface, fe-0/0/3.32767, for handling traffic that is not part of the aggregate, such as the Link Aggregation Control Protocol (LACP) traffic exchanged by the aggregated partners.

On the aggregated Ethernet interface, you see information about the bundle and traffic statistics:

```
aviva@router1> show interfaces ae0
Physical interface: ae0, Enabled, Physical link is Up
  Interface index: 302, SNMP ifIndex: 89
  Link-level type: Ethernet, MTU: 1518, Speed: 100mbps, Loopback: Disabled,
  Source filtering: Disabled, Flow control: Disabled, Minimum links needed: 1
  Device flags   : Present Running
  Interface flags: SNMP-Traps 16384
  Current address: 00:05:85:02:a7:f0, Hardware address: 00:05:85:02:a7:f0
  Last flapped   : Never
  Input rate     : 0 bps (0 pps)
  Output rate    : 0 bps (0 pps)

  Logical interface ae0.0 (Index 69) (SNMP ifIndex 211)
    Flags: SNMP-Traps 16384 VLAN-Tag [ 0x8100.1 ]  Encapsulation: ENET2
    Statistics        Packets        pps        Bytes          bps
    Bundle:
        Input :             0          0            0            0
        Output:             0          0            0            0
    Protocol inet, MTU: 1500
      Flags: None
      Addresses, Flags: Is-Preferred Is-Primary
        Destination: 10.10.10/24, Local: 10.10.10.1, Broadcast: 10.10.10.255
```

Notice that the VLAN tag on the aggregated Ethernet interface matches that of the fe-0/0/3.0 logical interface.

7.16 Configuring T1 Interfaces

Problem

You want to configure the T1 interface on your router.

Solution

Use the following commands to configure a T1 interface:

```
[edit interfaces]
aviva@RouterF# set t1-0/0/3 unit 0 family inet address 10.0.13.1/24
aviva@RouterF# set t1-0/0/3 description "J2300 T1 line in local office"
```

Discussion

The basic configuration to get a T1 interface is very straightforward. You just set the interface's IP address. T1 interfaces can handle 24 simultaneous connections, called channels or timeslots, running at a combined 1.544 Mbps. Each T1 or DS1 packet is 193 bits and consists of 24 8-bit frames that carry data, plus one framing bit. Each port on a T1 or DS1 PIC can have a maximum of 24 channels.

Once the interface is configured, check its status:

```
aviva@RouterF> show interfaces t1-0/0/3
Physical interface: t1-0/0/3, Enabled, Physical link is Up
  Interface index: 140, SNMP ifIndex: 38
  Description: J2300 T1 line in local office
  Link-level type: PPP, MTU: 1504, Clocking: Internal, Speed: T1,
  Loopback: None, FCS: 16, Framing: ESF
  Device flags   : Present Running
  Interface flags: Point-To-Point SNMP-Traps 16384
  Link flags     : Keepalives
  Keepalive settings: Interval 10 seconds, Up-count 1, Down-count 3
  Keepalive: Input: 164568 (00:00:06 ago), Output: 164561 (00:00:03 ago)
  LCP state: Opened
  NCP state: inet: Opened, inet6: Not-configured, iso: Not-configured, mpls:
  Not-configured
  CHAP state: Not-configured
  CoS queues     : 8 supported
  Last flapped   : 2005-04-15 21:13:25 PDT (5w3d 11:12 ago)
  Input rate     : 40 bps (0 pps)
  Output rate    : 48 bps (0 pps)
  DS1   alarms   : None
  DS1   defects  : None

  Logical interface t1-0/0/3.0 (Index 69) (SNMP ifIndex 40)
    Flags: Point-To-Point SNMP-Traps Encapsulation: PPP
    Protocol inet, MTU: 1500
      Flags: None
      Addresses, Flags: Is-Preferred Is-Primary
        Destination: 10.0.13/24, Local: 10.0.13.2, Broadcast: 10.0.13.255
```

This output shows some of the default settings on T1 interfaces. The first high-lighted line shows that the connection is point to point (PPP), the MTU size is 1,504 bytes, the clocking is internal, and the interface speed is T1, or 1.544 Mbps. The second line shows that loopback mode is disabled, the frame checksum size (FCS) is 16 bits, and the framing mode is extended superframe. Two other defaults not shown in the output are a byte encoding of 8 bites per byte (nx64) and B8ZS line encoding. In the last line of the output, you see the interface address that you configured.

To change the FCS to 32 bits to provide more reliable packet verification, use this command:

```
[edit interfaces t1-0/0/3]
aviva@RouterF# set t1-options fcs 32
```

T1 has two framing modes, D4 super frame (SF) and extended super frame (ESF). An SF frame consists of 192 data bits, arranged into 24 8-bit channels, and a single framing bit. That single framing bit is used as part of a 12-bit framing sequence. ESF extends the super frame from 12 frames to 24 frames. To change the framing mode to SF, use this command:

```
[edit interfaces t1-0/0/3]
aviva@RouterF# set t1-options framing sf
```

7.17   Performing a Loopback Test on a T1 Interface

Problem

A new T1 interface has been installed and configured, and you want to perform a loopback test to make sure the interface is operating properly.

Solution

Set up a T1 loopback configuration:

```
[edit interfaces t1-0/0/3]
aviva@RouterF# set t1-options loopback local
aviva@RouterF# set no-keepalives
aviva@RouterF# set encapsulation cisco-hdlc
aviva@RouterF# commit
```

Make sure the interface is up:

```
aviva@RouterF> show interfaces t1-0/0/3 terse
Interface            Admin Link Proto Local              Remote
t1-0/0/3             up    up
```

Then zero all the statistics on the interface:

```
aviva@RouterF> clear interfaces statistics t1-0/0/3
```

Run the loopback test, which sends 1,000 ping messages rapidly and reports the results in a single message:

```
aviva@RouterF> ping interface t1-0/0/3 10.0.13.2 bypass-routing count 1000 rapid
PING 10.0.13.2 (10.0.13.2): 56 data bytes
!!!!!!!!!!!!!!!!!!!!!!!!!!!!!!!!!!!!!!!!!!!!!!!!!!!!!!!!!!!!!!!!!!!!!!!!!!!!!!!
!!!!!!!!!!!!!!!!!!!!!!!!!!!!!!!!!!!!!!!!!!!!!!!!!!!!!!!!!!!!!!!!!!!!!!!!!!!!!!!
!!!!!!!!!!!!!!!!!!!!!!!!!!!!!!!!!!!!!!!!!!!!!!!!!!!!!!!!!!!!!!!!!!!!!!!!!!!!!!!
!!!!!!!!!!!!!!!!!!!!!!!!!!!!!!!!!!!!!!!!!!!!!!!!!!!!!!!!!!!!!!!!!!!!!!!!!!!!!!!
!!!!!!!!!!!!!!!!!!!!!!!!!!!!!!!!!!!!!!!!!!!!!!!!!!!!!!!!!!!!!!!!!!!!!!!!!!!!!!!
!!!!!!!!!!!!!!!!!!!!!!!!!!!!!!!!!!!!!!!!!!!!!!!!!!!!!!!!!!!!!!!!!!!!!!!!!!!!!!!
!!!!!!!!!!!!!!!!!!!!!!!!!!!!!!!!!!!!!!!!!!!!!!!!!!!!!!!!!!!!!!!!!!!!!!!!!!!!!!!
!!!!!!!!!!!!!!!!!!!!!!!!!!!!!!!!!!!!!!!!!!!!!!!!!!!!!!!!!!!!!!!!!!!!!!!!!!!!!!!
!!!!!!!!!!!!!!!!!!!!!!!!!!!!!!!!!!!!!!!!!!!!!!!!!!!!!!!!!!!!!!!!!!!!!!!!!!!!!!!
!!!!!!!!!!!!!!!!!!!!!!!!!!!!!!!!!!!!!!!!!!!!!!!!!!!!!!!!!!!!!!!!!!!!!!!!!!!!!!!
!!!!!!!!!!!!!!!!!!!!!!!!!!!!!!!!!!!!!!!!!!!!!!!!!!!!!!!!!!!!!!!!!!!!!!!!!!!!!!!
!!!!!!!!!!!!!!!!!!!!!!!!!!!!!!!!!!!!!!!!!!!!!!!
--- 10.0.13.2 ping statistics ---
1000 packets transmitted, 1000 packets received, 0% packet loss
round-trip min/avg/max/stddev = 2.376/19.102/369.920/35.795 ms
```

Discussion

To perform a loopback test on the T1 interface, first configure the T1 interface to use local loopback mode. Also include the encapsulation cisco-hdlc and no-keepalives statements to force the interface to stay up so you can run the ping loopback test. Then you need to create a physical loopback at the T1 port by connecting a T1 loopback plug to the T1 port. You can make a T1 loopback plug by connecting pin 1 to pin 4 and pin 2 to pin 5 on an RJ-48 plug.

The first commands in this recipe configure the loopback. After making sure the interface is up and zeroing all interfaces statistics, run the loopback test, which sends 1000 ping messages rapidly and reports the results in a single message. Include the bypass-routing option in the ping command to directly ping a system on an attached network, bypassing normal routing tables. This option forces the packets to be transmitted out the interface, because they have a local destination address and from an IP point of view, they are already at their destination.

If there are any problems on the link, you see input and output errors in the show interfaces extensive command output. This output also shows that 1,000 ping messages were sent (in Output packets) and 1,000 responses were received (in Input packets).

```
aviva@RouterF> show interfaces t1-0/0/3 extensive
Physical interface: t1-0/0/3, Enabled, Physical link is Up
  Interface index: 140, SNMP ifIndex: 38, Generation: 21
  Description: J2300 T1 line in local office
```

```
Link-level type: Cisco-HDLC, MTU: 1504, Clocking: Internal, Speed: T1,
Loopback: Local, FCS: 16, Framing: ESF
Device flags   : Present Running
Interface flags: Point-To-Point SNMP-Traps 16384
Link flags     : No-Keepalives
Hold-times     : Up 0 ms, Down 0 ms
CoS queues     : 8 supported
Last flapped   : 2005-05-25 20:57:42 PDT (00:02:13 ago)
Statistics last cleared: 2005-05-25 20:58:04 PDT (00:01:51 ago)
Traffic statistics:
 Input  bytes  :              84000              0 bps
 Output bytes  :              89000              0 bps
 Input  packets:               1000              0 pps
 Output packets:               1000              0 pps
Input errors:
  Errors: 0, Drops: 0, Framing errors: 0, Policed discards: 0,
  L3 incompletes: 0, L2 channel errors: 0, L2 mismatch timeouts: 0,
  HS link CRC errors: 0, SRAM errors: 0, Resource errors: 0
Output errors:
  Carrier transitions: 0, Errors: 0, Drops: 0, Aged packets: 0, MTU errors: 0,
  Resource errors: 0
Queue counters:    Queued packets  Transmitted packets    Dropped packets
  0 best-effort            1000                  1000                    0
  1 expedited-fo              0                     0                    0
  2 assured-forw              0                     0                    0
  3 network-cont           1284                  1284                    0
DS1   alarms   : None
DS1   defects  : None
T1  media:        Seconds      Count  State
  SEF                  0           0  OK
  BEE                  0           0  OK
  AIS                  0           0  OK
  LOF                  0           2  OK
  LOS                  0           1  OK
  YELLOW               2           1  OK
  BPV                  0           0
  EXZ                  1           1
  LCV                  1           1
  PCV                  0           0
  CS                   0           0
  LES                  1
  ES                   0
  SES                  0
  SEFS                 0
  BES                  0
  UAS                  0
  ...
```

The later part of the command output shows any active alarms and T1 media
defects, which you can also use to troubleshoot interface problems.

7.18   Setting Up a BERT Test on a T1 Interface

Problem

You want to run a bit error rate test (BERT) to test the quality of a T1 link.

Solution

First, configure the BERT test parameters on the local interface:

```
[edit interfaces t1-0/0/3]
aviva@RouterF# set t1-options bert-algorithm repeating-3-in-24
aviva@RouterF# set t1-options bert-period 180
aviva@RouterF# set disable
```

Then, put the interface at the far end of the link into loopback:

```
[edit interfaces t1-0/0/3]
aviva@RouterE# set t1-options loopback remote
```

Then run the BERT test on the local router:

```
aviva@RouterF> test interface t1-0/0/3 t1-bert-start
```

Use the following command to stop a BERT test:

```
aviva@RouterF> test interface t1-0/0/3 t1-bert-stop
```

Discussion

BERT testing checks the quality of a link by sending out a known bit pattern and verifying that the received pattern matches. Bit errors occur when the pattern doesn't match and indicates noise or other problems on the physical circuit. The higher the bit error rate, the worse the problem. The link you are testing is in loopback mode so the transmitted packets are looped back to the same interface.

This recipe shows how to configure BERT on a local T1 interface. You can also configure it similarly on other interfaces, including T3, E1, E3, DS, OC3, OC12, and STM1. Choose a bit pattern to send out in the set bert-algorithm command. There are about 20 patterns, including all ones, all zeros, alternating ones and zeros, and setting one bit out of a group of bits. Use the set t1-options bert-algorithm ? command to see the full list. In this recipe, we set 3 bits out of each 24 bits. By default, a BERT test runs for 10 seconds. We change this to 3 minutes (180 seconds). Finally, the T1 interface must be disabled for the BERT test to work.

On the remote end, the link must be in remote loopback mode. Verify that the remote end of the link is in remote loopback mode:

```
aviva@RouterE> show interfaces t1-0/0/3
Physical interface: t1-0/0/3, Enabled, Physical link is Up
  Interface index: 140, SNMP ifIndex: 38
  Link-level type: PPP, MTU: 1504, Clocking: Internal, Speed: T1,
  Loopback: Remote, FCS: 16, Framing: ESF
```

```
Device flags    : Present Running
Interface flags: Point-To-Point SNMP-Traps 16384
Link flags      : Keepalives
Keepalive settings: Interval 10 seconds, Up-count 1, Down-count 3
Keepalive: Input: 0 (never), Output: 0 (never)
LCP state: Conf-req-sent
NCP state: inet: Down, inet6: Not-configured, iso: Not-configured, mpls:
Not-configured
CHAP state: Not-configured
CoS queues      : 8 supported
Last flapped    : 2005-05-26 10:21:08 PDT (00:00:07 ago)
Input rate      : 0 bps (0 pps)
Output rate     : 72 bps (0 pps)
DS1   alarms    : None
DS1   defects   : None

Logical interface t1-0/0/3.0 (Index 69) (SNMP ifIndex 39)
  Flags: Hardware-Down Point-To-Point SNMP-Traps Encapsulation: PPP
  Protocol inet, MTU: 1500
    Flags: Protocol-Down
    Addresses, Flags: Dest-route-down Is-Preferred Is-Primary
      Destination: 10.0.13/24, Local: 10.0.13.1, Broadcast: 10.0.13.255
```

The physical interface is marked Loopback: Remote. In addition, a number of fields in the logical interface section indicate that the T1 interface at the remote side of the link is down.

Run the BERT test from operational mode. Because this is a T1 interface, use the t1-bert-start option. For other interfaces, use the test interface ? command to determine the proper option.

The show interfaces extensive command shows the results of the BERT test. Here, the test is in progress:

```
aviva@RouterF> show interfaces extensive t1-0/0/3 | find bert
  DS1 BERT configuration:
    BERT time period: 180 seconds, Elapsed: 96 seconds (in progress)
    Induced Error rate: 10e-0, Algorithm: 3 in 24, Repetitive (26)
    Bit count       :    146557240
    Error bit count:            0
  ...
```

The following output shows the results of the completed test, which found no bit errors on the T1 link:

```
aviva@RouterF> show interfaces extensive t1-0/0/3 | find bert
  DS1 BERT configuration:
    BERT time period: 180 seconds, Elapsed: 180 seconds (completed)
    Induced Error rate: 10e-0, Algorithm: 3 in 24, Repetitive (26)
    Bit count       :    273186232
    Error bit count:            0
  ...
```

You can configure an error rate to force errors in the bit stream:

```
[edit interfaces t1-0/0/3]
aviva@RouterF# set t1-options bert-error-rate 3
```

This configuration generates one error in every 1,000 packets (10e-3). The show interfaces command output shows the number of errors and the error rate:

```
aviva@RouterF> show interfaces t1-0/0/3 extensive | find bert
  DS1 BERT configuration:
    BERT time period: 10 seconds, Elapsed: 10 seconds (completed)
    Induced Error rate: 10e-3, Algorithm: 3 in 24, Repetitive (26)
    Bit count    :    15369016
    Error bit count:      15355
    Error rate: 10e-3.0
```

7.19 Configuring Frame Relay on a T1 Interface

Problem

You have a router that provides Frame Relay circuits to your customers. You want to set up a back-to-back connection between your router and that of a customer.

Solution

Use the following commands to configure Frame Relay:

```
[edit interfaces t1-0/0/3]
aviva@RouterF# set description "J2300 T1 line in local office"
aviva@RouterF# set encapsulation frame-relay
aviva@RouterF# set dce
aviva@RouterF# set unit 0 description "Customer A"
aviva@RouterF# set unit 0 dlci 100
aviva@RouterF# set unit 0 family inet address 10.0.13.2/24
```

Discussion

Frame Relay is a point-to-point technology that switches packets through a network instead of routing them. The paths through the network are called virtual circuits (VCs). Each VC is identified by a Data Link Connection Identifier (DLCI), which is a number from 0 to 1023. In the JUNOS software, DLCIs 0 through 15 are reserved, so you can use 16 through 1023 to carry traffic. Generally, you might want to configure Frame Relay on slower interfaces, such as T1, serial, or ISDN.

You configure each VC on a separate logical interface, setting a DLCI number and IP address. You also set the encapsulation to frame-relay on the physical interface itself. On the remote side of the VC, you configure a DLCI that has the same number. Because the two router interfaces are in a back-to-back configuration, include the set dce command on one end of the link to have the router look like a Frame Relay switch.

Use the show interfaces command to verify that the DLCI is up and running:

```
aviva@RouterF> show interfaces t1-0/0/3
Physical interface: t1-0/0/3, Enabled, Physical link is Up
  Interface index: 140, SNMP ifIndex: 38
  Description: J2300 T1 line in local office
  Link-level type: Frame-Relay, MTU: 1504, Clocking: Internal, Speed: T1,
  Loopback: None, FCS: 16, Framing: ESF
  Device flags   : Present Running
  Interface flags: Point-To-Point SNMP-Traps 16384
  Link flags     : No-Keepalives DCE
  ANSI LMI settings: n392dce 3, n393dce 4, t392dce 15 seconds
  LMI: Input: 0 (never), Output: 0 (never)
  CoS queues     : 8 supported
  Last flapped   : 2005-05-26 05:50:29 PDT (03:45:59 ago)
  Input rate     : 0 bps (0 pps)
  Output rate    : 0 bps (0 pps)
  DS1    alarms   : None
  DS1    defects  : None

  Logical interface t1-0/0/3.0 (Index 71) (SNMP ifIndex 40)
    Description: Customer A
    Flags: Point-To-Point SNMP-Traps Encapsulation: FR-NLPID
  Input packets : 0
  Output packets: 0
    Protocol inet, MTU: 1500
      Flags: None
      Addresses, Flags: Is-Preferred Is-Primary
        Destination: 10.0.13/24, Local: 10.0.13.2, Broadcast: 10.0.13.255
    DLCI 100
      Flags: Active
      Total down time: 0 sec, Last down: Never
      Input packets : 0
      Output packets: 0
```

The physical interface properties show the Frame Relay encapsulation on the link layer (Link-level type: Frame-Relay). Under logical interfaces, the logical interface is up (no flags are set; if it were down, you would see Device-Down) and the DLCI is operational (Flags: Active).

7.20   Configuring a SONET Interface

Problem

Your want to configure a SONET OC192 interface.

Solution

Use the following commands for a basic configuration:

```
[edit interfaces so-4/0/0]
aviva@t320# set description "JUNOS cookbook SONET OC192 interface"
aviva@t320# set unit 0 family inet address 192.0.4.1/24
```

Discussion

Synchronous Optical Network (SONET) is a high-speed fiber-optic transmission that was developed in the 1980s by Bellcore and is the American standard of the CCITT Synchronous Digital Hierarchy (SDH) standard for a hierarchy of optical transmission rates. SONET uses LEDs or lasers to transmit bits with pulses of light.

The basic building block of the SONET/SDH hierarchy in the optical domain is an OC1; in the electrical domain, it is an STS1. An OC1 operates at 51.840 Mbps. Common SONET speeds are OC3 (155.52 Mbps), OC12 (622.08 Mbps), OC48 (2.488 Gbps), and OC192 (9.953 Gbps), and the JUNOS software supports a variety of SONET PICs for all these interface speeds.

In this recipe, we are configuring the SONET OC192 PIC in slot 4 of a T320 router:

```
aviva@t320> show chassis hardware
Hardware inventory:
Item            Version  Part number  Serial number   Description
Chassis                               19086           T320
...
FPC 4           REV 01   710-005803   AZ2121          FPC Type 3
  CPU           REV 09   710-001726   AY4902          FPC CPU
  PIC 0         REV 01   750-004535   HC0276          1x OC-192 SM SR1
  PIC 1         REV 03   750-003336   HJ9955          4x OC-48 SONET, SMSR
  MMB 1         REV 01   710-005555   AZ2192          MMB-288mbit
...
```

The basic configuration is straightforward. You just need an IP address. Use the show interfaces terse command to check that the interface is up:

```
aviva@t320> show interfaces so-4/0/0 terse
Interface           Admin Link Proto    Local               Remote
so-4/0/0            up    up
so-4/0/0.0          up    up    inet    198.0.4.1/24
```

The output shows that both the physical and logical interfaces are up and running.

To verify the configuration and operation, look at the interface status:

```
aviva@t320> show interfaces so-4/0/0
Physical interface: so-4/0/0, Enabled, Physical link is Up
  Interface index: 131, SNMP ifIndex: 24
  Description: JUNOS cookbook SONET OC192 interface
  Link-level type: PPP, MTU: 4474, Clocking: Internal, SONET mode, Speed: OC192
  Loopback: None, FCS: 16, Payload scrambler: Enabled
  Device flags   : Present Running
  Interface flags: Point-To-Point SNMP-Traps 16384
  Link flags     : Keepalives
  Keepalive settings: Interval 10 seconds, Up-count 1, Down-count 3
  Keepalive: Input: 1688 (00:00:01 ago), Output: 1693 (00:00:05 ago)
  LCP state: Opened
  NCP state: inet: Opened, inet6: Not-configured, iso: Not-configured, mpls:
Opened
  CHAP state: Not-configured
```

```
    CoS queues      : 8 supported
    Last flapped    : 2005-05-26 10:41:53 PDT (07:29:52 ago)
    Input rate      : 40 bps (0 pps)
    Output rate     : 48 bps (0 pps)
    SONET alarms    : None
    SONET defects   : None

  Logical interface so-4/0/0.0 (Index 67) (SNMP ifIndex 22)
    Flags: Point-To-Point SNMP-Traps Encapsulation: PPP
    Protocol inet, MTU: 4470
      Flags: None
      Addresses, Flags: Is-Preferred Is-Primary
        Destination: 192.0.4/24, Local: 192.0.4.1, Broadcast: 192.0.4.255
```

Highlighted in this output are some of the default SONET interface settings. The link-level type is PPP, the default for interfaces with permanent virtual circuits. The default SONET media MTU for T320 routers is 4,474 bytes, and the default IPv4 MTU size (displayed in the logical interface section) is 4,470 bytes. SONET interfaces uses the router's internal stratum 3 clock as the default source of the transmit clock. The default FCS is 16 bites, and payload scrambling is enabled by default to improve link stability.

To see traffic statistics and debug issues with the SONET frames, use the show interfaces extensive command:

```
aviva@t320> show interfaces so-4/0/0 extensive
...
  Statistics last cleared: Never
  Traffic statistics:
   Input  bytes  :        2981660896              40 bps
   Output bytes  :      114715226202              48 bps
   Input  packets:          34674367               0 pps
   Output packets:        1333901910               0 pps
  Input errors:
    Errors: 0, Drops: 0, Framing errors: 0, Runts: 0, Giants: 0,
    Bucket drops: 0, Policed discards: 0, L3 incompletes: 0,
    L2 channel errors: 0, L2 mismatch timeouts: 0, HS link CRC errors: 0,
    HS link FIFO overflows: 0
  Output errors:
    Carrier transitions: 1, Errors: 0, Drops: 0, Aged packets: 0,
    HS link FIFO underflows: 0, MTU errors: 0
  Queue counters:       Queued packets  Transmitted packets    Dropped packets
    0 best-effort           1333890630           1333890630                  0
    1 expedited-fo                   0                    0                  0
    2 assured-forw                  0                    0                  0
    3 network-cont              11280                11280                  0
  SONET alarms   : None
  SONET defects  : None
  SONET PHY:           Seconds       Count  State
    PLL Lock                22           1  OK
    PHY Light               22           1  OK
  SONET section:
    BIP-B1                   0           0
```

```
               SEF              22        182  OK
               LOS              22          1  OK
               LOF              22          1  OK
               ES-S             22
               SES-S            22
               SEFS-S           22
     SONET line:
               BIP-B2            0          0
               REI-L             0          0
               RDI-L             0          0  OK
               AIS-L            22          1  OK
               BERR-SF           0          0  OK
               BERR-SD           0          0  OK
               ES-L             22
               SES-L            22
               UAS-L            12
               ES-LFE            0
               SES-LFE           0
               UAS-LFE           0
     SONET path:
               BIP-B3            0          0
               REI-P             0          0
               LOP-P             0          0  OK
               AIS-P            22          1  OK
               RDI-P             0          0  OK
               UNEQ-P            0          0  OK
               PLM-P             0          0  OK
               ES-P             22
               SES-P            22
               UAS-P            12
               ES-PFE            0
               SES-PFE           0
               UAS-PFE           0
     Received SONET overhead:
       F1     : 0x00, J0     : 0x01, K1     : 0x00, K2      : 0x00
       S1     : 0x00, C2     : 0xcf, C2(cmp) : 0xcf, F2      : 0x00
       Z3     : 0x00, Z4     : 0x00, S1(cmp) : 0x00
     Transmitted SONET overhead:
       F1     : 0x00, J0     : 0x01, K1     : 0x00, K2      : 0x00
       S1     : 0x00, C2     : 0xcf, F2     : 0x00, Z3      : 0x00
       Z4     : 0x00
     Received path trace: tercel so-3/1/0
       74 65 72 63 65 6c 20 73 6f 2d 33 2f 31 2f 30 00    tercel so-3/1/0.
       00 00 00 00 00 00 00 00 00 00 00 00 00 00 00 00    ................
       00 00 00 00 00 00 00 00 00 00 00 00 00 00 00 00    ................
       00 00 00 00 00 00 00 00 00 00 00 00 00 00 0d 0a    ................
     Transmitted path trace: neon so-4/0/0
       6e 65 6f 6e 20 73 6f 2d 34 2f 30 2f 30 00 00 00    neon so-4/0/0...
       00 00 00 00 00 00 00 00 00 00 00 00 00 00 00 00    ................
       00 00 00 00 00 00 00 00 00 00 00 00 00 00 00 00    ................
       00 00 00 00 00 00 00 00 00 00 00 00 00 00 00 00    ................
```

7.21 Using APS to Protect Against SONET Circuit Failures

Problem

One of your routers has two SONET interfaces that connect to the same add/drop multiplexer (ADM). You want to make sure that if one of the PICs or FPCs fails, the router does not lose its connection with the ADM.

Solution

To set up basic APS, first configure the working circuit:

```
[edit interfaces so-3/1/0 sonet-options]
aviva@t320# set aps working-circuit APS-at-my-colo
aviva@t320# set aps authentication-key $1991poPPi
```

Then configure the protect circuit:

```
[edit interfaces so-1/1/0 sonet-options]
aviva@t320# set aps protect-circuit APS-at-my-colo
aviva@t320# set aps authentication-key $1991poPPi
```

Discussion

APS allows a SONET circuit to switch over to a backup (protect) circuit in the event that the active (working) circuit fails. If the working circuit fails or degrades, the ADM and protect router switch the traffic to the protect circuit, which becomes active. JUNOS software uses APS 1+1 switching, which pairs a working circuit with a protect circuit. It supports both revertive and nonrevertive modes, but only bidirectional mode. The APS specification (GR-253-CORE, *SONET Transport Systems: Common Generic Criteria*) requires that the working and protect circuits transmit identical data, but the JUNOS software does not do this, which turns out to have no operational impact.

When protecting the PIC or FPC, configure two SONET interfaces on different FPCs. In this recipe, the working circuit is on FPC3 and the protect circuit is on FPC1. The APS group name, here APS-at-my-colo, and the authentication key must be the same to associate the two interfaces. On the ADM side, the router's working circuit must be connected to the ADM's working circuit, and the router's protect circuit must likewise be connected to the ADM's protect circuit.

When using APS to protect the entire router, use the same configuration on SONET interfaces in two different routers and also specify the address of the other router:

```
[edit interfaces so-3/1/0 sonet-options]
aviva@t320# set aps neighbor 192.0.8.2/24
```

Use the show aps command to check that the APS circuits are up:

```
aviva@t320> show aps
Interface   Group                      Circuit  Intf state
so-1/1/0    APS-at-my-colo             Protect  disabled, up
so-3/1/0    APS-at-my-colo             Working  enabled, up
```

The output shows that in the group APS-at-my-colo, the working circuit, so-3/0/1, is operational and the backup circuit, so-1/1/0, is down. You can also see this in the show interfaces command output:

```
aviva@t320> show interfaces so-1/1/0
Physical interface: so-1/1/0, Administratively down, Physical link is Up
...
  Logical interface so-1/1/0.0 (Index 67) (SNMP ifIndex 63)
    Flags: Hardware-Down Device-Down Point-To-Point SNMP-Traps
    Encapsulation: PPP
    Protocol inet, MTU: 4470
      Flags: Protocol-Down
      Addresses, Flags: Dest-route-down Is-Preferred Is-Primary
        Destination: 192.0.2/24, Local: 192.0.2.2, Broadcast: 192.0.2.255
```

This output shows that the physical link is up, but the physical interface is administratively down because you have configured it as a backup. The logical interface is also down.

The show aps group command gives detailed status of the two circuits:

```
aviva@t320> show aps group APS-at-my-colo
Interface   Group                      Circuit  Intf state
so-1/1/0    APS-at-my-colo             Protect  disabled, up
Neighbor 0.0.0.0, adj up,neighbor interface enabled,dead 2.912
  Channel state Working
  Working circuit is on interface so-3/1/0
local-mode bidirectional(5),neighbor-mode bidirectional(5)
  Req K1 0x00, rcv K1 0x00, xmit K1 0x00,nbr K1 0x00, nbr paired req 0
  Revert time 0, neighbor revert time 0
  Hello due in 0.632
so-3/1/0    APS-at-my-colo             Working  enabled, up
Neighbor 0.0.0.0, adj up,neighbor interface disabled,dead 2.672
  Channel state Working
  Protect circuit is on interface so-1/1/0
local-mode bidirectional(5),neighbor-mode bidirectional(5)
  Req K1 0x00, rcv K1 0x00, xmit K1 0x00,nbr K1 0x00, nbr paired req 0
  Revert time 0, neighbor revert time 0
  Hello due in 0.861
```

By default, APS is nonrevertive, which means that if the protect circuit becomes active, traffic is not switched back to the working circuit unless the protect circuit fails or you manually configure a switch to the working circuit. You can set the circuit to switch back after a specified amount of time, here 15 minutes:

```
[edit interfaces so-3/1/0 sonet-options]
aviva@t320# set aps revert-time 9000
```

The ADM must also be in revertive mode. You can also manually switch the circuit back to being the working circuit:

```
[edit interfaces so-3/1/0 sonet-options]
aviva@t320# set aps request working
```

See Also

GR-253-CORE, *SONET Transport Systems: Common Generic Criteria*

7.22 Configuring an ATM Interface

Problem

You need to get the ATM interface in your router up and running.

Solution

Set up the ATM interface with one virtual path identifier (VPI) and one virtual circuit identifier (VCI):

```
[edit interfaces at-1/0/0]
aviva@M10i# set atm-options pic-type atm2
aviva@M10i# set atm-options vpi 0
aviva@M10i# set unit 0 vci 0.32
aviva@M10i# set unit 0 family inet address 136.1.1.1/24
```

Discussion

ATM connections are set up over virtual paths and virtual circuits. The virtual path, represented by a VPI, establishes a route between two devices in a network. Each VPI can contain multiple virtual circuits, each with a VCI. There can be a maximum of 4,090 VCIs, starting at number 32. (Numbers 0 through 31 are reserved.) The VPI can range from 0 through 255. VPIs and VCIs are local to the router, so only the two devices connected by them need know the details of the connection.

This recipe sets up a basic ATM interface for a one-port ATM2 OC-12 PIC that is in slot 1. The ATM interface has a VPI of 0 and a VCI of 32. You configure the virtual circuit on the logical interface because, as the name implies, it's a virtual, not a physical, interface. It is also important to include the set atm-options command to explicitly configure the PIC as an ATM2 PIC type, not an ATM1. Some statements for configuring ATM PICs work either with the ATM1 PIC or the ATM2 PIC, but not both. If you do not use the set atm-options command, and if you use an ATM1-only statement with an ATM2 interface, the JUNOS software assumes that the PIC is an ATM1 and configures it accordingly, but the interface will not operate as you expect it to. The same thing happens if you use ATM2-only statements with an ATM1 interface. In either case, the JUNOS CLI provides no warning or commit error. If, however, you use the set atm-options command and include statements for the other type of ATM PIC, the configuration won't commit and JUNOS CLI error messages will tell you where the problem is.

This recipe is for the newer ATM2 PICs. The configuration for ATM1 PICs is more involved.

Use the show chassis hardware command to check the ATM PIC type:

```
aviva@M10i> show chassis hardware
Hardware inventory:
Item             Version  Part number  Serial number   Description
Chassis                                19155           M10i
...
FPC 1                                                  E-FPC
  PIC 0          REV 02   750-005718   BG0216          1x OC-12 ATM-II IQ, MM
  PIC 1          REV 09   750-008425   HX1881          Adaptive Services
  PIC 2          REV 02   750-003748   HC2155          2x OC-3 SONET, SMIR
  PIC 3          REV 05   750-005726   CC3987          1x OC-12 ATM-II IQ, MM
```

Use the show interfaces command to check that the ATM interface is correctly configured and is running:

```
aviva@M10i> show interfaces at-1/0/0
Physical interface: at-1/0/0, Enabled, Physical link is Up
  Interface index: 132, SNMP ifIndex: 49
  Link-level type: ATM-PVC, MTU: 4482, Clocking: Internal, SONET mode,
  Speed: OC12, Loopback: None, Payload scrambler: Enabled
  Device flags   : Present Running
  Link flags     : None
  CoS queues     : 4 supported
  Current address: 00:05:85:70:a4:7e
  Last flapped   : 2005-05-24 17:46:05 PDT (1d 05:11 ago)
  Input rate     : 0 bps (0 pps)
  Output rate    : 0 bps (0 pps)
  SONET alarms   : None
  SONET defects  : None
   VPI 0
     Flags: Active
     Total down time: 0 sec, Last down: Never
  Traffic statistics:
       Input  packets:           8918
       Output packets:           8999

  Logical interface at-1/0/0.0 (Index 66) (SNMP ifIndex 30)
    Flags: Point-To-Point SNMP-Traps 16384 Encapsulation: ATM-SNAP
  Input packets : 8918
  Output packets: 8999
    Protocol inet, MTU: 4470
      Flags: None
      Addresses, Flags: Is-Preferred Is-Primary
        Destination: 136.1.1/24, Local: 136.1.1.1, Broadcast: 136.1.1.255
    VCI 0.32
      Flags: Active, 1024
      Total down time: 0 sec, Last down: Never
```

```
        EPD threshold: 4259, Transmit weight cells: 0
        Input packets : 8918
        Output packets: 8999

    Logical interface at-1/0/0.32767 (Index 67) (SNMP ifIndex 29)
      Flags: Point-To-Multipoint No-Multicast SNMP-Traps 16384
      Encapsulation: ATM-VCMUX
    Input packets : 0
    Output packets: 0
      VCI 0.4
        Flags: Active, 1024
        Total down time: 0 sec, Last down: Never
        EPD threshold: 0, Transmit weight cells: 0
        Input packets : 0
        Output packets: 0
```

For the physical interface, the device flags Present, Running indicate that the physical ATM interface is operating properly. For the logical interface, the lack of a Down flag indicates that the logical portion of the interface is up. The Active flag under the VCI shows that the VCI is working.

The configuration of a basic ATM interface is straightforward, and the show interfaces command output illustrates some of the default ATM interface settings. The link-level type is ATM-PVC, the default for interfaces with permanent virtual circuits. The default SONET media MTU for M10i routers is 4,482 bytes, and the default IPv4 MTU size (displayed in the logical interfaces section) is 4,470 bytes. SONET interfaces use the router's internal stratum 3 clock as the default source of the transmit clock. Payload scrambling is also enabled by default to improve link stability.

7.23   Dealing with Nonconfigurable Interfaces

Problem

You see interfaces in the show interfaces command output that you didn't configure, and you want to know what to do with them.

Solution

The JUNOS software internally generates a number of interfaces that you cannot configure:

```
aviva@router1> show interfaces terse
Interface               Admin Link Proto Local                 Remote
dsc                     up    up
fxp0                    up    up
fxp0.0                  up    up   inet  192.168.71.246/21
fxp1                    up    up
fxp1.0                  up    up   inet  10.0.0.4/8
                                   tnp   4
```

```
gre                up
ipip               up
loo                up      up
loo.0              up      up    inet  127.0.0.1                 --> 0/0.
loo.16385          up      up    inet
                                 inet6 fe80::2a0:a5ff:fe12:3ed5
lsi                up      up
mtun               up      up
pimd               up      up
pime               up      up
tap                up      up
```

Description

Toward the end of the show interfaces output, you see a number of interfaces that don't correspond to any of the physical interfaces you have configured on the router. Most of these special interfaces are internal interfaces that are created and used by the JUNOS software to route traffic within the router. The fxp0 (the out-of-band management) and loopback (loo) interfaces, which are configurable, provide connection to the Routing Engine.

The fxp1 interface is an internal Ethernet interface that connects the Packet Forwarding Engine (all the chassis hardware components) to the Routing Engine, which handles all routing protocol operations. The output in this recipe shows that fxp1 has an internal IPv4 address of 10.0.0.5/8 and a Trivial Network Protocol (TNP) address of 5. JUNOS software uses the proprietary TNP internally to communicate between the forwarding and Routing Engines.

As a side note, the fxp0 and fxp1 interfaces take their names from the FreeBSD fxp Ethernet device driver.

On J-series routers, the Packet Forwarding Engine and Routing Engine functionality is on the same chip, so there is no fxp1 interface or its equivalent. Also, because the fe-0/0/0 serves the function of the fxp0 interface, it isn't listed at the end of the show interfaces terse command output with the nonconfigurable interfaces:

```
aviva@RouterA> show interfaces terse
Interface              Admin Link Proto Local                  Remote
fe-0/0/0               up    up
fe-0/0/0.0             up    up    inet  10.0.16.1/24
                                         172.19.121.142/24
gr-0/0/0               up    up
ip-0/0/0               up    up
ls-0/0/0               up    up
lt-0/0/0               up    up
mt-0/0/0               up    up
pd-0/0/0               up    up
pe-0/0/0               up    up
sp-0/0/0               up    up
sp-0/0/0.16383         up    up    inet
fe-0/0/1               up    up
```

```
fe-0/0/1.0              up    up    inet  10.0.15.2/24
se-0/0/2                up    down
se-0/0/3                up    up
se-0/0/3.0              up    up    inet  10.0.21.1/24
dsc                     up    up
gre                     up    up
ipip                    up    up
loo                     up    up
loo.0                   up    up    inet  192.168.42.1      --> 0/0
loo.16385               up    up    inet  10.0.0.1          --> 0/0
                                          10.0.0.16         --> 0/0
lsi                     up    up
mtun                    up    up
pimd                    up    up
pime                    up    up
ppo                     up    up
tap                     up    up
```

dsc is a virtual interface that is used to discard packets, which you might want to do if the router is experiencing a denial-of-service (DoS) attack. You can configure one discard interface. If you associate an output filter with the interface, you can log or count DoS traffic before discarding it to determine the source of the attack.

The remaining interfaces are created by the kernel and are used internally by the JUNOS software. Some have corresponding configurable interfaces for setting up tunnels on Tunnel Services PICs. You set up unicast tunnels with the gr- or ip- physical interfaces, in place of the nonconfigurable gre and ipip interfaces, to use generic route encapsulation or IP-IP encapsulation, respectively. PIM tunnels, used by PIM sparse mode, have two interfaces, pe- and pd-, for encapsulating and de-encapsulating PIM Register messages. When the router has a Tunnel Services PIC installed, the software automatically configures one multicast tunnel interface, mt- (corresponding to mtun), for each virtual private network (VPN) you configure.

The loo.16385 interface is created by the Internet Routing process (irsd) and is used for internal routing. The tap interface is used to copy discarded packets. lsi is a label-switched interface that is used by MPLS label-switched paths (LSPs).

7.24 Configuring Interfaces Before the PICs Are Installed

Problem

You are expecting new PICs and want to prepare the configuration file in advance.

Solution

Add the new interface to the router configuration but keep it deactivated:

```
[edit interfaces]
aviva@router1# set ge-1/1/0 unit 0 family inet address 172.19.121.3/24
aviva@router1# set ge-1/1/0 description "172.19.121.3/24; to router2's ge-0/0/1"
aviva@router1# deactivate ge-1/1/0
```

Use the following command to activate the interface:

```
[edit interfaces]
aviva@router1# activate ge-1/1/0
```

Discussion

When you are preparing the router for new hardware, either a new PIC or a new FPC with one or more PICs, or when you have a maintenance window in which you will be rearranging the FPCs or PICs in the router, you can preconfigure the interfaces before the hardware has arrived or is in the new location. This recipe shows how to configure a Gigabit Ethernet interface before the PIC is in the router.

The management process, MGD, ignores all inactive portions of the configuration when you issue a commit command. The deactivated configuration is effectively commented out of the configuration file, and the interface control daemons will not see the configuration data. One downside to this is that if there are mistakes in your configuration, you won't see the errors messages from MGD.

Because no physical hardware is installed in the router, you don't see this interface with any of the show interfaces commands. The only way to know that it's there is to look at the configuration. If you are outside the deactivated hierarchy, the CLI marks it with the string inactive:

```
[edit interfaces]
aviva@router1# show
inactive: ge-1/1/0 {
    description "172.19.121.3/24; to router2's ge-0/0/1";
    unit 0 {
        family inet {
            address 172.19.121.3/24;
        }
    }
}
```

If you issue the show command from a hierarchy that is within the deactivated statement, the CLI shows a three-line notice to catch your attention:

```
[edit interfaces]
aviva@router1# show ge-1/1/0
##
## inactive: interfaces ge-1/1/0
##
description "172.19.121.3/24; to router2's ge-0/0/1";
```

```
unit 0 {
    family inet {
        address 172.19.121.3/24;
    }
}
```

While you can set the ge-1/1/0 interface configuration without issuing the deactivate command, you are leaving yourself open for possible problems if someone installs the PIC unexpectedly.

Deactivating an interface's configuration rather than deleting is also a good practice when the hardware fails and you are waiting for a replacement PIC. When the new PIC arrives, you don't need to reconfigure the interface. Just reactivate it:

```
[edit interfaces]
aviva@router1# activate ge-1/1/0
```

For all interfaces, you can configure a disable statement. While this might look like a way to deactivate an interface, it actually does something quite different: it activates the interface, but treats it as being down or administratively disabled. When you commit a configuration that contains a disabled interface, the interface control daemon, DCD, sees the interface and the configuration data, but does not configure the interface. Here, you disable interface fe-0/0/0:

```
[edit interfaces]
aviva@router1# set fe-0/0/0 disable
```

The configuration shows this:

```
[edit interfaces]
aviva@router1# show fe-0/0/0
disable;
unit 0 {
    family inet {
        address 192.168.20.1/30;
    {
}
```

When you check the status of the interface, you see that the physical interface is administratively down, but the link to the remote side is up. The logical interface is also down.

```
aviva@router1> show interfaces fe-0/0/0 terse
Interface          Admin Link Proto Local                Remote
fe-0/0/0           down  up
fe-0/0/0.0         up    down inet  192.168.20.1/30
```

This output illustrates that when an interface is disabled instead of being deactivated, you see information about the interface in the show interfaces output instead of seeing nothing at all, which is the case with the deactivated interface.

To get the interface back up, you might think that it's logical to enable it:

```
[edit interfaces fe-0/0/0]
aviva@router1# set enable
```

While this does what you want, it may not be what you expect:

```
[edit interfaces]
aviva@router1# show fe-0/0/0
enable;
unit 0 {
    family inet {
        address 192.168.220.1/30;
    }
}
```

You generally don't need or want to explicitly enable an interface. The better way to get the interface back up is to remove the disable statement:

```
[edit interfaces fe-0/0/0]
aviva@router1# delete disable
edit interfaces]
aviva@router1# show fe-0/0/0
unit 0 {
    family inet {
        address 192.168.220.1/30;
    }
}
```

CHAPTER 8

IP Routing

8.0   Introduction

Routing is the act of forwarding packets toward a given destination from one network segment or interface to the next. *Routing tables*, also sometimes called routing information bases (RIBs), are the databases that routers use to route traffic toward their destination. These tables contain the network addresses and prefixes that have been learned from dynamic routing protocols such as RIP, IS-IS, OSPF, and BGP; that have been learned statically from static (configured) routing-table entries; and that have been learned from the router's network interfaces. Each address and prefix in a routing table has a next hop associated with it that takes the packet one hop closer to its destination.

Each IP packet that a router receives contains two types of information: the packet data itself (the packet's payload) and information that identifies the packet. In IP packets, the identifying information is at the beginning of the packet, in the header. One of these header fields is the source address, which states the packet's origin; another, which is key to the routing tables, is the destination address, which tells where the packet is going when the router uses standard destination-based forwarding. (Routing policy can alter the path toward a destination.) When the router is determining the path toward the destination, it checks the routing table for a route that matches the packet's destination and then sends the packet to the next hop associated with that route. If there is no exact match, the router locates a more general route, selecting the *longest match*, which is the route that matches the most bits in the network portion of the address. For example, if the packet's destination is 10.0.16.2 and the routing table contains a route to 10.0.16.2/32, which is the address of the specific host, the packet is sent using the next hop associated with that route. If the only matching routes in the table are 10.0.0.0/8 and 10.0.16.0/24, the latter route is used because it is the longest match.

If no match is found in the routing table, the *default route* of 0.0.0.0/0 is used if it exists. If no default route is configured or learned, the traffic is dropped.

When a single routing protocol provides equal-cost paths to a single prefix, the JUNOS default is to randomly choose one path on a per-prefix basis.

The JUNOS routing-protocol process (RPD) maintains a number of different routing tables to separate information learned from or used by different protocols. Table 8-1 lists the default routing tables that RPD maintains. You cannot rename the default routing tables or use them for different purposes but you can create routing tables for other purposes. All IPv4 routing tables are named inet.*n*, and all IPv6 routing tables are named inet6.*n*, where *n* is an integer.

Table 8-1. JUNOS default routing tables

Name	Description
inet.0	IPv4 unicast routes. BGP, IS-IS, OSPF, and RIP store their routing information in this table and use the routes in this table when advertising routes to their neighbors. Configured static routes are also stored in this table.
inet.1	Multicast forwarding cache. DVMRP and PIM store their routing information in this table.
inet.2	Used by MBGP to provide reverse path forwarding (RPF) checks.
inet.3	Traffic engineering paths. Stores path and label information.
inet6.0	IPv6 unicast routes.
iso.0	ISO routes for IS-IS.
mpls.0	MPLS label-switched path (LSP) next hops.

From the routes in each routing table, RPD determines active routes toward network destinations. For unicast routes, RPD chooses the route with the lowest preference value. For multicast traffic, RPD determines active routes based on traffic flow and other parameters specified by the multicast routing-protocol algorithms.

RPD installs the active routes into the Routing Engine's *forwarding table* (also sometimes called a forwarding information base, or FIB), and the Routing Engine's kernel copies this table to a forwarding table maintained by the Packet Forwarding Engine (PFE). This forwarding table maps each next-hop router IP address with the physical interface through which that router is reached. Forwarding-table entries are used to physically direct traffic out a router interface and toward its destination.

In addition to storing a superset of the routes that are installed into the forwarding tables, the routing-table routes also contain control information that is not relevant to forwarding. This information includes the metric, AS path, and BGP communities.

Juniper Networks M-series and T-series routers architecturally and physically separate the routing and forwarding processes. Routing is done by RPD, which runs on the Routing Engine, a small form-factor PC that is built into the router. The RE encompasses the *control plane* and performs all routing operations. *Routing* means discovering the network topology and sharing this information with neighboring routers. Routing protocols, both interior gateway protocols (IGPs) such as RIP, IS-IS, and OSPF, and the exterior gateway protocol (EGP) BGP, learn network topology by talking with other routers and advertising routing information to them. A number of other software modules run in the router's control plane, including the CLI and accounting processes such as SNMP. Each of these modules runs as a separate process in the JUNOS software, and, in some cases, multiple instances of a module might be running (for instance, if two users are logged in to the router, two CLI processes run).

The PFE is the router's *forwarding plane*, housing the forwarding table and handling most forwarding processing. *Forwarding* is the process of receiving a packet on an inbound interface, de-encapsulating it, executing a number of packet-processing activities (such as filtering, accounting, and next-hop determination), encapsulating it, and queuing it on the outbound interface toward the packet's destination. The PFE consists of custom ASICs and the router's input and output interfaces. The ASICs use the forwarding table to perform route lookup, looking up the IP address prefix and determining the output interface (next hop) for the packet. The link between the Routing Engine and the PFE is a standard Fast Ethernet link (the fxp1 interface).

On the smaller J-series routers, the control and data planes are handled by the same CPU, which runs the software for both the RE and PFE.

RPD installs all active routes from the routing tables into the forwarding table. The JUNOS kernel maintains a master copy of the forwarding table and copies the table to the PFE. The operation to update the forwarding table is done atomically, one route at a time. This ensures that the forwarding table always has a single view of how to forward traffic on the network.

IPv4 and IPv6 Addresses

IPv4 addresses are 32 bits long and are written in a dotted quad notation. Originally, IPv4 addresses were divided into four classes, Classes A, B, C, and D. This type of addressing is called *classful*. Classful addresses require an address and a network mask. The address consists of a *network portion* and a *host portion*. The *subnetwork mask* defines how to interpret the address bits in order to know which are being used for the network portion and which for the host portion.

The IETF developed *classless* addresses in the late 1990s with the introduction of Classless Interdomain Routing (CIDR). This was done as one way to increase the number of network addresses available on the Internet. All IPv4 addresses on JUNOS routers are expressed in CIDR format. Instead of network and host portions and subnetwork masks, CIDR addresses have a *prefix* that represents the network address, followed by a slash and the *prefix length*, which identifies the number of bits being used for the network address. For example, one of the groups of routers used as examples in this book has interface addresses in the network 10.0.1.0/24. Here, the prefix is 10.0.1.0, and 24 bits are used for the network prefix. The remaining 8 bits are available for host addresses, so this network can have up to 256 hosts.

IPv6 uses 128-bit addresses that consist of 8 groups of 16-bit hexadecimal values separated by colons, followed by a slash and a mask, or prefix length, that indicates which bits are the network address. An example of an address is fe80:0000:0205:85ff:feca:ca70/128. You can omit any leading zeros in a group, so you can shorten this address to fe80::205:85ff:feca:ca70/128.

A complete discussion of the structure of IP addresses is beyond the scope of this book. For more information, see *IP Routing* and *IPv6 Essentials* (both from O'Reilly).

Default Route Preferences

A route's *preference* is a value from 0 through 255 that ranks a route with respect to other routes to the same prefix. When RPD learns about routes to the same destination from different sources, including routing protocols, it chooses the one that has the lowest preference value as the active route and installs it in the forwarding table. The default preference value depends on how the route was learned (see Table 8-2).

Table 8-2. JUNOS default route preferences

How route is learned	Default preference value
Directly connected router or network	0
Static routes	5
MPLS	7
LDP	9
OSPF internal routes	10
IS-IS Level 1 internal routes	15
IS-IS Level 2 internal routes	18
SNMP	50
RIP, RIPng	100
PIM	105
DVMRP	110
Aggregate	130
OSPF external routes	150
IS-IS Level 1 external routes	160
IS-IS Level 2 external routes	165
BGP	170
MSDP	175

If more than one route exists with the same preference, secondary criteria are used to select which is the active one.

Selecting Active Routes

For each destination (prefix) in the routing table, RPD selects the best route, called the *active route*, and installs it into the forwarding table. The algorithm that RPD uses to select the active route is fairly involved, but there will be times when you will be analyzing the flow of traffic through your network and you will need to understand how and why RPD has chosen a particular path. The following is the JUNOS algorithm for selecting the active route:

1. Choose the route with the lowest preference value.

2. For BGP routes, prefer the one with the higher local preference value. Otherwise, choose the path with the lowest preference2 value. (This is a secondary preference you can set for some protocols to use as a tiebreaker when the primary preferences are identical.)

3. If the route includes an AS path:

   a. Prefer the route with a shorter AS path. (Confederation sequences are assigned a path length of 0, and AS and confederation sets have a path length of 1.)

   b. Prefer the route with the lower origin code. Routes learned from an IGP have a lower origin code than those learned from an EGP, and both have lower origin codes than incomplete routes (routes whose origin is unknown).

   c. If you are not using BGP nondeterministic routing-table path selection behavior, for paths with the same neighboring AS numbers at the beginning of the AS path, prefer the path with the lowest multiple exit discriminator (MED) metric. Confederation AS numbers are not considered when deciding what the neighbor AS number is.

   If you are using nondeterministic routing-table path selection behavior, prefer the path with the lowest MED metric.

   In both cases, confederations are not considered when determining neighboring ASs, and a missing metric is treated as a MED of 0.

4. Prefer strictly internal routes, which include IGP routes and locally generated routes (such as static and direct).

5. Prefer strictly EBGP routes over external paths learned through IBGP.

6. For BGP, prefer the route whose next hop is resolved through the IGP route with the lowest metric.

7. For BGP, prefer the route with the greatest number of BGP next hops.

8. For BGP, prefer the route with the shortest route reflection cluster list. Routes without a cluster list are considered to have a cluster list of length 0.

9. For BGP, prefer the route with the lowest IP address value for the BGP router ID.

10. Prefer the path that was learned from the neighbor with the lowest peer IP address.

8.1   Viewing the Routes in the Routing Table

Problem

You want to check the routing table to see that it contains the routes you expect to other routers in your domain and to routers in other ASs.

Solution

The show route command shows the contents of the routing table:

```
aviva@RouterA> show route
inet.0: 5 destinations, 5 routes (5 active, 0 holddown, 0 hidden)
+ = Active Route, - = Last Active, * = Both
10.0.16.0/24       *[Direct/0] 5d 17:37:05
                    > via fe-0/0/0.0
10.0.16.1/32       *[Local/0] 1w0d 15:51:30
                     Local via fe-0/0/0.0
10.0.21.0/24       *[Direct/0] 1w0d 17:32:48
                    > via se-0/0/3.0
10.0.21.1/32       *[Local/0] 1w0d 17:32:53
                     Local via se-0/0/3.0
192.168.42.1/32    *[Direct/0] 5d 18:02:37
                    > via lo0.0
__juniper_private1__.inet.0: 2 destinations, 2 routes (2 active, 0 holddown, 0
hidden)
+ = Active Route, - = Last Active, * = Both
10.0.0.1/32        *[Direct/0] 1w0d 19:02:26
                    > via lo0.16385
10.0.0.16/32       *[Direct/0] 1w0d 19:02:26
                    > via lo0.16385
```

If IPv6 is running on the router, the routing table contains its routes. These are listed at the end of the show route command, or you can display them separately with the following command:

```
aviva@RouterA> show route table inet6.0
inet6.0: 6 destinations, 8 routes (6 active, 0 holddown, 0 hidden)
+ = Active Route, - = Last Active, * = Both
9009:1::/64        *[Direct/0] 00:01:08
                    > via se-0/0/3.0
                     [Direct/0] 00:01:08
                    > via fe-0/0/0.0
9009:1::1/128      *[Local/0] 00:01:08
                     Local via fe-0/0/0.0
9009:1::3/128      *[Local/0] 00:01:08
                     Local via se-0/0/3.0
fe80::/64          *[Direct/0] 00:01:08
                    > via se-0/0/3.0
                     [Direct/0] 00:01:08
                    > via fe-0/0/0.0
fe80::205:85ff:feca:ca70/128
```

```
                    *[Direct/0] 00:01:08
                    > via lo0.0
    feee::10:255:71:4/128
                    *[Direct/0] 00:01:08
                    > via lo0.0
```

When the router is running IS-IS, the show route command lists entries in the ISO routing table, iso.0, or you can view them separately with this command:

```
aviva@RouterA> show route table iso.0
iso.0: 1 destinations, 1 routes (1 active, 0 holddown, 0 hidden)
+ = Active Route, - = Last Active, * = Both
49.0020.1921.6804.2001/72
                    *[Direct/0] 13:16:30
                    > via lo0.0
```

Discussion

The show route command is the basic command for listing routes in the routing table. The first command in this recipe, without any options, shows the contents of all the routing tables that RPD is currently using. This output shows the contents of two routing tables, inet.0, which is the default routing table for IPv4 unicast routes, and __juniper_private1__, which is an internal routing table used by the JUNOS software. If IPv6, IS-IS, multicast, or traffic engineering is configured on the router, the show route command lists the routes in the routing tables used by these protocols, including inet6.0, iso.0, inet.2, inet.3, and mpls.0.

The first two lines of the show route output summarize the entries in the inet.0 table:

```
inet.0: 5 destinations, 5 routes (5 active, 0 holddown, 0 hidden)
+ = Active Route, - = Last Active, * = Both
```

This table has five routes. Of these, five are active, none are in the hold-down state prior to being deleted from the routing table, and none are hidden as a result of a configured routing policy.

The left column of the table shows the IP addresses of the routing entries. The direct routes are those to the prefixes (subnetwork addresses) assigned to an interface on the router. In the inet.0 table, you see three direct routes: two are to physical interface subnetworks, 10.0.16.0/24 and 10.0.21.0/24, and one is to the router's loopback interface, 192.168.42.1/32. The local routes are the /32 interface addresses on the directly connected interfaces, and there are two in the routing table, 10.0.16.1/32 and 10.0.21.1/32.

The right column of the output gives some details about each route. The asterisk (*) indicates that the route is the active route, which is the route currently installed in the forwarding table.

The text within the square brackets indicates how the route was learned and the route's preference value. All routes in the inet.0 table are either local on the router or learned as a result of a direct network connection to a neighboring router. If a route is learned from a dynamic routing protocol, such as BGP or IS-IS, or is statically configured, you see this in the square brackets. Here is a static route:

```
192.168.12.1/32    *[Static/5] 3d 21:43:37
                    > to 10.0.16.1 via fe-1/0/0.0
```

Here is a route learned from IS-IS:

```
10.0.24.0/24       *[IS-IS/18] 22:53:36, metric 20
                    > to 10.0.1.1 via fe-0/0/1.0
```

The preference values shown in the output in this recipe are all default values.

The numbers following the brackets show how long the routing table has known about the route. The first route in the table has been known for 5 days, 17 hours, 37 minutes, and 5 seconds:

```
10.0.16.0/24       *[Direct/0] 5d 17:37:05
```

For routes learned from dynamic routing protocols, such as the IS-IS, the route's cost, or metric, is listed after the time. This value is calculated by the routing protocol.

The second line for each route shows the IP address of the next hop toward the destination and the router interface to use to reach that destination. Because no routing protocols are currently configured on the router, the routing table contains only local and direct routes, and you see only the router interface to the destination. If a routing protocol is running, the IP address precedes the interface, as you can see in the static and IS-IS routes shown above. The IP address doesn't always precede the interface. Exceptions include routes that point to unnumbered interfaces and routes with non-IP next hops, such as MPLS routes.

The second part of the show route output shows the routes for the other routing table RPD is currently using—the internal JUNOS routing table, __juniper_private1__. Both routes listed travel on interface loo.16385, which is an internal loopback interface created and used only by the JUNOS software.

To display only the IPv4 unicast routes without the internal JUNOS routes, use this command:

```
aviva@RouterA> show route table inet.0
inet.0: 5 destinations, 5 routes (5 active, 0 holddown, 0 hidden)
+ = Active Route, - = Last Active, * = Both
10.0.16.0/24       *[Direct/0] 5d 17:37:05
                    > via fe-0/0/0.0
10.0.16.1/32       *[Local/0] 1w0d 15:51:30
                    Local via fe-0/0/0.0
10.0.21.0/24       *[Direct/0] 1w0d 17:32:48
                    > via se-0/0/3.0
10.0.21.1/32       *[Local/0] 1w0d 17:32:53
                    Local via se-0/0/3.0
192.168.42.1/32    *[Direct/0] 5d 18:02:37
                    > via loo.0
```

For a quickly skimmable view of the routing-table entries, use the terse version of the show route command:

```
aviva@RouterA> show route terse
inet.0: 5 destinations, 5 routes (5 active, 0 holddown, 0 hidden)
+ = Active Route, - = Last Active, * = Both
A Destination       P Prf   Metric 1   Metric 2  Next hop         AS path
* 10.0.16.0/24      D  0                          >fe-0/0/0.0
* 10.0.16.1/32      L  0                          Local
* 10.0.21.0/24      D  0                          >se-0/0/3.0
* 10.0.21.1/32      L  0                          Local
* 192.168.42.1/32   D  0                          >lo0.0
__juniper_private1__.inet.0: 2 destinations, 2 routes (2 active, 0 holddown, 0
hidden)
+ = Active Route, - = Last Active, * = Both
A Destination       P Prf   Metric 1   Metric 2  Next hop         AS path
* 10.0.0.1/32       D  0                          >lo0.16385
* 10.0.0.16/32      D  0                          >lo0.16385
```

You may wonder how the router has any addresses in its routing tables when no routing protocols are running and you haven't configured any static routes. When you configure interfaces, the JUNOS software automatically puts routes in the routing table. For the routing-table examples in this recipe, the following interfaces and interface addresses are configured:

```
aviva@RouterA> show configuration interfaces
fe-0/0/0 {
    unit 0 {
        family inet {
            address 10.0.16.1/24;
        }
        family iso;
        family inet6 {
            address 9009:1::1/64;
        }
    }
}
se-0/0/3 {
    unit 0 {
        family inet {
            address 10.0.21.1/24;
        }
        family iso;
        family inet6 {
            address 9009:1::3/64;
        }
    }
}
lo0 {
    unit 0 {
        family inet {
            address 192.168.42.1/32;
        }
```

```
        family iso {
            address 49.0020.1921.6804.2001.00;
        }
        family inet6 {
            address feee::10:255:71:4/128;
        }
    }
}
```

Looking at the inet.0 routing table, you see it contains entries for each of these inter-faces and for the subnetworks (the /24 address) to which they are connected:

```
10.0.16.0/24      *[Direct/0] 5d 17:37:05
                   > via fe-0/0/0.0
10.0.16.1/32      *[Local/0] 1w0d 15:51:30
                    Local via fe-0/0/0.0
10.0.21.0/24      *[Direct/0] 1w0d 17:32:48
                   > via se-0/0/3.0
10.0.21.1/32      *[Local/0] 1w0d 17:32:53
                    Local via se-0/0/3.0
192.168.42.1/32   *[Direct/0] 5d 18:02:37
                   > via lo0.0
```

This output shows entries for the three configured interfaces. For fe-0/0/0, there is an entry for the interface itself (10.0.16.1/32) and an entry for a summary of all the addresses on the subnetwork (10.0.16.0/24). There are similar entries for the serial interface. A route to the loopback address, 192.168.42.1/32, which is the address of the router itself, is also included.

The opening lines of the show route output always indicate the number of hidden routes in a routing table. Because the routes are hidden, they are not listed in this output:

```
aviva@reflector> show route
inet.0: 163481 destinations, 163481 routes (163479 active, 0 holddown, 2 hidden)
+ = Active Route, - = Last Active, * = Both
```

Hidden routes are prefixes that cannot be used for routing. These routes have been rejected by an inbound routing policy (a policy applied with a set import com-mand), they may have an unresolvable next hop, or there may be a forwarding-table export filter that keeps them from being used. Hidden routes can never become the active route even if they are the best path toward a destination, so they can never be installed in the forwarding table. Hidden routes are marked as Unusable in the routing table:

```
aviva@Router3> show route hidden table inet.0
inet.0: 168242 destinations, 168253 routes (168240 active, 0 holddown, 2 hidden)
+ = Active Route, - = Last Active, * = Both
3.0.0.0/8          [BGP/170] 00:05:20, MED 0, localpref 100, from 172.158.5.125
                    AS path: 65500 65510 I
                    Unusable
172.16.10.0/24     [BGP/170] 00:05:20, MED 0, localpref 100, from 172.158.5.125
                    AS path: I
                    Unusable
```

To find out why the route is unusable, get more details about it:

```
aviva@Router3> show route hidden 172.16.0.0/24 extensive
inet.0: 168242 destinations, 168253 routes (168240 active, 0 holddown, 2 hidden)
172.16.10.0/24 (1 entry, 0 announced)
        BGP    Preference: 170/-101
               Next hop type: Unusable
               Next-hop reference count: 1
               State: <Hidden Int Ext>
               Local AS: 65000 Peer AS: 65000
               Age: 6:59      Metric: 0
               Task: BGP_65000.172.158.5.125+25464
               AS path: I
               Communities: 65500:340
               Localpref: 100
               Router ID: 172.158.5.125
               Indirect next hops: 1
                       Protocol next hop: 192.168.251.1
                       Indirect next hop: 0 -
```

The Next hop type: Unusable line of the output indicates that the route has been hidden because the next hop is unreachable. To find out why it's unreachable, check the network topology and network links. Consult the routing table for a route covering the next hop. If that route is not resolved, check that route's next hop. Recurse until you get to a directly connected next hop. Then determine whether the directly connected next hop's interface and address are up and reachable. Making this determination may require diagnosing the health of Layer 2 and Layer 1 connectivity.

Prefixes that have no active routes are marked as inactive:

```
aviva@Router3> show route inactive-prefix table inet.0
inet.0: 163307 destinations, 163307 routes (163305 active, 0 holddown, 2 hidden)
+ = Active Route, - = Last Active, * = Both
127.0.0.1/32       [Direct/0] 5w1d 23:32:04
                   > via lo0.0
207.16.0.0/14      [BGP/170] 4d 01:53:05, localpref 100, from 207.17.136.29
                     AS path: 14203 2914 701 I
                     Unusable
```

The inactive prefixes do not have an asterisk at the beginning of the second column of output. In this case, the inactive and hidden routes are the same, but this is just a coincidence. For both prefixes, the routing table has no active route that will reach either destination.

See Also

Recipes 14.2, 14.7, and 15.2

8.2 Viewing Routes to a Particular Prefix

Problem

You need to check to make sure the local router has a route to another router in the network.

Solution

Use the following version of the show route command:

```
aviva@RouterG> show route 10.0.8.1
inet.0: 18 destinations, 18 routes (18 active, 0 holddown, 0 hidden)
+ = Active Route, - = Last Active, * = Both
10.0.8.0/24        *[IS-IS/18] 00:11:18, metric 20
                    > to 10.0.0.2 via fe-1/0/1.0
```

Discussion

Often you may want to find out whether the local routing table has a route to a particular destination, such as when you are trying to figure out the path that traffic is taking toward a destination. If you include the destination's address in the show route command, you see only that route. This recipe shows the route to 10.0.8.1, which was learned from an IS-IS Level 2 internal route, has a metric value of 20, and goes through the next hop of 10.0.0.2 over the router's interface fe-1/0/1. The header lines for the inet.0 routing table are also displayed, so you see that this routing table has a total of 18 routes to 18 destinations.

For more information about the route, use the detail option:

```
aviva@RouterG> show route 10.0.8.1 detail
inet.0: 18 destinations, 18 routes (18 active, 0 holddown, 0 hidden)
10.0.8.0/24 (1 entry, 1 announced)
        *IS-IS  Preference: 18
                Level: 2
                Next-hop reference count: 4
                Next hop: 10.0.0.2 via fe-1/0/1.0, selected
                State: <Active Int>
                Age: 11:41      Metric: 20
                Task: IS-IS
                Announcement bits (1): 0-KRT
                AS path: I
```

This output shows a few more fields of interest. The Next hop field shows that this next hop has been selected for inclusion in the forwarding table. The State field shows that this route is active and is an interior route. The AS path field also shows that the route was learned internally.

The output in this recipe is straightforward because there is only one route to the destination and it is active. Some routes have multiple next hops:

```
aviva@RouterG> show route protocol 10.0.2.0/24
inet.0: 18 destinations, 18 routes (18 active, 0 holddown, 0 hidden)
+ = Active Route, - = Last Active, * = Both
10.0.2.0/24        *[IS-IS/18] 00:45:17, metric 20
                    > to 10.0.1.1 via fe-0/0/1.0
                      to 10.0.0.2 via fe-1/0/1.0
```

The destination 10.0.2.0/24 has two next hops, one reachable through interface fe-0/0/1 and the second through a different router interface, fe-1/0/1. The asterisk indicates that this route, learned from IS-IS, is active. The metric for both next hops is 20, so there are two equal-cost paths to 10.0.2.0/24. Because both routers have been learned from the same protocol, by default the JUNOS software randomly chooses one of them. The > indicates the path being used.

Routes can also be learned from multiple routing protocols:

```
aviva@Router3> show route 10.1.1.0/24
inet.0: 28 destinations, 48 routes (28 active, 0 holddown, 0 hidden)
Restart Complete
+ = Active Route, - = Last Active, * = Both
10.1.1.0/24        *[OSPF/10] 00:16:20, metric 65
                      via so-0/2/0.0
                    > via so-0/2/1.0
                     [IS-IS/18] 00:16:08, metric 126
                      to 10.1.2.1 via so-0/2/0.0
                    > to 10.1.6.1 via so-0/2/1.0
```

Here, both OSPF and IS-IS have learned routes to 10.1.1.0/24. The OSPF routes are chosen over the IS-IS ones because of the lower preference value (10 versus 18). The two routes learned by each protocol are both equal-cost paths to the destination, so the JUNOS software randomly chooses one of them, again indicating the selected path with a >.

If you expect a prefix to be in the routing table but it is not, look at the first two lines of the show route output to check for hidden routes. If the routing table contains some, check for the prefix with the show route hidden command. If the prefix is hidden, examine the router's routing policies to see if an inbound policy is rejecting the route. If necessary, set up policy tracing to log how policies are being evaluated (see Recipe 9.7). Another possibility is that there is no next hop toward the destination. Check the network topology and physical links between your network systems.

See Also

Recipe 9.7

8.3   Viewing Routes Learned from a Specific Protocol

Problem

You have configured a routing protocol and you want to make sure the router is learning routes from that protocol.

Solution

Include the protocol name in the show route command:

```
aviva@RouterG> show route protocol isis
inet.0: 18 destinations, 18 routes (18 active, 0 holddown, 0 hidden)
+ = Active Route, - = Last Active, * = Both
10.0.2.0/24        *[IS-IS/18] 00:45:17, metric 20
                    > to 10.0.1.1 via fe-0/0/1.0
                      to 10.0.0.2 via fe-1/0/1.0
10.0.8.0/24        *[IS-IS/18] 00:45:17, metric 20
                    > to 10.0.0.2 via fe-1/0/1.0
10.0.21.0/24       *[IS-IS/15] 00:45:17, metric 20
                    > to 10.0.16.1 via fe-1/0/0.0
10.0.24.0/24       *[IS-IS/18] 00:45:17, metric 20
                    > to 10.0.1.1 via fe-0/0/1.0
10.0.29.0/24       *[IS-IS/18] 00:45:17, metric 30
                    > to 10.0.1.1 via fe-0/0/1.0
192.168.14.1/32    *[IS-IS/18] 00:45:17, metric 20
                    > to 10.0.1.1 via fe-0/0/1.0
192.168.17.1/32    *[IS-IS/18] 00:45:17, metric 10
                    > to 10.0.0.2 via fe-1/0/1.0
192.168.18.1/32    *[IS-IS/18] 00:45:17, metric 10
                    > to 10.0.1.1 via fe-0/0/1.0
192.168.42.1/32    *[IS-IS/15] 00:45:17, metric 10
                    > to 10.0.16.1 via fe-1/0/0.0
```

Discussion

When you are setting up routing protocols on your network, use the show route protocol command to make sure that each router has a route to each other router and that the routes are being directed out the proper interface on the router. In this recipe, we are setting up an IS-IS network and checking that the local IS-IS router has learned routes to all IS-IS destinations.

8.4   Displaying the Routes in the Forwarding Table

Problem

You want to see the routes that RPD has installed in the forwarding table and that the router is actually using to forward packets.

Solution

Use the show route forwarding-table command to see the active routes in the Routing Engine's forwarding table:

```
aviva@RouterA> show route forwarding-table
Routing table: inet
Internet:
Destination          Type RtRef Next hop           Type Index NhRef Netif
default              user    1 0:10:db:ff:20:80     ucst   335     3 fe-0/0/0.0
default              perm    0                      rjct    14     1
10.17.214.0/26       intf    0                      rslv   329     1 fe-0/0/1.0
10.17.214.0/32       dest    0 10.17.214.0          recv   327     1 fe-0/0/1.0
10.17.214.27/32      intf    0 10.17.214.27         locl   328     2
10.17.214.27/32      dest    0 10.17.214.27         locl   328     2
10.17.214.63/32      dest    0 10.17.214.63         bcst   320     1 fe-0/0/1.0
172.19.121.0/24      intf    0                      rslv   326     1 fe-0/0/0.0
172.19.121.0/32      dest    0 172.19.121.0         recv   324     1 fe-0/0/0.0
172.19.121.1/32      dest    0 0:10:db:ff:20:80     ucst   335     3 fe-0/0/0.0
172.19.121.113/32    intf    0 172.19.121.113       locl   325     2
172.19.121.113/32    dest    0 172.19.121.113       locl   325     2
172.19.121.142/32    dest    0 0:5:85:ca:dd:60      ucst   336     1 fe-0/0/0.0
172.19.121.255/32    dest    0 172.19.121.255       bcst   323     1 fe-0/0/0.0
192.168.10.7/32      intf    0 192.168.10.7         locl   330     1
224.0.0.0/4          perm    0                      mdsc    13     1
224.0.0.1/32         perm    0 224.0.0.1            mcst     9     1
255.255.255.255/32   perm    0                      bcst    10     1


Routing table: __juniper_private1__.inet
Internet:
Destination          Type RtRef Next hop           Type Index NhRef Netif
default              perm    0                      rjct    46     1
10.0.0.1/32          intf    1 10.0.0.1             locl   321     2
10.0.0.16/32         intf    0 10.0.0.16            locl   322     1
224.0.0.0/4          perm    0                      mdsc    45     1
224.0.0.1/32         perm    0 224.0.0.1            mcst    41     1
255.255.255.255/32   perm    0                      bcst    42     1


Routing table: iso
ISO:
Destination          Type RtRef Next hop           Type Index NhRef Netif
default              perm    0                      rjct    38     1


Routing table: inet6
Internet6:
Destination          Type RtRef Next hop           Type Index NhRef Netif
default              perm    0                      rjct    22     1
ff00::/8             perm    0                      mdsc    21     1
ff02::1/128          perm    0 ff02::1              mcst    17     1


Routing table: __juniper_private1__.inet6
Internet6:
Destination          Type RtRef Next hop           Type Index NhRef Netif
default              perm    0                      rjct    54     1
```

```
ff00::/8          perm    0                     mdsc   53    1
ff02::1/128       perm    0 ff02::1             mcst   49    1

Routing table: mpls
MPLS:
Destination       Type RtRef Next hop          Type Index NhRef Netif
default           perm    0                     dscd   28    1
```

To see the forwarding entries that the PFE uses to forward packets, you must use the show pfe route command:

```
aviva@RouterA> show pfe route ip
IPv4 Route Table 0, default.0, 0x0:
Destination                            NH IP Addr       Type      NH ID Interface
-----------------------------------    ---------------  --------  ----- ---------
default                                172.19.121.1     Unicast   335 fe-0/0/0.0
10.17.214.0/26                                          Resolve   329 fe-0/0/1.0
10.17.214.0                            10.17.214.0      Receive   327 fe-0/0/1.0
10.17.214.27                           10.17.214.27     Local     328
10.17.214.63                                            Bcast     320 fe-0/0/1.0
172.19.121/24                                           Resolve   326 fe-0/0/0.0
172.19.121.0                           172.19.121.0     Receive   324 fe-0/0/0.0
172.19.121.1                           172.19.121.1     Unicast   335 fe-0/0/0.0
172.19.121.113                         172.19.121.113   Local     325
172.19.121.142                         172.19.121.142   Unicast   336 fe-0/0/0.0
172.19.121.255                                          Bcast     323 fe-0/0/0.0
192.168.10.7                           192.168.10.7     Local     330
224/4                                                   MDiscard  13
224.0.0.1                                               Mcast      9
255.255.255.255                                         Bcast     10

IPv4 Route Table 1, __juniper_private1__.1, 0x2:
Destination                            NH IP Addr       Type      NH ID Interface
-----------------------------------    ---------------  --------  ----- ---------
default                                                 Reject     46 .local..1
10.0.0.1                               10.0.0.1         Local     321 .local..1
10.0.0.16                              10.0.0.16        Local     322 .local..1
224/4                                                   MDiscard   45 .local..1
224.0.0.1                                               Mcast      41 .local..1
255.255.255.255                                         Bcast      42 .local..1
```

Discussion

Both the Routing Engine and the PFE maintain forwarding tables. The one on the Routing Engine contains the active routes that have been installed by RPD, and the show route forwarding-table command displays its contents. This command is similar to the FreeBSD netstat -rn command. The Routing Engine's kernel copies this table to the PFE. The PFE's forwarding table maps each next-hop router IP address with the physical interface through which that router is reached. The show pfe route command displays the contents of this forwarding table.

The show route forwarding-table output shows routes from all routing tables, so it includes IPv4, IPv6, ISO, and MPLS routes, as well as routes from the internal

JUNOS routing table. The output in this recipe shows sections for each type of routing table. You can also look at just the forwarding table for one of the routing families:

```
aviva@RouterA> show route forwarding-table family ?
Possible completions:
  inet               IP version 4 (IPv4)
  inet6              IP version 6 (IPv6)
  iso                International Standards Organization protocol
  mpls               Multiprotocol Label Switching
  tnp                Trivial Network Protocol
  unix               UNIX
```

The Destination column in each section lists network-layer addresses on which the router is forwarding traffic, and the last column, Netif, shows the interfaces that are being used to send traffic toward those addresses.

The Next hop column lists the next hop to the destination. If you compare the inet routing-table entries in the forwarding table to the entries in the routing table (see Recipe 8.1), which has routes to the interface addresses 10.0.16.0/24, 10.0.16.1/32, 10.0.21.0/24, and 10.0.21.1/32, and to the router (loopback) address 192.168.42.1/32, the forwarding table contains entries to reach all these destinations.

The first Type column immediately gives an indication of how the route was placed into the routing table. perm are permanent routes installed by the JUNOS kernel when the routing table is initialized, intf are routes learned when an interface was configured, and dest are remote addresses that are directly connected to an interface. When a routing protocol is running on the router, you also see the type ucst. Here, you see a route learned by IS-IS:

```
aviva@RouterA> show route 10.0.1.0/24
inet.0: 9 destinations, 9 routes (9 active, 0 holddown, 0 hidden)
+ = Active Route, - = Last Active, * = Both
10.0.1.0/24        *[IS-IS/15] 00:11:07, metric 20
                    > to 10.0.16.2 via fe-0/0/0.0

aviva@RouterA> show route forwarding-table destination 10.0.1.0/24
Routing table: inet
Internet:
Destination        Type RtRef Next hop        Type Index NhRef Netif
10.0.1.0/24        user    0 10.0.16.2        ucst  337     5 fe-0/0/0.0
```

A route that is unreachable is marked iddn if the interface to that destination is down.

The Next hop column is the address used to reach the next hop toward the destination, and the second Type column gives more information about the next hop. The last column shows the router's interface that will be used to send traffic toward the destination.

The actual forwarding tables that the router is using to forward traffic are in the PFE, so instead of a show route command, use a show pfe command to see the contents. Unlike the show route forwarding-table command, the show pfe route command lets you see only one forwarding table at a time:

```
aviva@RouterA> show pfe route ?
Possible completions:
  inet6               Show IP version 6 routing tables
  ip                  Show IP version 4 routing tables
  mpls                Show Multiprotocol Label Switching routing table
  summary             Show summary version of routing tables
```

The PFE has three tables, one each for IPv4, IPv6, and MPLS routes. All tables have a similar format and contents. The output in this recipe is for the IPv4 forwarding table. For each destination, the forwarding table shows the IP address of the next type, the type of route, and the interface out which traffic will be sent, which is pretty much the same information as in the Routing Engine's forwarding table.

You can also look at the entries for a particular destination:

```
aviva@RouterA> show route forwarding table destination 10.17.214.0/32
Routing table: inet
Internet:
Destination        Type RtRef Next hop           Type Index NhRef Netif
10.17.214.0/32     dest    0 10.17.214.0         recv  327     1 fe-0/0/1.0

aviva@RouterA> show pfe route ip prefix 10.17.214.0/32
IPv4 Route Table 0, default.0, 0x0:
Destination                        NH IP Addr        Type     NH ID Interface
--------------------------------   ---------------   -------- ----- ---------
10.17.214.0                        10.17.214.0       Receive    327 fe-0/0/1.0
```

8.5 Creating Static Routes

Problem

You want to be able to connect your router to the Internet.

Solution

Create a default static route:

```
[edit routing-options]
aviva@router1# set static route 0.0.0.0/0 next-hop 10.0.21.2
```

Discussion

Static routes are routes that you explicitly add to your routing table. Static routes are always available and do not change as a result of dynamic routing updates. For an enterprise network, a static route can be simply a default route that points to the ISP, as shown in this recipe. Here, you create a default route, 0.0.0.0/0. The next hop is the address of the interface to which you connect on the ISP's router. This route then forwards all Internet-bound traffic through the ISP and out to the Internet.

Check the routing table to see the route:

```
aviva@router1> show route table inet.0
inet.0: 20 destinations, 20 routes (19 active, 0 holddown, 1 hidden)
+ = Active Route, - = Last Active, * = Both
0.0.0.0/0          *[Static/5] 00:06:50
                    > to 10.0.21.2 via se-0/0/3
```

Another reason to use static routes is when your network connects to a router or other system outside the network and either that system can't run a routing protocol or you don't want to run a routing protocol on it. In this situation, create a static route from your edge router to the outside system and then, on the edge router, redistribute static routes into your IGP. Here's what the static route configuration might look like on the edge router:

```
[edit routing-options]
aviva@router1# set static route 172.168.17.6 next-hop 10.1.16.4
```

Here, 172.168.17.6 is the address of the system outside your network, and 10.1.16.4 is the address of the other router to which the interface on your router connects.

See Also

Recipes 11.8 and 12.10

8.6   Blackholing Routes

Problem

You don't want to route any traffic to particular networks.

Solution

Define static routes to these networks that discard the traffic:

```
[edit routing-options]
aviva@router1# set static route 1.0.0.0/8 discard
aviva@router1# set static route 2.0.0.0/8 discard
```

Discussion

There are some network addresses to which the router should never send traffic, and you never want routes to these networks to be installed in the routing table by one or all routing protocols. A good practice for dealing with these routes is to blackhole them. You do this by defining static routes to them with a next hop of discard. Packets being sent to these networks are then dropped. Also, the router does not send an ICMP (or ICMPv6) unreachable message in response to traffic sent to these networks, and the traffic to these networks is dropped silently. (When there is a reason to have the router send ICMP unreachable messages, use a next hop of reject instead.) Routes with a discard next hop are placed in the forwarding table with a next-hop type of dscd (discard).

Verify that the routes are in the routing table:

```
aviva@router1> show route
inet.0: 23 destinations, 23 routes (22 active, 0 holddown, 1 hidden)
+ = Active Route, - = Last Active, * = Both
1.0.0.0/8          *[Static/5] 00:03:41
                     Discard
2.0.0.0/8          *[Static/5] 00:00:02
                     Discard
```

They are installed in the forwarding table as discard routes:

```
aviva@router1> show route forwarding-table
Routing table: inet
Internet:
Destination        Type RtRef Next hop        Type Index NhRef Netif
1.0.0.0/8          user   0                    dscd   12    3
2.0.0.0/8          user   0                    dscd   12    3
```

A good security practice is to blackhole addresses that have not yet been allocated by one of the domain registries, such as ARIN or RIPE (see *http://www.iana.org/assignments/ipv4-address-space*). This recipe shows two of those addresses. For a complete list, see *http://www.cymru.com/gillsr/documents/junos-discard-routes.txt*. Because these addresses are not allocated and no traffic should be destined for them anyway, you might wonder why you should bother blackholing traffic to them. One reason is to limit a malicious hacker's ability to attack your router with a DoS attack from external spoofed sources. It also reduces the potential for outbound spoofing from your network. Certain spammers may also use unallocated space to send spam, first by announcing a prefix from unallocated space and sending their spam, then quickly withdrawing the route. Another reason to blackhole unallocated addresses is to reduce the possibility of prefix hijacking. For example, an AS might announce a /16, and the spammer can announce some unused (or even used) space within the /16.

As a note of caution, unallocated-addresses space changes from time to time as new allocations are made. You need to pay close attention to the changes and change your filters accordingly so as not to block legitimate traffic.

See Also

Internet Assigned Numbers Authority (IANA) (*http://www.iana.org/assignments/ipv4-address-space*) and Team Cymru (*http://www.cymru.com/gillsr/documents/junos-discard-routes.txt*)

8.7   Filtering Traffic Using Unicast Reverse-Path Forwarding

Problem

You want to more adequately filter traffic that is not coming through the proper interfaces to better prevent spoofing.

Solution

Turn on unicast reverse-path forwarding (RPF) on the router:

```
[edit routing-options]
aviva@router1# set forwarding-table unicast-reverse-path active-paths
```

Then enable it on the desired interface:

```
[edit interfaces so-0/0/0 unit 0 family inet]
aviva@router1# set rpf-check
```

Discussion

Unicast RPF is an extension of RPF, which is used by IP multicast routing protocols to prevent multicast routing loops. As the name implies, unicast RPF verifies unicast source addresses. When a router receives a packet, unicast RPF performs a route lookup on the source address to determine the interface closest to the source address (the reverse path to the source). If the receiving interface is not the closest interface, the packet is dropped.

Unicast RPF is one mechanism for dealing with *address-spoofing* DoS attacks. In these attacks, an intruder floods its target with packets that contain a spoofed source address, essentially impersonating another system's IP address. The flooding results in a DoS at the target, and because the source address is spoofed, the true source of the traffic is difficult to trace. UDP applications are more vulnerable to spoofing attacks than TCP applications because, though TCP uses sequence numbers and handshakes that require more than a single packet to establish and maintain a session, UDP applications perform their own internal verification to ensure that a given source is who it says it is and that the IP headers in the source of the packets have not been forged. rlogin and other Unix r-utilities and X Windows are commonly subject to spoofing attacks. DNS servers are also vulnerable to spoofing, because they regularly send queries to obtain the IP addresses of hosts, and cache this information, but do not authenticate the source of the answers they receive. This operation makes it possible for an attacker to send false or improper answers to DNS queries, thus poisoning the cache.

Figure 8-1 illustrates how a spoofing attack might work. The attacker, somewhere on the Internet at 10.0.0.1, sends packets through your router to one of your customers at 172.16.0.2.

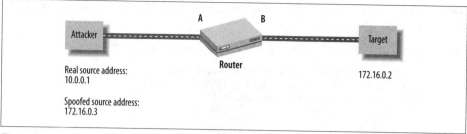

Figure 8-1. DoS attack scenario

In a normal packet, the source address in the packet's header would be 10.0.0.1. The attacker modifies the packet's header, spoofing the source address and changing it to 172.16.0.3. The attacker then floods your customer with spoofed packets. The flood can look like it's coming from several compromised hosts all spoofing random addresses, or the source addresses will remain. To protect your customer from attacks, you configure unicast RPF on the router's interface A.

Configuring unicast RPF is a two-step process. First, enable it on the router with the unicast-reverse-path statement in the [edit routing-options] hierarchy. With the active-paths option, unicast RPF considers all active routes in the routing table when checking how to reach the packet's destination. Use this option if the routing paths through your network are generally symmetrical. However, if paths are asymmetrical, unicast RPF might drop legitimate packets. In this case, use the feasible-paths option to consider both active and nonactive routes in the routing table.

Then, select the interfaces on which to run unicast RPF. Use the set rpf-check command when configuring the interface's address family. This command places unicast RPF in *strict mode*, which, as the name suggests, performs the most stringent examination of incoming packets. Strict-mode unicast RPF checks that the source address in each incoming packet matches a prefix in the routing table and verifies that the interface is the closest to the source address and is the interface the router would use when sending packets to that address. An interface drops any packets that do not meet both these criteria.

A second mode, *loose mode*, performs only one of these checks, making sure that the source address matches a routing-table prefix but not verifying that the incoming interface as the one closest to the source address:

```
[edit interfaces so-0/0/0 unit 0 family inet]
aviva@router1# set rpf-check mode loose
```

Loose-mode unicast RPF is good for filtering traffic that is sourced from bogon (invalid) address space and can be used in conjunction with or instead of routing policy filters that block specific bogon addresses. A key point to keep in mind when using loose-mode unicast RPF is whether your network uses a 0.0.0.0/0 (default) route. The router automatically accepts all packets when loose-mode unicast RPF is configured on interfaces that the default route uses, so it may not be a good fit in your network for this reason.

To verify the configuration, look at the statistics on the logical interface:

```
aviva@router1> show interfaces so-0/0/0.0 statistics
    Logical interface so-0/0/0.0 (Index 67) (SNMP ifIndex 41)
      Flags: Point-To-Point SNMP-Traps Encapsulation: PPP
      Protocol inet, MTU: 4470
        Flags: uRPF
        RPF Failures: Packets: 23, Bytes: 2492
        Addresses, Flags: Is-Preferred Is-Primary
          Destination: 10.1.12.0/30, Local: 10.1.12.1, Broadcast: 10.1.12.3
      Protocol iso, MTU: 4470
        Flags: Is-Primary
      Protocol mpls, MTU: 4458
        Flags: Is-Primary
```

The Flags field shows that unicast RPF is enabled, and the next line shows the number of packets and bytes dropped because of unicast RPF checks.

When you think the router is experiencing a DoS attack, set up a firewall filter to count the packets dropped by the interface. Create a separate filter to count the unicast RPF traffic:

```
[edit firewall]
aviva@router1# set filter rpf-filter term default then count rpf-failed-count
aviva@router1# set filter rpf-filter term default then reject
aviva@router1# show
filter rpf-filter {
    term default {
        then {
            count rpf-failed-count;
            reject;
        }
    }
}
```

This filter has no from clause, so it applies to all incoming packets. The then clause creates a file named *rpf-failed-count* and rejects all packets. Then apply the filter to the interface:

```
[edit interfaces so-0/0/0]
aviva@router1# set unit 0 family inet rpf-check fail-filter rpf-filter
```

Reference the filter you created in the fail-filter option of the rpf-check statement. Unicast RPF filters are not part of the normal firewall filter on an interface but are handled separately. They are evaluated after input filters and before output filters. Unicast RPF looks only in the inet.0 routing table for IPv4 packets and the inet6.0 table for IPv6 packets, so if an interface's input filter forwards packets to a different routing table, the unicast RPF check is not performed.

Check the firewall filter counts with the following command:

```
aviva@router1> show firewall filter rpf-failed-count
Filter: rpf-filter
Counters:
Name                                           Bytes              Packets
rpf-failed-count                               2492                    23
```

See Also

Recipe 9.8

8.8   Aggregating Routes

Problem

You want to aggregate some of the routes in the routing table to reduce the size of the tables and to minimize the amount of routing-information advertisements between routers.

Solution

Configure an aggregate route that covers the specific routes beneath it:

```
[edit routing-options]
aviva@router1# set aggregate route 10.20.8.0/21
```

Discussion

In this recipe, the routing table contains prefixes for 10.20.13.0/24 and 10.20.15.0/24, which aggregate as 10.20.8.0/21. Unlike static routes, you do not specify a next hop in the set aggregate route command, because aggregate routes are not "real" routes but rather are just route summaries. The default next hop is reject. Aggregate routes become active if a more specific route beneath them becomes active. For example, if 10.20.13.0/24 becomes active, the aggregate 10.20.8.0/21 also becomes active, and you then see it in the routing table:

```
aviva@RouterJ> show route
inet.0: 11 destinations, 11 routes (11 active, 0 holddown, 0 hidden)
+ = Active Route, - = Last Active, * = Both
10.20.8.0/21       *[Aggregate/130] 00:00:03
                      Reject
10.20.13.0/24      *[Direct/0] 00:01:30
                    > via fe-1/0/1.0
10.20.13.1/32      *[Local/0] 00:01:30
                      Local via fe-1/0/1.0
10.20.15.0/24      *[Direct/0] 00:01:30
                    > via fe-1/0/0.0
10.20.15.1/32      *[Local/0] 00:01:30
                      Local via fe-1/0/0.0
172.19.121.0/24    *[Direct/0] 1d 21:12:45
```

```
                         > via fe-0/0/0.0
    172.19.121.117/32   *[Local/0] 1d 21:12:45
                          Local via fe-0/0/0.0
    192.168.17.1/32     *[Direct/0] 00:01:30
                          > via loo.0
```

This output shows that the aggregate route has a default next hop of Reject, which drops any traffic addressed to it and sends an ICMP unreachable message back to the sender. If you are concerned about malicious hackers using the ICMP messages to gain information about your network and routers, change the next hop to discard so that no ICMP unreachable messages are sent:

```
[edit routing-options]
aviva@router1# set aggregate route 10.20.8.0/21 discard
```

Use the show route command to verify the change:

```
aviva@RouterJ> show route protocol aggregate
inet.0: 11 destinations, 11 routes (11 active, 0 holddown, 0 hidden)
+ = Active Route, - = Last Active, * = Both
10.20.8.0/21         *[Aggregate/130] 00:01:45
                      Discard
```

When the aggregate route is active, it is installed in the forwarding table as a discard route:

```
aviva@RouterJ> show route forwarding-table matching 10.20.8.0/21
Routing table: inet
Internet:
Destination        Type RtRef Next hop        Type  Index NhRef Netif
10.20.8.0/21       user  0                    dscd   12    1
10.20.13.0/24      intf  0                    rslv  338    1 fe-1/0/1.0
10.20.13.0/32      dest  0 10.20.13.0         recv  336    1 fe-1/0/1.0
10.20.13.1/32      intf  0 10.20.13.1         locl  337    2
10.20.13.1/32      dest  0 10.20.13.1         locl  337    2
10.20.13.255/32    dest  0 10.20.13.255       bcst  335    1 fe-1/0/1.0
10.20.15.0/24      intf  0                    rslv  334    1 fe-1/0/0.0
10.20.15.0/32      dest  0 10.20.15.0         recv  332    1 fe-1/0/0.0
10.20.15.1/32      intf  0 10.20.15.1         locl  333    2
10.20.15.1/32      dest  0 10.20.15.1         locl  333    2
10.20.15.255/32    dest  0 10.20.15.255       bcst  327    1 fe-1/0/0.0
```

8.9   Load-Balancing Traffic Flows

Problem

You want the JUNOS software to choose the path on a per-packet basis when there are multiple equal-cost paths to a destination.

Solution

Create a routing policy that load-balances traffic on a per-flow basis:

```
[edit policy-options]
aviva@router1# set policy-statement balance-traffic from route-filter 192.168.10.0/24
orlonger
aviva@router1# set policy-statement balance-traffic then load-balance per-packet
```

Then apply the policy to the forwarding table:

```
[edit routing-options]
aviva@router1# set forwarding-table export balance-traffic
```

Discussion

The routing protocols populate the routing table with the routes they know about and learn from their neighbors. For each prefix, or destination, RPD chooses one active route and installs its next hop into the forwarding table. If a route points to an indirect next hop, RPD downloads all the next hops of the indirect next hop, and the PFE selects a single next hop to use.

When there are multiple paths to a single destination, the routing protocols install the next hops for each path into the routing table. The protocols do have some degree of freedom when populating the routing table. A protocol can opt to install multiple routes, each with the same next hop, a single route with multiple next hops, or even multiple routes with multiple next hops. BGP, for example, can use any of these variations depending on how many peers advertise a prefix, how those peers can be reached, and whether BGP multipath is enabled.

When an active route has multiple equal-cost paths, the default behavior is for RPD to use a hash algorithm to choose a single gateway and install it into the forwarding table. If multiple prefixes have a common set of next hops, this gateway selection process should result in uniform distribution of prefixes across the next hops. For example, if prefixes A, B, C, and D all have gateways 1 and 2, RPD may install A and D with gateway 1 and B and C with gateway 2, so half the prefixes go through one link and half through the other.

To instead have RPD install all the next hops for a prefix into the forwarding table, you turn on load balancing for that prefix. Load balancing distributes the traffic to the prefix across all the paths, evening out the traffic flow across different interfaces and circuits.

Configuring load balancing is a two-step process. First, create a routing policy to define which packets to load-balance. In this recipe, the from clause matches the prefix 192.168.10.0/24 and any longer prefixes. The then clause has the load-balance per-packet action to turn on load balancing:

```
[edit policy-options]
aviva@router1# set policy-statement load-balance then load-balance per-packet
```

Even though the JUNOS CLI uses per-packet, the term is misnamed. This command is actually enabling *per-flow* load balancing.

The second step is to apply the policy to routes exported from the routing table to the forwarding engine. In the [edit routing-options] hierarchy, use a set export command:

```
[edit routing-options]
aviva@router1# set forwarding-table export balance-traffic
```

The result of this policy is that all equal-cost paths to destinations are installed in the forwarding table and traffic to these destinations is load-balanced on a per-flow basis. The exact balancing behavior depends on the ASICs in your router. For older routers with the Internet Processor I ASIC, load balancing uses a round-robin method across up to eight next hops. On newer routers with the Internet Processor II ASIC, packets for each individual flow are kept on a single interface and can be spread across up to 16 next hops.

A flow is defined as packets whose headers have the same source and destination addresses and the same protocol. Use the following commands to check for more information in the packet headers:

```
[edit forwarding-options]
aviva@router1# set hash-key family inet layer-3
aviva@router1# set hash-key family inet layer-4
```

With these two commands, the source and destination port numbers, source interface index, and type of service are also checked to determine whether packets are in the same flow. When you have more detailed knowledge of your network's traffic patterns and the network types, these two commands allow you to load-balance traffic flows more precisely.

See Also

Recipes 9.1 and 13.14

8.10 Adding Martian Addresses

Problem

You want to add a martian address to the JUNOS default martian list.

Solution

Specify the martian address in the [edit routing-options] hierarchy:

```
[edit routing-options]
aviva@router1# set martians 1.0.0.0/0 through 1.0.0.0/32
```

Discussion

Martian addresses are prefixes reserved for a specific purpose and not subject to future allocation by the IANA. You should never see traffic from these prefixes; if you do, it generally indicates that a system somewhere on the network is misconfigured. By default, the JUNOS software ignores all martian addresses and does not install them in the routing table. The JUNOS software maintains the following martian addresses by default:

```
aviva@router1> show route martians
inet.0:

        0.0.0.0/0 exact -- allowed
        0.0.0.0/8 orlonger -- disallowed
        127.0.0.0/8 orlonger -- disallowed
        128.0.0.0/16 orlonger -- disallowed
        191.255.0.0/16 orlonger -- disallowed
        192.0.0.0/24 orlonger -- disallowed
        223.255.255.0/24 orlonger -- disallowed
        240.0.0.0/4 orlonger -- disallowed
...
inet6.0:

        ::1/128 exact -- disallowed
```

These correspond to the all-zeros and all-ones classful network numbers, as well as the Class E network space. All of the former addresses were reserved by IANA (and many still are), and routing for the latter is undefined.

There is no permanent list of martian addresses because the address spaces that IANA chooses to reserve and make available for allocation change over time. Some martian addresses are not included in the JUNOS defaults, and some of the address blocks included in the JUNOS software default martian list have since been made available for allocation by IANA (see RFC 3330).

This recipe adds an address to the martian list on a router. Look at the martian routes in the routing table to verify that the address has been added:

```
aviva@router1> show route martians table inet.0
inet.0:

        0.0.0.0/0 exact -- allowed
        0.0.0.0/8 orlonger -- disallowed
        127.0.0.0/8 orlonger -- disallowed
        128.0.0.0/16 orlonger -- disallowed
        191.255.0.0/16 orlonger -- disallowed
        192.0.0.0/24 orlonger -- disallowed
        223.255.255.0/24 orlonger -- disallowed
        240.0.0.0/4 orlonger -- disallowed
        1.0.0.0/0 through 1.0.0.0/32-- disallowed
```

The disallowed keyword in the output means that the route is treated like a martian and is blocked.

As the IANA allocations change, you will want to remove some of the prefix blocks from the list to override the defaults. To change the JUNOS defaults so the only martians are 0.0.0.0/8 (addresses on this network), 127.0.0.0/8 (loopback address), and 240.0.0.0/4 (experimental address block, formerly the Class E addresses), configure the martian addresses to allow the remaining defaults:

```
[edit routing-options]
aviva@router1# set martians 128.0.0.0/16 orlonger allow
aviva@router1# set martians 191.255.0.0/16 orlonger allow
aviva@router1# set martians 192.0.0.0/24 orlonger allow
aviva@router1# set martians 223.255.255.0/24 orlonger allow
```

You can verify that these prefixes are now accepted:

```
aviva@router1> show route martians table inet.0
inet.0:
            0.0.0.0/0 exact -- allowed
            0.0.0.0/8 orlonger -- disallowed
            127.0.0.0/8 orlonger -- disallowed
            128.0.0.0/16 orlonger -- allowed
            191.255.0.0/16 orlonger -- allowed
            192.0.0.0/24 orlonger -- allowed
            223.255.255.0/24 orlonger -- allowed
            240.0.0.0/4 orlonger -- disallowed
```

The allowed keyword in the output means that the routes are now accepted.

RFC 3330, *Special-Use IPv4 Addresses*, describes specialized IPv4 address blocks that have been assigned to IANA to manage. Team Cymru maintains information about other prefixes that you might want to mark as martians (see *http://www.cymru.com/ gillsr/documents/junos-bgp-template.pdf* and *http://www.cymru.com/gillsr/documents/ junos-martians.txt*).

See Also

RFC 3330, *Special-Use IPv4 Addresses* and Team Cmyru (*http://www.cymru.com/ gillsr/documents/junos-bgp-template.pdf* and *http://www.cymru.com/gillsr/documents/ junos-martians.txt*)

8.11 Changing Route Preferences to Migrate to Another IGP

Problem

You are migrating the IGP on your network from OSPF to IS-IS and you want to do this in a controlled manner.

Solution

After configuring both OSPF and IS-IS on the routers you are migrating, change the route preference on the OSPF routes to be higher than the IS-IS preference:

```
[edit protocols ospf]
aviva@Router3# set preference 175
```

Discussion

While you can change the preference values for all dynamic routing protocols and user-configured routes using the set preference and set external-preference commands when configuring the protocols, it is generally not a good idea. The changes you make affect only the router you are configuring, and the local router will end up with a different idea of relative route preferences than the other routers on the network. Also, changing route preferences could affect which routes become active, which, in turn, would affect which routes are used to forward traffic.

However, one situation where you might want to change route preferences is when migrating IGPs. In this recipe, we are migrating from using OSPF as the IGP to using IS-IS. A preference of 175 for OSPF is greater than that of any IS-IS routes. From Table 8-2, you see that IS-IS internal routes have a preference of either 15 (for Level 1) or 18 (for Level 2), and external routes have a preference of 160 (for Level 1) or 165 (for Level 2).

The command shown in this recipe is actually the last step in an OSPF-to-IS-IS migration strategy. The first step is to configure IS-IS on the same interfaces that are running OSPF (see Recipe 11.1), then verify that IS-IS adjacencies are established on the same interfaces that have OSPF adjacencies:

```
aviva@Router3> show isis adjacency
Interface          System          L State      Hold (secs) SNPA
so-0/2/0.0         R1              2 Up               20
so-0/2/1.0         R2              2 Up               21
so-0/2/2.0         R4              2 Up               19
so-0/2/3.0         R10             2 Up               19

aviva@Router3> show ospf neighbor
  Address          Interface         State       ID            Pri  Dead
10.1.2.1           so-0/2/0.0        Full        10.10.255.1    128  36
10.1.6.1           so-0/2/1.0        Full        10.10.255.2    128  38
10.1.7.2           so-0/2/2.0        Full        10.10.255.4    128  34
10.1.8.2           so-0/2/3.0        Full        10.10.255.10   128  38
```

You then need to ensure that IS-IS calculates the same paths as OSPF. The default IS-IS metrics must be changed so that they give the same relative cost to each path as does OSPF. You can do this by manually assigning appropriate interface metrics or by configuring a reference bandwidth. (See Recipe 11.10 for IS-IS and Recipe 12.11 for OSPF.)

Unlike OSPF, for which the JUNOS software has an automatic costing algorithm based on interface bandwidth, for IS-IS JUNOS software assigns a default metric of 10 to all IS-IS interfaces. If this default is left unchanged, the shortest paths calculated by IS-IS are essentially shortest-hop paths.

With IS-IS enabled and metrics configured correctly, the routing table should have the same number of IS-IS entries as OSPF entries for each destination, and they should point to the same outgoing next hops. That is, if there is one OSPF route to a prefix, there should be one IS-IS route to the same prefix and with the same outgoing interface. If there are two OSPF routes to a prefix, there should be two IS-IS routes, and so on.

```
aviva@Router3> show route
inet.0: 28 destinations, 48 routes (28 active, 0 holddown, 0 hidden)
Restart Complete
+ = Active Route, - = Last Active, * = Both
10.1.1.0/24        *[OSPF/10] 00:16:20, metric 65
                      via so-0/2/0.0
                    > via so-0/2/1.0
                    [IS-IS/18] 00:16:08, metric 126
                      to 10.1.2.1 via so-0/2/0.0
                    > to 10.1.6.1 via so-0/2/1.0
10.1.3.0/24        *[OSPF/10] 00:16:20, metric 65
                      via so-0/2/0.0
                    > via so-0/2/2.0
                    [IS-IS/18] 00:16:08, metric 126
                    > to 10.1.2.1 via so-0/2/0.0
                      to 10.1.7.2 via so-0/2/2.0
...
```

The output shows that for each destination prefix, OSPF and IS-IS have the same number of routes and the same outgoing interfaces. The preferred route for each prefix (marked with an *) is the OSPF route. If there are equal-cost paths, the next hop chosen by OSPF (>) is not always the same as that chosen by IS-IS. This will not cause routing problems as long as the equal-cost paths are consistent between the protocols.

At this point, you change the route preference using the set protocols ospf preference command shown in this recipe. Here, you increase the OSPF preference to a value higher than any of the IS-IS preferences because OSPF is the protocol that you are migrating away from. You could instead change the IS-IS route preference so that its routes are more preferred than OSPF. However, leaving the IS-IS preference at its default value simplifies any future addition of routers to the network. Another alternative at this point would be to delete OSPF from the configuration altogether. However, you should leave it in for a short period of time to test the migration. If there are any problems and you need to back out of the migration, all you need to do is return to the default OSPF preference value:

```
[edit protocols ospf]
aviva@Router3# delete preference
aviva@Router3# commit
```

To verify the preference change, look at the routing table to check that IS-IS is the preferred protocol for all the routes:

```
aviva@Router3> show route
inet.0: 28 destinations, 48 routes (28 active, 0 holddown, 0 hidden)
Restart Complete
+ = Active Route, - = Last Active, * = Both
10.1.1.0/24        *[IS-IS/18] 00:32:24, metric 126
                     to 10.1.2.1 via so-0/2/0.0
                   > to 10.1.6.1 via so-0/2/1.0
                   [OSPF/175] 00:01:48, metric 65
                     via so-0/2/0.0
                   > via so-0/2/1.0
10.1.3.0/24        *[IS-IS/18] 00:32:24, metric 126
                   > to 10.1.2.1 via so-0/2/0.0
                     to 10.1.7.2 via so-0/2/2.0
                   [OSPF/175] 00:01:48, metric 65
                   > via so-0/2/0.0
                     via so-0/2/2.0
```

When you are sure that IS-IS is working properly, remove the OSPF configuration from the router:

```
[edit protocols]
aviva@Router3# delete ospf
aviva@Router3# commit
```

See Also

Recipes 11.1, 11.10, 12.1, and 12.11

8.12 Configuring Routing Protocols to Restart Without Losing Adjacencies

Problem

You want to control when routers calculate new paths so that temporary routing-protocol failures don't cause unnecessary recalculations.

Solution

Enable graceful restart for all routing protocols on the router:

```
[edit routing-options]
aviva@RouterG# set graceful-restart
```

Discussion

From time to time, something happens to interrupt the operation of the routing protocols. The interruption might be a planned reinstallation of the routing software to fix a problem. The interruption might also be unplanned because a routing protocol stops running or a network link goes down but is something you might be able to respond to and repair quickly. When this happens, the routing protocols stop sending keepalive messages to their neighbors. After a short while (the actual time depends on the protocol and how it's configured), the neighbor will declare that the local router is down and, because the network topology has changed, will start calculating new paths to network destinations. This recalculation floods a lot of protocol traffic, which can disrupt the operation of the network. If you know that the downtime for the routing protocols will generally be brief, you really don't want the routing protocols to recalculate paths, only to recalculate them again once the routing protocols are back up.

Graceful restart is a way to hide the fact that a routing protocol has restarted and thus prevent path recalculations. With graceful restart, if the router or routing protocol has to restart, it informs its adjacent neighbors and requests a grace period from them. During this grace period, the neighbor acts as a helper, masking the fact that the local router is down. The restarting router continues to forward traffic during the restart period, and convergence in the network is not disrupted. The restart is not visible to the portion of the network that is not communicating directly with the local router. The neighboring routers are aware of the restart. Also, the restarting router is not removed from the network topology. Because the network's topology is "frozen" during the restart period, you should use graceful restart only when you know that your topology is stable.

You turn on graceful restart globally, as shown in this recipe. You generally leave graceful restart running all the time in case of an unplanned failure. The global configuration applies to all routing protocols, including BGP, IS-IS, OSPF, PIM SM, RIP, and RIPng, and to all MPLS-related protocols, including RSVP, LDP, CCC, and TCC.

Configuring graceful restart is just a request. The JUNOS software honors the request only when the network topology is stable and the neighboring routers cooperate.

Now you see that graceful restart settings are different for the different protocols. For BGP, use the show bgp neighbor command:

```
aviva@RouterG> show bgp neighbor 10.0.0.2
Peer: 10.0.0.2+2098 AS 64555    Local: 10.0.0.1+179 AS 64550
  Type: External    State: Established    Flags: <Sync>
  Last State: OpenConfirm    Last Event: RecvKeepAlive
  Last Error: None
  Options: <Preference HoldTime GracefulRestart PeerAS Refresh>
  Holdtime: 90 Preference: 170
  Number of flaps: 1
  Error: 'Cease' Sent: 0 Recv: 1
  Peer ID: 10.0.0.1        Local ID: 192.168.19.1      Active Holdtime: 90
  Keepalive Interval: 30        Peer index: 0
  Local Interface: fe-1/0/1.0
  NLRI for restart configured on peer: inet-unicast
  NLRI advertised by peer: inet-unicast
  NLRI for this session: inet-unicast
```

```
  Peer supports Refresh capability (2)
  Restart time configured on the peer: 120
  Stale routes from peer are kept for: 300
  Restart time requested by this peer: 120
  NLRI that peer supports restart for: inet-unicast
  NLRI peer can save forwarding state: inet-unicast
  NLRI that peer saved forwarding for: inet-unicast
  NLRI that restart is negotiated for: inet-unicast
  NLRI of received end-of-rib markers: inet-unicast
  NLRI of all end-of-rib markers sent: inet-unicast
  Table inet.0 Bit: 10000
    RIB State: BGP restart is complete
    Send state: in sync
    Active prefixes:             0
    Received prefixes:           0
    Suppressed due to damping:   0
    Advertised prefixes:         0
  Last traffic (seconds): Received 19   Sent 19   Checked 19
  Input messages:  Total 3     Updates 1     Refreshes 0     Octets 97
  Output messages: Total 3     Updates 0     Refreshes 0     Octets 116
```

The Options line shows that graceful restart is enabled. The two Restart time lines and the Stale routes line show the default graceful restart parameters. Here, the router allows a grace period of 120 seconds for a neighboring router to restart and requests a grace period of 120 seconds from its neighbors. The router will continue to advertise stale routes from the down neighbors for 300 seconds. The NLRI lines indicate which routing tables are involved in the graceful restart operation.

For IS-IS, you see the graceful restart settings in the show isis adjacency detail output:

```
aviva@RouterF> show isis adjacency detail
RouterF
  Interface: fe-0/0/1.0, Level: 2, State: Up, Expires in 7 secs
  Priority: 64, Up/Down transitions: 1, Last transition: 00:01:05 ago
  Circuit type: 3, Speaks: IP, IPv6, MAC address: 0:5:85:c4:72:d1
  Topologies: Unicast
  Restart capable: Yes
  LAN id: RouterF.02, IP addresses: 10.0.8.1
```

The Restart capable line indicates that graceful restart is configured.

For OSPF, there is no specific command to see that graceful restart is configured.

For all protocols, there are two commands that show that graceful restart is configured. The first is the show route command:

```
aviva@RouterF> show route
inet.0: 9 destinations, 9 routes (9 active, 0 holddown, 0 hidden)
Restart Complete
+ = Active Route, - = Last Active, * = Both
```

The Restart line at the top of the output shows that graceful restart is enabled.

The second command is show route instance detail:

```
aviva@RouterF> show route instance detail
master:
  Router ID: 192.168.12.1
  Type: forwarding          State: Active
  Restart State: Pending  Path selection timeout: 300
  Tables:
    inet.0                  : 8 routes (8 active, 0 holddown, 0 hidden)
    Restart Complete
    iso.0                   : 1 routes (1 active, 0 holddown, 0 hidden)
    Restart Complete
```

The Restart State: Pending entry tells you that graceful restart is enabled and that the router is ready to perform a graceful restart operation, if necessary. When the router is in the process of restarting, you can see the routing component that is restarting. For IS-IS, here is the restart operation in progress:

```
aviva@RouterF> show route instance detail
master:
  Router ID: 10.0.0.1
  Type: forwarding          State: Active
  Restart State: Pending  Path selection timeout: 300
  Tables:
    inet.0                  : 8 routes (8 active, 0 holddown, 0 hidden)
    Restart Pending: IS-IS
    iso.0                   : 1 routes (1 active, 0 holddown, 0 hidden)
    Restart Pending: IS-IS
```

For OSPF, the output is similar:

```
aviva@RouterF> show route instance detail
master:
  Router ID: 10.0.0.1
  Type: forwarding          State: Active
  Restart State: Pending  Path selection timeout: 300
  Tables:
    inet.0                  : 10 routes (9 active, 1 holddown, 0 hidden)
    Restart Pending: OSPF(TED done)
    iso.0                   : 1 routes (1 active, 0 holddown, 0 hidden)
    Restart Complete
```

When the restart operation completes, the output changes to Restart Complete:

```
aviva@RouterF> show route instance detail
master:
  Router ID: 10.0.0.1
  Type: forwarding          State: Active
  Restart State: Pending  Path selection timeout: 300
  Tables:
    inet.0                  : 8 routes (8 active, 0 holddown, 0 hidden)
    Restart Complete
    iso.0                   : 1 routes (1 active, 0 holddown, 0 hidden)
    Restart Complete
```

This recipe shows how to enable graceful restart for all routing protocols. If you do not want to use it on a particular protocol, disable it for that protocol. Here's how to disable it for IS-IS:

```
[edit protocols isis]
aviva@RouterF# set graceful-restart disable
```

See Also

RFC 3478, *Graceful Restart Mechanism for LDP*; RFC 3623, *Graceful OSPF Restart*; RFC 3847, *Restart signaling for IS-IS*; Internet draft *draft-ietf-idr-restart-10.txt, Graceful Restart Mechanism for BGP* (expires December 2004); Internet draft *draft-ietf-mpls-bgp-mpls-restart-03.txt, Graceful Restart Mechanism for BGP with MPLS* (expires August 2004) at *http://www.ietf.org*

CHAPTER 9
Routing Policy and Firewall Filters

9.0 Introduction

The JUNOS software policy framework provides a mechanism for controlling the flow of traffic into and out of the router. The policy framework has two broad components:

Routing policy
> Controls routing information that routing protocols place into the routing and forwarding tables and advertise based on the routes in the routing table.

Firewall filters
> Control packets passing through a router's interface, either coming into the router or being transmitted out.

The architectural design and configuration of JUNOS routing policy and firewall filters and how you configure them are nearly identical, so we discuss them together in a single chapter. However, because they are so similar, it's sometimes easy to confuse the two. The most important point to remember is that routing policy applies to routing protocols and affects how routes are stored in the routing table and how routes are advertised to peers, while firewall filters affect which packets a router's interfaces accept and send.

The process for configuring policies and filters always has two basic steps:

1. Define the policy or filtering conditions in one part of the configuration ([edit policy-options] for routing policies and [edit firewall] for firewall filters).
2. Apply the conditions by referencing them when configuring either a specific routing protocol or a specific interface.

Separating the specification of policy and firewall conditions from their actual application means that you can set up common policy and firewall conditions that encompass your organization's business, security, and peering policies. You can then apply the same conditions to different peers, customers, or interfaces.

Because the policy and filter conditions are referenced, you don't have to repeat the same information in many places throughout a configuration but can instead modify the conditions in a single place and reuse them as needed. This modularity is useful, especially when you consider that for larger ISPs, the routing policy and firewall filter sections of the JUNOS configuration file make up a very large percentage of the router's configuration, sometimes 50 percent or more.

Defining Policies and Filters

In the JUNOS configuration, routing policies and firewall filters have the same basic structure:

Name

Identifies each policy and filter. You specify and use this name to reference the policy or filter when configuring a routing protocol or interface. You set the name like this:

```
[edit policy-options]
aviva@router1# edit policy-statement add-community
```

```
[edit firewall]
aviva@router1# edit filter incoming-to-me
```

Here, the edit policy-statement command creates a routing policy named add-community, and the edit filter command creates a filter called incoming-to-me.

Term

Groups match conditions with corresponding actions. Policies and filters can have one or more terms, which are evaluated in order. Terms are also identified by name, such as:

```
[edit policy-options filter incoming-to-me]
aviva@router1# edit term allow-snmp-from-nms-systems
```

The edit term command creates a term called allow-snmp-from-nms-system.

Match conditions

For policies, the match conditions apply to routes; for firewall filters, they apply to packets. Match conditions are generally identified by a from clause to indicate information in the received route or packet. Here, the from clause matches UDP packets:

```
[edit policy-options filter incoming-to-me term allow-snmp-from-nms-systems]
aviva@router1# set from protocol udp
```

Match conditions sometimes have a to clause to match information about the route or packet destination.

Action

Specifies what to do when a match occurs. The action is identified by a then clause:

```
[edit policy-options filter incoming-to-me term allow-snmp-from-nms-systems]
aviva@router1# set then accept
```

Here, the action is to accept the packet.

If the route or packet does not match any of the conditions when the end of the policy or filter is reached, a default action is taken.

A routing policy can have several match conditions, with multiple conditions in a single term, with several terms in the same policy, or with several policies chained together. Similarly, a firewall filter can have a number of match conditions. However, you can apply only one firewall filter on an input or output interface. To have a series of match conditions, you define multiple matches in a term or multiple terms in a single filter.

Applying Policies and Filters

After defining a policy or filter, you apply it to a protocol or interface. For a policy, you use import and export statements. An import policy applies when the router is evaluating routes received from a routing protocol before placing them into the routing table. An export policy applies when an active route in the routing table is sent in a routing-protocol advertisement. For a firewall filter, you use filter input and filter output statements for incoming and outgoing traffic on an interface.

9.1   Creating a Simple Routing Policy

Problem

You want to advertise configured static routes to adjacent OSPF neighbors, going beyond the OSPF default of advertising only the routes learned from an OSPF neighbor.

Solution

To modify the route advertisement behavior, create and apply a routing policy. First, create the policy:

```
[edit]
aviva@router1# set policy-options policy-statement send-statics term 1 from protocol
static
aviva@router1# set policy-options policy-statement send-statics term 1 then accept
```

Then, apply it to OSPF:

```
[edit]
aviva@router1# set protocols ospf export send-statics
```

Here's what the policy looks like in the configuration:

```
[edit]
aviva@router1# show
policy-options {
    policy-statement send-statics {
        term 1 {
            from protocol static;
```

```
                then accept;
            }
        }
    }
    protocols {
        ospf {
            export send-statics;
        }
    }
}
```

Discussion

From a structural point of view, this routing policy is very straightforward and illustrates the basic components of how to configure a policy. The JUNOS policy language is similar to standard programming languages or pseudocode, so you can read through the show output in this recipe to get the gist of the policy. If you are not a programmer, you can read the policy language as if it were a paragraph written in an outline format. Looking through the show output in this recipe, you see it creates a policy named send-statics that looks for static routes and accepts them. OSPF applies the policy to routes it advertises to its OSPF neighbors. Rephrased, this recipe allows OSPF to advertise static routes in addition to the default OSPF behavior, which is to advertise routes learned from OSPF.

Before looking at the policy configuration, one question you might ask is why you need to create routing policies at all. What happens if you don't configure any? By default, all routing protocols accept any routes they learn from their protocol neighbors or peers and place them into one of the routing tables (see Table 9-1). This means that without a routing policy, BGP accepts all routes from all its BGP neighbors, IS-IS accepts all routes from all its IS-IS neighbors, OSPF from all its OSPF neighbors, and so on. Routing policy is how you modify this behavior. In most cases, you use routing policy with BGP to enforce peering agreements and your company's administrative policies because they provide explicit control over which routes are installed in the routing table. These routes are eligible to become active routes, which are used for forwarding traffic. Routing policy also provides explicit control over which routes are advertised to the router's neighbors.

Table 9-1. Default routing-policy actions

Protocol	Routing table	Default import action	Default export action
BGP	inet.0	Accept all BGP routes. Do not modify BGP route properties.	Accept and export active BGP routes. Do not modify BGP route properties.
DVMRP	inet.1	Accept all DVMRP routes.	Accept and export active DVMRP routes.
IS-IS	inet.0 and inet6.0	Accept all IS-IS routes. Policy cannot be modified because IS-IS requires that all routers in an area have the same link-state database to maintain a stable, loop-free network.	Reject everything (IS-IS uses LSPs to advertise its routes).

Table 9-1. Default routing-policy actions (continued)

Protocol	Routing table	Default import action	Default export action
LDP	inet.3	Accept all LDP routes.	Accept and export active LDP routes.
MPLS	inet.3	Accept all MPLS routes.	Accept and export active MPLS routes.
OSPF	inet.0	Accept all OSPF routes. Policy cannot be modified because OSPF requires that all routers in an area have the same link-state database to maintain a stable, loop-free network.	Reject everything (OSPF uses LSAs to advertise its routes).
PIM dense mode	inet.1	Accept all PIM DM routes.	Accept and export active PIM DM routes.
PIM sparse mode	inet.1	Accept all PIM SM routes.	Accept and export active PIM SM routes.
RIP	inet.0	Accept all RIP routes learned from RIP neighbors.	Reject everything.
RIPng	inet6.0	Accept all RIPng routes learned from RIPng neighbors.	Reject everything.
Direct and static routes	inet.0	Accept all routes.	Do not export.

What are some reasons to modify the default routing-policy behavior? This recipe illustrates one reason, which is to redistribute routes learned from one protocol (here, static routes) to another protocol (here, OSPF). This type of policy affects which routes the protocol advertises (or exports) from the routing table, so you configure it with a set export command. Another reason is to keep a route out of the routing table so that it can never become the active route. Active routes are placed in the forwarding table and are used to forward traffic. For these types of policy, you use a set import command to control the routes placed into (imported into) the routing table. Another reason specific to BGP is to change the BGP properties associated with a route, such as the AS path and community, and to configure route flap damping. Depending on your purposes, you use the set import or set export commands to apply policies.

For the link-state IGPs (IS-IS and OSPF), you should never modify the default policy behavior for incoming routes (with a set import command). These protocols use link-state databases to keep track of their routes, and the databases on all routers in an area must be identical for the protocol to work properly.

Now let's look at this recipe to understand how the policy is configured. The policy, being a simple one, has only one term, called 1. While you could name the term with a text string that describes what the term does, it is common practice to use a number to name the term, especially in simple policies. The term name is not referenced by other parts of the configuration. It is, however, used in logfiles created when tracing routing-policy operation (see Recipe 9.7), so, for more complex networks and policies, identify each term with a meaningful name so you can identify them in the logfiles.

The first command in the recipe defines the policy match condition. The `from` clause, `from protocol static`, looks for routes from the static protocol—in other words, static routes that are configured on the local router. Routing policies can match various routing information (see Table 9-2).

Table 9-2. Routing-information match conditions used in routing policies

Match term	Match description
area *area-id*	Routes learned from an OSPF area.
as-path *as-path-string*	Routes containing the BGP AS path, which you specify as a regular expression.
community [*names*]	One or more BGP communities.
external [type *metric*]	OSPF external routes.
interface *name* interface *address*	In a `from` clause, routes received on an interface or address. In a `to` clause, routes advertised out of an interface or to an address. Do not use with BGP.
level *level*	In a `from` clause, routes from an IS-IS level. In a `to` clause, routes advertised to an IS-IS level.
local-preference *value*	BGP LOCAL_PREF attribute.
metric *value* metric2 *value*	Routes with the metric value. For BGP, metric is the MED and metric2 is the IGP metric of the BGP next hop.
neighbor *address*	In a `from` clause, routes from a neighbor. In a `to` clause, routes advertised to a neighbor.
origin *value*	BGP ORIGIN attribute.
preference *value*	Preference value.
protocol *name*	Sending protocol (aggregate, bgp, direct, dvmrp, isis, local, ospf, pim-dense, pim-sparse, rip, ripng, or static).
tag *value* tag2 *value*	Tag and tag2 values in OSPF external LSAs.

A single term can match one or several conditions. Here's an example of a term with two conditions:

```
[edit policy-options policy-statement ospf-policy term 1]
aviva@router1# set from area 0.0.0.1
aviva@router1# set from metric 1
```

For a route to match this term, it must match both conditions. OSPF must have learned it from area 0.0.0.1, and it must have a metric value of 1. This operation is similar to a logical AND operation.

The second command in the recipe specifies the action to take when a match occurs. Here, the action is to accept the packet (set then accept). Table 9-3 lists possible policy actions.

Table 9-3. General actions to take on matching routes

Action term	Description	Additional action taken
accept	Accept the route and propagate it.	Evaluation of the policy statement ends. If the policy has more terms, they are ignored. If the policy is part of a chain of policies, any subsequent policies are ignored.
reject	Reject the route and do not propagate it.	Evaluation of the policy statement ends. If the policy has more terms, they are ignored. If the policy is part of a chain of policies, any subsequent policies are ignored.
next term	Take any actions in the then clause that modify the route properties.	Any accept or reject action is ignored, and evaluation of the policy statement jumps to the next term in the policy.
next policy	Take any actions in the then clause that modify the route properties.	Any accept or reject action is ignored, any subsequent terms in the policy are ignored, and evaluation of the policy statement jumps to the next policy in the chain.

Because the policy in this recipe has one term, if the packet matches all the conditions (similar to a logical AND action), the action is taken. If there are no actions or if a route does not match all the conditions, the default accept or reject action is taken, which for OSPF is to reject the route and not advertise it. If a routing policy has multiple terms, they are evaluated sequentially. As soon as the route matches a term, the action in that term is taken and policy evaluation completes. If the route does not match any of the terms, the default action for that protocol is taken.

The then clause can include additional actions that modify the route properties. These are discussed in Recipe 9.2.

The third command in the recipe, set export send-statics, applies the policy to OSPF, referencing it by name. The set export command affects routes that OSPF advertises to its peers. By default, OSPF advertises only routes learned from other OSPF routers. This policy configures OSPF to also advertise any static routes configured on the local router.

Use the show policy command to see which policies are configured:

```
aviva@router1> show policy
Configured policies:
send-statics
```

For just one policy, the output is not very interesting. However, if the configuration contains a number of routing policies, this command is a good way to get a quick list of the policies.

Because all routing policies are in a common place in the configuration (in the [edit policy-options] hierarchy), you can refer to them more than once when configuring a routing protocol. For example, you can use the policy in this recipe to redistribute static routes into an EBGP group. Because the policy is already defined, you need to just reference the EBGP group:

```
[edit]
aviva@router1# set protocols bgp group external group export send-statics
```

It's worthwhile to take a moment to comment on the style you use to type configuration statements for routing policies (and also for firewall filters). In this recipe, you are at the [edit] configuration hierarchy level, which is the very top level of the hierarchy, so you have to type the full hierarchy to the statement as well as the statement itself. This recipe has a fairly deep hierarchy level, as do most policy and firewall configurations, so the method shown here involves a lot of typing:

```
[edit]
aviva@router1# set policy-options policy-statement send-statics term 1 from protocol
static
aviva@router1# set policy-options policy-statement send-statics term 1 then accept
```

You may find it a better practice to move to that hierarchy level, both so you have less typing to do and so you have a better sense of where you are in the configuration. For this recipe, you could type most of the configuration commands from the [edit policy-options policy-statement send-statics term 1] hierarchy level:

```
[edit]
aviva@router1# edit policy-options policy-statement send-statics term 1
[edit policy-options policy-statement send-statics term 1]
aviva@router1# set from protocol static
aviva@router1# set then accept
```

Another configuration shortcut to minimize typing is to use the keystroke sequences listed in Table 1-1. Ctrl-p (or sometimes the up arrow on the keyboard) displays the previous CLI command:

```
[edit]
aviva@router1# set policy-options policy-statement send-statics term 1 from protocol
static
aviva@router1# Ctrl-p
[edit]
aviva@router1# set policy-options policy-statement send-statics term 1 from protocol
static
```

Then delete from protocol static and type **then accept**. To delete the previous statements, use the Backspace key or the sequence Ctrl-b to move back one character or Esc-b to move back one word, along with Ctrl-k to delete all characters from the cursor to the end of the line:

```
[edit]
aviva@router1# set policy-options policy-statement send-statics term 1 backspace to here
aviva@router1# set policy-options policy-statement send-statics term 1 then accept
```

See Also

Recipes 9.2 and 9.7

9.2   Changing a Route's Routing Information

Problem

You want to enforce your company's BGP peering relationships and control the traffic you receive from BGP peers by modifying the BGP LOCAL_PREF attribute and associating a community with certain BGP routes.

Solution

Another function of routing policy is to modify the routing information associated with BGP routes. First, match the routes to be affected:

```
[edit policy-options policy-statement from-my-customers term 1]
aviva@router1# set from neighbor 10.0.31.2/32
```

Use the then clause to modify the route's routing information:

```
[edit policy-options policy-statement from-my-customers term 1]
aviva@router1# set then local-preference 300
aviva@router1# set then community set 65500:12345
aviva@router1# set then accept
```

Finally, apply the policy to a BGP group:

```
[edit protocols bgp]
aviva@router1# set group external-group import from-my-customers
```

Discussion

For BGP routes, routing policy allows you to modify the BGP routing information associated with each route, including the BGP local preference, community, and origin attributes, and the AS paths in each route. You typically do this to manage customer traffic and peering arrangements with other ISPs. Table 9-4 lists the actions you can include in a policy to change a route's routing information. Most of these actions are specific to BGP.

Table 9-4. Actions that change routing information in matching routes

Action term	Description
as-path-prepend *path*	Add AS numbers to the beginning of the BGP AS path.
as-path-expand last-as count *number*	Add the last AS number to the BGP AS path the specified number of times before adding the local AS number.
community +*names* community add *names*	Add BGP community names.
community -*names* community delete *names*	Delete BGP community names.
community =*names* community set *names*	Set the specific BGP community name.
damping *name*	Configure BGP route flap damping.

Table 9-4. Actions that change routing information in matching routes (continued)

Action term	Description
external type *metric*	External metric for exported OSPF routes.
local-preference *value*	Set the value of the BGP LOCAL_PREF attribute.
local-preference add *number* local-preference subtract *number*	Increment or decrement the BGP LOCAL_PREF value.
metric *value* metric2 *value*	Set the metric value. For BGP, metric is MED and metric2 is the IGP metric of the BGP next hop.
metric igp *value* metric minimum-igp *value*	Change the MED by the specified value for EBGP routes being exported.
origin *value*	Set the BGP ORIGIN attribute.
preference *value*	Set the preference value.
tag *value* tag2 *value*	Set the tag and tag2 values in OSPF external LSAs.
tag add *number* tag subtract *number* tag2 add *number* tag2 subtract *number*	Increment or decrement the OSPF tag or tag2 value.

This recipe changes two attributes in a BGP route, the local preference and community. The first command in the then clause sets the LOCAL_PREF attribute to 300. The second command changes the community string in the route to 65500:12345. The policy affects all routes received from the BGP neighbor at 10.0.31.2/32 (configured with the set from neighbor command). The last command in the recipe applies the policy to the BGP group external.

9.3 Filtering Routes by IP Address

Problem

You need to reject all routes to certain IP addresses because you don't want to install them into the routing table.

Solution

Create a list of all the IP address prefixes:

```
[edit policy-options]
aviva@router1# set prefix-list PREFIX-LIST-1 10.0.0.1/24
aviva@router1# set prefix-list PREFIX-LIST-1 10.10.0.0/16
aviva@router1# show
prefix-list PREFIX-LIST-1 {
    10.0.0.1/24;
    10.10.0.0/16;
}
```

Then create a policy that references the list of prefixes:

```
[edit policy options policy-statement addresses-to-reject]
aviva@router1# set term 1 from prefix-list PREFIX-LIST-1
aviva@router1# set term 1 then reject
```

Finally, apply the policy to a protocol, here to EBGP:

```
[edit protocols bgp]
aviva@router1# set group external-group import addresses-to-reject
```

Discussion

One of the most common uses of routing policies is to filter routes based on the IP address prefix. You create a *prefix list* and then reference it in the from clause of a routing policy. Instead of looking at the protocol information in routes, the policy examines the route prefix itself. This provides you with fine-grained control for identifying routes that you want to act on. A prefix list is simply a list, so it contains no information about what actions to take. You can create various lists in the [edit policy-options] hierarchy and then reference them as needed in different routing policies and also in firewall filters.

Prefix lists are a great way to reuse IP addresses in a JUNOS configuration. They are handy for keeping lists of all your customers or separate lists of customers to whom you apply the same routing policies. For firewall filters, prefix lists are handy for listing network servers, such as DNS, NTP, and RADIUS or TACACS+ servers, in a single place. They are also handy for keeping a single list of your BGP peers and SNMP systems. Because the lists are defined only once, they help restrict the number of places you have to change, add, or manipulate IP addresses for network management and other tasks. Both routing policies and firewall filters can reference the same prefix lists.

This recipe creates a list of prefixes that are rejected when they are received from EBGP peers. They are prefixes BGP should never install in the routing table or advertise to its peers. As a first step, create a list of prefixes by creating a named prefix list in the [edit policy-options] hierarchy. In this recipe, the prefix list named PREFIX-LIST-1 has two prefixes.

Then define a policy that references the prefix list and specifies the action to take when a match occurs. This recipe creates a policy named addresses-to-reject. The from clause references the prefix list, which consists of the prefixes to match. If the prefix in a received packet exactly matches one of the prefixes, the action in the then clause is taken. This behavior is similar to a logical OR operation and differs from how matching is done for routing information, where all the conditions in the from clause have to match before an action is taken (similar to a logical AND operation). With a prefix list, when the packet's prefix matches one of the listed prefixes, the action in the then clause is taken. When the JUNOS software evaluates a prefix to see if it matches one in the list, it searches through the entire list for the longest prefix (called *longest-match lookup*), so the order of the prefixes in the list does not matter. This is different from how the JUNOS software handles policy evaluation, which is to look at policy terms and chained policies in order, from beginning to end, and perform the action immediately when a match occurs.

The then clause in this recipe has a reject action, which rejects the route. When applying this policy with a set import command, the routes will not be installed into the routing table. When applying it with a set export command, the routes will not be advertised to peer routers. The set import command in this recipe applies the policy to routes received from neighbors in an EBGP peer group, so the routes are not installed in the inet.0 routing table.

9.4   Filtering Long Prefixes

Problem

You do not want to install IP address prefixes longer than 172.18.20.0/19 in the routing table.

Solution

Create a filter that identifies the long prefixes:

```
[edit policy-options policy-statement long-prefixes term 1]
aviva@router1# set from route-filter 172.18.20.0/19 longer
aviva@router1# set then reject
```

Then apply the policy to an EBGP group:

```
[edit protocols bgp]
aviva@router1# set group external-group import long-prefixes
```

Discussion

A second way to filter routes based on their IP address prefixes is to create a *route list*. Unlike prefix lists, route lists are embedded in the routing policy, not maintained in a separate list, so it can be somewhat harder to maintain them because the same prefixes may be used in different policies. This recipe creates a simple policy that an EBGP group uses to reject all incoming prefixes longer than 172.18.20.0/19. This policy keeps longer prefixes out of the routing table and is somewhat similar to aggregating routes.

In the recipe, the set from route-filter command defines the prefix (172.18.20.0/19) and how to match it (longer). The set then command is a simple action clause to reject matching prefixes. We apply the policy with a set import command to an EBGP group to prevent BGP from installing the long prefixes into the routing table.

Route lists have two advantages over prefix lists. The first is that route lists match prefix ranges instead of the exact matching performed by prefix lists. This recipe uses the longer option to match all prefixes longer than 172.18.20.0/19—for example, 172.18.20.0/24. A variation of this uses the orlonger keyword instead of the longer keyword to match the specified prefix and all longer prefixes:

```
[edit policy-options policy-statement long-prefixes term 1]
aviva@router1# set route-filter 172.18.20.0/19 orlonger
```

The difference between this command and the one in the recipe is that this command will match 172.18.20.0/19, while the set from route-filter 172.18.20.0/19 longer command will not.

There are two other ways to specify address ranges. The upto keyword is, in some sense, the opposite of the longer and orlonger keywords, looking at the high-order bits of the IP address instead of the low-order bits:

```
[edit policy-options policy-statement prefixes-to-exclude term 1]
aviva@router1# set route-filter 0.0.0.0/0 upto /7
```

The following command matches prefixes 0.0.0.0/0, 0.0.0.0/1, and so on, up to 0.0.0.0/7. The final keyword is prefix-length-range:

```
[edit policy-options policy-statement prefixes-to-exclude term 1]
aviva@router1# set route-filter 0.0.0.0/0 prefix-length-range /25-/30
```

The following command matches IP prefixes in the range 0.0.0.0/25, 0.0.0.0/26, 0.0.0.0/27, 0.0.0.0/28, 0.0.0.0/29, and 0.0.0.0/30 only.

Route lists can also match exactly one prefix, just as prefix lists can:

```
[edit policy-options policy-statement long-prefixes term 1]
aviva@router1# set route-filter 172.18.20.0/24 exact
```

A second advantage of route lists over prefix lists is that each prefix can include an action. When a match occurs, the action is taken immediately instead of waiting to reach the then clause. (The action can be any of those listed in Table 9-3.) When the list of prefixes is long, this speeds up the processing of routing traffic. The following simple policy illustrates how this works:

```
[edit policy-options policy-statement prefix-policy term 1]
aviva@router1# set from route-filter 0.0.0.0/0 upto /7 accept
aviva@router1# set from route-filter 0.0.0.0/0 or longer
aviva@router1# set then reject
```

This policy accepts prefixes up to /7 and rejects everything longer.

You can also use route lists as another way to manipulate the routing information in a route. Instead of screening routes by protocol or by other routing information they contain, you filter by destination prefix:

```
[edit policy-statement set-metric-igp]
aviva@router1# set term 1 from route-filter 10.12.0.0/16 exact
aviva@router1# set term 1 from route-filter 172.64.0.0/16 exact
aviva@router1# set term 1 from route-filter 192.168.0.0/24 exact
aviva@router1# set term 1 then local-preference 300
aviva@router1# set term 1 then accept
```

```
aviva@router1# set term 2 then reject
aviva@router1# show
policy-statement set-metric-igp {
    term 1 {
        from {
            route-filter 10.12.0.0/16 exact;
            route-filter 172.64.0.0/16 exact;
            route-filter 192.168.0.0/24 exact;
        }
        then {
            preference 300;
            accept;
        }
    }
    term 2 {
        then reject;
    }
}
```

This configuration sets the BGP local preference value on three specific prefixes and rejects any other prefixes.

9.5   Filtering Unallocated Prefix Blocks

Problem

You do not want to accept prefixes from address spaces that have not yet been allocated by IANA.

Solution

Define a policy that rejects routes from unallocated address space:

```
[edit policy-options policy-statement no-bogons term 1]
aviva@router1# set route-filter 1.0.0.0/8 orlonger reject
aviva@router1# set route-filter 2.0.0.0/8 orlonger reject
aviva@router1# set route-filter 5.0.0.0/8 orlonger reject
aviva@router1# set route-filter 7.0.0.0/8 orlonger reject
aviva@router1# set route-filter 23.0.0.0/8 orlonger reject
...
```

Then apply the policy to a BGP group:

```
[edit protocols bgp]
aviva@router1# set group external-group import no-bogons
```

Discussion

Bogons are prefixes in the IP address space that have not been allocated by IANA or that have been allocated but are marked as being reserved. About 40 percent of the total possible IPv4 address space is bogon. One subset of addresses that are reserved, and thus bogon, are the RFC 1918 private IPv4 addresses 10.0.0.0/8, 172.16.0.0/12, and `192.168.0.0/16`. *Malware*, which is malicious software designed to damage or disrupt network equipment, often targets random IP addresses and chooses bogon prefixes to launch or propagate network attacks. Because of this, and because you should never receive legitimate traffic from unallocated prefixes, it is good preventive security practice to put in place routing policies that reject bogon routes so that they are never added to the routing table.

This recipe shows a snippet of a routing policy that uses route lists to identify each unallocated bogon prefix. Each `set route-filter` command includes a `reject` action to quickly and immediately reject any matching incoming prefix. The recipe applies this policy to an EBGP group with an `import` command so that the policy is evaluated when incoming routes are received by the EBGP group.

The bogon filter in this example uses routing policy. Another way to filter them is with firewall filters (see Recipe 9.8), providing bogon filters on the network's ingress and egress interfaces. Firewall filters let you log and syslog traffic (see Recipe 9.13) and maintain SNMP counters about traffic that comes from bogon space (see Recipe 9.12), giving you data to graph network attacks that come from bogon space, which is a very common occurrence, and helping you be more aware of what's happening on your network. With a firewall filter, you can do bogon filtering by referring to bogon prefixes in prefix lists and then counting and discarding any matches.

Over time, the list of bogons changes, mostly because IANA allocates IP prefixes and less often because of changes to reserved addresses. If a configuration includes a policy to filter bogons, you must update it to keep it in sync with current address allocations. Every time a bogon is allocated, many people, including big ISPs, forget to update their filters for some reason or another and they often need specific reminders sent directly to them. If you do not actively monitor for bogon changes on a regular basis, you will be blocking future allocations from functioning properly. One way to update the bogon list automatically is to peer with Team Cymru, which maintains a current list of JUNOS bogon route lists, as well as a list of reserved prefixes. See *http://www.cymru.com/BGP/bogon-rs.html* for information about the BGP bogon project.

One caveat in using the Team Cymru bogon lists is that you should examine the prefixes to make sure they are not blocking traffic that you want to receive. For example, one of the bogon lists, *http://www.cymru.com/Documents/bogon-bn-agg.txt*, contains `224.0.0.0/3` as an entry. If you do not specify that your firewall terms are for unicast IPv4 traffic only, using this prefix in a prefix list for a firewall filter will break OSPF, because this is the OSPF multicast address and must be present for OSPF to operate (see Recipe 12.1).

See Also

IANA, *http://www.iana.org/assignments/ipv4-address-space*; Team Cymru, *http://www.cymru.com/gillsr/documents/junos-bogon-route-filters.txt* and *http://www.cymru.com/gillsr/documents/junos-reserved-prefix-list.txt*; Recipes 9.8, 9.12, 9.13, and 12.1

9.6   Creating a Chain of Routing Policies

Problem

You need to perform a series of actions on routes.

Solution

The JUNOS routing-policy language has several different ways of chaining policies together. One way is to list more than one policy in the import or export command:

```
[edit protocols bgp group external-group]
aviva@router1# set export [ block-private remove-communities send-statics ]
```

A second way is to configure policy evaluation so that it explicitly jumps to the next policy when a match occurs:

```
[edit policy-options policy-statement from-my-customers term 1]
aviva@router1# set then local-preference 300
aviva@router1# set then community set 65500:12345
aviva@router1# set then next policy
```

Discussion

Larger networks typically require a number of routing policies to handle an ISP's peer and customer relationship or to handle different organizations within a large enterprise network. You have to make the design decision about whether to create longer policies with many terms or whether to create a number of smaller policies and chain them together. Because policy language is so critical to the operation of your network and your business, and because policy language can get complex quickly and might have unexpected results, it is good practice to design policies to be as straightforward as possible.

This recipe illustrates two ways of creating a number of smaller policies and chaining them together. The first command, set export, chains together three policies that have been configured in the [edit policy-options] hierarchy when configuring a BGP group. The JUNOS policy language evaluates the three policies in order. If a route does not match the conditions in block-private, evaluation continues with the remove-communities policy. If a route does not match the conditions in remove-communities, the policy language looks at the send-statics policy. When a route does match the conditions in one of the policies, the action is taken immediately. If a route matches none of the policies, no action is taken.

Let's take a look at the three routing policies to see how they are evaluated when chained together:

```
[edit]
aviva@router1> show configuration policy-options
policy-statement block-private {
    term 1 {
        from {
            route-filter 0.0.0.0/0 upto /7;
            route-filter 0.0.0.0/0 prefix-length-range /25-/32;
            route-filter 10.0.0.0/8 orlonger;
            route-filter 127.0.0.0/8 orlonger;
            route-filter 172.16.0.0/12 orlonger;
            route-filter 192.168.0.0/16 orlonger;
            route-filter 224.0.0.0/4 orlonger;
        }
        then reject;
        }
    }
}
policy-statement remove-communities {
    term 1 {
        then {
            community delete all-communities;
        }
    }
}
policy-statement send-statics {
    term 1 {
        from protocol [ static direct ];
        then accept;
    }
}
community all-communities members *:*;
```

For routes being exported by the BGP group external-group, the policy evaluation first checks against the prefix ranges listed in the block-private policy, which keeps private addresses from being advertised to external ASs. Routes matching any one of the prefixes are rejected, and policy evaluation stops. Otherwise, routes are checked against the remove-communities policy. This policy has no match conditions, so all routes match and all community strings are removed from the route. Because this policy has no action that terminates policy evaluation (accept or reject), the evaluation continues with the next policy in the chain, send-statics, which redistributes static and direct routes to the BGP peers. At this point, if a route does not match any of the three routing policies, the default BGP export action is taken, which is to export only those routes learned from BGP and reject everything else.

You can also design routing policies that are implicitly chained together. If a policy has no flow control action (then accept, then reject, then next term, or then next policy) and has no more terms, policy evaluation automatically continues with the next policy if one is configured. The second two policies, remove-communities and send-statics, illustrate how this works. After the remove-communities policy removes the community string from the route, no action is taken and evaluation automatically continues with the send-statics policy, which has an accept action to terminate policy evaluation.

When chaining policies together in this way, make sure that the last policy in the chain has a terminating action (either then accept or then reject). One trick for ensuring that there's always a terminating action is to create a policy that is nothing more than the action itself and place it at the end of the chain:

```
[edit policy-options policy-statement final-accept]
aviva@router1# set then accept
[edit protocols bgp group external-group]
aviva@router1# set export [ block-private remove-communities send-statics final-
accept ]
```

You would no longer need the set then accept command at the end of the send-statics policy, so the configured policies would look like this:

```
[edit]
aviva@router1> show configuration policy-options
policy-statement remove-communities {
    term 1 {
        then {
            community delete all-communities;
        }
    }
}
policy-statement send-statics {
    term 1 {
        from protocol [ static direct ];
    }
}
policy-statement final-accept {
    term 1 {
        then accept;
    }
}
community all-communities members *:*;
```

The second configuration in this recipe chains policies using the next policy action in a then clause. This forces policy evaluation to continue with the next policy after a match occurs. The next policy action is optional because it is the default action that the policy evaluation takes when a match occurs; when you do not include an accept, reject, or next term action; and when there are no more terms in the routing policy. However, using it can speed up policy evaluation when a policy contains several terms and the import or export command references a number of policies.

It is also possible to explicitly jump to the next term in a policy when a match occurs:

```
[edit policy-options policy-statement from-my-customers]
aviva@router1# set term 1 from protocol direct
aviva@router1# set term 1 then local-preference 300
aviva@router1# set term 1 then community set 65500:12345
```

```
aviva@router1# set term 1 then next term
aviva@router1# set term 2 from protocol static
aviva@router1# set term 2 then local-preference 300
aviva@router1# set term 2 then community set 65500:10300
aviva@router1# set term 2 then next term
aviva@router1# set final-term then reject
```

Once again, explicitly configuring this action is optional because it is the default when a match occurs and you haven't specified an accept, reject, or next term action.

9.7   Making Sure a Routing Policy Is Functioning Properly

Problem

You want to ensure that a configured policy is working as intended by logging its actions.

Solution

There are two steps to setting up tracing to see how a configured routing policy is being applied to routes. First, include a trace action in the policy's then clause:

```
[edit policy-options policy-statement outbound-policy term 1]
aviva@Router3# set then trace
```

Then, set up a tracing file for capturing the output:

```
[edit routing-options]
aviva@Router3# set traceoptions file policy-trace-log size 10m files 10
aviva@Router3# set traceoptions flag policy
```

Discussion

When checking whether a routing policy is working, the first and easiest step is to check the entries in the routing table. Use the show route command on the local router to verify the effects of an imported routing policy and use the command on the neighboring router to check the effect of an export policy (see Recipe 8.1). This command shows the real-time effect of the configured routing policies. If, in examining the routing tables, you find routes you don't expect or that routes are missing, use the JUNOS tracing function to keep a log of which routes a policy has analyzed and taken action on. This is a common way to debug problems that appear to be caused by a routing policy not being applied or not being applied properly.

This recipe shows how to set up policy tracing. The set then trace command adds a tracing action to the policy. This command is part of a larger policy that is being used to verify that the router is matching prefixes on its outbound EBGP links. This policy is already in place on the router, and the trace action is added to help with debugging:

```
[edit policy-options policy-statement outbound-policy term peer-routes]
aviva@Router3# show
from {
    route-filter 192.168.0.0/16 exact;
    route-filter 192.168.72.0/21 exact;
    route-filter 192.168.194.0/21 orlonger;
    route-filter 192.168.157.0/24 exact;
    route-filter 192.168.228.0/24 exact;
    }
then {
    as-path-prepend "65520 65520";
    trace;
    accept;
}
```

The set traceoptions command configures a logging file to receive the policy-tracing information. Because routing policy is handled by RPD, you set up a general routing-protocol trace file in the [edit routing-options] hierarchy, not in the [edit policy-options] hierarchy. This recipe creates a 10 MB file named *policy-trace-log*. The flag policy is necessary to trace the routing-policy operations. You can also use the all flag, which traces all RPD-related operations, but this can quickly fill the logfile with many messages not related to policy.

The logfile shows the routes that the policy is evaluating:

```
aviva@Router3> show log policy-trace-log
Sep  2 20:13:10 trace_on: Tracing to "/var/log/policy-trace-log" started
Sep  2 20:13:10 export: Dest 172.16.32.0 proto BGP
Sep  2 20:13:10 policy_match_qual_or: Qualifier proto Sense: 0
Sep  2 20:13:10 policy_match_qual_or: Qualifier proto Sense: 0
Sep  2 20:13:10 export: Dest 192.168.0.0 proto BGP
Sep  2 20:13:10 policy_match_qual_or: Qualifier community Sense: 0
Sep  2 20:13:10 policy_match_qual_or: Qualifier community Sense: 0
Sep  2 20:13:10 policy_match_qual_or: Qualifier community Sense: 0
Sep  2 20:13:10 policy_export_trace: Prefix 192.168.0.0/16 term peer-routes -->
accept
```

This output shows an evaluation of two export policies that have been applied to BGP. No routes match the first export policy, but 192.168.0.0/16 matches. The policy_export_trace line shows the policy term that the route matches and the action that was taken (here, accept) as a result of the match.

See Also

Recipe 8.1

9.8 Creating a Simple Firewall Filter that Matches Packet Contents

Problem

The default router interface behavior is to allow connections from anywhere on the network, but you want to restrict access so connections can be made only from known subnetworks.

Solution

Use firewall filters to control which packets an interface allows to enter the router. You know that connections to the router use Telnet or SSH, so create a filter that checks for these packets. First, create the firewall filter:

```
[edit firewall]
aviva@router1# set filter incoming-to-me term restrict-telnet-ssh from protocol tcp
aviva@router1# set filter incoming-to-me term restrict-telnet-ssh from destination-
port [ telnet ssh ]
aviva@router1# set filter incoming-to-me term restrict-telnet-ssh from source-address
10.0.0.0/8
aviva@router1# set filter incoming-to-me term restrict-telnet-ssh then accept
```

Then, apply the filter to the router's interface:

```
[edit interfaces]
aviva@router1# set fe-0/0/0 unit 0 family inet filter input incoming-to-me
```

Here's what the firewall filter looks like in the configuration:

```
[edit]
aviva@router1# show
firewall {
    filter incoming-to-me {
        term restrict-telnet-ssh {
            from {
                protocol tcp;
                destination-port [ telnet ssh ];
                source-address {
                    10.0.0.0/8;
                }
            }
            then accept;
        }
    }
}
interfaces {
    fe-0/0/0 {
        unit 0 {
            family inet {
                filter input incoming-to-me;
```

```
        }
      }
    }
  }
```

Discussion

Placing firewall filters on the router's interfaces is one of the most critical actions you can take to protect the security of the router and the integrity of traffic received and sent by the router. Firewall filters also provide a mechanism for counting different types of packets received or sent over an interface. What happens if you don't configure a firewall filter? By default, interfaces accept all incoming traffic and transmit all outgoing traffic.

Unlike routing policy, which is part of RPD running on the Routing Engine and which looks at routing-protocol traffic, firewall filters look at all traffic on router interfaces, working as part of the PFE.

The firewall filter in this recipe has the same basic structure and components as a routing policy. It uses the same JUNOS policy language, and you can read through the show command output to understand what the firewall filter does.

The configuration creates a filter named incoming-to-me that has one term named restrict-telnet-ssh. This term accepts TCP packets if the IP packet header has a destination port or either Telnet (port 23) or SSH (port 22) and a source address that falls in the subnetwork 10.0.0.0/8. By default, this filter rejects all other packets. This recipe applies the filter to all IPv4 traffic on one of the router's physical interfaces, fe-0/0/0.

It's important to remember that this recipe shows only one term in a longer firewall filter as a way of illustrating how to configure a firewall filter. (Recipe 9.15 shows a complete filter.) If you were to apply only this filter to an interface, you would be able to use the interface only for Telnet and SSH connections from subnet 10.0.0.0/8, and all other incoming traffic would be dropped. Although it's possible that this is what you might want to do, it's not likely that you would want to do exactly this. However, this recipe does illustrate the point that you need to very carefully design and construct firewall files so that they do what you want and what you expect.

Because firewall filters apply to logical interfaces, not physical interfaces, each address family on an interface can have one filter for incoming traffic and one for outgoing traffic. This means you can have different filters for different logical interfaces. For this recipe, it also means that if this is the only interface on which you restrict SSH and Telnet access, using them to access the router through any other interfaces is unrestricted. This might be exactly the action you want. However, if your intent is to restrict SSH and Telnet access for all interfaces on the router, you must apply this firewall filter to all the router's interfaces. Again, you have a design choice to make here. You can certainly apply the filter to all the interfaces—or to any number of interfaces. Another option in this case is to associate this filter with the router's loopback interface, lo0, which filters traffic going to the Routing Engine:

```
[edit interfaces]
aviva@router1# set lo0 unit 0 family inet filter input incoming-to-me
```

Because SSH requests are handled by the Routing Engine, instead of applying the filter to many or all of the router's physical interfaces, you can effect the same filtering by setting it on the loopback interface.

As defined, this filter works only on IPv4 traffic, because you configure it at the [edit firewall] level. To have it work for IPv6 traffic, you need to configure the filter at the [edit firewall family inet6] hierarchy:

```
[edit firewall family inet6]
aviva@router1# set filter incoming-to-me term restrict-telnet-ssh from protocol tcp
...
```

Then apply the filter to IPv6 traffic when configuring the interface's IPv6 address family:

```
[edit]
aviva@router1# set interfaces fe-0/0/0 unit 0 family inet6 filter input incoming-to-me
```

If your router has filters for both IPv4 and IPv6 traffic, you should define the IPv4 firewall filters at the [edit firewall family inet] hierarchy so it will be clear to someone reading through the configuration which filters apply to IPv4 and which apply to IPv6:

```
[edit firewall family inet]
aviva@router1# set filter ipv4-incoming-to-me term restrict-telnet-ssh from protocol tcp
[edit firewall family inet6]
aviva@router1# set filter ipv6-incoming-to-me term restrict-telnet-ssh from protocol tcp
```

The first three commands in the recipe, which form the from clause, set the filter's match conditions, defining which fields in the packet headers to examine. Firewall filters can match various fields in the headers (see Table 9-5).

Table 9-5. Header match conditions used in firewall filters

Match term	Match description
Address matches	
address *prefix*	IP address in the source or destination field.
destination-address *prefix*	IP address in the destination field.
source-address *prefix*	IP address in the source field.
destination-prefix-list *prefix-list*	IP destination address of one of the prefixes in the prefix list.

Table 9-5. Header match conditions used in firewall filters (continued)

Match term	Match description
`source-prefix-list` `prefix-list`	IP source address of one of the prefixes in the prefix list.
`prefix-list` *prefix-list*	IP source or destination address of one of the prefixes in the prefix list.
Port matches	
`destination-port` *number* `destination-port` *name*	TCP or UDP destination port field, specified as a number or name. Use with the `protocol` match condition to determine the protocol being used on a port.
	Port names and numbers: afs, bgp, biff (512), bootpc (68), bootps (67), cmd (514), cvspserver (2401), dhcp (67), domain (53), eklogin (2105), ekshell (2106), exec (512), finger (79), ftp (21), ftp-data (20), http (80), https (443), ident, imap, kerberos-sec (88), klogin (543), kpasswd (761), krb-prop (754), krbupdate (760), kshell (544), ldap (389), login (513), mobileip-agent (434), mobilip-mn (435), msdp (639), netbios-dgm, netbios-ns, netbios-ssn, nfsd (2049), nntp, ntalk (518), ntp pop3, pptp, printer (515), radacct, radius, rip (520), rkinit (2108), smtp (25), snmp, snmptrap, snpp (444), socks, ssh (22), sunrpc, syslog (514), tacacs-ds (65), talk (517), telnet(23), tftp (69), timed (525), who (513), xdmcp, zephyr-clt (2103), zephyr-hm (2104)
`source-port` *number* `source-port` *name*	TCP or UDP source port field, specified as a number or name. Use with the `protocol` match condition to determine the protocol being used on a port.
	Port names and numbers same as those listed for `destination-port`.
Protocol and packet matches	
`icmp-type` *number* `icmp-type` *name*	ICMP packet type field, specified as a number or name. Use with the `protocol` match condition to determine the protocol being used on a port.
	Type names and numbers: echo-reply (0), echo-request (8), info-reply, info-request, mask-request, mask-reply, parameter-problem, redirect (5), router-advertisement (9), router-solicit, source-quench (4), time-exceeded, timestamp, timestamp-reply, unreachable (3)
`packet-length` *bytes*	Length of the IP portion of the packet, including the header but excluding Layer 2 encapsulation overhead.
`protocol` *number* `protocol` *name*	IP protocol field, specified as a number or name.
	Names and numbers: ah, egp (8), esp (50), gre (47), icmp, igmp (2), ipip (4), ipv6 (41), ospf (89), pim, rsvp (46), tcp (6), udp
Packet field matches	
`fragment-flags` *number*	IP fragmentation flag field, specified as a number or name.
	Flag names and numbers: dont-fragment (0x4000), more-fragments (0x2000), reserved (0x8000)
`fragment-offset` *number*	Fragment offset from the beginning of the original packet, in 8-byte units. Use to identify all fragmented packets. The More Fragments (MF) flag is set for all fragmented packets except the last. To identify fragments, set `fragment offset != 0` (or more-fragments=1).
`ip-options` *number*	IP option field, specified as a number or name.
	Option names and numbers: loose-source-route, record-route (7), router-alert, strict-source-route, timestamp (68)

Table 9-5. Header match conditions used in firewall filters (continued)

Match term	Match description
tcp-flags *number*	TCP flag field, specified as a number or name. Use with the protocol match condition to determine the protocol being used on a port.
	Flag names and numbers: ack (0x10), fin (0x01), push (0x08), rst (0x04), syn (0x02), urgent (0x20)
first-fragment	First fragment of a fragmented packet.
is-fragment	Packet fragment other than the first one.
tcp-established	TCP packets other than the first one in a connection (equivalent to "(ack | rst)"). Use with protocol tcp to match TCP packets.
tcp-initial	First packet of a TCP connection (equivalent to "(syn & !ack)"). Use with protocol tcp to match TCP packets.
Packet field operators	
& or +	Logical AND
| or ,	Logical OR
!	Negation
( )	Grouping

The fourth command in the recipe is the then clause, which specifies the action to take when a route matches the condition (or conditions) in the from clause, which is to accept the packet (then accept). Table 9-6 lists the actions you can use in a firewall filter.

Table 9-6. Actions to take on matching packets

Action term	Description
accept	Accept the packet and send it to its destination. This is the default action.
reject	Do not accept the packet and send an ICMP unreachable message. Rejected packets can be logged.
discard	Discard a packet silently, without sending an ICMP unreachable message. Discarded packets can be counted but not logged.
next term	Evaluate the next term in the filter.
counter *name*	Count the packet, keeping track of the count in the named counter.
log	Log the packet's header.
policer *name*	Rate-limit traffic on an interface.
syslog	Keep a record of the packet in a system logfile.

As with routing policy, the JUNOS software evaluates a firewall filter term by term, and, when a term matches, the action is taken and evaluation ends. If the packet matches none of the terms, the default action is to discard the packet, which is equivalent to the following:

```
aviva@RouterF# set term last-term then discard
```

The default firewall action, to discard packets, is the opposite of the default policy action of accepting routes. You would not be alone in thinking that this behavior is counterintuitive. However, understanding this behavior is critical in designing filters and tracing problems if the router stops receiving certain types of traffic. Be especially careful when implementing filters that limit access to the router to ensure that you don't lock yourself out of the router. A common mistake is to block Telnet access to the router. One way to protect against lockout is to use the commit confirmed command.

The default time to revert to the previous configuration is 10 minutes. Choose a rollback time of one minute to minimize how long you have to wait to reconnect to the router if you lock yourself out:

```
[edit firewall]
aviva@RouterF# commit confirmed 1
commit confirmed will be automatically rolled back in 1 minutes unless confirmed
commit complete
```

When using the commit confirmed command, especially with firewall filters, another good practice is to include a comment, which is saved to the router's commit logfile:

```
[edit firewall]
aviva@RouterF# commit confirmed 1 comment "added filter to discard remaining packets"
commit confirmed will be automatically rolled back in 1 minutes unless confirmed
commit complete
```

Use the show system commit command to see the comments:

```
aviva@RouterF> show system commit
0   2005-11-07 20:31:03 UTC by aviva via cli
    added filter to discard remaining packets
1   2005-11-02 23:42:38 UTC by root via cli
2   2005-11-02 23:35:11 UTC by root via cli
```

Adding a comment is a handy way to keep track of reasons for commits if for some reason you lock yourself out of the router.

Another counterintuitive behavior of JUNOS firewalls is that filters do not have a then clause to accept packets that match the from conditions. To verify this, create a one-term filter with no action:

```
[edit firewall]
aviva@RouterF# set filter one-term-filter term bgp-peers from destination-address 10.
0.31.1/24
```

Look in the file /var/etc/filters/dfwc.out to see the actions taken by the term:

```
aviva@RouterF> file show /var/etc/filters/dfwc.out
rule "bgp-peers" matches 3
    match destination-port unreferenced type range
        ranges 1
        179
    match source-address unreferenced type addrmask
        number of address-masks: 1
        10.0.8/24
    match action unreferenced type action
        accept
```

The output shows the filter (or rule) bgp-peers matched and accepted three packets.

See Also

The firewall match conditions and how you specify them are far too numerous to include in this book. For a complete list, see the *JUNOS Policy Framework Configuration Guide* at *http://www.juniper.net/techpubs;* Recipes 1.5, 1.16, and 9.12.

9.9   Creating a Firewall Filter that Negates a Match

Problem

The default router interface behavior is to allow connections from anywhere on the network, but you want to restrict access so connections can be made fom all subnetworks except for a particular one.

Solution

Allow Telnet and SSH connections from all subnetworks except 10.0.0.0/8:

```
[edit firewall filter incoming-to-me]
aviva@router1# set term restrict-telnet-ssh from source-address 10.0.0.0/8 except
aviva@router1# set term restrict-telnet-ssh then accept
```

Then apply the filter to the router's interface:

```
[edit interfaces]
aviva@router1# set fe-0/0/0 unit 0 family inet filter input incoming-to-me
```

Discussion

When you want to be less restrictive with a filter's conditions, instead of defining the address, port, or protocol to match, you can do the inverse and define what not to match. This recipe, which is a variation of Recipe 9.8, adds the except keyword to the from term to allow Telnet and SSH connections from all subnetworks *except* 10.0.0.0/8.

You can use the except keyword to negate all firewall match terms. Sometimes, you use a separate keyword, as shown in this recipe. Other times, the keyword is built into the match condition, as in the following example, which matches packets from all protocols except TCP, counts them so you can determine the rate of this type of traffic, and then accepts the packets:

```
[edit firewall filter incoming-to-me term not-TCP]
aviva@RouterF# set from protocol-except tcp
aviva@RouterF# set then count packets-not-tcp
aviva@RouterF# set then accept
```

The filter looks like this:

```
[edit firewall filter incoming-to-me term not-TCP]
aviva@RouterF# show
from {
```

```
        protocol-except tcp;
    }
    then {
        count packets-not-tcp;
        accept;
    }
```

The best way to determine when to use a separate except keyword or whether there is a built-in keyword is to use the CLI online help:

```
[edit firewall filter incoming-filter term 1]
aviva@router1# set from ?
Possible completions:
> address              Match IP source or destination address
+ ah-spi               Match IPSec AH SPI value
+ ah-spi-except        Do not match IPSec AH SPI value
+ apply-groups         Groups from which to inherit configuration data
+ apply-groups-except  Don't inherit configuration data from these groups
> destination-address  Match IP destination address
+ destination-class    Match destination class
+ destination-class-except  Do not match destination class
+ destination-port     Match TCP/UDP destination port
+ destination-port-except  Do not match TCP/UDP destination port
> destination-prefix-list  Match IP destination prefixes in named list
+ dscp                 Match Differentiated Services (DiffServ) code point
+ dscp-except          Do not match Differentiated Services (DiffServ) code point
+ esp-spi              Match IPSec ESP SPI value
+ esp-spi-except       Do not match IPSec ESP SPI value
  first-fragment       Match if packet is the first fragment
+ forwarding-class     Match forwarding class
+ forwarding-class-except  Do not match forwarding class
  fragment-flags       Match fragment flags
+ fragment-offset      Match fragment offset
+ fragment-offset-except  Do not match fragment offset
+ icmp-code            Match ICMP message code
+ icmp-code-except     Do not match ICMP message code
+ icmp-type            Match ICMP message type
+ icmp-type-except     Do not match ICMP message type
> interface            Match interface name
+ interface-group      Match interface group
+ interface-group-except  Do not match interface group
> interface-set        Match interface in set
+ ip-options           Match IP options
+ ip-options-except    Do not match IP options
  is-fragment          Match if packet is a fragment
+ packet-length        Match packet length
+ packet-length-except  Do not match packet length
+ port                 Match TCP/UDP source or destination port
+ port-except          Do not match TCP/UDP source or destination port
+ precedence           Match IP precedence value
+ precedence-except    Do not match IP precedence value
> prefix-list          Match IP source or destination prefixes in named list
```

```
+ protocol              Match IP protocol type
+ protocol-except       Do not match IP protocol type
> source-address        Match IP source address
+ source-class          Match source class
+ source-class-except   Do not match source class
+ source-port           Match TCP/UDP source port
+ source-port-except    Do not match TCP/UDP source port
> source-prefix-list    Match IP source prefixes in named list
  tcp-established       Match packet of an established TCP connection
  tcp-flags            Match TCP flags
  tcp-initial          Match initial packet of a TCP connection
```

You use the separate keyword with all match conditions that do not have an -except version.

9.10   Reordering Firewall Terms

Problem

You want to change the order of terms in a firewall filter.

Solution

Use the CLI insert command to rearrange the terms in a firewall filter:

```
[edit firewall filter incoming-to-me]
aviva@RouterF# insert term restrict-bgp before term restrict-telnet-ssh
```

Discussion

One difference between routing policies and firewall filters is that while you can apply several routing policies to a routing protocol, chaining them together as necessary, you can apply only one incoming and one outgoing firewall filter to an interface. This means that firewall filters generally contain a large number of terms.

As with routing policies, the order of the terms in a firewall filter is significant. Packets are tested against each term in the order. For performance and packet-handling efficiency, design each filter so the most important or time-critical packets are processed first. When you add a term to an existing filter, it appears at the end:

```
[edit firewall filter incoming-to-me]
aviva@router1# set term restrict-bgp from protocol tcp
aviva@router1# set term restrict-bgp from port bgp
aviva@router1# set term restrict-bgp from source-address 10.0.31.0/24
aviva@router1# set term restrict-bgp then accept
aviva@router1# show
term restrict-telnet-ssh {
    from {
        source-address {
            10.0.0.0/8;
        }
```

```
            protocol tcp;
            destination-port [ telnet ssh ];
        }
        then accept;
    }
    term restrict-bgp {
        from {
            source-address {
                10.0.31.0/24;
            }
            protocol tcp;
            port bgp;
        }
        then accept;
    }
}
```

Use the insert command to rearrange the terms. The command in this recipe moves the restrict-bgp term so that it precedes the restrict-telnet-ssh term. Check that the order is what you expect:

```
[edit firewall filter incoming-to-me]
aviva@RouterF# show
term restrict-bgp {
    from {
        source-address {
            10.0.31.0/24;
        }
        protocol tcp;
        port bgp;
    }
    then accept;
}
term restrict-telnet-ssh {
    from {
        source-address {
            10.0.0.0/8;
        }
        protocol tcp;
        destination-port [ telnet ssh ];
    }
    then accept;
}
```

9.11   Filtering Traffic Transiting the Router

Problem

For traffic transiting through the router, you want to accept packets only from trusted hosts and routers.

Solution

Create a firewall filter for all incoming traffic to the router that will be used on interfaces facing the Internet. The filter contains a number of terms for different types of packets and for specific addresses.

The first term discards unwanted traffic from specific addresses:

```
[edit firewall incoming-to-me]
aviva@RouterF# set term reject-addresses from source-address 172.68.0.0/16
aviva@RouterF# set term reject-addresses from source-address 192.168.0.0/24
aviva@RouterF# set term reject-addresses then discard
```

The second term accepts traffic from BGP peers:

```
[edit firewall filter incoming-to-me]
aviva@RouterF# set term bgp-peers from destination-address 10.0.31.0/24
aviva@RouterF# set term bgp-peers from protocol tcp
aviva@RouterF# set term bgp-peers from port bgp
aviva@RouterF# set term bgp-peers from tcp-established
aviva@RouterF# set term bgp-peers then accept
```

The third term accepts all ICMP traffic:

```
[edit firewall filter incoming-to-me]
aviva@RouterF# set term icmp from protocol icmp
aviva@RouterF# set term icmp then accept
```

The last term accepts all other packets:

```
[edit firewall filter incoming-to-me]
aviva@RouterF# set term final-accept then accept
```

For the filter to take effect, apply it to an Internet-facing interface:

```
[edit interfaces t1-0/0/3]
aviva@RouterF# set unit 0 family inet filter input incoming-to-me
```

Discussion

There are two basic ways to design a firewall filter. One way is to block packets and traffic that the router shouldn't receive and accept everything else, which is how the filter in this recipe operates. This type of filter design is fairly intuitive and, as you can see from this recipe, these filters are reasonably short and fairly easy to configure. One downside to this approach is that if you forget to block a particular type of traffic, you are opening yourself up to security breaches. The second design philosophy, of accepting only desired traffic and blocking everything else, is discussed in Recipe 9.15.

This recipe is for an EBGP edge router that connects to the Internet. The filter is very straightforward, accepting all packets except for traffic coming from a few IP prefixes.

Firewall filter terms are evaluated in order, so place the terms at the beginning of the filter that you want executed first. The first term in this recipe, reject-addresses, looks for packets from two networks that you never want to accept traffic from and immediately discards them, dropping them without sending any notification to the sender. Placing this term at the top of the filter improves the packet-processing efficiency of the interface.

The second term, bgp-peers, accepts BGP traffic only from the specified peer. The conditions in this term look for TCP protocol traffic from the BGP port and match TCP connections that have been established. Again, all BGP traffic is accepted by the final term, so including a separate term for the router's BGP peer just speeds up the processing of traffic from the peer.

The final term, ospf, accepts all OSPF traffic. You might wonder why you need this term when the final term will also accept OSPF traffic. The only reason to do this is that you want OSPF traffic to be handled more quickly than the other remaining traffic. If other operations on your network are time-critical, include them early in the filter. If you are going to apply this filter to a high-speed interface or to traffic flowing at a high rate, you gain efficiency from this type of firewall filter design.

The last term in the filter accepts all other traffic. It is important to note that you must be very cognizant of what you are enabling and what the other protocols are that run on the router when you design firewall filters that, as a last term, accept all other traffic. While this example illustrates a way to design filters that is easy and intuitive, it is generally better practice to explicitly accept what you want and discard everything else. Recipe 9.15 illustrates this firewall filter design approach.

As the last step in the configuration, apply the filter to an interface, here the t1-0/0/3 interface. The set filter input command applies the filter to incoming traffic. To apply a filter to traffic going out of the interface, use the set filter output command.

Here's the entire configuration to show all the contents together:

```
[edit firewall]
aviva@RouterF# show
filter incoming-to-me {
    term reject-addresses {
        from {
            source-address {
                172.68.0.0/16;
                192.168.0.0/24;
            }
        }
        then {
            discard;
        }
    }
    term ospf {
        from {
            protocol ospf;
        }
    }
```

```
                then accept;
        }
        term bgp-peers {
            from {
                destination-address {
                    10.0.31.0/24;
                }
                protocol tcp;
                port bgp;
                tcp-established;
            }
            then accept;
        }
        term final-accept {
            then accept;
        }
    }
}
[edit interfaces]
t1-0/0/3 {
    unit 0 {
        family inet {
            filter {
                input incoming-to-me;
            }
            address 10.0.31.2/24;
        }
    }
}
```

Use the show interfaces command to check that the filter is configured:

```
aviva@RouterF> show interfaces t1-0/0/3.0 detail
  Logical interface t1-0/0/3.0 (Index 70) (SNMP ifIndex 40) (Generation 24)
    Flags: Point-To-Point SNMP-Traps Encapsulation: PPP
    Protocol inet, MTU: 1500, Generation: 31, Route table: 0
      Flags: None
      Filters: Input: incoming-to-me
      Addresses, Flags: Is-Preferred Is-Primary
        Destination: 10.0.31/24, Local: 10.0.31.2, Broadcast: 10.0.31.255,
        Generation: 63
```

Looking at the logical interface, which is where information about the address family is displayed, you can see which firewall filters are applied to the interface.

See Also

Recipe 9.15

9.12 Using a Firewall Filter to Count Traffic on an Interface

Problem

You want to find out how much traffic is passing through an interface.

Solution

To check how much traffic is successfully passing through an interface, add the count option to a then clause that accepts traffic:

```
[edit firewall filter incoming-to-me]
aviva@RouterF# set term final-accept then count incoming-accepted
aviva@RouterF# set term final-accept then accept
```

To track unwanted traffic, use the count option and a then clause that discards traffic:

```
[edit firewall filter incoming-to-me]
aviva@RouterF# set term reject-addresses then count bad-addresses
aviva@RouterF# set term final-accept then discard
```

To look at the counters, use the show firewall filter command:

```
aviva@RouterF> show firewall filter incoming-to-me
Filter: incoming-to-me
Counters:
Name                                      Bytes              Packets
incoming-accepted                           246                    4
```

Discussion

Either as part of your standard network practices or while tracking a problem, you often want to know how much traffic has either successfully passed through an interface or how much traffic attempted but failed to pass through an interface. You do this by counting the packets that match each term in a firewall filter.

The first command in this recipe counts all the traffic accepted by the interface other than the ICMP and BGP traffic. Each counter is identified by name, and this counter is called incoming-accepted.

Use the show firewall filter command to see the counters. The output is very straightforward, showing how many bytes and packets have matched the final-accept term in the filter.

The second command in this recipe shows how to count unwanted traffic. As a general point, you rarely just reject a firewall term without also either counting the rejections or logging or syslogging it (see Recipe 9.13). Tracking the rejections is useful for documenting abuse of your router, attacks on the router, or even misconfigurations.

As with routing policy, you define firewall filters in a common location in the configuration and then apply them where needed. Designing filters that apply to several interfaces in the router can help minimize your administrative overhead. If you do use the same filter on more than one interface, the packet counts from the two interfaces are stored in the same counter. Use the following configuration command to create separate counters for packets from the different interfaces:

```
[edit firewall filter incoming-to-me]
aviva@RouterF# set interface-specific
```

Again, use the show firewall filter command to see the counters:

```
aviva@RouterF> show firewall filter ?
Possible completions:
  counter                Counter name
  incoming-to-me-fe-0/0/1.0-i
  incoming-to-me-t1-0/0/3.0-i
aviva@RouterF> show firewall filter incoming-to-me-t1-0/0/3.0-i
Filter: incoming-to-me-t1-0/0/3.0-i
Counters:
Name                                         Bytes          Packets
incoming-accepted-t1-0/0/3.0-i               6474               105
```

The interface name and –i are appended to the filter name to separate the counters into two different buckets.

9.13 Logging the Traffic on an Interface

Problem

You want to keep a log of the traffic passing through an interface.

Solution

In the then clause, include the log option to capture information about filter activity:

```
[edit firewall filter incoming-to-me]
aviva@RouterF# set term final-accept then log
aviva@RouterF# set term final-accept then accept
```

Use the show firewall log command to display the firewall logs:

```
aviva@RouterF> show firewall log
Log :
Time      Filter   Action Interface      Protocol Src Addr
          Dest Addr
04:59:13  pfe      A      t1-0/0/3.0     TCP      10.0.31.1
          10.0.31.2
04:59:11  pfe      A      t1-0/0/3.0     TCP      10.0.31.1
          10.0.31.2
04:58:43  pfe      A      t1-0/0/3.0     TCP      10.0.31.1
          10.0.31.2
```

```
   04:58:41  pfe      A      t1-0/0/3.0    TCP      10.0.31.1
           10.0.31.2
```

You can also save the activity records to a standard system logfile:

```
[edit firewall filter incoming-to-me]
aviva@RouterF# set term final-accept then syslog
aviva@RouterF# set term final-accept then accept
```

Then configure a system logfile to accept the log messages:

```
[edit system syslog]
aviva@RouterF# set file messages firewall any
```

Discussion

You can log the activity of a term in a firewall filter using the log facility that is built into the firewall filter software itself. Configure this with a set then log command. You can log accepted and rejected packets but not discarded ones. This configuration stores all the activity in real time on the router, not in a file, so use it when you want to actively watch traffic or debug a problem.

The show firewall log command displays the firewall logs. The detail option of this command shows an expanded version of the same information:

```
aviva@RouterF> show firewall log detail
Time of Log: 2005-09-07 05:00:13 UTC, Filter: pfe, Filter action: accept, Name of
interface: t1-0/0/3.0
Name of protocol: TCP, Packet Length: 71, Source address: 10.0.31.1:1390, Destination
address: 10.0.31.2:179
Time of Log: 2005-09-07 05:00:11 UTC, Filter: pfe, Filter action: accept, Name of
interface: t1-0/0/3.0
Name of protocol: TCP, Packet Length: 52, Source address: 10.0.31.1:1390, Destination
address: 10.0.31.2:179
Time of Log: 2005-09-07 04:59:43 UTC, Filter: pfe, Filter action: accept, Name of
interface: t1-0/0/3.0
Name of protocol: TCP, Packet Length: 71, Source address: 10.0.31.1:1390, Destination
address: 10.0.31.2:179
Time of Log: 2005-09-07 04:59:41 UTC, Filter: pfe, Filter action: accept, Name of
interface: t1-0/0/3.0
Name of protocol: TCP, Packet Length: 52, Source address: 10.0.31.1:1390, Destination
address: 10.0.31.2:179
```

In the output, the first field shows when the packet was received. Looking at the times in this output, you see that the firewall log facility places the latest messages at the beginning of the output. This is the opposite of system logfiles, which have the newest entries at the end. The Filter field shows pfe, which means that the packet was handled by the JUNOS PFE. The Action and Filter action fields show the fate of the packet. In this output, all packets were accepted (in the standard output, this shows as an A). Packets can also be Discard (D) or Reject (R).

The next two fields show the interface on which the filter is configured and the protocol type of the packet. The last two fields show the packet's source and destination addresses. In the detail output, the address also includes the port number being used.

You can also save the activity records to a standard system logfile with a set then syslog command. Then configure a system logfile to accept the log messages. This recipe places all firewall logging messages in the *messages* file. The firewall facility captures firewall-related messages. Use the show log command to view the messages:

```
aviva@RouterF> show log messages
Sep  7 04:59:13  RouterF fwdd[2498]: PFE_FW_SYSLOG_IP: FW: t1-0/0/3.0   A  tcp
 172.19.121.114 172.17.28.108  5888 18695 (1 packets)
Sep  7 04:59:13  RouterF last message repeated 5 times
Sep  7 04:59:13  RouterF fwdd[2498]: PFE_FW_SYSLOG_IP: FW: t1-0/0/3.0   A  tcp
 192.168.14.1 192.168.18.1 54532 45824 (1 packets)
```

The fwdd after the router name means that the message was generated by the JUNOS forwarding process (daemon). The message code for firewall logs is PFE_FW_SYSLOG_IP, and the FW: indicates that the message is present in the logs as the result of a firewall configuration. Some of the remaining information in the system log message is similar to what is displayed by the show firewall log command. First is the interface name, followed by an A to report that the packet was accepted, and tcp, which is the type of packet. The two IP addresses are the packet's source and destination addresses, respectively, and the last two numbers are the source and destination ports.

See Also

Recipe 5.1

9.14 Limiting Traffic on an Interface

Problem

You want to throttle traffic to make sure that the Routing Engine and protocol adjacencies won't go down because the router is being overwhelmed by other types of traffic.

Solution

Create a policer to limit the rate of traffic:

```
[edit firewall]
aviva@RouterF# set policer limit-icmp if-exceeding bandwidth-limit 1m
aviva@RouterF# set policer limit-icmp if-exceeding burst-size-limit 50k
aviva@RouterF# set policer limit-icmp then discard
```

Then apply the policer to a filter term:

```
[edit firewall filter incoming-to-me]
aviva@RouterF# set term icmp then policer limit-icmp
```

Discussion

A more secure way to protect an interface is to rate-limit the incoming traffic, especially the nonessential traffic. Rate limiting is an additional mechanism that prioritizes which traffic is more important and which traffic should just be discarded when congestion occurs. It also provides protection against DoS attacks. You set up packet rate limiting by configuring *policers* that define the conditions under which traffic is dropped.

This recipe sets up rate limiting for ICMP traffic. These policers traffic can be dropped if the flow exceeds a set bandwidth or if a burst of packets exceeds a certain size. The first command accepts ICMP traffic flowing at a sustained rate of up to 1 Mbps and drops all packets when this rate is exceeded (if-exceeding bandwidth-limit 1m).

The second command accepts traffic bursts up to 50 Kbps and drops all packets when this rate is exceeded (if-exceeding burst-size-limit 50k). When the flow of ICMP packets exceeds either limit, all ICMP traffic will be discarded until the flow rate subsides. To verify the configuration and see if any traffic has been discarded, use the show firewall filter command:

```
aviva@RouterF> show firewall filter incoming-to-me
Filter: incoming-to-me
Counters:
Name                                    Bytes              Packets
incoming-accepted                        160                  2
Policers:
Name                                    Packets
limit-icmp-icmp                            0
```

The policer counters are shown at the end of the output. The policer name is a concatenation of the policer name (limit-icmp) and the term in which it is used (icmp). At this point, no congestion has occurred, so no packets have been discarded as a result of the policer.

Before configuring a policer, you need to have some idea of what normal traffic loads are on your network and on your router. You generally do this with your network traffic management tools. You can also gather some of this data from the router itself by configuring counters for each term in the firewall filter over a representative period of time, generally several days or weeks. The following command adds a counter to the icmp term:

```
[edit firewall filter incoming-to-me]
aviva@RouterF# set term icmp then count icmp-counter
```

Then use the show firewall filter command to see the statistics:

```
aviva@RouterF> show firewall filter incoming-to-me
Filter: incoming-to-me
Counters:
Name                                    Bytes              Packets
icmp-counter                              0                  0
incoming-accepted                       1680                 25
```

A disadvantage of this method is that you have to log in to each router and no timestamp information is included, but it is a useful way to supplement your other management tools.

If you don't have tools to determine the size and duration of traffic bursts, as a first-order approximation you can select a value by multiplying the interface bandwidth by the burst duration. The maximum value for the burst-size limit is 100 Mbps.

How you select the thresholds at which to start dropping traffic is a function of your business and network design models. Some factors might include how variable the traffic flow is, how critical the traffic is or how damaging an excess of it could be, and how conservative or liberal you want to be about controlling the flow.

You need to define a policer for each type of traffic you want to rate-limit and then reference the policer in the proper term.

9.15   Protecting the Local Routing Engine

Problem

You want to protect the Routing Engine by ensuring that it accepts traffic only from trusted network systems.

Solution

Protecting the Routing Engine involves filtering incoming routing protocol traffic on the router's lo0 interface. The first step is to create the filter:

```
[edit firewall]
aviva@RouterF# edit filter protect-RE
```

This filter contains terms for the different protocols running on the router. The first terms allow the router to accept routing-protocol traffic from BGP peers and OSPF neighbors:

```
[edit firewall filter protect-RE]
aviva@RouterF# edit term bgp-peers
[edit firewall filter protect-RE term bgp-peers]
aviva@RouterF# set from source-address 10.0.8.0/24
aviva@RouterF# set from source-address 10.0.13.0/24
aviva@RouterF# set from destination-port bgp
aviva@RouterF# set then accept
aviva@RouterF# up
[edit firewall filter protect-RE]
aviva@RouterF# edit term ospf-neighbors
[edit firewall filter protect-RE term ospf-neighbors]
aviva@RouterF# set from source-address 10.0.8.0/24
aviva@RouterF# set from source-address 10.0.13.0/24
aviva@RouterF# set from protocol ospf
aviva@RouterF# set then accept
```

The next term allows TCP traffic:

```
[edit firewall filter protect-RE]
aviva@RouterF# edit term tcp-traffic
[edit firewall filter protect-RE term tcp-traffic]
aviva@RouterF# set from source-address 10.0.0.0/8
aviva@RouterF# set from protocol tcp
aviva@RouterF# set then accept
```

The following term allows DNS traffic:

```
[edit firewall filter protect-RE]
aviva@RouterF# edit term dns-servers
[edit firewall filter protect-RE term dns-servers]
aviva@RouterF# set from source-address 10.0.0.0/8
aviva@RouterF# set from protocol udp
aviva@RouterF# set from port domain
aviva@RouterF# set then accept
```

The next two terms allow RADIUS, SSH, and Telnet connections to the router:

```
[edit firewall filter protect-RE]
aviva@RouterF# edit term radius
[edit firewall filter protect-RE term radius]
aviva@RouterF# set from source-address 10.1.0.1/32
aviva@RouterF# set from source-address 10.3.0.1/32
aviva@RouterF# set from source-port radius
aviva@RouterF# set then accept
[edit firewall filter protect-RE term radius]
aviva@RouterF# up
[edit firewall filter protect-RE]
aviva@RouterF# edit term ssh-telnet
[edit firewall filter protect-RE term ssh-telnet]
aviva@RouterF# set from source-address 10.0.8.0/24
aviva@RouterF# set from source-address 10.0.13.0/24
aviva@routerF# set from destination-port [ ssh telnet ]
aviva@RouterF# set then accept
```

Two terms accept traffic from SNMP NMS systems:

```
[edit firewall filter protect-RE]
aviva@RouterF# edit term xnm-from-nms
[edit firewall filter protect-RE term xnm-from-nms]
aviva@RouterF# set from source-address 10.0.0.1/32
aviva@RouterF# set from source-address 10.0.5.1/32
aviva@RouterF# set from protocol tcp
aviva@RouterF# set then accept
aviva@RouterF# up
[edit firewall filter protect-RE]
aviva@RouterF# edit term allow-snmp-from-nms
[edit firewall filter protect-RE term allow-snmp-from-nms]
aviva@RouterF# set from source-address 10.0.0.1/32
aviva@RouterF# set from source-address 10.0.5.1/32
aviva@RouterF# set from protocol udp
aviva@RouterF# set from destination-port snmp
aviva@RouterF# set then accept
```

Two terms accept traffic from the network's NTP servers and from ICMP:

```
[edit firewall filter protect-RE]
aviva@RouterF# edit term allow-ntp
[edit firewall filter protect-RE term allow-ntp]
aviva@RouterF# set from source-address 10.10.0.1/32
aviva@RouterF# set from source-address 10.10.5.1/32
aviva@RouterF# set from port ntp
aviva@RouterF# set then accept
aviva@RouterF# up
[edit firewall filter protect-RE]
aviva@RouterF# edit term allow-icmp
[edit firewall filter protect-RE term allow-icmp]
aviva@RouterF# set from protocol icmp
aviva@RouterF# set from icmp-type [ echo-request echo-reply unreachable time-exceeded
source-quench ]
aviva@RouterF# set then accept
```

The last term explicitly rejects all other traffic:

```
[edit firewall filter protect-RE]
aviva@RouterF# edit term allow-nothing-else
[edit firewall filter protect-RE term allow-nothing-else]
aviva@RouterF# set then count reject-counter
aviva@RouterF# set then log
aviva@RouterF# set then syslog
aviva@RouterF# set then reject
```

Create a system logfile for the messages that will be generated by the set then syslog command:

```
[edit system syslog]
aviva@RouterF# set file messages firewall any
```

Finally, apply the filter to the router's loopback interface:

```
[edit interfaces lo0]
aviva@RouterF# set unit 0 family inet filter input protect-RE
```

Discussion

This recipe illustrates the second broad firewall filter design philosophy mentioned in Recipe 9.11—that of creating a filter that allows only the desired traffic and blocks everything else. This design requires more planning than the reverse strategy of blocking traffic that the router should not receive first and then allowing everything else, but it ensures maximum security. You need to spend time up front looking at your network and router configurations and analyzing the flow of traffic through your network to determine the types of traffic the router should expect to receive and the addresses and ports from which it should receive the traffic. Another factor working in favor of improving the security of this design is that, by default, if a packet does not match any term in a firewall filter, it is discarded.

This "allow known, block everything else" design is good practice for protecting the router's Routing Engine. Because the JUNOS routing-protocol software runs on the

Routing Engine, you want to make sure that all the traffic it receives is from known and trusted sources.

This recipe is for a router running the routing protocols BGP and OSPF. The router can be accessed by SSH and Telnet, and by DNS, RADIUS, and NMS servers. The firewall filter has a term that handles each type of protocol traffic. A design decision you have to make is the order of the terms in the filter. As with routing policy, the terms in the firewall filter are evaluated in the order in which they appear in the configuration, so the placement affects the efficiency of the filter. You need to decide which packet-filtering operations need to be performed quickly and which are not so time-critical. Generally, protocol packets and possibly address resolution should be handled quickly so that the actual process of routing traffic occurs efficiently. The terms for other less important or background tasks, such as user connections to the router and SNMP polling, are placed towards the end of the filter.

The first terms in this firewall filter accept BGP and OSPF protocol traffic. The AS has two subnetworks, 10.0.8.0/24 and 10.0.13.0/24, so the filter allows protocol traffic only from these specific addresses. For OSPF, we can match on the protocol, but there is no BGP protocol option, so you need to match packets destined for a BGP port. The third term accepts TCP traffic. Because BGP runs over TCP, this term ensures that TCP connections can be set up.

The term dns-servers filters DNS traffic for resolving hostnames and addresses. DNS runs over UDP and uses the domain source port, and the filter uses this information to identify DNS traffic. DNS traffic can come from any server on the 10.0.0.0/8 subnetwork. The terms radius and ssh-telnet accept traffic from the network's RADIUS servers and from SSH and Telnet connections. Both these filters identify packets by looking at their destination port. The RADIUS servers are on two subnetworks, 10.1.0.1/32 and 10.3.0.1/32, and SSH and Telnet sessions are allowed on the 10.0.8.0/24 and 10.0.13.0/24 subnetworks.

The terms xnm-from-nms and allow-snmp-from-nms allow the network's two management systems, 10.0.0.1/32 and 10.0.5.1/32, to access the router. These two servers are both running JUNOScript software, which establishes TCP-based SSL connections to the router, and SNMP. The xnm-from-nms term accepts SSL connections from the JUNOScript software, and the second term accepts SNMP queries.

The final term in the filter, allow-nothing-else, drops all other packets. In this case, we want to know how many packets are dropped, so nonmatching packets are counted in the counter named reject-counter. The set then log command logs these packets to the firewall counter, and the set then syslog command logs them to a system logfile. The recipe configures the system logfile messages to contain the system log messages, using the firewall facility to capture firewall-related messages.

Use the show firewall log command to see how many packets are being rejected or look in the logfile with the show low messages command. You can also look in the file

/var/etc/filters/dfwc.out to see the actions taken by the different terms in the filter. The following is some of the output for the protect-RE filter:

```
aviva@RouterF> file show /var/etc/filters/dfwc.out
**************************************************************
* filter "protect-RE" protocol ip: 8 rules, 24 matches
* Stage: after match reduction and useless match elimination
* Optimizations: max-reduction,skip,flatness,level-compress,
*                max-level-compress,branch,action-elimination
**************************************************************
    rule "ospf-neighbors" matches 3
    match protocol unreferenced type range
        ranges 1
        89
    match source-address unreferenced type addrmask
        number of address-masks: 2
        10.0.8/24
        10.0.13/24
    match action unreferenced type action
        accept
  rule "dns-servers" matches 4
    match protocol unreferenced type range
        ranges 1
        17
    match port unreferenced type range
        ranges 1
        53
    match source-address unreferenced type addrmask
        number of address-masks: 1
        10/8
    match action unreferenced type action
        accept
```

The header shows the name of the filter and the number of rules (terms) it has, along with the number of packets that have matched:

```
* filter "protect-RE" protocol ip: 8 rules, 24 matches
```

Again, because the firewall filter is fairly complicated, here is the complete configuration so you can see the structure:

```
[edit firewall]
aviva@RouterF# show
filter protect-RE {
    term bgp-peers {
        from {
            source-address {
                10.0.8.0/24;
                10.0.13.0/24;
            }
            destination-port bgp;
        }
        then accept;
    }
    term ospf-neighbors {
```

```
                from {
                    source-address {
                        10.0.8.0/24;
                        10.0.13.0/24;
                    }
                    protocol ospf;
                }
                then accept;
            }
            term tcp-traffic {
                from {
                    source-address 10.0.0.0/8;
                    protocol tcp;
                }
                then accept:
            }
            term dns-servers {
                from {
                    source-address {
                        10.0.0.0/8;
                    }
                    protocol udp;
                    port domain;
                }
                then accept;
            }
            term radius {
                from {
                    source-address {
                        10.1.0.1/32;
                        10.3.0.1/32;
                    }
                    destination-port radius;
                }
                then accept;
            }
            term ssh-telnet {
                from {
                    source-address {
                        10.0.8.0/24;
                        10.0.13.0/24;
                    }
                    destination-port [ ssh telnet ];
                }
                then accept;
            }
            term xnm-from-nms {
                from {
                    source-address {
                        10.0.0.1/32;
                        10.0.5.1/32;
                    }
                    protocol tcp;
                }
```

```
            then accept;
        }
        term allow-ntp {
            from {
                source-address {
                    10.10.0.1/32;
                    10.10.5.1/32;
                }
                port ntp;
            }
            then accept;
        }
        term allow-icmp {
            from {
                protocol icmp;
                icmp-type [ echo-request echo-reply unreachable time-exceeded source-
quench ];
            }
            then accept;
        }
        term allow-snmp-from-nms {
            from {
                source-address {
                    10.0.0.1/32;
                    10.0.5.1/32;
                }
                protocol udp;
                destination-port snmp;
            }
            then accept;
        }
        term allow-nothing-else {
            then {
                count reject-counter;
                log;
                syslog;
                reject;
            }
        }
    }
}

[edit interfaces]
lo0 {
    unit 0 {
        family inet {
            filter input protect-RE;
            address 192.168.16.1
        }
    }
}
```

9.16 Rate-Limiting Traffic Flow to the Routing Engine

Problem

You need to ensure the availability of the Routing Engine during times of heavy traffic.

Solution

Configure policers to use with the firewall filter that you apply to the Routing Engine. First, create policers for control and low-priority traffic. The first policer is for SSH connections to the Routing Engine:

```
[edit firewall]
aviva@RouterF# set policer ssh if-exceeding bandwidth-limit 1m
aviva@RouterF# set policer ssh if-exceeding burst-size-limit 100k
aviva@RouterF# set policer ssh then discard
```

Two additional policers limit ICMP and TCP traffic:

```
[edit firewall]
aviva@RouterF# set policer icmp if-exceeding bandwidth-limit 1m
aviva@RouterF# set policer icmp if-exceeding burst-size-limit 100k
aviva@RouterF# set policer icmp then discard
aviva@RouterF# set policer tcp if-exceeding bandwidth-limit 1m
aviva@RouterF# set policer tcp if-exceeding burst-size-limit 100k
aviva@RouterF# set policer tcp then discard
```

A final policer affects various background applications, including SNMP, NTP, and RADIUS:

```
[edit firewall]
aviva@RouterF# set policer utility if-exceeding bandwidth-limit 3m
aviva@RouterF# set policer utility if-exceeding burst-size-limit 300k
aviva@RouterF# set policer utility then discard
```

Then, apply the policers in the then clause of the firewall terms that affect TCP, SSH, ICMP, SNMP, NTP, and RADIUS packets:

```
[edit firewall filter protect-RE2]
aviva@RouterF# set term tcp from source-prefix-list ssh-prefixes
aviva@RouterF# set term tcp from source-prefix-list bgp-prefixes
aviva@RouterF# set term tcp from protocol tcp
aviva@RouterF# set term tcp from tcp-flags "(syn & !ack) | fin | rst"
aviva@RouterF# set term tcp then policer tcp
aviva@RouterF# set term tcp then accept
aviva@RouterF# set term ssh from prefix-list ssh-prefixes
aviva@RouterF# set term ssh from protocol tcp
aviva@RouterF# set term ssh from destination-port ssh
aviva@RouterF# set term ssh then policer ssh
aviva@RouterF# set term ssh then accept
aviva@RouterF# set term utility from source-prefix-list utility-prefixes
aviva@RouterF# set term utility from protocol udp
aviva@RouterF# set term utility from port [ snmp ntp radius ]
aviva@RouterF# set term utility then policer utility
```

```
aviva@RouterF# set term utility then accept
aviva@RouterF# set term icmp from protocol icmp
aviva@RouterF# set term icmp from icmp-type [ echo-request echo-reply unreachable
time-exceeded source-quench ]
aviva@RouterF# set term icmp then policer icmp
aviva@RouterF# set term icmp then accept
```

A final term in the filter counts and discards all remaining traffic:

```
[edit firewall filter protect-RE2]
aviva@RouterF# set term final-term then count discarded-packets
aviva@RouterF# set term final-term then discard
```

To have the filter take effect, apply it to the router's lo0 interface:

```
[edit interfaces]
aviva@RouterF# set lo0 unit 0 family inet filter input protect-RE2
```

Discussion

It is considered good practice to apply policers to Routing Engine firewall filter terms to keep unwanted traffic and possible attacks from overwhelming the routing-protocol software, which runs on the Routing Engine. You want to police control traffic and traffic that is not time-dependent and you don't want to police critical traffic, such as BGP protocol exchanges. This section provides a second example of a Routing Engine firewall filter that includes policers. It is based on a JUNOS secure template publicly available from Team Cymru at *http://www.cymru.com*.

First, create policers for control and low-priority traffic. The first policer, configured with the set policer ssh commands, discards all SSH traffic when the bandwidth exceeds 1 MB or when the traffic burst size is greater than 100 Kbps. The second and third policers provide similar limits for ICMP and TCP traffic.

The terms of the first three policers are the same, so you might wonder why you should bother creating separate policers. You could use just one, which is fine if you know that you will always want to use the same bandwidth and burst-size limits for these three types of traffic. However, if you think you might need to tweak the policers individually, this will be easier to do if you create separate policers initially. When you change the values, you will just need to reconfigure the policer. Otherwise, you will have to reconfigure both the policer and the firewall term in which the policer is used.

The last policer in this recipe, configured with the set policer utility commands, is for background applications, including SNMP, NTP, and RADIUS. This policer drops traffic when the bandwidth is greater than 3 MB or a traffic burst exceeds 300 Kbps.

You then apply the policers in the then clause of the firewall terms. You need a term for each type of traffic. The first term, configured with the set term tcp commands, accepts TCP control traffic only from trusted sources and rate-limits this traffic. The first two commands match prefix lists defined in the [edit policy] section of the configuration. As with the routing-policy prefix lists, you use these to keep a single list of IP addresses in one place in the configuration. The ssh-prefixes list has all the SSH servers in your network, and the bgp-prefixes list has all your BGP peers. The last from clause command matches bits found in TCP control traffic. The first option, (syn & !ack), matches TCP synchronize packets that are being used to establish connections. For connections that are already established and operating normally, these packets also have the ACK bit set, so we exclude these packets from the policer limits. The RST option is present in packets resetting a TCP session, and FIN indicates that a session has closed and there is no more data from the sender. You must enclose the bits in quotation marks so the CLI interprets them correctly. The final two commands in this term configure the action. The first command applies the tcp policer, and the second accepts the packets.

After the tcp term, you should add the following filter term to accept BGP traffic from trusted sources:

```
[edit firewall filter protect-RE2]
aviva@RouterF# set term bgp from source-prefix-list bgp-prefixes
aviva@RouterF# set term bgp from protocol tcp
aviva@RouterF# set term bgp from port bgp
aviva@RouterF# set term bgp then accept
```

The first three commands match packets from a prefix list configured in the [edit policy] section that lists the router's BGP peers, and this traffic is TCP protocol traffic sent from the BGP port. The then clause accepts these packets. You don't rate-limit BGP traffic, because it must be received and handled by the Routing Engine.

The ssh, utility, and icmp terms in the filter are similar, accepting and rate-limiting SSH, SNMP, NTP, RADIUS, and ICMP packets. The last term, final-term, counts and discards all remaining traffic.

Finally, to have the filter take effect, apply it to the lo0 interface.

9.17 Using Counters to Determine Whether a Router Is Under Attack

Problem

You want to count traffic on an interface to help determine whether a router is under attack.

Solution

If you suspect that an attack includes TCP packets, add a counter to the firewall term that counts all TCP traffic:

```
[edit firewall filter protect-RE2]
aviva@RouterF# set term tcp then count tcp-counter
```

To have the counter take effect, apply the firewall filter to the router's lo0 interface:

```
[edit interfaces]
aviva@RouterF# set lo0 unit 0 family inet filter input protect-RE2
```

For more fine-grained counting of the TCP traffic, define additional filter terms:

```
[edit firewall filter tcp-flooding]
aviva@RouterF# set term syn from protocol tcp
aviva@RouterF# set term syn from tcp-flags syn
aviva@RouterF# set term syn then count packets-syn
aviva@RouterF# set term syn then log
aviva@RouterF# set term syn then accept
aviva@RouterF# set term rst from protocol tcp
aviva@RouterF# set term rst from tcp-flags rst
aviva@RouterF# set term rst then count packets-rst
aviva@RouterF# set term rst then log
aviva@RouterF# set term rst then accept
aviva@RouterF# set term fin from protocol tcp
aviva@RouterF# set term fin from tcp-flags fin
aviva@RouterF# set term fin then count packets-fin
aviva@RouterF# set term fin then log
aviva@RouterF# set term fin then accept
aviva@RouterF# set term tcp then count packets-tcp
aviva@RouterF# set term tcp then accept
```

Discussion

If the router comes under attack, the best way to spot the attack is by watching network flows and sampling traffic if necessary. Firewall filters also provide some clues about what is happening. If the attack packets match one of the rate-limited terms, the router will start dropping traffic. If they don't match any term, you will see a sudden increase in any counters that reject traffic (in Recipe 9.16, this is the discarded-packets counter). To determine what types of attack packets the router is receiving, add a counter to the appropriate firewall term.

If your traffic sampling indicates that the attack includes TCP packets, start by counting all the TCP packets. The set term tcp then count tcp-counter command in this recipe adds a counter to the tcp term in Recipe 9.16.

If you determine that a TCP flooding attack of some kind might be underway, you can replace the tcp term with a series of terms that count each type of TCP control packet or you can create a separate filter that does this and apply it to the interface instead—here, the filter tcp-flooding. The first term, configured with the set term syn commands, matches, counts, logs, and accepts TCP SYN packets. The second and third terms do the same for TCP RST and FIN packets. A final term accepts and counts all the TCP packets.

To help you figure out what's going on with the attack, look at the amount of TCP SYN, RST, and FIN packets received as a percentage of all TCP traffic received (counted in the packets-tcp counter). If the router already has a number of established TCP connections and you suddenly see that TCP RST, FIN, or SYN packets start to make up more than 10 percent of the total TCP packet, this is an indication of unusual and unexpected router activity. You should also check the rate at which the counters are changing. If you use a filter like this to monitor your standard day-to-day traffic when you are not under attack, you will have a better handle on what the normal and unusual TCP packet ratios are on the router.

See Also

Recipe 9.16

CHAPTER 10

RIP

10.0 Introduction

The Routing Information Protocol (RIP) is an interior gateway protocol (IGP) that was developed as part of the ARPANET project and was included in the Unix BSD operating system in the early 1980s. RIP was widely deployed in the 1980s and became the industry standard for interior routing. It was standardized by the IETF in 1988, in RFC 1058. This version is referred to as RIP Version 1. RIP Version 2, defined in RFC 2453, added support for Classless Interdomain Routing (CIDR) and authentication. RIP Version 2 MD5 authentication is defined in RFC 2082. RFCs 2080 and 2081 define RIPng, which is designed for IPv6 networks. JUNOS software supports RIP Versions 1 and 2, and RIPng.

RIP is a relatively simple protocol. It uses a distance-vector algorithm (also called the Bellman-Ford algorithm) to determine the best route to a destination. The distance is measured in hops, which is the number of routers that a packet must pass through to reach the destination. The best route is the one with the shortest number of hops. In the routing table, the router maintains two basic pieces of information for RIP routes: the IP address of the destination network or host and the hop count (metric) to that destination.

Every 30 seconds, devices on a RIP network broadcast RIP route information, which describes their view of the network topology and generates a lot of traffic on the network. RIP uses two techniques to reduce the amount of traffic:

Split horizon
> A device receives a route advertisement on an interface but does not retransmit that advertisement back on the same interface. This limits the amount of RIP traffic by eliminating information that its RIP neighbor has already learned.

Poison reverse
> If a RIP device learns from an interface that a device is no longer connected or reachable, it advertises that device's route back on the same interface, setting the number of hops to 16, which means infinite or unreachable. Poison reverse improves the convergence time on a RIP network.

By default, the JUNOS software implements both split horizon and poison reverse.

For service provider networks that use Juniper Networks routers, IS-IS or OSPF are generally used for the IGP because they are more powerful routing protocols and have more features for the larger service provider networks. You might have to use RIP for part of your network if it still has devices running RIP or for one of your customers if they still have devices running RIP. You might choose to use RIP because it is a relatively simple protocol, has very few advanced features, and is relatively straightforward to configure and manage. RIP can be useful in a small, reasonably homogeneous network, which might be served by some of the newer, smaller J-series routers.

This chapter discusses how to enable RIP on the router, how to set it up to receive and send both Version 1 and Version 2 protocol update packets, how to set up some simple routing policies to filter the traffic that RIP sends and receives, and how to perform basic troubleshooting of RIP traffic.

If you use RIP, you should remember that the protocol itself has some inherent limitations. RIP can be used only in small networks because the maximum number of hops to a destination is 16. If a RIP device is more than 15 hops away, it is considered to be unreachable. In practice, this is often a serious limitation. From a route convergence point of view, you should use RIP only if your network is small, with no devices more than four hops from each other. If the network diameter is larger than this, the route convergence time increases to about two to four minutes, which can lead to network instabilities and routers becoming unreachable. In comparison, OSPF and IS-IS typically converge in about 40 seconds. Although it is possible to influence the convergence times by altering RIP timers, if you find yourself having to do this, you should consider using OSPF or IS-IS instead of RIP.

RIP Version 1 has two additional limitations. First, it uses only classful routing, so it cannot handle subnet and network mask information. Second, it uses clear-text password authentication, which is vulnerable to attack. RIP Version 2 was developed to address these two limitations, supporting CIDR and MD5 authentication. However, the hop-count limit of 15 was retained to maintain interoperability with Version 1.

The JUNOS implementation of RIP also has a design point of note. By default, the JUNOS RIP only listens to RIP updates. The router does not send RIP updates unless you explicitly tell RIP to do so. You do this by creating a routing policy, which can be a fairly simple policy, to advertise the routes.

10.1 Configuring RIP

Problem

You want network devices running RIP Version 2 to be able to communicate with the rest of your network.

Solution

You configure basic RIP functionality on your router:

```
[edit protocols]
aviva@RouterA# set rip group alpha-rip-group neighbor fe-0/0/0
aviva@RouterA# show
protocols {
    rip {
        group alpha-rip-group {
            neighbor fe-0/0/0.0;
        }
    }
}
```

Discussion

To have your RIP systems communicate with the rest of your network, you enable RIP on each interface that is directly connected to a RIP neighbor. You do this by defining a group in which you identify each RIP device by the name of the interface that is directly connected to the RIP device. In this example, the Fast Ethernet interface fe-0/0/0 is the connection to your RIP device.

For the connection to the RIP neighbor to work, you must configure an IPv4 address on the interface that is connected to the neighbor (see Recipe 7.5).

We said that we were configuring RIP Version 2, but nowhere in this configuration is there any mention of the RIP version. By default, the JUNOS software configures both versions of RIP when you enable RIP. Most modern devices support and run RIP Version 2, so this shouldn't be an issue.

Why does the JUNOS software force you to put your RIP neighbors in groups instead of just letting you just define them individually? There are a few reasons for this. First, if one of your customers has multiple links to their site or sites, groups let you keep all these links together. Second, if you need to set up different authentication passwords or routing policies, or if you need to control traffic flow differently across different parts of the RIP network by modifying metrics or route preferences, it can be easier for you to configure these changes for an entire group of RIP neighbors rather than for individual neighbors.

If you have a number of RIP devices, you configure each interface that is connected to a RIP neighbor:

```
[edit protocols]
aviva@RouterA# set rip group alpha-rip-group neighbor fe-0/0/1
aviva@RouterA# set rip group alpha-rip-group neighbor se-0/0/3
protocols {
    rip {
        group alpha-rip-group {
            neighbor se-0/0/3.0;
        }
    }
}
```

```
                neighbor fe-0/0/0.0;
                neighbor fe-0/0/1.0;
        }
    }
}
```

After you have configured RIP, you can see that the connections to the RIP neighbors are active:

```
aviva@RouterA> show rip neighbor
                      Source        Destination   Send   Receive   In
Neighbor       State  Address       Address       Mode   Mode      Met
--------       -----  -------       -----------   ----   -------   ---
fe-0/0/1.0     Up     10.0.15.2     224.0.0.9     mcast  both      1
fe-0/0/0.0     Up     10.0.16.1     224.0.0.9     mcast  both      1
se-0/0/3.0     Up     10.0.21.1     224.0.0.9     mcast  both      1
```

You see the three RIP neighbors that you configured. The first column shows the interface that is directly connected to the RIP neighbor. The second column shows that the interface to the neighbor is operational, or Up, and is listening to RIP traffic. The source address is the IPv4 address of the interface, and the destination address is the address of the neighbor's RIP interface. Here, the destination address is the well-known multicast group assigned to RIP Version 2, which is 224.0.0.9.

The Send Mode column tells how the router's RIP update packets are sent and received. The JUNOS implementation of RIP can multicast or broadcast both Version 1 and Version 2 packets (multicast is the default) or can broadcast only Version 1 packets. You should always use the default multicast mode to reduce the amount of RIP protocol update packets traveling on your network. The Receive Mode column indicates which type of RIP update packets the router can receive: Version 1, Version 2, or both (the default).

The last column shows the inbound metric, which is how many hops away the neighbor is. Here, each neighbor is directly connected and is one hop away, so the inbound metrics are 1. The metric value is included in the RIP route to the neighbor that is placed in the routing table.

If the interface to the RIP neighbor is not operational, the Source Address and Destination Address columns would show Dn (down):

```
aviva@RouterA> show rip neighbor
                      Source        Destination   Send   Receive   In
Neighbor       State  Address       Address       Mode   Mode      Met
--------       -----  -------       -----------   ----   -------   ---
fe-0/0/1.0     Up     10.0.15.2     224.0.0.9     mcast  both      1
fe-0/0/0.0     Up     10.0.16.1     224.0.0.9     mcast  both      1
se-0/0/3.0     Dn     (null)        (null)        mcast  both      1
```

To find out what the problem is, first check whether the interface to the neighbor is running:

```
[edit interfaces]
aviva@RouterE# run ping 10.0.15.1 count 5
PING 10.0.15.1 (10.0.15.1): 56 data bytes
ping: sendto: No route to host
```

The ping command here shows that no IPv4 address is configured on the interface. If the interface is configured properly on the local router, log in to the neighboring router and make sure that RIP is enabled and configured properly.

After RIP is running on the local router, you can check whether it is learning routes from its neighbors:

```
[edit]
aviva@RouterA# run show rip statistics
RIPv2 info: port 520; update interval 30s; holddown 180s; timeout 120s.
    rts learned  rts held down  rqsts dropped  resps dropped
           6              0              0              0
fe-0/0/1.0:  4 routes learned; 0 routes advertised
Counter                     Total  Last 5 min  Last minute
-------                 ----------- ----------- -----------
Updates Sent                    0           0           0
Triggered Updates Sent          0           0           0
Responses Sent                  0           0           0
Bad Messages                    0           0           0
RIPv1 Updates Received          0           0           0
RIPv1 Bad Route Entries         0           0           0
RIPv1 Updates Ignored           0           0           0
RIPv2 Updates Received         14          11           2
RIPv2 Bad Route Entries         0           0           0
RIPv2 Updates Ignored           0           0           0
Authentication Failures         0           0           0
RIP Requests Received           0           0           0
RIP Requests Ignored            0           0           0
```

From this output, you see that RIP has learned six routes and that the fe-0/0/1 interface has learned four routes. The other two routes have been learned by one or both of the other two interfaces, but we have abridged the command output to save space.

One thing to notice from this output is that RIP has not sent any protocol update messages. The values in the Updates Sent line are all 0. This is the default JUNOS RIP behavior. With the basic RIP configuration of this recipe, RIP only listens to updates but does not send any.

You can find out which routes RIP learned by looking in the unicast routing table:

```
aviva@RouterA> show route table inet.0
inet.0: 13 destinations, 14 routes (14 active, 0 holddown, 0 hidden)
+ = Active Route, - = Last Active, * = Both
0.0.0.0/0          *[Static/5] 2w4d 23:08:21
                    > to 172.19.121.1 via fe-0/0/0.0
```

```
10.0.0.0/24       *[Direct/0] 2w4d 23:05:23
                   > via fe-0/0/1.0
10.0.0.2/32       *[Local/0] 2w4d 23:05:23
                    Local via fe-0/0/1.0
10.0.1.0/24       *[RIP/100] 00:04:40, metric 2, tag 0
                   > to 10.0.2.1 via fe-0/0/0.0
                    to 10.0.0.1 via fe-0/0/1.0
10.0.2.0/24       *[Direct/0] 2w4d 23:05:23
                   > via fe-0/0/1.0
10.0.2.2/32       *[Local/0] 2w4d 23:05:23
                    Local via fe-0/0/1.0
10.0.8.0/24       *[Direct/0] 2w4d 23:08:59
                   > via fe-0/0/0.0
10.0.8.1/32       *[Local/0] 2w4d 23:08:59
                    Local via fe-0/0/0.0
10.0.16.0/24      *[RIP/100] 00:02:48, metric 2, tag 0
                   > to 10.0.0.1 via fe-0/0/1.0
10.0.24.0/24      *[RIP/100] 00:04:40, metric 2, tag 0
                   > to 10.0.2.1 via fe-0/0/0.0
192.168.0.1/32    *[RIP/100] 00:02:48, metric 2, tag 0
                   > to 10.0.0.1 via fe-0/0/1.0
192.168.2.1/32    *[RIP/100] 00:04:40, metric 2, tag 0
                   > to 10.0.2.1 via fe-0/0/0.0
192.168.5.1/32    *[Direct/0] 2w4d 19:43:23
                   > via lo0.0
224.0.0.9/32      *[RIP/100] 02:02:08, metric 1
                    MultiRecv
```

The route entries starting with [RIP/100] are those learned from RIP. The router has learned six routes from RIP:

- 10.0.1.0/24, 10.0.16.0/24, and 10.0.24.0/24, which are subnetworks
- 192.168.0.1/32 and 192.168.2.1./32, which are router loopback addresses
- The RIP Version 2 multicast address

The value of 100 in the brackets is the JUNOS default value for the RIP administrative distance, also called the preference, which is used to select which route is installed in the forwarding table when several protocols calculate routes to the same destination. You can change the preference value by configuring the preference statement for the RIP group. The numbers following the brackets show how long the routing table has known about the route. The metric value (either 1 or 2) indicates the distance (number of hops) to this address. Understanding the routing table is discussed in more detail in Recipe 8.1.

You might find it strange that a multicast address, 224.0.0.9/32, is present in the inet.0 routing table, which is the unicast routing table. This is simply a result of a JUNOS design decision. Instead of establishing a separate routing table for the few multicast routes used by routing protocols, which are well-known addresses, the JUNOS software places these routes in the unicast routing table.

See Also

Recipes 7.5 and 8.1

10.2 Having RIP Advertise Its Routes

Problem

You want your RIP-enabled router to share routes with its neighbors and learn routes from them.

Solution

To have RIP advertise RIP routes to its neighbors, you need to configure a routing policy that accepts all RIP packets:

```
[edit policy-options]
aviva@RouterA# set policy-statement advertise-rip-routes term 1 from protocol direct
aviva@RouterA# set policy-statement advertise-rip-routes term 1 from protocol rip
aviva@RouterA# set policy-statement advertise-rip-routes term 1 then accept
user@router1# show
policy-options {
    policy-statement advertise-rip-routes {
        term 1 {
            from protocol [ direct rip ];
            then accept;
        }
    }
}
```

Then you apply the policy to all updates sent by RIP:

```
[edit protocols rip]
aviva@RouterA# set group alpha-rip-group export advertise-rip-routes
```

Discussion

When you simply enable RIP, the default JUNOS behavior is to only receive RIP traffic but not learn any of the routes or send any RIP routes. To have RIP send routing information to its neighbors, you need to configure a routing policy that has RIP export routes to its neighbors. An easy way to do this is to have RIP send both the direct and the RIP routes it knows about. Sending the RIP routes is obvious, but why do you need to send the direct routes? Direct routes, which are routes directly to a subnet, are automatically created when you configure the subnet on an interface address. Because RIP does not exchange routes by default, when you first configure RIP on your network, your routers might not have learned any RIP routes. You use the direct routes to catalyze the route-learning process. Once the RIP routers have exchanged direct routes, they can start to exchange their RIP routes.

The routing policy you set up is a simple one. It has one term, which accepts all direct routes and all RIP routes. You apply the policy on the entire group of RIP neighbors, using an export statement to apply the policy to all outgoing RIP traffic. You can apply a RIP export policy only on an entire group of neighbors, so when you are designing your network and have decided which neighbors to place in which group, you need to consider that you have to apply the same routing policies to the entire group.

You see that RIP is now advertising routes to its neighbors. The fe-0/0/1 interface has sent two updates and has advertised four routes:

```
[edit protocols rip]
aviva@RouterA# run show rip statistics
RIPv2 info: port 520; update interval 30s; holddown 180s; timeout 120s.
    rts learned  rts held down  rqsts dropped  resps dropped
              6              0              0              0
fe-0/0/1.0:  4 routes learned; 4 routes advertised
Counter                      Total  Last 5 min  Last minute
-------                      -----------  -----------  -----------
Updates Sent                     2           1           1
Triggered Updates Sent           1           1           1
Responses Sent                   0           0           0
Bad Messages                     0           0           0
RIPv1 Updates Received           0           0           0
RIPv1 Bad Route Entries          0           0           0
RIPv1 Updates Ignored            0           0           0
RIPv2 Updates Received          16          11           2
RIPv2 Bad Route Entries          0           0           0
RIPv2 Updates Ignored            0           0           0
Authentication Failures          0           0           0
RIP Requests Received            0           0           0
RIP Requests Ignored             0           0           0
```

For RIP to work properly on your network, you need to configure this same routing policy on all the RIP neighbors.

See Also

Recipe 9.1

10.3 Configuring RIP for IPv6

Problem

You want to add a JUNOS router running RIP to your IPv6 network.

Solution

The configuration for the IPv6 version of RIP, called RIPng, is basically the same as for the IPv4 version of RIP. RIPng has a separate configuration hierarchy:

```
[edit protocols ripng]
aviva@RouterH# set group v6-rip-group neighbor t1-4/0/0.0
aviva@RouterH# set group v6-rip-group neighbor fe-1/0/1.0
```

You also need to configure the interfaces to support IPv6 traffic:

```
[edit interfaces]
aviva@RouterH# set t1-r/0/0 unit 0 family inet6
aviva@RouterH# set fe-1/0/1 unit 0 family inet6
```

To have the router advertise RIPng routes to its neighbors, configure a routing policy and apply it to the RIPng group:

```
[edit policy-options]
aviva@RouterH# set policy-statement advertise-rip-routes term 1 from protocol direct
aviva@RouterH# set policy-statement advertise-rip-routes term 1 from protocol rip
aviva@RouterH# set policy-statement advertise-rip-routes term 1 then accept

[edit protocols ripng]
aviva@RouterH# set group v6-rip-group neighbor export advertise-rip-routes
```

Discussion

JUNOS RIPng configuration for IPv6 networks is almost identical to the IPv4 RIP configure configuration. You configure the protocol with set ripng commands instead of set rip commands and use show ripng commands instead of show rip commands to check the RIP status. Also, make sure to set the IPv6 address with the inet6 family on the interfaces running RIPng and on the loopback interface, lo0.

To have RIPng advertise its RIPng routes, you create a routing policy as you did with RIPv4. This recipe uses the same policy configured in Recipe 10.2.

To check that the RIPng configuration is working and the router knows about its neighbors, use the show ripng neighbor command:

```
aviva@RouterG> show ripng neighbor
                        Source                  Dest            In
Neighbor     State  Address                 Address  Send Recv Met
--------     -----  -------                 -------  ---- ---- ---
fe-1/0/1.0     Up  fe80::205:85ff:fec2:2ef5  ff02::9  yes yes   1
t1-4/0/0.0     Up  fe80::205:85ff:fec2:2ed0  ff02::9  yes yes   1
```

This output shows the two configured RIPng interfaces. The first column shows the interface that connects to the neighbor, and the second column shows that the neighbor is operational, or Up, and is listening to RIPng traffic. The Send and Recv columns indicate that the router is both sending RIPng packets to and receiving packets from its neighbors. The last column shows the inbound metric, which is how many hops away the neighbor is. Here, each neighbor is directly connected and is one hop away, so the inbound metrics are 1. The metric value is included in the RIPng route to that neighbor that is placed in the routing table.

Check that the router has learned RIPng routes:

```
aviva@RouterG> show route table inet6 protocol ripng
inet6.0: 7 destinations, 8 routes (7 active, 0 holddown, 0 hidden)
+ = Active Route, - = Last Active, * = Both
1080::8:800:200c:2/128
                   *[RIPng/100] 00:13:36, metric 2, tag 0
                    > to fe80::205:85ff:fec4:72d0 via t1-4/0/0.0
1080::8:800:200c:3/128
                   *[RIPng/100] 00:12:43, metric 2, tag 0
                    > to fe80::205:85ff:fec1:d1f5 via fe-1/0/1.0
ff02::9/128        *[RIPng/100] 00:12:03, metric 1
                    MultiRecv
```

Finally, verify that RIPng is sending protocol updates to and receiving updates from its neighbors:

```
aviva@RouterG> show ripng statistics
RIPng info: port 521; update interval 30s; holddown 180s; timeout 120s.
    rts learned   rts held down   rqsts dropped   resps dropped
        2             0               0               0
fe-1/0/1.0:  1 routes learned; 1 routes advertised
Counter                    Total    Last 5 min   Last minute
-------                    -----    ----------   -----------
Updates Sent                30          11           2
Triggered Updates Sent       0           0           0
Responses Sent               0           0           0
Bad Messages                 0           0           0
Updates Received            32          11           2
Bad Route Entries            0           0           0
Updates Ignored              0           0           0
RIPng Requests Received      1           0           0
RIPng Requests Ignored       0           0           0

t1-4/0/0.0:  1 routes learned; 1 routes advertised
Counter                    Total    Last 5 min   Last minute
-------                    -----    ----------   -----------
Updates Sent                30          11           2
Triggered Updates Sent       0           0           0
Responses Sent               0           0           0
Bad Messages                 0           0           0
Updates Received            34          11           2
Bad Route Entries            0           0           0
Updates Ignored              0           0           0
RIPng Requests Received      0           0           0
RIPng Requests Ignored       0           0           0
```

See Also

Recipe 7.6

10.4 Enabling RIP Authentication

Problem

You want to ensure that all RIP protocol traffic your router accepts comes from devices known to you so that only trusted routers participate in determining how traffic is routed through your network.

Solution

Configure MD5 authentication for RIP:

```
aviva@RouterA> configure
[edit protocols]
aviva@RouterA# set rip authentication-type md5
aviva@RouterA# set rip authentication-key 123456
rip {
    authentication-type md5;
    authentication-key "$9$CuWOtBIhSrc8XcS24JGiH"; ## SECRET-DATA
    group alpha-rip-group {
        neighbor fe-0/0/0.0;
    }
}
```

Discussion

It is a good security measure to authenticate all RIP protocol exchanges to ensure that only trusted routers participate in your RIP network and in the exchange of traffic and protocol updates. RIP authentication was added to Version 2 of the protocol standard, so you cannot authenticate RIP Version 1 traffic.

This example shows how to configure RIP to use MD5 authentication. You do this with two statements, one to set the authentication type and another to set the key, or password, that is included in all transmitted RIP packets. MD5 creates an encoded checksum that is included in the transmitted RIP packets. The receiving router verifies this checksum before accepting the packet.

When you display the router's configuration after you have typed the password, the password is displayed in encrypted form. This ensures that someone casually glancing through the configuration does not see the actual password.

You can also configure a simple password for RIP authentication, which includes a plain-text password in the transmitted RIP packets. Plain-text passwords are easy to break by devices that sniff network traffic, so you should never use them when your goal is network security.

For authentication to work across your entire RIP network, you need to configure MD5 authentication and the same password on all your routers in the same way as we show in this recipe. Once you have the encrypted version of the password, you

---

can use it in the authentication-key statement instead of the password itself. This is one way to minimize the number of people who see the actual password.

```
aviva@RouterB# set rip authentication-key "$9$CuWOtBIhSrc8XcS24JGiH"
```

10.5 Routing RIP Traffic over Faster Interfaces

Problem

You want to force RIP to route traffic over a faster physical link even if using that link has more hops than a slower link.

Solution

Use the following command to make the path through the slower interface less preferable:

```
[edit protocols rip]
aviva@RouterA# set group alpha-rip-group neighbor se-0/0/3.0 metric-in 2
```

Discussion

By default, each directly connected neighbor in a RIP network has a metric value of 1. If there are two equal-cost routes to a destination, RIP considers them equivalent and uses one or the other at any given time. You cannot control RIP's choice of paths. If all the links on your network are the same speed, the path taken by RIP traffic is not an issue and you can leave the default metric values unchanged. However, if one of the paths includes a slower or faster link, you probably want to route the RIP traffic along the faster path. In our example, all routers are linked with faster Ethernet interfaces except for one, which has a slower serial link (see Figure 10-1).

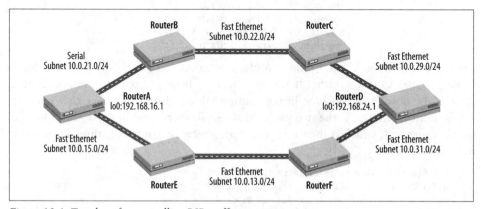

Figure 10-1. Topology for controlling RIP traffic

If you are controlling the path taken by RIP traffic from RouterA to RouterD, you want to make sure it never goes through RouterB but always goes through RouterE and RouterF. If you do not change the default metric configuration, RIP traffic can go along either path. You can check the path it has chosen at this moment, which is the path through RouterB:

```
aviva@RouterA> traceroute 192.168.24.1
traceroute to 192.168.24.1 (192.168.24.1), 30 hops max, 40 byte packets
 1  10.0.21.2 (10.0.21.2)  23.712 ms  29.928 ms  31.495 ms
 2  10.0.22.2 (10.0.22.2)  49.921 ms  68.857 ms  100.153 ms
 3  192.168.24.1 (192.168.24.1)  100.107 ms  100.417 ms  99.953 ms
```

To control the path selected between RouterA and RouterD, you set the inbound metric on RouterA's serial interface to 2. Whenever RouterA receives a route on the se-0/0/3 interface, it sets the metric in that route to 2:

```
aviva@RouterA> show rip neighbor
                        Source        Destination   Send   Receive   In
Neighbor        State   Address       Address       Mode   Mode      Met
--------        -----   -------       -----------   ----   -------   ---
fe-0/0/1.0      Up      10.0.15.2     224.0.0.9     mcast  both      1
se-0/0/3.0      Up      10.0.21.1     224.0.0.9     mcast  both      2
```

You use the traceroute command again to see that you are forcing traffic through RouterE:

```
aviva@RouterA> traceroute 192.168.24.1
traceroute to 192.168.24.1 (192.168.24.1), 30 hops max, 40 byte packets
 1  10.0.15.1 (10.0.15.1)  20.245 ms  11.334 ms  17.559 ms
 2  10.0.13.2 (10.0.13.2)  19.916 ms  19.534 ms  18.065 ms
 3  192.168.24.1 (192.168.24.1)  21.769 ms  29.599 ms  19.960 ms
```

You check the routing table to see that the route to RouterD through RouterB has a metric of 4, while the route through RouterE has a metric of 3:

```
aviva@RouterA> show route table inet.0
10.0.29.0/24       *[RIP/100] 00:16:27, metric 4, tag 0
                      to 10.0.15.1 via fe-0/0/1.0
                    > to 10.0.21.2 via se-0/0/3.0
10.0.31.0/24       *[RIP/100] 02:56:55, metric 3, tag 0
                    > to 10.0.15.1 via fe-0/0/1.0
```

Changing the inbound metric on a router's interface modifies only how the local router, RouterA, sends traffic. It has no effect on how any remote routers control their traffic flow. You can look in the routing table of RouterD to see that when it sends traffic to RouterA, the two paths (through RouterC and RouterF) both have a metric value of 3, which is the value you expect because RouterA is three hops away from RouterD:

```
aviva@RouterD> show route table inet.0
10.0.15.0/24       *[RIP/100] 03:39:30, metric 3, tag 0
                    > to 10.0.31.2 via t1-0/0/2.0
10.0.21.0/24       *[RIP/100] 03:41:18, metric 3, tag 0
                    > to 10.0.29.1 via fe-0/0/1.0
```

10.6   Sending Version 1 Update Messages

Problem

You want your router to send route updates that can be understood by legacy RIP Version 1 devices.

Solution

You configure RIP to send update messages that the RIP Version 1 routers can understand:

```
[edit protocols]
aviva@RouterA# set rip group alpha-rip-group neighbor fe-0/0/0 send broadcast
```

Discussion

When you enable RIP on an interface, the router receives both RIP Version 1 and Version 2 update messages but sends only RIP Version 2 updates. If you have devices in your network that are still using RIP Version 1, you want them to be able to receive update messages. The send broadcast configuration statement sets RIP to send both Version 1 and Version 2 update packets.

When you look at the RIP interfaces now, you see that the send mode for interface fe-/0/00 has changed from mcast to bcast:

```
aviva@RouterA> show rip neighbor fe-0/0/0
                        Source          Destination     Send    Receive  In
Neighbor        State   Address         Address         Mode    Mode     Met
--------        -----   -------         -----------     ----    -------  ---
fe-0/0/0.0         Up   10.0.16.1       10.0.16.255     bcast   both      1
```

You can verify that the neighboring router is receiving RIP Version 1 updates by issuing the show rip statistics command on the RIP neighbor:

```
aviva@RouterE> run show rip statistics fe-1/0/0.0
RIPv2 info: port 520; update interval 30s; holddown 180s; timeout 120s.
    rts learned  rts held down  rqsts dropped  resps dropped
            18            0              0              0
fe-1/0/0.0:  4 routes learned; 17 routes advertised
Counter                   Total   Last 5 min  Last minute
-------                   -----   ----------  -----------
Updates Sent               2690       11           2
Triggered Updates Sent       10        0           0
Responses Sent                0        0           0
Bad Messages                  2        1           1
RIPv1 Updates Received        2        1           1
RIPv1 Bad Route Entries       0        0           0
RIPv1 Updates Ignored         0        0           0
RIPv2 Updates Received     2753       10           1
RIPv2 Bad Route Entries      57        0           0
```

```
RIPv2 Updates Ignored            0          0          0
Authentication Failures          0          0          0
RIP Requests Received            0          0          0
RIP Requests Ignored             0          0          0
```

10.7   Tracing RIP Protocol Traffic

Problem

You are setting up RIP on your network and want to keep a running log of RIP protocol updates that the router is sending to help you track any problems that might occur during the configuration process.

Solution

You set up a trace file that captures all information about RIP protocol update messages:

```
[edit protocols rip]
aviva@RouterA# set traceoptions file rip-update-log
aviva@RouterA# set traceoptions flag update
aviva@RouterA# show
traceoptions {
    file rip-update-log;
    flag update;
}
```

Discussion

When you need to debug RIP operations, you can use the JUNOS tracing facility to track the packets that RIP is sending. You specify the name of the file to which you want to collect the information and the type of information you want to trace. In this example, we are logging RIP update traffic information in the file named *rip-update-log*, which is on the router's hard disk in the directory */var/log*.

To see the RIP protocol update messages, look at the contents of the file:

```
aviva@RouterA> show log rip-update-log
Mar 31 10:10:47 trace_on: Tracing to "/var/log/rip-update-log" started
Mar 31 10:10:51 received response: command 2, version 2, mbz: 0; 5 routes.
Mar 31 10:11:00 received response: command 2, version 2, mbz: 0; 8 routes.
Mar 31 10:11:13 Preparing to send RIPv2 updates.
Mar 31 10:11:13 Update job: sending 20 msgs; group: alpha-rip-group.
Mar 31 10:11:13         nbr se-0/0/3.0; msgp: 0x866ee00.
Mar 31 10:11:13                 sending msg 0x866ee04, 6 rtes
Mar 31 10:11:13         nbr se-0/0/3.0 done.
Mar 31 10:11:13     Group alpha-rip-group done.
Mar 31 10:11:13     New group beta-rip-group.
Mar 31 10:11:13         New nbr fe-0/0/1.0; msgp 0x8672000.
Mar 31 10:11:13                 sending msg 0x8672004, 8 rtes
Mar 31 10:11:13         nbr fe-0/0/1.0 done.
```

```
Mar 31 10:11:13      Group beta-rip-group done.
Mar 31 10:11:13 Update job done!
Mar 31 10:11:20 received response: command 2, version 2, mbz: 0; 5 routes.
```

What you are seeing here is the standard RIP message update process. Every 30 seconds, RIP sends an unsolicited update message that contains the complete routing table to every neighboring router. This router has two RIP neighbors, reachable through interfaces se-0/0/3 and fe-0/0/1. In this update, the router sends six routes to the neighbor on the serial interface and eight routes to the neighbor of the Fast Ethernet interface. The second and third lines of the file show that the local router has received two updates from its two RIP neighbors, one with five and the other with eight routes.

Over time, logfiles can get very large. RIP is a very chatty protocol. You can see from the timestamps in this example that tracing has been on for about 40 seconds. Similar information is added to the file every 30 seconds. If you want to save the logfile for future analysis, you can copy the file to a server:

```
aviva@RouterA> file copy /var/log/rip-update-log server1:rip-update-log-20050227
```

If you no longer need the information in the file, you can delete the contents:

```
aviva@RouterA> clear log rip-update-log
```

Deleting the file's contents does not turn off tracing. To stop the tracing altogether, you need to either deactivate or remove the traceoptions statement from the configuration:

```
[edit protocols rip]
aviva@RouterA# deactivate traceoptions
aviva@RouterA# show protocols rip
inactive: traceoptions {
    file rip-update-log;
    flag update;
}
```

or:

```
[edit protocols rip]
aviva@RouterA# delete traceoptions
```

When debugging RIP, you can set one or more of the following trace flags to capture RIP information:

```
[edit protocols rip traceoptions]
aviva@RouterA# set flag ?
Possible completions:
  all                 Trace everything
  auth                Trace RIP authentication
  error               Trace RIP errors
  expiration          Trace RIP route expiration processing
  general             Trace general events
  holddown            Trace RIP hold-down processing
  normal              Trace normal events
```

packets	Trace all RIP packets
policy	Trace policy processing
request	Trace RIP information packets
route	Trace routing information
state	Trace state transitions
task	Trace routing protocol task processing
timer	Trace routing protocol timer processing
trigger	Trace RIP triggered updates
update	Trace RIP update packets

See Also

Recipe 5.10

## CHAPTER 11

IS-IS

11.0 Introduction

The Intermediate System-to-Intermediate System (IS-IS) protocol is an IGP that routes packets within a single autonomous system (AS), or domain. IS-IS is based on the DECNET Phase V network technology, which was developed at Digital Equipment Corporation (DEC) in the 1980s and was initially standardized by ANSI as the International Organization for Standardization (ISO) intradomain protocol in ISO/IEC 10589. The first version of IS-IS was designed to work on the OSI Connectionless Network Protocol (CNLP). RFC 1195, published in 1990, added extensions to support IP routes.

As an IGP, IS-IS works within a routing domain, which usually corresponds to an administrative boundary, and focuses on determining the most efficient routes to destinations within a domain. This is in contrast with EGPs, whose primary focus is on policy rather than on the most efficient routing. An IS-IS routing domain consists of *end systems*, which send and receive packets, and *intermediate systems* (the ISO term for a router), which receive and forward packets.

IS-IS is a link-state protocol and uses link-state protocol data units (link-state PDUs, or LSPs) to describe the network topology. Each IS-IS router generates LSPs that describe the topology, along with IP routes, checksums, and other information, and floods the LSPs throughout the domain. Each router ends up with a link-state database that describes the same network topology. Once the router has the complete network topology, it runs the Dijkstra shortest-path first (SPF) calculation to determine the shortest path to each destination in the network. The calculation results in destination/next-hop pairs that are placed in the IS-IS routing database. Each router performs the SPF calculation independently, and each IS-IS router has an identical database as a result.

Unlike other IP routing protocols, IS-IS runs directly on the data link layer (Layer 2 of the OSI model) and does not need addresses on each interface, just on the router itself. This makes IS-IS configuration simpler.

Because IS-IS was developed as part of the OSI network protocols, not as part of TCP/IP, it uses a different network-addressing scheme. Instead of the IP 32-bit addresses, IS-IS addresses, called *network entity titles* (NETs), are generally 10 bytes long (they can be from 8 to 20 bytes long) and are written as shown in the following example:

    49.0001.1921.6801.9001.00

The first three bytes of the address (here, 49.0001) form the *area identifier*, or area ID. The area ID can be up to 13 bytes long. The first byte of the area ID is the *address family identifier* (AFI) of the authority, which is the space assigned to a particular enterprise (equivalent to an IP address space that is assigned to an enterprise). The value of 49 is the well-known AFI used for private addressing, which is the equivalent of RFC 1918 addressing for IP protocols. The last two bytes in the area ID identify an IS-IS area within the AS, here 0001, or area 1.

The next six bytes (here, 1921.6801.9001) are the system identifier, which identifies each node (router) on the network. Although IS-IS supports a variable-length system field, in practice this field is always six bytes. The method of allocating system identifiers is up to the network designer. One of the simpler methods, and the one used in this chapter, is binary-coded decimal (BCD), which takes the router's IP address (the lo0 address), fills in all the leading zeros, and repositions the decimal points to form three two-byte numbers. Here, the router's lo0 address is 192.168.19.1. Adding the leading zeros gives 192.168.019.001, and rearranging the decimal points gives 1921.6801.9001. A second common method is to use the router's media access control (MAC) address, regrouping the six-byte address into three groups. For a router with a MAC address of 00:05:85:c2:2e:d0, the system identifier would be 0005.85c2.2ed0. (To see the router's MAC address, use the show chassis mac-address command.)

The final two bytes of the NET are the NET selector (NSEL) and, for IS-IS, they must always be zero to indicate "this system."

IS-IS divides each AS into one or more smaller segments called *areas*. Each area is a set of networks and hosts that are administratively grouped together. Routers within an area run the link-state algorithm in parallel and store the results in their link-state databases. They share this information with each other by exchanging LSPs and thus have identical link-state databases. They can also inject a summary of that area's routes into other areas.

Routers within an IS-IS area are divided into two types. Level 1 systems route within an area, and Level 2 systems route between areas and toward other ASs. When a Level 1 router needs to route a packet to a destination outside its area, it sends the packet toward a Level 2 system. Systems that run both Level 1 and Level 2 are similar to OSPF area border routers (ABRs). One difference between IS-IS and OSPF is that an IS-IS router resides completely within an area, and the area borders are on the links; while with OSPF, the ABR is a router that connects to all the areas on its boundary. This means that the IS-IS Level 2 systems have to maintain only two link-state databases, one for the Level 1 area and the second for the Level 2 area, as compared to the OSPF ABR, which maintains a link-state database for each connected area.

On broadcast, multiaccess networks, IS-IS elects a designated intermediate system (DIS), also referred to as a designated router (DR), which advertises links to all routers in the level. IS-IS elects a separate DIS for Level 1 and Level 2 areas (although they could be on the same router). DIS election is based on priority, which is a number between 0 and 127, with the router with the highest value becoming the DIS. IS-IS does not have a backup designated router.

For more background information about IS-IS, see *The Complete IS-IS Routing Protocol* (Springer) and *OSPF and IS-IS: A Comparative Anatomy* (*http://www.nanog.org/mtg-0006/katz.html*).

11.1 Configuring IS-IS

Problem

You want to configure IS-IS on a JUNOS router.

Solution

There are three steps to setting up IS-IS. First, define the interfaces on which IS-IS will run and the levels to which the interfaces will be attached:

```
[edit protocols isis]
aviva@RouterG# set interface fe-0/0/1
aviva@RouterG# set interface fe-1/0/0 level 2 disable
aviva@RouterG# set interface lo0.0
```

Second, enable the ISO protocol family on the interfaces:

```
[edit interfaces]
aviva@RouterG# set fe-0/0/1 unit 0 family iso
aviva@RouterG# set fe-1/0/0 unit 0 family iso
```

Finally, configure a NET on the lo0 interface:

```
[edit interfaces]
aviva@RouterG# set lo0 unit 0 family iso address 49.0020.1921.6801.9001.00
```

Discussion

The basic setup to get IS-IS up and running on your router is straightforward. Enable the protocol on all router interfaces that will participate in the IS-IS domain and specify the level at which they should run. This recipe configures the IS-IS on the router topology shown in Figure 11-1. Here, because interface fe-0/0/1 is a border node between areas 20 and 30, you need to specify only the interface name because, by default, all IS-IS interfaces are both Level 1 and Level 2 interfaces.

The other interface, fe-1/0/0, is only in area 20, so it is a Level 1 router. For this interface, you disable Level 2 operation.

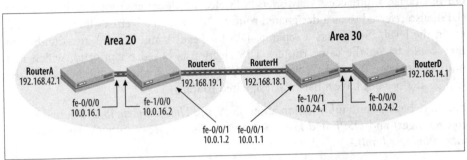

Figure 11-1. IS-IS network topology with one area

In addition to the network interfaces, you should also run IS-IS on the lo0.0 interface because this is the most straightforward way to ensure that your loopback address (or addresses) is advertised into IS-IS. IS-IS automatically treats the loopback interface as passive, which means that the interface advertises its direct addresses but does not form adjacencies. (In older versions of JUNOS software, you had to include the passive statement on the loopback interface to have the interface be passive, but this has changed in newer versions.) However, to have other interfaces be passive, you must configure them explicitly by including the passive statement; for example:

```
[edit protocols isis]
aviva@RouterG# set interface fe-1/0/1.0 level 2 passive
```

In the interfaces portion of the configuration, configure the interfaces that will be running IS-IS, here fe-0/0/1 and fe-1/0/0, so that they recognize and accept ISO packets. Do this by including family iso in the logical interface. Interfaces can have multiple address families on them, as you can see for fe-0/0/1:

```
aviva@RouterG> show configuration interfaces fe-0/0/1
unit 0 {
    family inet {
        address 10.0.1.2/24;
    }
    family iso;
}
```

Also, you must set a NET for the router. Technically, you can set this address on any interface but, in practice, you set it on the router's loopback interface, lo0. This address is stable, and, as long as the router is up, this interface is accessible. If you assign the NET on a network interface and that interface goes down, IS-IS will stop functioning on the router. You can assign multiple NETs to the lo0 interface, which might be useful when migrating two previously independent IS-IS domains into a single domain.

After this simple configuration, the IS-IS protocol takes over. You do not have to configure neighbors. IS-IS automatically discovers them and establishes adjacencies with its neighbors by first sending IS-IS Hello (IIH) packets to ensure that the two ends of the link can communicate.

To check that IS-IS is running on the router interfaces, use the show isis interface command:

```
aviva@RouterG> show isis interface
IS-IS interface database:
Interface         L  CirID Level 1 DR    Level 2 DR     L1/L2 Metric
fe-0/0/1.0        3  0x2 RouterG.02      RouterG.02         10/10
fe-1/0/0.0        1  0x3 RouterG.03      Disabled           10/10
lo0.0             0  0x1 Passive         Passive             0/0
```

This output shows the two Fast Ethernet interfaces we configured for IS-IS, as well as the lo0 interface. The second column, L, shows that fe-0/0/1 is a Level 1–Level 2 interface (represented by the number 3) and fe-1/0/0 is a Level 1 interface. The loopback address is also listed because a NET is configured on it but it does not participate in any IS-IS level (shown as 0 in the L column). The two DR columns show the name of the router that has been elected as the DIS for that level. Interface fe-1/0/0 has no Level 2 DR (Disabled) because it is a Level 1 interface. You may wonder how IS-IS discovers the name of the neighbor because it is not an IP routing protocol and hence doesn't support DNS. The answer is that the JUNOS software supports dynamic mapping of ISO system identifiers to the hostname. If you have configured a router name with the set system host-name command, this name, and not the router's NET, is displayed in all IS-IS output. The JUNOS implementation of IS-IS includes the hostname in the LSP, using the dynamic hostname TLV, type 137, to cache the symbolic name of the router.

In the DR columns for the lo0.0 interface, the interface is shown as Passive, which is the default when you configure IS-IS on the loopback interface.

The last column shows the link's Layer 1 and Layer 2 metrics, which are 10 by default.

You can see a brief summary of the adjacencies the router has established with the show isis adjacencies command:

```
aviva@RouterG> show isis adjacency
Interface         System      L State      Hold (secs) SNPA
fe-0/0/1.0        RouterH     2 Up              21  0:5:85:c1:d1:d1
fe-1/0/0.0        RouterA     1 Up               6  0:5:85:ca:ca:70
```

The output shows the two interfaces we configured. The interface fe-0/0/1 participates in a Level 2 area, connecting to RouterH, and interface fe-1/0/0 connects to RouterA. Notice that the lo0 interface is not listed because it doesn't form any adjacencies. The State column shows that both adjacencies are operational (Up). The Hold column shows the amount of time remaining before the router closes the adjacency. By default, IS-IS sends Hello packets, which act as adjacency keepalives, every three seconds for DIS routers and every nine seconds for Level 1 routers. Non-DIS routers send Hello packets less frequently in case IS-IS needs to re-elect a DIS. While a DIS is being elected, there is likely to be traffic loss. Having a longer hello timer interval on the non-DIS systems remedies this problem. The default hold time is three times the hello interval, or 9 seconds, and 27 seconds for DIS and Level 1 routers, respectively. The SNPA column shows the subnetwork point of attachment, which is the MAC address of the next hop.

The detail version of this command gives a bit more insight into the adjacencies:

```
aviva@RouterG> show isis adjacency detail
RouterH
    Interface: fe-0/0/1.0, Level: 2, State: Up, Expires in 21 secs
    Priority: 64, Up/Down transitions: 1, Last transition: 17:16:43 ago
    Circuit type: 3, Speaks: IP, IPv6, CLNS, MAC address: 0:5:85:c1:d1:d1
    Topologies: Unicast
    Restart capable: Yes
    LAN id: RouterG.02, IP addresses: 10.0.1.1
RouterA
    Interface: fe-1/0/0.0, Level: 1, State: Up, Expires in 7 secs
    Priority: 64, Up/Down transitions: 1, Last transition: 16:57:54 ago
    Circuit type: 1, Speaks: IP, IPv6, MAC address: 0:5:85:ca:ca:70
    Topologies: Unicast
    Restart capable: Yes
    LAN id: RouterA.02, IP addresses: 10.0.16.1
```

The output shows the other two IS-IS routers. RouterG reaches RouterH over interface fe-0/0/1, and it connects to RouterA over interface fe-1/0/0. The State field shows that the adjacencies are operational (Up), and the Expires field shows the amount of time remaining before the router closes the adjacency. The second line shows the router's DR priority, how many times the adjacency has gone down and come back up, and when the last up-down transition occurred. The third line shows the Circuit type, which is the IS-IS level. A value of 3 indicates the router is a Level 1–Level 2 router, a value of 2 is a Level 2–only router, and a value of 1 is a Level 1–only router. The Speaks field shows the protocols that the router is running, and the MAC address field shows the subnetwork point of attachment, which is the MAC address of the next hop. The last line shows the IS-IS identifier of the router on the LAN and the router's IP address.

If the IS-IS adjacency doesn't come up, there are a few things to check when troubleshooting. First, make sure the physical interface is operational. Here, the adjacency with RouterH is down:

```
aviva@RouterG> show isis adjacency
```

```
Interface                System        L State      Hold (secs) SNPA
fe-0/0/1.0               RouterH        2 Down             0   0:5:85:c1:d1:d1
fe-1/0/0.0               RouterA        1 Up               8   0:5:85:ca:ca:70
```

RouterG's interface to RouterH is up:

```
aviva@RouterG> show interfaces fe-0/0/1 terse
Interface                Admin Link Proto Local              Remote
fe-0/0/1                 up    up
fe-0/0/1.0               up    up    inet  10.0.1.2/24
                                     iso
```

but the interface on RouterH is not:

```
aviva@RouterH> show interfaces fe-0/0/1 terse
Interface                Admin Link Proto Local              Remote
fe-0/0/1                 down  up
fe-0/0/1.0               up    down  inet  10.0.1.1/24
                                     iso
```

Checking the configuration, you see that the interface has been disabled:

```
aviva@RouterH> show configuration interfaces fe-0/0/1
disable;
unit 0 {
    family inet {
        address 10.0.1.1/24;
    }
    family iso;
}
```

Delete the disable statement to activate the interface.

Next, check that all interfaces in a Level 1 area are configured with the same area
identifier. You can check this on the local router:

```
aviva@RouterG> show interfaces terse lo0.0
Interface                Admin Link Proto Local              Remote
lo0.0                    up    up    inet  192.168.19.1        --> 0/0
                                     iso   49.0020.1921.6801.9001
```

Also check on the Level 1 neighbor:

```
aviva@RouterA> show interfaces terse lo0.0
Interface                Admin Link Proto Local              Remote
lo0.0                    up    up    inet  192.168.42.1        --> 0/0
                                     iso   49.0020.1921.6804.2001
```

You see that both routers are in area 20.

You can also find the area identifier in the IS-IS TLV field in the database:

```
aviva@RouterG> show isis database extensive level 1
IS-IS level 1 link-state database:
RouterG.00-00 Sequence: 0x63, Checksum: 0xfe33, Lifetime: 549 secs
...
```

```
    TLVs:
      Area address: 49.0020 (3)
  ...
```

Check the interface's MTU to make sure that it is at least 1,492 bytes:

```
aviva@RouterG> show interfaces fe-0/0/1.0
  Logical interface fe-0/0/1.0 (Index 64) (SNMP ifIndex 40)
    Flags: SNMP-Traps Encapsulation: ENET2
    Protocol inet, MTU: 1500
      Flags: None
      Addresses, Flags: Is-Preferred Is-Primary
        Destination: 10.0.1/24, Local: 10.0.1.2, Broadcast: 10.0.1.255
    Protocol iso, MTU: 1497
      Flags: Is-Primary
```

Another common mistake that results in adjacency being down is that the IP addresses on either end of the connection are in different subnets and do not match. An example is having one router interface with an IP address of 192.168.0.1/24 connect to another router with an interface IP address of 192.168.1.2/24.

Finally, check that each interface includes an ISO family and that the lo0 interface has an NET address:

```
aviva@RouterG> show interfaces terse
Interface          Admin Link Proto Local               Remote
...
fe-0/0/1.0         up    up   inet  10.0.1.2/24
                              iso

fe-1/0/0           up    up
fe-1/0/0.0         up    up   inet  10.0.16.2/24
                              iso

...
lo0.0              up    up   inet  192.168.19.1        --> 0/0
                              iso   49.0020.1921.6801.9001

...
```

11.2 Viewing the IS-IS Link-State Database

Problem

You want to look at each router's link-state database to make sure that all the IS-IS routers know about each other.

Solution

Use the show isis database command to view the contents of the link-state database:

```
aviva@RouterG> show isis database
IS-IS level 1 link-state database:
LSP ID                        Sequence Checksum Lifetime Attributes
RouterG.00-00                   0x65    0xfa35    851 L1 L2 Attached
RouterA.00-00                   0x5e    0xf289    661 L1 L2
```

```
RouterA.02-00                           0x59   0xeda9     632 L1 L2
  3 LSPs
IS-IS level 2 link-state database:
LSP ID                           Sequence Checksum Lifetime Attributes
RouterH.00-00                           0x61   0xa315     923 L1 L2
RouterG.00-00                           0x61   0x125e     741 L1 L2
RouterG.02-00                           0x5e   0x79f0     741 L1 L2
  3 LSPs
```

Discussion

IS-IS routers exchange LSPs that describe each individual router's view of the network topology and they store the LSPs in a link-state database. The SPF algorithm then runs on the link-state database to create the IS-IS routing table. Use the show isis database command to look at the contents of the link-state database. In this recipe, RouterG is a Level 1–Level 2 router, so you see two link-state databases, one for each level.

The first part of the output shows that the Level 1 link-state database has three LSPs. The entry for RouterG includes the attach bit (Attached), which indicates that it is connected to another IS-IS area. From the configuration, you know that this router is connected to area 30.

If you check on the other Level 2 router, its Level 2 database is identical to that of RouterG:

```
aviva@RouterH> show isis database level 2
IS-IS level 2 link-state database:
LSP ID                           Sequence Checksum Lifetime Attributes
RouterH.00-00                           0x61   0xa315     988 L1 L2
RouterG.00-00                           0x61   0x125e     802 L1 L2
RouterG.02-00                           0x5e   0x79f0     802 L1 L2
  3 LSPs
```

Use the extensive version of the show isis database command to see all the information carried in the LSP:

```
aviva@RouterG> show isis database extensive level 2 RouterH.00-00
IS-IS level 2 link-state database:
RouterH.00-00 Sequence: 0x62, Checksum: 0xa116, Lifetime: 1121 secs
   IS neighbor: RouterG.02                    Metric:      10
   IP prefix: 10.0.1.0/24                     Metric:      10 Internal Up
   IP prefix: 10.0.24.0/24                    Metric:      10 Internal Up
  Header: LSP ID: RouterH.00-00, Length: 134 bytes
    Allocated length: 284 bytes, Router ID: 192.168.18.1
    Remaining lifetime: 1121 secs, Level: 2, Interface: 64
    Estimated free bytes: 170, Actual free bytes: 150
    Aging timer expires in: 1121 secs
    Protocols: IP, IPv6
  Packet: LSP ID: RouterH.00-00, Length: 134 bytes, Lifetime : 1198 secs
    Checksum: 0xa116, Sequence: 0x62, Attributes: 0x3 <L1 L2>
    NLPID: 0x83, Fixed length: 27 bytes, Version: 1, Sysid length: 0 bytes
    Packet type: 20, Packet version: 1, Max area: 0
```

```
TLVs:
  Area address: 49.0030 (3)
  Speaks: IP
  Speaks: IPv6
  IP router id: 192.168.18.1
  IP address: 192.168.18.1
  Hostname: RouterH
  IP prefix: 10.0.24.0/24, Internal, Metric: default 10, Up
  IP prefix: 10.0.1.0/24, Internal, Metric: default 10, Up
  IP extended prefix: 10.0.24.0/24 metric 10 up
  IP extended prefix: 10.0.1.0/24 metric 10 up
  IS neighbor: RouterG.02, Internal, Metric: default 10
  IS extended neighbor: RouterG.02, Metric: default 10
      IP address: 10.0.1.1
No queued transmissions
```

The first section of the output shows the entries (IS-IS neighbors and IP prefixes) in the link-state database:

```
RouterH.00-00 Sequence: 0x62, Checksum: 0xa116, Lifetime: 1121 secs
  IS neighbor: RouterG.02          Metric:      10
  IP prefix: 10.0.1.0/24           Metric:      10 Internal Up
  IP prefix: 10.0.24.0/24          Metric:      10 Internal Up
```

RouterG has one IS-IS neighbor, RouterH, and the metric to reach this neighbor is 10 (the default). RouterG has learned two prefixes, both from a Level 1 (internal) IS-IS area, and both prefixes have the default metric cost of 10. Any routes learned from outside the area would be marked External.

The remaining three sections correspond to portions of the LSP. The Header section shows the packet length, the router ID (which is the address configured on the lo0 interface), and various timer information. The Packet section shows the PDU length, remaining lifetime, checksum, sequence number, and other information. The TLV section shows the TLV information carried in the LSP. The first line shows TLV 1, the address of the area in which the router is located:

```
Area address: 49.0030 (3)
```

RouterH is in area 49.0030. The next two lines list the protocols that RouterH supports (TLV 129):

```
Speaks: IP
Speaks: IPv6
```

The router is running both IPv4 and IPv6. Next, you see two router IDs:

```
IP router id: 192.168.18.1
IP address: 192.168.18.1
```

The first line corresponds to TLV 134, the traffic-engineering router ID (defined in RFC 3784), and the second is TLV 132, which is defined as the interface address. In the JUNOS IS-IS implementation, the IP address field shows the configured router ID, not all interface addresses. The sixth line shows the router's dynamic (symbolic) hostname:

```
Hostname: RouterH
```

The next four lines show the IP prefixes in the LSP:

```
IP prefix: 10.0.24.0/24, Internal, Metric: default 10, Up
IP prefix: 10.0.1.0/24, Internal, Metric: default 10, Up
IP extended prefix: 10.0.24.0/24 metric 10 up
IP extended prefix: 10.0.1.0/24 metric 10 up
```

The first two prefixes map to TLV 128, IP internal reachability, and are the IP addresses within the routing domain that are directly reachable through RouterH interfaces. This TLV can carry metrics in the range of 0 through 63. The second two prefixes map to TLV 135, the extended reachability TLV, defined in RFC 3784. This TLV can carry metric values greater than 63.

The last two lines provide information about reaching IS-IS neighbors:

```
IS neighbor: RouterG.02, Internal, Metric: default 10
IS extended neighbor: RouterG.02, Metric: default 10
   IP address: 10.0.1.1
```

The first line, IS neighbor, corresponds to TLV 2, which carries IS reachability information, including the one-octet default metric. The second line maps to TLV 22, for extended IS reachability information (also defined in RFC 3784). This TLV carries three-octet metric values.

11.3 Viewing Routes Learned by IS-IS

Problem

You want to check the routes that are being generated by the link-state algorithm to make sure that the router is learning the expected routes.

Solution

Use the show isis route command to see the contents of the IS-IS routing table:

```
aviva@RouterG> show isis route
  IS-IS routing table              Current version: L1: 85 L2: 85
  IPv4/IPv6 Routes
  ----------------
  Prefix          L Version  Metric Type Interface    Via
  10.0.24.0/24    2     85       20 int  fe-0/0/1.0   RouterH
```

Discussion

IS-IS uses the information in its link-state database to calculate the best route to a destination and places these routes in its routing table. The show isis route command displays what's in the IS-IS routing table. In this recipe, the output shows that IS-IS has learned one route, to network 10.0.24.0/24, the interface to which RouterH is connected. This is an internal route accessible over interface fe-0/0/1, and the next hop is RouterH (shown in the Via column). The Metric column shows the cost of the route.

You can find out which routes the router has learned from IS-IS by looking in the unicast routing table:

```
aviva@RouterG> show route
inet.0: 11 destinations, 11 routes (11 active, 0 holddown, 0 hidden)
+ = Active Route, - = Last Active, * = Both
10.0.0.0/24        *[Direct/0] 3d 19:05:01
                    > via fe-1/0/1.0
10.0.0.1/32        *[Local/0] 3d 19:05:01
                     Local via fe-1/0/1.0
10.0.1.0/24        *[Direct/0] 3d 19:05:01
                    > via fe-0/0/1.0
10.0.1.2/32        *[Local/0] 3d 19:05:01
                     Local via fe-0/0/1.0
10.0.16.0/24       *[Direct/0] 3d 18:41:06
                    > via fe-1/0/0.0
10.0.16.2/32       *[Local/0] 3d 18:41:06
                     Local via fe-1/0/0.0
10.0.24.0/24       *[IS-IS/18] 22:53:36, metric 20
                    > to 10.0.1.1 via fe-0/0/1.0
172.19.121.0/24    *[Direct/0] 3d 19:05:01
                    > via fe-0/0/0.0
172.19.121.119/32  *[Local/0] 3d 19:05:01
                     Local via fe-0/0/0.0
192.168.18.1/32    *[IS-IS/18] 22:53:36, metric 10
                    > to 10.0.1.1 via fe-0/0/1.0
192.168.19.1/32    *[Direct/0] 3d 19:05:01
                    > via lo0.0

__juniper_private1__.inet.0: 2 destinations, 2 routes (2 active, 0 holddown, 0
hidden)
+ = Active Route, - = Last Active, * = Both
10.0.0.1/32        *[Direct/0] 3d 19:05:01
                    > via lo0.16385
10.0.0.16/32       *[Direct/0] 3d 19:05:01
                    > via lo0.16385

iso.0: 1 destinations, 1 routes (1 active, 0 holddown, 0 hidden)
+ = Active Route, - = Last Active, * = Both
49.0020.1921.6801.9001/72
                   *[Direct/0] 1d 20:46:39
                    > via lo0.0
```

This output shows the contents of three routing tables. The first is inet.0, which is the unicast routing table. The second, __juniper_private1__inet.0, is a table of private routes within the router itself. The third is the ISO routing table, iso.0.

In the inet.0 table, the route entries starting with [IS-IS/18] are learned from IS-IS. The router has learned one route from IS-IS, to network 10.0.24.0, which we also saw in the IS-IS routing table. The value of 18 in the brackets is the JUNOS default value for the external IS-IS administrative distance, also called the preference, which is used to select which route is installed in the forwarding table when several protocols calculate routes to the same destination. You can change the preference value by configuring the preference statement for the IS-IS level. The numbers following the brackets indicate how long the routing table has known about the route. The metric value is the cost to this address. The default IS-IS metric is 10. For example, in the route to 10.0.24.0, the metric is 20 because that network is two hops away.

The inet.0 table also contains a route to 192.168.19.1/32, which is this router's loopback address. This route appears in the routing table because you configured IS-IS on the router's loopback interface, lo0.0.

The ISO address family creates a separate routing table, iso.0, which is for the ISO routes to the NET destinations. Here, this table contains one route, to the Level 2 neighbor, which is the only NET destination in the network.

You can also see just the routes learned by IS-IS:

```
aviva@RouterG> show route protocol isis
inet.0: 11 destinations, 11 routes (11 active, 0 holddown, 0 hidden)
+ = Active Route, - = Last Active, * = Both
10.0.24.0/24        *[IS-IS/18] 22:58:48, metric 20
                     > to 10.0.1.1 via fe-0/0/1.0
192.168.18.1/32     *[IS-IS/18] 22:58:48, metric 10
                     > to 10.0.1.1 via fe-0/0/1.0
```

See Also

Recipe 9.1

11.4 Configuring IS-IS for IPv6

Problem

You want to use IS-IS on an IPv6 network.

Solution

The IS-IS configuration for an IPv6 network is the same as for IPv4. Configure the interfaces, enable ISO on the IS-IS interfaces, and configure a NET on lo0:

```
[edit protocols isis]
aviva@RouterG# set interface fe-0/0/1
aviva@RouterG# set interface fe-1/0/1
aviva@RouterG# set interface lo0.0

[edit interfaces]
aviva@RouterG# set fe-0/0/1 unit 0 family iso
aviva@RouterG# set fe-1/0/1 unit 0 family iso
aviva@RouterG# set lo0 unit 0 family iso address 49.0020.1921.6801.9001.00
```

Discussion

Because IS-IS runs directly on the data-link layer (Layer 2), from an IS-IS point of view, there is nothing different or special about configuring it for an IPv6 environment. The only thing you do differently is set IPv6 addresses on the physical interfaces instead of IPv4 addresses. This recipe configures a router that connects to two other Level 1–Level 2 IS-IS routers.

Again, use the show isis interface command to see the configured IS-IS interfaces:

```
aviva@RouterG> show isis interface
IS-IS interface database:
Interface        L CirID Level 1 DR    Level 2 DR    L1/L2 Metric
fe-0/0/1.0       3  0x2  RouterG.02    RouterG.02       10/10
fe-1/0/1.0       3  0x3  RouterJ.03    RouterJ.03       10/10
loo.0            0  0x1  Passive       Passive           0/0
```

When looking at the adjacencies, you can see the IPv6 addresses configured on the router:

```
aviva@RouterG> show isis adjacency detail
RouterH
   Interface: fe-0/0/1.0, Level: 2, State: Up, Expires in 19 secs
   Priority: 64, Up/Down transitions: 1, Last transition: 00:18:55 ago
   Circuit type: 3, Speaks: IP, IPv6, CLNS, MAC address: 0:5:85:c1:d1:d1
   Topologies: Unicast
   Restart capable: Yes
   LAN id: Incredible-Hulk.02, IP addresses: 192.168.18.1
   IPv6 addresses: fe80::205:85ff:fec1:d1d1
...
```

The IS-IS database output is also unchanged. If you look at the detail version of the output, you now see the IPv6 address prefixes:

```
aviva@RouterG> show isis database level 2 detail
IS-IS level 2 link-state database:

RotuerJ.00-00 Sequence: 0x5, Checksum: 0x9645, Lifetime: 647 secs
   IS neighbor: RouterJ.02          Metric:      10
   IS neighbor: RouterJ.03          Metric:      10
   V6 prefix: 9009:1::/64           Metric:      10 Internal Up
   V6 prefix: 9009:2::/64           Metric:      20 Internal Up
   V6 prefix: 9009:3::/64           Metric:      10 Internal Up
...
```

See Also

Recipes 7.6 and 11.1

11.5 Configuring a Level 1–Only Router

Problem

You want to set up the Level 1–only routers.

Solution

For routers that participate only in a Level 1 area, disable Level 2 on the router:

```
[edit protocols isis]
aviva@RouterA# set level 2 disable
aviva@RouterA# set interface fe-0/0/0.0
aviva@RouterA# set interface lo0.0
```

Discussion

To configure routers that are only in a Level 1 area, just disable Level 2 routing for all of IS-IS, not for a specific interface. The configuration looks like this:

```
[edit protocols]
aviva@RouterA# show
isis {
    level 2 disable;
    interface fe-0/0/0.0;
    interface lo0.0;
}
```

These routers have only a Level 1 link-state database:

```
aviva@RouterA> show isis database
IS-IS level 1 link-state database:
LSP ID                      Sequence Checksum Lifetime Attributes
RouterG.00-00                 0x198   0x3ea3    2389 L1 L2 Attached
RouterA.00-00                 0x1ad   0xee5f    1190 L1
RouterA.02-00                 0x1a6   0x4efc    1190 L1
  3 LSPs
IS-IS level 2 link-state database:
  0 LSPs
```

The Level 1 link-state database has three LSPs, while the Level 2 database is empty.

Level 1 IS-IS routers know only about paths to routers within their level. For routes outside the level, they install a default route that points to the closest Level 1–Level 2 router. To confirm that the router knows about other levels, first check the link-state database for an LSP that has the Attached (ATT) bit set. The show isis database output above shows that RouterG is connected to another level:

```
LSP ID                      Sequence Checksum Lifetime Attributes
RouterG.00-00                 0x198   0x3ea3    2389 L1 L2 Attached
```

Then check that the default route is installed:

```
aviva@RouterA> show isis route
 IS-IS routing table              Current version: L1: 328 L2: 322
 IPv4/IPv6 Routes
 ----------------
 Prefix           L Version  Metric Type Interface   Via
 0.0.0.0/0        1    328       10 int  fe-0/0/0.0  RouterG
 10.0.0.0/24      1    328       20 int  fe-0/0/0.0  RouterG
 10.0.1.0/24      1    328       20 int  fe-0/0/0.0  RouterG
 192.168.12.1/32  1    328       10 int  fe-0/0/0.0  RouterG
 192.168.19.1/32  1    328       10 int  fe-0/0/0.0  RouterG
```

You see from this output that all the routes are Level 1 routes and the default route 0.0.0.0/0 is directed to RouterG, which is the nearest Level 1–Level 2 router. (In this example, it also happens to be the only Level 1–Level 2 router in area 20.)

Also check that the default route is installed in the main routing table, inet.0:

```
aviva@RouterA> show route table inet.0
inet.0: 10 destinations, 10 routes (10 active, 0 holddown, 0 hidden)
+ = Active Route, - = Last Active, * = Both
0.0.0.0/0          *[IS-IS/15] 00:30:06, metric 10
                   > to 10.0.16.2 via fe-0/0/0.0
10.0.0.0/24        *[IS-IS/15] 00:30:06, metric 20
                   > to 10.0.16.2 via fe-0/0/0.0
10.0.1.0/24        *[IS-IS/15] 00:30:06, metric 20
                   > to 10.0.16.2 via fe-0/0/0.0
10.0.16.0/24       *[Direct/0] 2d 20:28:21
                   > via fe-0/0/0.0
10.0.16.1/32       *[Local/0] 4d 18:42:46
                     Local via fe-0/0/0.0
10.0.21.0/24       *[Direct/0] 4d 20:24:04
                   > via se-0/0/3.0
10.0.21.1/32       *[Local/0] 4d 20:24:09
                     Local via se-0/0/3.0
192.168.12.1/32    *[IS-IS/160] 00:30:06, metric 10
                   > to 10.0.16.2 via fe-0/0/0.0
192.168.19.1/32    *[IS-IS/15] 00:30:06, metric 10
                   > to 10.0.16.2 via fe-0/0/0.0
192.168.42.1/32    *[Direct/0] 2d 20:53:53
                   > via lo0.0
```

The output above shows that the static route via interface fe-0/0/0 goes to RouterG (10.0.16.2) and was learned from IS-IS. The default route is advertised as an internal Layer 1 route and has a default routing preference value of 15 rather than 18, which is the default for external Layer 2 routes. Because the JUNOS software chooses routes with the lowest preference, it will select an IS-IS internal route over an external one.

In both the show isis route and show route command outputs, the only routes included are those with the area. There is no information about links outside the area.

11.6 Controlling DIS Election

Problem

You want to force IS-IS to use a specific router as the designated router.

Solution

Increase the priority on the desired router:

```
[edit protocols isis]
aviva@RouterH# set interface fe-0/0/1 level 2 priority 65
```

Discussion

With the IS-IS configuration we have shown in previous recipes, all IS-IS routers have the default priority value (64), which IS-IS uses to elect the DR in each area. In this situation, the router with the higher MAC address is elected as the DR.

In the previous recipes, RouterG is elected DR because it has a higher MAC address (0:5:85:c2:2e:d1, compared to 0:5:85:c1:d1:d1 for RouterH):

```
aviva@RouterG> show isis adjacency
Interface            System            L State     Hold (secs) SNPA
fe-0/0/1.0           RouterH           2 Up                  7 0:5:85:c1:d1:d1
fe-1/0/0.0           Captain-Caveman1  Up                   7 0:5:85:ca:ca:70

aviva@RouterH> show isis adjacency
Interface            System            L State     Hold (secs) SNPA
fe-0/0/1.0           RouterG           2 Up                 20 0:5:85:c2:2e:d1
fe-1/0/1.0           RouterA           1 Up                  7 0:5:85:ca:e7:d0
```

Looking at the IS-IS interfaces, you see the default priority value of 64 for all interfaces at both Level 1 and Level 2 and that RouterG is the DR for the Level 2 area:

```
aviva@RouterG> show isis interface detail
IS-IS interface database:
fe-0/0/1.0
  Index: 64, State: 0x6, Circuit id: 0x2, Circuit type: 3
  LSP interval: 100 ms, CSNP interval: 10 s
  Level Adjacencies Priority Metric Hello (s) Hold (s) Designated Router
    1            0      64     10    9.000       27
    2            1      64     10    3.000        9 RouterG.02 (us)
fe-1/0/0.0
  Index: 68, State: 0x6, Circuit id: 0x3, Circuit type: 1
  LSP interval: 100 ms, CSNP interval: 10 s
  Level Adjacencies Priority Metric Hello (s) Hold (s) Designated Router
    1            1      64     10    9.000       27 RouterA.02
      (not us)
lo0.0
  Index: 70, State: 0x6, Circuit id: 0x1, Circuit type: 0
  LSP interval: 100 ms, CSNP interval: disabled
```

```
Level Adjacencies Priority Metric Hello (s) Hold (s) Designated Router
     1           0       64        0 Passive
     2           0       64        0 Passive
```

Unlike OSPF, which has a "sticky" DR, in IS-IS, if a new router with a higher priority than the existing DR becomes active, or if the new router has an equal priority and a higher MAC address, it becomes the new DR. In this recipe, for RouterH to become the DR, its priority needs to be greater than 64. After changing the value, you see that RouterH has become the Level 2 DR:

```
aviva@RouterG> show isis interface
IS-IS interface database:
Interface           L CirID Level 1 DR        Level 2 DR        L1/L2 Metric
fe-0/0/1.0          3   0x2 RouterG.02        RouterH.02            10/10
fe-1/0/0.0          1   0x3 RouterA.02 Disabled          10/10
loo.0               0   0x1 Passive            Passive              0/0
```

Looking at RouterH, you see it has a DR priority of 65:

```
aviva@RouterH> show isis interface fe-0/0/1 detail
IS-IS interface database:
fe-0/0/1.0
  Index: 67, State: 0x6, Circuit id: 0x2, Circuit type: 3
  LSP interval: 100 ms, CSNP interval: 10 s
  Level Adjacencies Priority Metric Hello (s) Hold (s) Designated Router
     1           0       64     10     9.000      27
     2           1       65     10     3.000       9 RouterH.02 (us)
```

11.7 Enabling IS-IS Authentication

Problem

You want to ensure that all IS-IS protocol traffic that your router accepts comes from devices known to you so that only trusted routers participate in determining the contents of the IS-IS routing database.

Solution

Configure MD5 authentication for IS-IS:

```
[edit protocols isis]
aviva@RouterG# set level 2 authentication-type md5
aviva@RouterG# set level 2 authentication-key $1991poPPi
```

Discussion

It is a good security measure to authenticate IS-IS protocol packet exchanges to ensure that only trusted routers participate in the IS-IS network and in the exchange of LSA packets.

This recipe shows how to configure IS-IS to use MD5 authentication for the Level 2 area. First you configure MD5 authentication for the entire area, then you set the key, or password, for each interface. MD5 creates an encoded checksum that is included in all transmitted IS-IS packets. The receiving router verifies this checksum before accepting the packet. By default, the JUNOS implementation of IS-IS authenticates all PDU types, including link-state PDUs (LSPs), IIH PDUs, and complete and partial sequence number PDUs (CSNPs and PSNPs). This is why the software has only one command for establishing authentication.

To configure authentication for all Level 1 areas that the router participates in, use the following commands:

```
[edit protocols isis]
aviva@RouterG# set level 1 authentication-type md5
aviva@RouterG# set level 1 authentication-key $SuMPasswRD
```

You cannot configure authentication for IS-IS Level 2 and Level 1 areas globally with a single command. You must configure the two authentications separately.

When you display the router's configuration after you have typed the password, you do not see the password itself but the encrypted form of the password. This safeguard means that someone casually glancing through the configuration does not see the actual password.

You can also configure a simple password for IS-IS authentication, which includes a plain-text password in the transmitted IS-IS packets. Plain-text passwords are easy to break by devices that sniff network traffic, so you should never use them when your goal is network security.

For authentication to work across the entire IS-IS domain, you need to configure MD5 authentication and the same password on all IS-IS interfaces in the same way as shown in this recipe. Once you have the encrypted version of the password, you can use it in the authentication-key statement instead of the password itself. This is one way to minimize the number of people who see the actual password.

```
aviva@RouterG# set interface fe-1/0/1 authentication-key
"$9$dEbgoZUjqP5GUApO1hcgoaJHq"
```

When you are looking at the configuration contents, pipe the output to hide the passwords:

```
[edit protocols isis]
aviva@RouterG# show | except SECRET-DATA
level 2 {
}
interface fe-0/0/1.0;
interface fe-1/0/0.0 {
    level 2 disable;
}
interface lo0.0 {
    passive;
}
```

If the same authentication type and password are not configured across the area, IS-IS cannot establish adjacencies and you will see errors. Here, Level 2 authentication is configured on RouterH but not on RouterG:

```
aviva@RouterH> show isis adjacency extensive
RouterG
   Interface: fe-0/0/1.0, Level: 2, State: Down, Expires in 0 secs
   Priority: 64, Up/Down transitions: 2, Last transition: 00:00:37 ago
   Circuit type: 3, Speaks: IP, IPv6, MAC address: 0:5:85:c2:2e:d1
   Topologies: Unicast
   Restart capable: Yes
   LAN id: RouterH.02, IP addresses: 10.0.1.2
   Transition log:
   When                State     Event          Down reason
   Tue Jun 21 19:51:33 Up        Seenself
   Tue Jun 21 23:51:01 Down      Error          Bad Hello
RouterA
   Interface: fe-1/0/1.0, Level: 1, State: Up, Expires in 7 secs
   Priority: 64, Up/Down transitions: 1, Last transition: 21:37:54 ago
   Circuit type: 1, Speaks: IP, IPv6, MAC address: 0:5:85:ca:e7:d0
   Topologies: Unicast
   Restart capable: Yes
   LAN id: RouterA.02, IP addresses: 10.0.24.2
   Transition log:
   When                State     Event          Down reason
   Tue Jun 21 02:13:44 Up        Seenself
```

For tighter security, you can also define separate authentication passwords for the IS-IS Hello packet exchanges on interfaces. The following commands set the hello password on interface fe-0/0/1:

```
[edit protocols isis interface fe-0/0/1.0]
aviva@RouterG# set level 2 hello-authentication-type md5
aviva@RouterG# set level 2 hello-authentication-key $NutherPaSSwd
```

11.8 Redistributing Static Routes into IS-IS

Problem

You have a single, low-speed link to a small customer and instead, of having the customer run IS-IS (or even RIP), you want to set up a static route to the customer.

Solution

Create a routing policy to redistribute static routes into IS-IS:

```
[edit policy-options]
aviva@RouterG# set policy-statement export-statics term 1 from protocol static
aviva@RouterG# set policy-statement export-statics term 1 then accept
aviva@RouterG# show
policy-statement export-statics {
    term 1 {
```

```
        from protocol static;
        then accept;
    }
}
```

Then apply the policy to IS-IS:

```
[edit protocols isis]
aviva@RouterG# set export export-statics
```

Discussion

Routing policy is normally applied to BGP to filter the entries in the routing table rather than to IS-IS or another IGP. This is because the main purpose of an IGP is to determine the best route to a destination. However, occasionally you need to use routing policies with an IGP, generally to redistribute routes into that IGP from another protocol. For example, this might be done for a small customer who doesn't need to run a dynamic routing protocol, such as IS-IS, but just connect to you using a static route. You create a routing policy to redistribute these customer's routes into your IS-IS network. This recipe creates a simple routing policy to do this, accepting all static routes. For the policy to take effect, you must apply it to IS-IS.

RouterG has one configured static route:

```
aviva@RouterG> show route protocol static table inet.0
inet.0: 12 destinations, 12 routes (12 active, 0 holddown, 0 hidden)
+ = Active Route, - = Last Active, * = Both
192.168.12.1/32    *[Static/5] 00:10:41
                    > to 10.0.16.1 via fe-1/0/0.0
```

When the static route is redistributed into IS-IS, it is incorporated into the IS-IS link-state database and is marked as being an external prefix:

```
aviva@RouterG> show isis database extensive
IS-IS level 1 link-state database:
RouterG.00-00 Sequence: 0xe5, Checksum: 0x912c, Lifetime: 492 secs
    IP prefix: 10.0.1.0/24                   Metric:      10 Internal Up
    IP prefix: 10.0.16.0/24                  Metric:      10 Internal Up
    IP prefix: 192.168.12.1/32               Metric:       0 External Up
    IP prefix: 192.168.19.1/32               Metric:       0 Internal Up
  Header: LSP ID: RouterG.00-00, Length: 175 bytes
    Allocated length: 1492 bytes, Router ID: 192.168.19.1
    Remaining lifetime: 492 secs, Level: 1,Interface: 0
    Estimated free bytes: 1317, Actual free bytes: 1317
    Aging timer expires in: 492 secs
    Protocols: IP, IPv6
  Packet: LSP ID: RouterG.00-00, Length: 175 bytes, Lifetime : 1200 secs
    Checksum: 0x912c, Sequence: 0xe5, Attributes: 0xb <L1 L2 Attached>
    NLPID: 0x83, Fixed length: 27 bytes, Version: 1, Sysid length: 0 bytes
    Packet type: 18, Packet version: 1, Max area: 0
  TLVs:
    Area address: 49.0020 (3)
    Speaks: IP
    Speaks: IPv6
```

```
IP router id: 192.168.19.1
IP address: 192.168.19.1
Hostname: RouterG
IP prefix: 10.0.1.0/24, Internal, Metric: default 10, Up
IP prefix: 10.0.16.0/24, Internal, Metric: default 10, Up
IP prefix: 192.168.19.1/32, Internal, Metric: default 0, Up
IP extended prefix: 10.0.1.0/24 metric 10 up
IP extended prefix: 10.0.16.0/24 metric 10 up
IP extended prefix: 192.168.19.1/32 metric 0 up
IP external prefix: 192.168.12.1/32, Internal, Metric: default 0, Up
IP extended prefix: 192.168.12.1/32 metric 0 up
Authentication data: 17 bytes
  No queued transmissions
...
```

The show isis database extensive command output shows that the metric for the
static route redistributed into IS-IS is 0. To lower the preference for the route, change
the metric in the routing policy to increase the cost. Here, we increase the metric to
500:

```
[edit policy-options]
aviva@RouterG# set policy-statement export-statics term 1 then metric 500
```

The policy now looks like this:

```
aviva@RouterG# show
policy-statement export-statics {
    term 1 {
        from protocol static;
        then {
            metric 500;
            accept;
        }
    }
}
```

Looking in the IS-IS link-state database shows that the metric value has changed
from 0:

```
aviva@RouterG> show isis database extensive
IS-IS level 1 link-state database:
RouterG.00-00 Sequence: 0xe5, Checksum: 0x912c, Lifetime: 492 secs
    IP prefix: 10.0.1.0/24              Metric:        10 Internal Up
    IP prefix: 10.0.16.0/24            Metric:        10 Internal Up
    IP prefix: 192.168.12.1/32         Metric:        63 External Up
    IP prefix: 192.168.19.1/32         Metric:         0 Internal Up
```

It's true that the metric has changed, but instead of being 500, it's 63. Looking in the
routing table on the neighboring router shows that it has learned the static route:

```
aviva@RouterA> show route
inet.0: 6 destinations, 7 routes (6 active, 0 holddown, 0 hidden)
+ = Active Route, - = Last Active, * = Both
192.168.12.1/32      *[IS-IS/160] 00:14:56, metric 73
                      > via se-0/0/3.0
```

Again, we expect the metric to change from the default of 10 to 500, but it's showing a metric of 73. Why isn't the metric value changing to 500? The reason is because
IS-IS uses two kinds of metrics, narrow and wide. By default, the JUNOS software
uses the IS-IS narrow metrics, which are defined in the original IS-IS standards documents as 8-bit values. With narrow metrics, the router can't advertise a metric
greater than 63. If it receives a metric value greater than 63, IS-IS clips it to 63. This is
why the link-state database shows a metric of 63 and the neighbor's routing table
shows a metric of 73 (the default metric of 10 plus 63). To resolve this problem, configure IS-IS to use wide metrics:

```
[edit protocols isis]
aviva@RouterG# set level 1 wide-metrics-only
```

Wide metrics, defined in RFC 3784, can be values greater than 63. Looking again at
the link-state database shows that IS-IS is now advertising the metric value of 500:

```
aviva@RouterG> show isis database extensive
IS-IS level 1 link-state database:
RouterG.00-00 Sequence: 0xe5, Checksum: 0x912c, Lifetime: 492 secs
    IP prefix: 10.0.1.0/24                   Metric:        10 Internal Up
    IP prefix: 10.0.16.0/24                  Metric:        10 Internal Up
    IP prefix: 192.168.12.1/32               Metric:       500 External Up
    IP prefix: 192.168.19.1/32               Metric:         0 Internal Up
  TLVs:
  ...
        IP external prefix: 192.168.12.1/32, Internal, Metric: 500, Up
```

The neighbor's routing table also reflects the change:

```
aviva@RouterA> show route
inet.0: 6 destinations, 7 routes (6 active, 0 holddown, 0 hidden)
+ = Active Route, - = Last Active, * = Both
192.168.12.1/32    *[IS-IS/160] 00:14:56, metric 500
                    > via se-0/0/3.0
```

11.9   Leaking IS-IS Level 2 Routes into Level 1

Problem

Your IS-IS network has several areas, some which have multiple exit points to your
core area, and you want to increase the routing efficiency of your Level 1 routers.

Solution

On the Level 1–Level 2 router, create a policy to leak a specific Level 2 route into the
Level 1 link-state database:

```
[edit policy-options policy-statement level2-leaking term 1]
aviva@RouterJ# set from protocol isis
aviva@RouterJ# set from level 2
aviva@RouterJ# set from route-filter 10.0.21.0/24 prefix-length-range /32-/32
```

```
aviva@RouterJ# set to protocol isis
aviva@RouterJ# set to level 1
aviva@RouterJ# set then accept
aviva@RouterJ# show
term 1 {
    from {
        protocol isis;
        level 2;
        route-filter 10.0.21.0/24 prefix-length-range /32-/32;
    }
    to {
        protocol isis;
        level 1;
    }
    then accept;
}
```

Then apply the policy to IS-IS:

```
[edit protocols isis]
aviva@RouterJ# set export level2-leaking
```

Discussion

Unlike OSPF, which combines all routes from all areas into a single link-state data-base, IS-IS keeps separate databases for its Level 2 and Level 1 routes. Because a Level 1 router knows only about the routers in its area, it routes traffic that is des-tined for another area to the nearest Level 1–Level 2 router, and that router then for-wards the traffic to the external area. Under most circumstances, this is what you want to happen because it minimizes the number of routes on which the SPF calcula-tion needs to be performed. In some situations, however, this behavior results in traf-fic going through more links than necessary as it travels from a Level 1 router to its destination. Figure 11-2 shows such a case. To reduce the number of links, you can inject, or leak, an external route from the Level 2 link-state database into an area's Level 1 database.

In this network, traffic sent from the Level 1 RouterH to RouterE, which is in an external network, goes through RouterF because it is the closest Level 1–Level 2 router. You can see this in the RouterH routing table:

```
aviva@RouterH> show route 10.0.21.2
inet.0: 11 destinations, 11 routes (11 active, 0 holddown, 0 hidden)
+ = Active Route, - = Last Active, * = Both
0.0.0.0/0          *[IS-IS/15] 00:31:53, metric 10
                    > to 10.0.8.1 via fe-0/0/1.0
```

RouterF then routes the traffic through all three routers in Area 1, taking a total of seven hops for the packet to travel from RouterH to RouterE. If you could route the traffic from RouterH to RouterG, which is the other Level 1–Level 2 router in Area 2, the path would be only four hops.

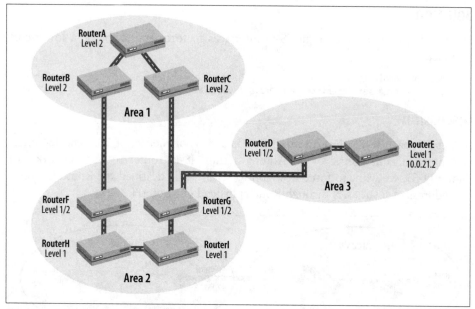

Figure 11-2. IS-IS topology for leaking routes from Level 2 to Level 1

You do this is by creating a routing policy on RouterG that leaks the route to the external network 10.0.21.0/24 into the Level 1 routers in Area 2. The policy in this recipe contains a route filter that matches all /32 addresses in this external network and redistributes all IS-IS Level 2 routes from the network into IS-IS Level 1. Matching the /32 addresses captures all the addresses you are interested in, which are the loopback addresses. After you apply the policy on the Level 1–Level 2 router, you see on RouterH, the Level 1 router, that the route to 10.0.21.0/24 has leaked into its routing table:

```
aviva@RouterH> show route 10.0.21.2
inet.0: 12 destinations, 12 routes (12 active, 0 holddown, 0 hidden)
+ = Active Route, - = Last Active, * = Both
10.0.21.0/24      *[IS-IS/18] 00:00:09, metric 40
                   > to 10.0.8.1 via fe-0/0/1.0
```

Instead of having a cost of 15, which is the default cost of an intra-area IS-IS route, the route has a cost of 18, which is the default for an interarea IS-IS route.

11.10 Adjusting IS-IS Link Costs

Problem

You want to direct traffic within an IS-IS area toward a particular router.

Solution

Increase the cost on one of the IS-IS interfaces to force traffic to use a lower-cost interface:

```
[edit protocols isis]
aviva@RouterG# set interface fe-0/0/1.0 level 2 metric 30
```

Discussion

By default, each IS-IS physical interface has a cost, or metric, of 10. (The lo0 interface has a default metric of 0.) Adding a third IS-IS router to our network (see Figure 11-3), we want to force RouterG to send traffic destined for RouterD (interface address of 10.0.24.2) through RouterJ instead of RouterH.

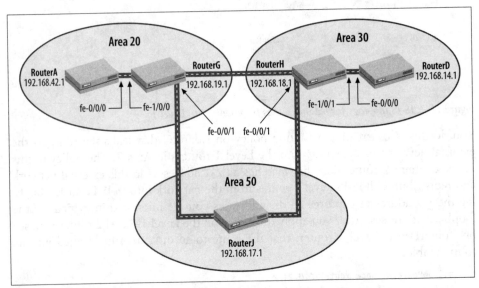

Figure 11-3. OSFP network topology with three areas

With the default metric values, the cost through RouterH is 20 (a cost of 10 for each interface transited) while the cost through RouterJ is 30 (a cost of 10 for each of the three interfaces), so the router chooses the path through RouterH:

```
aviva@RouterG> show route 10.0.24.2
inet.0: 14 destinations, 14 routes (14 active, 0 holddown, 0 hidden)
+ = Active Route, - = Last Active, * = Both
10.0.24.0/24       *[IS-IS/18] 00:04:10, metric 20
                    > to 10.0.1.1 via fe-0/0/1.0
```

Use the traceroute command to confirm the path taken:

```
aviva@RouterG> traceroute 10.0.24.2
traceroute to 10.0.24.2 (10.0.24.2), 30 hops max, 40 byte packets
 1  10.0.1.1 (10.0.1.1)  10.977 ms  9.131 ms  29.827 ms
 2  10.0.24.2 (10.0.24.2)  9.763 ms  9.670 ms  29.863 ms
```

Increasing the IS-IS cost of RouterG's fe-0/0/1 interface to 30 reroutes the traffic through RouterJ. Here, we see that the cost to 10.0.24.0/24 has increased from 20 to 30:

```
aviva@RouterG> show route 10.0.24.2
inet.0: 14 destinations, 14 routes (14 active, 0 holddown, 0 hidden)
+ = Active Route, - = Last Active, * = Both
10.0.24.0/24       *[IS-IS/18] 00:00:06, metric 30
                    > to 10.0.0.2 via fe-1/0/1.0
```

This increase occurs because traffic is now going via RouterJ, across three interfaces that each have a metric of 10:

```
aviva@RouterG> traceroute 10.0.24.2
traceroute to 10.0.24.2 (10.0.24.2), 30 hops max, 40 byte packets
 1  10.0.0.2 (10.0.0.2)  11.747 ms   8.741 ms  10.099 ms
 2  10.0.2.1 (10.0.2.1)   9.783 ms  19.964 ms  19.541 ms
 3  10.0.24.2 (10.0.24.2)  20.068 ms  19.382 ms  20.051 ms
```

If the IS-IS interfaces are running at significantly different speeds, each interface still has the same default metric of 10. When there are equal-cost paths to the same destination, instead of traffic being routed across the fastest interface, the default behavior is to equally distribute traffic across the different interfaces in a round-robin fashion. To have IS-IS calculate interface metrics that accurately reflect the actual interface speeds, you need to configure a *reference bandwidth* value. Instead of using the default metric, IS-IS uses the following formula to calculate the metric on each interface:

$$\text{metric} = \frac{\text{reference bandwidth}}{\text{interface bandwidth}}$$

For IS-IS, the default reference bandwidth value is 10 Mbps, which is the speed of a regular Ethernet interface. To illustrate how the reference bandwidth affects the metric, consider a router that has Fast Ethernet and Gigabit Ethernet interfaces running IS-IS. For IS-IS to choose the best path, you can set the reference bandwidth to 1 Gbps:

```
[edit protocols isis]
aviva@RouterJ# set reference-bandwidth 1g
```

With this configuration, IS-IS assigns the Fast Ethernet interface a metric of 10 and the Gigabit Ethernet interface a metric of 1. Because the Gigabit Ethernet interface has the lowest metric, IS-IS selects it when routing traffic.

11.11 Improving IS-IS Convergence Times

Problem

You want to speed convergence of IS-IS routes in case a path fails with no hardware indication, which might happen on an Ethernet network.

Solution

Have IS-IS perform the SPF calculation more often:

```
[edit protocols isis]
aviva@RouterG# set spf-delay 100
```

Discussion

One of the most important factors that affects the convergence of IS-IS routes is how often the software performs the SPF calculation. By default, IS-IS performs the SPF calculation 200 milliseconds after a topology change is detected. The command in this recipe halves the time to 100 milliseconds:

```
[edit protocols isis]
aviva@RouterG# set spf-delay 100
```

Another way to improve link failure detection times is to use the Bidirectional Forwarding Protocol (BFD), which provides a mechanism to detect communication failures with a forwarding-plane next hop. BFD is a simple hello protocol. A pair of systems exchange BFD packets periodically, and if a system stops receiving the packets for long enough, some component in that particular bidirectional path to the neighboring system is assumed to have failed. If you want to shorten the IS-IS link failure detection time to about 1 second, set the BFD packet exchange interval to 333 milliseconds:

```
[edit protocols isis]
aviva@RouterG# set interface fe-0/0/1 bfd-liveness-detection minimum-interval 333
```

By default, BFD multiplies the packet-exchange interval by three to determine the link detection failure time. Configuring an interval of 333 milliseconds results in a failure time of just under 1 second.

You also need to configure BFD using the same command on the interface at the other end of the link. Use the show bfd session command to see BFD information:

```
aviva@RouterG> show bfd session detail
Address            State    Interface      Detect Time  Interval  Multiplier
10.0.1.1           Up       fe-0/0/1.0         0.999     0.333      3
  Client ISIS L2, TX interval 0.300, RX interval 0.300, multiplier 3
  Session up time 00:00:37
  Local diagnostic None, remote diagnostic None
  Remote heard, hears us
1 sessions, 1 clients
Cumulative transmit rate 3.0 pps, cumulative receive rate 3.0 pps
```

If the link goes down, the BFD session fails and you no longer see the link:

```
aviva@RouterG> show bfd session detail
                                               Transmit
Address            State    Interface      Detect Time  Interval  Multiplier
0 sessions, 0 clients
Cumulative transmit rate 0.0 pps, cumulative receive rate 0.0 pps
```

11.12 Moving IS-IS Traffic off a Router

Problem

You are getting ready to perform router maintenance and you want to move all IS-IS traffic off the router.

Solution

Configure the router so that it appears to be overloaded with IS-IS traffic:

```
[edit protocols isis]
aviva@RouterG# set overload
```

Discussion

As you are preparing to perform maintenance on a router in a production network, you want to move traffic off that router so that network services are not interrupted during your maintenance window. The set overload command tricks the router into believing that it is overloaded and can't handle any more IS-IS transit traffic, and the result is that IS-IS transit traffic is sent to other routers. IS-IS traffic destined to interfaces directly attached to the local router continues to reach the router.

To check that the IS-IS traffic has moved off the router, use show interfaces commands to verify that traffic has moved off the upstream interfaces. The detail and extensive versions of this command report traffic statistics for most interface types. If the router is part of an LSP, use the show mpls lsp transit command to verify that transit LSPs have moved off the router.

11.13 Disabling IS-IS on an Interface

Problem

You want to temporarily turn off IS-IS on an interface.

Solution

Disable IS-IS on the interface:

```
[edit protocols isis]
aviva@RouterG# set interface fe-1/0/1 disable
```

To start IS-IS again, remove the disable statement from the configuration:

```
[edit protocols isis]
aviva@RouterG# delete disable
aviva@RouterG# commit
```

Discussion

To remove an interface from the IS-IS network, you can disable it. Because you are only removing the interface temporarily, you don't want to remove the configuration statements entirely. You see that the interface is down:

```
aviva@RouterG> show isis interface
IS-IS interface database:
Interface          L CirID Level 1 DR    Level 2 DR        L1/L2 Metric
fe-0/0/1.0         3   0x2 RouterG.02    RouterG.02           10/10
fe-1/0/0.0         1   0x3 RouterA.02    Disabled             10/10
fe-1/0/1.0         3   0x1 Disabled      Disabled             10/10
lo0.0              0   0x1 Passive       Passive               0/0
```

Also, the adjacency to the neighbor is down:

```
aviva@RouterG> show isis adjacency
Interface          System        L State      Hold (secs) SNPA
fe-0/0/1.0         RouterH       2 Up                  26  0:5:85:c1:d1:d1
fe-1/0/0.0         RouterA       1 Up                   6  0:5:85:ca:ca:70
fe-1/0/1.0         RouterJ       2 Down                 0  0:5:85:c4:72:f5
```

Another way to disable IS-IS on an interface is with the deactivate command:

```
[edit protocols isis]
aviva@RouterG# deactivate interface fe-1/0/1.0
aviva@RouterG# commit
aviva@RouterG# show
interface fe-0/0/1.0;
interface fe-1/0/0.0 {
    level 2 disable;
}
inactive: interface fe-1/0/1.0;
interface lo0.0;
}
```

To start IS-IS again on the interface, reactivate it:

```
[edit protocols isis]
aviva@RouterG# activate interface fe-1/0/1
aviva@RouterG# commit
```

You can also temporarily disable OSPF on the router:

```
[edit protocols isis]
aviva@RouterG# set disable
aviva@RouterG# commit and-quit
aviva@RouterG> show isis interface
IS-IS instance is not running
```

11.14 Tracing IS-IS Protocol Traffic

Problem

You are setting up IS-IS on your network and want to keep a running log of IS-IS protocol packets that the router is sending to help you track any problems that might occur during the configuration process.

Solution

Set up a tracing file that captures information about IS-IS protocol operations:

```
[edit protocols isis]
aviva@RouterJ# set traceoptions file isis-logs
aviva@RouterJ# set traceoptions flag error
aviva@RouterJ# set traceoptions flag general
aviva@RouterJ# set traceoptions flag normal
```

To stop the tracing, remove the traceoptions statement from the configuration:

```
[edit protocols isis]
aviva@RouterJ# delete traceoptions
```

Discussion

To debug IS-IS operations, use the JUNOS tracing facility to track the packets that IS-IS is sending and receiving. You specify the name of the file to which you want to collect the information and the type of information you want to trace. In this example, we set three flags to track normal operations and errors in the file *isis-logs*, which is on the router's hard disk in the directory */var/log* (on M-series and T-series routers) and */cf/var/log* (on J-series routers).

When you are first bringing up an IS-IS network, you may find that an adjacency is not establishing between two Level 1 routers:

```
aviva@RouterJ> show isis adjacency
Interface         System      L State      Hold (secs) SNPA
fe-0/0/1.0        RouterF     1 Down               0   0:5:85:c1:86:31
fe-1/0/0.0        RouterH     2 Up               22   0:5:85:c1:d1:f4
fe-1/0/1.0        RouterG     2 Up               24   0:5:85:c2:2e:f5
```

The logfile shows where the problem is:

```
aviva@RouterJ> show log isis-logs | last
Jun 25 12:47:15 ERROR: IIH from RouterG with no matching areas, interface fe-1/0/1.0
Jun 25 12:47:15     local area  49.0050
Jun 25 12:47:15     remote area 49.0020 (3 bytes)
Jun 25 12:47:15 ERROR: IIH from RouterF with no matching areas, interface fe-0/0/1.0
Jun 25 12:47:15     local area  49.0050
Jun 25 12:47:15     remote area 49.0051 (3 bytes)
```

The second error shows that the adjacency to the Level 1 router RouterF is down because RouterJ is in Area 50, while RouterF has been accidentally misconfigured to be in Area 51. You might wonder why we are not concerned with the first error in the file, which also reports an area mismatch. We don't care about this because RouterG is another Level 2 router and is in a different area (Area 20), so it's fine for it to have a different area number.

Over time, the IS-IS logfiles can become very large and fill up the router's hard disk. To save the logfile for future analysis, you can copy the file to a server:

```
aviva@RouterJ> file copy /cf/var/log/isis-logs server1:isis-logs-20050625
```

If you no longer need the information in the file, you can delete the contents:

```
aviva@RouterJ> clear log isis-logs
```

Deleting the file's contents does not turn off tracing.

To stop the tracing altogether, you can remove the traceoptions statement from the configuration with the delete traceoptions command or you can leave the statements in the configuration and simply deactivate them so that they do not take effect when you commit the configuration:

```
[edit protocols isis]
aviva@RouterJ# deactivate traceoptions
```

To delete the logfiles and the rolled-over version of the file, use the file delete command:

```
aviva@RouterJ> file delete isis-logs*
```

When debugging IS-IS, you can set one or more of the following trace flags to capture IS-IS information:

```
[edit protocols isis traceoptions]
aviva@RouterA# set flag ?
Possible completions:
  all                Trace everything
  csn                Trace complete sequence number (CSN) packets
  error              Trace errored packets
  general            Trace general events
  graceful-restart   Trace graceful restart events
  hello              Trace hello packets
  lsp                Trace link-state packets
  lsp-generation     Trace LSP generation
  normal             Trace normal events
  packets            Trace IS-IS packets
  policy             Trace policy processing
  psn                Trace partial sequence number (PSN) packets
  route              Trace routing information
  spf                Trace SPF events
  state              Trace state transitions
  task               Trace routing protocol task processing
  timer              Trace routing protocol timer processing
```

Using some of the other flags, you can see IS-IS protocol packet exchanges:

```
Jun 25 13:06:31 Sending L2 CSN on interface fe-1/0/0.0
Jun 25 13:06:31     LSP range 0000.0000.0000.00-00 to ffff.ffff.ffff.ff-ff
Jun 25 13:06:31     packet length 131
Jun 25 13:06:31 Received L1 LAN IIH, source id RouterH on fe-1/0/0.0
Jun 25 13:06:31 ERROR: IIH from RouterH with no matching areas, interface fe-1/0/0.0
Jun 25 13:06:31     local area  49.0050
Jun 25 13:06:31     remote area 49.0030 (3 bytes)
Jun 25 13:06:31 ISIS L2 periodic xmit to 01:80:c2:00:00:15 interface fe-1/0/1.0
Jun 25 13:06:31 ISIS L2 periodic xmit to 01:80:c2:00:00:15 interface fe-1/0/0.0
Jun 25 13:06:31 ISIS L2 hello from RouterH interface fe-1/0/0.0 absorbed
Jun 25 13:06:32 Sending L2 CSN on interface fe-1/0/1.0
Jun 25 13:06:32     LSP range 0000.0000.0000.00-00 to ffff.ffff.ffff.ff-ff
Jun 25 13:06:32     packet length 131
Jun 25 13:06:32 Sending L1 CSN on interface fe-0/0/1.0
Jun 25 13:06:32     LSP range 0000.0000.0000.00-00 to ffff.ffff.ffff.ff-ff
Jun 25 13:06:32     packet length 83
Jun 25 13:06:32 Received L1 LAN IIH, source id RouterG on fe-1/0/1.0
Jun 25 13:06:32 ERROR: IIH from RouterG with no matching areas, interface fe-1/0/1.0
Jun 25 13:06:32     local area  49.0050
Jun 25 13:06:32     remote area 49.0020 (3 bytes)
Jun 25 13:06:33 ISIS L1 hello from RouterF interface fe-0/0/1.0 absorbed
Jun 25 13:06:33 ISIS L1 periodic xmit to 01:80:c2:00:00:14 interface fe-0/0/1.0
Jun 25 13:06:33 ISIS L2 hello from RouterG interface fe-1/0/1.0 absorbed
```

This logfile snippet shows that IS-IS exchanges complete sequence number (CSN) LSPs with one of its Level 2 and one of its Level 1 neighbors. You also see the periodic transmission of IS-IS Hello packets.

See Also

Recipe 5.10

CHAPTER 12

OSPF

12.0 Introduction

The Open Shortest Path First (OSPF) protocol is an IGP that routes packets within a single AS, or domain. The IETF began work on OSPF in the late 1980s to develop a replacement for RIP, which was the only routing protocol at the time, because people felt that a stronger routing protocol was needed and the link-state algorithm looked promising. OSPF was implemented by router vendors in the early 1990s and was eventually standardized by the IETF in 1997 as OSPF Version 1. The current standard is Version 2, defined in RFC 2328. Much of the OSPF design was lifted from IS-IS, which is an ISO routing-protocol standard developed at the same time. OSPF was designed specifically for TCP/IP and explicitly supports IP subnetting and the tagging of externally derived routing information. OSPF also provides for the authentication of routing updates. RFC 2740 defines OSPF for IPv6.

As an IGP, OSPF works within a domain, which usually corresponds to an administrative boundary and focuses on determining the most efficient routes to destinations within a domain. EGPs, on the other hand, primarily focus on policy rather than on the most efficient routing.

OSPF is a link-state protocol and uses link-state advertisements (LSAs) to describe the network topology. Each OSPF router generates LSAs that describe the topology it sees and floods the LSAs throughout the domain. As a result, each router ends up with a link-state database that describes the same network topology. Once the router has the complete network topology, it runs the Dijkstra SPF calculation to determine the shortest path to each destination in the network. The calculation results in destination/next-hop pairs that are placed in the OSPF routing database. Each router performs the SPF calculation independently, and the result is that each OSPF router has an identical routing database (though each router has different next hops for the destinations).

OSPF runs directly over IP, using IP protocol 89. It does not use a transport layer protocol such as TCP or UDP.

OSPF views routers as nodes, which are named by a router ID (one per router) that is unique within the domain. The router ID is a 32-bit number written in dotted decimal notation that looks a lot like an IP address but isn't necessarily one. The router ID need not be a routable IP address (although it can be) and is typically the lo0 interface address.

OSPF divides each AS into one or more smaller segments called *areas*. Each area is a set of networks and hosts that are administratively grouped together. Routers in an area run the link-state algorithm in parallel and store the results in their link-state databases. They share this information with each other by exchanging LSAs and thus have identical link-state databases.

To exchange routing information between areas, OSPF has *area border routers* (ABRs), which are routers connected to two or more areas. ABRs run a separate SPF calculation and maintain a separate link-state database for each area to which they are connected. ABRs summarize link-state information from one area before passing it to the next, which increases the overall stability of the network. An OSPF ABR is similar to an IS-IS router that is a Level 1–Level 2 system. However, one difference is that for OSPF, the router itself is at the area boundary, while for IS-IS the link between two routers is the area boundary.

Routers that exchange routing information with other ASs are called AS *boundary routers* (ASBRs). They advertise externally learned routes throughout the AS.

On each multiaccess network, OSPF elects a DR, which originates network LSAs on behalf of the network and establishes adjacencies with all routers on the network, thus participating in synchronizing the link-state databases. DR election is based on priority, which is an number between 0 and 255, with the router with the highest value becoming the DR. For OSPF, DR election is sticky. This means that once a couple of routers have agreed on a DR, if you add another router with higher priority to the network, it will not become the DR. If two routers have equal priority, the one with the lower router ID is selected. OSPF also elects a backup designated router (BDR).

OSPF defines several different types of areas. The core of an OSPF network is the *backbone area*, which is the area 0 (written as the 32-bit 0.0.0.0). All ABRs are attached to the backbone area, as are any networks that have an area ID of 0.0.0.0. The backbone area is a transit area that distributes traffic between other areas. The routers that make up the backbone must be physically contiguous. If they are not, you create OSFP *virtual links* so that the backbone routers appear to be contiguous.

In a straightforward OSPF network, all areas connect directly to the backbone area. All these areas, including the backbone, are referred to as *regular areas*.

OSPF *stub areas* are areas through which or into which AS external advertisements are not flooded. A stub area receives detailed or summarized routing information about other areas but receives no information about external ASs. It can receive a default summary from an ABR to reach external ASs. Because a stub area has no external routes, it cannot connect to an external area (that is, it cannot contain an ASBR) and you cannot redistribute routes from another protocol into the stub area. You might use stub areas when much of the topological database consists of AS external advertisements because it reduces the size of the topological databases and therefore the amount of memory required on the internal routers in the stub area. Another restriction on stub areas is that you cannot create a virtual link through them.

Not-so-stubby areas (NSSAs) are a variant of stub areas that allows a stub area to connect to an external network. This allows external routes originated by ASBRs within the areas to be flooded in Type 7 LSAs and then leaked into other areas. However, external routes from other areas are not flooded into the NSSA.

For more background information about OSPF, see *OSPF and IS-IS: A Comparative Anatomy* at *http://www.nanog.org/mtg-0006/katz.html*.

12.1 Configuring OSPF

Problem

Your want to configure OSPF on a JUNOS router.

Solution

You enable OSPF by defining the interfaces on which it will run and the area to which the interfaces will be attached:

```
[edit protocols]
aviva@RouterG# set ospf area 0.0.0.0 interface fe-0/0/1.0
aviva@RouterG# set ospf area 0.0.0.0 interface fe-1/0/1.0
```

Discussion

The basic setup for configuring a single OSPF area is straightforward. Enable the protocol on all router interfaces that will participate in the OSPF domain and specify which area the interfaces are in. In this recipe, area 0 has three routers (see Figure 12-1).

In this recipe, we configure OSPF on two interfaces of a router that is in the backbone area, which has an area identifier of 0.0.0.0. In addition, the router must have a router ID to identify the router from which OSPF packets originate. In this recipe, we don't set one explicitly because we have configured a unicast IP address on the router's lo0 interface and this address is used as the router ID:

```
aviva@RouterG> show configuration interfaces lo0
unit 0 {
    family inet {
        address 192.168.19.1/32;
    }
}
```

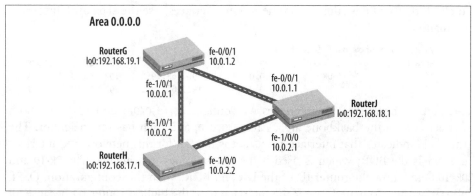

Figure 12-1. OSPF single-area topology

You do not need to explicitly configure OSPF to run on lo0, because the JUNOS software automatically configures lo0 as a stub network if the router ID is the same as the address on the lo0 interface (which is what is recommended). Use the following command to set the router ID:

```
[edit routing-options]
aviva@RouterG# set router-id 192.168.19.1
```

In this recipe, using the lo0 as the router ID is implicit. Having the router ID be the same as the lo0 address provides a way for OSPF packets to get to the Routing Engine. If the router ID is different from the lo0 address, OSPF does not automatically run on the router's lo0 interface. The result is that LSAs will use the router ID as the originator, but the routing table will have a route to the lo0 address but not to the router ID.

However, it is good practice to configure the lo0 interface as a passive interface:

```
[edit protocols]
aviva@RouterG# set ospf area 0.0.0.0 interface lo0.0 passive
```

Passive interfaces advertise their addresses but do not form adjacencies.

With this simple configuration, the OSPF protocol takes over. You do not have to configure neighbors; OSPF automatically discovers them. (The exception to this is running OSPF on multipoint nonbroadcast, multiaccess [NBMA] networks, such as ATM and Frame Relay. For these, you must explicitly configure neighbors.) OSPF then establishes adjacencies with its neighbors, first sending OSPF Hello packets to ensure that the two ends of the link can communicate. All point-to-point neighbors become adjacent to each other, and, on LANs, all interfaces become adjacent to the DR and BDR. In the process of establishing adjacencies, the routers synchronize their link-state databases. Once the adjacencies are established, OSPF floods LSAs to establish consistent routing databases.

To check that OSPF is running on the router interfaces, use the show ospf interface command:

```
aviva@RouterG> show ospf interface
Interface              State    Area           DR ID          BDR ID         Nbrs
fe-0/0/1.0             DR       0.0.0.0        192.168.19.1   192.168.18.1    1
fe-1/0/1.0             BDR      0.0.0.0        192.168.17.1   192.168.19.1    1
```

This output shows the two interfaces we configured, fe-0/0/1 and fe-1/0/1. Both interfaces are in the backbone area, Area 0.0.0.0, and each has one neighbor. The State field indicates that interface fe-/0/0/1 is the DR for this network and interface fe-1/0/1 is the BDR, which is used if the DR becomes unavailable. The DR-ID and BDR-ID fields show the router ID of the DR and BDR. With this configuration, OSPF chooses as the designated router the interface with the highest router ID because all routers are using the default priority (which you see with the show ospf neighbor command, described below). If the router has not yet determined which router is the DR, the state is Waiting:

```
aviva@RouterJ> show ospf interface
Interface              State    Area           DR ID          BDR ID         Nbrs
fe-1/0/0.0             BDR      0.0.0.0        192.168.18.1   192.168.17.1    1
fe-1/0/1.0             Waiting  0.0.0.0        0.0.0.0        0.0.0.0          0
```

Use the show ospf neighbor command to see who the OSPF neighbors are:

```
aviva@RouterG> show ospf neighbor
  Address        Interface         State     ID            Pri  Dead
  10.0.1.1       fe-0/0/1.0        Full      192.168.18.1  128   34
  10.0.0.2       fe-1/0/1.0        Full      192.168.17.1  128   34
```

The Interface column lists the two interfaces we configured. Interface fe-0/0/1 connects to the neighbor's interface address 10.0.1.1, and this neighbor has a router ID of 192.168.18.1. The other interface, fe-1/0/1, goes to the neighbor's interface at IP address 10.0.0.2, and this neighbor has a router ID of 192.168.17.1. You see from this output that both neighbors have a router priority of 128, which is the default OSPF priority. OSPF uses this value to select the DR, choosing the router with the highest priority to be the DR. In the event of a tie, OSPF chooses the router with the highest router ID.

The State column shows the state of each OSPF neighbor. When OSPF network connectivity has established and the network is up and running, the state is Full. As OSPF connectivity is establishing, you may see Attempt, Init, or 2way in this field. (If either end of an adjacency on a LAN is not a DR or a BDR, the final state is 2Way.) If the state does not show as Full after about 30 seconds, check that the OSPF connectivity between the two neighbors is working correctly. Use the show interfaces command to make sure that the interface is operational. On the neighboring router, use the show configuration protocols ospf command to make sure that OSPF is configured, properly, and use the show ospf neighbor and show ospf interface commands to verify that OSPF is running on the interfaces.

Another common problem in establishing adjacencies is an MTU mismatch between the end points of the adjacency. This causes the adjacency to get stuck in the ExState state. The show interfaces command shows the MTU sizes for the physical and logical interfaces.

The last column of the output shows the OSPF dead interval, which is the amount of time remaining before the router closes the adjacency with its neighbor. OSPF sends Hello packets, which act as adjacency keepalives, every 10 seconds (this is the default). If there are no problems with the connection or the routers, the dead interval never drops below 31 seconds. The default dead time is four times the hello interval, or 40 seconds.

In the show ospf interface output, you can see that OSPF has automatically chosen DRs and a BDR:

```
aviva@RouterG> show ospf interface
Interface          State    Area       DR ID          BDR ID         Nbrs
fe-0/0/1.0         DR       0.0.0.0    192.168.19.1   192.168.18.1   1
fe-1/0/1.0         BDR      0.0.0.0    192.168.17.1   192.168.19.1   1
```

How does OSPF elect the DR? It chooses the DR based on the priority. However, the default priority value (128) is the same for all OSPF interfaces, and we haven't changed it in the configuration:

```
aviva@RouterG> show ospf neighbor
Address      Interface       State    ID             Pri  Dead
10.0.1.1     fe-0/0/1.0      Full     192.168.18.1   128  34
10.0.0.2     fe-1/0/1.0      Full     192.168.17.1   128  34
```

When an OSPF interface comes up, one of the things it checks is whether the network already has a DR. If it does, the interface simply accepts that DR regardless of its own router priority. In other words, the assignment of the DR is sticky. This is done by design because it's relatively traumatic for the network to switch DRs (except to promote the BDR). So, even if you were to configure a DR priority (the priority can be a value from 1 to 255, with a higher number taking priority), it is effectively ignored once a DR is elected. Typically, there is no reason to care which router is the DR, because all JUNOS routers are powerful enough to handle the LSA load.

12.2 Viewing Routes Learned by OSPF

Problem

You want to check the routes that are being generated by the Dijkstra SPF calculation to make sure that the router is learning the expected routes.

Solution

Use the show ospf route command to see the contents of the OSPF routing table:

```
aviva@RouterG> show ospf route
Prefix             Path    Route     NH    Metric  NextHop      Nexthop
                   Type    Type      Type          Interface    addr/label
192.168.17.1       Intra   Router    IP    1       fe-1/0/1.0   10.0.0.2
192.168.18.1       Intra   Router    IP    1       fe-0/0/1.0   10.0.1.1
10.0.0.0/24        Intra   Network   IP    1       fe-1/0/1.0
10.0.1.0/24        Intra   Network   IP    1       fe-0/0/1.0
10.0.2.0/24        Intra   Network   IP    2       fe-0/0/1.0   10.0.1.1
                                                   fe-1/0/1.0   10.0.0.2
192.168.17.1/32    Intra   Network   IP    1       fe-1/0/1.0   10.0.0.2
192.168.18.1/32    Intra   Network   IP    1       fe-0/0/1.0   10.0.1.1
```

Discussion

OSPF routers perform an SPF calculation to determine the best route to a destination and places these routes in its routing table. The show ospf route command displays what's in the OSPF routing table. The Prefix column shows the destinations on the network, and you also see the interface used to reach the next hop toward the destination and the IP address of that next hop.

You can find out which routes the router has learned from OSPF by checking the unicast routing table:

```
aviva@RouterG> show route table inet.0
inet.0: 11 destinations, 11 routes (11 active, 0 holddown, 0 hidden)
+ = Active Route, - = Last Active, * = Both
10.0.0.0/24        *[Direct/0] 3d 01:42:24
                    > via fe-1/0/1.0
10.0.0.1/32        *[Local/0] 3d 01:42:24
                     Local via fe-1/0/1.0
10.0.1.0/24        *[Direct/0] 3d 01:42:24
                    > via fe-0/0/1.0
10.0.1.2/32        *[Local/0] 3d 01:42:24
                     Local via fe-0/0/1.0
10.0.2.0/24        *[OSPF/10] 00:18:28, metric 2
                     to 10.0.1.1 via fe-0/0/1.0
                    > to 10.0.0.2 via fe-1/0/1.0
10.0.16.0/24       *[Direct/0] 3d 01:42:24
                    > via fe-1/0/0.0
10.0.16.2/32       *[Local/0] 3d 01:42:24
                     Local via fe-1/0/0.0
192.168.17.1/32    *[OSPF/10] 00:18:28, metric 1
                    > to 10.0.0.2 via fe-1/0/1.0
192.168.18.1/32    *[OSPF/10] 00:18:28, metric 1
                    > to 10.0.1.1 via fe-0/0/1.0
192.168.19.1/32    *[Direct/0] 3d 01:40:56
                    > via lo0.0
224.0.0.5/32       *[OSPF/10] 2d 20:52:32, metric 1
                     MultiRecv
```

The route entries starting with [OSPF/10] are those learned from OSPF. The router has learned four routes from OSPF:

- 192.168.17.1/32 and 192.168.18.1./32 are router loopback addresses that are the two OSPF neighbors we saw in the OSPF routing table.
- 10.0.2.0/24 is a subnetwork that is the subnet between our two neighbors (which we also saw in the OSPF database).
- 224.0.0.5/32 is the OSPF multicast address.

The routes to the two loopback addresses show up in the routing table because the router ID is configured on the routers' loo addresses, not with the set routing-options router-id command.

The value of 10 in the brackets is the JUNOS default value for the OSPF administrative distance, also called the routing preference, which is used to select what route is installed in the forwarding table when several protocols calculate routes to the same destination. A preference of 10 is the default for internal OSPF routes, which are those within the domain. The preference value for routes outside the domain that OSPF advertises is 150. You can change the preference value by configuring the preference statement for the OSPF area. The numbers following the brackets show how long the routing table has known about the route. The metric value (either 1 or 2) is the cost to this address. Understanding the routing table is discussed more in Recipe 9.1.

You might find it strange that a multicast address, 224.0.0.5/32, is present in the inet.0 routing table, which is the unicast routing table. This is simply a result of a JUNOS design decision. Instead of establishing a separate routing table for the few multicast routes used by routing protocols for receiving protocol packets, which are well-known addresses, the JUNOS software places these routes in the unicast routing table.

You can also see just the routes learned by OSPF:

```
aviva@RouterG> show route protocol ospf table inet.0
inet.0: 14 destinations, 14 routes (14 active, 0 holddown, 0 hidden)
+ = Active Route, - = Last Active, * = Both
10.0.2.0/24        *[OSPF/10] 00:00:26, metric 2
                     to 10.0.1.1 via fe-0/0/1.0
                   > to 10.0.0.2 via fe-1/0/1.0
192.168.17.1/32    *[OSPF/10] 00:00:26, metric 1
                   > to 10.0.0.2 via fe-1/0/1.0
192.168.18.1/32    *[OSPF/10] 00:00:31, metric 1
                   > to 10.0.1.1 via fe-0/0/1.0
224.0.0.5/32       *[OSPF/10] 00:00:42, metric 1
                     MultiRecv
```

12.3   Viewing the OSPF Link-State Database

Problem

You want to look at the router's link-state database to make sure that all the OSPF routers know about each other.

Solution

Use the show ospf database command to view the contents of the link-state database:

```
aviva@RouterG> show ospf database
OSPF link state database, area 0.0.0.0
 Type      ID               Adv Rtr         Seq      Age  Opt  Cksum  Len
 Router    192.168.17.1     192.168.17.1    0x800000d0  986  0x2  0xebd2  60
 Router    192.168.18.1     192.168.18.1    0x80000083  986  0x2  0xbd4a  60
 Router   *192.168.19.1     192.168.19.1    0x8000009f  656  0x2  0x46a5  60
 Network  *10.0.0.1         192.168.19.1    0x80000010   56  0x2  0x9b2e  32
 Network  *10.0.1.2         192.168.19.1    0x80000030  356  0x2  0x5353  32
 Network   10.0.2.1         192.168.18.1    0x80000005 1454  0x2  0x993b  32
```

Discussion

OSPF routers exchange LSAs that describe that router's view of the network topology, and the routers store the LSAs in a link-state database. The SPF algorithm then runs on the link-state database to create the OSPF routing table, which contains the shortest path to each destination.

Use the show ospf database command to look at the OSPF LSAs in the link-state database. Table 12-1 explains the different types OSPF LSAs.

Table 12-1. OSPF LSA types

Type	Name	Description
1	Router	All routers originate these LSAs, flooding them within a single area, to describe the state and cost of router interfaces within the area.
2	Network	DRs originate these LSAs, flooding them within a single area, to describe all routers attached to the network, including the DR.
3	Summary (network)	ABRs originate a single Summary LSA for each known interarea destination, flooding them within a single domain. Type 3 Summary LSAs are sent when the destination is an IP network.
4	Summary (ASBR)	ABRs originate a single Summary LSA for each known interarea destination, flooding them within a single domain. Type 4 summary LSAs are sent when the destination is an ASBR.
5	AS External	ASBRs originate these LSAs to describe destinations external to the OSPF domain (AS).
7	NSSA External	NSSA ASBRs originate these LSAs, flooding them within the NSSA, to describe destinations in the other parts of the OSPF domain.

In the command output in this recipe, the database has three Router (Type 1) and three Network (Type 2) LSAs. The lines with an asterisk in the ID are database entries that originated from the local router. The router also knows about its two neighbors, 192.168.17.1 and 192.168.18.1, and about the subnetwork that connects these two neighbors (10.0.2.1).

If you check on the other two routers in the area, you see that they have identical databases:

```
aviva@RouterJ> show ospf database
     OSPF link state database, area 0.0.0.0
 Type     ID              Adv Rtr           Seq       Age  Opt  Cksum  Len
 Router  *192.168.17.1    192.168.17.1      0x8000010a 170  0x2  0x760e  60
 Router   192.168.18.1    192.168.18.1      0x800000ae 377  0x2  0x6775  60
 Router   192.168.19.1    192.168.19.1      0x80000007 372  0x2  0xdf32  48
 Network  10.0.0.1        192.168.19.1      0x80000002 372  0x2  0xb720  32
 Network  10.0.1.2        192.168.19.1      0x80000002 378  0x2  0xaf25  32
 Network  10.0.2.1        192.168.18.1      0x8000002a 481  0x2  0x4f60  32

aviva@RouterH> show ospf database
     OSPF link state database, area 0.0.0.0
 Type     ID              Adv Rtr           Seq       Age  Opt  Cksum  Len
 Router   192.168.17.1    192.168.17.1      0x8000010a  45  0x2  0x760e  60
 Router  *192.168.18.1    192.168.18.1      0x800000ae 250  0x2  0x6775  60
 Router   192.168.19.1    192.168.19.1      0x80000007 247  0x2  0xdf32  48
 Network  10.0.0.1        192.168.19.1      0x80000002 247  0x2  0xb720  32
 Network  10.0.1.2        192.168.19.1      0x80000002 251  0x2  0xaf25  32
 Network *10.0.2.1        192.168.18.1      0x8000002a 354  0x2  0x4f60  32
```

The only thing different is which LSAs are marked as originated from the router.

Use the following version of the show ospf database command to get a quick summary of the entries LSA database:

```
aviva@RouterG> show ospf database summary
Area 0.0.0.0:
   3 Router LSAs
   3 Network LSAs
Externals:
Interface fe-0/0/1.0:
Interface fe-1/0/0.0:
```

12.4 Configuring OSPF for IPv6

Problem

You want to use OSPF on an IPv6 network.

Solution

The configuration for OSPFv3 is the same as for OSPFv2, the IPv4 version of OSPF, except that you use set ospf3 commands instead of set ospf commands:

```
[edit protocols]
aviva@RouterJ# set ospf3 area 0.0.0.0 interface fe-1/0/0.0
aviva@RouterJ# set ospf3 area 0.0.0.0 interface lo0.0 passive
```

Discussion

JUNOS OSPFv3 configuration for IPv6 networks is basically identical to OSPFv2 configuration. You configure the protocol with set ospf3 commands instead of set ospf commands and use show ospf3 commands instead of show ospf commands to check on the OSPF status. Also, make sure to set IPv6 address on the interfaces running OSPFv3 and on the loopback interface, lo0.

This recipe shows how to configure an OSPFv3 backbone router. All backbone routers have the same basic configuration. As with OSPFv2, define which interfaces are in the area. Again, include the lo0 interface, configured as a passive interface, so that it advertises its address into OSPF.

To check that OSPF is running on the router interfaces, use the show ospf3 interface command:

```
aviva@RouterH> show ospf3 interface
Interface          State     Area          DR-ID         BDR-ID      Nbrs
fe-1/0/0.0         DR        0.0.0.0       192.168.18.1  10.0.0.1    1
lo0.0              DRother   0.0.0.0       0.0.0.0       0.0.0.0     0
```

The output shows that OSPFv3 is running on the configured interfaces, fe-1/0/0 and lo0, and that the Fast Ethernet interface is the DR. The DR-ID and BDR-ID columns show the OSPF router ID of the DR and BDR routers.

Use the following command to see the neighbors with which the router has formed OSPFv3 adjacencies:

```
aviva@RouterH> show ospf3 neighbor
ID                 Interface            State    Pri   Dead
10.0.0.1           fe-1/0/0.0           Full     128   36
     Neighbor-address fe80::205:85ff:fec4:72f4
```

You see one adjacency, with the router ID 10.0.0.1, which is the neighbor via interface fe-1/0/0. As with OSPFv2, Full in the State column indicates that the OSPFv3 adjacency is up and running. The neighbor has a default priority of 128, the same default as OSPFv2, which is used to elect the DR.

To see the OSPF routing table on the router, use the show ospf3 route command:

```
aviva@RouterH> show ospf3 route
Prefix                                       Path    Route       NH    Metric
                                             type    type        type
10.0.0.1                                     Intra   Router      IP    1
     NH-interface fe-1/0/0.0, NH-addr fe80::205:85ff:fec4:72f4
192.168.18.1;0.0.0.3                         Intra   Transit     IP    1
     NH-interface fe-1/0/0.0
9009:3::/64                                  Intra   Network     IP    1
     NH-interface fe-1/0/0.0
```

The prefix column shows the routes to the other Area 0 router. One difference in the output for OSPFv3 is that the loopback address, 192.168.18.1, shows up as type Transit instead of as Network to indicate that the loopback address is not on a real

OSPF network. Route 192.168.18.1:0.0.0.3 actually represents a route to the pseudonode corresponding to the fe-1/0/0 link. (In OSPFv3, a LAN link is called a transit link.) Any multiaccess link, such as a LAN or an NBMA link, is represented by a fake node, or pseudonode, in the IGP. This route is used for debugging and is not installed in the forwarding table.

The OSPFv3 link-state database contains more information than for OSPFv2:

```
aviva@RouterH> show ospf3 database
      OSPF3 link state database, area 0.0.0.0
 Type       ID           Adv Rtr          Seq         Age  Cksum  Len
 Router     0.0.0.0      10.0.0.1         0x80000422  933  0x3338 40
 Router    *0.0.0.0      192.168.18.1     0x80000013  327  0x1fee 40
 Router     0.0.0.0      192.168.19.1     0x80000012  3399 0x98e4 56
 Network   *0.0.0.3      192.168.18.1     0x80000003  27   0x31ee 32
 Network    0.0.0.1      192.168.19.1     0x8000000e  3399 0x4352 36
 IntraArPfx *0.0.0.4     192.168.18.1     0x80000002  932  0x2602 44
 IntraArPfx 0.0.0.2      192.168.19.1     0x8000000d  3399 0xe937 44

      OSPF3 Link-Local link state database, interface fe-1/0/0.0
 Type       ID           Adv Rtr          Seq         Age  Cksum  Len
 Link       0.0.0.4      10.0.0.1         0x80000001  933  0xd6af 56
 Link      *0.0.0.3      192.168.18.1     0x80000005  627  0x3f76 56
```

In addition to listing the entries in this area, Area 0.0.0.0, the second part of the output shows the entries in the link-local, link-state database for this interface. These are the database entries learned over the specific OSPFv3 interface and they are visible only by nodes that are directly on this link.

See Also

Recipes 7.6 and 12.1

12.5   Configuring a Multiarea OSPF Network

Problem

Your OSPF network has a number of physical and departmental boundaries, and, for administrative purposes and for scalability, you want to divide the network into a number of areas.

Solution

Configure a second OSPF area on the router:

```
[edit protocols]
aviva@RouterG# set ospf area 0.0.0.1 interface fe-1/0/0.0
```

Discussion

To create additional areas in the OSPF network, configure the second area on the router's interface (or interfaces) that connects to the second area. In this recipe, we configure the second area, Area 0.0.0.1, on our router. This router acts as the ABR between the backbone area and Area 0.0.0.1. See Figure 12-2.

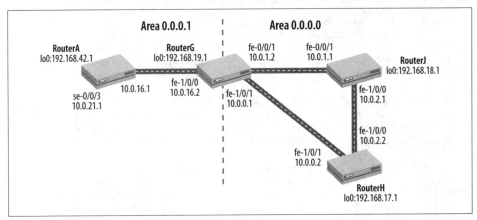

Figure 12-2. OSPF two-area topology

Check that the interface is configured:

```
aviva@RouterG> show ospf interface
Interface        State   Area         DR ID          BDR ID          Nbrs
fe-0/0/1.0       DR      0.0.0.0      192.168.19.1   192.168.18.1    1
fe-1/0/1.0       BDR     0.0.0.0      192.168.17.1   192.168.19.1    1
fe-1/0/0.0       BDR     0.0.0.1      192.168.42.1   192.168.19.1    1
```

You see that interface fe-1/0/0 is up and is in Area 0.0.0.1.

Again, check that the neighbor is active:

```
aviva@RouterG> show ospf neighbor detail
  Address         Interface         State      ID           Pri  Dead
  10.0.1.1        fe-0/0/1.0        Full       192.168.18.1  128  33
    area 0.0.0.0, opt 0x42, DR 10.0.1.2, BDR 10.0.1.1
    Up 01:11:30, adjacent 01:11:30
  10.0.0.2        fe-1/0/1.0        Full       192.168.17.1  128  39
    area 0.0.0.0, opt 0x42, DR 10.0.0.1, BDR 10.0.0.2
    Up 01:11:30, adjacent 01:11:25
  10.0.16.1       fe-1/0/0.0        Full       192.168.42.1  128  31
    area 0.0.0.1, opt 0x42, DR 10.0.16.1, BDR 10.0.16.2
    Up 00:00:55, adjacent 00:00:55
```

In addition to showing that the neighbor is up (State is Full), the detail version of the show ospf neighbor command shows how long the interface and adjacency have been up, as well as the area number and the router IDs of the DR and BDR for the area.

Checking on RouterA at the other end of the connection, you see the connection to our router, RouterG, and that it is the designated router for Area 0.0.0.1:

```
aviva@RouterA> show ospf neighbor detail
  Address        Interface          State      ID          Pri  Dead
  10.0.16.2       fe-0/0/0.0         Full     192.168.19.1   128   39
    area 0.0.0.1, opt 0x42, DR 10.0.16.1, BDR 10.0.16.2
    Up 00:03:56, adjacent 00:03:56
  10.0.21.2       se-0/0/3.0         Full     192.168.12.1   128   33
    area 0.0.0.1, opt 0x42, DR 0.0.0.0, BDR 0.0.0.0
    Up 03:24:41, adjacent 03:24:41
```

OSPF collects topology information for each of the areas in their respective databases:

```
aviva@RouterG> show ospf database
    OSPF link state database, area 0.0.0.0
 Type       ID              Adv Rtr           Seq      Age  Opt  Cksum  Len
 Router    192.168.17.1    192.168.17.1    0x800000d0  1481  0x2  0xebd2  60
 Router    192.168.18.1    192.168.18.1    0x80000083  1481  0x2  0xbd4a  60
 Router   *192.168.19.1    192.168.19.1    0x800000a1    78  0x2  0x45a3  60
 Network  *10.0.0.1        192.168.19.1    0x80000010   551  0x2  0x9b2e  32
 Network  *10.0.1.2        192.168.19.1    0x80000030   851  0x2  0x5353  32
 Network   10.0.2.1        192.168.18.1    0x80000005  1949  0x2  0x993b  32
 Summary  *10.0.16.0       192.168.19.1    0x80000002    77  0x2  0xa81b  28
 Summary  *10.0.21.0       192.168.19.1    0x80000001    77  0x2  0xebc7  28
 Summary  *10.0.22.0       192.168.19.1    0x80000001    77  0x2  0x594d  28
 Summary  *172.19.121.0    192.168.19.1    0x80000001    77  0x2  0x69e   28
 Summary  *172.100.1.0     192.168.19.1    0x80000001   319  0x2  0x6368  28
 Summary  *192.168.12.1    192.168.19.1    0x80000001    77  0x2  0x1646  28
 Summary  *192.168.42.1    192.168.19.1    0x80000001    77  0x2  0x52f7  28

    OSPF link state database, area 0.0.0.1
 Type       ID              Adv Rtr           Seq      Age  Opt  Cksum  Len
 Router    192.168.12.1    192.168.12.1    0x80000054  1223  0x2  0x1540  72
 Router   *192.168.19.1    192.168.19.1    0x80000002    77  0x2  0x771a  48
 Router    192.168.42.1    192.168.42.1    0x8000005b    78  0x2  0x870d  96
 Network   10.0.16.1       192.168.42.1    0x80000001    78  0x2  0x5147  32
 Summary  *10.0.0.0        192.168.19.1    0x80000001    77  0x2  0x5b79  28
 Summary  *10.0.1.0        192.168.19.1    0x80000001    77  0x2  0x5083  28
 Summary  *10.0.2.0        192.168.19.1    0x80000001    77  0x2  0x4f82  28
 Summary  *192.168.17.1    192.168.19.1    0x80000001    77  0x2  0x66fc  28
 Summary  *192.168.18.1    192.168.19.1    0x80000001    77  0x2  0x5b07  28
```

Notice that the link-state database now contains summary advertisements, which summarize routing information from one area into another.

The OSPF routing table now shows destinations in Area 0.0.0.1:

```
aviva@RouterG> show ospf route
 Prefix            Path   Route    NH  Metric  NextHop      Nexthop
                   Type   Type     Type        Interface    addr/label
 192.168.12.1      Intra  Router   IP   13     fe-1/0/0.0   10.0.16.1
 192.168.17.1      Intra  Router   IP    1     fe-1/0/1.0   10.0.0.2
 192.168.18.1      Intra  Router   IP    1     fe-0/0/1.0   10.0.1.1
 192.168.42.1      Intra  Router   IP    1     fe-1/0/0.0   10.0.16.1
```

```
10.0.0.0/24        Intra  Network  IP  1    fe-1/0/1.0
10.0.1.0/24        Intra  Network  IP  1    fe-0/0/1.0
10.0.2.0/24        Intra  Network  IP  2    fe-0/0/1.0   10.0.1.1
                                            fe-1/0/1.0   10.0.0.2

10.0.16.0/24       Intra  Network  IP  1    fe-1/0/0.0
10.0.21.0/24       Intra  Network  IP  13   fe-1/0/0.0   10.0.16.1
10.0.22.0/24       Intra  Network  IP  25   fe-1/0/0.0   10.0.16.1
172.19.121.0/24    Intra  Network  IP  2    fe-1/0/0.0   10.0.16.1
172.100.1.0/24     Intra  Network  IP  2    fe-1/0/0.0   10.0.16.1
192.168.12.1/32    Intra  Network  IP  13   fe-1/0/0.0   10.0.16.1
192.168.17.1/32    Intra  Network  IP  1    fe-1/0/1.0   10.0.0.2
192.168.18.1/32    Intra  Network  IP  1    fe-0/0/1.0   10.0.1.1
192.168.42.1/32    Intra  Network  IP  1    fe-1/0/0.0   10.0.16.1
```

These routes are also in the router's routing table:

```
aviva@RouterG> show route table inet.0
inet.0: 19 destinations, 20 routes (19 active, 0 holddown, 0 hidden)
+ = Active Route, - = Last Active, * = Both
0.0.0.0/0           *[Static/5] 5w4d 20:51:01
                     > to 172.19.121.1 via fe-0/0/0.0
10.0.0.0/24         *[Direct/0] 3d 01:53:17
                     > via fe-1/0/1.0
10.0.0.1/32         *[Local/0] 3d 01:53:17
                      Local via fe-1/0/1.0
10.0.1.0/24         *[Direct/0] 3d 01:53:17
                     > via fe-0/0/1.0
10.0.1.2/32         *[Local/0] 3d 01:53:17
                      Local via fe-0/0/1.0
10.0.2.0/24         *[OSPF/10] 00:05:31, metric 2
                     > to 10.0.1.1 via fe-0/0/1.0
                       to 10.0.0.2 via fe-1/0/1.0
10.0.16.0/24        *[Direct/0] 3d 01:53:17
                     > via fe-1/0/0.0
10.0.16.2/32        *[Local/0] 3d 01:53:17
                      Local via fe-1/0/0.0
10.0.21.0/24        *[OSPF/10] 00:05:31, metric 13
                     > to 10.0.16.1 via fe-1/0/0.0
10.0.22.0/24        *[OSPF/10] 00:05:31, metric 25
                     > to 10.0.16.1 via fe-1/0/0.0
172.19.121.0/24     *[Direct/0] 5w4d 20:51:01
                     > via fe-0/0/0.0
                      [OSPF/10] 00:05:31, metric 2
                     > to 10.0.16.1 via fe-1/0/0.0
172.19.121.119/32   *[Local/0] 5w4d 20:51:04
                      Local via fe-0/0/0.0
172.100.1.0/24      *[OSPF/10] 00:07:48, metric 2
                     > to 10.0.16.1 via fe-1/0/0.0
192.168.12.1/32     *[OSPF/10] 00:05:31, metric 13
                     > to 10.0.16.1 via fe-1/0/0.0
192.168.17.1/32     *[OSPF/10] 00:05:31, metric 1
                     > to 10.0.0.2 via fe-1/0/1.0
192.168.18.1/32     *[OSPF/10] 00:05:31, metric 1
                     > to 10.0.1.1 via fe-0/0/1.0
```

```
192.168.19.1/32    *[Direct/0] 3d 01:51:49
                    > via lo0.0
192.168.42.1/32    *[OSPF/10] 00:05:31, metric 1
                    > to 10.0.16.1 via fe-1/0/0.0
224.0.0.5/32       *[OSPF/10] 2d 21:03:25, metric 1
                    MultiRecv
```

12.6 Setting Up Stub Areas

Problem

You want to optimize OSPF performance in an area that connects only to the OSPF backbone.

Solution

Configure the area as a stub area:

```
[edit protocols ospf]
aviva@RouterE# set area 0.0.0.3 interface t1-0/0/3.0
aviva@RouterE# set area 0.0.0.3 stub
```

Discussion

When some areas of your network have no external connections, you can make them into stub areas. This reduces the amount of OSPF protocol traffic that is flooded through the area, which improves performance on the router by decreasing the size of the OSPF routing database and thus decreasing the amount of CPU needed to perform the SPF calculations. Another common reason to set up a stub area is to allow legacy routers that don't have enough memory or CPU horsepower to participate in the OSPF network. A stub area receives OSPF routing-database information from all the other areas in the network. However, instead of receiving all AS external advertisements, the stub area gets only a default summary (0.0.0.0/0) from ABRs to reach external destinations and gets summaries for destinations in other OSPF areas.

You configure each router in the stub area as a stub router by including the stub statement when configuring the area. In our recipe, Area 0.0.0.3 is a stub area (see Figure 12-3). Configure the stub area on each router that is part of this area.

Check that the stub area is up and running:

```
aviva@RouterE> show ospf interface detail
Interface          State   Area          DR ID        BDR ID      Nbrs
t1-0/0/3.0         PtToPt  0.0.0.3       0.0.0.0      0.0.0.0       1
Type: P2P, Address: 0.0.0.0, Mask: 0.0.0.0, MTU: 1500, Cost: 65
  Adj count: 1
Hello: 10, Dead: 40, ReXmit: 5, Stub
Auth type: None
```

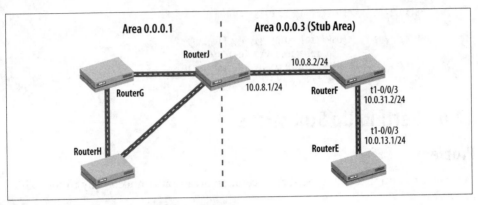

Figure 12-3. OSPF stub area topology

Type 4 (ASBR Summary) and Type 5 (AS External) LSAs are not flooded into stub areas. When Area 0.0.0.3 is a regular area, not a stub area, the routers in that area receive Type 4 and Type 5 LSAs. Here are the entries in RouterE's link-state database:

```
aviva@RouterE> show ospf database summary
Area 0.0.0.3:
    3 Router LSAs
    1 Network LSAs
    9 Summary LSAs
    1 ASBRSum LSAs
Externals:
    2 Extern LSAs
Interface loo.0:
Interface t1-0/0/3.0:
Interface t1-0/0/3.0:
```

The output shows one ASBR Summary and two External LSAs. After you configure the area as a stub, these routes are no longer sent from Area 0.0.0.0 so are not in the router's link-state database:

```
aviva@RouterE> show ospf database summary
Area 0.0.0.3:
    3 Router LSAs
    1 Network LSAs
    9 Summary LSAs
Externals:
Interface loo.0:
Interface t1-0/0/3.0:
Interface t1-0/0/3.0:
```

You can further reduce the number of LSA packets flooded through the stub area by configuring the ABR so that it does not flood Type 3 (Network Summary) LSAs to the routers in the stub area:

```
[edit protocols ospf]
aviva@RouterJ# set area 0.0.0.3 stub no-summaries
```

The routers in the stub area no longer receive the Type 3 LSAs:

```
aviva@RouterE> show ospf database summary
Area 0.0.0.3:
   3 Router LSAs
   1 Network LSAs <-- No Type 3 LSAs are listed after the Type 2 LSAs
Externals:
Interface t1-0/0/3.0:
Interface t1-0/0/3.0:
```

12.7 Creating a Not-So-Stubby Area

Problem

You want to configure a stub area for an area that has an ASBR to connect it to an external network. This area already sends AS External LSAs to the backbone area and doesn't need to receive them from the backbone.

Solution

Configure the area as an NSSA. Include this configuration on each router in the NSSA area.

```
[edit protocols ospf]
aviva@RouterJ# set area 0.0.0.3 nssa
```

Discussion

The configuration for NSSA is similar to that for stub areas. Include the nssa statement when configuring each area. Once you commit the configuration, you can see that the router is in an NSSA:

```
aviva@RouterJ> show ospf interface fe-0/0/1.0 detail
Interface           State     Area          DR ID          BDR ID        Nbrs
fe-0/0/1.0          BDR       0.0.0.3       192.168.16.1   192.168.17.1    1
Type: LAN, Address: 10.0.8.1, Mask: 255.255.255.240, MTU: 1500, Cost: 1
DR addr: 10.0.8.2, BDR addr: 10.0.8.1, Adj count: 1, Priority: 128
Hello: 10, Dead: 40, ReXmit: 5, Stub NSSA
Auth type: None
```

Before you configure the stub area, the OSPF link-state database contains two Type 5 (AS External) LSAs for the external routes that are coming from the ASBR, which is RouterE (192.168.15.1):

```
aviva@RouterJ> show ospf database area 0.0.0.3
   OSPF link state database, area 0.0.0.3
 Type        ID              Adv Rtr         Seq        Age  Opt  Cksum   Len
Router    192.168.15.1     192.168.15.1    0x80000004   163  0x2  0x4156   60
Router    192.168.16.1     192.168.16.1    0x80000007    49  0x2  0xbd74   84
Router   *192.168.17.1     192.168.17.1    0x80000004   290  0x2  0x47ea   36
Network  *10.0.8.1         192.168.17.1    0x80000002   699  0x2  0x4e86   32
Summary  *10.0.0.0         192.168.17.1    0x80000003   289  0x2  0xe7ac   28
```

```
    Summary *10.0.0.1          192.168.17.1    0x80000002  289  0x2  0x5830  28
    Summary *10.0.1.0          192.168.17.1    0x80000007   22  0x2  0xdeaf  28
    Summary *10.0.2.0          192.168.17.1    0x80000002  289  0x2  0xd3bf  28
    Summary *10.0.16.0         192.168.17.1    0x80000002  289  0x2  0xb1c7  28
    Summary *192.168.13.1      192.168.17.1    0x80000002  289  0x2  0x9982  28
    Summary *192.168.17.1      192.168.17.1    0x80000002  289  0x2  0x68fc  28
    Summary *192.168.18.1      192.168.17.1    0x80000002  289  0x2  0xe939  28
    Summary *192.168.19.1      192.168.17.1    0x80000002  289  0x2  0xde43  28
       OSPF AS SCOPE link state database
    Type     ID            Adv Rtr           Seq        Age  Opt  Cksum  Len
    Extern   0.0.0.0       192.168.15.1    0x80000001   590  0x2  0x67f1  36
    Extern   172.19.121.0  192.168.15.1    0x80000001   590  0x2  0x859a  36
```

With the NSSA configured, these Type 5 routes are injected into the area as Type 7 (NSSA) LSAs:

```
aviva@RouterJ> show ospf database area 0.0.0.3
    OSPF link state database, area 0.0.0.3
    Type      ID            Adv Rtr           Seq        Age  Opt  Cksum  Len
    Router   192.168.15.1   192.168.15.1    0x80000002   29  0x0  0x6338  60
    Router   192.168.16.1   192.168.16.1    0x80000004    2  0x0  0xe155  84
    Router  *192.168.17.1   192.168.17.1    0x80000003    1  0x0  0x6dc5  36
    Network *10.0.8.1       192.168.17.1    0x80000001    1  0x0  0x6e69  32
    Summary *10.0.0.0       192.168.17.1    0x80000001   55  0x0  0xa8e   28
    Summary *10.0.0.1       192.168.17.1    0x80000001   55  0x0  0x7813  28
    Summary *10.0.1.0       192.168.17.1    0x80000002    1  0x0  0x78e   28
    Summary *10.0.2.0       192.168.17.1    0x80000001   55  0x0  0xf3a2  28
    Summary *10.0.16.0      192.168.17.1    0x80000001   55  0x0  0xd1aa  28
    Summary *192.168.13.1   192.168.17.1    0x80000001   55  0x0  0xb965  28
    Summary *192.168.17.1   192.168.17.1    0x80000001   55  0x0  0x88df  28
    Summary *192.168.18.1   192.168.17.1    0x80000001   55  0x0  0xa1c   28
    Summary *192.168.19.1   192.168.17.1    0x80000001   55  0x0  0xfe26  28
    NSSA     0.0.0.0        192.168.15.1    0x80000001   29  0x8  0xf2e4  36
    NSSA     172.19.121.0   192.168.15.1    0x80000001   29  0x8  0x118d  36
       OSPF AS SCOPE link state database
    Type      ID            Adv Rtr           Seq        Age  Opt  Cksum  Len
    Extern   0.0.0.0        192.168.15.1    0x80000001  711  0x2  0x67f1  36
    Extern   172.19.121.0   192.168.15.1    0x80000001  711  0x2  0x859a  36
```

The output shows that the Type 7 NSSAs still originate from the ASBR, RouterE (192.168.15.1).

As with stub areas, you can configure the ABR in the NSSA to not flood Type 3 (Network Summary) LSAs to the routers in the stub area:

```
[edit protocols ospf]
aviva@RouterJ# set area 0.0.0.3 nssa no-summaries
```

Looking at a router in Area 0.0.0.3, where before its link-state database would have contained Type 3 (Summary) LSAs:

```
aviva@RouterE> show ospf database
    OSPF link state database, area 0.0.0.3
    Type      ID            Adv Rtr           Seq        Age  Opt  Cksum  Len
    Router  *192.168.15.1   192.168.15.1    0x80000004  429  0x0  0x4167  60
```

```
Router    192.168.16.1    192.168.16.1    0x8000000b     7  0x0  0x94d3  72
Router    192.168.17.1    192.168.17.1    0x80000006     8  0x0  0xd8ca  48
Network   10.0.8.2        192.168.16.1    0x80000006     7  0x0  0xbd6   32
Summary   10.0.0.0        192.168.17.1    0x80000002     8  0x0  0x8552  28
Summary   10.0.1.0        192.168.17.1    0x80000002     8  0x0  0x8451  28
Summary   10.0.2.0        192.168.17.1    0x80000002     8  0x0  0x795b  28
Summary   192.168.18.1    192.168.17.1    0x80000001    17  0x0  0x91d3  28
NSSA      *10.0.15.0      192.168.15.1    0x80000001   429  0x8  0xcaf3  36
NSSA      *172.19.121.0   192.168.15.1    0x80000001   429  0x8  0x118d  36
NSSA      *192.168.15.1   192.168.15.1    0x80000001   429  0x8  0x91cc  36
```

The Summary LSAs are no longer present:

```
aviva@RouterE> show ospf database
     OSPF link state database, area 0.0.0.3
 Type      ID              Adv Rtr          Seq         Age  Opt  Cksum  Len
Router    *192.168.15.1    192.168.15.1    0x80000004   338  0x0  0x4167  60
Router    192.168.16.1     192.168.16.1    0x80000008   283  0x0  0x9ad0  72
Router    192.168.17.1     192.168.17.1    0x80000004   278  0x0  0xdcc8  48
Network   10.0.8.2         192.168.16.1    0x80000004   283  0x0  0xfd4   32
NSSA      *10.0.15.0       192.168.15.1    0x80000001   338  0x8  0xcaf3  36
NSSA      *172.19.121.0    192.168.15.1    0x80000001   338  0x8  0x118d  36
NSSA      *192.168.15.1    192.168.15.1    0x80000001   338  0x8  0x91cc  36
```

12.8   Summarizing Routes in OSPF

Problem

You want to minimize the size of a backbone router's link-state database by summarizing the routes sent to the backbone area.

Solution

Summarize the routes that are flooded into the backbone area by the ABR:

```
[edit protocols ospf]
aviva@RouterJ# set area 0.0.0.3 area-range 10.0.0.0/16
```

Discussion

OSPF route summarization aggregates routes sent by nonbackbone areas to the backbone routers so that the size of their link-state databases is reduced. In this recipe, the networks in Area 0.0.0.3 are 10.0.8.1/28, 10.0.8.2/28, 10.0.13.1/28, and 10.0.13.2/28 (see Figure 12-3), which can be summarized as 10.0.0.0/24.

If we check on one of the backbone routers before configuring route summarization, we see four Type 3 (Summary) LSAs in the link-state database:

```
aviva@RouterG> show ospf database
     OSPF link state database, area 0.0.0.0
 Type      ID              Adv Rtr          Seq         Age  Opt  Cksum  Len
Router    192.168.17.1     192.168.17.1    0x80000189    16  0x2  0x926e  60
```

```
Router    192.168.18.1      192.168.18.1      0x80000124  2601  0x2  0x97cd  60
Router   *192.168.19.1      192.168.19.1      0x8000009c   126  0x2  0xb4c7  48
Network  *10.0.0.1          192.168.19.1      0x80000090   726  0x2  0x9aae  32
Network  *10.0.1.2          192.168.19.1      0x80000090   426  0x2  0x92b3  32
Network   10.0.2.1          192.168.18.1      0x8000009b  1651  0x2  0x6cd1  32
Summary   10.0.8.0          192.168.17.1      0x80000009    16  0x2  0xa62f  28
Summary   10.0.13.0         192.168.17.1      0x80000002    16  0x2  0xa8c   28
Summary   192.168.15.1      192.168.17.1      0x80000002    16  0x2  0x1510  28
Summary   192.168.16.1      192.168.17.1      0x80000002    16  0x2  0x7de7  28
ASBRSum   192.168.15.1      192.168.17.1      0x80000002    16  0x2  0x71d   28
     OSPF AS SCOPE link state database
Type      ID                Adv Rtr           Seq          Age  Opt  Cksum   Len
Extern    10.0.15.0         192.168.15.1      0x80000001   161  0x2  0x3f01  36
Extern    172.19.121.0      192.168.15.1      0x80000001   161  0x2  0x859a  36
Extern    172.19.121.0      192.168.17.1      0x80000003   472  0x2  0x73a8  36
Extern    192.168.15.1      192.168.15.1      0x80000001   161  0x2  0x6d9   36
Extern    192.168.17.1      192.168.17.1      0x80000003   240  0x2  0xddfb  36
```

After the ABR for Area 0.0.0.3 begins aggregating the routes, the number of Type 3 LSAs sent to the backbone area decreases to three, and two LSAs from that area, 10.0.8.0 and 10.0.13.0, are combined into one, 10.0.0.0:

```
aviva@RouterG> show ospf database
     OSPF link state database, area 0.0.0.0
Type      ID                Adv Rtr           Seq          Age  Opt  Cksum   Len
Router    192.168.17.1      192.168.17.1      0x8000018c    20  0x2  0x8c71  60
Router    192.168.18.1      192.168.18.1      0x80000124  2842  0x2  0x97cd  60
Router   *192.168.19.1      192.168.19.1      0x8000009c   367  0x2  0xb4c7  48
Network  *10.0.0.1          192.168.19.1      0x80000091    67  0x2  0x98af  32
Network  *10.0.1.2          192.168.19.1      0x80000090   667  0x2  0x92b3  32
Network   10.0.2.1          192.168.18.1      0x8000009b  1892  0x2  0x6cd1  32
Summary   10.0.0.0          192.168.17.1      0x80000001    20  0x2  0xf59f  28
Summary   192.168.15.1      192.168.17.1      0x80000005    20  0x2  0xf13   28
Summary   192.168.16.1      192.168.17.1      0x80000005    20  0x2  0x77ea  28
ASBRSum   192.168.15.1      192.168.17.1      0x80000005    20  0x2  0x120   28
     OSPF AS SCOPE link state database
Type      ID                Adv Rtr           Seq          Age  Opt  Cksum   Len
Extern    10.0.15.0         192.168.15.1      0x80000002    10  0x2  0x3d02  36
Extern    172.19.121.0      192.168.15.1      0x80000001   402  0x2  0x859a  36
Extern    172.19.121.0      192.168.17.1      0x80000004   117  0x2  0x71a9  36
Extern    192.168.15.1      192.168.15.1      0x80000001   402  0x2  0x6d9   36
Extern    192.168.17.1      192.168.17.1      0x80000003   481  0x2  0xddfb  36
```

12.9   Enabling OSPF Authentication

Problem

You want to ensure that all OSPF protocol traffic that your router accepts comes from devices known to you so that only trusted routers participate in determining the contents of the OSPF routing database.

Solution

You configure MD5 authentication for OSPF:

```
[edit protocols ospf area 0.0.0.0]
aviva@RouterG# set authentication-type md5
aviva@RouterG# set interface fe-0/0/1 authentication md5 1 key $1991poPPi
aviva@RouterG# set interface fe-1/0/1 authentication md5 1 key $1991poPPi
aviva@RouterG# show
authentication-type md5;
interface fe-0/0/1.0 {
    authentication {
        md5 1 key "$9$dEbgoZUjqP5GUApO1hcgoaJHq"; ## SECRET-DATA
    }
}
interface fe-1/0/1.0 {
    authentication {
        md5 1 key "$9$dEbgoZUjqP5GUApO1hcgoaJHq"; ## SECRET-DATA
    }
}
```

Discussion

It is a good security measure to authenticate OSPF protocol packet exchanges to ensure that only trusted routers participate in the OSPF network and in the exchange of Hello and LSA packets.

This recipe shows how to configure OSFP to use MD5 authentication. First, configure MD5 authentication for the entire area, then set the key, or password, for each interface. Each key has an identifier; here, it is 1. MD5 creates an encoded checksum that is included in all transmitted OSPF packets. The receiving router verifies this checksum before accepting the packet.

When you display the router's configuration after you have typed the password, you do not see the password itself, only the encrypted form of the password. Someone casually glancing through the configuration would not see the actual password.

You can also configure a simple password for OSPF authentication, which includes a plain-text password in the transmitted OSPF packets. Plain-text passwords are easy to break by devices that sniff network traffic, so you should never use them when your goal is network security.

For authentication to work across the entire OSPF domain, you need to configure MD5 authentication with the same key identifier and the same password on all OSPF interfaces, as shown in this recipe. Once you have the encrypted version of the password, you can use it in the authentication-key statement instead of the password itself. This is one way to minimize the number of people who see the actual password.

```
aviva@RouterG# set interface fe-1/0/1 authentication 1 key
"$9$dEbgoZUjqP5GUApO1hcgoaJHq"
```

When you are looking at the configuration contents, pipe the output to hide the passwords:

```
[edit]
aviva@RouterG# show protocols ospf | except SECRET-DATA
area 0.0.0.0 {
    authentication-type md5;
    interface fe-0/0/1.0 {
        authentication {
        }
    }
    interface fe-1/0/1.0 {
        authentication {
        }
    }
}
```

You can do the same thing in operational mode:

```
aviva@RouterG> show configuration protocols ospf | except SECRET-DATA
area 0.0.0.0 {
    authentication-type md5;
    interface fe-0/0/1.0 {
        authentication {
        }
    }
    interface fe-1/0/1.0 {
        authentication {
        }
    }
}
```

As part of your security measures, you may, from time to time, want to transition from using one MD5 key to another. You can do this by configuring multiple MD5 keys, each with a unique key ID, and setting the date and time to switch to the new key. Here, the new keys take effect at 12:01 a.m. on the first day of the month for the next several months:

```
[edit protocols ospf area 0.0.0.0]
aviva@RouterG# set interface fe-0/0/1 authentication md5 1 key $1991poPPi
aviva@RouterG# set interface fe-0/0/1 authentication md5 2 key NeWpsswdFEB start-time
2006-02-01.00:01
aviva@RouterG# set interface fe-0/0/1 authentication md5 3 key NeWpsswdMAR start-time
2006-03-01.00:01
aviva@RouterG# set interface fe-0/0/1 authentication md5 4 key NeWpsswdAPR start-time
2006-04-01.00:01
```

The start time specifies the time at which the router starts using the MD5 key for transmission. When receiving packets, the router accepts packets with any MD5 key as long as the key ID specified in the packet corresponds to a currently configured key, regardless of the key's start time.

Use the show ospf interface detail command to see which key is currently active:

```
aviva@RouterG# run show ospf interface detail
Interface             State     Area              DR ID         BDR ID        Nb
rs
t1-0/2/1.0            PtToPt    0.0.0.0           0.0.0.0       0.0.0.0
0
Type P2P, address 0.0.0.0, mask 0.0.0.0, MTU 1500, cost 2604
  adj count 0
Hello 10, Dead 40, ReXmit 5, Not Stub
Auth type MD5, Active key id 3, Start time 2002 Nov 19 10:00:00 PST

t1-0/2/1.0            PtToPt    0.0.0.0           0.0.0.0       0.0.0.0
0
Type P2P, address 192.168.37.16, mask 255.255.255.255, MTU 1500, cost 2604
  adj count 0,  Passive
Hello 10, Dead 40, ReXmit 5, Not Stub
Auth type MD5, Active key id 3, Start time 2006 Mar 1 00:01:00 PST
```

12.10 Redistributing Static Routes into OSPF

Problem

You have a single, low-speed link to a small-size customer and, instead of having the customer run OSPF (or even RIP), you want to set up a static route to the customer.

Solution

Create a routing policy to redistribute static routes into OSPF:

```
[edit policy-options]
aviva@RouterG# set policy-statement export-statics term 1 from protocol static
aviva@RouterG# set policy-statement export-statics term 1 then accept
aviva@RouterG# show
policy-statement export-statics {
    term 1 {
        from protocol static;
        then accept;
    }
}
```

Then apply the policy to OSPF:

```
[edit protocols ospf]
aviva@RouterG# set export export-statics
```

Discussion

If you have small-size customers who don't need to run a dynamic routing protocol, such as OSPF or RIP, and only need to connect to you using a static route, you create a routing policy to get their routes into your OSPF network.

As an ISP, you might use static routes to represent your customer links and networks, especially for small-size customers that you connect to with just a single link or a low-speed link. In these cases, you want to redistribute these static links into your OSPF network. Create a simple routing policy that accepts all static routes and then apply it as an export policy to OSPF. This adds Type 7 (AS External) routes to the link-state database:

```
aviva@RouterG> show ospf database
    OSPF link state database, area 0.0.0.0
 Type       ID            Adv Rtr         Seq      Age  Opt  Cksum  Len
 Router  192.168.17.1  192.168.17.1  0x800001c6  1633  0x2  0x13b3  60
 Router  192.168.18.1  192.168.18.1  0x8000015f   384  0x2  0xf833  60
 Router *192.168.19.1  192.168.19.1  0x800000f3    11  0x2  0x180b  48
 Network 10.0.0.2      192.168.17.1  0x80000004  1633  0x2  0xbf17  32
 Network 10.0.1.1      192.168.18.1  0x80000004    84  0x2  0xc014  32
 Network 10.0.2.1      192.168.18.1  0x800000b4   684  0x2  0x3aea  32
    OSPF AS SCOPE link state database
 Type       ID            Adv Rtr         Seq      Age  Opt  Cksum  Len
 Extern  *0.0.0.0      192.168.19.1  0x80000001    11  0x2  0x4b0a  36
 Extern  *192.168.42.1 192.168.19.1  0x80000001    11  0x2  0xbf01  36
```

The only drawback is that if the link between the customer and the ISP goes down, the network still appears to be reachable to the world, and you would need to stop advertising it if this occurred. However, short links between a customer and an ISP should rarely or never fail.

12.11 Adjusting OSPF Link Costs

Problem

You want to direct traffic within an OSPF area toward a particular interface.

Solution

Increase the cost on one interface to have OSPF use a different interface:

```
[edit protocols ospf area 0.0.0.0]
aviva@RouterJ# set interface fe-1/0/0.0 metric 3
```

Discussion

When choosing paths to a destination, OSPF uses the one with the lowest metric. By default, all links faster than 100 Mbps have a metric of 1. This recipe shows how to adjust the metric in our three-router backbone area so that traffic from RouterH always goes through RouterG instead of directly to RouterJ. You might want to do this if the interface between RouterH and RouterJ is congested with other traffic (see Figure 12-1).

With the default metric, traffic from RouterH to RouterJ goes out interface fe-1/0/0, which is one hop away:

```
aviva@RouterJ> show route 192.168.18.1
inet.0: 12 destinations, 12 routes (12 active, 0 holddown, 0 hidden)
+ = Active Route, - = Last Active, * = Both
192.168.18.1/32    *[OSPF/10] 00:26:19, metric 1
                    > to 10.0.2.1 via fe-1/0/0.0
```

Use the traceroute command to verify this:

```
[edit protocols ospf area 0.0.0.0 interface fe-1/0/0.0]
aviva@RouterJ# run traceroute 192.168.18.1
traceroute to 192.168.18.1 (192.168.18.1), 30 hops max, 40 byte packets
 1  192.168.18.1 (192.168.18.1)  10.905 ms  9.060 ms  9.807 ms
```

If you change the metric value on the fe-1/0/0 interface to 2, you create an equal-cost path to RouterH:

```
[edit protocols ospf area 0.0.0.0]
aviva@RouterJ# show
interface fe-1/0/1.0;
interface fe-1/0/0.0 {
    metric 2;
}
```

The cost is 2, whether packets go through interface fe-1/0/0 or interface fe-1/0/1:

```
[edit protocols ospf area 0.0.0.0]
aviva@RouterJ# run show route 192.168.18.1
inet.0: 12 destinations, 12 routes (12 active, 0 holddown, 0 hidden)
+ = Active Route, - = Last Active, * = Both
192.168.18.1/32    *[OSPF/10] 00:00:08, metric 2
                      to 10.0.2.1 via fe-1/0/0.0
                    > to 10.0.0.1 via fe-1/0/1.0
```

Because we want traffic to always go through RouterG, we need to set the metric to something greater than 2, so in this recipe we set it to 3. The traffic now goes along the desired path:

```
[edit protocols ospf area 0.0.0.0]
aviva@RouterJ# run show route 192.168.18.1
inet.0: 12 destinations, 12 routes (12 active, 0 holddown, 0 hidden)
+ = Active Route, - = Last Active, * = Both
192.168.18.1/32    *[OSPF/10] 00:00:06, metric 2
                    > to 10.0.0.1 via fe-1/0/1.0
```

The traceroute shows the path through interface 10.0.0.1 on RouterG:

```
[edit protocols ospf area 0.0.0.0 interface fe-1/0/0.0]
aviva@RouterJ# run traceroute 192.168.18.1
traceroute to 192.168.18.1 (192.168.18.1), 30 hops max, 40 byte packets
 1  10.0.0.1 (10.0.0.1)  12.170 ms  8.826 ms  9.798 ms
 2  192.168.18.1 (192.168.18.1)  10.313 ms  15.829 ms  13.332 ms
```

The interfaces in this recipe are all Fast Ethernet interfaces (100 Mbps), so their default metric is 1. This metric is assigned by OSPF using the following formula:

$$\text{metric} = \frac{\text{reference bandwidth}}{\text{interface bandwidth}}$$

OSPF uses this formula for all "real" interfaces, which are interfaces that correspond to a physical PIC. In the formula, the default reference bandwidth value is 100 Mbps, which is why Fast Ethernet interfaces have a default metric of 1. For a 10 Mbps Ethernet interface, OSPF assigns a default metric of 10 based on this formula. For interfaces faster than 100 Mbps, OSPF assigns a metric of 1 to them all because the calculated value is a fraction that is less than 1 and OSPF rounds up to 1. Here's the calculation for a Gigabit Ethernet (1,000 Mbps) interface:

$$\frac{100\ \text{Mbps}}{1,000\ \text{Mbps}} = 0.1$$

The calculation for a SONET OC-192 interface looks like this:

$$\frac{100\ \text{Mbps}}{10\ \text{Gbps}} = 0.01$$

OSPF would assign a default metric of 1 to both these interfaces because all fractions less than 1 are rounded up to 1.

Having the same default metric is not necessarily a problem if all the interfaces are running at the same speed. But if they operate at different speeds, when there are equal-cost paths to the same destination, instead of traffic being routed across the fastest interface, the default behavior is to equally distribute traffic across the different interfaces in a round-robin fashion. To have the interface metrics that OSPF calculates accurately reflect the actual speeds of the interfaces, modify the default reference bandwidth value. As an example, if your router has Fast Ethernet, Gigabit Ethernet, and OC192 interfaces running OSPF, you can set the reference bandwidth to 10 Gbps:

```
[edit protocols ospf]
aviva@RouterJ# set reference-bandwidth 10g
```

With this configuration, OSPF assigns the Fast Ethernet interface a metric of 100, the Gigabit Ethernet interface a metric of 10, and the OC192 interface a metric of 1. Because the OC192 interface has the lowest metric, OSPF selects it when routing traffic.

12.12 Improving OSPF Convergence Times

Problem

You want to speed up convergence of OSPF routes in case a path fails with no hardware indication, which might happen on an Ethernet network.

Solution

Reduce the interval at which OSPF exchanges Hello messages and, in parallel, decrease the dead interval:

```
[edit protocols ospf area 0.0.0.0]
aviva@RouterG# set interface fe-0/0/1 hello-interval 2
aviva@RouterG# set interface fe-0/0/1 dead-interval 8
aviva@RouterG# set interface fe-1/0/1 hello-interval 2
aviva@RouterG# set interface fe-1/0/1 dead-interval 8
```

Discussion

The OSPF protocol specifications were developed when routers and network interfaces were slower to allow enough time for LSAs to reach all nodes and for the SPF calculation to run on all routers. Modern routers and interfaces are much faster, so one strategy for speeding up route convergence is to modify the default OSPF timers. The base JUNOS OSPF code already optimizes convergence times by doing fast link detection and flooding, by quickly regenerating LSAs, and by quickly scheduling SPF calculations, so you don't often need to modify the timers.

When changing OSPF timers, you must modify each interface, changing the hello timer and dead timer intervals. The default timer settings, as defined in the OSPF specification, are 10 seconds for sending periodic Hello packets and 40 seconds for declaring the adjacency dead, or down (four times the hello interval):

```
aviva@RouterG> show ospf interface detail
Interface          State    Area        DR ID          BDR ID        Nbrs
fe-0/0/1.0           DR      0.0.0.0     192.168.19.1   192.168.18.1    1
Type: LAN, Address: 10.0.1.2, Mask: 255.255.255.0, MTU: 1500, Cost: 1
DR addr: 10.0.1.2, BDR addr: 10.0.1.1, Adj count: 1, Priority: 128
Hello: 10, Dead: 40, ReXmit: 5, Not Stub
Auth type: None
fe-1/0/1.0           DR      0.0.0.0     192.168.19.1   192.168.17.1    1
Type: LAN, Address: 10.0.0.1, Mask: 255.255.255.0, MTU: 1500, Cost: 1
DR addr: 10.0.0.1, BDR addr: 10.0.0.2, Adj count: 1, Priority: 128
Hello: 10, Dead: 40, ReXmit: 5, Not Stub
Auth type: None
```

This recipe lowers the hello timer interval to two seconds and the dead timer interval to eight seconds. You have to change the timers on each interface and on all routers in the area because adjacencies can be established only between systems with the same timer values (as required by the OSPF specifications). If you do not change the timers on all interfaces, OSPF cannot establish the adjacency. Here, you see that the adjacency to the router at 10.0.1.1 through interface fe-0/0/1 has broken because the timers are different:

```
aviva@RouterG> show ospf neighbor
  Address          Interface          State     ID              Pri Dead
  10.0.0.2         fe-1/0/1.0         Full      192.168.17.1    128  38
```

When the timers are the same, the adjacency comes back up:

```
aviva@RouterG> show ospf neighbor
  Address          Interface          State     ID              Pri Dead
  10.0.1.1         fe-0/0/1.0         Full      192.168.18.1    128  33
  10.0.0.2         fe-1/0/1.0         Full      192.168.17.1    128  37
```

For data traveling at gigabit rates, even decreasing the OSPF hello timer may not detect failures fast enough. An alternative to adjusting the OSPF timer intervals is to use the BFD, which detects communication failures with a forwarding-plane next hop. BFD is useful on interfaces where you can't detect failure quickly, such as Ethernet interfaces. Other interface types, such as SONET interfaces, already have built-in failure detection, so you don't need to use BFD.

BFD is a simple hello protocol. A pair of systems exchange BFD packets periodically, and if a system stops receiving the packets for long enough, some component in that particular bidirectional path to the neighboring system is assumed to have failed. If you want to shorten the OSPF link failure detection time to 1.5 seconds, set the BFD packet exchange interval to 500 milliseconds:

```
[edit protocols ospf area 0.0.0.0]
aviva@RouterG# set interface fe-0/0/1 bfd-liveness-detection minimum-interval 500
```

By default, BFD multiplies the packet exchange interval by three to determine the link detection failure time. Configuring an interval of 500 milliseconds results in a failure time of 1.5 seconds.

You also need to configure BFD on the interface at the other end of the link. Unlike the OSPF timers, you do not have to enable BFD on all interfaces in the area. Use the show bfd session command to see BFD information:

```
aviva@RouterG> show bfd session detail
                                                    Transmit
  Address           State     Interface    Detect Time Interval  Multiplier
  10.0.1.1          Up        fe-0/0/1.0        1.500    0.500         3
    Client OSPF, TX interval 0.500, RX interval 0.500, multiplier 3
    Session up time 00:13:02
    Local diagnostic None, remote diagnostic None
    Remote heard, hears us
  10.0.0.2             Up     fe-1/0/1.0        1.500    0.500         3
    Client OSPF, TX interval 0.500, RX interval 0.500, multiplier 3
    Session up time 00:01:25
    Local diagnostic None, remote diagnostic CtlExpire
    Remote heard, hears us
  2 sessions, 2 clients
  Cumulative transmit rate 4.0 pps, cumulative receive rate 4.0 pps
```

This output shows two BFD sessions on the router's two interfaces. The BFD client is OSPF, and the timers that we configured are shown. The last line for each interface, Remote heard, hears us, indicates that the OSPF link is operating properly. If the link fails, neither side initially hears the other:

```
aviva@RouterG> show bfd session detail
                                              Transmit
Address              State    Interface    Detect Time  Interval  Multiplier
10.0.1.1             Up       fe-0/0/1.0        1.500     0.500     3
   Client OSPF, TX interval 0.500, RX interval 0.500, multiplier 3
   Session up time 00:16:55
   Local diagnostic None, remote diagnostic None
   Remote heard, hears us
10.0.0.2             AdminDown fe-1/0/1.0       3.000     1.000     3
   Session down time 00:00:09, previous up time 00:05:09
   Local diagnostic NbrSignal, remote diagnostic AdminDown
   Remote not heard, doesn't hear us
```

Once the link is completely down and the BFD session fails, the link is no longer shown:

```
aviva@RouterG> show bfd session detail
                                              Transmit
Address              State    Interface    Detect Time  Interval  Multiplier
10.0.1.1             Up       fe-0/0/1.0        1.500     0.500     3
   Client OSPF, TX interval 0.500, RX interval 0.500, multiplier 3
   Session up time 00:18:10
   Local diagnostic None, remote diagnostic None
   Remote heard, hears us
1 sessions, 1 clients
Cumulative transmit rate 2.0 pps, cumulative receive rate 2.0 pps
```

12.13 Moving OSPF Traffic off a Router

Problem

You are getting ready to perform router maintenance and you want to move all OSPF traffic off the router.

Solution

Configure the router so that it appears to be overloaded with OSPF traffic:

```
[edit protocols ospf]
aviva@RouterG# set overload
```

Discussion

As you are preparing to perform maintenance on a router in a production network, you want to move traffic off that router so that network services are not interrupted during your maintenance window. The set overload command tricks the router into believing that it is overloaded and can't handle any more OSPF transit traffic, and the result is that OSPF transit traffic is sent to other routers. OSPF traffic destined to interfaces directly attached to the local router continues to reach the router.

To check that the OSPF traffic has moved off the router, use show interfaces commands to verify that traffic has moved off the upstream interfaces. The detail and extensive versions of this command report traffic statistics for most interface types. If the router is part of an LSP, use the show mpls lsp transit command to verify that transit LSPs have moved off the router.

12.14 Disabling OSPF on an Interface

Problem

You want to temporarily turn off OSPF on an interface.

Solution

Disable OSPF on the interface:

```
[edit protocols ospf]
aviva@RouterG# set area 0.0.0.0 interface fe-0/0/1.0 disable
```

To start OSPF again, remove the disable statement from the configuration:

```
[edit protocols ospf]
aviva@RouterG# delete area 0.0.0.0 interface fe-0/0/1.0 disable
aviva@RouterG# commit
```

Discussion

To remove an interface from the OSPF network, you can disable it. Because you are removing the interface only temporarily, you don't want to remove the configuration statements entirely. You see that the adjacency to that interface's neighbor is no longer listed:

```
aviva@RouterG> show ospf neighbor
  Address        Interface        State     ID            Pri  Dead
  10.0.0.2       fe-1/0/1.0       Full      192.168.17.1  128   32
```

Also, the metric to that neighbor has increased from 1 to 2 because the neighbor is no longer directly connected, and that traffic is being directed out the router's only active OSPF interface, fe-1/0/1:

```
aviva@RouterG> show route table inet.0 show route table inet.0 192.168.18.1
192.168.18.1/32    *[OSPF/10] 00:00:45, metric 2
                    > to 10.0.0.2 via fe-1/0/1.0
```

Another way to disable OSPF on an interface is with the deactivate command:

```
[edit protocols ospf]
aviva@RouterG# deactivate area 0.0.0.0 interface fe-0/0/1.0
```

```
aviva@RouterG# commit
aviva@RouterG# show
area 0.0.0.0 {
    inactive: interface fe-0/0/1.0;
    interface fe-1/0/1.0;
}
```

To start OSPF again on the interface, reactivate it:

```
[edit protocols ospf]
aviva@RouterG# activate area 0.0.0.0 interface fe-0/0/1.0
aviva@RouterG# commit
```

You can also temporarily disable OSPF on the router:

```
[edit protocols ospf]
aviva@RouterG# set disable
aviva@RouterG# commit and-quit
aviva@RouterG> show ospf neighbor
OSPF instance is not running
```

12.15 Tracing OSPF Protocol Traffic

Problem

You are setting up OSPF on your network and want to keep a running log of OSPF protocol packets that the router is sending to help track any problems that might occur during the configuration process.

Solution

Set up a tracing file that captures information about OSPF protocol operations:

```
[edit protocols ospf]
aviva@RouterG# set traceoptions file ospf-log
aviva@RouterG# set traceoptions flag hello
aviva@RouterG# set traceoptions flag error
aviva@RouterG# set traceoptions flag general
```

To stop the tracing, remove the traceoptions statement from the configuration:

```
[edit protocols ospf]
aviva@RouterG# delete traceoptions
```

Discussion

To debug OSPF operations, use the JUNOS tracing facility to track the packets that OSPF is sending. You specify the name of the file to which you want to collect the information and the type of information you want to trace. In this example, we are logging general OSPF traffic information as well as Hello packets and errors in the *ospf-log* file, which is on the router's hard disk in the directories */var/log* (on M-series and T-series routers) and */cf/var/log* (on J-series routers).

Some things you see in the logfile are Hello packets sent to and received from neighbors:

```
Jun 14 21:49:36 OSPF rcvd Hello 10.0.16.2 -> 224.0.0.5 (fe-0/0/0.0, IFL 0x42)
Jun 14 21:49:36   Version 2, length 48, ID 192.168.19.1, area 0.0.0.1
Jun 14 21:49:36   checksum 0x0, authtype 0
Jun 14 21:49:36   mask 255.255.255.0, hello_ivl 10, opts 0x2, prio 128
Jun 14 21:49:36   dead_ivl 40, DR 10.0.16.1, BDR 10.0.16.2
Jun 14 21:49:36 OSPF sent Hello 10.0.16.1 -> 224.0.0.5 (fe-0/0/0.0, IFL 0x42)
Jun 14 21:49:36   Version 2, length 48, ID 192.168.42.1, area 0.0.0.1
Jun 14 21:49:36   checksum 0x0, authtype 0
Jun 14 21:49:36   mask 255.255.255.0, hello_ivl 10, opts 0x2, prio 128
Jun 14 21:49:36   dead_ivl 40, DR 10.0.16.1, BDR 10.0.16.2
```

This log shows the values for two of the OSPF timers, the hello interval of 10 seconds (hello_ivl 10) and the dead interval of 40 seconds (dead_ivl 40), as well as the address of the DR and BDR and the priority to become the DR (128).

You also see changes to the adjacency changes when neighbors come up:

```
Jun 14 21:49:36 RPD_OSPF_NBRUP: OSPF neighbor 10.0.16.2 (fe-0/0/0.0) state changed
from Loading to Full due to OSPF loading done
Jun 14 21:49:36 CHANGE    10.0.0.0/24       gw 10.0.16.2      OSPF     pref 10/0
metric 2/0 fe-0/0/0.0 <Active Int>
Jun 14 21:49:36 ADD       10.0.0.0/24       gw 10.0.16.2      OSPF     pref 10/0
metric 2/0 fe-0/0/0.0 <Active Int>
Jun 14 21:49:36 CHANGE    10.0.1.0/24       gw 10.0.16.2      OSPF     pref 10/0
metric 2/0 fe-0/0/0.0 <Active Int>
Jun 14 21:49:36 ADD       10.0.1.0/24       gw 10.0.16.2      OSPF     pref 10/0
metric 2/0 fe-0/0/0.0 <Active Int>
Jun 14 21:49:36 CHANGE    10.0.2.0/24       gw 10.0.16.2      OSPF     pref 10/0
metric 4/0 fe-0/0/0.0 <Active Int>
Jun 14 21:49:36 ADD       10.0.2.0/24       gw 10.0.16.2      OSPF     pref 10/0
metric 4/0 fe-0/0/0.0 <Active Int>
```

Here are the adjacency changes when neighbors go down:

```
Jun 14 22:00:26 RPD_OSPF_NBRDOWN: OSPF neighbor 10.0.16.2 (fe-0/0/0.0) state changed
from Full to Down due to Kill all neighbors
Jun 14 22:00:26 RPD_OSPF_NBRDOWN: OSPF neighbor 10.0.21.2 (se-0/0/3.0) state changed
from Full to Down due to Kill all neighbors
Jun 14 22:00:26 OSPF:  multicast address 224.0.0.5/32, route ignored
Jun 14 22:00:26 OSPF:  multicast address 224.0.0.5/32, route ignored
Jun 14 22:00:26 CHANGE    10.0.0.0/24       gw 10.0.16.2      OSPF     pref 10/0
metric 2/0 fe-0/0/0.0 <Delete Int>
Jun 14 22:00:26 CHANGE    10.0.1.0/24       gw 10.0.16.2      OSPF     pref 10/0
metric 2/0 fe-0/0/0.0 <Delete Int>
Jun 14 22:00:26 CHANGE    10.0.2.0/24       gw 10.0.16.2      OSPF     pref 10/0
metric 4/0 fe-0/0/0.0 <Delete Int>
Jun 14 22:00:26 RELEASE   10.0.21.0/24      gw (null)         OSPF     pref 10/0
metric 12/0 se-0/0/3.0 <Release Int>
Jun 14 22:00:26 CHANGE    10.0.22.0/24      gw (null)         OSPF     pref 10/0
metric 24/0 se-0/0/3.0 <Delete Int>
Jun 14 22:00:26 CHANGE    192.168.12.1/32   gw (null)         OSPF     pref 10/0
metric 12/0 se-0/0/3.0 <Delete Int>
```

```
Jun 14 22:00:26 CHANGE    192.168.17.1/32    gw 10.0.16.2      OSPF      pref 10/0
metric 2/0 fe-0/0/0.0 <Delete Int>
Jun 14 22:00:26 CHANGE    192.168.18.1/32    gw 10.0.16.2      OSPF      pref 10/0
metric 2/0 fe-0/0/0.0 <Delete Int>
Jun 14 22:00:26 rt_close: 8/11 routes proto OSPF
Jun 14 22:00:26
Jun 14 22:00:26 CHANGE    224.0.0.5/32       OSPF      pref 10/0 metric 1/0 <Delete
NoReadvrt Int>
Jun 14 22:00:26 rt_close: 1/1 route proto OSPF
Jun 14 22:00:26
Jun 14 22:00:26 Terminating OSPFv2 I/O
```

Over time, the OSPF logfiles can become very large and fill the router's hard disk. To save a logfile for future analysis, you can copy the file to a server:

```
aviva@RouterG> file copy /cf/var/log/ospf-log server1:ospf-log-20050614
```

If you no longer need the information in the file, you can delete the contents:

```
aviva@RouterG> clear log ospf-log
```

Deleting the file's contents does not turn off tracing.

To stop the tracing altogether, you can remove the traceoptions statement from the configuration with the delete traceoptions command or leave the statements in the configuration and simply deactivate them so that they do not take effect when you commit the configuration:

```
[edit protocols ospf]
aviva@RouterG# deactivate traceoptions
```

To delete the logfiles and the rolled-over version of the file, use the file delete command:

```
aviva@RouterG> file delete ospf-log*
```

When debugging OSPF, you can set one or more of the following trace flags to capture OSPF information:

```
[edit protocols ospf traceoptions]
aviva@RouterG# set flag ?
Possible completions:
  all                   Trace everything
  database-description  Trace database description packets
  error                 Trace errored packets
  event                 Trace OSPF state machine events
  flooding              Trace LSA flooding
  general               Trace general events
  hello                 Trace hello packets
  lsa-ack               Trace LSA acknowledgement packets
  lsa-request           Trace LSA request packets
  lsa-update            Trace LSA update packets
  normal                Trace normal events
  packet-dump           Dump the contents of selected packet types
  packets               Trace all OSPF packets
  policy                Trace policy processing
```

route	Trace routing information
spf	Trace SPF calculations
state	Trace state transitions
task	Trace routing protocol task processing
timer	Trace routing protocol timer processing

Using some of these other flags, you can debug adjacencies to see whether they come up:

```
Jun 14 22:22:02 OSPF rcvd LSUpdate 10.0.16.1 -> 224.0.0.5 (fe-1/0/0.0, IFL 0x44)
Jun 14 22:22:02  Version 2, length 124, ID 192.168.42.1, area 0.0.0.1
Jun 14 22:22:02  checksum 0x0, authtype 0
Jun 14 22:22:02  adv count 1
Jun 14 22:22:02  id 192.168.42.1, type Router (0x1), age 3
Jun 14 22:22:02  options 0x2
Jun 14 22:22:02  adv rtr 192.168.42.1, seq 0x80000015, cksum 0x8c54, len 96
Jun 14 22:22:02    bits 0x0, link count 6
Jun 14 22:22:02    id 10.0.16.2, data 10.0.16.1, type Transit (2)
Jun 14 22:22:02    TOS count 0, TOS 0 metric 1
Jun 14 22:22:02    id 172.19.121.0, data 255.255.255.0, type Stub (3)
Jun 14 22:22:02    TOS count 0, TOS 0 metric 1
Jun 14 22:22:02    id 172.100.1.0, data 255.255.255.0, type Stub (3)
Jun 14 22:22:02    TOS count 0, TOS 0 metric 1
Jun 14 22:22:02    id 192.168.12.1, data 10.0.21.1, type PointToPoint (1)
Jun 14 22:22:02    TOS count 0, TOS 0 metric 12
Jun 14 22:22:02    id 10.0.21.0, data 255.255.255.0, type Stub (3)
Jun 14 22:22:02    TOS count 0, TOS 0 metric 12
Jun 14 22:22:02    id 192.168.42.1, data 255.255.255.255, type Stub (3)
Jun 14 22:22:02    TOS count 0, TOS 0 metric 0
```

You can also check that the SPF calculation is performed:

```
Jun 13 16:55:20  OSPF SPF start, area 0.0.0.0
Jun 13 16:55:20  OSPF add LSA Router (192.168.19.1, 192.168.19.1) distance 0 to SPF
list
Jun 13 16:55:20  Considering router link Transit 10.0.1.2 10.0.1.2
Jun 13 16:55:20  Examining network link 192.168.19.1
Jun 13 16:55:20  Back link found
Jun 13 16:55:20  Added to candidate list at distance 1
Jun 13 16:55:20  No nexthops, parent is root
Jun 13 16:55:20  Network LSA, adding interface nexthop
Jun 13 16:55:20  IP Nexthop #1 (null):0.0.0.0 (fe-0/0/1.0) added
Jun 13 16:55:20  Considering router link Transit 10.0.0.1 10.0.0.1
Jun 13 16:55:20  Examining network link 192.168.19.1
Jun 13 16:55:20  Back link found
Jun 13 16:55:20  Added to candidate list at distance 1
Jun 13 16:55:20  No nexthops, parent is root
Jun 13 16:55:20  Network LSA, adding interface nexthop
Jun 13 16:55:20  IP Nexthop #1 (null):0.0.0.0 (fe-1/0/1.0) added
Jun 13 16:55:20  Adding SPF route 10.0.1.0/24
Jun 13 16:55:20  IP Nexthop #1 (null):0.0.0.0 (fe-0/0/1.0) added
Jun 13 16:55:20  IP Route added with cost 1 (fresh)
...
Jun 13 16:55:20  SPF elapsed time 0.002172s
Jun 13 16:55:20  Adding stub route 192.168.19.1/32
```

```
Jun 13 16:55:20      IP Route added with cost 0
Jun 13 16:55:20      IP Nexthop #1 10.0.1.1:0.0.0.0 (fe-0/0/1.0) added
...
Jun 13 16:55:20  Stub elapsed time 0.000567s
Jun 13 16:55:20  Interarea elapsed time 0.000007s
Jun 13 16:55:20  External elapsed time 0.000003s
Jun 13 16:55:20  NSSA elapsed time 0.000002s
Jun 13 16:55:20    Route 10.0.0.0/24 is unchanged
Jun 13 16:55:20    Route 10.0.1.0/24 is unchanged
Jun 13 16:55:20 CHANGE    10.0.2.0/24        gw 10.0.1.1        OSPF      pref 10/0
metric 10001/0 fe-0/0/1.0 <Delete Int>
Jun 13 16:55:20 CHANGE    10.0.2.0/24        gw 10.0.0.2        OSPF      pref 10/0
metric 2/0 fe-1/0/1.0 <Active Int>
Jun 13 16:55:20 ADD       10.0.2.0/24        gw 10.0.0.2        OSPF      pref 10/0
metric 2/0 fe-1/0/1.0 <Active Int>
Jun 13 16:55:20    Route 10.0.2.0/24 has changed
Jun 13 16:55:20    Considering autosummary for 10.0.2.0/24, summary possible=1
Jun 13 16:55:20    Considering NSSA autosummary for 10.0.2.0/24
Jun 13 16:55:20 CHANGE    192.168.17.1/32    gw 10.0.1.1        OSPF      pref 10/0
metric 10001/0 fe-0/0/1.0 <Delete Int>
Jun 13 16:55:20 CHANGE    192.168.17.1/32    gw 10.0.0.2        OSPF      pref 10/0
metric 1/0 fe-1/0/1.0 <Active Int>
Jun 13 16:55:20 ADD       192.168.17.1/32    gw 10.0.0.2        OSPF      pref 10/0
metric 1/0 fe-1/0/1.0 <Active Int>
Jun 13 16:55:20    Route 192.168.17.1/32 has changed
Jun 13 16:55:20    Considering autosummary for 192.168.17.1/32, summary possible=1
Jun 13 16:55:20    Considering NSSA autosummary for 192.168.17.1/32
Jun 13 16:55:20    Route 192.168.18.1/32 is unchanged
Jun 13 16:55:20    Route 192.168.19.1/32 has been deleted
Jun 13 16:55:20    Considering autosummary for 192.168.19.1/32, summary possible=0
Jun 13 16:55:20     All autosummaries deleted
Jun 13 16:55:20    Considering NSSA autosummary for 192.168.19.1/32
Jun 13 16:55:20    Route 192.168.17.1 has changed
Jun 13 16:55:20    Considering autosummary for 192.168.17.1, summary possible=0
Jun 13 16:55:20     All autosummaries deleted
Jun 13 16:55:20    Considering NSSA autosummary for 192.168.17.1
Jun 13 16:55:20    Route 192.168.18.1 is unchanged
Jun 13 16:55:20 rt_close: 4/3 routes proto OSPF
Jun 13 16:55:20
Jun 13 16:55:20  Cleanup elapsed time 0.001236s
Jun 13 16:55:20    Total elapsed time 0.004206s
```

See Also

Recipe 5.10

CHAPTER 13

BGP

13.0 Introduction

The IGPs OSPF, IS-IS, and RIP maintain the mapping for the topology within a single administrative domain or AS, along with the set of best paths between systems within the domain. Each AS uses one or more common IGPs and common metrics to determine how to route packets within the AS. The administration of an AS appears to other ASs to have a single coherent interior routing scheme and presents a consistent picture of what destinations are reachable through it.

To handle inter-AS routing, IGPs use an EGP. EGPs keep track of how routing domains are connected to each other and the sequence of domains that must be traversed to reach a particular destination. Although a number of EGPs were developed in the late 1980s, the Border Gateway Protocol (BGP) is the only one currently being used on IP networks and the Internet. Version 1 of BGP was introduced in 1989, and the current iteration, Version 4, is defined in RFC 1771 and has been in use since 1995. A number of additional RFCs define extensions to the base BGP protocol (see *http://www.bgp4.as/rfc*).

BGP is the routing protocol that holds the Internet together, providing the mesh-like connectivity of Internet service provider (ISP) networks that forms what we call the Internet. ISPs use BGP to connect to each other, forming the virtual backbone of the Internet. Large enterprises also sometimes use BGP to connect to their ISPs, as well as to connect portions of their internal corporate network.

BGP uses a path vector algorithm to determine network topology and paths to destinations. This algorithm defines a route as a pairing between a destination and the attributes of the path to that destination. It considers multiple attributes of the path in order to choose the best route to the destination. In comparison, a distance-vector protocol uses a single distance metric to choose the best route. BGP routing updates carry path information, which is a full list of the transit ASs that must be traversed between the AS receiving the update and the AS that can deliver the packet using its IGP. BGP uses this list to eliminate loops in the path because a router can check the list of ASs to see whether a route has already passed through it. BGP treats each AS equally when considering the path, no matter how big or small it is. BGP does not know how many routers or what type of links are in an AS.

BGP uses TCP port 179 for transport. BGP relies on basic TCP connections to reach its peers, using the fragmentation, retransmission, acknowledgment, and sequencing functions in TCP. If two routers cannot establish a TCP connection between them, they will not be able to establish BGP peering.

BGP requires that all peering sessions be configured explicitly between BGP neighbors. There are two types of BGP peerings, *external BGP* (EBGP) and *internal BGP* (IBGP). The basic distinction between them is that an EBGP peering is between two ASs that have different AS numbers and an IBGP peering is within a single AS so the peers have the same AS number. An EBGP peering is between two BGP routers that are directly connected to each other. IBGP peerings can be among multiple routers within an AS. IBGP routers must create a full mesh of IBGP peering sessions to communicate BGP routing information with each other. This full mesh can be physical connections, where all IBGP routers are directly connected and adjacent to each other. Typically, though, the full mesh is virtual, created in the router software configuration, and the connectivity is provided by an IGP. A third type of BGP peering, called *multihop* or *EBGP multihop*, allows BGP to set up sessions with neighbors in other ASs that are not directly connected.

BGP requires that each AS have a 16-bit AS number. AS numbers range from 0 through 65535 and are globally unique across the Internet. BGP uses the AS number to prevent routing loops. AS numbers are doled out in blocks to each of the regional Internet registries (ARIN, APNIC, RIPE, AfriNIC, and LatNIC), and the regional registries assign AS numbers to individual organizations. The AS numbers 64512 through 65534 are reserved for private use, but you can use these on internal enterprise networks as long as the numbers are unique within your network. The examples in this chapter use private AS numbers as well as RFC 1918 private IP addresses. This is purely for demonstration purposes—you should never allow private AS numbers or private IP addresses to reach the public Internet.

By default, BGP routers accept all BGP information from EBGP peers and advertise all BGP information to all EBGP peers. BGP routers advertise all BGP information to IBGP peers if it comes from an EBGP peer and advertise paths learned from IBGP peers only to external peers. BGP does not advertise its internal paths to IBGP peers. This is done instead by IGP. To prevent routing loops, a BGP router does not, by default, accept routes that contain its own AS number.

BGP makes extensive use of routing policy to allow ISPs to enforce administrative policies. The JUNOS software provides both inbound and outbound policy controls at different levels: for all BGP peers, for groups of peers, and for individual peers. A policy with a narrower scope overrides one with a broader scope. Stated another way, a policy applied to a group overrides a BGP-wide policy, and a policy applied to a peer overrides both a group and BGP-wide policy.

Multiprotocol BGP (MBGP), defined in RFC 2858, is an extension to BGP that supports other protocols, including IPv6, MPLS, and VPNs.

In choosing routes toward a destination, if there is more than one route to the same destination, BGP uses an algorithm to select a single route to use (see the Introduction to Chapter 8). Note that other router vendors may follow a slightly different set of rules to determine the active route.

For more information about BGP, see *BGP4: Inter-Domain Routing in the Internet* (Addison-Wesley).

BGP Attributes

BGP routers exchange routes, or NLRI, with their neighbors. An NLRI consists of a route prefix and the BGP *attributes* associated with the route. Attributes contain information about a route, such as where it came from and how to reach it, that BGP uses to choose the best path to a destination. A number of attributes were defined in the original BGP specification, and, over time, attributes have been added to extend the functionality of BGP. Compared to IGP routes, which generally just carry the route, a next hop, metric, and an optional tag, BGP routes typically have about a dozen attributes associated with them.

There are several types of attributes. *Well-known attributes* are supported by all BGP implementations. *Mandatory attributes* are included with every prefix. If they are missing, the receiving BGP router will generate an error message. *Discretionary attributes* are those that BGP routers must recognize and support but don't have to be included with every prefix. When a BGP router passes a prefix to its peers, it includes all well-known, mandatory, and discretionary attributes associated with the prefix, either in the state they were received or in the state after they were modified when they passed through the local AS.

BGP routers can also include *optional attributes* with prefixes, or those that are not necessarily supported by all BGP routers. Optional attributes can be *transitive*, which means that BGP must include the information when sending the prefix to another router even if the sending router doesn't understand the option, or *nontransitive*, which allows a router that doesn't understand the option to silently drop it when advertising the prefix.

The following are some of the common BGP attributes. Most BGP implementations understand these attributes.

ORIGIN (well-known, mandatory)
    Designates how BGP learned about the route. It can be one of the following:

    I
        Route was originally learned from an IGP in the originating AS.

E

    Route was originally learned from an EGP.

Incomplete

    Route's source is unknown or BGP doesn't have complete knowledge of its origin.

AS_PATH (well-known, mandatory)

Contains a list of AS numbers that form the path to a destination network. There are two types of AS path attributes. The AS_SEQUENCE attribute indicates the networks that the route has transited from the originating AS to the local AS. When advertising a prefix to an EBGP peer, a BGP router modifies the AS path, *prepending* its AS by adding it to the beginning of the list. The last AS in the path sequence is the originator of the route. For example, in the AS path 65500 65505 65100, the route originated at AS 65100 and the last AS it passed through was 65500. BGP uses the AS path for loop avoidance among ASs. The second type of AS path attribute is AS_SET, which is an unordered list of AS numbers along the path to the destination.

NEXT_HOP (well-known, mandatory)

Contains the IP address of the BGP router that is the next hop toward the destination. The BGP router selects the next hop based on its local routing table. For routes learned from a different AS, the next hop is the IP address of the physical interface to a remote router. If the advertising and receiving routers are in the same AS and the route is in the same AS, the BGP next hop is the IP address of the advertising router. If the route is in a different AS, the BGP next hop is the IP address of a remote BGP router.

LOCAL_PREF (well-known, optional)

Indicates the degree of preference for routes learned by IBGP within an AS. BGP uses this information to choose or favor an exit point from the AS. The higher the preference, the more preferred a route is. This attribute is distributed only in IBGP routing updates.

MED or MULTI_EXIT_DESC (optional, nontransitive)

The multiple exit discriminator is used to determine the exit point from one AS to another AS when there are multiple equivalent paths between the ASs and when all other factors in determining the exit point are equal. The MED is effectively the BGP metric and is a common way for one ISP to make another ISP use the desired link between the two ISPs. Because the MED is nontransitive, it is sent only to adjacent ASs.

ATOMIC_AGGREGATE (well-known, optional)

Indicates that the route is an aggregate of several route prefixes. BGP sets this attribute to indicate that some route information has been lost in the aggregation process.

AGGREGATOR (optional, transitive)
Indicates that the BGP router has summarized a range of prefixes.

COMMUNITY (optional, transitive)
Identifies an administrative or logical grouping of routes that share routing policies. Communities are represented by an identifier that includes the 16-bit AS
number and a 16-bit community number. For example, in 65500:1001, the AS
number is 65500 and the community number is 1001. BGP has three well-known
communities:

NO_EXPORT
Routes cannot be advertised to EBGP peers but can be advertised within a
BGP confederation.

NO_ADVERTISE
Routes cannot be advertised at all.

LOCAL_AS
Routes cannot be advertised to EBGP peers, even if the peers are in the same
confederation.

MP_REACH_NLRI and MP_UNREACH_NLRI (optional, nontransitive)
Carry IPv6 NLRI information in MBGP.

ORIGINATOR_ID (optional, nontransitive)
Identifies a route reflector for IBGP. It is a 32-bit value that indicates the originator of the route within an AS.

CLUSTER_LIST (optional, nontransitive)
Lists route reflection identifiers of the clusters through which the route has
passed. If a cluster sees its own identifier in the list, a loop has occurred and the
route is ignored.

13.1 Configuring a BGP Session Between Routers in Two ASs

Problem

You want to configure BGP on the border routers that connect the two different ASs.

Solution

Configure the autonomous system number and router ID on each router:

```
[edit routing-options]
aviva@RouterF# set autonomous-system 65500
aviva@RouterF# set router-id 192.168.16.1
```

Then configure an EBGP session to the border router in the other AS:

```
[edit protocols bgp]
aviva@RouterF# set group session-to-AS65505 type external
aviva@RouterF# set group session-to-AS65505 peer-as 65505
aviva@RouterF# set group session-to-AS65505 neighbor 10.0.31.1
[edit protocols]
aviva@RouterF# show
bgp {
    group session-to-AS65505 {
        type external;
        peer-as 65505;
        neighbor 10.0.31.1;
    }
}
```

Discussion

The basic configuration of EBGP is very straightforward, and the configuration of the two EBGP peers is pretty much identical. This recipe shows how to configure a session between the two border routers shown in Figure 13-1.

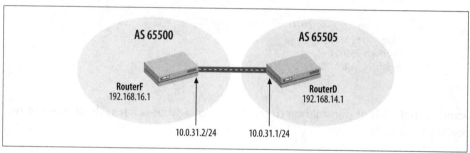

Figure 13-1. EBGP network

You define the router's AS number and its router ID. You don't configure these in the [edit protocols bgp] hierarchy but rather in the [edit routing-options] hierarchy because these two properties are not specific to BGP and can be used by other routing protocols. BGP includes the 32-bit router ID in Open messages when establishing a BGP connection. If you don't manually set the router ID, the JUNOS software uses the IP address on the lo0 interface. However, it is good practice to configure the router ID so the address included in Open messages is always clear.

For an EBGP peering connection, the AS numbers must be different on the two routers. In this recipe, RouterF is in AS 65500 and RouterD is in AS 65505.

In the JUNOS BGP configuration, you place BGP neighbors into *peer groups* so you can apply the same policies and other characteristics to an entire group of neighbors. Each peer group is identified by a name. In this recipe, the group name is session-to-AS65505. While multiple peers can be members of the same group, it is good practice to configure a separate group for each external peer, especially if the external peer is untrusted.

Within a group, you need to configure three things to set up the EBGP session:

1. Use the type external statement to define the session as an external one.
2. Set the AS number of the remote peer AS (here, 65505).
3. Specify the address of the neighboring border router (here, 10.0.31.1).

For EBGP sessions, use the peer router's interface address. You can use the interface address instead of the router's lo0 address because, in most cases, the link between ASs is a point-to-point WAN link. If this link goes down, the peer router is unreachable anyway, so the remote AS would also be unreachable.

To establish the EBGP session, configure a similar EBGP group on the other border router:

```
[edit routing-options]
aviva@RouterD# show
router-id 192.168.14.1;
autonomous-system 65505;

[edit protocols]
aviva@RouterD# show
bgp {
    group session-to-AS65500 {
        type external;
        peer-as 65500;
        neighbor 10.0.31.2;
    }
}
```

Another useful bit of information to set for each neighbor is a text description of the peering session:

```
[edit protocols bgp]
aviva@RouterF# set group session-to-AS65505 description "EBGP to Customer A"
```

This is especially useful to help identify peering sessions when many sessions are configured on a single router.

After you have configured the two peer routers, check that they have established a BGP connection:

```
aviva@RouterF> show bgp neighbor
Peer: 10.0.31.1+1778 AS 65505  Local: 10.0.31.2+179 AS 65500
  Description: EBGP to Customer A
  Type: External    State: Established    Flags: <Sync>
  Last State: OpenConfirm   Last Event: RecvKeepAlive
  Last Error: None
  Options: <Preference HoldTime PeerAS Refresh>
  Holdtime: 90 Preference: 170
  Number of flaps: 0
  Peer ID: 192.168.14.1    Local ID: 192.168.16.1    Active Holdtime: 90
  Keepalive Interval: 30        Peer index: 0
  Local Interface: t1-0/0/3.0
  NLRI advertised by peer: inet-unicast
```

```
NLRI for this session: inet-unicast
Peer supports Refresh capability (2)
Table inet.0 Bit: 10000
  RIB State: BGP restart is complete
  Send state: in sync
  Active prefixes:              0
  Received prefixes:            0
  Suppressed due to damping:    0
  Advertised prefixes:          0
Last traffic (seconds): Received 19    Sent 19    Checked 19
Input messages:  Total 12    Updates 0      Refreshes 0    Octets 254
Output messages: Total 13    Updates 0      Refreshes 0    Octets 273
Output Queue[0]: 0
```

The third line of the output shows that the session has been established. The current state of the BGP connection is Established. If the connection isn't up, but is in the process of establishing itself, this field shows the current state of the BGP session. These states correspond to the session establishment states defined in RFC 1771:

Idle

> This is the initial stage of establishing a connection, when BGP is waiting for a start event.

Connect

> BGP is waiting for TCP to establish its connection between the two peers.

Active

> BGP is actively attempting to connect to its peer.

OpenSent

> The local BGP peer has sent an open request to the peer and is waiting to receive an open message back.

OpenConfirm

> BGP acknowledges that it has received an open message from the peer and is waiting to receive a keepalive message.

When a BGP session doesn't get established, the state often remains as Connect or Active. To troubleshoot the problem, use the show interfaces terse and show interfaces commands to check that the interfaces between the two routers are up and configured properly. Check the BGP configuration on both routers, making sure that the AS numbers are correct. Also, check the current state of the TCP session with the show system connections extensive command (see Recipe 13.3).

The remainder of the third line and the next two lines provide additional information about the session. The Last State field shows the previous state of the BGP session, which is OpenConfirm, the BGP message the two peers exchange when they have confirmed that they will indeed establish a connection.

This command also shows other information about the BGP session. The first line shows the addresses and AS number of the peer border router and the address and AS number of the local router:

```
Peer: 10.0.31.1+1778 AS 65505   Local: 10.0.31.2+179 AS 65500
```

The number following the remote peer's address is the TCP port number used for the connection. The second line shows the peer description that you configured with the set description command.

The Options line shows the BGP options that the peers have agreed to use for the session:

```
Options: <Preference HoldTime PeerAS Refresh>
```

The next lines of the output show the specific values of options and other information about the session:

```
Holdtime: 90 Preference: 170
```

Holdtime is the hold timer value, which is the maximum length of time that one peer will wait to get a BGP message from the other side (either an update or a keepalive message) before assuming that this session is down. RPD uses the Preference value to select among routes learned from different sources (see Table 8-2). These two output fields report the values configured with the hold-time and preference statements. Because we haven't configured these values, both fields show the default values: 170 for the route preference and 90 seconds for the hold time (three times the default keepalive message interval of 30 seconds).

A few lines down in the output, you see the keepalive interval. The Number of flaps field tells you whether the BGP session has gone down and come back up:

```
Number of flaps: 0
```

Because we just established the session, the value is 0. You can use this field to track whether the session has been interrupted. The Peer ID and Local ID fields show the router ID of each peer, which are configured with the set routing-options router-id command. The Active Holdtime field is the hold timer that has been negotiated between the BGP peers and is actually being used on the session.

```
Peer ID: 192.168.14.1     Local ID: 192.168.16.1     Active Holdtime: 90
```

The next several lines show the NLRI learned from the BGP update messages sent on this session. These two lines show the address family that is being advertised by the peer and used by the session, which can be either unicast (as shown here) or multicast:

```
NLRI advertised by peer: inet-unicast
NLRI for this session: inet-unicast
```

The route refresh line shows that the peer supports the BGP route refresh capability, defined in RFC 2918, which allows BGP peers to readvertise their prefixes to the peer. Route refresh facilitates nondisruptive routing-policy changes.

Next is information about routes learned from BGP in the inet.0 routing table:

```
Table inet.0 Bit: 10000
    RIB State: BGP restart is complete
    Send state: in sync
    Active prefixes:              0
    Received prefixes:            0
    Suppressed due to damping:    0
    Advertised prefixes:          0
```

The last few lines show traffic statistics for the session:

```
Last traffic (seconds): Received 19   Sent 19    Checked 19
  Input messages:  Total 12    Updates 0     Refreshes 0    Octets 254
  Output messages: Total 13    Updates 0     Refreshes 0    Octets 273
  Output Queue[0]: 0
```

The show bgp summary command also shows information about the BGP connection that you can use to determine whether the session has been established:

```
aviva@RouterF> show bgp summary
Groups: 1 Peers: 1 Down peers: 0
Table          Tot Paths  Act Paths Suppressed    History Damp State    Pending
inet.0                 0          0          0          0         0           0
Peer            AS      InPkt     OutPkt    OutQ   Flaps Last Up/Dwn State|#A
ctive/Received/Damped...
10.0.31.1       65505      29        30       0       0    13:56 0/0/0
                0/0/0
```

The first line shows the number of groups configured (here, 1) and the number of peers that are up (1) and down (0). Because our router currently has just one peer, this line tells us that the peer is up. The Table portion of the output provides a summary of the BGP route information in each routing table. This output shows that the inet.0 routing table doesn't yet have any BGP routes.

The Peer portion of the output shows the address of the BGP peer (10.0.31.1), its AS number (65505), and traffic statistics for the session. The State column shows three values separated by slashes that correspond to the states Active/Received/Damped. If the session with the neighbor is actively establishing itself but is not yet up, the State column shows Active. If the state is Connect or Idle and has remained that way for more than several minutes (the Last Up/Dwn field tells how long the neighbor has been in the particular state), this is a sign that the connection is not establishing. Use the show interfaces terse command to check that the physical connection to the peer is physically up and the show chassis hardware command to make sure that the network interface card is still installed and present in your router. If you determine that the Layer 1 and Layer 2 portions of the connection are functioning, move up the protocol stack. Try pinging the remote IP address to help identify if any filters are in place that might block the connection. You can also try ICMP tests and a Telnet test from the local IP address to port 179 on the remote IP address to determine whether you can establish a socket between the two IP addresses.

When the State column shows three numbers separated by slashes, the BGP session is up. The values are the number of routes received from the neighbor, the number of routes accepted as active and being used in the forwarding table, and the number of routes that have been damped. The current state is 0/0/0, and the previous state of the session, on the second line of output, is 0/0/0.

The remaining columns for the peer show the number of packets received from (InPkt) and sent to (OutPkt) the peer; the number of packets queued to be sent to the peer (OutQ), which is usually 0 because the queue is emptied quickly; the number of times the BGP session has flapped (gone down and then come back up); and how long it has been since the neighbor was established (Last Up/Dwn).

Why does the State column show that there are no BGP routes? Looking at the routing table confirms that the router hasn't learned any routes from BGP:

```
aviva@RouterF> show route
inet.0: 10 destinations, 10 routes (10 active, 0 holddown, 0 hidden)
+ = Active Route, - = Last Active, * = Both
0.0.0.0/0          *[Static/5] 1w0d 22:18:02
                    > to 172.19.121.1 via fe-0/0/0.0
10.0.8.0/24        *[Direct/0] 1w0d 22:17:55
                    > via fe-0/0/1.0
10.0.8.2/32        *[Local/0] 1w0d 22:18:05
                    Local via fe-0/0/1.0
10.0.13.0/24       *[Direct/0] 05:30:25
                    > via t1-0/0/2.0
10.0.13.2/32       *[Local/0] 05:30:27
                    Local via t1-0/0/2.0
10.0.31.0/24       *[Direct/0] 05:30:27
                    > via t1-0/0/3.0
10.0.31.2/32       *[Local/0] 05:30:27
                    Local via t1-0/0/3.0
172.19.121.0/24    *[Direct/0] 1w0d 22:18:02
                    > via fe-0/0/0.0
172.19.121.116/32  *[Local/0] 1w0d 22:18:05
                    Local via fe-0/0/0.0
192.168.16.1/32    *[Direct/0] 1d 22:22:13
                    > via lo0.0
```

Sure enough, no routes have been learned from BGP. You need a routing policy to redistribute the desired information from AS 65505 into the local AS. Create a routing policy on each peer so that it exports static routes into BGP:

```
[edit policy-options policy-statement send-statics]
aviva@RouterF# set term 1 from protocol static
aviva@RouterF# set term 1 then accept
```

Then apply this policy to the EBGP group:

```
[edit protocols bgp group session-to-AS65505]
aviva@RouterG# set export send-statics
```

Looking at the remote peer router, you now see routes learned from BGP:

```
aviva@RouterD> show route
inet.0: 11 destinations, 15 routes (11 active, 0 holddown, 0 hidden)
+ = Active Route, - = Last Active, * = Both
0.0.0.0/0           *[Static/5] 1w0d 22:33:16
                    > to 172.19.121.1 via t1-0/0/3.0
                    [BGP/170] 00:07:27, localpref 100
                      AS path: 65500 I
                    > to 10.0.31.2 via t1-0/0/3.0
10.0.24.2/32        *[Local/0] 1d 23:00:04
                      Reject
10.0.29.0/24        *[Direct/0] 05:31:20
                    > via fe-0/0/1.0
10.0.29.2/32        *[Local/0] 05:31:20
                      Local via fe-0/0/1.0
10.0.31.0/24        *[Direct/0] 05:31:20
                    > via t1-0/0/3.0
                    [BGP/170] 00:05:02, localpref 100
                      AS path: 65500 I
                    > to 10.0.31.2 via t1-0/0/3.0
10.0.31.1/32        *[Local/0] 05:31:20
                      Local via t1-0/0/3.0
172.19.121.0/24     *[Direct/0] 4d 20:23:23
                    > via fe-0/0/0.0
                    [BGP/170] 16:47:48, localpref 100
                      AS path: 65505 I
                    > to 10.0.31.1 via t1-0/0/3.0
172.19.121.116/32   *[Local/0] 4d 20:23:23
                      Local via fe-0/0/0.0
192.168.14.1/32     *[Direct/0] 1w0d 22:33:44
                    > via lo0.0
192.168.16.1/32     *[BGP/170] 00:05:02, localpref 100
                      AS path: 65500 I
                    > to 10.0.31.2 via t1-0/0/3.0
```

The BGP route entries start with [BGP/170], and the router has learned four routes from BGP:

- 10.0.31.0/24 is the subnet that the BGP session is running on.
- 192.168.16.1/32 is the peer's loopback address.
- 0.0.0.0/0 is the default gateway address.
- 172.19.121.1 goes to another network internal to the lab.

Each BGP route also contains specific BGP information. localpref is the value of the BGP local preference (LOCAL_PREF) attribute, which is the metric that BGP assigns to the route. Because BGP learned these routes as a result of the send-statics policy, which you defined to export static routes into BGP, the JUNOS BGP software assigns them a local preference of 100 by default. If these routes were learned from BGP and already had a local preference value, that value would not be changed.

The AS path line lists all AS paths from the AS_PATH attribute, which shows the ASs through which the announcement for the prefix has traveled. The first AS in the path is the most recent AS, and the last AS is the originating AS. All routes in this output have come directly from the peer AS, so there is just one AS number in the path, AS 65500.

Following the path is the information from the BGP ORIGIN attribute, which indicates how BGP learned the prefix. The I here means that the prefix was learned from an IGP. Routes learned from an EGP peer would have an E, and those learned some other way would show as INCOMPLETE. The final line for each BGP route entry shows the next hop toward the destination and the interface the router will use to reach that next hop. Of the three BGP routes, the one to 192.168.16.1/32 is active and is marked with an asterisk.

Checking the BGP connection status on the peer, you now see the BGP routes:

```
aviva@RouterD> show bgp summary
Groups: 1 Peers: 1 Down peers: 0
Table          Tot Paths  Act Paths Suppressed    History Damp State    Pending
inet.0             4          1          0          0         0            0
Peer             AS     InPkt    OutPkt   OutQ   Flaps Last Up/Dwn State|#A
ctive/Received/Damped...
10.0.31.2      65500      721       718      0       0   5:57:50 1/4/0
                0/0/0
```

The Table section of the output shows that the inet.0 routing table has four BGP routes, which matches what we saw in the routing-table entries above. In the Peer section, the State column indicates that four BGP routes have been received from peer 10.0.31.2 and that one is active. Again, this corresponds with the routing-table entries.

Another way to find out about BGP routes is to look at what the routing table has received from BGP:

```
aviva@RouterD> show route receive-protocol bgp 10.0.31.2
inet.0: 11 destinations, 15 routes (11 active, 0 holddown, 0 hidden)
  Prefix                 Nexthop          MED    Lclpref    AS path
  0.0.0.0/0              10.0.31.2                           65500 I
  10.0.31.0/24          10.0.31.2                           65500 I
  172.19.121.0/24       10.0.31.2                           65500 I
* 192.168.16.1/32       10.0.31.2                           65500 I
```

Again, you see the four routes learned from BGP but in a format that is much easier to scan. For each route, you also see the value of four BGP attributes: NEXT_HOP, MED, LOCAL_PREF, and AS_PATH. The active route is marked with an asterisk.

Use the following command to see which routes the router has advertised:

```
aviva@RouterF> show route advertising-protocol bgp 10.0.31.1
inet.0: 6 destinations, 6 routes (6 active, 0 holddown, 0 hidden)
  Prefix                 Nexthop          MED    Lclpref    AS path
* 0.0.0.0/0             Self                                I
```

```
* 10.0.31.0/24        Self                        I
* 172.19.121.0/24     Self                        I
* 192.168.16.1/32     Self                        I
```

See Also

Recipe 13.3

13.2 Configuring BGP on Routers Within an AS

Problem

You want to propagate the routes learned by your EBGP peering sessions to your
IBGP routers.

Solution

Configure IBGP on the border router and on all the routers within your AS. On each
router, configure an IBGP group:

```
[edit protocols bgp]
aviva@RouterF# set group internal-within-AS65500 type internal
aviva@RouterF# set group internal-within-AS65500 local-address 192.168.16.1
aviva@RouterF# set group internal-within-AS65500 neighbor 192.168.15.1
aviva@RouterF# set group internal-within-AS65500 neighbor 192.168.17.1
```

Discussion

Once you have set up an external BGP connection that runs between two different
ASs, the two border routers are able to exchange routing information, but you still
need a way to propagate these routes within your AS. One way to do this is to inject
all the external routes into your IGP. Generally, you do not want to use this
approach, especially if you are an ISP and are carrying the full Internet routing table;
there are too many routes (on the order of 170,000 and climbing), and they change
too often, so you would end up overwhelming the IGP. The standard way to inject
external routes into your AS is to set up IBGP sessions on all routers in your AS. The
connections between all IBGP routers must be fully meshed to prevent routing loops
within the AS. This full mesh is a virtual mesh, completely independent of any actual
physical connections. To do this, you create an IBGP group in which you list as
neighbors all the IBGP routers in the AS. You must also use an IGP, such as OSPF or
IS-IS, to distribute the IBGP routing information to all the routers in the AS. This recipe configures the routers shown in Figure 13-2.

The configuration for IBGP is very similar to that for EBGP. You create a BGP group
with the set protocols bgp group command. This time, however, the type is internal,
not external. Because the group is within the AS, you do not need to configure the
peer's AS number. In the group, you list all the IBGP peers, one in each neighbor
statement. These are all the IBGP routers in the AS, both the ones that the router is

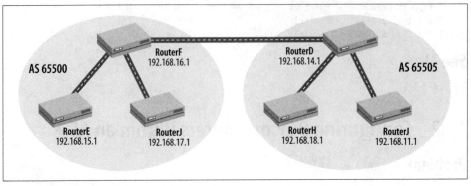

Figure 13-2. IBGP network

directly connected to and the ones that it is not directly connected to. These neighbor statements effectively create the full-mesh peering among all the IBGP routers. For IBGP peers, when you specify the addresses, you don't use the physical interface but rather the loopback address of the router. You can do this because even if a link to the router is down, it might still be reachable through the IGP. Finally, the local-address statement sets the loopback address as the source address of all IP packets sent by BGP to all destination routers.

The configuration for all the IBGP routers is basically the same, with each router using the appropriate local address and listing all the other IBGP routers in the AS as neighbors.

Define the AS number and router ID on each IBGP router just as you did on the border router:

```
[edit routing-options]
aviva@RouterE# set autonomous-system 65500
aviva@RouterE# set router-id 192.168.15.1
```

Be sure to configure the same AS number on all the IBGP routers.

Finally, an IGP must run among all the IBGP routers. For the examples in this chapter, we use a simple OSPF configuration. Here is the configuration on RouterF, the border router:

```
[edit protocols]
aviva@RouterF# show ospf
area 0.0.0.0 {
    interface lo0.0 {
        passive;
    }
    interface t1-0/0/2.0;
    interface fe-0/0/1.0;
}
```

When all routers are configured for the IBGP mesh, use the show bgp summary command to check that all the sessions are up and running. Here's what you see on one of the internal routers:

```
aviva@RouterE> show bgp summary
Groups: 1 Peers: 2 Down peers: 0
Table          Tot Paths  Act Paths Suppressed    History Damp State    Pending
inet.0               5         5          0           0        0          0
Peer            AS     InPkt    OutPkt    OutQ   Flaps Last Up/Dwn State|#A
ctive/Received/Damped...
192.168.16.1   65500   1985     1977       0       1   16:27:39 5/5/0
               0/0/0
192.168.17.1   65500     15       17       0       0    7:36 0/0/0
               0/0/0
```

The first line of output shows that this IBGP router has one BGP group and two peers, which are both up. The Table portion shows five active BGP paths in the inet.0 routing table. The Peer portion shows that the router received these routes from 192.168.16.1, which is the border router. Use the show route command to verify this. The summary version provides an overview of routes learned from BGP and other protocols:

```
aviva@RouterE> show route summary
Autonomous system number: 65500
Router ID: 192.168.15.1
inet.0: 15 destinations, 16 routes (15 active, 0 holddown, 0 hidden)
              Direct:     3 routes,      3 active
               Local:     2 routes,      2 active
                OSPF:     5 routes,      4 active
                 BGP:     5 routes,      5 active
              Static:     1 routes,      1 active
```

The show route protocol bgp command gives more detail about the routes learned from BGP:

```
aviva@RouterE> show route protocol bgp
inet.0: 15 destinations, 16 routes (15 active, 0 holddown, 0 hidden)
+ = Active Route, - = Last Active, * = Both
10.0.24.0/24      *[BGP/170] 00:07:14, localpref 100, from 192.168.16.1
                    AS path: 65505 I
                  > to 172.19.121.1 via fe-0/0/0.0
10.0.29.0/24      *[BGP/170] 00:07:14, localpref 100, from 192.168.16.1
                    AS path: 65505 I
                  > to 172.19.121.1 via fe-0/0/0.0
192.168.11.1/32   *[BGP/170] 00:07:14, MED 1, localpref 100, from 192.168.16.1
                    AS path: 65505 I
                  > to 172.19.121.1 via fe-0/0/0.0
192.168.14.1/32   *[BGP/170] 00:07:14, localpref 100, from 192.168.16.1
                    AS path: 65505 I
                  > to 172.19.121.1 via fe-0/0/0.0
192.168.18.1/32   *[BGP/170] 00:07:14, MED 65, localpref 100, from 192.168.16.1
                    AS path: 65505 I
                  > to 172.19.121.1 via fe-0/0/0.0
```

The five BGP routes are marked with an asterisk to indicate that they are active routes. These routes are all to systems in the remote AS, 65505. The 192.168/32 addresses are the loopback addresses of the BGP routers (192.168.14.1 is the border router, and 192.168.11.1 and 192.168.14.1 are its IBGP peers), and the two 10.0/24 prefixes are the subnets connecting the remote IBGP peers.

Notice that from BGP, the router learns only about destinations in the remote AS. It learns routes to destinations within the local AS from OSPF:

```
aviva@RouterE> show route protocol ospf
inet.0: 15 destinations, 16 routes (15 active, 0 holddown, 0 hidden)
+ = Active Route, - = Last Active, * = Both
10.0.8.0/24        *[OSPF/10] 00:12:15, metric 66
                    > via t1-0/0/3.0
10.0.13.0/24       [OSPF/10] 00:12:15, metric 65
                    > via t1-0/0/3.0
192.168.16.1/32    *[OSPF/10] 00:12:15, metric 65
                    > via t1-0/0/3.0
192.168.17.1/32    *[OSPF/10] 00:12:15, metric 66
                    > via t1-0/0/3.0
224.0.0.5/32       *[OSPF/10] 17:32:17, metric 1
                    MultiRecv
```

OSPF has routes to the two internal subnets, 10.0.8.0/24 and 10.0.13.0/24, and to the loopback addresses of the other two routers in the AS (the 192.168 addresses).

Looking at the BGP sessions on the border router, here's what you see:

```
aviva@RouterF> show bgp summary
Groups: 2 Peers: 3 Down peers: 0
Table          Tot Paths  Act Paths Suppressed    History Damp State    Pending
inet.0                 8          5          0          0         0           0
Peer             AS      InPkt      OutPkt    OutQ   Flaps Last Up/Dwn State|#A
ctive/Received/Damped...
192.168.15.1   65500     1994        2006       0       0    16:37:18 0/0/0
                    0/0/0
192.168.17.1   65500       37          44       0       0       18:19 0/0/0
                    0/0/0
10.0.31.1      65505     2002        2006       0       0    16:37:26 5/8/0
                    0/0/0
```

The Groups line shows that this router has two BGP groups (one for the EBGP session, the second for the IBGP peerings) and has three peers that are all up. The Table section shows that the router has eight BGP routes in the inet.0 table. The Peer section shows where the router is learning the BGP routes, which is only from its EBGP peer, 10.0.31.1. It is not receiving any routes from its IBGP peers, 192.168.15.1 and 192.168.17.1, as expected. Looking in the routing table confirms that the only routes learned from BGP are those from the remote AS:

```
aviva@RouterF> show route protocol bgp
inet.0: 18 destinations, 22 routes (18 active, 0 holddown, 0 hidden)
+ = Active Route, - = Last Active, * = Both
0.0.0.0/0          [BGP/170] 15:23:37, localpref 100
                    AS path: 65505 I
                    > to 10.0.31.1 via t1-0/0/3.0
10.0.24.0/24       *[BGP/170] 01:23:48, localpref 100
                    AS path: 65505 I
```

```
                           > to 10.0.31.1 via t1-0/0/3.0
10.0.29.0/24     *[BGP/170] 01:19:38, localpref 100
                              AS path: 65505 I
                           > to 10.0.31.1 via t1-0/0/3.0
10.0.31.0/24      [BGP/170] 15:23:37, localpref 100
                              AS path: 65505 I
                           > to 10.0.31.1 via t1-0/0/3.0
172.19.121.0/24   [BGP/170] 15:23:37, localpref 100
                              AS path: 65505 I
                           > to 10.0.31.1 via t1-0/0/3.0
192.168.11.1/32  *[BGP/170] 01:18:52, MED 1, localpref 100
                              AS path: 65505 I
                           > to 10.0.31.1 via t1-0/0/3.0
192.168.14.1/32  *[BGP/170] 15:23:37, localpref 100
                              AS path: 65505 I
                           > to 10.0.31.1 via t1-0/0/3.0
192.168.18.1/32  *[BGP/170] 01:23:38, MED 65, localpref 100
                              AS path: 65505 I
                           > to 10.0.31.1 via t1-0/0/3.0
```

The BGP routes in the routing table now include the value of the BGP multiple exit discriminator (MED) attribute that was advertised with the prefix:

```
192.168.11.1/32  *[BGP/170] 01:18:52, MED 1, localpref 100
                              AS path: 65505 I
                           > to 10.0.31.1 via t1-0/0/3.0
192.168.18.1/32  *[BGP/170] 01:23:38, MED 65, localpref 100
                              AS path: 65505 I
                           > to 10.0.31.1 via t1-0/0/3.0
```

The output shows the MED in the prefixes to the IBGP routers in the immediately adjacent AS. The MED is the BGP metric and is used as a tie-breaker to pick the path to an AS when there are multiple equivalent paths between the ASs and when all other factors in determining the exit point are equal.

The show bgp group command shows information about the two BGP groups on the router:

```
aviva@RouterF> show bgp group
Group Type: External                        Local AS: 65500
  Name: session-to-AS65505 Index: 0         Flags: <>
  Export: [ send-statics ]
  Total peers: 1        Established: 1
  10.0.31.1+179
  inet.0: 5/8/0
Group Type: Internal    AS: 65500           Local AS: 65500
  Name: internal-within-AS65500 Index: 1    Flags: <Export Eval>
  Total peers: 2        Established: 2
  192.168.15.1+179
  192.168.17.1+179
  inet.0: 0/0/0
Groups: 2  Peers: 3    External: 1   Internal: 2    Down peers: 0   Flaps: 0
Table          Tot Paths Act Paths Suppressed   History Damp State   Pending
inet.0             8         5         0            0        0          0
```

The first group is the external group session-to-AS65505, and the second is the IBGP group internal-within-AS65500. The output shows the local AS number and the export policies that have been applied to this group (here, send-statics). Because a group is a collection of peers with the same export characteristics, the show bgp group command shows just the configured export policy. Any import policies you might have configured are not displayed, because each peer in a group can have a different import policy. This command also shows the number of peers in the group and their addresses, and the number of routes active and received from this peer. This group has one peer, which is the remote border router 10.0.31.1, and it has received six routes from the peer, three of which are active (3/6/0).

The last three lines of the output summarize the BGP groups and the routes that have been placed into the routing table. It shows the two groups (one external and one internal) and three peers that are up and have never gone down. The routing table has learned eight total paths from its BGP peers and five of them are active in the inet.0 routing table.

13.3 Diagnosing TCP Session Problems

Problem

You want to figure out why the BGP session is not being established.

Solution

Start by looking at the current state of the TCP sessions on the router:

    aviva@RouterF> show system connections extensive

Also look at the information in the system logging files:

    aviva@RouterF> show log messages

Check that the TCP session can pass Internet control packets:

    aviva@RouterF> ping tos 0xc0 *RouterD*

Discussion

When two BGP peers have a problem establishing a BGP session, one of the first indications is that you see BGP hold-time expired error messages on the routers in the router's system logging files. You also see that the State field in the show bgp neighbor command output is not Established and that the State field in the show bgp summary command is Active or Connect, indicating that the BGP session is not established.

The hold-time expired errors usually occur because the TCP session between a pair of peers cannot effectively transmit data between the routers, not because of a problem with BGP itself. When the TCP session doesn't work properly, the BGP session times out, and BGP signals the problem by sending hold-time expired messages and generating a BGP Notification message to the remote peer. Notification messages are logged at the system logging severity level warning.

Some of the most frequent causes of hold-time expired errors are MTU issues on a directly connected link, issues related to forwarding of Internet control packets, and IGP failures on IBGP sessions.

Looking at the TCP MTU path behavior, first let's look at the TCP session. By default, a TCP session transmits 576 bytes in a single packet to minimize the chances that the packet will be fragmented at a device along the path to the destination. Most links use an MTU of at least 1,500 bytes. Path MTU discovery, which is disabled by default in the JUNOS BGP, allows BGP to dynamically determine how large the packets can be in a TCP session without being fragmented. This means that BGP tries to use 576-byte packets for the TCP sessions. However, on directly connected EBGP sessions, TCP uses MTU-sized packets. If there is an MTU mismatch between the two sides of the TCP connection, the BGP session cannot be established. One workaround is to enable path MTU discovery within the BGP group:

```
[edit protocols bgp group external]
aviva@RouterF# set mtu-discovery
```

When path MTU discovery is enabled, the don't fragment (DF) bit is set on all TCP packets sent by the BGP session.

When you are testing session connectivity, in addition to the standard ping command, send packets in which the Internet control CoS bit is set:

```
aviva@RouterF> ping tos 0xc0 RouterD
```

If the QoS parameters are misconfigured on a transit router, TCP connectivity can work for regular best-effort traffic but will break for Internet control traffic. The same behavior can happen when you are testing new software or new PICs.

Another way to get information about the TCP session and what might be malfunctioning is to look at the current state of TCP sessions:

```
aviva@RouterF> show system connections extensive | find tcp
tcp4      0     2  192.168.70.143.23        172.17.28.108.3350       ESTABLISHED
     sndsbcc:            2 sndsbmbcnt:          256  sndsbmbmax:    266432
  sndsblowat:         2048 sndsbhiwat:        33304
     rcvsbcc:            0 rcvsbmbcnt:            0  rcvsbmbmax:    463360
  rcvsblowat:            1 rcvsbhiwat:        57920
         iss: 2677798142       sndup: 2677853922         sndcc:         0
      snduna: 2677853922      sndnxt: 2677853924        sndwnd:     57920
      sndmax: 2677853924     sndcwnd:       65535 sndssthresh: 1073725440
         irs: 1577022682       rcvup: 1577023284         rcvcc:         0
      rcvnxt: 1577023292      rcvadv: 1577081212        rcvwnd:     57920
```

```
rtt:  200130618      srtt:        301       rttv:        12
rttmin:         100  duration:        0       mss:       1448
   flags: REQ_SCALE RCVD_SCALE REQ_TSTMP RCVD_TSTMP [0x1e0]
```

Also, use the information in the system logging files, which is very extensive and is similar to the output of the show system connections extensive command:

```
Aug 24 13:15:46 RouterF rpd[2797]: bgp_traffic_timeout: NOTIFICATION sent to 192.168.
14.1 (Internal AS 3356): code 4 (Hold Timer Expired Error), Reason: holdtime expired
for 192.168.14.1 (Internal AS 3356), socket buffer sndcc: 0 rcvcc: 0 TCP state: 4,
snd_una: 1404695285 snd_nxt: 1404695285 snd_wnd: 16384 rcv_nxt: 4086106368 rcv_adv:
4086157473, keepalive timer 0
```

You can learn a lot of information about the TCP connection from the socket buffer information in the system logging message, which is a subset of BSD transmission control block (TCB) parameters:

sndcc
> Bytes on send buffer. A full send buffer typically means that packets from this host are not being acknowledged.

rcvcc
> Bytes on receive buffer. Expect 0 bytes here because RPD should not declared a hold time expired if information is available about the buffer.

snd_una
snd_nxt
> The difference between these two (snd_nxt − snd_una) is the amount of unacknowledged data on the TCP session.

snd_wnd
> Size of the window advertised by the peer.

rcv_adv
rcv_nxt
> The difference between these two (rcv_adv − rcv_nxt) is the size of the window advertised by the local TCP stack.

It is important to try to collect the information on both sides of the session. This gives an indication about whether the data path failure is unidirectional, bidirectional, or dependent on packet size.

If you are seeing hold-time expired errors between IBGP peers, check the IGP logs. If this correlates to a link failure in your IGP, this should probably be your starting point for diagnostics.

See Also

For information about BSD TCBs, see *TCP/IP Illustrated* (Addison-Wesley).

13.4   Adjusting the Next-Hop Attribute

Problem

Your IBGP routers need to be able to resolve the BGP next hop of routes that are in external ASs.

Solution

To have IBGP routers reach addresses in external ASs, you change the BGP next-hop attribute on routes when it is distributed from EBGP into IBGP so that the routes always point to a next-hop address inside the local AS. You do this with a routing policy that defines the next hop as self (that is, this router):

```
[edit policy-options]
aviva@RouterF# set policy-statement next-hop-self term 1 from protocol bgp
aviva@RouterF# set policy-statement next-hop-self term 1 then next-hop self
```

Then apply the policy as an export policy in the IBGP group on the border router:

```
[edit protocols bgp]
aviva@RouterF# set group internal-within-AS65500 export next-hop-self
```

Discussion

When an EBGP route arrives from another AS, it contains the physical address of the remote interface as the BGP next hop. If the EBGP router advertises this route within its IBGP network, the IGP routing table may not know about that next hop because it is a physical interface in another AS and might not have a way to reach it. Setting up a next-hop self policy allows the EBGP router that is advertising the route to IBGP to use itself as the next hop for the EBGP routes.

This recipe creates a simple routing policy that takes all BGP routes and defines the next hop of the route as self, which is the router on which the route resides. As with all JUNOS routing policies, you need to apply it—here, to the IBGP peer group as an export policy. It would be a mistake to apply the policy as an import policy in the EBGP group, because then all EBGP routes would be installed in the routing table with the local router as the BGP next hop, which would make the routes unusable.

See Also

Recipe 9.1

13.5 Adjusting Local Preference Values

Problem

You want to change the value of the BGP local preference attribute to control which routes the router uses.

Solution

There are two ways to change the local preference value. The first method changes the value for all routes distributed into IBGP from the router:

```
[edit protocols bgp]
aviva@RouterF# set group internal-within-AS65500 local-preference 140
```

The second method allows you to change the preference of specific routes:

```
[edit policy-options policy-statement set-local-pref]
aviva@RouterF# set from route-filter 192.168.14.1/32 exact
aviva@RouterF# set then local-preference 140
aviva@RouterF# set then accept

[edit protocols bgp group session-to-AS65505]
aviva@RouterF# set import set-local-pref
```

Discussion

When IBGP routers exchange prefix information, one of the attributes associated with each prefix is its local preference (LOCAL_PREF) value. This attribute is not advertised to EBGP peers. IBGP routers use the local preference value as a metric to decide which routes should exit the AS, choosing the route with the highest local preference value. The default local preference value is 100. BGP includes the local preference value only when advertising prefixes to IBGP peers. It is not advertised to EBGP peers.

When the router is determining the active route to a destination (see the Introduction to Chapter 8), one of the first things it considers is the BGP local preference, so changing the local preference is a useful way to manipulate route selection. By selecting from multiple routes to a destination, the local preference is the first BGP path attribute checked, even before the AS path length, the origin, and the MED.

Don't confuse the BGP local preference with the JUNOS software routing-protocol preference (see Table 8-2). The JUNOS routing preference is local to each router, and the software uses it to choose the active route when there are a number of paths to the same prefix. The BGP local preference is used only by BGP, and only by IBGP routers within an AS. Also, the choice is between two different types of preference values that are the reverse of each other. For the JUNOS routing-protocol preference, the route with the lowest value is chosen, but with the BGP local preference, the route with the highest value is chosen.

The first configuration in this recipe changes the local preference for all routes in the IBGP group to 140, making them more preferred over unaltered routes, which have a default local preference of 100. The second configuration creates a routing policy that changes the local preference value just on the one route, 192.168.14.1/32. Another variation of this policy is to change the value on all routes coming from a particular AS:

```
[edit policy-options]
aviva@RouterF# set as-path local-pref-path "65505 .*"
aviva@RouterF# set policy-statement AS-local-pref from as-path local-pref-path
aviva@RouterF# set policy-statement AS-local-pref then local-preference 140
aviva@RouterF# set policy-statement AS-local-pref then accept
```

This policy modifies the preference only for routes that have 65505 as the first AS in the AS path. No other BGP routes are affected by this routing policy.

Looking again at the original policy in this recipe, before applying the policy, the route has the default local preference of 100:

```
[edit policy-options]
aviva@RouterF> show route 192.168.14.1/32
inet.0: 24 destinations, 28 routes (24 active, 0 holddown, 0 hidden)
+ = Active Route, - = Last Active, * = Both
192.168.14.1/32    *[BGP/170] 00:05:48, localpref 100
                        AS path: 65505 I
                      > to 10.0.31.1 via t1-0/0/3.0
```

After applying the policy, the local preference changes to 140:

```
aviva@RouterF> show route 192.168.14.1/32
inet.0: 24 destinations, 28 routes (24 active, 0 holddown, 0 hidden)
+ = Active Route, - = Last Active, * = Both
192.168.14.1/32    *[BGP/170] 00:08:15, localpref 140
                        AS path: 65505 I
                      > to 10.0.31.1 via t1-0/0/3.0
```

See Also

The Introduction to Chapter 8

13.6   Removing Private AS Numbers from the AS Path

Problem

You are using private AS numbers within your AS and want to remove them on advertisements going out to the public Internet.

Solution

Configure the border router to remove private AS numbers:

```
[edit protocols bgp]
aviva@Router3# set group ISP remove-private
```

Discussion

When BGP advertises prefixes to remote systems, it includes the AS_PATH attribute, which lists all the ASs along the path to the prefix. BGP routers use this information to determine the path to the route's origin. As a route passes through each AS, the BGP router adds its AS number to the beginning of the AS path. In this way, each AS is a single hop in the path. The BGP specification prohibits removing information from the AS path attribute. However, if on your internal network you are using private AS numbers (numbers in the range from 64512 through 65534), you shouldn't be passing these numbers to the Internet because they are reserved for private use only. If another network happens to be using the same private AS numbers, the two ASs will not be able communicate with each other because BGP will see the same AS numbers and conclude that there is a routing loop.

Use the set remove-private command to remove private AS numbers when the local border router advertises its prefixes to remote border routers. One case when you might want to do this is if your customers are using private AS numbers within the networks and, as the ISP, you want to remove the private AS numbers from the path. You include this configuration in the EBGP group that faces the Internet or other EBGP peers.

Looking in the routing table of the receiving router before the remove-private configuration, you see that the routes contain private AS numbers. The following route contains the private number 64555:

```
aviva@Router3> show route advertising-protocol bgp 172.0.0.34
inet.0: 164830 destinations, 164838 routes (164829 active, 0 holddown, 1 hidden)
  Prefix               Nexthop          MED     Lclpref    AS path
* 172.0.0.0/24         Self             0                  64555 65534 I
  172.0.0.0/24         *[BGP/170] 00:04:55, MED 0, localpref 100, from 172.0.0.127
                         AS path: 64555 65534 I
                       > to 172.0.0.11 via ge-1/3/0.2
```

After the configuration is applied, BGP strips the private AS number from the AS path, and the receiving router no longer sees it in the routing table:

```
aviva@Router3> show route advertising-protocol bgp 172.0.0.34
inet.0: 164830 destinations, 164838 routes (164829 active, 0 holddown, 1 hidden)
  Prefix               Nexthop          MED     Lclpref    AS path
* 172.0.0.0/24         Self             0                  65534 I
  172.0.0.0/24         *[BGP/170] 00:04:55, MED 0, localpref 100, from 172.0.0.127
                         AS path: 65534 I
                       > to 172.0.0.11 via ge-1/3/0.2
```

The remove-private statement removes only leading private AS numbers. If the path had been 3937 64555, the private AS would remain in the path. As another example, the path 64555 64555 64555 65300 64590 65534 would be sent as *local-AS* 65300 64590 65534.

13.7 Prepending AS Numbers to the AS Path

Problem

You want to extend the number of values in the AS path to make that path appear to be less preferable.

Solution

In the JUNOS software, you prepend paths to the AS path using routing policy. First, create a policy the defines the AS path string to prepend:

```
[edit policy-options]
aviva@RouterF# set policy-statement prepend-as-path then prepend-as-path "65500 65500
65500"
```

Then, apply the policy to the EBGP group:

```
[edit bgp]
aviva@RouterF# set group session-to-AS65505 export prepend-as-path
```

Discussion

When ASs have multiple connections between them, you might want to make the remote AS prefer one of those paths when it is sending traffic to your AS. An easy way to force external routers to choose a particular path is to adjust the AS path attribute. Early on in the process of determining the active route to a destination (see the Introduction to Chapter 8), a BGP router looks at the AS path and chooses the prefix with the shorter path. If you lengthen the path for routes that use a particular EBGP connection, the remote network will reach you using a different connection. There still might be times when the route with the lengthened AS path is used because it is the shorter path, so you can prepend the same AS number several times to lengthen the path even more.

This recipe prepends the local AS number to BGP prefixes exported on this BGP connection. To do this, you create a routing policy. Because you want the policy to match all BGP prefixes, you don't need a from clause. If you want to prepend the AS numbers only to certain prefixes, list them in a from clause. Then apply the policy to the EBGP group.

Looking at the remote AS before applying this policy, you see that the AS path for each prefix in AS 65500 lists the AS only once:

```
aviva@RouterD> show route protocol bgp
inet.0: 19 destinations, 25 routes (19 active, 0 holddown, 0 hidden)
+ = Active Route, - = Last Active, * = Both
0.0.0.0/0          [BGP/170] 00:00:13, localpref 100
                     AS path: 65500 I
                   > to 10.0.31.2 via t1-0/0/3.0
10.0.8.0/24        *[BGP/170] 00:00:13, localpref 100
                     AS path: 65500 I
```

```
                              > to 10.0.31.2 via t1-0/0/3.0
10.0.13.0/24          *[BGP/170] 00:00:13, localpref 100
                        AS path: 65500 I
                              > to 10.0.31.2 via t1-0/0/3.0
10.0.31.0/24           [BGP/170] 00:00:13, localpref 100
                        AS path: 65500 I
                              > to 10.0.31.2 via t1-0/0/3.0
172.19.121.0/24        [BGP/170] 00:00:13, localpref 100
                        AS path: 65500 I
                              > to 10.0.31.2 via t1-0/0/3.0
192.168.15.1/32       *[BGP/170] 00:00:13, MED 65, localpref 100
                        AS path: 65500 I
                              > to 10.0.31.2 via t1-0/0/3.0
192.168.16.1/32       *[BGP/170] 00:00:13, localpref 100
                        AS path: 65500 I
                              > to 10.0.31.2 via t1-0/0/3.0
192.168.17.1/32       *[BGP/170] 00:00:13, MED 1, localpref 100
                        AS path: 65500 I
                              > to 10.0.31.2 via t1-0/0/3.0
```

After the policy is applied, you see the lengthened AS paths for these prefixes:

```
aviva@RouterD> show route protocol bgp
inet.0: 19 destinations, 25 routes (19 active, 0 holddown, 0 hidden)
+ = Active Route, - = Last Active, * = Both
0.0.0.0/0              [BGP/170] 00:01:06, localpref 100
                        AS path: 65500 65500 65500 65500 I
                              > to 10.0.31.2 via t1-0/0/3.0
10.0.8.0/24           *[BGP/170] 00:01:06, localpref 100
                        AS path: 65500 65500 65500 65500 I
                              > to 10.0.31.2 via t1-0/0/3.0
10.0.13.0/24          *[BGP/170] 00:01:06, localpref 100
                        AS path: 65500 65500 65500 65500 I
                              > to 10.0.31.2 via t1-0/0/3.0
10.0.31.0/24           [BGP/170] 00:01:06, localpref 100
                        AS path: 65500 65500 65500 65500 I
                              > to 10.0.31.2 via t1-0/0/3.0
172.19.121.0/24        [BGP/170] 00:01:06, localpref 100
                        AS path: 65500 65500 65500 65500 I
                              > to 10.0.31.2 via t1-0/0/3.0
192.168.15.1/32       *[BGP/170] 00:01:06, MED 65, localpref 100
                        AS path: 65500 65500 65500 65500 I
                              > to 10.0.31.2 via t1-0/0/3.0
192.168.16.1/32       *[BGP/170] 00:01:06, localpref 100
                        AS path: 65500 65500 65500 65500 I
                              > to 10.0.31.2 via t1-0/0/3.0
192.168.17.1/32       *[BGP/170] 00:01:06, MED 1, localpref 100
                        AS path: 65500 65500 65500 65500 I
                              > to 10.0.31.2 via t1-0/0/3.0
```

13.8 Filtering BGP Routes Based on AS Paths

Problem

You want to filter the BGP routes that you send or receive based on the AS path information in the routes.

Solution

To filter the routes, create a routing policy that acts on a route's AS path information. The first step is to define a regular expression that matches the AS path information:

```
[edit policy-options]
aviva@RouterD# set as-path from-AS-65500 "65500{4}"
```

Then reference the AS path information in a routing policy:

```
[edit policy-options policy-statement match-AS65500]
aviva@RouterD# set term 1 from as-path from-AS-65500
aviva@RouterD# set term 1 then reject
aviva@RouterD# set term accept-others then accept
```

Finally, apply the policy to a BGP group:

```
[edit protocols bgp]
aviva@RouterD# set group session-to-AS65500 import match-AS65500
```

Discussion

It it often useful to develop routing policies based on information within the AS path information. You can then use these policies to enforce your network's administrative policy with respect to a customer or peer. Instead of looking for many prefixes or routes individually, it can be easier to use the AS path. The AS path attribute lets you filter all routes that originated from or transited through a particular AS, all routes announced by a particular neighboring AS, and routes that originated in the local AS.

To match information in the AS path attribute, you first create a *regular expression* that identifies the match conditions. In this recipe, the set as-path command creates the regular expression from-AS-65500, which matches exactly four occurrences of the string 65500.

A regular expression (also sometimes called a *regex*) is a pattern-matching tool that applies to strings in AS paths. It has two components, a term and an operator. The *term* matches an AS number or an AS path, or it can be a wildcard character. If the term includes any spaces, enclose it in quotation marks. The *operator* indicates how to match the term, typically how many times to match a specific term. In this recipe, 65500 is the term and {4} is the operator. Table 13-1 describes the regular expression operators.

Table 13-1. AS path regular expression operators

Operator	Description	Match example
{m,n}	Match at least *m* and at most *n* repetitions of term.	65500{2,3}—Match only "65500 65500" and "65500 65500 65500".
?	Match zero or one repetition of term; equivalent to {0,1}.	65500?—Match only "65500" and "65500 65500".
{m}	Match exactly *m* repetitions of term.	65500{2}—Match only "65500 65500".
{m,}	Match *m* or more repetitions of term.	65500{2,}—Match "65500 65500", "65500 65500 65500", "65500 65500 65500 65500", and so on.
*	Match zero or more repetitions of term; equivalent to {0,}.	65500*—Match "65500", "65500 65500", and so on; also match a path that does not contain "65500".
+	Match one or more repetitions of term; equivalent to {1,}.	65500+—Match "65500", "65500 65500", and so on.
. (dot)	Match any single instance of any term.	65500.—Match 65500 if it appears anywhere in the AS path. A more exact way to create this match is ".* 65500 .*".
|	Match one of the terms on either side of the pipe; the terms can include other operators.	(65500 | 65505)—Match either "65500" or "65505".
()	Match a group of terms enclosed in the parentheses.	
–	Match a range; the terms can include other operators.	65500-65505—Match 65500, 65501, 65502, 65503, 65504, or 65505.
"()"	Match a null AS path.	
^	Indicates the character at the beginning of an AS path.	
$	Indicates the character at the end of an AS path.	

You must include the term when defining the pattern to match, but the operator is optional. When you leave out an operator, the AS path exactly matches what you type for the term.

The JUNOS regular expressions for AS paths are, for the most part, identical to Unix regular expressions. There are, however, a few differences. The main difference is that the basic unit of matching is an *entire* AS number, not an individual character. This means that the JUNOS regular expression treats 65500 as a single entity when it performs any matching operations, not as the five individual digits 6, 5, 5, 0, and 0. In other words, the AS number is effectively a single integer. A second difference is that with Unix, you need to type the operators ^ (which matches the beginning of a string) and $ (which matches the end of a string), but in the JUNOS regular expressions, these operators are always assumed to be present. So, with Unix you would type **^65500$** to match the string 65500, but in the AS path regular expression you just need to type **65500**.

Looking back at our recipe, the AS path match term and operator are:

```
65500{4}
```

Translated, this match looks for four adjacent occurrences of the AS path 65500. It would match a path of 65500 65500 65500 65500. Examples of AS paths that this regular expression would not match are 65500 65500 65500, which has only three occurrences of the AS number, and 65500 65525 65500 65500 65500, which doesn't have four consecutive occurrences of the AS number.

After you define the match criteria in the set as-path command, you then need to incorporate them into a routing policy. In this recipe, the policy match-AS65500 rejects all routes whose AS path matches the regular expression but accepts all other routes.

As a final step, apply the policy to your BGP group as an import policy.

To verify that the policy is working, look at the BGP routes in the routing table. Before applying the policy, routes containing the AS path 65500 65500 65500 65500 are present:

```
aviva@RouterD> show route protocol bgp
inet.0: 25 destinations, 31 routes (25 active, 0 holddown, 0 hidden)
+ = Active Route, - = Last Active, * = Both

10.0.8.0/24        *[BGP/170] 01:42:26, localpref 100
                      AS path: 65500 65500 65500 65500 I
                   > to 10.0.31.2 via t1-0/0/3.0
...
```

The route to 10.0.8.0/24 is active (indicated by the asterisk). After applying the policy, the route is no longer in the routing table:

```
aviva@RouterD> show route 10.0.8.0/24
inet.0: 25 destinations, 31 routes (14 active, 0 holddown, 14 hidden)
```

This output shows that there are now 14 hidden routes. This is where you find the routes that your policy rejected:

```
aviva@RouterD> show route 10.0.8.0/24 hidden
inet.0: 25 destinations, 31 routes (14 active, 0 holddown, 14 hidden)
+ = Active Route, - = Last Active, * = Both
10.0.8.0/24         [BGP ] 01:44:48, localpref 100
                      AS path: 65500 65500 65500 65500 I
                   > to 10.0.31.2 via t1-0/0/3.0
```

Because the route is hidden, there is no preference associated with it. The route is marked as [BGP] instead of [BGP/170].

Routes that originate within your AS do not yet have an AS path associated with them. To find them with an as-path policy, create a match condition based on the null AS path:

```
[edit policy-options]
aviva@RouterF# set as-path local-as "()"
[edit policy-options policy-statement null-path]
aviva@RouterF# set term accept-null-path from protocol bgp
aviva@RouterF# set term accept-null-path from as-path local-as
```

```
aviva@RouterF# set term accept-null-path then accept
aviva@RouterF# set term else-reject then reject
```

This policy accepts all routes learned from BGP and that have no AS path, and rejects all other routes. A policy like this is useful when the only routes you want to advertise to a particular EBGP peer are those that originated in your AS. For instance, if another AS is advertising routes to you and you don't want to readvertise them, you can apply this null AS path policy with a set export null-path command.

13.9 Restricting the Number of Routes Advertised to a BGP Peer

Problem

You want to control the number of routes that your peers send you.

Solution

Set the maximum number of routes that you will accept from each of your peers:

```
[edit protocols bgp group session-to-AS65505 neighbor 10.0.31.1]
aviva@RouterF# set family inet unicast prefix-limit maximum 7500
aviva@RouterF# set family inet unicast prefix-limit teardown
```

Discussion

As an ISP, you keep track of how many routes each of your peers and customers normally send you. This number generally increases slowly over time. To place a limit on the number of routes a peer or customer can send you, set a maximum number of routes to accept. This type of administrative policy guards against an inadvertent policy misconfiguration, which, in the worst case, could result in a peer or customer redistributing the full Internet routing table to you. You decide on the maximum number of prefixes you accept based on the normal number of routes exchanged with the peer, and, when the limit is reached, BGP tears down the session with the peer. Typically, you take the current number of routes exchanged and add about 50 percent.

In this recipe, we know that neighbor 10.0.31.1 typically sends 5,000 prefixes, so we set the limit to 7,500 prefixes. For example, if the peer tries to send the entire Internet routing table (on the order of 170,000 prefixes), BGP on the local router will shut down the peering session with the neighbor. This shutdown tells both you and the peer that something has gone wrong at his end.

To verify the configuration, look at the BGP neighbor's information:

```
aviva@RouterF> show bgp neighbor 10.0.31.1
Peer: 10.0.31.1+4051 AS 65505  Local: 10.0.31.2+179 AS 65500
  Description: EBGP to Customer A
```

```
Type: External     State: Established     Flags: <Sync>
Last State: OpenConfirm    Last Event: RecvKeepAlive
Last Error: None
Export: [ send-statics ]
Options: <Preference HoldTime AddressFamily PeerAS PrefixLimit Refresh>
Address families configured: inet-unicast
Holdtime: 90 Preference: 170
Number of flaps: 2
Peer ID: 192.168.14.1     Local ID: 192.168.16.1     Active Holdtime: 90
Keepalive Interval: 30        Peer index: 0
Local Interface: t1-0/0/3.0
NLRI advertised by peer: inet-unicast
NLRI for this session: inet-unicast
Peer supports Refresh capability (2)
Table inet.0 Bit: 10000
  RIB State: BGP restart is complete
  Send state: in sync
  Active prefixes:              5
  Received prefixes:           8
  Suppressed due to damping:   0
  Advertised prefixes:         8
Last traffic (seconds): Received 3    Sent 28    Checked 28
Input messages:  Total 253    Updates 4     Refreshes 0     Octets 4967
Output messages: Total 261    Updates 12    Refreshes 0     Octets 5411
Output Queue[0]: 0
```

On the Options line, the option PrefixLimit indicates that the number of prefixes this neighbor can send has been limited.

When the prefix limit is reached and the EBGP session is torn down, a message is logged to the system logging files:

```
Aug 6 22:19:21 M20-R7 rpd[2254]: 10.1.6.2 (External AS 65501): Configured maximum
prefix-limit(10) exceeded for inet-unicast nlri: 13
```

If you want some advanced warning that the peer is nearing the maximum number of prefixes you will accept from it, you can have BGP log a message when the peer has sent some percentage of the maximum allowed prefixes. The following example uses a percentage that is about halfway between the normal number of prefixes and the maximum:

```
[edit protocols bgp group session-to-AS65505 neighbor 10.0.31.1]
aviva@RouterF# set family inet unicast prefix-limit teardown 85
```

After the session is torn down, it will be re-established a short time later. In most cases, this behavior is fine. You might want to force the session to stay down for a fixed amount of time to give you time to investigate what might be causing the prefix overflow or to contact the administrator of the remote AS. This command keeps the session down for 5 minutes (300 seconds):

```
[edit protocols bgp group session-to-AS65505 neighbor 10.0.31.1]
aviva@RouterF# set family inet unicast prefix-limit idle-timeout 300
```

Under extreme conditions, you might want the session to stay down until you manually restart it:

```
[edit protocols bgp group session-to-AS65505 neighbor 10.0.31.1]
aviva@RouterF# set family inet unicast prefix-limit idle-timeout forever
```

Use the clear bgp neighbor command to restart the session:

```
aviva@RouterF> clear bgp neighbor 10.0.31.1
Cleared 1 connections
```

After the session is reestablished, the Error line in the show bgp neighbor output reports Cease to indicate that the session was cleared:

```
aviva@RouterF> show bgp neighbor 10.0.31.1
Peer: 10.0.31.1 AS 65505        Local: 10.0.31.2 AS 0
  Description: EBGP to Customer A
  Type: External     State: Active        Flags: <>
  Last State: Idle          Last Event: Start
  Last Error: Cease
  Export: [ send-statics ]
  Options: <Preference HoldTime AddressFamily PeerAS PrefixLimit Refresh>
  Address families configured: inet-unicast
  Holdtime: 90 Preference: 170
  Number of flaps: 3
  Error: 'Cease' Sent: 1 Recv: 0
  ...
```

See Also

Recipe 13.15

13.10 Authenticating BGP Peers

Problem

You want to ensure that all BGP protocol traffic that your router accepts from external ASs comes from devices known to you.

Solution

Configure MD5 authentication for your EBGP sessions:

```
[edit protocols bgp group session-to-AS65505]
aviva@RouterF# set authentication-key 1991$pOppi
```

Discussion

Many external attacks launched against routing protocols are directed at BGP. Authenticating BGP packet exchanges on EBGP sessions prevents the router from accepting any authorized packets. The JUNOS BGP software supports MD5 cryptographic authentication.

This recipe configures MD5 authentication on the EBGP session to AS 65505. You simply need to configure an MD5 key in the EBGP group. The peer router in this EBGP session must have the same key. Because the peer router is in another AS that is likely under the control of a different administrator or ISP, you need to agree on the authentication key with the remote administrator beforehand. From the key, MD5 creates an encoded checksum that is included in all transmitted BGP packets. The receiving router verifies this checksum before accepting the packet.

You can configure BGP authentication globally, per group, or per peer. It is a good practice to use per-peer authentication for external peers, with a unique key for each customer. This prevents the possibility of a single leaked key compromising all customer peering points.

Another good practice is to change authentication keys periodically, on the order of every three to six months, to prevent the key from leaking either intentionally or accidentally.

If your IBGP peer routers are all within your domain and are trusted routers, you can choose not to enable BGP authentication on them. Otherwise, you should configure authentication for all IBGP sessions, in the same way as for EBGP sessions, to prevent any attacks by dropping BGP packets that do not contain the correct authentication parameters.

When you display the router's configuration after you have typed the password, you see only the encrypted form of the password. Someone casually glancing through the configuration would not see the actual password.

```
[edit protocols bgp group session-to-AS65505]
aviva@RouterF# show
group session-to-AS65505 {
    type external;
    description "EBGP to Customer A";
    authentication-key "$9$FBDdnApO1RSlKB1dbYgJZApuOhS"; ## SECRET-DATA
    peer-as 65505;
    neighbor 10.0.31.1 {
...
```

Looking at the BGP information about the neighbor shows that authentication is configured:

```
aviva@RouterF> show bgp neighbor 10.0.31.1
Peer: 10.0.31.1+179 AS 65505   Local: 10.0.31.2+2259 AS 65500
  Description: EBGP to Customer A
  Type: External    State: Established     Flags: <Sync>
  Last State: OpenConfirm   Last Event: RecvKeepAlive
  Last Error: None
  Export: [ send-statics ]
  Options: <Preference HoldTime AuthKey AddressFamily PeerAS PrefixLimit Refresh>
  Authentication key is configured
...
```

To hide the keys when you are looking at the configuration contents, pipe the output:

```
aviva@RouterF> show configuration protocols bgp | except SECRET-DATA
group session-to-AS65505 {
    type external;
    description "EBGP to Customer A";
    peer-as 65505;
    neighbor 10.0.31.1 {
...
```

Notice that the entire authentication-key statement is not displayed because all the authentication information is on one line in the configuration.

See Also

RFC 2385, *Protection of BGP Sessions via the TCP MD5 Signature Option*

13.11 Setting Up Route Reflectors

Problem

Your local AS has a large number of IBGP routers, and you want to reduce the number of IBGP sessions that you need to configure and maintain.

Solution

Configure one of the IBGP routers to be the route reflector for a route reflection cluster:

```
[edit protocols bgp]
aviva@RouterG# set group internal-within-AS65500 cluster 192.168.19.1
```

Discussion

The configuration in Recipe 13.2, in which all BGP systems within the AS are fully meshed, is a standard IBGP implementation. The full mesh results from listing all IBGP peers in a peering group rather than from having them all be physically connected and from using an IGP within the AS to distribute BGP routes. The full mesh is necessary so that external routing information can be redistributed among all routers within the AS with the help of the IGP running in the AS. As you can imagine, as the number of IBGP routers increases, you have to configure many BGP neighbor commands in each router's configuration, and there is a lot of overhead because a large number of TCP connections need to be maintained for each IBGP peering.

There are two common ways to deal with this scaling issue. One is route reflection, which provides one means of decreasing BGP control traffic and minimizing the number of update messages sent within the AS. The second method is confederations.

With normal BGP route redistribution rules, IBGP peers are not allowed to advertise routes learned from IBGP rules. Route reflection works by bending this rule. Each route reflector system has a set of *client peers* that are arranged in a *cluster*. The clients send their routes to the route reflector, and the route reflector advertises these routes to the other clients in the cluster and to other IBGP peers outside of the cluster (*nonclient peers*). The route reflector is not allowed to change any of the route's attributes, which is one way of preventing routing loops. When the route reflector learns routes from nonclient peers, it advertises them to its clients and to no one else. For routes learned from EBGP, the route reflector follows normal BGP route advertisement rules, advertising these routes to both clients and nonclients.

In this recipe, RouterG is the route reflector (see Figure 13-3). The only configuration needed is to add the cluster identifier to the IBGP group with the set cluster command. The cluster identifier is a 32-bit number. You can use the router identifier or any 32-bit number. When the router reflector forwards a route from one of its client routers to a nonclient router, the cluster identifier is prepended to the cluster list. If a route reflector ever receives a BGP update that contains its own cluster identifier, it ignores the update because it knows a routing loop has occurred.

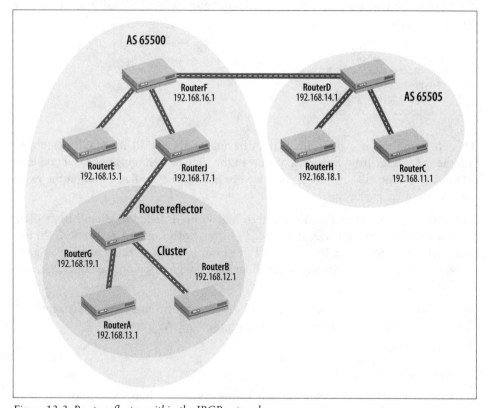

Figure 13-3. Route reflector within the IBGP network

Here's the complete IBGP group configuration on RouterG:

```
[edit protocols bgp]
aviva@RouterG# show
group internal-within-AS65500 {
    type internal;
    local-address 192.168.19.1;
    cluster 192.168.19.1;
    neighbor 192.168.13.1;
    neighbor 192.168.12.1;
    neighbor 192.168.17.1;
    neighbor 192.168.15.1;
    neighbor 192.168.16.1;
}
```

You still need to configure all the IBGP neighbors, both those within the cluster (192.168.13.1 and 192.168.12.1) and the three IBGP peers outside the cluster. For the nonclient routers, those outside the cluster, you include the route reflector in the IBGP group but don't need to have neighbor statements for the routers within the cluster. On the client routers, you need to configure only one IBGP peer, the route reflector 192.168.19.1:

```
[edit protocols bgp]
aviva@RouterA# show
group cluster-within-AS65500 {
    type internal;
    local-address 192.168.13.1;
    neighbor 192.168.19.1;
}
```

This configuration is a lot simpler than having to specify all the IBGP neighbors. Another advantage from the point of view of the routers' configurations is if you later add routers to the cluster, you do not need to change the configuration on the existing client routers in the cluster.

The nonclient routers in the AS, RouterE and RouterF, need to establish an IBGP session with RouterG but they don't need sessions with RouterA or RouterB. In this small network, this is a savings of four TCP sessions and four IBGP peerings. Again, if you add routers to the cluster, the IBGP group configuration on the nonclient routers doesn't need to change.

All the client routers in the cluster and all the nonclient routers are in the same AS, so make sure that you configure them all with the same AS number:

```
[edit routing-options]
aviva@RouterB# show
autonomous-system 65500;
```

Looking at the routes that RouterB has learned, you see that it still knows how to reach routes in AS 65505:

```
aviva@RouterB> show route protocol bgp
inet.0: 21 destinations, 22 routes (21 active, 0 holddown, 0 hidden)
+ = Active Route, - = Last Active, * = Both
```

```
10.0.24.0/24      *[BGP/170] 00:18:38, localpref 100, from 192.168.19.1
                     AS path: 65505 I
                   > via se-0/0/2.0
10.0.29.0/24      *[BGP/170] 00:18:38, localpref 100, from 192.168.19.1
                     AS path: 65505 I
                   > via se-0/0/2.0
192.168.11.1/32   *[BGP/170] 00:18:38, MED 1, localpref 100, from 192.168.19.1
                     AS path: 65505 I
                   > via se-0/0/2.0
192.168.14.1/32   *[BGP/170] 00:18:38, localpref 100, from 192.168.19.1
                     AS path: 65505 I
                   > via se-0/0/2.0
192.168.18.1/32   *[BGP/170] 00:18:38, MED 65, localpref 100, from 192.168.19.1
                     AS path: 65505 I
                   > via se-0/0/2.0
```

A detailed look at one of these routes shows information about the cluster:

```
aviva@RouterB> show route 10.0.24.0/24 extensive
inet.0: 21 destinations, 22 routes (21 active, 0 holddown, 0 hidden)
10.0.24.0/24 (1 entry, 1 announced)
TSI:
KRT in-kernel 10.0.24.0/24 -> {indirect(291)}
        *BGP    Preference: 170/-101
                Next-hop reference count: 15
                Source: 192.168.19.1
                Next hop: via se-0/0/2.0, selected
                Protocol next hop: 192.168.16.1 Indirect next hop: 8670300 291
                State: <Active Int Ext>
                Local AS: 65500 Peer AS: 65500
                Age: 25:44      Metric2: 90
                Task: BGP_65500.192.168.19.1+1106
                Announcement bits (2): 0-KRT 4-Resolve tree 1
                AS path: 65505 I (Originator) Cluster list:  192.168.19.1
                AS path:  Originator ID: 192.168.16.1
                Localpref: 100
                Router ID: 192.168.19.1
                Indirect next hops: 1
                        Protocol next hop: 192.168.16.1 Metric: 90 Indirect next hop:
8670300 291
                        Indirect path forwarding next hops: 1
                Next hop:       via se-0/0/2.0
                        192.168.16.1/32 Originating RIB: inet.0
                          Metric: 90                    Node path count: 1
                          Forwarding nexthops: 1
                            Nexthop: via se-0/0/2.0
```

The Cluster list field shows the cluster ID of the route reflector. This line shows the
32-bit value that we configured on RouterG. The address of the route reflector that
originally sent the route is in the Originator ID field.

This recipe illustrates a simple route reflection setup. One problem is that the route reflector is a single point of failure. If it goes down, its two peers lose their connection to the IBGP network. It is a common practice to configure two route reflectors for each cluster to provide backup.

Another less commonly used way to subdivide a large IBGP network into more manageable groups is create sub-ASs within your AS and link them together as a BGP confederation. On each IBGP router in the sub-AS, define the sub-AS number and the confederation group:

```
[edit routing-options]
aviva@RouterG# set autonomous-system 65502
aviva@RouterG# set confederation 65500 members [ 65501 65502 ]
```

Here, the main AS number is 65500 and the two sub-ASs are 65501 and 65502. This router is in the 65502 sub-AS. The set autonomous-system command defines the sub-AS number, and the set confederation command identifies all the sub-ASs in the main AS.

From BGP's point of view, each sub-AS is a separate AS because each has a different AS number. So, you configure each sub-AS as you would an EBGP connection, setting up border routers between the sub-ASs. On each of these routers, create an external group to connect the two sub-ASs. The following commands configure the EBGP group on the border router in sub-AS 65502:

```
[edit protocols bgp]
aviva@RouterG# set group to-subAS65501 type external
aviva@RouterG# set group to-subAS65501 neighbor 192.168.17.1
aviva@RouterG# set group to-subAS65501 peer-as 65501
```

The set peer-as command identifies the sub-AS number. The border router also has an IBGP group to create peerings with the IBGP routers in the sub-AS:

```
[edit protocols bgp]
aviva@RouterG# show
group internal-within-subAS65502 {
    type internal;
    export next-hop-self;
    local-address 192.168.19.1;
    neighbor 192.168.13.1;
    neighbor 192.168.12.1;
}
```

Just like with the EBGP sessions between ASs, you need a next-hop-self policy in the IBGP group for the sub-AS border router (see Recipe 13.4).

As with route reflectors, BGP confederations (see Figure 13-4) reduce the number of peering sessions you need to configure and the number of TCP sessions that the routers need to establish to maintain full-mesh connections between all IBGP routers.

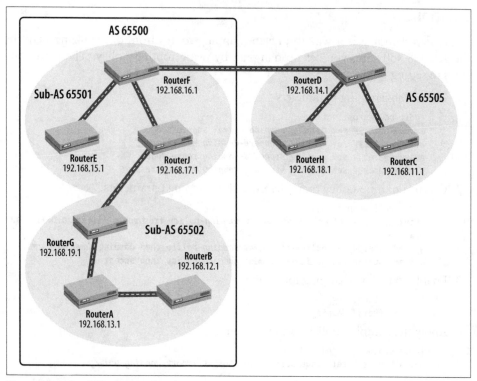

Figure 13-4. Confederation within the AS

See Also

RFC 1965, *Autonomous System Confederations for BGP*; RFC 1966, *BGP Route Reflection: An Alternative to Full-Mesh IBGP*; RFC 2796, *BGP Route Reflection*; RFC 3065, *Autonomous System Confederations for BGP*

13.12 Mitigating Route Instabilities with Route Flap Damping

Problem

You want to deal with potential route instabilities caused by routes being withdrawn in a series of BGP Update messages only to be readvertised as active routes a few minutes later when an intermittently failing link is restored.

Solution

Route flap damping is a way to prevent flapping routes from destabilizing BGP. In the JUNOS software, you set up damping by using routing policy. There are four steps in setting up damping:

1. Define the damping parameters:

   ```
   [edit policy-options]
   aviva@Router3# set damping damping-normal suppress 6000
   aviva@Router3# set damping standard-damping half-life 15
   aviva@Router3# set damping standard-damping reuse 3000
   aviva@Router3# set damping standard-damping max-suppress 30
   ```

2. Create a routing policy that references the damping parameters:

   ```
   [edit policy-options]
   aviva@Router3# set policy-statement damping-policy from route-filter 10.0.31.1/32
   exact
   aviva@Router3# set policy-statement damping-policy then damping damping-normal
   aviva@Router3# set policy-statement damping-policy then accept
   ```

3. Enable route flap damping for BGP:

   ```
   [edit protocols bgp]
   aviva@Router3# damping
   ```

4. Apply the damping policy to a BGP group:

   ```
   [edit protocols bgp]
   aviva@Router3# set group session-to-AS65505 import damping-policy
   ```

Discussion

If a link on the network is intermittently failing, routes can be withdrawn and re-advertised in quick succession as the link goes down and then comes back up. This *route flapping* forces BGP to change any next hops that use the failed interface each time the link goes down. BGP then has to update its routing tables and propagate the new routing information. If many routes are being recalculated, the flapping link could make BGP very unstable.

Route damping is a mechanism for preventing flapping routes from destabilizing a BGP network. Damping slows or stops the "vibrations," or rapid changes, in the routing table. When a route flaps, it is given a specified number of demerits. The route's accumulated demerits are reduced over time according to a configured decay rate. If the route's accumulated demerits exceed a configured threshold, the route is suppressed until the number of demerits decays below a second configured threshold.

Route damping is most useful in large service provider networks that have many attached peers and that carry many prefixes—a scenario in which the chances of one or more routes flapping at any given time is high.

In the first part of the configuration, you set four damping parameters that are used to calculate a *figure of merit*, which controls how long a route can be suppressed. The figure-of-merit value correlates to the probability of a route's future instability, and the value decays exponentially over time. BGP suppresses routes with higher figure-of-merit values for longer periods of time.

For a new route, BGP assigns a figure-of-merit value of 0. If the route experiences any instability, the value is increased based on the following rules:

- If the route is withdrawn by the EBGP peer, the value increases by 1,000.
- If the route is readvertised by the EBGP peer, the value increases by 1,000.
- If the BGP attributes for the route change in a new Update message from the EBGP peer, the value increases by 500.

The points, or demerits, given to a route decrease over time and decay exponentially. This time is the *half-life* of the route. If the demerits decay faster than the figure-of-merit value increases, the route will not be suppressed. When the figure-of-merit value increases beyond a cutoff value, called the *suppression threshold* (also called the *cutoff threshold*), the route is suppressed and is considered unusable. The router will ignore any new information about the route received from its peers and will not install it into the forwarding table or forward the route to any other routing protocols. The figure-of-merit value continues to decay based on the half-life. When the value drops below the *reuse threshold*, it is unsuppressed and again considered usable.

The damping parameters that you configure play into the figure of merit. The suppress statement controls the suppression threshold. By default, when a route's figure-of-merit value reaches 3,000, it is suppressed. The figure-of-merit value decays exponentially over the half-life that you set with the half-life statement. The default half-life is 15 minutes. To illustrate how the decay works, if a route has a figure-of-merit value of 1,000 and no incidents occur, the value decays to 500 after 15 minutes, then to 250 after another 15 minutes. You set the reuse threshold with the reuse statement. The default is 750. As the figure-of-merit value continues to decay, when it drops below the reuse threshold, the route becomes usable again. The maximum amount of time a route can be suppressed is 60 minutes by default, which you can modify with the max-suppress statement.

The first step in configuring damping parameters is to create a named parameter list. In this recipe, the list is named damping-normal, which sets up a standard set of damping parameters. The figure-of-merit value decays over 15 minutes, which is the default half-life. Routes are suppressed when their figure of merit reaches a value of 6,000 (instead of the default 3,000) and are unsuppressed at half that value (3,000) instead of at the default value (750). Finally, in the recipe, routes remain suppressed for a maximum of 30 minutes instead of the default 60 minutes.

The figure of merit doesn't increase forever but stops when it reaches the *merit ceiling*, ε_c, which is a value that is calculated based on the reuse threshold (ε_r); half-life (λ), in minutes; and maximum suppression time (t), in minutes:

$$\varepsilon_c \leq \varepsilon_r * e^{(t/l)\,(\ln 2)}$$

Using the default reuse threshold of 750, a maximum suppression time of 60 minutes, and a half-life of 30 minutes, the calculation looks like this:

$$\varepsilon_c \leq 750 * e^{(60/30)\,(\ln 2)}$$
$$\varepsilon_c \leq 3000$$

In this case, a route's figure-of-merit value will stop increasing when it reaches 3,000. If you change the default damping parameter values, use this formula to make sure that the suppression threshold is not greater than the merit ceiling. If it is, routes will never be suppressed and route flap damping will never occur.

After setting the damping parameters, you are ready to create the routing policy for route flap damping. In this recipe, the policy named damping-policy applies to a particular peer, 10.0.31.1.

In larger networks, it is common to set up different degrees of damping policy to apply to different types of routes. In addition to the normal damping parameters set in this recipe, you can also set up parameters to suppress routes for longer periods of time:

```
[edit policy-options damping damping-medium]
aviva@Router3# show
half-life 15;
reuse 1500;
suppress 6000;
max-suppress 45;

[edit policy-options damping damping-high]
aviva@Router3# show
half-life 30;
reuse 1640;
suppress 6000;
max-suppress 60;
```

The damping-medium parameters increase the decay half-life from 10 to 15 minutes and the maximum suppression time from 30 to 45 minutes, and the damping-high parameters increase the half-life to 30 minutes and maximum suppression to 60 minutes. You apply these two damping parameters to routes that flap a bit more than normal or severely more than normal. Then, instead of applying the policy to specific BGP peers, you can apply it to a range of prefixes:

```
[edit policy-options policy-statement flap-damping]
aviva@Router3# show
from {
    route-filter 0.0.0.0/0 upto /21 damping damping-normal;
    route-filter 0.0.0.0/0 upto /23 damping damping-medium;
    route-filter 0.0.0.0/0 orlonger damping damping-high;
}
then accept;
```

Once the routing policy is set up, enable damping for BGP with the set damping command. Then apply the damping policy to the EBGP group with an import statement so the damping policy is applied to all routes before they are placed into the routing table.

Verify the damping configuration with the show policy damping command:

```
aviva@Router3> show policy damping
Default damping information:
  Halflife: 15 minutes
  Reuse merit: 750 Suppress/cutoff merit: 3000
  Maximum suppress time: 60 minutes
  Computed values:
    Merit ceiling: 12110
    Maximum decay: 6193
Damping information for "damping-high":
  Halflife: 30 minutes
  Reuse merit: 1640 Suppress/cutoff merit: 6000
  Maximum suppress time: 60 minutes
  Computed values:
    Merit ceiling: 6577
    Maximum decay: 24933
Damping information for "damping-medium":
  Halflife: 15 minutes
  Reuse merit: 1500 Suppress/cutoff merit: 6000
  Maximum suppress time: 45 minutes
  Computed values:
    Merit ceiling: 12049
    Maximum decay: 12449
Damping information for "damping-normal":
  Halflife: 15 minutes
  Reuse merit: 3000 Suppress/cutoff merit: 6000
  Maximum suppress time: 30 minutes
  Computed values:
    Merit ceiling: 12017
    Maximum decay: 24963
```

The output shows the default damping information and the three configured sets of parameters. The first portion of the output lists the default damping parameters. The Computed values fields show the merit ceiling value calculated from the damping parameters. In the default policy, you can see that the merit ceiling of 12,110 is well above the suppression threshold of 3,000.

The show bgp summary command output shows whether any BGP routes have been damped:

```
aviva@Router3> show bgp summary
Groups: 2 Peers: 3 Down peers: 0
Table          Tot Paths  Act Paths Suppressed    History Damp State    Pending
inet.0                8          5          0          0         1          0
Peer             AS    InPkt    OutPkt    OutQ   Flaps Last Up/Dwn State|#A
ctive/Received/Damped...
192.168.15.1   65500      503       517       0       0   4:11:20 0/0/0
```

```
                  0/0/0
192.168.17.1      65500      501      515      0      0      4:10:25 0/0/0
                  0/0/0
10.0.31.1         65505      181      182      0      3      1:27:46 4/8/1
                  0/0/0
```

The Damp State field in the first line shows that one route in the inet.0 routing table has been damped. Farther down in the output, you see that a connection to BGP peer 10.0.31.1 in AS 65505 is established because the State field shows that the router has received eight routes from that peer and four of them are active. The third number in the State field shows that one route is currently suppressed as a result of the damping policy.

The show route damping command provides more information about damped routes. The suppressed detail option shows specific prefixes that are or have been suppressed:

```
aviva@Router3> show route damping suppressed detail
inet.0: 173318 destinations, 1533437 routes (172602 active, 11 holddown, 108105
hidden)
10.4.10.0/19 (1 entry, 0 announced)
        BGP                    /-101
                Next-hop reference count: 18064
                Source: 192.168.106.33
                Next hop: 192.168.106.33 via so-6/3/0.0, selected
                State: <Hidden Ext>
                Local AS: 65000 Peer AS:  65530
                Age: 1:36
                Task: BGP_65530.192.168.106.33+179
                AS path: 65530 65531 65532 I ()
                Communities: 65501:390 65501:2000 65501:3000 65504:6453
                Localpref: 100
                Router ID: 192.168.103.240
                Merit (last update/now): 12866/11594
                damping-parameters: damping-normal
                Last update:      00:01:36 First update:  1w3d 03:00:51
                Flaps: 13718
                Suppressed. Reusable in:      00:19:40
                Preference will be: 170
```

Here, the prefix 10.4.10.0/19 is suppressed. While suppressed, the prefix is not active in the forwarding table, so there is no asterisk next to BGP on the second line of the output, and the prefix is hidden (noted in the State field) and is not exported to any BGP peers. The last several lines show the damping information. The damping-parameters line indicates that this route is being damped with the damping-normal parameters. The current figure-of-merit value is 11,594, which is above the reuse threshold of 3,000 that is set for damping-normal. The third line gives an idea of how long the prefix has been unusable. First update shows when the path attributes for the route were first changed (here, more than a week ago) and when they were last updated (about 1.5 hours ago). The next lines show that the route has flapped a total of 13,718 times. If the route remains stable and the path information for it does not change, the router will unsuppress this route and reuse it in 19 minutes 40 seconds, and with a preference of 170, which is the default JUNOS preference for routes learned from BGP.

You can also check to see the routes that have flapped but have not been suppressed:

```
aviva@Router3> show route damping decayed detail
inet.0: 173319 destinations, 1533668 routes (172625 active, 4 holddown, 108083
hidden)
10.0.111.0/24 (7 entries, 1 announced)
        *BGP    Preference: 170/-101
                Next-hop reference count: 151973
                Source: 172.23.2.129
                Next hop: via so-1/2/0.0
                Next hop: via so-5/1/0.0, selected
                Next hop: via so-6/0/0.0
                Protocol next hop: 172.23.2.129
                Indirect next hop: 89a1a00 264185
                State: <Active Ext>
                Local AS: 65000 Peer AS:   65490
                Age: 3:28       Metric2: 0
                Task: BGP_65490.172.23.2.129+179
                Announcement bits (6): 0-KRT 1-RT 4-KRT 5-BGP.0.0.0.0+179 6-Resolve
tree 2 7-Resolve tree 3
                AS path: 65490 65520 65525 65525 65525 65525 I ( )
                Communities: 65501:390 65501:2000 65501:3000 65504:701
                Localpref: 100
                Router ID: 172.23.2.129
                Merit (last update/now): 1934/1790
                damping-parameters: damping-high
                Last update:         00:03:28 First update:       00:06:40
                Flaps: 2
```

The prefix 10.0.111.0/24 is using the damping-high parameters, which have a suppression threshold of 6,000. This route currently has not yet crossed this threshold but has a nonzero figure of merit of 1,790. The asterisk before BGP on the second line and the Active in the State field both indicate that this route is still active.

The show route damping history command shows whether any routes have been withdrawn:

```
aviva@Router3> show route damping history
inet.0: 173320 destinations, 1533529 routes (172624 active, 6 holddown, 108122
hidden)
+ = Active Route, - = Last Active, * = Both
10.108.0.0/15      [BGP ] 2d 22:47:58, localpref 100
                     AS path: 65220 65501 65502 I
                   > to 192.168.60.85 via so-3/1/0.0
```

The prefix 10.108.0.0/15 has been withdrawn. Use the detail option to get more information:

```
aviva@Router3> show route damping history detail
```

```
inet.0: 173319 destinations, 1533435 routes (172627 active, 2 holddown, 108105
hidden)
10.108.0.0/15 (3 entries, 1 announced)
        BGP                     /-101
                Next-hop reference count: 69058
                Source: 192.168.60.85
                Next hop: 192.168.60.85 via so-3/1/0.0, selected
                State: <Hidden Ext>
                Inactive reason: Unusable path
                Local AS: 65000 Peer AS:  65220
                Age: 2d 22:48:10
                Task: BGP_65220.192.168.60.85+179
                AS path: 65220 65501 65502 I ( )
                Communities: 65501:390 65501:2000 65501:3000 65504:3561
                Localpref: 100
                Router ID: 192.168.80.25
                Merit (last update/now): 1000/932
                damping-parameters: set-normal
                Last update:        00:01:05 First update:        00:01:05
                Flaps: 1
                History entry.  Expires in:        00:22:20
```

This output is similar to the show route damping suppressed detail command. It also
shows in the Inactive reason line that the path is hidden because it is unusable.
Unusable path can mean one of three things: that the route was rejected as the result
of an import routing policy, that the route has been damped (which is the case here),
or that the next hop to the route cannot be resolved.

Checking the routing table entries for 10.108.0.0/15 confirms that the route is
unusable:

```
aviva@Router3> show route 10.108.0.0/15 exact all
inet.0: 173321 destinations, 1533468 routes (172617 active, 14 holddown, 108123
hidden)
+ = Active Route, - = Last Active, * = Both
10.108.0.0/15        *[BGP/170] 02:59:16, localpref 120, from 172.24.250.123
                        AS path: (64603) 65503 65503 65503 I
                      > via so-2/0/0.0, label-switched-path 1
                        via so-2/0/0.0, label-switched-path 2
                       [BGP/170] 5w3d 11:43:01, localpref 100, from 172.24.20.129
                        AS path: 65520 65521 I
                        via so-1/2/0.0
                      > via so-5/1/0.0
                        via so-6/0/0.0
                       [BGP ] 2d 22:49:33, localpref 100
                        AS path: 65220 65501 65502  I
                      > to 192.168.60.85 via so-3/1/0.0
```

The third route to 10.108.0.0/15, using the SONET interface so-3/1/0.0, is the one
that is suppressed. You can confirm this because no preference value is associated
with the route. You see [BGP] instead of [BGP/170].

See Also

RFC 2439, *BGP Route Flap Damping*; Recipe 9.1

13.13 Adding a BGP Community to Routes

Problem

You want to add a BGP community to routes so you can apply common routing policy to the routes.

Solution

BGP communities are a way to group routes so you can apply the same policy to them. To use them in a routing policy, first define the community members and an AS path string:

```
[edit policy-options]
aviva@RouterF# set community customer members 65500:1234
aviva@RouterF# set as-path AS65505-path "65505 .*"
```

Then include the community in the routing policy:

```
[edit policy-options policy-statement community-add]
aviva@RouterF# set term match-route from protocol bgp
aviva@RouterF# set term match-route from as-path AS65505-path
aviva@RouterF# set then community add customer
aviva@RouterF# set then accept
```

To have the policy take effect, apply it with an import statement to an EBGP group:

```
[edit protocols bgp]
aviva@RouterF# set group session-to-AS65505 import community-add
```

Discussion

BGP communities are a way to group routes so that the same routing policy can be applied to them. This recipe shows a simple application of BGP communities that adds the community 65500:1234 to all received BGP routes that have the AS number 65505 in their AS path.

Creating the routing policy is a two-step process. First, define the members in your community with the set community statement. Each member has a community identifier, which looks like *AS-number:community-value*. The *AS-number* portion of the identifier is the local AS number. The *community-value* is a number from 1 through 65535 that you assign to identify the community. How you choose this number is a function of your internal administrative policies. Because the first part of the community identifier is your AS number, the identifier is unique across the network.

In the community identifier, you can use regular expressions to specify matches for the AS number and member identifier. The regular expressions have the same format as those for AS paths, consisting of a term and an operator, and they use the same operators as AS paths (see Table 13-1).

Because the routing policy in the recipe matches an AS number, we need the set as-path command to define which ASs to look for.

The second part of the process is creating a routing policy that references the community. The routing policy checks for BGP routes that have 65505 in their AS path and adds the community customer to any that match. Here's what the policy-options portion of the configuration looks like:

```
[edit policy-options]
aviva@RouterF# show
policy-statement community-add {
    term match-route {
        from {
            protocol bgp;
            as-path AS65505-path;
        }
        then {
            community add customer;
            accept;
        }
    }
}
community customer members 65500:1234;
as-path AS65505-path "65505 .*";
```

As with all policies, to have it take affect, apply it to BGP. Here, we apply it with an import statement on routes being learned from the EBGP peer to AS 65505.

The detail option of the show route command lists the community attributes associated with a route:

```
aviva@RouterF> show route detail 192.168.18.1
inet.0: 18 destinations, 22 routes (18 active, 0 holddown, 0 hidden)
192.168.18.1/32 (1 entry, 1 announced)
        *BGP    Preference: 170/-101
                Next-hop reference count: 18
                Source: 10.0.31.1
                Next hop: 10.0.31.1 via t1-0/0/3.0, selected
                State: <Active Ext>
                Local AS: 65500 Peer AS: 65505
                Age: 2d 18:35:30       Metric: 65
                Task: BGP_65505.10.0.31.1+2079
                Announcement bits (3): 0-KRT 3-BGP.0.0.0.0+179 4-Resolve tree 1
                AS path: 65505 I
                Communities: 65500:1234
                Localpref: 100
                Router ID: 192.168.14.1
```

You see that the route to 192.168.18.1, which is in AS 65505, has been marked with the configured community 65500:1234.

The rest of this section provides a more detailed example of using BGP communities and shows a configuration that updates the bogon prefixes on your router automatically whenever they change. Bogons are prefixes that should never appear in the Internet routing table. (The term *bogon* refers to something that is bogus.) There are two types of bogons: *martian prefixes*, which are private (RFC 1918) and reserved addresses (multicast and loopback), and *unallocated prefixes*, which are address spaces that have not yet been assigned to a routing information registry (RIR) by IANA. Although you can use bogon addresses in a private network, they should never leak out to the public Internet.

A good security policy on edge routers that face the Internet is to filter bogons. If you are using private address space inside your private network, you don't want these addresses to leak out to the public Internet because traffic to or from these prefixes should not be seen on the public Internet. Also, if your network receives bogons from the Internet, you want to ignore them. Some common occurrences of bogons on the Internet include spoofed attacks, prefix hijacking, and simple configuration mistakes.

One way to filter bogons is to create a route prefix list that lists all the bogons and then reference this list in a routing policy. However, because the list of bogon addresses changes as unallocated space is allocated and as definitions of martian routes change, you would manually need to change the prefix lists. To avoid this administrative overhead, you can set up the configuration to automatically update the bogon list from the Team Cymru bogon route server project, which maintains a current list of bogons (see *http://www.cymru.com/BGP/bogon-rs.html*). This configuration, which is based on a suggested Team Cymru configuration, sets up an EBGP session with Team Cymru to automatically update the bogon list when it changes. This configuration also ties together many of the individual BGP configuration commands discussed in this chapter.

This configuration creates the community 65333:888 that is used to filter all bogons:

```
[edit policy-options]
aviva@RouterF# set community cymru-bogon-community members [ no-export 65333:888 ]
```

This community includes the no-export member to attach the BGP NO_EXPORT attribute to the community to ensure that the router does not advertise the route beyond the local AS. The JUNOS software also allows you to attach the BGP NO_ADVERTISE and NO_EXPORT_SUBCONFED attributes to a community, with the no-advertise and no-export-subconfed options.

The routing policy also uses a second community:

```
[edit policy-options]
aviva@RouterF# set community dont-announce members 65500:1234
```

This configuration assumes that you use community 65500:1234 as a standard way to suppress announcements of these routes outside your AS. The community is included as a precaution to provide a backup method to make sure that the routes stay within your AS in case, for some reason, the NO_EXPORT action fails.

Then define a simple regular expression to match the Team Cymru private AS number:

```
[edit policy-options]
aviva@RouterF# set as-path cymru-private-asn 65333
```

The following routing policy for the EBGP peering session accepts the bogon route updates:

```
[edit policy-options]
aviva@RouterF# edit policy-statement cymru-bogon-list
[edit policy-options policy-statement cymru-bogon-list]
aviva@RouterF# set term 1 from protocol bgp
aviva@RouterF# set term 1 from as-path cymru-private-asn
aviva@RouterF# set term 1 from community cymru-bogon-community
aviva@RouterF# set term 1 then community add dont-announce
aviva@RouterF# set term 1 then next-hop 192.0.2.1
aviva@RouterF# set term 1 then accept
aviva@RouterF# set then reject
```

The from clause matches BGP routes from the AS path defined in cymru-private-asn (that is, from AS number 65333) and that contain the community string defined in cymru-bogon-community (that is, 65333:888). The then clause performs two actions on any matching routes before accepting them. The set then community add dont-announce command attaches the community string 65500:1234 to the routes to ensure that the routes are never forwarded outside the local AS. (This is the community you defined with the set community dont-announce command.) The second action in the then clause sets the route's next hop to 192.0.1.2, which is a reserved network prefix. This next hop maps the bogons to a remotely triggered black hole, which acts as a filter for the bogons, discarding them and explicitly stating that they are never to be readvertised. You define this prefix as a static route in the routing table:

```
[edit routing-options]
aviva@RouterF# set static route 192.0.2.1/32 discard
aviva@RouterF# set static route 192.0.2.1/32 no-readvertise
aviva@RouterF# set static route 192.0.2.1/32 retain
```

The discard option on the static route prevents it from being forwarded, no-readvertise prevents it from being readvertised to anyone else, and retain keeps the route in the forwarding table if the JUNOS routing process restarts normally.

If you are using the default JUNOS martians, 192.0.2.1/32 is a martian and will be rejected, so you need to explicitly allow the routing table to accept it:

```
[edit routing-options]
aviva@RouterF# set martians 192.0.2.1/32 exact allow
```

When setting up policies, also create a second one for the EBGP peering session to make sure your network doesn't forward any routing information back to Team Cymru:

```
[edit policy-options]
aviva@RouterF# set policy-statement deny-all then reject
```

Now you have all the pieces in place to configure the EBGP peering session with Team Cymru so you can receive the automatic bogon updates. As with establishing a peering session with any remote AS, you need to contact the AS administrator to set up the peering terms and to provide your AS number, the IP address of the router's interface that will be used for peering, and your MD5 password. With this information you can configure the EBGP peer. The basic configuration establishes the external peering, sets a description for the peer, defines the peer's AS number and the remote IP address used for the peering session, and sets a mutually agreed upon MD5 key:

```
[edit protocols bgp group cymru-peering]
aviva@RouterF# set type external
aviva@RouterF# set description "bogon update peering with team cymru"
aviva@RouterF# set peer-as 65333
aviva@RouterF# set neighbor 10.0.31.1
aviva@RouterF# set authentication-key "$9$D8imfQFnCpOzFreM87Nmf5T/C"
```

Apply the routing policies:

```
[edit protocols bgp group cymru-peering]
aviva@RouterF# set import cymru-bogon-list
aviva@RouterF# set export deny-all
```

The import policy accepts the bogon list, and the export policy prevents the router from sending any routing updates to Team Cymru.

Because Team Cymru is more than one BGP hop away from your network, the EBGP peering needs to be a multihop session:

```
[edit protocols bgp group cymru-peering]
aviva@RouterF# set multihop ttl 255
```

The time to live (TTL) specifies how many hops your router is from the EBGP neighbor. For an EBGP session where the external neighbor is directly connected, the TTL is 1. For multihop sessions, the default TTL is 64. This configuration sets the TTL to the maximum allowable value of 255 to ensure that the peering succeeds. BGP places the TTL value in the packet's IP header.

A final portion of the EBGP peer configuration restricts the number of routes Team Cymru can advertise to you, to guard against a misconfiguration or an inadvertent advertisement of the entire Internet routing table:

```
[edit protocols bgp group cymru-peering]
aviva@RouterF# set family inet unicast prefix-limit maximum 100
aviva@RouterF# set family inet unicast prefix-limit teardown 100
```

As of this writing, the bogon list contains 95 prefixes, so you use a prefix limit slightly higher than this.

This is a fairly involved configuration, so it's worth summarizing it all in one place:

```
[edit]
aviva@RouterF# show
routing-options {
    static {
        route 192.0.2.1/32 {
            discard;
            retain;
            no-readvertise;
        }
    }
    martians {
        192.0.2.1/32 exact allow;
    }
    router-id 192.168.16.1;
    autonomous-system 65500;
}
protocols {
    bgp {
        group cymru-peering {
            type external;
            description "bogon update peering with team cymru";
            multihop {
                ttl 255;
            }
            import cymru-bogon-list;
            family inet {
                unicast {
                    prefix-limit {
                        maximum 100;
                        teardown 100;
                    }
                }
            }
            authentication-key "$9$D8imfQFnCpOzFreM87Nmf5T/C"; ## SECRET-DATA
            export deny-all;
            peer-as 65333;
            neighbor 10.0.31.1;
        }
    }
}
policy-options {
    policy-statement cymru-bogon-list {
        term 1 {
            from {
                protocol bgp;
                as-path cymru-private-asn;
                community cymru-bogon-community;
            }
            then {
                community add dont-announce;
```

```
                next-hop 192.0.2.1;
                accept;
            }
        then reject;
    }
    policy-statement deny-all {
        then reject;
    }
    community cymru-bogon-community members [ no-export 65333:888 ];
    community dont-announce members 65500:1234;
    as-path cymru-private-asn 65333;
}
```

See Also

RFC 1997, *BGP Communities Attribute*; RFC 1998, *An Application of the BGP Community Attribute in Multihome Routing*; Team Cymru's bogon route server project, *http://www.cymru.com/BGP/bogon-rs.html*; Recipe 9.1

13.14 Load-Balancing BGP Traffic

Problem

A customer is multihomed to two different routers in your point of presence (POP). Instead of having BGP send all traffic across one of the links, which is the default behavior, you want to load-balance the EBGP traffic from the customer across the two links.

Solution

To enable load balancing across multiple EBGP peerings, configure the BGP group to use multipath:

```
[edit protocols bgp group external-group]
aviva@Router1# set type external
aviva@Router1# set peer-as 65505
aviva@Router1# set multipath
aviva@Router1# set neighbor 192.168.1.1
aviva@Router1# set neighbor 192.168.1.3
```

For the load balancing to happen, configure a load-balancing policy:

```
[edit policy-options]
aviva@router1# set policy-statement LoadBalance from route-filter 192.168.1.0/24
orlonger
aviva@Router1# set policy-statement LoadBalance then load-balance per-packet

[edit routing-options]
aviva@Router1# set forwarding-table export LoadBalance
```

Discussion

Multihomed connections from a customer's network to the ISP's POP provide redundant Internet connectivity. If one of the links goes down—for example, because a fiber was cut—the second connection provides backup. If the paths from both connections are equal-cost, the default BGP behavior is to select the single best route to a destination. The result is that BGP uses only one of the links to forward traffic. As long as both links are up, the customer wants to use both, spreading the traffic between them to increase the bandwidth available for sending traffic to the Internet. Multipath BGP allows the traffic to be load-balanced across the two links.

Figure 13-5 shows a network topology with redundant peerings. Router1 in AS 65500 has EBGP peerings with two routers in AS 65505. If Router1 receives two paths from Router3 and Router4 for a prefix in the remote AS, and if all route parameters are the same except for the router ID, BGP will pick the path with the lower router ID. The result is that only one of the paths (either through Router3 or Router4) will be used for traffic from Router1 to a customer in AS 65505.

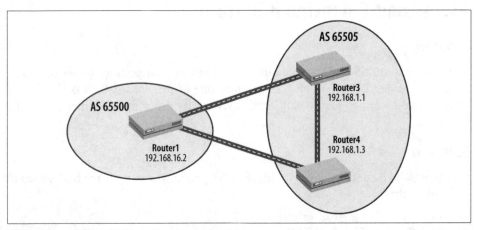

Figure 13-5. Multiple BGP peerings to another AS

Multipath BGP overrides the default BGP behavior and allows both links to be used for forwarding traffic. The result is equal-cost load balancing between the two links, which allows Router1 to send traffic both to Router3 and Router4.

Multipath BGP works by allowing a path other than the best one to be placed into the forwarding table to be used as an alternative. When BGP evaluates multiple routes to determine the best path to a prefix, if all the conditions are the same except for the router ID, which is the last route property that BGP considers as a tie-breaker, BGP installs all the equal-cost routes into the forwarding table (see the Introduction to Chapter 8).

Another restriction for multipath BGP is that both neighboring routers must be in the same AS. This is necessary because BGP can advertise only a single path, and it makes assumptions regarding the forwarding path matching the routing information.

This recipe creates an EBGP group external-group on Router1, in AS 65500, with two neighbors in AS 65505 (configured with the set peer-as 65505 command) (see Figure 13-5). The set multipath command configures BGP multipath. However, for BGP multipath to work, you must also set up a load-balancing routing policy that is applied to the router's forwarding table.

Looking in the routing table, you see the routes learned from both routers:

```
aviva@Router1> show route 172.16.14.0/24
inet.0: 176580 destinations, 1421698 routes (176272 active, 1 holddown, 79688 hidden)
+ = Active Route, - = Last Active, * = Both
172.16.14.0/24    *[BGP/170] 3w4d 05:01:06, MED 0, localpref 100
                     AS path: (65505) 65510 65520 ?
                   > to 192.168.1.1 via ge-0/1/0.0
                     to 192.168.1.3 via ge-1/1/0.0
                    [BGP/170] 3w4d 05:01:15, MED 0, localpref 100
                     AS path: (65505) 65510 65520 ?
                   > to 192.168.1.3 via ge-1/1/0.0
```

The routing table shows two paths to this destination, the first goes through Router3 (192.168.1.1) and the ge-0/1/0 interface, and the second goes through Router4 (192.168.1.3) and the ge-1/1/0 interface. The first path is active (marked with an asterisk) because it was learned from the router with the lower router ID (192.168.1.1 is lower than 192.168.1.3). The second path is the alternate next hop. The first path lists two next hops:

```
                   > to 192.168.1.1 via ge-0/1/0.0
                     to 192.168.1.3 via ge-1/1/0.0
```

The first hop is learned from 192.168.1.1, and the second is learned from 192.168.1.3. The second next hop has been copied from the second path up to the first one.

The detail version of the show route command gives more information about the two paths:

```
aviva@Router1> show route 172.16.14.0/24 detail
inet.0: 176576 destinations, 1426247 routes (176265 active, 4 holddown, 79690 hidden)
172.16.14.0/24 (12 entries, 1 announced)
        *BGP    Preference: 170/-101
                Next-hop reference count: 14184
                Source: 192.168.1.1
                Next hop: 192.168.1.1 via ge-0/1/0.0, selected
                Next hop: 192.168.1.3 via ge-1/1/0.0
                Protocol next hop: 192.168.1.1
                Indirect next hop: ac0a200 524714
                Protocol next hop: 192.168.1.3
                Indirect next hop: 24479700 524586
                State: <Active Int Ext>
                Local AS: 65000 Peer AS: 65505
                Age: 3w4d 5:08:45      Metric: 0      Metric2: 0
```

```
            Task: BGP_65505.192.168.1.1+3718
            Announcement bits (6): 0-KRT 1-RT 5-KRT 6-BGP.0.0.0.0+179 7-Resolve
tree 3 8-Resolve tree 4
            AS path: (65505) 65510 65520 ? (Atomic) Aggregator: 2468 192.168.246.3
            Communities: 65500:390 65500:2400 65505:3400
            Localpref: 100
            Router ID: 192.168.16.5
       BGP  Preference: 170/-101
            Next-hop reference count: 12709
            Source: 192.168.1.3
            Next hop: 192.168.1.3 via ge-1/1/0.0, selected
            Protocol next hop: 192.168.1.3
            Indirect next hop: 24479700 524586
            State: <NotBest Int Ext>
            Inactive reason: Router ID
            Local AS: 65000 Peer AS: 65505
            Age: 3w4d 5:08:54       Metric: 0       Metric2: 0
            Task: BGP_65505.192.168.1.3+179
            AS path: (65505) 65510 65520 ? (Atomic) Aggregator: 2468 192.168.246.3
            Communities: 65500:390 65500:2400 65505:3400
            Localpref: 100
            Router ID: 192.168.1.6
```

The Source field shows the router from which the path was learned. The first path is learned from Router3 (192.168.1.1) and the second is from Router4 (192.168.1.3). The Next hop field repeats the information in the standard show route output, showing the next-hop IP address and the interface toward the destination.

The Protocol next hop field is the next-hop information that BGP learned from its peers. Because BGP learns only about routers in the network, not in the interface, this IP address is listed without a corresponding interface on the local router. The indirect next hop is an internal RPD address of the next hop. The second number in this field is the kernel's index of the indirect next hop. You will see this index when you look at the contents of the forwarding table.

The State field gives additional information about the path. For the first path to 172.168.14.0/24, this field shows that the path is active. For the second path, this field lists the path as an alternate (NotBest) and indicates that it was not chosen as the active path because it does not have the lowest router ID:

```
State: <NotBest Int Ext>
Inactive reason: Router ID
```

Both next hops are installed in the Routing Engine's forwarding table:

```
aviva@Router1> show route forwarding-table destination 172.16.14.0/24
Routing table: inet
Internet:
Destination        Type RtRef Next hop           Type Index NhRef Netif
172.16.14.0/24     user    0                     ulst 526570 3545
                                                 indr 524714  523
                         192.168.1.1             ucst   336    17 ge-0/1/0.0
                                                 indr 524586 1864
                         192.168.1.3             ucst   340    13 ge-1/1/0.0
```

This forwarding table is then copied to the PFE's forwarding table:

```
aviva@Router1> show pfe route ip prefix 172.16.14.0/24
Slot 0
IPv4 Route Table 0, default.0, 0x0:
Destination                         NH IP Addr      Type     NH ID Interface
--------------------------------    --------------- -------- ----- ---------
172.16.14/24                                        Unilist 526570 ge-0/1/0.0
Slot 1
IPv4 Route Table 0, default.0, 0x0:
Destination                         NH IP Addr      Type     NH ID Interface
--------------------------------    --------------- -------- ----- ---------
172.16.14/24                                        Unilist 526570 ge-0/1/0.0
```

Both the routes are of type Unilist, which means that they are in the list of unicast next hops maintained by the Packet Forwarding Engine. The NH ID field shows the kernel's index of the indirect next hop, which matches what you saw in the show route detail output.

Even though multipath BGP selects multiple paths for forwarding and installs two paths in the forwarding table, BGP advertises only one path to its peers, which is the best path toward the destination. This is the same path that BGP would advertise if BGP load balancing were not configured.

You can also use multipath BGP across IBGP peerings. An additional restriction is that the IGP metric distance to the two IBGP peers must be identical. A scenario for doing this might be to load-balance traffic across redundant paths within a POP.

See Also

Recipes 8.9 and 9.1

13.15 Tracing BGP Protocol Traffic

Problem

You want to keep a running log of BGP protocol information so you can track any problems with your BGP peers.

Solution

When performing ongoing monitoring of BGP operations, set up tracing options (or traceoptions for short) to track BGP state changes globally for all BGP groups:

```
[edit protocols bgp]
aviva@RouterF# set traceoptions flag state detail
aviva@RouterF# set traceoptions file bgp-trace world-readable
```

To turn off BGP tracing, remove the traceoptions statement from the configuration:

```
[edit protocols bgp]
aviva@RouterF# delete traceoptions
```

You can also deactivate the statement:

```
[edit protocols bgp]
aviva@RouterF# deactivate traceoptions
```

Discussion

It's good practice to trace high-level BGP operations on an ongoing basis. If and when a problem arises, you can examine the resulting log to get the necessary information about the source of the problem. Then you can enable more detailed traceoptions flags to pinpoint the causes.

This recipe sets up tracing of BGP peer state exchanges, saving them to the file *bgp-trace*. The word-readable option allows anyone logged in to the router to read the file. This file is created on the router's hard disk in the directories */var/log* (on M-series and T-series routers) and */cf/var/log* (on J-series routers). The detail option provides additional information about abnormal events. This configuration creates 10 logfiles (the default) and uses the default trace file size of 10 MB, which is generally a useful size for logging events over a long period of time. If your BGP network is large, you might want to increase the file size so that you have time to review or archive the logfiles before the files start overwriting each other:

```
[edit protocols bgp]
aviva@RouterF# set traceoptions file size 100M
aviva@RouterF# show
traceoptions {
    file bgp-trace size 100m world-readable;
    flag state detail;
    flag open;
}
```

The following output shows the log results when a BGP peer drops and then re-establishes a session:

```
aviva@RouterF> show log bgp-trace
Aug  6 19:07:18 trace_on: Tracing to "/var/log/bgp-trace" started
Aug  6 19:07:53 bgp_recv: peer 10.0.31.1 (External AS 65505): received unexpected EOF
Aug  6 19:07:53 bgp_peer_close: closing peer 10.0.31.1 (External AS 65505), state is
6 (Established)
Aug  6 19:07:53 bgp_event: peer 10.0.31.1 (External AS 65505) old state Established
event Closed new state Idle
Aug  6 19:07:53 bgp_event: peer 10.0.31.1 (External AS 65505) old state Idle event
Start new state Active
Aug  6 19:07:57 bgp_event: peer 10.0.31.1 (External AS 65505) old state Active event
Open new state OpenSent
Aug  6 19:07:57 bgp_event: peer 10.0.31.1 (External AS 65505) old state OpenSent
event RecvOpen new state OpenConfirm
Aug  6 19:07:57 bgp_event: peer 10.0.31.1 (External AS 65505) old state OpenConfirm
event RecvKeepAlive new state Established
```

The first line shows the abnormal event receive unexpected EOF when the BGP peer connection drops. The following lines show the transition through various states as

---

BGP establishes the connection, from Idle, to Active, OpenSent, and OpenConfirm, and finally to Established.

Another useful tracing flag for ongoing monitoring of BGP is open, used to track when peer connections are established and torn down:

```
[edit protocols bgp]
aviva@RouterF# set traceoptions flag open
```

When the BGP peer session drops and re-establishes, the log contains traces of the BGP Open messages:

```
aviva@RouterF> show log bgp-trace
Aug  6 19:17:45 trace_on: Tracing to "/var/log/bgp-trace" started
Aug  6 19:18:05 bgp_recv: peer 10.0.31.1 (External AS 65505): received unexpected EOF
Aug  6 19:18:05 bgp_peer_close: closing peer 10.0.31.1 (External AS 65505), state is
6 (Established)
Aug  6 19:18:05 bgp_event: peer 10.0.31.1 (External AS 65505) old state Established
event Closed new state Idle
Aug  6 19:18:05 bgp_event: peer 10.0.31.1 (External AS 65505) old state Idle event
Start new state Active
Aug  6 19:18:09
Aug  6 19:18:09 BGP RECV 10.0.31.1+4379 -> 10.0.31.2+179
Aug  6 19:18:09 BGP RECV message type 1 (Open) length 45
Aug  6 19:18:09 bgp_event: peer 10.0.31.1 (External AS 65505) old state Active event
Open new state OpenSent
Aug  6 19:18:09 bgp_send: sending 45 bytes to 10.0.31.1 (External AS 65505)
Aug  6 19:18:09
Aug  6 19:18:09 BGP SEND 10.0.31.2+179 -> 10.0.31.1+4379
Aug  6 19:18:09 BGP SEND message type 1 (Open) length 45
Aug  6 19:18:09 bgp_event: peer 10.0.31.1 (External AS 65505) old state OpenSent
event RecvOpen new state OpenConfirm
Aug  6 19:18:09 bgp_event: peer 10.0.31.1 (External AS 65505) old state OpenConfirm
event RecvKeepAlive new state Established
```

When debugging BGP, you can set one or more of the following trace flags to monitor BGP information:

```
[edit protocols bgp]
aviva@RouterF# show traceoptions flag ?
Possible completions:
  all            Trace everything
  damping        Trace BGP damping information
  general        Trace general events
  keepalive      Trace BGP keepalive packets
  normal         Trace normal events
  open           Trace BGP open packets
  packets        Trace all BGP protocol packets
  policy         Trace policy processing
  refresh        Trace BGP refresh packets
  route          Trace routing information
  state          Trace state transitions
  task           Trace routing protocol task processing
  timer          Trace routing protocol timer processing
  update         Trace BGP update packets
```

You can configure BGP traceoptions globally, per group, or per peer. For ongoing monitoring, enable them at the global level, as in this recipe. For more focused traceoptions for when you're troubleshooting a known problem, enable tracing at the appropriate level, either for an IBGP or EBGP group or for a specific peer. For example, the following commands log route changes from an EBGP peer:

```
[edit protocols bgp]
aviva@RouterF# set group session-to-AS65505 traceoptions file bgp-log-CustomerA
world-readable
aviva@RouterF# set group session-to-AS65505 traceoptions flag route
aviva@RouterF# set group session-to-AS65505 traceoptions flag state
aviva@RouterF# show
group session-to-AS65505 {
    type external;
    traceoptions {
        file bgp-log-CustomerA world-readable;
        flag route;
        flag state;
    }
    description "EBGP to Customer A";
...
```

The JUNOS software also provides a BGP configuration command, log-updown, to log peer state transitions to a standard system logging file (the default file is named *messages*):

```
[edit protocols bgp]
aviva@RouterF# set log-updown
```

This command enables the logging globally, but you can also set it for an individual BGP group or peer. This is a useful way to keep basic system logging information in one file so you have to look only in one place to check router status. One disadvantage of this, however, is that BGP log entries are mixed into a system-wide logfile, so the BGP-specific messages can be buried in many other messages.

If you need to disable BGP tracing, either remove the traceoptions statement from the configuration with the delete configuration mode command or simply deactivate it. Deactivation leaves the statements in the configuration, but they are ignored when you issue a commit command. When you need to turn on BGP tracing again, restoring a deactivated portion of the configuration is very quick:

```
[edit protocols bgp]
aviva@RouterF# activate traceoptions
aviva@RouterF# commit
```

See Also

Recipe 5.10

## CHAPTER 14

MPLS

14.0 Introduction

Multiprotocol Label Switching (MPLS), as its name implies, is a switching protocol developed by the IETF to incorporate some of the benefits of network switching devices into an IP network. MPLS is designed to work with standard IP routing protocols—BGP, OSPF, and IS-IS—which have been extended to support MPLS.

Work on MPLS started as a response to the development of the Asynchronous Transfer Mode (ATM) protocol by the ITU and the ATM Forum in the late 1980s and early 1990s, and the propagation of ATM switches. By the early 1990s, the performance of ATM switches exceeded that of IP routers, but the architectural model, which is based on virtual circuits (a connection model) fundamentally differed from the IP connectionless model. In the early 1990s, it seemed that ATM-based applications might become dominant. However, when TCP/IP-based applications, such as the World Wide Web, became standard, the ATM Forum and the IP standards bodies designed a number of schemes, sometimes fairly complex, that allowed ATM and IP protocols to interoperate. The IETF borrowed a number of ATM switching design features when designing MPLS.

In response to ATM, several router vendors developed switching technologies compatible with IP routing. IPsilon, a now defunct startup, created IP Switching, Toshiba developed a Cell Switching Router (CSR), IBM introduced an approach called Aggregate Route-based IP Switching (ARIS), and Cisco Systems had Tag Switching. Cisco pursued standardization of Tag Switching with the IETF, which led to the formation of the MPLS working group in early 1997.

The first RFCs from the working group, RFCs 3031 and 3032, released in 2001, define the basic MPLS architectural framework, describing labels and label operations for passing MPLS traffic across *label-switched paths* (LSPs) through the network. Later RFCs defined the signaling protocols used by MPLS. The Label Distribution Protocol (LDP, RFC 3036) was specifically designed for distributing labels to set up LSPs. An already existing protocol, the Resource Reservation Protocol

(RSVP), originally designed as a general protocol for reserving bandwidth for network flows, was extended to set up LSPs, assign and manage labels, and reserve bandwidth for the LSP.

Since the introduction of MPLS, many new services have been developed that use MPLS, including Layer 3 VPNs, Virtual Private LAN Services (VPLS), and Differentiated Services Traffic Engineering (DiffServ TE).

For more detailed information about how MPLS works, see *MPLS: Technology and Applications* (Morgan Kaufmann) and *MPLS-Enabled Applications* (Wiley UK).

LSPs

MPLS assigns labels to network packets that describe how to forward them through the network. A label is a short, fixed-length numeric identifier. The labeled traffic is forwarded along LSPs, which are unidirectional tunnels through the IP network. LSPs are connections similar to ATM or Frame Relay virtual circuits. LSPs have an entry point, called an *ingress router*, and an exit point, called an *egress router*. LDP-signaled LSPs have multiple ingress points and a single egress point. RSVP-signaled LSPs have one ingress point and one egress point and optional intermediate routers called *transit routers*.

A signaling protocol establishes the physical path taken by the LSP between the ingress and egress routers. Once the paths are established, the ingress router *pushes* a fixed-length label onto packets traveling through the LSP. Each transit router swaps the label, removing the incoming label and replacing it with an outgoing label, and forwards the packets to the next hop. At the egress router (or typically at the penultimate hop, which is the router immediately prior to the egress router), the label is *popped*, or removed, from the packet, and the egress router continues forwarding the packet using the standard IP routing longest-match lookup algorithm. MPLS maintains a label forwarding table that it uses to determine the next hop in an LSP. The next-to-last router in the LSP, the *penultimate router*, usually performs a label *pop operation*, removing the MPLS label before sending the packet to the egress router. This is called *penultimate hop popping* (PHP).

LSPs are established either manually or dynamically using a signaling protocol.

MPLS Header and Labels

Packets traveling along an LSP are identified by a label, which is part of a 4-byte MPLS header that is inserted as a *shim* between the packet's link-level (Layer 2) header and its network layer (Layer 3) data (see Figure 14-1).

Multiple MPLS headers can be stacked in the packet's header. The newest header is placed at the beginning (top) of the stack.

The first 20 bits of the MPLS header are the MPLS label value, a numeric identifier that the LSP uses to forward packets. The label itself has no internal structure, unlike

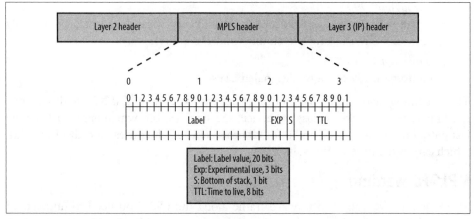

Figure 14-1. MPLS header

IP addresses, which are structured as a prefix (network portion) and prefix length (subnetwork or host portion). The ingress router assigns a label to each packet as it enters an LSP, pushing the label onto the packet's label stack. When a router receives a labeled packet, it looks up the label value at the top of the stack to learn the next hop to which to forward the packet and any operation to be performed on the label stack before forwarding the packet. Common label operations are to swap (replace) the top label stack entry with another label and to pop (remove) the top label from the stack.

Label values range from 0 through 1,048,575 (2^{20}). Values 0 through 15 are reserved by the IETF, and all others are available for use. Of the 16 label values reserved by the IETF, a few have well-defined meanings:

0   IPv4 Explicit Null label indicates that the label must be popped when the packet is received. Packet forwarding then continues using longest-match lookup based on the contents of the IPv4 packet.

1   Router Alert label delivers the packet to the local router's software for processing.

2   IPv6 Explicit Null label indicates that the label must be popped when the packet is received. Packet forwarding then continues using longest-match lookup based on the contents of the IPv6 packet.

3   Implicit Null label is used by a signaling protocol (in JUNOS software, either LDP or RSVP) to request that the downstream router pop the label.

The JUNOS software allocates the remaining labels as follows:

16 through 1,023
    Used for mapping labels for VPN VRF routing tables

1,024 through 9,999
    Reserved for future use

10,000 through 99,999

For manually configured static LSPs (JUNOS software does not automatically allocate labels in this range to eliminate label conflict)

100,000 through 1,048,575

For automatically configured signaled LSPs

The remaining fields in the MPLS header are the experimental (EXP) field, which is used for setting a packet's class of service; the stack (S) bit, which is set to 1 for the last entry on the label stack and 0 for all other label stack entries; and the TTL field, which carries the time-to-live value.

MPLS Forwarding

MPLS uses packet labels to forward traffic along the LSP. You need to understand how the labels are applied on the different routers in an LSP to configure and monitor an MPLS network.

Starting at the head end of an LSP, let's follow an IPv4 packet whose destination is downstream of RouterF (192.168.16.1). When the packet arrives at the ingress router (RouterG), this router checks its routing table and finds a route for this destination with a next hop of the LSP. The router inserts an MPLS header with a label of 100000 into the packet's header then forwards the packet to the next downstream router on the path (see Figure 14-2).

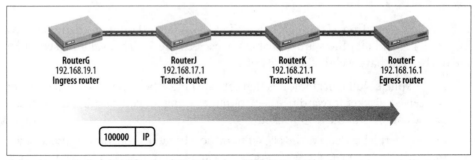

Figure 14-2. Ingress router adds MPLS header with label to IPv4 packet

The transit router (RouterJ) receives the labeled packet and performs a lookup in its label forwarding table. The router then performs a swap operation, removing the received label 100000 and replacing it with label 100032 from its switching table (see Figure 14-3).

RouterK, the penultimate router, also performs a lookup in its switching table. Because the egress router signaled the label 3, RouterK pops the label from the packet and forwards the remaining data to the egress router. This data is a native IPv4 packet, so the egress router (RouterF) performs a route lookup and forwards the packet to the appropriate next hop (see Figure 14-4).

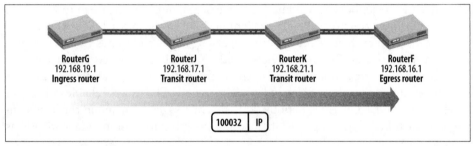

Figure 14-3. Transit router swaps labels in the MPLS header

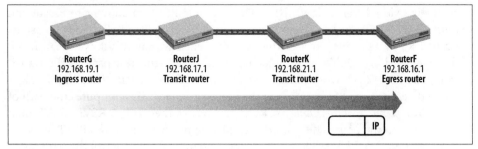

Figure 14-4. Penultimate router pops label

MPLS Routing and Forwarding Tables

For standard routing operations, the JUNOS routing software uses the inet.0 unicast routing table, which contains prefixes learned from IGPs. For MPLS forwarding operations, by default the JUNOS software stores prefixes learned from a signaling protocol (either LDP or RSVP) in a separate routing table, inet.3. MPLS consults this table when making forwarding decisions.

MPLS also creates another table, mpls.0, that contains the labels received and used by the local router to forward packets to the next-hop router.

Signaling Protocols

Labels are allocated and distributed throughout an MPLS network either manually or using a signaling protocol. It is time-intensive to set up and maintain static (manual) LSPs, so they are rarely used and are not discussed in this book. The JUNOS software supports two signaling protocols, LDP and RSVP.

LDP was designed by the MPLS working group in the IETF to set up LSPs and distribute labels throughout an MPLS network. LDP relies on an IGP (either OSPF or IS-IS) for all routing decisions, and the LSPs it sets up always follow the IGP's shortest path and change when the IGP's path changes. These LSPs use the IGP to avoid loops. Because LDP is dependent on an IGP, LDP-signaled LSPs are limited in scope to the IGP's domain and cannot cross AS boundaries.

LDP discovers neighbors by sending Hello messages, multicasting them to 224.0.0.2 on UDP port 646. After discovering a neighbor, LDP establishes a TCP connection to the neighbor and exchanges information regarding labels and routes (called *forwarding equivalence classes* [FRCs]) associated with the labels. All packets associated with the same FEC are treated in the same way by the router. In general, this means that the packets are sent to the same next hop. The use of TCP ensures reliable delivery of label information. LDP sends periodic keepalive messages to maintain the TCP connection. Each LDP router updates its forwarding-path information independently as it tracks the state of the IGP.

RSVP was developed before MPLS and was designed to create bandwidth reservations for individual traffic flows. RFC 3209 extends RSVP to allow it to create and maintain MPLS LSPs and to reserve the bandwidth needed for LSPs. The extensions are called RSVP-TE. In the rest of this chapter, when we say RSVP, we mean RSVP with TE extensions. Unlike LDP, which uses the IGP's shortest path as the transit path for the LSP, RSVP works with the *Constrained Shortest Path First* (CSPF) algorithm to determine the LSP's path. On the ingress router, CSPF computes the path of the LSP (the *Explicit Route Object* [ERO]) and passes the path to RSVP. RSVP then signals to set up the path. This path-determination mechanism allows RSVP-signaled LSPs to be used in MPLS-based traffic engineering to explicitly control the path taken by traffic between specific points in the network. Unlike LDP, which is limited to a single IGP domain, RSVP-signaled LSPs can cross AS boundaries.

When the ingress router initiates an RSVP-signaled LSP, it sends an RSVP Path message with the destination address of the egress router. This message also contains several objects, including the:

Label Request Object (LRO)
    Requests an MPLS label for the path

ERO
    Contains the addresses of the routers along the LSP

Record Route Object (RRO)
    Records the path of the LSP

Sender TSpec
    Requests a bandwidth reservation for the LSP

The egress router responds to a Path message by sending a Resv message that contains the label to be used for the LSP (in the label object) and a record of the path taken by the Resv message. In turn, the penultimate router sends a Resv message to its upstream router containing the label value of its choice inside the label object, because each hop to the downstream router chooses the label value to be used by the upstream router to forward packets on that hop. This message-exchange scheme means that an RSVP-signaled LSP requires configuration only on the ingress router. RSVP periodically sends Path and Resv messages along the LSP to maintain its state.

The main difference between LDP and RSVP is that for LDP, any router in the path can be the ingress for traffic destined to the LSP tail end, while for RSVP, only the head-end router can push traffic onto the LSP.

When deciding which signaling protocol to use, you should consider configuration complexity and features. From a configuration point of view, LDP is easier to configure. For the initial configuration, you enable LDP on the router's interfaces and, when adding new routers to the network, you configure only the new box. For initial RSVP configuration, you must explicitly configure the LSP on the ingress router and, when adding a new router, you must explicitly configure all LSPs originating at that router. Because LSPs are unidirectional, they must also be configured from each of the other routers toward the new one. From a feature point of view, only RSVP supports traffic engineering and fast reroute. If these are not required by your network, LDP is a better choice.

CSPF

RSVP uses the CSPF algorithm when computing paths for LSPs. CSPF is based on the SPF algorithm used in OSPF and IS-IS route calculations. In addition to network topology, CSPF considers other factors constraining the LSP computation—such as link attributes, bandwidth requirements, current bandwidth reservations, and hop limitations—when choosing paths that minimize congestion, balance traffic, and avoid node failures.

CSPF uses the router's *traffic engineering database* (TED) when computing paths. The TED maintains information about network topology and current link state. It learns this information from an IGP, either IS-IS or OSPF, that has been extended to carry additional information, such as available link bandwidth, that is used in the CSPF calculation. In the JUNOS IS-IS implementation, traffic engineering extensions are enabled by default; for OSPF, you must explicitly enable them.

14.1 Configuring LSPs Using LDP as the Signaling Protocol

Problem

You want to set up an LSP path through an IP network. Instead of setting up the path manually, you want to use LDP as the signaling protocol to establish and maintain the path.

Solution

For each LDP-signaled LSP, configure the ingress, transit, and egress routers on the path. On the ingress router, first configure the interface to support the MPLS address family:

```
[edit interfaces]
aviva@RouterG# set t1-4/0/0 unit 0 family mpls
```

Then enable the MPLS protocol on the interface:

```
[edit protocols]
aviva@RouterG# set mpls interface t1-4/0/0
```

Finally, turn on LDP as the signaling protocol:

```
[edit protocols]
aviva@RouterG# set ldp interface t1-4/0/0
```

On the transit and egress routers, turn on MPLS and LDP in a similar fashion.
RouterF is the egress router:

```
[edit interfaces]
aviva@RouterF# set fe-0/0/1 unit 0 family mpls

[edit protocols]
aviva@RouterF# set mpls interface fe-0/0/1
aviva@RouterF# set ldp interface fe-0/0/1
```

RouterJ is the transit router:

```
[edit interfaces]
aviva@RouterJ# set fe-1/0/1 unit 0 family mpls
aviva@RouterJ# set t1-5/0/0 unit 0 family mpls

[edit protocols]
aviva@RouterJ# set mpls interface t1-5/0/0
aviva@RouterJ# set mpls interface fe-1/0/1
aviva@RouterJ# set ldp interface t1-5/0/0
aviva@RouterJ# set ldp interface fe-1/0/1
```

Discussion

For MPLS to run on the routers in your network, you configure MPLS and a signaling protocol. This recipe uses LDP as the signaling protocol and the topology shown
in Figure 14-5. Because LDP depends on an IGP when creating LSPs, interfaces running MPLS must also be running either IS-IS or OSPF.

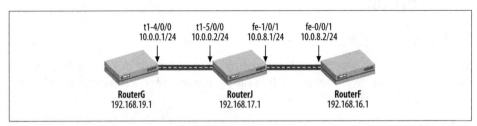

Figure 14-5. MPLS with LDP topology

The first step in the configuration is to enable the MPLS address family on the logical interfaces of all the interfaces that are running MPLS. This family allows the interface to process labeled packets. On the ingress router, RouterG, add the MPLS

family to the t1-4/0/0 interface; on the transit router, RouterJ, add it to the t1-5/0/0 and fe-1/0/1 interfaces; and on the egress router, RouterF, add it to the fe-0/0/1 interface. The interface configuration now has two families, IPv4 (inet) and MPLS:

```
aviva@RouterG> show configuration interfaces
t1-4/0/0 {
    unit 0 {
        family inet {
            address 10.0.0.1/24;
        }
        family mpls;
    }
}
lo0 {
    unit 0 {
        family inet {
            address 192.168.19.1/32;
        }
    }
}
```

The output shows the MPLS family on the t1-4/0/0 interface on the ingress router but not on the loopback interface. Because the loopback interface isn't a transit interface and never carries labeled packets, you don't need to configure it for the MPLS family.

Use the show interfaces terse command to verify that the MPLS family is configured on all expected interfaces. Here's the output for the transit router:

```
aviva@RouterJ> show interfaces terse
Interface            Admin Link Proto Local                 Remote
fe-0/0/0             up    up
fe-0/0/0.0           up    up   inet  172.19.121.117/24
fe-1/0/1             up    up
fe-1/0/1.0           up    up   inet  10.0.8.1/24
                                mpls
t1-5/0/0             up    up
t1-5/0/0.0           up    up   inet  10.0.0.2/24
                                mpls
lo0                  up    up
lo0.0                up    up   inet  192.168.17.1          --> 0/0
lo0.16385            up    up   inet  10.0.0.1              --> 0/0
                                      10.0.0.16             --> 0/0
```

This output confirms that the two MPLS interfaces, fe-1/0/1 and t1-5/0/0, are configured with the MPLS family and have IPv4 addresses, and that the loopback interface, lo0.0, has only an IPv4 address and is not configured for the MPLS family.

Next, configure the router to run the MPLS protocol. The basic configuration is very simple. In the [edit protocols mpls] section of the configuration hierarchy, list the router interfaces on which MPLS will run. For the ingress router, configure MPLS on the interface that leads toward the far end of the LSP:

```
[edit protocols]
aviva@RouterG# set mpls interface t1-4/0/0
```

If you are configuring MPLS on all the router's interfaces, use the following shortcut:

```
[edit protocols]
aviva@RouterG# set mpls interface all
```

For M-series and T-series routers, it's also considered good practice to disable MPLS on the fxp0 interface. This is true in particular for configurations where you configure MPLS on all interfaces instead of enabling it interface by interface.

```
[edit protocols]
aviva@router1# set mpls interface fxp0.0 disable
```

For J-series routers, you can disable MPLS on the equivalent interface, the fe-0/0/0 out-of-band interface:

```
[edit protocols]
aviva@routerJ# set mpls interface fe-0/0/0 disable
```

After configuring MPLS, confirm the configuration:

```
aviva@RouterG> show mpls interface
Interface        State        Administrative groups
t1-4/0/0.0       Up           <none>
```

The output shows that MPLS is up and running on interface t1-4/0/0 on the ingress router, RouterG. If you don't see the interface, make sure that the MPLS address family is configured on the interface:

```
aviva@RouterG> show interfaces terse t1-4/0/0
Interface                Admin Link Proto Local                 Remote
t1-4/0/0                 up    up
t1-4/0/0.0               up    up    inet  10.0.0.1/24
```

This output shows that the interface is configured for the IPv4 address, but not for the MPLS family. Use the set family mpls command to configure this family:

```
[edit interfaces]
aviva@RouterG# set t1-4/0/0 unit 0 family mpls
aviva@RouterG# commit and-quit
```

Then verify the configuration:

```
aviva@RouterG> show configuration interfaces t1-4/0/0
unit 0 {
    family inet {
        address 10.0.0.1/24;
    }
    family mpls;
}
```

The show interfaces terse output now indicates that the interfaces recognize the MPLS family:

```
aviva@RouterG> show interfaces terse t1-4/0/0
Interface                Admin Link Proto Local                 Remote
t1-4/0/0                 up    up
t1-4/0/0.0               up    up    inet  10.0.0.1/24
                                     mpls
```

Also verify the MPLS-enabled interfaces on the other routers. The transit router has two, one each to the ingress and egress routers:

```
aviva@RouterJ> show mpls interface
Interface       State        Administrative groups
t1-5/0/0.0      Up           <none>
fe-1/0/1.0      Up           <none>
```

The egress router has one MPLS-enabled interface:

```
aviva@RouterF> show mpls interface
Interface       State        Administrative groups
fe-0/0/1.0      Up           <none>
```

If you misconfigure MPLS, either by forgetting to include the interface in the [edit protocols mpls] hierarchy or omitting the MPLS family from the interface, the show mpls interface output doesn't list the interface. If MPLS and the interface are configured properly but the interface is not operational for some reason, the State column shows that the MPLS interface is down:

```
aviva@RouterG> show mpls interface
Interface       State        Administrative groups
t1-4/0/0.0      Dn           <none>
```

As the next configuration step, set up LDP as the signaling protocol. As with MPLS, just list all the router interfaces that will be running LDP. These are the same interfaces that run MPLS. Use the set ldp interface command to configure these interfaces in the [edit protocols] hierarchy. As with MPLS, you don't include the lo0 loopback interface in the list of interfaces running LDP because it is not a transit interface for labeled traffic. (LDP does use the lo0 interface, however, when sending targeted Hello messages to discover LDP peers that are not directly connected to the local router. LDP depends on these Hello messages to set up and maintain its sessions.)

Again, you are configuring LDP on all interfaces, so you can use the following shortcut:

```
[edit protocols]
aviva@RouterG# set ldp interface all
```

It's also considered good practice to disable LDP on the fxp0 interface on M-series and T-series routers. This is true in particular for configurations where you configure LDP on all interfaces instead of enabling it interface by interface.

```
[edit protocols]
aviva@router1# set ldp interface fxp0.0 disable
```

For J-series routers, you can disable LDP on the equivalent interface—the fe-0/0/0 out-of-band interface:

```
[edit protocols]
aviva@routerJ# set mpls interface fe-0/0/0 disable
```

Once LDP is turned on on all the routers, the protocol automatically builds multipoint-to-point LSPs, each ending on a different router in the network.

Use the show ldp interface command to check that LDP is up and running on the expected interfaces:

```
aviva@RouterG> show ldp interface
Interface          Label space ID        Nbr count   Next hello
t1-4/0/0.0         192.168.19.1:0           1            2

aviva@RouterF> show ldp interface
Interface          Label space ID        Nbr count   Next hello
fe-0/0/1.0         192.168.16.1:0           1            3
```

The output of these two show commands indicates that LDP is running on one interface on the ingress and egress routers. On the transit router, LDP is running on the two interfaces connected to the ingress and egress routers:

```
aviva@RouterJ> show ldp interface
Interface          Label space ID        Nbr count   Next hello
fe-1/0/1.0         192.168.17.1:0           1            1
t1-5/0/0.0         192.168.17.1:0           1            2
```

You see that each LDP interface is operational and has learned about one neighbor.

The LDP session between two routers runs over TCP, so after LDP is running on an interface, you expect to see that the TCP connection is established and operational:

```
aviva@RouterG> show ldp session
  Address          State         Connection    Hold time
  192.168.17.1     Operational   Open             26
```

The session information for the ingress router shows that the session to RouterJ at 192.168.17.1 is operational and the connection is open. The session hold time is how long LDP should wait to receive keepalive messages from its peer before closing the session. (LDP considers any LDP message to be a keepalive.) The JUNOS default hold time is 30 seconds, and the output shows that 26 seconds remain on this timer. Use the detail form of this command to see the session parameters:

```
aviva@RouterG> show ldp session detail
Address: 192.168.17.1, State: Operational, Connection: Open, Hold time: 23
  Session ID: 192.168.19.1:0--192.168.17.1:0
  Next keepalive in 3 seconds
  Active, Maximum PDU: 4096, Hold time: 30, Neighbor count: 1
  Keepalive interval: 10, Connect retry interval: 1
  Local address: 192.168.19.1, Remote address: 192.168.17.1
  Up for 1d 21:52:42
  Local - Restart: disabled, Helper mode: enabled
  Remote - Restart: disabled, Helper mode: enabled
  Local maximum recovery time: 240000 msec
  Next-hop addresses received:
    t1-4/0/0.0
    10.0.8.1
    10.0.0.2
```

The first line of the output shows that the LDP session is up and running—this is essentially the same information as the basic show ldp session command. The second line reports the LDP session ID, which is a concatenation of the LDP IDs for the local router and its LDP neighbor. Each router creates a 6-byte LDP ID. The first four bytes are the router ID or IP address of the router itself. The next two bytes define the type of labels that LDP is allocating. The value 0 is the default and means that LDP assigns labels on a per-router basis rather than on a per-interface basis.

The Next keepalive field shows how long before the LDP sends a keepalive message to its neighbors. A couple of lines down, you see that keepalive messages are sent every 10 seconds, which is the LDP default. The fourth line indicates that the session is active and can carry packets up to 4,096 bytes long. The last two fields show the default hold time and how many neighbors are participating in this LDP session.

The next several lines provide information about the session to the LDP peer, including the IP addresses and how long the session has been up. The Local, Remote, and Local maximum recovery time lines report provide information about graceful restart (see Recipe 8.12). The last section lists the next-hop addresses that the router has learned from the LDP session. You see that the router has learned the address to interface t1-4/0/0, the address of the subnet to the neighbor (10.0.0.2), and the address of the subnet between the neighbor and the egress router (10.0.8.1).

A reliable way to check that the LSP is up is to look for a route for the FEC:

```
aviva@RouterG> show route protocol ldp table inet.3
inet.3: 2 destinations, 2 routes (2 active, 0 holddown, 0 hidden)
+ = Active Route, - = Last Active, * = Both
192.168.16.1/32    *[LDP/9] 1d 21:53:52, metric 1
                    > via t1-4/0/0.0, Push 100000
192.168.17.1/32    *[LDP/9] 1d 21:53:52, metric 1
                    > via t1-4/0/0.0
```

These two routes are the LDP FECs, and there is one for each LDP neighbor. By default, the JUNOS LDP software advertises an FEC for its loopback address. The first FEC is to the LSP's egress point, 192.168.16.1/32, through the t1-4/0/0/0 interface. The second line also shows the label value and operation associated with this FEC. The label value is 100000, and LDP pushes this label onto the label stack of all packets destined for 192.168.16.1/32. Recipe 14.2 describes the contents of the inet.3 and mpls.0 routing tables.

LDP also keeps track of its FECs in a database. Here are the entries on the egress router:

```
aviva@RouterF> show ldp database
Input label database, 192.168.16.1:0--192.168.17.1:0
  Label      Prefix
  100000     192.168.16.1/32
       3     192.168.17.1/32
  100032     192.168.19.1/32
Output label database, 192.168.16.1:0--192.168.17.1:0
  Label      Prefix
```

```
      3      192.168.16.1/32
 100000      192.168.17.1/32
 100032      192.168.19.1/32
```

The Input label database section shows the labels received from the LDP peers, and the Output label database section shows the labels that this router has advertised. Here, RouterF has advertised a label value of 3 to RouterJ. This reserved label indicates that RouterF has signaled RouterJ to perform penultimate-hop popping to remove the top label on the stack before forwarding packets to RouterF.

To verify correct forwarding along the LSP, ping the egress router from the ingress router. For this to work, you need to configure a loopback address of 127.0.0.1 on the egress router:

```
[edit]
aviva@RouterF# set interfaces lo0 unit 0 family inet address 127.0.0.1/32
```

The egress router uses this address to send echo replies to echo requests sent by the ping command. Then send an MPLS ping request from the ingress router along the LSP:

```
aviva@RouterG> ping mpls ldp 192.168.16.1
!!!!!
--- lsping statistics ---
5 packets transmitted, 5 packets received, 0% packet loss
```

The ping echo replies include the label that the ingress router added to the packet when putting it into the LSP. The ping mpls command uses port 3503 for MPLS echo requests instead of the UDP port 7, which is used by the standard ping command.

This recipe shows only the commands you need to set up MPLS and LDP. Because LDP depends on the routing information provided by an IGP, the routers must be running either IS-IS or OSPF and IPv4 addresses must be configured on all interfaces running LDP and the IGP. For the ingress router in this recipe, here are the parts of the configuration related to setting up the LDP-signaled LSP:

```
aviva@RouterG> show configuration interfaces
t1-4/0/0 {
    unit 0 {
        family inet {
            address 10.0.0.1/24;
        }
    family mpls;
    }
}
lo0 {
    unit 0 {
        family inet {
            address 192.168.19.1/32;
        }
    }
}

aviva@RouterG> show configuration routing-options
router-id 192.168.19.1;
```

```
aviva@RouterG> show configuration protocols
mpls {
    interface t1-4/0/0.0;
}
ospf {
    area 0.0.0.0 {
        interface lo0.0 {
            passive;
        }
        interface t1-4/0/0.0;
    }
}
ldp {
    interface t1-4/0/0.0;
}
```

See Also

Recipes 8.12 and 14.2

14.2   Viewing Information and LDP-Signaled LSPs in the Routing Tables

Problem

After you have configured MPLS and LDP on your router, you want to look at the information in the router's routing tables.

Solution

Look in the inet.3 routing table to view the LDP routes:

```
aviva@RouterG> show route table inet.3
inet.3: 2 destinations, 2 routes (2 active, 0 holddown, 0 hidden)
+ = Active Route, - = Last Active, * = Both
192.168.16.1/32    *[LDP/9] 1d 23:02:21, metric 1
                    > via t1-4/0/0.0, Push 100000
192.168.17.1/32    *[LDP/9] 1d 23:02:21, metric 1
                    > via t1-4/0/0.0
```

Look in the mpls.0 table to see the router's label information:

```
aviva@RouterG> show route table mpls.0
mpls.0: 6 destinations, 6 routes (6 active, 0 holddown, 0 hidden)
+ = Active Route, - = Last Active, * = Both

0                  *[MPLS/0] 2d 01:59:47, metric 1
                    Receive
1                  *[MPLS/0] 2d 01:59:47, metric 1
                    Receive
2                  *[MPLS/0] 2d 01:59:47, metric 1
                    Receive
```

```
100064              *[LDP/9] 1d 23:02:36, metric 1
                      > via t1-4/0/0.0, Pop
100064(S=0)         *[LDP/9] 1d 23:02:36, metric 1
                      > via t1-4/0/0.0, Pop
100080              *[LDP/9] 1d 23:02:36, metric 1
                      > via t1-4/0/0.0, Swap 100000
```

Discussion

After configuring MPLS and LDP, if you look in the default JUNOS routing table, inet.0, you don't see any of the MPLS or LSP routes and you don't see any routers learned from LDP:

```
aviva@RouterG> show route table inet.0
inet.0: 12 destinations, 13 routes (12 active, 0 holddown, 0 hidden)
+ = Active Route, - = Last Active, * = Both
0.0.0.0/0           *[Static/5] 2d 19:44:09
                      > to 172.19.121.1 via fe-0/0/0.0
10.0.0.0/24         *[Direct/0] 1d 23:01:58
                      > via t1-4/0/0.0
                     [OSPF/10] 1d 23:01:57, metric 65
                      > via t1-4/0/0.0
10.0.0.1/32         *[Local/0] 3d 02:43:04
                      Local via t1-4/0/0.0
10.0.8.0/24         *[OSPF/10] 1d 23:01:49, metric 66
                      > via t1-4/0/0.0
10.0.13.0/24        *[OSPF/10] 1d 23:01:49, metric 131
                      > via t1-4/0/0.0
172.19.121.0/24     *[Direct/0] 1w3d 21:48:23
                      > via fe-0/0/0.0
172.19.121.119/32   *[Local/0] 1w3d 21:48:26
                      Local via fe-0/0/0.0
192.168.15.1/32     *[OSPF/10] 1d 23:01:49, metric 131
                      > via t1-4/0/0.0
192.168.16.1/32     *[OSPF/10] 1d 23:01:49, metric 66
                      > via t1-4/0/0.0
192.168.17.1/32     *[OSPF/10] 1d 23:01:49, metric 65
                      > via t1-4/0/0.0
192.168.19.1/32     *[Direct/0] 3d 02:18:53
                      > via lo0.0
224.0.0.5/32        *[OSPF/10] 2d 02:31:29, metric 1
                      MultiRecv
```

This routing table shows only the unicast routes, listing the routes learned from OSPF, which is the IGP we configured in the previous recipe, and the directly connected routes. In the JUNOS software, MPLS and LDP store their routing and forwarding information in two other routing tables, inet.3 and mpls.0. The inet.3 table contains the LDP FECs:

```
aviva@RouterG> show route table inet.3
inet.3: 2 destinations, 2 routes (2 active, 0 holddown, 0 hidden)
+ = Active Route, - = Last Active, * = Both
192.168.16.1/32     *[LDP/9] 5d 00:51:17, metric 1
```

```
                   > via t1-4/0/0.0, Push 100000
192.168.17.1/32    *[LDP/9] 5d 00:51:17, metric 1
                   > via t1-4/0/0.0
```

This output shows two LDP FECs (routes) to the two LDP neighbors. The first FEC is to the LSP's egress router, 192.168.16.1/32 (RouterF), and the second is to the transit router. Both FECs have a route preference of 9 and a metric of 1, which are the default JUNOS values for LDP. Both routes use the t1-4/0/0 interface, which is what you expect. The end of the second line of the FEC for 192.168.16.1/32 shows a push operation and a label value. When forwarding packets, LDP pushes a label of 100000 onto the packet. LDP stores all the labels being used in LDP-signaled LSPs, which you can display with the following command:

```
aviva@RouterF> show ldp database
Input label database, 192.168.16.1:0--192.168.17.1:0
  Label       Prefix
  100000      192.168.16.1/32
       3      192.168.17.1/32
  100032      192.168.19.1/32
Output label database, 192.168.16.1:0--192.168.17.1:0
  Label       Prefix
       3      192.168.16.1/32
  100000      192.168.17.1/32
  100032      192.168.19.1/32
```

The inet.3 table on RouterF shows similar FECs:

```
aviva@RouterF> show route table inet.3

inet.3: 2 destinations, 2 routes (2 active, 0 holddown, 0 hidden)
+ = Active Route, - = Last Active, * = Both

192.168.17.1/32    *[LDP/9] 5d 03:33:23, metric 1
                   > to 10.0.8.1 via fe-0/0/1.0
192.168.19.1/32    *[LDP/9] 5d 00:57:15, metric 1
                   > to 10.0.8.1 via fe-0/0/1.0, Push 100032
```

When the router is forwarding packets on this LSP, LDP pushes a label value, this time 100032, onto all packets entering the LSP.

The second JUNOS routing table, mpls.0, stores label values for MPLS and for LDP. Here's the mpls.0 table on RouterG:

```
aviva@RouterG> show route table mpls.0
mpls.0: 6 destinations, 6 routes (6 active, 0 holddown, 0 hidden)
+ = Active Route, - = Last Active, * = Both

0                  *[MPLS/0] 5d 03:58:02, metric 1
                      Receive
1                  *[MPLS/0] 5d 03:58:02, metric 1
                      Receive
2                  *[MPLS/0] 5d 03:58:02, metric 1
```

```
                        Receive
100064                  *[LDP/9] 5d 01:00:51, metric 1
                        > via t1-4/0/0.0, Pop
100064(S=0)             *[LDP/9] 5d 01:00:51, metric 1
                        > via t1-4/0/0.0, Pop
100080                  *[LDP/9] 5d 01:00:51, metric 1
                        > via t1-4/0/0.0, Swap 100000
```

This table is the MPLS label-swapping table and is actually a switching table rather than a routing table. Instead of a prefix in the first column, you see a label value. In this output, the first three entries correspond to reserved labels, defined in RFC 3032. These three entries are learned from MPLS (as indicated by [MPLS/0] in the second column) and are always in the mpls.0 routing table. The remaining three entries are for incoming labels that MPLS assigns to each upstream neighbor. Label 100064 has two entries because the stack value in the MPLS header can be different in different packets. In the first entry label, 100064, the S (stack) bit is 1, so this label matches packets that have only one label on their stacks. The second entry, 100064(S=0), has the stack bit set to 0 and is used when the stack depth is not 1. That is, it is used when the packet is carrying more than one label. For both labels, the operation pops the top label off the stack. The third label, 100080, has a swap operation associated with it.

You can quickly check all the routes learned from LDP with the show route protocol ldp command:

```
aviva@RouterG> show route protocol ldp
inet.0: 12 destinations, 13 routes (12 active, 0 holddown, 0 hidden)
inet.3: 2 destinations, 2 routes (2 active, 0 holddown, 0 hidden)
+ = Active Route, - = Last Active, * = Both
192.168.16.1/32    *[LDP/9] 1d 23:03:35, metric 1
                   > via t1-4/0/0.0, Push 100000
192.168.17.1/32    *[LDP/9] 1d 23:03:35, metric 1
                   > via t1-4/0/0.0

__juniper_private1__.inet.0: 2 destinations, 2 routes (2 active, 0 holddown, 0
hidden)

mpls.0: 6 destinations, 6 routes (6 active, 0 holddown, 0 hidden)
+ = Active Route, - = Last Active, * = Both
100064             *[LDP/9] 1d 23:03:35, metric 1
                   > via t1-4/0/0.0, Pop
100064(S=0)        *[LDP/9] 1d 23:03:35, metric 1
                   > via t1-4/0/0.0, Pop
100080             *[LDP/9] 1d 23:03:35, metric 1
                   > via t1-4/0/0.0, Swap 100000
```

This output displays the routes for the LDP FECs, stored in inet.3, and the label-switching state stored in mpls.0.

Use the show route forwarding-table mpls command to see the active MPLS routes in the Routing Engine's forwarding table:

```
aviva@RouterG> show route forwarding-table family mpls
Routing table: mpls
MPLS:
Destination        Type RtRef Next hop      Type Index NhRef Netif
default            perm  0                   dscd   28    1
0                  user  0                   recv   27    3
1                  user  0                   recv   27    3
2                  user  0                   recv   27    3
100064             user  0                   Pop             t1-4/0/0.0
100064(S=0)        user  0                   Pop             t1-4/0/0.0
100080             user  0                   Swap 100000     t1-4/0/0.0
```

The Destination column lists labels that the router is using to forward traffic, and the last column, Netif, shows the interfaces that are being used to send the labeled traffic. For the nonreserved labels, the second Type column shows the operation performed on matching packets. For packets with label 100064, the label is popped, and packets with label 100080 have their label swapped for 100000.

To see the forwarding entries used by the Packet Forwarding Engine to forward MPLS packets, use the following version of the show pfe route command:

```
aviva@RouterG> show pfe route mpls
MPLS Route Table 0, MPLS.0, 0x0:
Destination              Type      ID NhRef
----------------------- -------- ----- -----
default   Discard    28   1
0         Receive    27   3
1         Receive    27   3
2         Receive    27   3
100064    Unicast   330   1 t1-4/0/0.0
100064(S=0)   Unicast   332    1 t1-4/0/0.0
100080    Unicast   333   1 t1-4/0/0.0
```

Looking at this output, you can see that it shows pretty much the same information as the Routing Engine's forwarding table.

See Also

Recipe 8.1

14.3   Verifying that an LDP-Signaled LSP Is Carrying Traffic

Problem

You want to check that traffic is using an LDP-signaled LSP.

Solution

Look at the LSP traffic statistics:

```
aviva@RouterJ> show ldp traffic-statistics
FEC                  Type              Packets           Bytes    Shared
  192.168.16.1/32    Transit               15             1260    No
                     Ingress                0                0    No
  192.168.19.1/32    Transit                0                0    No
                     Ingress                0                0    No
```

Discussion

To make sure that traffic is using the LSP, look at the traffic statistics on the LDP sessions with the show ldp traffic-statistics commands. The Packets column shows the number of packets that have been sent, and the Bytes column gives the total byte count of all the packets. In this recipe, RouterJ carried 15 packets (1,260 bytes) from RouterG (192.168.16.1), acting as the transit router for this traffic.

14.4   Enabling LDP Authentication

Problem

You want to ensure that all LDP protocol traffic that your router accepts comes from devices known to you so that only trusted routers participate in determining the contents of the LDP database.

Solution

Configure MD5 authentication for each LDP session on the router. For authentication to work across all LDP peers, you need to configure MD5 authentication with the same password on all LDP sessions on all LDP routers. First, configure the session on the ingress router, RouterG:

```
[edit protocols ldp]
aviva@RouterG# set session 192.168.17.1 authentication-key $1991poPPi
```

Then, configure the LDP session on the egress router:

```
[edit protocols ldp]
aviva@RouterF# set session 192.168.17.1 authentication-key $1991poPPi
```

Finally, configure both LDP sessions on the transit router:

```
[edit protocols ldp]
aviva@RouterJ# set session 192.168.16.1 authentication-key $1991poPPi
aviva@RouterJ# set session 192.168.19.1 authentication-key $1991poPPi
```

Discussion

It's a good security measure to authenticate the TCP connection used for LDP sessions to ensure against spoofing on the TCP connection. The JUNOS implementation LDP uses an MD5 signature for authentication.

This recipe shows how to configure MD5 authentication for LDP. You configure MD5 authentication for each session and set a key, or password. From the key, MD5 creates an encoded checksum that is included in all transmitted LDP packets. The receiving router verifies this checksum before accepting the packet. LDP routers establish sessions with each of their LDP neighbors. Because LDP authentication is always between a pair of neighbors, not end to end, you can use a different key on each session. For example, you could set a one key for the RouterG–RouterJ session and a different one for the RouterJ–RouterF session.

Use the show ldp session command to list the established sessions. You see that RouterG has one LDP session:

```
aviva@RouterG> show ldp session
   Address           State           Connection      Hold time
   192.168.17.1      Operational     Open                 24
```

The LDP session is established with the immediate neighbor, RouterJ (191.168.17.1). So, when you configure authentication, specify the address of the session to RouterJ. RouterF also has one session, to its neighbor RouterJ:

```
aviva@RouterF> show ldp session
   Address           State           Connection      Hold time
   192.168.17.1      Operational     Open                 29
```

The router in the middle, RouterJ, has one session to each LDP peer:

```
aviva@RouterJ> show ldp session
   Address           State           Connection      Hold time
   192.168.16.1      Operational     Open                 24
   192.168.19.1      Operational     Open                 21
```

One way to verify whether authentication is configured is to look at the configuration:

```
aviva@RouterG> show configuration protocols ldp
interface t1-4/0/0.0;
session 192.168.17.1 {
    authentication-key "$9$c3pyvWX7-w24x7k.fT3nvW8LVw"; ## SECRET-DATA
}
```

This output confirms that authentication is configured. As a security measure, the CLI shows only the encrypted form of the password to stop anyone from casually glancing through the configuration and seeing the actual password. You can also protect the password by using the encrypted form instead of the text form when configuring authentication on additional routers:

```
[edit protocols ldp session 192.168.17.1]
aviva@RouterF# set authentication-key $9$c3pyvWX7-w24x7k.fT3nvW8LVw
```

Another way to check that authentication is configured is to look at the LDP session:

```
aviva@RouterG> show ldp session detail
Address: 192.168.17.1, State: Connecting, Connection: Opening, Hold time: 0
   Session ID: 192.168.19.1:0--192.168.17.1:0
   Active, Maximum PDU: 4096, Hold time: 30, Neighbor count: 1
```

```
Keepalive interval: 10, Connect retry interval: 1
Local address: 192.168.19.1, Remote address: 192.168.17.1
Last down 00:00:09 ago; Reason: connect time expired
Authentication type: MD5
Local - Restart: disabled, Helper mode: enabled
Remote - Restart: disabled, Helper mode: enabled
Local maximum recovery time: 240000 msec
Next-hop addresses received:
   t1-4/0/0.0
```

The Authentication type line shows that the LDP session is using MD5 authentication.

14.5   Tracing LDP Operations

Problem

You want to check that LDP is properly exchanging messages with its neighbors.

Solution

Set up a tracing file to capture information about the exchange of LDP protocol packets:

```
[edit protocols ldp]
aviva@RouterG# set traceoptions file ldp-log
aviva@RouterG# set traceoptions flag packets
```

Discussion

One tool for troubleshooting LDP operation is the JUNOS tracing facility. If an LDP session that was operating properly suddenly stops working, you can trace the router's LDP packet exchanges with its neighbors to help track down the source of the problem. This recipe sets up an LDP-specific tracing file named *ldp-log* that captures all LDP packet exchanges with neighboring routers.

Use the show log command to see the file contents:

```
aviva@RouterG> show log ldp-log
Oct 5 19:25:46 Incredible-Hulk clear-log[15758]: logfile cleared
Oct  5 19:25:48 LDP sent UDP PDU 10.0.0.1 -> 224.0.0.2 (t1-4/0/0.0)
Oct  5 19:25:48 ver 1, pkt len 42, PDU len 38, ID 192.168.19.1:0
Oct  5 19:25:48   Msg Hello (0x100), len 28, ID 396082
Oct  5 19:25:48     TLV HelloParms (0x400), len 4
Oct  5 19:25:48     TLV XportAddr (0x401), len 4
Oct  5 19:25:48     TLV ConfSeq (0x402), len 4
Oct  5 19:25:49 LDP rcvd UDP PDU 10.0.0.2 -> 224.0.0.2 (t1-4/0/0.0)
Oct  5 19:25:49 ver 1, pkt len 42, PDU len 38, ID 192.168.17.1:0
Oct  5 19:25:49   Msg Hello (0x100), len 28, ID 397238
Oct  5 19:25:49     TLV HelloParms (0x400), len 4
Oct  5 19:25:49     TLV XportAddr (0x401), len 4
Oct  5 19:25:49     TLV ConfSeq (0x402), len 4
Oct  5 19:25:52 LDP sent UDP PDU 10.0.0.1 -> 224.0.0.2 (t1-4/0/0.0)
Oct  5 19:25:52 ver 1, pkt len 42, PDU len 38, ID 192.168.19.1:0
```

```
Oct  5 19:25:52   Msg Hello (0x100), len 28, ID 396083
Oct  5 19:25:52     TLV HelloParms (0x400), len 4
Oct  5 19:25:52     TLV XportAddr (0x401), len 4
Oct  5 19:25:52     TLV ConfSeq (0x402), len 4
Oct  5 19:25:52   LDP sent TCP PDU 192.168.19.1 -> 192.168.17.1 (none)
Oct  5 19:25:52   ver 1, pkt len 18, PDU len 14, ID 192.168.19.1:0
Oct  5 19:25:52     Msg Keepalive (0x201), len 4, ID 396084
Oct  5 19:25:52   LDP rcvd TCP PDU 192.168.17.1 -> 192.168.19.1 (none)
Oct  5 19:25:52   ver 1, pkt len 18, PDU len 14, ID 192.168.17.1:0
Oct  5 19:25:52     Msg Keepalive (0x201), len 4, ID 397241
Oct  5 19:25:53   LDP rcvd UDP PDU 10.0.0.2 -> 224.0.0.2 (t1-4/0/0.0)
Oct  5 19:25:53   ver 1, pkt len 42, PDU len 38, ID 192.168.17.1:0
Oct  5 19:25:53     Msg Hello (0x100), len 28, ID 397242
Oct  5 19:25:53       TLV HelloParms (0x400), len 4
Oct  5 19:25:53       TLV XportAddr (0x401), len 4
Oct  5 19:25:53       TLV ConfSeq (0x402), len 4
```

This log shows normal LDP operation. LDP is sending and receiving UDP and TCP messages with its neighboring routers. LDP multicasts UDP Hello messages to 224.0.0.2 to discover its neighbors. The log output shows that LDP is sending UDP hellos out the connection to the local subnet (10.0.0.1) and receiving hellos from the other end of the connection (10.0.0.2). LDP establishes TCP connections to exchange label and FEC information and sends periodic keepalive messages (every 10 seconds, by default) to its neighbors to keep the TCP session established. The logfile also shows that LDP is sending and receiving TCP keepalives from 192.168.17.1, the neighboring LDP router. All the entries in this logfile are what you would expect to see when an LDP session is operating properly.

When debugging LDP, you can set one or more of the following trace flags to capture LDP-related information:

```
[edit protocols ldp]
aviva@RouterG# set traceoptions flag ?
Possible completions:
  address           Trace address packets
  all               Trace everything
  binding           Trace label binding state
  error             Trace errored packets
  event             Trace LDP state machine events
  general           Trace general events
  initialization    Trace initialization packets
  label             Trace label packets
  normal            Trace normal events
  notification      Trace notification packets
  packets           Trace all LDP packets
  path              Trace label path state
  periodic          Trace periodic (hello and keepalive) packets
  policy            Trace policy processing
  route             Trace routing information
  state             Trace state transitions
  task              Trace routing protocol task processing
  timer             Trace routing protocol timer processing
```

See Also

Recipe 5.10

14.6   Setting Up RSVP-Signaled LSPs

Problem

You want to use RSVP as the signaling protocol so you can implement some of the traffic engineering features available only with RSVP, including protecting traffic links.

Solution

For each MPLS LSP, configure the ingress, transit, and egress routers on the path. On the ingress router, first configure the interface to support MPLS addressing:

```
[edit interfaces]
aviva@R1# set so-0/0/2 unit 0 family mpls
```

Then enable the MPLS protocol on the interface:

```
[edit protocols]
aviva@R1# set mpls interface so-0/0/2
aviva@R1# set mpls interface fxp0.0 disable
```

Finally, turn on RSVP as the signaling protocol:

```
[edit protocols]
aviva@R1# set rsvp interface so-0/0/2
```

On the transit and egress routers, turn on MPLS and RSVP in a similar fashion. R6 is the egress router:

```
[edit interfaces]
aviva@R6# set so-0/0/3 unit 0 family mpls

[edit protocols]
aviva@R6# set mpls interface so-0/0/3
aviva@R6# set mpls interface fxp0.0 disable
aviva@R6# set rsvp interface so-0/0/3
aviva@R6# set rsvp interface fxp0.0 disable
```

R3 is the transit router:

```
[edit interfaces]
aviva@R3# set so-0/0/2 unit 0 family mpls
aviva@R3# set so-0/0/3 unit 0 family mpls

[edit protocols]
aviva@R3# set mpls interface so-0/0/2
aviva@R3# set mpls interface so-0/0/3
aviva@R3# set mpls interface fxp0.0 disable
aviva@R3# set rsvp interface so-0/0/2
aviva@R3# set rsvp interface so-0/0/3
```

```
aviva@R3# set rsvp interface fxp0.0 disable
```

Then, on the ingress router, set up the LSP:

```
[edit protocols mpls]
aviva@R1# set mpls label-switched-path R1-to-R6 to 10.0.0.6
```

Also set up a return LSP from R6 to R1 so that the LSP is bidirectional and traffic can travel from the egress router back to the ingress router:

```
[edit protocols]
aviva@R6# set mpls label-switched-path R6-to-R1 to 10.0.0.1
```

Discussion

This recipe shows how to use RSVP as the signaling protocol for MPLS, based on the topology shown in Figure 14-6. Interfaces running MPLS must also be running BGP and an IGP (either IS-IS or OSPF). In this topology, all interfaces are running IS-IS and OSPF.

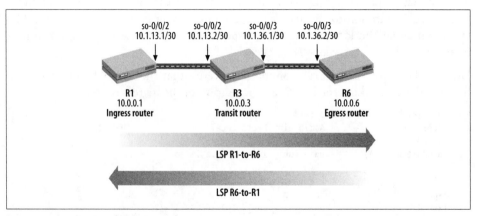

Figure 14-6. MPLS with RSVP topology

As with the LDP configuration, first configure the MPLS address family on the logical interfaces so the interface can process labeled packets. On the ingress router, R1, set the MPLS family on the so-0/0/2 interface. On the transit router, R3, add it to the so-0/0/2 and so-0/0/3 interfaces. On the egress router, R6, configure it on the so-0/0/3 interface. The configuration for each physical interface now has three families, IPv4 (inet), iso (for IS-IS), and MPLS:

```
aviva@R1> show configuration interfaces
so-0/0/2 {
    unit 0 {
        family inet {
            address 10.1.13.1/30;
        }
        family iso;
        family mpls;
    }
}
```

```
        }
        fxp0 {
            unit 0 {
                family inet {
                    address 192.168.70.143/21;
                }
            }
        }
        lo0 {
            unit 0 {
                family inet {
                    address 10.0.0.1/32;
                }
                family iso {
                    address 49.0004.1000.0000.0001.00;
                }
            }
        }
    }
```

You see that on physical interface so-0/0/2 on the ingress router, the MPLS family is configured in addition to the inet and iso families. You don't configure the MPLS family on either the loopback (lo0) or fxp0 interfaces because they are not transit interfaces and never carry labeled packets.

Use the show interfaces terse command to verify that the MPLS family is configured on all expected interfaces. Here's the output for the ingress router:

```
aviva@R1> show interfaces terse
Interface              Admin Link Proto Local                 Remote
so-0/0/2               up    up
so-0/0/2.0             up    up   inet  10.1.13.1/30
                                  iso
                                  mpls
fxp0                   up    up
fxp0.0                 up    up   inet  192.168.70.143/21
lo0                    up    up
lo0.0                  up    up   inet  10.0.0.1              --> 0/0
                                  iso   49.0004.1000.0000.0001.00
lo0.16385              up    up   inet
                                  inet6 fe80::2a0:a5ff:fe56:189
```

Here's the output for the transit router:

```
aviva@R3> show interfaces terse
Interface              Admin Link Proto Local                 Remote
so-0/0/2               up    up
so-0/0/2.0             up    up   inet  10.1.13.2/30
                                  iso
                                  mpls
so-0/0/3               up    up
so-0/0/3.0             up    up   inet  10.1.36.1/30
                                  iso
                                  mpls
```

```
fxp0                          up    up
fxp0.0                        up    up    inet  192.168.70.145/21
lo0                           up    up
lo0.0                         up    up    inet  10.0.0.3              --> 0/0
                                          iso   49.0002.1000.0000.0003.00
lo0.16385                     up    up    inet
                                          inet6 fe80::2a0:a5ff:fe56:416
```

On both routers, you see that the MPLS family is enabled on the appropriate logical interfaces (so-0/0/2 on the ingress router, and so-0/0/2 and so-0/0/3 on the transit router). You also see that the inet and iso families are configured on these interfaces and on the routers' lo0 interfaces.

Next, configure the three routers that will form the LSP to run MPLS. The basic configuration is very simple. In the [edit protocols mpls] section of the configuration hierarchy, list the router interfaces on which MPLS will run. For the ingress router, configure MPLS on the interface that leads toward the transit router in the LSP and disable MPLS on the router's fxp0 interface:

```
aviva@R1> show configuration protocols mpls
interface so-0/0/2.0;
interface fxp0.0 {
    disable;
}
```

The SONET interface so-0/0/2 connects from the ingress router to the transit router. This lab setup uses M7i routers, so we disable MPLS on the fxp0 interface, which, while not required, is considered to be good practice.

After configuring the MPLS interfaces, check that MPLS is running on the interfaces. Here's the status on the ingress router:

```
aviva@R1> show mpls interface
Interface       State       Administrative groups
so-0/0/2.0      Up          <none>
```

The output shows that MPLS is up and running on interface so-0/0/2. Also, confirm MPLS status on the transit and egress routers:

```
aviva@R3> show mpls interface
Interface       State       Administrative groups
so-0/0/2.0      Up          <none>
so-0/0/3.0      Up          <none>

aviva@R6> show mpls interface
Interface       State       Administrative groups
so-0/0/3.0      Up          <none>
```

You see that all required MPLS interfaces are up and running.

The next step in the configuration is to set up RSVP as the signaling protocol. The basic configuration is similar to that for MPLS: you list all router interfaces that will be running RSVP. These are the same interfaces that you configured for MPLS. Use the set rsvp interface command to configure these interfaces in the [edit protocols] hierarchy. As with MPLS, do not include the loo and fxp0 interfaces in the list of RSVP interfaces because they do not carry labeled traffic. Also, as with MPLS, it is considered good practice to disable RSVP on the fxp0 interface. Use the following command to verify the configuration:

```
aviva@R1> show configuration protocols rsvp
interface so-0/0/2.0;
interface fxp0.0 {
    disable;
}
```

The show rsvp version command shows you whether RSVP is running on the router:

```
aviva@R1> show rsvp version
Resource ReSerVation Protocol, version 1. rfc2205
    RSVP protocol                   = Enabled
    R(refresh timer)                = 30 seconds
    K(keep multiplier)              = 3
    Preemption                      = Normal
    Soft-preemption cleanup         = 30 seconds
    Graceful deletion timeout       = 30 seconds
    Graceful restart                = Disabled
    Restart helper mode             = Enabled
    Maximum helper restart time    = 20000 msec
    Maximum helper recovery time = 180000 msec
    Restart time                    = 0 msec
```

The first line of the output shows that the JUNOS software is running RSVP Version 1 (defined in RFC 2205). The second line shows that RSVP is enabled on the router. The remaining lines show the settings for various RSVP parameters, which are the default values because we haven't configured anything other than basic RSVP functionality at this point. The refresh timer of 30 seconds determines how often RSVP sends periodic messages to its neighbors. The JUNOS software multiplies this value by 1.5 and sends RSVP messages every 45 seconds by default. The keep multiplier indicates the number of RSVP messages that can be lost on a connection before the software considers an RSVP state to be stale.

The fifth line, Preemption, shows the default session preemption type of Normal. RSVP uses preemption to accommodate additional sessions when a link does not have sufficient bandwidth to carry all sessions. Normal preemption means that only new better-priority RSVP sessions can preempt existing ones. (Recipe 14.14 explains how to modify the default preemption behavior.) Normally, sessions are torn down immediately when they are preempted. However, if soft preemption is configured, RSVP attempts for 30 seconds to establish a new session before tearing down the existing one. This is called soft-preemption cleanup. As part of tearing down an LSP, by default, RSVP waits 30 seconds to gracefully time out the session. The last five lines apply to graceful restart, which is disabled on the router.

Next, check that RSVP is up and running on the router's interfaces. Here's the output for the ingress router:

```
aviva@R1> show rsvp interface
RSVP interface: 1 active
                  Active Subscr- Static      Available    Reserved   Highwater
Interface   State resv   iption  BW          BW           BW         mark
so-0/0/2.0  Up        0   100%   155.52Mbps  155.52Mbps   0bps       0bps
```

The second column, State, shows that RSVP is running on the so-0/0/2 interface.

Finally, you are ready to configure the LSP between R1 and R6 with the following command. On the ingress router, R1, verify the configuration:

```
[edit protocols mpls]
aviva@R1# set label-switched-path R1-to-R6 to 10.0.0.6
```

Then check that the LSP is up:

```
aviva@R1> show mpls lsp
Ingress LSP: 1 sessions
To              From            State Rt ActivePath      P     LSPname
10.0.0.6        10.0.0.1        Up    1                  *     R1-to-R6
Total 1 displayed, Up 1, Down 0

Egress LSP: 0 sessions
Total 0 displayed, Up 0, Down 0

Transit LSP: 0 sessions
Total 0 displayed, Up 0, Down 0
```

The output shows one LSP, R1-to-R6, configured on R1 and that this is an ingress LSP. To verify that the LSP is up on all the routers, use the same command to check LSP status. Here's the command output on the transit router:

```
aviva@R3> show mpls lsp
Ingress LSP: 0 sessions
Total 0 displayed, Up 0, Down 0

Egress LSP: 0 sessions
Total 0 displayed, Up 0, Down 0

Transit LSP: 1 sessions
To              From            State  Rt Style Labelin Labelout LSPname
10.0.0.6        10.0.0.1        Up     1  1 FF   103488       3 R1-to-R6
Total 1 displayed, Up 1, Down 0
```

You see that it has one transit LSP from the ingress, 10.0.0.1, to the expected egress at 10.0.0.6. This is LSP R1-to-R6, which is the one we expect. Here's the output on the egress router:

```
aviva@R6> show mpls lsp
Ingress LSP: 0 sessions
Total 0 displayed, Up 0, Down 0

Egress LSP: 1 sessions
To              From            State  Rt Style Labelin Labelout LSPname
10.0.0.6        10.0.0.1        Up     0  1 FF   3            - R1-to-R6
Total 1 displayed, Up 1, Down 0
```

```
Transit LSP: 0 sessions
Total 0 displayed, Up 0, Down 0
```

This output correctly shows the one LSP we have configured.

For the three routers in the LSP, the show mpls lsp output differs slightly. The P column for R1, the ingress router, contains an asterisk to indicate that LSP R1-to-R6 is the primary LSP between the two routers. The output on the transit and egress routers shows information about the RSVP reservation style and label values.

The command output for the transit router shows that received packets have a label value of 103488 and it uses a label value of 3 on the record for outgoing packets. A label value of 3 is one of the reserved values, used to request that the downstream router pop the label. The transit router is the penultimate-hop router, and the egress router has advertised a label value of 3 to R3 so that it performs penultimate-hop popping to remove the top label on the stack before forwarding packets to R6.

The Rt column in the output on all three routers shows the number of active prefixes installed in the routing table as a result of the RSVP session. Recipe 14.7 explains how to view these routes.

The extensive version of the show mpls lsp command provides additional information about the LSP, including a log of the LSP's history:

```
aviva@R1> show mpls lsp extensive
Ingress LSP: 1 sessions
10.0.0.6
  From: 10.0.0.1, State: Up, ActiveRoute: 1, LSPname: R1-to-R6
  ActivePath: (primary)
  LoadBalance: Random
  Encoding type: Packet, Switching type: Packet, GPID: IPv4
 *Primary                         State: Up
    Computed ERO (S [L] denotes strict [loose] hops): (CSPF metric: 20)
  10.1.13.2 S 10.1.36.2 S
    Received RRO (ProtectionFlag 1=Available 2=InUse 4=B/W 8=Node 10=SoftPreempt):
          10.1.13.2 10.1.36.2
    5 Oct  4 13:31:06 Selected as active path
    4 Oct  4 13:31:06 Record Route:  10.1.13.2 10.1.36.2
    3 Oct  4 13:31:06 Up
    2 Oct  4 13:31:06 Originate Call
    1 Oct  4 13:31:06 CSPF: computation result accepted
  Created: Tue Oct  4 13:31:05 2005
Total 1 displayed, Up 1, Down 0
```

This command works only on the ingress router because this router is responsible for establishing and maintaining the LSP. The transit and egress routers have no details about the LSP's state. The first line of the output confirms what we already know about the LSP: that it is named R1-to-R6, runs from 10.0.0.1 to 10.0.0.6, and is up. The highlighted lines show the history of the LSP, from most current to oldest events. The last line in the log tells you that the LSP was created at 13:31:05. RSVP used CSPF to determine a path for the LSP (this is the default JUNOS RSVP behavior), and by 13:31:06 the LSP was up and running and was selected as the active path. Consult the LSP's log to help determine the causes of MPLS errors in the network.

You may be wondering why RSVP is using CSPF when setting up the LSP when we haven't included anything about turning on CSPF in the configuration. By default, JUNOS RSVP uses CSPF to calculate paths. The data that RSVP uses for the CSPF calculation comes from an IGP, either IS-IS or OSPF. Extensions to both protocols allow them to collect information about the network topology and available bandwidth on network links. The JUNOS implementations of both IGPs support the extensions. This network data for CSPF is stored in a TED on each router. In the JUNOS IS-IS software, these extensions are on by default. Because IS-IS is running as one of the IGPs in our network, it automatically carries the traffic-engineering information. Here's how you can disable the IS-IS support for TE:

```
[edit protocols isis]
aviva@R1# set traffic-engineering disable
```

In the JUNOS OSPF, the extensions are off by default. You must explicitly configure OSPF support of the CSPF computation:

```
[edit protocols ospf]
aviva@R1# set traffic-engineering
```

Use the following command to see what information IS-IS and OSPF have added to the TED database:

```
aviva@R1> show ted database
TED database: 3 ISIS nodes 3 INET nodes
ID                            Type Age(s) LnkIn LnkOut Protocol
R1.00(10.0.0.1)                Rtr    239     1      1 IS-IS(2)
    To: R3.00(10.0.0.3), Local: 10.1.13.1, Remote: 10.1.13.2
ID                            Type Age(s) LnkIn LnkOut Protocol
                                                        OSPF(0.0.0.0)
    To: R3.00(10.0.0.3), Local: 10.1.13.1, Remote: 10.1.13.2
ID                            Type Age(s) LnkIn LnkOut Protocol
R3.00(10.0.0.3)                Rtr    468     2      2 IS-IS(2)
    To: R1.00(10.0.0.1), Local: 10.1.13.2, Remote: 10.1.13.1
    To: R6.00(10.0.0.6), Local: 10.1.36.1, Remote: 10.1.36.2
ID                            Type Age(s) LnkIn LnkOut Protocol
R6.00(10.0.0.6)                Rtr    431     1      1 IS-IS(2)
    To: R3.00(10.0.0.3), Local: 10.1.36.2, Remote: 10.1.36.1
```

This output shows three entries and that both IS-IS and OSPF are contributing to the TED database (listed in the Protocol column). All three entries were learned from routers (shown in the Type column). You see that R1 (the ingress router) has one link in and one link out, R2 (the transit router) has two links in either direction, and R3 (the egress router) has one link in and one out, which matches the LSP. The To: lines show the router IDs that correspond to the three routers in the LSP.

The extensive version of this command shows additional information about reservable and available bandwidth on networks links that IS-IS and OSPF have collected for use by CSPF:

```
aviva@R1> show ted database 10.0.0.1 extensive
TED database: 3 ISIS nodes 3 INET nodes
NodeID: R1.00(10.0.0.1)
  Type: Rtr, Age: 621 secs, LinkIn: 1, LinkOut: 1
  Protocol: IS-IS(2)
    To: R3.00(10.0.0.3), Local: 10.1.13.1, Remote: 10.1.13.2
      Color: 0 <none>
      Metric: 10
      Static BW: 155.52Mbps
      Reservable BW: 155.52Mbps
      Available BW [priority] bps:
          [0] 155.52Mbps   [1] 155.52Mbps   [2] 155.52Mbps   [3] 155.52Mbps
          [4] 155.52Mbps   [5] 155.52Mbps   [6] 155.52Mbps   [7] 155.52Mbps
      Interface Switching Capability Descriptor(1):
        Switching type: Packet
        Encoding type: Packet
        Maximum LSP BW [priority] bps:
          [0] 155.52Mbps   [1] 155.52Mbps   [2] 155.52Mbps   [3] 155.52Mbps
          [4] 155.52Mbps   [5] 155.52Mbps   [6] 155.52Mbps   [7] 155.52Mbps
  Protocol: OSPF(0.0.0.0)
    To: R3.00(10.0.0.3), Local: 10.1.13.1, Remote: 10.1.13.2
      Color: 0 <none>
      Metric: 1
      Static BW: 155.52Mbps
      Reservable BW: 155.52Mbps
      Available BW [priority] bps:
          [0] 155.52Mbps   [1] 155.52Mbps   [2] 155.52Mbps   [3] 155.52Mbps
          [4] 155.52Mbps   [5] 155.52Mbps   [6] 155.52Mbps   [7] 155.52Mbps
      Interface Switching Capability Descriptor(1):
        Switching type: Packet
        Encoding type: Packet
        Maximum LSP BW [priority] bps:
          [0] 155.52Mbps   [1] 155.52Mbps   [2] 155.52Mbps   [3] 155.52Mbps
          [4] 155.52Mbps   [5] 155.52Mbps   [6] 155.52Mbps   [7] 155.52Mbps
```

The last step in setting up the RSVP-signaled LSP is to create a return LSP from R6 to R1 on router R6:

```
[edit protocols mpls]
aviva@R6# set label-switched-path R6-to-R1 to 10.0.0.1
```

To confirm the configuration, use the show mpls lsp command on R6:

```
aviva@R6> show mpls lsp
Ingress LSP: 1 sessions
To              From            State Rt ActivePath       P    LSPname
10.0.0.1        10.0.0.6        Up    1                   *    R6-to-R1
Total 1 displayed, Up 1, Down 0

Egress LSP: 1 sessions
To              From            State  Rt Style Labelin Labelout LSPname
```

```
10.0.0.6        10.0.0.1        Up       0  1 FF     3          - R1-to-R6
Total 1 displayed, Up 1, Down 0
```

You see that R6 now has both an ingress and egress LSP session. R1, the router at the far end of the LSP, also has two similar LSP sessions, and R3, the router in the middle, has two transit sessions:

```
aviva@R3> show mpls lsp
Transit LSP: 2 sessions
To              From            State    Rt Style Labelin Labelout LSPname
10.0.0.1        10.0.0.6        Up       1  1 FF   103504         3 R6-to-R1
10.0.0.6        10.0.0.1        Up       1  1 FF   103488         3 R1-to-R6
Total 2 displayed, Up 2, Down 0
```

This output shows that R3 is using two different labels for the two LSPs, which is what you expect because the two traffic flows are separate.

Another way to verify that the RSVP-signaled LSP is up is to examine the RSVP session. Let's look at R1, the ingress router for the R1-to-R6 LSP:

```
aviva@R1> show rsvp session detail
Ingress RSVP: 1 sessions
10.0.0.6
  From: 10.0.0.1, LSPstate: Up, ActiveRoute: 1
  LSPname: R1-to-R6, LSPpath: Primary
  Suggested label received: -, Suggested label sent: -
  Recovery label received: -, Recovery label sent: 103536
  Resv style: 1 FF, Label in: -, Label out: 103536
  Time left:    -, Since: Tue Oct  4 14:36:13 2005
  Tspec: rate 0bps size 0bps peak Infbps m 20 M 1500
  Port number: sender 2 receiver 12077 protocol 0
  PATH rcvfrom: localclient
  Adspec: sent MTU 1500
  Path MTU: received 1500
  PATH sentto: 10.1.13.2 (so-0/0/2.0) 1886 pkts
  RESV rcvfrom: 10.1.13.2 (so-0/0/2.0) 1894 pkts
  Explct route: 10.1.13.2 10.1.36.2
  Record route: <self> 10.1.13.2 10.1.36.2
Total 1 displayed, Up 1, Down 0

Egress RSVP: 1 sessions
10.0.0.1
  From: 10.0.0.6, LSPstate: Up, ActiveRoute: 0
  LSPname: R6-to-R1, LSPpath: Primary
  Suggested label received: -, Suggested label sent: -
  Recovery label received: -, Recovery label sent: -
  Resv style: 1 FF, Label in: 3, Label out: -
  Time left: 119, Since: Tue Oct  4 14:35:46 2005
  Tspec: rate 0bps size 0bps peak Infbps m 20 M 1500
  Port number: sender 1 receiver 49792 protocol 0
  PATH rcvfrom: 10.1.13.2 (so-0/0/2.0) 1886 pkts
  Adspec: received MTU 1500
  PATH sentto: localclient
  RESV rcvfrom: localclient
  Record route: 10.1.36.2 10.1.13.2 <self>
Total 1 displayed, Up 1, Down 0
```

The ingress router now has two RSVP sessions. The first two lines of the output for each session confirm the head and tail ends of the RSVP sessions, the LSP pathname, and that the LSP is operational. For the first session, from 10.0.0.1 to 10.0.0.6, R1 is the ingress router and the output shows that RSVP is using label 103536 on outgoing packets. Check the transit router to confirm that it is receiving this label:

```
aviva@R3> show rsvp session detail name R1-to-R6
Transit LSP: 2 sessions
10.0.0.6
  From: 10.0.0.1, LSPstate: Up, ActiveRoute: 1
  LSPname: R1-to-R6, LSPpath: Primary
  Suggested label received: -, Suggested label sent: -
  Recovery label received: -, Recovery label sent: 3
  Resv style: 1 FF, Label in: 103536, Label out: 3
  Time left:  157, Since: Tue Oct  4 14:15:42 2005
  Tspec: rate 0bps size 0bps peak Infbps m 20 M 1500
  Port number: sender 2 receiver 12077 protocol 0
  PATH rcvfrom: 10.1.13.1 (so-0/0/2.0) 1904 pkts
  Adspec: received MTU 1500 sent MTU 1500
  PATH sentto: 10.1.36.2 (so-0/0/3.0) 1908 pkts
  RESV rcvfrom: 10.1.36.2 (so-0/0/3.0) 1904 pkts
  Explct route: 10.1.36.2
  Record route: 10.1.13.1 <self> 10.1.36.2
Total 1 displayed, Up 1, Down 0
```

Back to the output for R1, the Record route field shows the route being used for this session as reported in the RSVP RRO:

```
Record route: <self> 10.1.13.2 10.1.36.2
```

The RSVP session starts at <self>, which is the local router, then proceeds through 10.1.31.2 to the egress router at 10.1.36.2. This matches the LSP illustrated in Figure 14-6. The record route on the transit router shows the following:

```
Record route: 10.1.13.1 <self> 10.1.36.2
```

Here, the transit router, <self>, is placed between the ingress and egress routers, which again matches the network topology.

See Also

Recipes 14.7 and 14.14

14.7   Viewing Information About RSVP-Signaled LSPs in the Routing Tables

Problem

You want to check the routing tables to verify that an RSVP-signaled LSP has been established and is being used.

Solution

On the ingress router, look in the inet.3 routing table to view the RSVP routes:

```
aviva@R1> show route table inet.3
inet.3: 1 destinations, 1 routes (1 active, 0 holddown, 0 hidden)
+ = Active Route, - = Last Active, * = Both
10.0.0.6/32        *[RSVP/7] 00:17:28, metric 2
                    > via so-0/0/2.0, label-switched-path R1-to-R6
```

On the transit router, look in the mpls.0 table to see the router's label information:

```
aviva@R3> show route table mpls.0
mpls.0: 7 destinations, 7 routes (7 active, 0 holddown, 0 hidden)
+ = Active Route, - = Last Active, * = Both
0                  *[MPLS/0] 06:28:10, metric 1
                    Receive
1                  *[MPLS/0] 06:28:10, metric 1
                    Receive
2                  *[MPLS/0] 06:28:10, metric 1
                    Receive
100048             *[RSVP/7] 05:55:24, metric 1
                    > via so-0/0/2.0, label-switched-path R6-to-R1
100048(S=0)        *[RSVP/7] 05:55:24, metric 1
                    > via so-0/0/2.0, label-switched-path R6-to-R1
100064             *[RSVP/7] 00:18:59, metric 1
                    > via so-0/0/3.0, label-switched-path R1-to-R6
100064(S=0)        *[RSVP/7] 00:18:59, metric 1
                    > via so-0/0/3.0, label-switched-path R1-to-R6
```

Discussion

MPLS and RSVP store their routing and forwarding information in two routing tables, inet.3 and mpls.0. The inet.3 table contains the routers learned from the signaling protocol, RSVP (and also LDP), which MPLS uses to make forwarding decisions. The show route table inet.3 command lists the routes to RSVP-signaled LSP. You can also use the show route protocol rsvp command to display the same information:

```
aviva@R1> show route protocol rsvp
inet.0: 14 destinations, 18 routes (14 active, 0 holddown, 0 hidden)
inet.3: 1 destinations, 1 routes (1 active, 0 holddown, 0 hidden)
+ = Active Route, - = Last Active, * = Both
10.0.0.6/32        *[RSVP/7] 00:32:04, metric 2
                    > via so-0/0/2.0, label-switched-path R1-to-R6
```

The inet.0 unicast routing table doesn't contain any routes learned from RSVP, and the inet.3 table has one route, to 10.0.0.6, the LSP's egress router. The second line of the routing entry shows that the path to the egress router goes out the so-0/0/2 interface and travels along LSP R1-to-R6. The detail version of both show route commands gives more information about the route and LSP:

```
aviva@R1> show route table inet.3 detail
inet.3: 1 destinations, 1 routes (1 active, 0 holddown, 0 hidden)
10.0.0.6/32 (1 entry, 1 announced)
```

```
            State: <FlashAll>
*RSVP    Preference: 7
            Next-hop reference count: 7
            Next hop: via so-0/0/2.0 weight 0x1, selected
            Label-switched-path R1-to-R6
            Label operation: Push 100064
            State: <Active Int>
            Local AS: 65432
            Age: 23:52        Metric: 2
            Task: RSVP
            Announcement bits (2): 2-Resolve tree 1 3-Resolve tree 2
            AS path: I
```

The first highlighted line shows the name of the LSP, while the Label operation line shows the label operation performed by this route, here a push operation, and the label value that is placed into the MPLS header.

The inet.3 routing table is only on the ingress router because this is the only router that can place traffic into the LSP. This is important to remember when trouble-shooting RSVP-signaled LSPs, so you don't become confused when looking for routes on different routers. Checking the transit router confirms that the inet.3 table is not present:

```
aviva@R3> show route table inet.3
aviva@R3>
```

The second routing table used by RSVP is mpls.0, which stores the label bindings for the LSPs:

```
aviva@R3> show route table mpls.0
mpls.0: 7 destinations, 7 routes (7 active, 0 holddown, 0 hidden)
+ = Active Route, - = Last Active, * = Both
0                    *[MPLS/0] 06:50:42, metric 1
                        Receive
1                    *[MPLS/0] 06:50:42, metric 1
                        Receive
2                    *[MPLS/0] 06:50:42, metric 1
                        Receive
100048               *[RSVP/7] 06:17:56, metric 1
                        > via so-0/0/2.0, label-switched-path R6-to-R1
100048(S=0)          *[RSVP/7] 06:17:56, metric 1
                        > via so-0/0/2.0, label-switched-path R6-to-R1
100064               *[RSVP/7] 00:41:31, metric 1
                        > via so-0/0/3.0, label-switched-path R1-to-R6
100064(S=0)          *[RSVP/7] 00:41:31, metric 1
                        > via so-0/0/3.0, label-switched-path R1-to-R6
```

Recipe 14.3 explains how to interpret the entries in the mpls.0 table.

The JUNOS software maintains the mpls.0 table on all routers along the LSP, but only the table on the transit router contains information about the labels being used

---

for LSP signaling. On the egress and egress routers, the mpls.0 table lists only the reserved labels:

```
aviva@R1> show route table mpls.0
mpls.0: 3 destinations, 3 routes (3 active, 0 holddown, 0 hidden)
+ = Active Route, - = Last Active, * = Both
0                    *[MPLS/0] 07:01:51, metric 1
                        Receive
1                    *[MPLS/0] 07:01:51, metric 1
                        Receive
2                    *[MPLS/0] 07:01:51, metric 1
                        Receive
```

Again, this is important to remember when monitoring and troubleshooting LSPs.

Because BGP is also configured on the MPLS routers, when the BGP next hop is the same as the LSP egress address, the JUNOS default behavior uses the LSP for the BGP traffic. You see this in the routing-table entry:

```
aviva@R1> show route protocol bgp
inet.0: 14 destinations, 18 routes (14 active, 0 holddown, 0 hidden)
+ = Active Route, - = Last Active, * = Both
100.100.6.0/24     *[BGP/170] 4w6d 02:45:37, localpref 100, from 10.0.0.6
                      AS path: I
                    > via so-0/0/2.0, label-switched-path R1-to-R6
```

Here, the route to 100.100.6.0, learned by BGP, is the route over the R1-to-R6 LSP.

The JUNOS software installs the active routes from the inet.3 and mpls.0 table into the Routing Engine's forwarding table. On the ingress router, the IPv4 forwarding table includes the following routes:

```
aviva@R1> show route forwarding-table family inet
Routing table: inet
Internet:
Destination        Type RtRef Next hop          Type Index NhRef Netif
10.0.0.3/32        user    1                     ucst   330     6 so-0/0/2.0
10.0.0.6/32        user    1                     ucst   330     6 so-0/0/2.0
100.100.6.0/24     user    0                     indr 262142     2
                                                 Push 100064       so-0/0/2.0
```

The destinations to the transit and egress routers, 10.0.0.3 and 10.0.0.6, show up simply as unicast routes. The destination 100.100.6.0, learned from BGP and by using the LSP, shows as type indr (indirect) and you see the label (100064) and label operation (Push).

On the transit router, the MPLS forwarding table lists the labels used to forward the MPLS packets:

```
aviva@R3> show route forwarding-table family mpls
Routing table: mpls
MPLS:
Destination        Type RtRef Next hop          Type Index NhRef Netif
default            perm    0                     dscd    28     1
0                  user    0                     recv    27     3
```

```
1                    user      0              recv    27    3
2                    user      0              recv    27    3
100048               user      0              Pop           so-0/0/2.0
100048(S=0)          user      0              Pop           so-0/0/2.0
100064               user      0              Pop           so-0/0/3.0
100064(S=0)          user      0              Pop           so-0/0/3.0
```

These labels match what you see in the show route mpls.0 output on the transit router. These labels are installed into the Packet Forwarding Engine's forwarding table:

```
aviva@R3> show pfe route mpls
MPLS Route Table 0, MPLS.0, 0x0:
Destination                    Type     ID NhRef
---------------------- -------- ----- -----
default     Discard    28      1
0           Receive    27      3
1           Receive    27      3
2           Receive    27      3
100048      Unicast    336      1 so-0/0/2.0
100048(S=0)    Unicast    337       1 so-0/0/2.0
100064      Unicast    334      1 so-0/0/3.0
100064(S=0)    Unicast    335       1 so-0/0/3.0
```

On the ingress and egress routers, the output of the show route forwarding-table family mpls and show pfe route mpls commands on the ingress and egress route lists only the reserved labels.

See Also

Recipes 8.1 and 14.3

14.8 Verifying Packet Labels

Problem

After configuring an RSVP-signaled LSP, you want to verify which labels are being used when packets are forwarded along the LSP.

Solution

The easiest way to see all the labels being used as a packet traverses an LSP is to run the traceroute command on the ingress router:

```
aviva@R1> traceroute 100.100.6.0
traceroute to 100.100.6.0 (100.100.6.0), 30 hops max, 40 byte packets
 1   10.1.13.2 (10.1.13.2)  0.858 ms   0.751 ms   0.701 ms
     MPLS Label=103536 CoS=0 TTL=1 S=1
 2   10.1.36.2 (10.1.36.2)  0.598 ms !N  0.591 ms !N  0.554 ms !N
```

Discussion

There are several ways to find out which labels packets carry as they pass through the routers in an LSP. To see all the labels used by all the routers along the LSP with a single command, issue a traceroute command on the ingress router. Traceroute works when the inet.0 routing table has a route to the destination that has the LSP as the next hop. This recipe shows the output of this command. For the first hop (line 1), the second line shows the MPLS label value of 103536. It also shows the other value in the MPLS header. The CoS (experimental) bits are not set (they are 0), and the Stack bit is 1 because this is the last label in the stack.

The LSP in this recipe is short, so the traceroute output shows only the one label. Here's what the output looks like for a longer LSP:

```
aviva@R1> traceroute 100.100.6.1
traceroute to 100.100.6.1 (100.100.6.1), 30 hops max, 40 byte packets
 1  10.1.12.2 (10.1.12.2)  0.861 ms  0.718 ms  0.679 ms
    MPLS Label=100048 CoS=0 TTL=1 S=1
 2  10.1.24.2 (10.1.24.2)  0.822 ms  0.731 ms  0.708 ms
    MPLS Label=100016 CoS=0 TTL=1 S=1
 3  10.1.46.2 (10.1.46.2)  0.571 ms !N  0.547 ms !N  0.532 ms !N
```

The ingress router uses the label 100048 to reach the next hop in the LSP, and the first transit router replaces that label with 100016.

Other JUNOS commands show the labels used on individual routers or on adjacent routers; however, you need to log in to each router to use these commands. The show mpls lsp command on any router in an LSP shows the labels the router is receiving on incoming packets and using on outgoing packets. Here's an example from a transit router:

```
aviva@R3> show mpls lsp
Transit LSP: 2 sessions
To              From        State   Rt Style Labelin Labelout LSPname
10.0.0.1        10.0.0.6    Up      1  1 FF  100048        3 R6-to-R1
10.0.0.6        10.0.0.1    Up      1  1 FF  100064        3 R1-to-R6
Total 2 displayed, Up 2, Down 0
```

To verify that the LSP label operations are working properly, check the transit router's labels against those on the ingress and egress routers:

```
aviva@R1> show rsvp session
Ingress RSVP: 1 sessions
To              From        State   Rt Style Labelin Labelout LSPname
10.0.0.6        10.0.0.1    Up      1  1 FF        -  100064 R1-to-R6
Total 1 displayed, Up 1, Down 0

aviva@R6> show rsvp session
Ingress RSVP: 1 sessions
To              From        State   Rt Style Labelin Labelout LSPname
10.0.0.1        10.0.0.6    Up      1  1 FF        -  100048 R6-to-R1
Total 1 displayed, Up 1, Down 0
```

On R1, the router's outgoing label on LSP R1-to-R6 is 100064, which matches what the transit router is receiving. On R6, the outgoing label on the R6-to-R1 LSP is 100048, which matches the incoming label on the transit router.

The show mpls lsp detail command also lists the labels. The mpls.0 routing table on the transit routers also lists the labels for the LSPs:

```
aviva@R3> show route table mpls.0
mpls.0: 7 destinations, 7 routes (7 active, 0 holddown, 0 hidden)
+ = Active Route, - = Last Active, * = Both
0                      *[MPLS/0] 00:48:54, metric 1
                         Receive
1                      *[MPLS/0] 00:48:54, metric 1
                         Receive
2                      *[MPLS/0] 00:48:54, metric 1
                         Receive
100032                 *[RSVP/7] 00:16:43, metric 1
                       > via so-0/0/3.0, label-switched-path R1-to-R6
100032(S=0)            *[RSVP/7] 00:16:43, metric 1
                       > via so-0/0/3.0, label-switched-path R1-to-R6
100048                 *[RSVP/7] 00:16:08, metric 1
                       > via so-0/0/2.0, label-switched-path R6-to-R1
100048(S=0)            *[RSVP/7] 00:16:08, metric 1
                       > via so-0/0/2.0, label-switched-path R6-to-R1
```

To verify correct forwarding along the LSP, ping the egress router from the ingress router. For this to work, you need to configure a loopback address of 127.0.0.1 on the egress router:

```
[edit]
aviva@R6# set interfaces lo0 unit 0 family inet address 127.0.0.1/32
```

The egress router uses this address to send echo replies to echo requests sent by the ping command. You then send an MPLS ping request from the ingress router along the LSP:

```
aviva@R1> ping mpls rsvp R1-to-R6
!!!!!
--- lsping statistics ---
5 packets transmitted, 5 packets received, 0% packet loss
```

The ping echo replies include the label that the ingress router added to the packet when putting it into the LSP. The ping mpls command uses port 3503 for MPLS echo requests instead of UDP port 7, which is used by the standard ping command.

14.9 Verifying that the RSVP-Signaled LSP Is Carrying Traffic

Problem

You want to know that traffic is actually using an RSVP-signaled LSP that you've configured.

Solution

Look at the LSP traffic statistics:

```
aviva@R3> show mpls lsp statistics transit
Transit LSP: 2 sessions
To              From            State     Packets          Bytes LSPname
10.0.0.1        10.0.0.6        Up             0              0 R6-to-R1
10.0.0.6        10.0.0.1        Up            25           2400 R1-to-R6
Total 2 displayed, Up 2, Down 0
```

Discussion

To make sure that traffic is using the LSP, look at the traffic statistics. This recipe shows the show mpls lsp statistics commands. You can also use the show rsvp session statistics command to get the same output.

The Packets column shows the number of packets that have followed a particular LSP, and the Bytes column gives the total byte count of all the packets. In this recipe, LSP R1-to-R6 has carried 25 packets, for a total of 2,400 bytes.

14.10 Configuring RSVP Authentication

Problem

You want to verify that all RSVP traffic that the router accepts comes from trusted routers to ensure the security of the LSP and the data it carries.

Solution

Configure MD5 authentication for each interface running RSVP:

```
[edit protocols rsvp]
aviva@R1# set interface so-0/0/2 authentication-key 1991$poPPi
aviva@R1# show
interface so-0/0/2.0 {
    authentication-key "$9$GoDqm5QF/ApTQSrKMXxqmPfn/"; ## SECRET-DATA
}
```

Discussion

It is a good security measure to authenticate RSVP exchanges to ensure that only trusted routers participate in the LSP. This recipe shows how to configure RSVP authentication. You configure a key for each interface on the router that is running RSVP. MD5 creates an encoded checksum that is included in all transmitted RSVP packets. The receiving router verifies this checksum before accepting the packet.

Use the following command to check that RSVP authentication is configured:

```
aviva@R1> show rsvp interface detail
RSVP interface: 1 active
so-0/0/2.0 Index 69, State Ena/Up
  Authentication, NoAggregate, NoReliable, NoLinkProtection
  HelloInterval 9(second)
  Address 10.1.13.1, 10.0.0.1
  ActiveResv 1, PreemptionCnt 0, Update threshold 10%
  Subscription 100%, StaticBW 155.52Mbps, AvailableBW 155.52Mbps
  ReservedBW [0] 0bps[1] 0bps[2] 0bps[3] 0bps[4] 0bps[5] 0bps[6] 0bps[7] 0bps
  PacketType              Total                  Last 5 seconds
                    Sent      Received       Sent      Received
  Path              1588          35            0            0
  PathErr              0           0            0            0
  PathTear             3           1            0            0
  Resv                34        1586            0            0
  ResvErr              0           0            0            0
  ResvTear             0           0            0            0
  Hello             8526        8527            1            1
  Ack                  0           0            0            0
  Srefresh             0           0            0            0
  EndtoEnd RSVP        0           0            0            0
```

Configure the same authentication key on all interfaces participating in the LSP. If you do not configure the same password, the LSP cannot be established and is marked as Dn (down) in the show mpls lsp command output:

```
aviva@R1> show mpls lsp
Ingress LSP: 1 sessions
To              From            State Rt ActivePath      P      LSPname
10.0.0.6        10.0.0.1        Dn     0 -                      R1-to-R6
Total 1 displayed, Up 0, Down 1
```

This LSP is not operating because authentication is not configured on R6, the egress router:

```
aviva@R6> show rsvp interface detail
RSVP interface: 1 active
so-0/0/3.0 Index 66, State Ena/Up
  NoAuthentication, NoAggregate, NoReliable, NoLinkProtection
  HelloInterval 9(second)
  Address 10.1.36.2, 10.0.0.6
  ActiveResv 0, PreemptionCnt 0, Update threshold 10%
  Subscription 100%, StaticBW 155.52Mbps, AvailableBW 155.52Mbps
  ReservedBW [0] 0bps[1] 0bps[2] 0bps[3] 0bps[4] 0bps[5] 0bps[6] 0bps[7] 0bps
```

14.11 Protecting an LSP's Path

Problem

You want to protect an LSP's traffic in the event of a link or router failure to ensure that it always arrives at the egress end of the LSP.

Solution

When you create an LSP, RSVP establishes a single path between the ingress and egress routers. One way to protect the LSP's path is to establish an end-to-end secondary path for the LSP. First, explicitly set up the primary LSP:

```
[edit protocols mpls]
aviva@R1# set label-switched-path R1-to-R5 to 10.0.0.5
aviva@R1# set label-switched-path R1-to-R5 bandwidth 50m
aviva@R1# set label-switched-path R1-to-R5 primary primary-path-R1-to-R5
aviva@R1# set path primary-path-R1-to-R5
```

Then, configure a secondary path to the same egress router:

```
[edit protocols mpls]
aviva@R1# set label-switched-path R1-to-R5 secondary secondary-path-R1-to-R5 standby
aviva@R1# set path secondary-path-R1-to-R5
```

Discussion

When you create a basic LSP on the ingress router, one route is set up to reach the egress router and all the LSP's traffic is forwarded along this route. If a failure occurs along the path—for instance, if a router's interface goes offline, if an entire router goes down, or if the physical link between two routers is cut—the ingress router recalculates the LSP's path and re-establishes the LSP if possible. However, until the ingress route learns of the LSP failure and recalculates a new LSP, all traffic going into the LSP is dropped and never reaches the egress. Depending on the length of the LSP, the speeds of the interfaces, and other factors, it can take some seconds for the new LSP to become operational. One way to provide a redundant path is to set up a secondary path in advance and have it always be on call in case the primary path fails so that it can immediately take over forwarding the LSP's traffic. An optimal secondary LSP takes a completely different path through the network so that there are no common links or routers shared by the two LSPs. For this recipe, the network topology is extended to six routers (see Figure 14-7).

The first part of this recipe sets up the primary path on the ingress router, R1. The first command names the LSP and specifies the address of the egress router, R5. The second command reserves bandwidth for the LSP, here requesting 50 Mbps. The third command creates the primary LSP and names it `primary-path-R1-to-R5`. The final command, the set path command, tells MPLS about the name of the path.

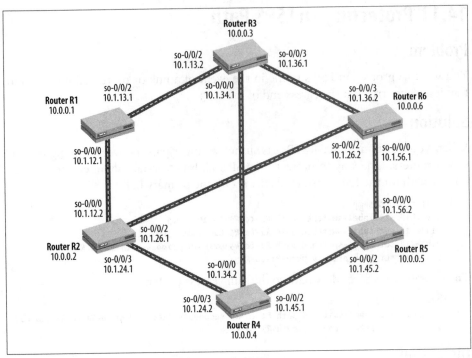

Figure 14-7. Six-router topology for RSVP-signaled LSPs

At this point in the configuration, you can verify that the primary path has been established:

```
aviva@R1> show mpls lsp ingress extensive
Ingress LSP: 1 sessions
10.0.0.5
  From: 10.0.0.1, State: Up, ActiveRoute: 0, LSPname: R1-to-R5
  ActivePath: primary-path-R1-to-R5 (primary)
  LoadBalance: Random
  Encoding type: Packet, Switching type: Packet, GPID: IPv4
 *Primary   primary-path-R1-to-R5 State: Up
    Bandwidth: 50Mbps
    SmartOptimizeTimer: 180
    Received RRO (ProtectionFlag 1=Available 2=InUse 4=B/W 8=Node 10=SoftPreempt):
          10.1.13.2 10.1.34.2 10.1.45.2
    5 Oct  7 09:15:34 Selected as active path
    4 Oct  7 09:15:34 Record Route:  10.1.13.2 10.1.34.2 10.1.45.2
    3 Oct  7 09:15:34 Up
    2 Oct  7 09:15:34 Originate Call
    1 Oct  7 09:15:05 Path name undefined or disabled[3 times]
   Created: Fri Oct  7 09:14:36 2005
  Total 1 displayed, Up 1, Down 0
```

This output shows that the LSP to 10.0.0.5, the egress router, is up (State: Up) and is the primary path to the egress router. The Bandwidth field indicates that the requested bandwidth reservation of 50 Mbps has been honored and allocated. The

RSVP RRO in the path calculation log (line 4 in the log) contains the path being followed by the primary LSP. This LSP goes first to R3 (10.1.31.2) and then to R4 (10.1.34.2) before reaching the egress at R5 (10.1.45.2). The following command shows that RSVP has reserved the bandwidth:

```
aviva@R1> show rsvp interface
RSVP interface: 2 active
                 Active Subscr- Static     Available  Reserved  Highwater
Interface  State resv  iption BW          BW         BW        mark
so-0/0/0.0 Up        0   100%  155.52Mbps  155.52Mbps 0bps      0bps
so-0/0/2.0 Up        1   100%  155.52Mbps  105.52Mbps 50Mbps    50Mbps
```

For interface so-0/0/2, which connects to R3, the first router in the LSP, the output shows that 50 Mbps have been reserved and 105.52 Mbps are still available.

Next in the configuration is to set up a secondary path. There are two commands for this. The first command creates the secondary path in the LSP, and the second defines the path for MPLS. This recipe uses the standby option in the secondary path so the path is established when the primary path is set up and remains up at all times. This means that the secondary path is always available to take over immediately if the primary path fails. The result is that no traffic is dropped during the time it takes for CSPF to calculate a new route and RSVP to signal a new path.

Look at the LSP again to check that the secondary path has been set up. A quick glance shows two RSVP sessions for the R1-to-R5 LSP:

```
aviva@R1> show rsvp session ingress
Ingress RSVP: 2 sessions
To               From           State  Rt Style Labelin Labelout LSPname
10.0.0.5         10.0.0.1       Up     0  1 FF          -  100144 R1-to-R5
10.0.0.5         10.0.0.1       Up     0  1 FF          -  100160 R1-to-R5
Total 2 displayed, Up 2, Down 0
```

A detailed look at the LSP shows more information about the two paths:

```
aviva@R1> show mpls lsp ingress extensive
Ingress LSP: 1 sessions
10.0.0.5
  From: 10.0.0.1, State: Up, ActiveRoute: 0, LSPname: R1-to-R5
  ActivePath: primary-path-R1-to-R5 (primary)
  LoadBalance: Random
  Encoding type: Packet, Switching type: Packet, GPID: IPv4
 *Primary   primary-path-R1-to-R5 State: Up
    Bandwidth: 50Mbps
    SmartOptimizeTimer: 180
    Received RRO (ProtectionFlag 1=Available 2=InUse 4=B/W 8=Node 10=SoftPreempt):
          10.1.13.2 10.1.34.2 10.1.45.2
    5 Oct  7 09:15:34 Selected as active path
    4 Oct  7 09:15:34 Record Route:  10.1.13.2 10.1.34.2 10.1.45.2
    3 Oct  7 09:15:34 Up
    2 Oct  7 09:15:34 Originate Call
    1 Oct  7 09:15:05 Path name undefined or disabled[3 times]
  Standby   secondary-path-R1-to-R5 State: Up
```

```
        Bandwidth: 50Mbps
        SmartOptimizeTimer: 180
        Received RRO (ProtectionFlag 1=Available 2=InUse 4=B/W 8=Node 10=SoftPreempt):
              10.1.13.2 10.1.36.2 10.1.56.1
          3 Oct  7 09:26:07 Record Route:  10.1.12.2 10.1.24.2 10.1.45.2
          2 Oct  7 09:26:07 Up
          1 Oct  7 09:26:07 Originate Call
        Created: Fri Oct  7 09:14:37 2005
       Total 1 displayed, Up 1, Down 0
```

In addition to the primary path, the LSP now has the secondary, standby path, which is up and for which 50 Mbps of bandwidth have been reserved. Check RSVP again to verify the bandwidth reservation:

```
aviva@R1> show rsvp interface
RSVP interface: 2 active
                  Active Subscr- Static      Available  Reserved  Highwater
Interface  State resv    iption  BW          BW         BW        mark
so-0/0/0.0 Up        1   100%    155.52Mbps  105.52Mbps 50Mbps    50Mbps
so-0/0/2.0 Up        1   100%    155.52Mbps  105.52Mbps 50Mbps    100Mbps
```

The output shows that RSVP has reserved 50 Mbps for the secondary LSP on the router's other interface, so-0/0/0.

The difference between the primary and secondary paths is the path itself. The Record Route fields, which contain the information in the RSVP RRO, show the two paths. The primary path goes along 10.1.13.2 to R3, then along 10.1.34.2 to R4, and finally along 10.1.45.2 to reach the egress router, R5:

```
   4 Oct  7 09:15:34 Record Route:  10.1.13.2 10.1.34.2 10.1.45.2
```

The secondary path goes out 10.0.12.1 to R2, then along 10.1.24.2 to R4 to reach R5:

```
   3 Oct  7 09:26:07 Record Route:  10.1.12.2 10.1.24.2 10.1.45.2
```

The two paths from R1 to R5 are completely separate and nonoverlapping, so the secondary path provides nonredundant backup in case the primary LSP fails. Because the LSP is being signaled and set up automatically, the secondary path might share routers with the primary path. However, the JUNOS CSPF calculation tries to ensure that the primary and secondary paths do not overlap where possible; the calculation of the secondary path by CSPF takes the path of the primary into account. Let's look at an example where this happens. First, look at the interfaces on which RSVP has reserved bandwidth:

```
aviva@R1> show rsvp interface
RSVP interface: 2 active
                  Active Subscr- Static      Available  Reserved  Highwater
Interface  State resv    iption  BW          BW         BW        mark
so-0/0/0.0 Up        0   100%    155.52Mbps  155.52Mbps 0bps      50Mbps
so-0/0/2.0 Up        2   100%    155.52Mbps  55.52Mbps  100Mbps   100Mbps
```

The configuration allocates 50 Mbps for the primary path, and this output shows that RSVP has set aside 100 Mbps on a single interface, so-0/0/2, so you know that both the primary and secondary LSPs are being routed toward R3. To check this, look at the LSP's record route:

```
aviva@R1> show mpls lsp ingress extensive
Ingress LSP: 1 sessions
10.0.0.5
  From: 10.0.0.1, State: Up, ActiveRoute: 0, LSPname: R1-to-R5
  ActivePath: primary-path-R1-to-R5 (primary)
  LoadBalance: Random
  Encoding type: Packet, Switching type: Packet, GPID: IPv4
 *Primary    primary-path-R1-to-R5 State: Up
    Bandwidth: 50Mbps
    SmartOptimizeTimer: 180
    Received RRO (ProtectionFlag 1=Available 2=InUse 4=B/W 8=Node 10=SoftPreempt):
        10.1.13.2 10.1.34.2 10.1.45.2
   22 Oct 12 14:53:24 Selected as active path
   21 Oct 12 14:53:24 Record Route:   10.1.13.2 10.1.34.2 10.1.45.2
   20 Oct 12 14:53:24 Up
   19 Oct 12 14:53:24 Originate Call
  ...
  Standby   secondary-path-R1-to-R5 State: Up
    Bandwidth: 50Mbps
    SmartOptimizeTimer: 180
    Received RRO (ProtectionFlag 1=Available 2=InUse 4=B/W 8=Node 10=SoftPreempt):
        10.1.13.2 10.1.36.2 10.1.56.1
   35 Oct 12 14:55:56 Record Route:   10.1.13.2 10.1.36.2 10.1.56.1
   34 Oct 12 14:55:56 Up
   33 Oct 12 14:55:55 Originate Call
  ...
Total 1 displayed, Up 1, Down 0
```

This output confirms that RSVP has routed both the primary and secondary LSPs through R3 (10.1.13.2). You can force one of the LSPs to go through R2 instead by manually configuring the LSP's next hop. The following command explicitly configures the first next hop for the secondary LSP:

```
[edit protocols mpls]
aviva@R1# set path secondary-path-R1-to-R5 10.1.12.2
```

Checking the RSVP bandwidth reservation confirms the change:

```
aviva@R1> show rsvp interface
RSVP interface: 2 active
                     Active Subscr- Static      Available   Reserved   Highwater
Interface   State resv iption  BW          BW          BW         mark
so-0/0/0.0  Up       1    100%  155.52Mbps  105.52Mbps  50Mbps     50Mbps
so-0/0/2.0  Up       1    100%  155.52Mbps  105.52Mbps  50Mbps     100Mbps
```

RSVP has reserved 50 Mbps on each of the two outgoing interfaces. Looking at the LSP paths shows that the two paths are indeed different:

```
aviva@R1> show mpls lsp ingress extensive
Ingress LSP: 1 sessions
10.0.0.5
```

```
From: 10.0.0.1, State: Up, ActiveRoute: 0, LSPname: R1-to-R5
ActivePath: primary-path-R1-to-R5 (primary)
LoadBalance: Random
Encoding type: Packet, Switching type: Packet, GPID: IPv4
 *Primary    primary-path-R1-to-R5 State: Up
   Bandwidth: 50Mbps
   SmartOptimizeTimer: 180
   Received RRO (ProtectionFlag 1=Available 2=InUse 4=B/W 8=Node 10=SoftPreempt):
         10.1.13.2 10.1.34.2 10.1.45.2
  22 Oct 12 14:53:24 Selected as active path
  21 Oct 12 14:53:24 Record Route:  10.1.13.2 10.1.34.2 10.1.45.2
  20 Oct 12 14:53:24 Up
  19 Oct 12 14:53:24 Originate Call
 ...
   Standby   secondary-path-R1-to-R5 State: Up
   Bandwidth: 50Mbps
   SmartOptimizeTimer: 180
   Received RRO (ProtectionFlag 1=Available 2=InUse 4=B/W 8=Node 10=SoftPreempt):
         10.1.12.2 10.1.24.2 10.1.45.2
  39 Oct 12 15:07:10 Record Route:  10.1.12.2 10.1.24.2 10.1.45.2
  38 Oct 12 15:07:10 Up
  37 Oct 12 15:07:10 Originate Call
  36 Oct 12 15:07:10 Clear Call
 ...
Total 1 displayed, Up 1,
```

The show rsvp interface output illustrates an important point about secondary paths, which is that the secondary path inherits the same properties as the primary path. In the output, you see that RSVP has reserved the same amount of bandwidth (50 Mbps) for both the secondary and primary paths, so 100 Mbps total are reserved for the primary and secondary LSPs. This points out one of the drawbacks of having a secondary LSP that is on standby. Even though the secondary path is used only rarely, bandwidth resources must always be set aside for it so that the secondary path is always available. If your network's link resources are constrained in any way, you should consider different methods of protecting LSPs, such as fast reroute (see Recipe 14.12) and autobandwidth (see Recipe 14.13).

When setting up secondary paths, be careful not to overallocate resources accidentally. For the SONET link in this example, if you set aside 80 Mbps for the primary LSP, RSVP can establish the LSP just fine:

```
[edit protocols mpls]
aviva@R1# set label-switched-path R1-to-R5 bandwidth 80m
aviva@R1# commit and-quit
commit complete
Exiting configuration mode
aviva@R1> show rsvp interface
RSVP interface: 2 active
                    Active Subscr- Static      Available   Reserved   Highwater
Interface   State  resv  iption  BW          BW          BW         mark
so-0/0/0.0  Up        0   100%  155.52Mbps  155.52Mbps  0bps       0bps
so-0/0/2.0  Up        1   100%  155.52Mbps  75.52Mbps   80Mbps     100Mbps
```

However, RSVP cannot establish the secondary LSP:

```
aviva@R1> show mpls lsp ingress extensive
Ingress LSP: 1 sessions
10.0.0.5
  From: 10.0.0.1, State: Up, ActiveRoute: 0, LSPname: R1-to-R5
  ActivePath: primary-path-R1-to-R5 (primary)
  LoadBalance: Random
  Encoding type: Packet, Switching type: Packet, GPID: IPv4
 *Primary    primary-path-R1-to-R5 State: Up
    Bandwidth: 80Mbps
    SmartOptimizeTimer: 180
    Received RRO (ProtectionFlag 1=Available 2=InUse 4=B/W 8=Node 10=SoftPreempt):
          10.1.13.2 10.1.36.2 10.1.56.1
    9 Oct  7 09:32:15 Record Route:  10.1.13.2 10.1.36.2 10.1.56.1
    8 Oct  7 09:32:15 Up
    7 Oct  7 09:32:15 Originate Call
    6 Oct  7 09:32:15 Clear Call
    5 Oct  7 09:15:34 Selected as active path
    4 Oct  7 09:15:34 Record Route:  10.1.13.2 10.1.34.2 10.1.45.2
    3 Oct  7 09:15:34 Up
    2 Oct  7 09:15:34 Originate Call
    1 Oct  7 09:15:05 Path name undefined or disabled[3 times]
  Standby    secondary-path-R1-to-R5 State: Dn
    Bandwidth: 80Mbps
    SmartOptimizeTimer: 180
    6 Oct  7 09:33:18 Requested bandwidth unavailable[14 times]
    5 Oct  7 09:32:15 Originate Call
    4 Oct  7 09:32:15 Clear Call
    3 Oct  7 09:26:07 Record Route:  10.1.13.2 10.1.36.2 10.1.56.1
    2 Oct  7 09:26:07 Up
    1 Oct  7 09:26:07 Originate Call
  Created: Fri Oct  7 09:14:36 2005
Total 1 displayed, Up 1, Down 0
```

This output shows that the secondary path is down because of insufficient bandwidth on the link. The interface has 155.52 Mbps total bandwidth, but the two LSPs need 160 Mbps. To not have RSVP double-count the bandwidth, you can make the secondary LSP *adaptive*:

```
[edit protocols mpls]
aviva@R1# set label-switched-path R1-to-R5 adaptive
```

In adaptive mode, the bandwidth reservation for the secondary path is shared with that for the primary path, so RSVP is now able to establish the secondary LSP. Checking the LSP again:

```
aviva@R1> show mpls lsp ingress extensive
Ingress LSP: 1 sessions
10.0.0.5
  From: 10.0.0.1, State: Up, ActiveRoute: 0, LSPname: R1-to-R5
  ActivePath: primary-path-R1-to-R5 (primary)
  LoadBalance: Random
  Encoding type: Packet, Switching type: Packet, GPID: IPv4
```

```
*Primary    primary-path-R1-to-R5 State: Up
    Bandwidth: 80Mbps
    SmartOptimizeTimer: 180
    Received RRO (ProtectionFlag 1=Available 2=InUse 4=B/W 8=Node 10=SoftPreempt):
          10.1.13.2 10.1.36.2 10.1.56.1
    4 Oct   7 09:34:29 Selected as active path
    3 Oct   7 09:34:29 Record Route:  10.1.13.2 10.1.36.2 10.1.56.1
    2 Oct   7 09:34:29 Up
    1 Oct   7 09:34:28 Originate Call
 Standby    secondary-path-R1-to-R5 State: Up
    Bandwidth: 80Mbps
    SmartOptimizeTimer: 180
    Received RRO (ProtectionFlag 1=Available 2=InUse 4=B/W 8=Node 10=SoftPreempt):
          10.1.13.2 10.1.36.2 10.1.56.1
    3 Oct   7 09:34:57 Record Route:  10.1.13.2 10.1.36.2 10.1.56.1
    2 Oct   7 09:34:57 Up
    1 Oct   7 09:34:57 Originate Call
  Created: Fri Oct  7 09:34:28 2005
Total 1 displayed, Up 1, Down 0
```

The output verifies that the secondary LSP has been established.

Another option is not to reserve bandwidth at all for the secondary path, which gives protection but without any guarantees.

In addition to needing to reserve bandwidth for rarely used secondary paths, secondary LSPs have two other disadvantages that may cause you to consider using different protection methods. One is that this configuration creates a single secondary standby for each protected path. If both paths fail, the desired protection is not provided. Although you can create more than one secondary path, you are again faced with the problem of reserving bandwidth for several rarely used paths. A second disadvantage is that the secondary LSP takes effect only when the ingress router learns of the failure in the path, so some traffic in the LSP will be lost. Methods such as fast reroute kick in when routers along the LSP learn of a failure, resulting in less loss of traffic.

See Also

Recipes 14.12 and 14.13

14.12 Using Fast Reroute to Reduce Packet Loss Following a Link Failure

Problem

You want to reduce packet loss when a link along an LSP fails.

Solution

Fast reroute reduces packet loss when a link in the LSP fails. You configure fast reroute on the ingress router only:

```
[edit protocols mpls]
aviva@R1# set label-switched-path R1-to-R5 to 10.0.0.5
aviva@R1# set label-switched-path R1-to-R5 fast-reroute
```

Discussion

A basic function of IP routing protocols is to reroute traffic changes that occur in the network, such as a link or router node failure. Because the IP routing protocols are distributed across the network devices and because all routers must have a consistent view of the network, it can take some time for the routes to converge after a topology change. In a large network, convergence times can be on the order of several seconds, which may be unacceptable for your service-level agreements (SLAs).

MPLS fast reroute provides a solution to the convergence problem by rerouting traffic around a point of failure in an LSP. Fast reroute sets up a *protection LSP* around a point of failure in advance to protect an individual link between two routers. Each router in the LSP sets up protection LSPs when the ingress router signals the initial setup of the LSP. When a link along an LSP fails, the router upstream of the failure switches to the protection LSP as soon as it detects the failure. No route calculations need to be done because the protection LSP is signaled and set up in advance, and the routing protocols don't need to converge, so the move to a path that circumvents the point of failure can happen quickly. Following a failure, the ingress router is notified and can compute a new path at its leisure. Traffic is protected in the meantime.

Fast reroute does not eliminate packet loss; it merely minimizes it. When a path fails and MPLS switches to the protection LSP, the MPLS routers still need some small amount of time to detect the failure and switch to the alternate path. The ingress router can then recalculate the LSP if necessary. During the switchover, the LSP will continue forwarding traffic while a new LSP is established.

You configure fast reroute only on the ingress router. You do not need to configure it on the LSP's transit and egress routers. As this recipe shows, the configuration is straightforward: just include the fast-reroute statement in the LSP's configuration. Once the LPS is running fast reroute, the ingress router signals all downstream routers that fast reroute has been requested and indicate which link requires protection, and each downstream router does its best to set up detours for the LSP. If a downstream router does not support fast reroute, it ignores the request to set up detours but continues to support the LSP. A router that does not support fast reroute will cause some of the detours to fail but otherwise has no impact on the LSP.

To check that fast reroute is configured and working properly, first verify that the ingress router has created an operational LSP:

```
aviva@R1> show mpls lsp ingress extensive
Ingress LSP: 1 sessions
10.0.0.5
  From: 10.0.0.1, State: Up, ActiveRoute: 0, LSPname: R1-to-R5
  ActivePath: primary-path-R1-to-R5 (primary)
  FastReroute desired
  LoadBalance: Random
  Encoding type: Packet, Switching type: Packet, GPID: IPv4
 *Primary    primary-path-R1-to-R5 State: Up
    SmartOptimizeTimer: 180
    Computed ERO (S [L] denotes strict [loose] hops): (CSPF metric: 30)
  10.1.13.2 S 10.1.36.2 S 10.1.56.1 S
    Received RRO (ProtectionFlag 1=Available 2=InUse 4=B/W 8=Node 10=SoftPreempt):
        10.1.13.2(flag=9) 10.1.36.2(flag=1) 10.1.56.1
    8 Oct 12 15:15:31 Fast-reroute Detour Up
    7 Oct 12 15:15:22 Record Route:  10.1.13.2(flag=9) 10.1.36.2(flag=1) 10.1.56.1
    6 Oct 12 15:15:22 Record Route:  10.1.13.2(flag=9) 10.1.36.2 10.1.56.1
    5 Oct 12 15:15:19 Selected as active path
    4 Oct 12 15:15:19 Record Route:  10.1.13.2 10.1.36.2 10.1.56.1
    3 Oct 12 15:15:18 Up
    2 Oct 12 15:15:18 Originate Call
    1 Oct 12 15:15:18 CSPF: computation result accepted
  Created: Wed Oct 12 15:15:18 2005
 Total 1 displayed, Up 1, Down 0
```

This output shows the details of the LSP on the ingress router, R1. The LSP goes to 10.0.0.5 from 10.0.0.1, which is correct, and the state is Up, so the LSP is operational. The line FastReroute desired tells you that the ingress router has signaled the routers that might participate in the LSP to use fast reroute. This indicates that the fast reroute configuration has taken effect. Line 8 in the LSP log for the LSP indicates that a fast reroute detour has been set up. The Record Route for the LSP shows that the LSP is routed through R3 (10.1.13.2) and R6 (10.1.36.2).

Looking at the RSVP session shows more information about the detour:

```
aviva@R1> show rsvp session ingress detail
Ingress RSVP: 1 sessions
10.0.0.5
  From: 10.0.0.1, LSPstate: Up, ActiveRoute: 0
  LSPname: R1-to-R5, LSPpath: Primary
  Suggested label received: -, Suggested label sent: -
  Recovery label received: -, Recovery label sent: 100480
  Resv style: 1 FF, Label in: -, Label out: 100480
  Time left:    -, Since: Mon Oct 10 13:15:17 2005
  Tspec: rate 0bps size 0bps peak Infbps m 20 M 1500
  Port number: sender 1 receiver 39233 protocol 0
  FastReroute desired
  PATH rcvfrom: localclient
  Adspec: sent MTU 1500
  Path MTU: received 1500
```

```
    PATH sentto: 10.1.13.2 (so-0/0/2.0) 12 pkts
    RESV rcvfrom: 10.1.13.2 (so-0/0/2.0) 9 pkts
    Explct route: 10.1.13.2 10.1.36.2 10.1.56.1
    Record route: <self> 10.1.13.2 10.1.36.2 10.1.56.1
      Detour is Up
      Detour Tspec: rate 0bps size 0bps peak Infbps m 20 M 1500
      Detour adspec: sent MTU 1500
      Path MTU: received 1500
      Detour PATH sentto: 10.1.12.2 (so-0/0/0.0) 8 pkts
      Detour RESV rcvfrom: 10.1.12.2 (so-0/0/0.0) 4 pkts
      Detour Explct route: 10.1.12.2 10.1.26.2 10.1.56.1
      Detour Record route: <self> 10.1.12.2 10.1.26.2 10.1.56.1
      Detour Label out: 100192
Total 1 displayed, Up 1, Down 0
```

The record route shows the primary path of the LSP, from R1 out interface so-0/0/2, to R3, then to R5 and ending at R6 (10.1.56.1). The Detour Record route shows the detour path, from R1 out a different interface, so-0/0/0, to R2 (10.1.12.1), then to R4 (10.1.26.2), and finally to R6. This detour goes around R3, providing protection if the link between R1 and R3 fails or if R3 itself fails.

Next, look on the transit routers to make sure they are aware of the detour. First, look at Router R3, which is the first router in the primary path:

```
aviva@R3> show rsvp session transit detail
Transit RSVP: 1 sessions
10.0.0.5
  From: 10.0.0.1, LSPstate: Up, ActiveRoute: 1
  LSPname: R1-to-R5, LSPpath: Primary
  Suggested label received: -, Suggested label sent: -
  Recovery label received: -, Recovery label sent: 100112
  Resv style: 1 FF, Label in: 100480, Label out: 100112
  Time left:   119, Since: Mon Oct 10 13:09:14 2005
  Tspec: rate 0bps size 0bps peak Infbps m 20 M 1500
  Port number: sender 1 receiver 39233 protocol 0
  FastReroute desired
  PATH rcvfrom: 10.1.13.1 (so-0/0/2.0) 18 pkts
  Adspec: received MTU 1500 sent MTU 1500
  PATH sentto: 10.1.36.2 (so-0/0/3.0) 15 pkts
  RESV rcvfrom: 10.1.36.2 (so-0/0/3.0) 15 pkts
  Explct route: 10.1.36.2 10.1.56.1
  Record route: 10.1.13.1 <self> 10.1.36.2 10.1.56.1
    Detour is Up
    Detour Tspec: rate 0bps size 0bps peak Infbps m 20 M 1500
    Detour adspec: received MTU 1500 sent MTU 1500
    Path MTU: received 1500
    Detour PATH sentto: 10.1.34.2 (so-0/0/0.0) 14 pkts
    Detour RESV rcvfrom: 10.1.34.2 (so-0/0/0.0) 10 pkts
    Detour Explct route: 10.1.34.2 10.1.45.2
    Detour Record route: 10.1.13.1 <self> 10.1.34.2 10.1.45.2
    Detour Label out: 100160
Total 1 displayed, Up 1, Down 0
```

Router R3's record route for the primary R1-to-R5 LSP shows:

```
Record route: 10.1.13.1 <self> 10.1.36.2 10.1.56.1
```

This matches the record route on the ingress router:

```
Record route: <self> 10.1.13.2 10.1.36.2 10.1.56.1
```

The only difference here is that for R3, <self> is between 10.1.13.1 and 10.1.36.2, while for R1, <self> is at the beginning of the path, before 10.1.13.2. Next, look at the detour that R3 has set up:

```
Detour Record route: 10.1.13.1 <self> 10.1.34.2 10.1.45.2
```

This detour protects the downstream link from R3, which is the connection to R5. If this link fails, the detour goes to R4 (10.1.34.2), then to R5, the egress router.

The next transit router to check is R2, which is not in the primary LSP but is part of the protection LSP that R1 has set up if its link to R3 goes down:

```
aviva@R2> show rsvp session transit detail
Transit RSVP: 1 sessions
10.0.0.5
  From: 10.0.0.1, LSPstate: Up, ActiveRoute: 1
  LSPname: R1-to-R5, LSPpath: Primary
  Suggested label received: -, Suggested label sent: -
  Recovery label received: -, Recovery label sent: 100464
  Resv style: 1 FF, Label in: 100432, Label out: 100464
  Time left: 158, Since: Wed Oct 12 15:24:45 2005
  Tspec: rate 0bps size 0bps peak Infbps m 20 M 1500
  Port number: sender 5 receiver 39275 protocol 0
  Detour branch from 10.1.12.1, to skip 10.0.0.3, Up
    Tspec: rate 0bps size 0bps peak Infbps m 20 M 1500
    Adspec: received MTU 1500
    Path MTU: received 0
    PATH rcvfrom: 10.1.12.1 (so-0/0/0.0) 8 pkts
    Adspec: received MTU 1500 sent MTU 1500
    PATH sentto: 10.1.24.2 (so-0/0/3.0) 4 pkts
    RESV rcvfrom: 10.1.24.2 (so-0/0/3.0) 4 pkts
    Explct route: 10.1.24.2 10.1.45.2
    Record route: 10.1.12.1 <self> 10.1.24.2 10.1.45.2
    Label in: 100432, Label out: 100464
Total 1 displayed, Up 1, Down 0
```

The first few lines of the output confirm that this is LSP R1-to-R5, from 10.0.0.1 to 10.0.0.5. The Detour branch line indicates that this router is a fast-reroute detour that will be used if R3 (10.0.0.3) fails.

What happens when the link on one of the transit routers goes down? When R3 goes down, R1 can no longer direct the primary LSP out the so-0/0/2 interface to R3:

```
aviva@R1> show rsvp interface
RSVP interface: 2 active
                    Active Subscr- Static     Available  Reserved  Highwater
Interface   State resv  iption  BW          BW         BW        mark
so-0/0/0.0  Up       2   100%   155.52Mbps  155.52Mbps 0bps      50Mbps
so-0/0/2.0  Down     0   100%   155.52Mbps  155.52Mbps 0bps      100Mbps
```

The RSVP interface status shows that the so-0/0/2 link is down and has no active RSVP sessions, and all RSVP sessions have been moved to so-0/0/0. Next, look at the LSP on the ingress router:

```
aviva@R1> show mpls lsp ingress extensive
Ingress LSP: 1 sessions
10.0.0.5
  From: 10.0.0.1, State: Up, ActiveRoute: 0, LSPname: R1-to-R5
  ActivePath: primary-path-R1-to-R5 (primary)
  FastReroute desired
  LoadBalance: Random
  Encoding type: Packet, Switching type: Packet, GPID: IPv4
 *Primary   primary-path-R1-to-R5 State: Up
    SmartOptimizeTimer: 180
    Computed ERO (S [L] denotes strict [loose] hops): (CSPF metric: 30)
  10.1.12.2 S 10.1.26.2 S 10.1.56.1 S
    Received RRO (ProtectionFlag 1=Available 2=InUse 4=B/W 8=Node 10=SoftPreempt):
          10.1.12.2(flag=9) 10.1.26.2(flag=1) 10.1.56.1
   21 Oct 12 15:23:03 Record Route:  10.1.12.2(flag=9) 10.1.26.2(flag=1) 10.1.56.1
   20 Oct 12 15:23:03 Record Route:  10.1.12.2(flag=9) 10.1.26.2 10.1.56.1
   19 Oct 12 15:23:00 Record Route:  10.1.12.2 10.1.26.2 10.1.56.1
   18 Oct 12 15:23:00 Up
   17 Oct 12 15:23:00 Originate make-before-break call
   16 Oct 12 15:23:00 CSPF: computation result accepted
   15 Oct 12 15:23:00 CSPF: link down/deleted: 10.1.13.1(R1.00/10.0.0.1)->10.1.13.
2(R3.00/10.0.0.3)
   14 Oct 12 15:23:00 Originate make-before-break call
   13 Oct 12 15:23:00 CSPF: computation result accepted
   12 Oct 12 15:23:00 Tunnel local repaired
   11 Oct 12 15:23:00 Record Route:  10.1.12.2 10.1.26.2 10.1.56.1
   10 Oct 12 15:23:00 Tunnel local repaired
    9 Oct 12 15:23:00 Down
 ...
Total 1 displayed, Up 1, Down 0
```

Line 9 of the LSP log shows when the link broke and the primary LSP went down. Line 10 shows R1 repairing the LSP, and line 11 shows that R1 has switched to the protection LSP, redirecting traffic out so-0/0/0 (10.1.12.2) to R2. In lines 13 and 14, CSPF verifies that the protection LSP is up before tearing down the primary LSP (shown in line 15). By line 18, the new LSP is fully up, and line 19 shows its path (record route) through R2 and then R4, and then to R5.

Line 12 indicates that the ingress router received a PathErr message with an indication that the LSP was locally repaired by the fast reroute backup LSP. This message triggers a recomputation for the primary LSP itself, and line 13 reports that the computation succeeded. Line 14 shows that signaling has been initiated for the make-before-break path. (This path is not up yet.) Line 15 indicates that the IGP deleted the listed link shown in the TE database, which triggers another path recomputation (line 16) and the initiation of another make-before-break operation (line 17), which overrides the previous one that is not yet up. The LSP finally comes up in line 18, with the path (record route) through R2 and then R4, and then to R5, as shown in lines 19, 20, and 21.

Lines 10 through 17 log the reoptimization of the LSP after fast reroute kicks in. The times shown are when the operation was recorded by the ingress router. They are not indicative of how long it took to switch over from the primary LSP to the protection path.

When the link between R3 and R1 breaks, R3 is no longer participating in the LSP:

```
aviva@R3> show mpls lsp transit extensive
Transit LSP: 0 sessions
Total 0 displayed, Up 0, Down 0
```

This output shows that R3 has no knowledge of being the transit router for any LSPs.

Finally, check the transit router R2:

```
aviva@R2> show mpls lsp transit extensive
Transit LSP: 1 sessions
10.0.0.5
  From: 10.0.0.1, LSPstate: Up, ActiveRoute: 1
  LSPname: R1-to-R5, LSPpath: Primary
  Suggested label received: -, Suggested label sent: -
  Recovery label received: -, Recovery label sent: 100320
  Resv style: 1 FF, Label in: 100416, Label out: 100320
  Time left:  158, Since: Wed Oct 12 15:12:01 2005
  Tspec: rate 0bps size 0bps peak Infbps m 20 M 1500
  Port number: sender 3 receiver 39275 protocol 0
  FastReroute desired
  PATH rcvfrom: 10.1.12.1 (so-0/0/0.0) 109 pkts
  Adspec: received MTU 1500 sent MTU 1500
  PATH sentto: 10.1.26.2 (so-0/0/2.0) 11 pkts
  RESV rcvfrom: 10.1.26.2 (so-0/0/2.0) 10 pkts
  Explct route: 10.1.26.2 10.1.56.1
  Record route: 10.1.12.1 <self> 10.1.26.2 10.1.56.1
    Detour is Up
    Detour Tspec: rate 0bps size 0bps peak Infbps m 20 M 1500
    Detour adspec: received MTU 1500 sent MTU 1500
    Path MTU: received 1500
    Detour PATH sentto: 10.1.24.2 (so-0/0/3.0) 10 pkts
    Detour RESV rcvfrom: 10.1.24.2 (so-0/0/3.0) 7 pkts
    Detour Explct route: 10.1.24.2 10.1.45.2
    Detour Record route: 10.1.12.1 <self> 10.1.24.2 10.1.45.2
    Detour Label out: 100416
Total 1 displayed, Up 1, Down 0
```

The Record route line confirms that the LSP has been detoured to R2 and that R2 is now the second hop in the R1-to-R5 LSP.

See Also

RFC 4090, *Fast Reroute Extensions to RSVP-TE for LSP Tunnels*

14.13 Automatically Allocating Bandwidth

Problem

You want an automatic way to optimize the amount of bandwidth allocated to each LSP to minimize or eliminate any contention for the available bandwidth on the shared links.

Solution

MPLS can automatically allocate bandwidth for an LSP and can automatically adjust the allocation as necessary from time to time. The configuration has two parts. First, MPLS must gather bandwidth statistics:

```
[edit protocols mpls]
aviva@R1# set statistics auto-bandwidth
aviva@R1# set statistics file mpls-bandwidth-stats world-readable
```

Second, configure the LSP to automatically allocate and adjust the bandwidth for an LSP:

```
[edit protocols mpls]
aviva@R1# set label-switched-path R1-to-R5 auto-bandwidth minimum-bandwidth 50m
```

Discussion

In a network with bandwidth constraints, it can be difficult for RSVP to set up LSPs when insufficient bandwidth is available. If you choose to allocate LSP bandwidth manually (see Recipe 14.11), it can be challenging to figure out how much bandwidth to set aside for an individual LSP or for a series of LSPs so that they are always available to carry your customer's traffic. MPLS autobandwidth is a JUNOS mechanism that automatically allocates bandwidth for an LSP. It works by monitoring the rate of traffic flow through an LSP and periodically resizing the allocated bandwidth to match the flow rate. In effect, autobandwidth adaptively requests bandwidth reservations based on actual LSP usage.

When MPLS resizes the bandwidth, it calculates and sets up a new LSP and sets it up in a make-before-break fashion, then tears down the old LSP after the new one is established. To avoid double-counting of resources, the LSP is set up as adaptive. Thus, the new and old LSPs share bandwidth over common links. In this process, the LSP might be rerouted. If this happens, all traffic already in the existing LSP continues to the egress router and any new traffic entering the LSP travels along the newly established path.

You turn on autobandwidth at the ingress router. No configuration is necessary on the other routers in the LSP. As a first step, enable MPLS statistics collection (with the set statistics auto-bandwidth command) and create a logfile to track actual bandwidth usage on the LSP. This recipe creates a file named *mpls-bandwidth-stats*.

The second step is to configure autobandwidth on the LSP itself. In this recipe, we set autobandwidth on the R1-to-R5 LSP, specifying that RSVP always allocates a minimum of 50 Mbps for the LSP.

To verify the autobandwidth configuration, look at the LSP on the ingress router:

```
aviva@R1> show mpls lsp detail ingress
Ingress LSP: 1 sessions
10.0.0.5
  From: 10.0.0.1, State: Up, ActiveRoute: 0, LSPname: R1-to-R5
  ActivePath: (primary)
  LoadBalance: Random
  Autobandwidth
  MinBW: 50Mbps
  AdjustTimer: 86400 secs
  Max AvgBW util: 0bps, Bandwidth Adjustment in 86368 second(s).
  Encoding type: Packet, Switching type: Packet, GPID: IPv4
 *Primary                    State: Up
    SmartOptimizeTimer: 180
    Computed ERO (S [L] denotes strict [loose] hops): (CSPF metric: 30)
  10.1.12.2 S 10.1.26.2 S 10.1.56.1 S
    Received RRO (ProtectionFlag 1=Available 2=InUse 4=B/W 8=Node 10=SoftPreempt):
          10.1.12.2 10.1.26.2 10.1.56.1
Total 1 displayed, Up 1, Down 0
```

The first highlighted line shows that autobandwidth is operational, and the second line reflects the configured minimum bandwidth of 50 Mbps. The AdjustTimer line is how often MPLS automatically recalculates the LSP's bandwidth. Here, the default time is 86,400 seconds (24 hours). Use the following command to change the interval:

```
[edit protocols mpls]
aviva@R1# set label-switched-path R1-to-R5 auto-bandwidth adjust-interval 28800
```

This configuration changes the recalculation interval to 12 hours.

Next, verify that RSVP has reserved bandwidth for the LSP:

```
aviva@R1> show rsvp interface
RSVP interface: 2 active
                Active Subscr- Static     Available  Reserved  Highwater
Interface   State resv  iption  BW         BW         BW        mark
so-0/0/0.0  Up       1   100%  155.52Mbps 155.52Mbps 0bps      0bps
so-0/0/2.0  Up       1   100%  155.52Mbps 105.52Mbps 50Mbps    80Mbps
```

RSVP has reserved 50 Mbps for the LSP in interface so-0/0/2.

You might wonder whether the LSP goes down each time RSVP recalculates the bandwidth requirements. The answer here is no. The whole point of autobandwidth is that the LSP stays up during the entire process and RSVP makes the bandwidth changes without dropping any traffic traveling along the LSP. This occurs because RSPV sets up the new LSP before tearing down the existing one—make-before-break. You can confirm this by forcing RSVP to recompute the allocated bandwidth:

```
aviva@R1> request mpls lsp adjust-autobandwidth
```

Then examine the history of the LSP:

```
aviva@R1> show mpls lsp ingress extensive
Ingress LSP: 1 sessions
10.0.0.5
  From: 10.0.0.1, State: Up, ActiveRoute: 0, LSPname: R1-to-R5
  ActivePath: (primary)
  LoadBalance: Random
  Autobandwidth
  MinBW: 50Mbps
  AdjustTimer: 86400 secs
  Max AvgBW util: 0bps, Bandwidth Adjustment in 86089 second(s).
  Encoding type: Packet, Switching type: Packet, GPID: IPv4
 *Primary                    State: Up
    Bandwidth: 50Mbps
    SmartOptimizeTimer: 180
    Computed ERO (S [L] denotes strict [loose] hops): (CSPF metric: 30)
  10.1.13.2 S 10.1.34.2 S 10.1.45.2 S
    Received RRO (ProtectionFlag 1=Available 2=InUse 4=B/W 8=Node 10=SoftPreempt):
          10.1.13.2 10.1.34.2 10.1.45.2
   10 Oct 10 13:44:54 Record Route:   10.1.13.2 10.1.34.2 10.1.45.2
    9 Oct 10 13:44:54 Up
    8 Oct 10 13:44:54 Manual Autobw adjustment succeeded
    7 Oct 10 13:44:54 Originate make-before-break call
    6 Oct 10 13:44:54 CSPF: computation result accepted
    5 Oct 10 13:39:48 Selected as active path
    4 Oct 10 13:39:48 Record Route:   10.1.12.2 10.1.26.2 10.1.56.1
    3 Oct 10 13:39:48 Up
    2 Oct 10 13:39:47 Originate Call
    1 Oct 10 13:39:47 CSPF: computation result accepted
  Created: Mon Oct 10 13:39:47 2005
Total 1 displayed, Up 1, Down 0
```

Line 4 of the history shows the initial path calculated for the LSP. Line 7 gives the first indication of the autobandwidth recalculation triggered by the request mpls lsp adjust-autobandwidth command. At this point, RSVP starts setting up the new LSP. When it is ready, RSVP then tears down the existing LSP. Line 8 shows that the auto-bandwidth adjustment was successful. Line 9 shows that the new LSP is up, and line 10 shows the new path.

See Also

Recipe 14.11

14.14 Prioritizing LSPs

Problem

You want to give higher priority to the more important LSPs so that they can always be established.

Solution

Configure the more important LSP so that it is more likely to be set up and remain up:

```
[edit protocols mpls]
aviva@R1# set label-switched-path R1-to-R5 priority 0 0
```

Then configure intermediate priority LSPs, those less likely to be set up and remain up:

```
[edit protocols mpls]
aviva@R1# set label-switched-path R1-to-R6 priority 1 3
aviva@R1# set label-switched-path R1-to-R4 priority 4 5
```

Finally, set up the least important LSP, the one least like to be set up and most likely to be torn down if there is insufficient bandwidth:

```
[edit protocols mpls]
aviva@R1# set label-switched-path R1-to-R5-low priority 7 7
```

Discussion

When you offer a higher level of service for some customers, you want RSVP to be able to establish those customers' LSP at all times, even when there might not be enough bandwidth available on some links because other LSPs are already established. To provide this level of service, you can prioritize each customer's LSP so that some are more important than others. Then, when RSVP calculates the path and sets up the LSP, RSVP will always be able to establish the more important LSPs, even at the cost of tearing down a less important LSP. The relative LSP priorities are determined in advance, when RSVP is establishing the LSP, not when traffic is being forwarded. If a link has insufficient bandwidth, RSVP establishes the more important (higher-priority) LSPs first and tears down lower-priority LSPs if necessary.

This recipe prioritizes the four LSPs that originate on router R1. To configure an LSP's priority, you include two values in the priority statement, the setup priority and the hold priority. You express these two priorities with a number from 0 through 7, where 0 is best and 7 is worst. A setup priority of 0 means that this LSP can preempt any other LSP whose hold priority is worse than 0. Similarly, a hold priority of 0 means that once the LSP is set up, it cannot be preempted. A hold priority of 1 means that it can be preempted only by an LSP with a setup priority of 0. The default setup priority is 7, which means that one LSP cannot preempt another. The default hold priority is 0, which means that another LSP cannot preempt this one.

The four LSPs configured in this recipe have different priorities. The LSP R1-to-R5 is the one being used for the most important customer. It will always be set up (setup priority of 0) and can never be preempted (hold priority of 0) when RSVP is setting up another LSP. The other three LSPs, in order from highest to lowest priority, are R1-to-R6 (setup priority of 1, hold priority of 3), R1-to-R4 (setup priority of 4, hold priority of 5), and R1-to-R5-low (setup priority of 7, hold priority of 7). The setup and hold priority values for the different LSP are all evaluated relative to each other.

To understand how preemption works, set up LSPs sequentially and observe how they are established. First, set up the lowest-priority LSP, R1-to-R5-low:

```
[edit protocols mpls]
aviva@R1# set label-switched-path R1-to-R5-low to 10.0.0.5
aviva@R1# set label-switched-path R1-to-R5-low bandwidth 80m
aviva@R1# set label-switched-path R1-to-R5-low to priority 7 7
```

Because this is the first and only LSP on the ingress router, you expect RSVP to set it up even though it has the lowest setup priority. Look at the LSP to check that RSVP has set it up:

```
aviva@R7# show mpls lsp
Ingress LSP: 1 sessions
To               From            State Rt ActivePath       P     LSPname
10.0.0.5         10.0.0.1        Up     0                  *     R1-to-R5-low
Total 1 displayed, Up 1, Down 0
```

The State column confirms that the LSP is up. Then check that RSVP has reserved the requested bandwidth for the LSP:

```
aviva@R7# show rsvp interface
RSVP interface: 2 active
                       Active Subscr- Static      Available  Reserved  Highwater
Interface    State resv  iption BW         BW         BW        mark
so-0/0/0.0   Up      1    100%  155.52Mbps 75.52Mbps  80Mbps    80Mbps
so-0/0/2.0   Up      0    100%  155.52Mbps 155.52Mbps 0bps      100Mbps
```

You see that RSVP has reserved 80 Mbps on the so-0/0/0 interface for this LSP. Finally, look at the details about the LSP:

```
aviva@R7# show mpls lsp ingress extensive
Ingress LSP: 1 sessions
10.0.0.5
  From: 10.0.0.1, State: Up, ActiveRoute: 0, LSPname: R1-to-R5-low
  ActivePath:  (primary)
  LoadBalance: Random
  Encoding type: Packet, Switching type: Packet, GPID: IPv4
 *Primary                    State: Up
    Priorities: 7 7
    Bandwidth: 80Mbps
    SmartOptimizeTimer: 180
    Computed ERO (S [L] denotes strict [loose] hops): (CSPF metric: 30)
 10.1.12.2 S 10.1.26.2 S 10.1.56.1 S
    Received RRO (ProtectionFlag 1=Available 2=InUse 4=B/W 8=Node 10=SoftPreempt):
        10.1.12.2 10.1.26.2 10.1.56.1
   10 Oct 14 10:39:39 Record Route:  10.1.12.2 10.1.26.2 10.1.56.1
    9 Oct 14 10:39:39 Up
    8 Oct 14 10:39:39 Originate Call
    ...
  Created: Fri Oct 14 10:35:55 2005
Total 1 displayed, Up 1, Down 0
```

This output confirms that the LSP is up and shows the configured priority values and bandwidth request.

Next, configure the higher-priority LSP R1-to-R4:

```
[edit protocols mpls]
aviva@R1# set label-switched-path R1-to-R4 to 10.0.0.4
aviva@R1# set label-switched-path R1-to-R4 to priority 4 4
aviva@R1# set label-switched-path R1-to-R4 bandwidth 90m
```

Check that the second LSP is set up:

```
aviva@R7# show mpls lsp ingress
Ingress LSP: 2 sessions
To              From            State Rt ActivePath      P      LSPname
10.0.0.4        10.0.0.1        Up    0                  *      R1-to-R4
10.0.0.5        10.0.0.1        Up    0                  *      R1-to-R5-low
Total 2 displayed, Up 2, Down 0
```

This output confirms that RSVP was able to establish both LSPs. Then, look at the bandwidth reservations:

```
aviva@R7# show rsvp interface
RSVP interface: 2 active
                    Active Subscr- Static      Available   Reserved   Highwater
Interface   State resv  iption BW          BW          BW         mark
so-0/0/0.0  Up       1   100%  155.52Mbps  75.52Mbps   80Mbps     80Mbps
so-0/0/2.0  Up       1   100%  155.52Mbps  65.52Mbps   90Mbps     100Mbps
```

You see here that RSVP has reserved 90 Mbps for LSP R1-to-R4 on the so-0/0/2 inter-face and has left the previously established reservation for LSP R1-to-R5-low of 80 Mbps on unchanged. The two SONET interfaces on the router have sufficient band-width for both LSPs, so RSVP can create both without preempting one of them. Check the details of the two LSPs to see the paths that RSVP has established for them:

```
aviva@R7# show mpls lsp ingress extensive
Ingress LSP: 2 sessions
10.0.0.4
  From: 10.0.0.1, State: Up, ActiveRoute: 0, LSPname: R1-to-R4
  ActivePath:  (primary)
  LoadBalance: Random
  Encoding type: Packet, Switching type: Packet, GPID: IPv4
 *Primary                    State: Up
    Priorities: 4 4
    Bandwidth: 90Mbps
    SmartOptimizeTimer: 180
    Computed ERO (S [L] denotes strict [loose] hops): (CSPF metric: 20)
 10.1.13.2 S 10.1.34.2 S
    Received RRO (ProtectionFlag 1=Available 2=InUse 4=B/W 8=Node 10=SoftPreempt):
          10.1.13.2 10.1.34.2
    5 Oct 14 10:43:13 Selected as active path
    4 Oct 14 10:43:13 Record Route:  10.1.13.2 10.1.34.2
    3 Oct 14 10:43:13 Up
    2 Oct 14 10:43:13 Originate Call
    1 Oct 14 10:43:13 CSPF: computation result accepted
  Created: Fri Oct 14 10:43:12 2005
```

```
10.0.0.5
  From: 10.0.0.1, State: Up, ActiveRoute: 0, LSPname: R1-to-R5-low
  ActivePath:  (primary)
  LoadBalance: Random
  Encoding type: Packet, Switching type: Packet, GPID: IPv4
 *Primary                    State: Up
    Priorities: 7 7
    Bandwidth: 80Mbps
    SmartOptimizeTimer: 180
    Computed ERO (S [L] denotes strict [loose] hops): (CSPF metric: 30)
  10.1.12.2 S 10.1.26.2 S 10.1.56.1 S
    Received RRO (ProtectionFlag 1=Available 2=InUse 4=B/W 8=Node 10=SoftPreempt):
          10.1.12.2 10.1.26.2 10.1.56.1
   10 Oct 14 10:39:39 Record Route:  10.1.12.2 10.1.26.2 10.1.56.1
    9 Oct 14 10:39:39 Up
    8 Oct 14 10:39:39 Originate Call
  Created: Fri Oct 14 10:35:55 2005
  Total 2 displayed, Up 2, Down 0
```

The record route objects in this output confirm that RSVP has directed the LSP R1-to-R5-low to R2 (12.1.12.2), over the so-0/0/0 interface, and has set up LSP R1-to-R4 to R3 (12.1.13.2), over so-0/0/2.

Finally, configure an even higher-priority LSP on the ingress router, R1-to-R6:

```
[edit protocols mpls]
aviva@R1# set label-switched-path R1-to-R6 to 10.0.0.6
aviva@R1# set label-switched-path R1-to-R6 to priority 2 2
aviva@R1# set label-switched-path R1-to-R6 bandwidth 90m
```

You are requesting 90 Mbps for this LSP, in addition to the 80 Mbps for LSP R1-to-R5-low and 90 Mbps for LSP R1-to-R4. At this point, not enough bandwidth is available on the router, because each of the two SONET interfaces can carry only 155.52 Mbps. To see how RSVP handles this, first look at the status of the LSPs on the ingress router:

```
aviva@R7# show mpls lsp ingress
Ingress LSP: 3 sessions
To          From        State Rt ActivePath      P     LSPname
10.0.0.4    10.0.0.1    Up    0                  *     R1-to-R4
10.0.0.5    10.0.0.1    Dn    0  -                     R1-to-R5-low
10.0.0.6    10.0.0.1    Up    1                  *     R1-to-R6
Total 3 displayed, Up 2, Down 1
```

You see that while MPLS has created three LSPs, RSVP has established only two of them, R1-to-R4 and R1-to-R6. The LSP R1-to-R5-low is down. Check how RSVP has reserved bandwidth for the two LSPs:

```
aviva@R7# show rsvp interface
RSVP interface: 2 active
                 Active Subscr- Static    Available  Reserved  Highwater
Interface   State resv  iption  BW        BW         BW        mark
so-0/0/0.0  Up    1     100%    155.52Mbps 65.52Mbps  90Mbps    90Mbps
so-0/0/2.0  Up    1     100%    155.52Mbps 65.52Mbps  90Mbps    100Mbps
```

Use the show mpls lsp ingress extensive command to look at the LSPs on the ingress router to see what has happened. First, look at LSP R1-to-R6, which has the highest priority of the three LSPs:

```
aviva@R7# show mpls lsp ingress extensive
Ingress LSP: 3 sessions
...
10.0.0.6
  From: 10.0.0.1, State: Up, ActiveRoute: 1, LSPname: R1-to-R6
  ActivePath: (primary)
  LoadBalance: Random
  Encoding type: Packet, Switching type: Packet, GPID: IPv4
 *Primary                    State: Up
    Priorities: 2 2
    Bandwidth: 90Mbps
    SmartOptimizeTimer: 180
    Computed ERO (S [L] denotes strict [loose] hops): (CSPF metric: 20)
  10.1.13.2 S 10.1.36.2 S
    Received RRO (ProtectionFlag 1=Available 2=InUse 4=B/W 8=Node 10=SoftPreempt):
          10.1.13.2 10.1.36.2
    5 Oct 14 10:51:20 Selected as active path
    4 Oct 14 10:51:20 Record Route:  10.1.13.2 10.1.36.2
    3 Oct 14 10:51:20 Up
    2 Oct 14 10:51:20 Originate Call
    1 Oct 14 10:51:20 CSPF: computation result accepted
  Created: Fri Oct 14 10:51:20 2005
Total 3 displayed, Up 2, Down 1
```

RSVP has set up this LSP with the requested bandwidth of 90 Mbps, routing it through 10.1.13.2 (R3) on interface so-0/0/2. Next, look at the medium-priority LSP, R1-to-R4:

```
aviva@R7# show mpls lsp ingress extensive
Ingress LSP: 3 sessions
...
10.0.0.4
  From: 10.0.0.1, State: Up, ActiveRoute: 0, LSPname: R1-to-R4
  ActivePath: (primary)
  LoadBalance: Random
  Encoding type: Packet, Switching type: Packet, GPID: IPv4
 *Primary                    State: Up
    Priorities: 4 4
    Bandwidth: 90Mbps
    SmartOptimizeTimer: 180
    Computed ERO (S [L] denotes strict [loose] hops): (CSPF metric: 20)
  10.1.12.2 S 10.1.24.2 S
    Received RRO (ProtectionFlag 1=Available 2=InUse 4=B/W 8=Node 10=SoftPreempt):
          10.1.12.2 10.1.24.2
    15 Oct 14 10:51:20 Selected as active path
    14 Oct 14 10:51:20 Record Route:  10.1.12.2 10.1.24.2
    13 Oct 14 10:51:20 Up
    12 Oct 14 10:51:20 Originate Call
    11 Oct 14 10:51:20 Clear Call
    10 Oct 14 10:51:20 CSPF: computation result accepted
```

```
    9 Oct 14 10:51:20 Deselected as active
    8 Oct 14 10:51:20 Requested bandwidth unavailable
    7 Oct 14 10:51:20 Session preempted
    6 Oct 14 10:51:20 Down
    5 Oct 14 10:43:13 Selected as active path
    4 Oct 14 10:43:13 Record Route:  10.1.13.2 10.1.34.2
    3 Oct 14 10:43:13 Up
    2 Oct 14 10:43:13 Originate Call
    1 Oct 14 10:43:13 CSPF: computation result accepted
  Created: Fri Oct 14 10:43:12 2005
  ...
Total 3 displayed, Up 2, Down 1
```

Line 4 of the LSP history shows the original route of the LSP, through 10.1.13.2 (out of interface so-0/0/2). When you configure the higher-priority R1-to-R6 LSP, RSVP preempted LSP R1-to-R4 because of insufficient bandwidth (shown in lines 7 and 8 of this history). However, the LSP was reestablished later (reflected in lines 13 and 14), when RSVP determined it could route the LSP through 10.1.12.2, out of interface so-0/0/0.

Finally, look at the lowest-priority LSP, R1-to-R5-low, which is now down:

```
aviva@R7# show mpls lsp ingress extensive
Ingress LSP: 3 sessions
...
10.0.0.5
  From: 10.0.0.1, State: Dn, ActiveRoute: 0, LSPname: R1-to-R5-low
  ActivePath: (none)
  LoadBalance: Random
  Encoding type: Packet, Switching type: Packet, GPID: IPv4
  Primary                 State: Dn
    Priorities: 7 7
    Bandwidth: 80Mbps
    SmartOptimizeTimer: 180
    Will be enqueued for recomputation in 24 second(s).
   16 Oct 14 10:52:18 CSPF failed: no route toward 10.0.0.5[3 times]
   15 Oct 14 10:51:20 Clear Call
   14 Oct 14 10:51:20 Deselected as active
   13 Oct 14 10:51:20 Requested bandwidth unavailable
   12 Oct 14 10:51:20 Session preempted
   11 Oct 14 10:51:20 Down
   10 Oct 14 10:39:39 Record Route:  10.1.12.2 10.1.26.2 10.1.56.1
    9 Oct 14 10:39:39 Up
    8 Oct 14 10:39:39 Originate Call
  Created: Fri Oct 14 10:35:55 2005
  ...
Total 3 displayed, Up 2, Down 1
```

Lines 12 and 13 show that the LSP was preempted by a higher-priority one because not enough bandwidth was available for all the LSPs. Line 16 indicates that CSPF made three attempts to calculate a path for the LSP but was unable to compute one, which means that RSVP could not establish the LSP.

14.15 Allowing IGP Traffic to Use an LSP

Problem

You want to configure IS-IS and OSPF so they can also use the LSPs on the ingress router.

Solution

Configure OSPF and IS-IS so that the LSP is advertised into the IGP. For OSPF, configure the area with the following command:

```
[edit protocols ospf area 0.0.0.0]
aviva@R1# set label-switched-path R1-to-R6
```

The configuration for IS-IS is similar:

```
[edit protocols isis]
aviva@R1# set label-switched-path R1-to-R6
```

Discussion

One of the main reasons that you configure LSPs on your network is to control the shortest path between two points on the network. If enough bandwidth is available on the LSP, you might also want to have your IGP traffic routed along the LSP instead of having it use the default best-effort routing. To configure this, set up OSPF and IS-IS so that the LSP is advertised into the IGP. For OSPF, use the set label-switched-path command for each OSPF area, and for IS-IS, use this command at the top of the IS-IS configuration. In this recipe, R1-to-R6 is the name of the LSP configured on the ingress router R1. Because only the ingress router is aware of the LSP and because this is the only router that can place packets into the LSP tunnel, you can configure this only on the ingress router.

Let's look at the effect of this configuration. Before configuring OSPF to use the LSP, check which routes have been learned from OSPF:

```
aviva@R1> show route protocol ospf
inet.0: 14 destinations, 18 routes (14 active, 0 holddown, 0 hidden)
+ = Active Route, - = Last Active, * = Both
10.0.0.3/32        *[OSPF/10] 00:00:07, metric 1
                    > via so-0/0/2.0
10.0.0.6/32        *[OSPF/10] 00:00:07, metric 2
                    > via so-0/0/2.0
10.1.13.0/30        [OSPF/10] 00:00:07, metric 1
                    > via so-0/0/2.0
10.1.36.0/30       *[OSPF/10] 00:00:07, metric 2
                    > via so-0/0/2.0
224.0.0.5/32       *[OSPF/10] 01:56:46, metric 1
                    MultiRecv
```

The router knows how to reach its immediate neighbor R3 (router ID of 10.0.0.3/32 and subnet of 10.1.31.0/30) and the next downstream neighbor, R6 (router ID of 10.0.0.6/32 and subnet of 10.1.36.0/30). R1 has one OSPF neighbor, 10.1.13.2, which is the immediately adjacent router:

```
aviva@R1> show ospf neighbor
   Address       Interface        State     ID          Pri  Dead
   10.1.13.2     so-0/0/2.0       Full      10.0.0.3     128   35
```

After you advertise the LSP into OSPF, check the neighbors again:

```
aviva@R1> show ospf neighbor
   Address       Interface        State     ID          Pri  Dead
   10.0.0.6      R1-to-R6         Full      10.0.0.6      0    0
   10.1.13.2     so-0/0/2.0       Full      10.0.0.3     128   36
```

The output shows that R1 now has a second neighbor, 10.0.0.6, which is R6, that is reachable not over a physical interface but rather over the LSP.

Looking at the routing table shows a route to 10.0.0.6/32 that uses the LSP:

```
aviva@R1> show route table inet.0 protocol ospf
inet.0: 14 destinations, 18 routes (14 active, 0 holddown, 0 hidden)
+ = Active Route, - = Last Active, * = Both
10.0.0.3/32        *[OSPF/10] 00:01:50, metric 1
                    > via so-0/0/2.0
10.0.0.6/32        *[OSPF/10] 00:01:50, metric 1
                    > via so-0/0/2.0, label-switched-path R1-to-R6
10.1.13.0/30        [OSPF/10] 00:01:50, metric 1
                    > via so-0/0/2.0
10.1.36.0/30       *[OSPF/10] 00:01:50, metric 2
                    > via so-0/0/2.0
224.0.0.5/32       *[OSPF/10] 02:00:33, metric 1
                    MultiRecv
```

You verify the IS-IS configuration in the same way, checking the IS-IS interfaces and adjacencies to confirm that IS-IS is aware of the LSP:

```
aviva@R1> show isis interface
IS-IS interface database:
Interface          L CirID Level 1 DR      Level 2 DR       L1/L2 Metric
R1-to-R6           2  0x1 Disabled         Point to Point        10/10
lo0.0              0  0x1 Passive          Passive                0/0
so-0/0/2.0         2  0x1 Disabled         Point to Point        10/10

aviva@R1> show isis adjacency
Interface          System        L State       Hold (secs) SNPA
R1-to-R6           R6            0 One-way            0
so-0/0/2.0         R3            2 Up               18
```

Both outputs show that IS-IS treats the LSP as an IS-IS interface and considers it an adjacency.

14.16 Installing LSPs into the Unicast Routing Table

Problem

You want to install the routes from the label forwarding table, inet.3, into the unicast routing table, inet.0, so that applications such as ping can use LSPs.

Solution

Configure MPLS to install the LSP routes into the inet.0 unicast routing table:

```
[edit protocols mpls]
aviva@R1# set traffic-engineering bgp-igp
```

Discussion

One of the main reasons that you configure LSPs on your network is to control the shortest path between two points on the network. By default, the JUNOS MPLS software stores the LSP routes in the inet.3 routing table, which can be used by MPLS and BGP. Applications such as ping and traceroute, which use the routes in the inet.0 table, cannot take advantage of the LSP routes.

You can confirm the default behavior by looking at the two routing tables. One LSP is configured on router R1, and the inet.3 table contains the RSVP route for that LSP:

```
aviva@R1> show route table inet.3
inet.3: 1 destinations, 1 routes (1 active, 0 holddown, 0 hidden)
+ = Active Route, - = Last Active, * = Both
10.0.0.6/32        *[RSVP/7] 00:00:07, metric 2
                    > via so-0/0/2.0, label-switched-path R1-to-R6
```

The inet.0 routing table contains the expected unicast routes from IS-IS, OSPF, and BGP:

```
aviva@R1> show route table inet.0
inet.0: 14 destinations, 18 routes (14 active, 0 holddown, 0 hidden)
+ = Active Route, - = Last Active, * = Both
0.0.0.0/0          *[Static/5] 5w0d 05:51:43
                    Discard
10.0.0.1/32        *[Direct/0] 5w0d 05:51:43
                    > via lo0.0
10.0.0.3/32        *[OSPF/10] 00:00:14, metric 1
                    > via so-0/0/2.0
                    [IS-IS/18] 00:00:14, metric 10
                    > to 10.1.13.2 via so-0/0/2.0
10.0.0.6/32        *[OSPF/10] 00:00:14, metric 2
                    > via so-0/0/2.0
                    [IS-IS/18] 00:00:14, metric 20
                    > to 10.1.13.2 via so-0/0/2.0
10.1.13.0/30       *[Direct/0] 00:16:20
                    > via so-0/0/2.0
                    [OSPF/10] 00:00:14, metric 1
                    > via so-0/0/2.0
```

```
10.1.13.1/32        *[Local/0] 2d 20:39:51
                      Local via so-0/0/2.0
10.1.36.0/30        *[OSPF/10] 00:00:14, metric 2
                      > via so-0/0/2.0
                     [IS-IS/18] 00:00:14, metric 20
                      > to 10.1.13.2 via so-0/0/2.0
100.100.6.0/24      *[BGP/170] 00:15:37, localpref 100, from 10.0.0.6
                       AS path: I
                      > via so-0/0/2.0, label-switched-path R1-to-R6
192.168.0.0/16      *[Static/5] 4d 16:57:10
                      > to 192.168.71.254 via fxp0.0
192.168.64.0/21     *[Direct/0] 4d 16:57:10
                      > via fxp0.0
192.168.70.143/32   *[Local/0] 5w0d 05:51:43
                      Local via fxp0.0
224.0.0.5/32        *[OSPF/10] 5w0d 05:51:44, metric 1
                      MultiRecv
```

This recipe configures the router to install the routes from the inet.3 routing table into the inet.0 unicast routing table so they are accessible to ping and traceroute. Simply use the set traffic-engineering bgp-igp command to modify where the routes are installed. To check the effect, first look at the inet.3 routing table:

```
aviva@R1> show route table inet.3
aviva@R1>
```

This command shows that this routing table is empty. Then look at the unicast routing table:

```
aviva@R1> show route table inet.0
inet.0: 14 destinations, 19 routes (14 active, 0 holddown, 0 hidden)
+ = Active Route, - = Last Active, * = Both
0.0.0.0/0           *[Static/5] 5w0d 05:53:28
                      Discard
10.0.0.1/32         *[Direct/0] 5w0d 05:53:28
                      > via lo0.0
10.0.0.3/32         *[OSPF/10] 00:00:05, metric 1
                      > via so-0/0/2.0
                     [IS-IS/18] 00:00:05, metric 10
                      > to 10.1.13.2 via so-0/0/2.0
10.0.0.6/32         *[RSVP/7] 00:00:05, metric 2
                      > via so-0/0/2.0, label-switched-path R1-to-R6
                     [OSPF/10] 00:00:05, metric 2
                      > via so-0/0/2.0
                     [IS-IS/18] 00:00:05, metric 20
                      > to 10.1.13.2 via so-0/0/2.0
10.1.13.0/30        *[Direct/0] 00:18:05
                      > via so-0/0/2.0
                     [OSPF/10] 00:00:05, metric 1
                      > via so-0/0/2.0
10.1.13.1/32        *[Local/0] 2d 20:41:36
                      Local via so-0/0/2.0
10.1.36.0/30        *[OSPF/10] 00:00:05, metric 2
                      > via so-0/0/2.0
```

```
                        [IS-IS/18] 00:00:05, metric 20
                        > to 10.1.13.2 via so-0/0/2.0
    100.100.6.0/24      *[BGP/170] 00:17:22, localpref 100, from 10.0.0.6
                          AS path: I
                        > via so-0/0/2.0, label-switched-path R1-to-R6
    192.168.0.0/16      *[Static/5] 4d 16:58:55
                        > to 192.168.71.254 via fxp0.0
    192.168.64.0/21     *[Direct/0] 4d 16:58:55
                        > via fxp0.0
    192.168.70.143/32   *[Local/0] 5w0d 05:53:28
                          Local via fxp0.0
    224.0.0.5/32        *[OSPF/10] 5w0d 05:53:29, metric 1
                          MultiRecv
```

The LSP route to 10.0.0.6, which is learned from RSVP and had been in the inet.3 routing table, is now installed in the inet.0 table.

See Also

Recipe 8.1

14.17 Tracing RSVP Operations

Problem

You want to keep a running log of RSVP events that occur on the router in case any problems arise and you need to debug problems with RSVP or your LSPs.

Solution

When performing ongoing monitoring of RSVP operations, set up tracing options to track RSVP events that occur on the router:

```
[edit protocols rsvp]
aviva@R1# set traceoptions file rsvp-trace-log world-readable
aviva@R1# set traceoptions flag packets detail
```

Discussion

It's a good practice to trace high-level RSVP operations on an ongoing basis so that if a problem occurs, you can examine the logs as part of your troubleshooting process. Then you can enable more detailed traceoptions flags to help pinpoint the causes.

This recipe sets up tracing of RSVP packets that are sent and received by the router, saving them to the file *rsvp-trace-log*. The world-readable option allows anyone logged in to the router to read the file. This file is created on the router's hard disk in the directories */var/log* (on M-series and T-series routers) and */cf/var/log* (on J-series routers). The detail option provides additional information about the packets. Here's what the file contains when existing RSVP sessions are cleared and then restarted:

```
aviva@R1> clear log rsvp-trace-log
aviva@R1> clear rsvp sessions
aviva@R1> show log rsvp-trace-log
Nov  4 16:47:41 R1 clear-log[22684]: logfile cleared
Nov  4 16:47:47 RSVP send PathErr 10.1.13.1->10.1.13.2 Len=188 so-0/0/2.0
Nov  4 16:47:47   Integty  Len 36 flag 0x0 key 0x0000010d010a seq 0x2c016c435db8
0b00 digest 0x53682741 0x68419a28 0x340b7b1d 0x8bdc0112
Nov  4 16:47:47   Session7 Len 16 10.0.0.1(port/tunnel ID 51620 Ext-ID 10.0.0.6)
  Proto 0
Nov  4 16:47:47   Error    Len 12 Session preempted flag 0 by 10.1.13.1
Nov  4 16:47:47   Sender7  Len 12 10.0.0.6(port/lsp ID  1)
Nov  4 16:47:47   Tspec    Len 36 rate 0bps size 0bps peak Infbps m 20 M 1500
Nov  4 16:47:47   ADspec   Len 48 MTU 1500
Nov  4 16:47:47   RecRoute Len 20  10.1.13.2 10.1.36.2
Nov  4 16:47:47 RSVP send ResvTear 10.1.13.1->10.1.13.2 Len=92 so-0/0/2.0
Nov  4 16:47:47   Integty  Len 36 flag 0x0 key 0x0000010d010a seq 0x33016c434b6b
0200 digest 0x3c6b90bf 0x3d4bc125 0x5cb3da5d 0x42518ffc
Nov  4 16:47:47   Session7 Len 16 10.0.0.1(port/tunnel ID 51620 Ext-ID 10.0.0.6)
  Proto 0
Nov  4 16:47:47   Hop      Len 12 10.1.13.1/0x0869a660
Nov  4 16:47:47   Style    Len  8 FF
Nov  4 16:47:47   Filter7  Len 12 10.0.0.6(port/lsp ID  1)
Nov  4 16:47:47 RSVP send PathTear 10.0.0.1->10.0.0.6 Len=120 so-0/0/2.0
Nov  4 16:47:47   Integty  Len 36 flag 0x0 key 0x0000010d010a seq 0x33016c43456d
0200 digest 0x582dab2c 0x3801d98c 0x7dbf2854 0x8f8ea32e
Nov  4 16:47:47   Session7 Len 16 10.0.0.6(port/tunnel ID 39357 Ext-ID 10.0.0.1)
  Proto 0
Nov  4 16:47:47   Hop      Len 12 10.1.13.1/0x086dd770
Nov  4 16:47:47   Sender7  Len 12 10.0.0.1(port/lsp ID  2)
Nov  4 16:47:47   Tspec    Len 36 rate 0bps size 0bps peak Infbps m 20 M 1500
Nov  4 16:47:47 RSVP recv Path 10.0.0.6->10.0.0.1 Len=244 so-0/0/2.0
Nov  4 16:47:47   Integty  Len 36 flag 0x0 key 0x0000020d010a seq 0xbbfe6b43793e
0800 digest 0x1a36b6f1 0xf3d0cd4d 0x0c3ffc31 0x6f587cf9
Nov  4 16:47:47   Session7 Len 16 10.0.0.1(port/tunnel ID 51620 Ext-ID 10.0.0.6)
  Proto 0
Nov  4 16:47:47   Hop      Len 12 10.1.13.2/0x0869a660
Nov  4 16:47:47   Time     Len  8 30000 ms
Nov  4 16:47:47   SrcRoute Len 12  10.1.13.1 S
Nov  4 16:47:47   LabelRequest Len  8 EtherType 0x800
Nov  4 16:47:47   Properties Len 12 Primary path
Nov  4 16:47:47   SessionAttribute Len 16 Prio (7,0) flag 0x0 "R6-to-R1"
Nov  4 16:47:47   Sender7  Len 12 10.0.0.6(port/lsp ID  1)
Nov  4 16:47:47   Tspec    Len 36 rate 0bps size 0bps peak Infbps m 20 M 1500
Nov  4 16:47:47   ADspec   Len 48 MTU 1500
Nov  4 16:47:47   RecRoute Len 20  10.1.13.2 10.1.36.2
Nov  4 16:47:47 RSVP send Resv 10.1.13.1->10.1.13.2 Len=156 so-0/0/2.0
Nov  4 16:47:47   Integty  Len 36 flag 0x0 key 0x0000010d010a seq 0x33016c43e07d
0200 digest 0x976571f8 0x06983f40 0x7a9bb90d 0xfdf51c42
Nov  4 16:47:47   Session7 Len 16 10.0.0.1(port/tunnel ID 51620 Ext-ID 10.0.0.6)
  Proto 0
Nov  4 16:47:47   Hop      Len 12 10.1.13.1/0x0869a660
Nov  4 16:47:47   Time     Len  8 30000 ms
Nov  4 16:47:47   Style    Len  8 FF
Nov  4 16:47:47   Flow     Len 36 rate 0bps size 0bps peak Infbps m 20 M 1500
```

```
Nov  4 16:47:47   Filter7  Len 12 10.0.0.6(port/lsp ID  1)
Nov  4 16:47:47   Label    Len 8  3
Nov  4 16:47:47   RecRoute Len 12  10.1.13.1
Nov  4 16:47:49 RSVP recv Hello New 10.1.13.2->10.1.13.1 Len=68 so-0/0/2.0
Nov  4 16:47:49   Integty  Len 36 flag 0x0 key 0x0000020d010a seq 0xbbfe6b43793e
0800 digest 0x0a523b8a 0x89b1162e 0x18a9feab 0x901053f2
Nov  4 16:47:49   HelloReq Len 12
Nov  4 16:47:49   RestartCap Len 12 restart time 0, recovery time 0
Nov  4 16:47:49 RSVP send Hello New 10.1.13.1->10.1.13.2 Len=68 so-0/0/2.0
Nov  4 16:47:49   Integty  Len 36 flag 0x0 key 0x0000010d010a seq 0x35016c43dd51
0c00 digest 0xfc4c9304 0xe69e24ee 0xd219ef33 0x6a5f31e5
Nov  4 16:47:49   HelloRply Len 12
Nov  4 16:47:49   RestartCap Len 12 restart time 0, recovery time 0
```

The first RSVP packet sent is a PathErr, which indicates that some type of error has occurred on the LSP. When RSVP clears the sessions, it sends two PathTear messages to tear down the session, one message to the interface link between 10.1.13.1 and 10.1.13.2, and the second message to the link between the loopback addresses of the ingress router (10.0.0.1) and the egress router (10.0.0.6). As RSVP re-establishes the LSP, it exchanges Path and Resv messages. Once the RSVP session is set up again, RSVP exchanges periodic Hello messages. The information logged for the RSVP Path packets is similar to the show rsvp session detail command output:

```
aviva@R1> show rsvp session detail
Ingress RSVP: 1 sessions
10.0.0.6
  From: 10.0.0.1, LSPstate: Up, ActiveRoute: 1
  LSPname: R1-to-R6, LSPpath: Primary
  Suggested label received: -, Suggested label sent: -
  Recovery label received: -, Recovery label sent: 100128
  Resv style: 1 FF, Label in: -, Label out: 100128
  Time left:    -, Since: Fri Nov  4 16:52:15 2005
  Tspec: rate 0bps size 0bps peak Infbps m 20 M 1500
  Port number: sender 4 receiver 39357 protocol 0
  PATH rcvfrom: localclient
  Adspec: sent MTU 1500
  Path MTU: received 1500
  PATH sentto: 10.1.13.2 (so-0/0/2.0) 4 pkts
  RESV rcvfrom: 10.1.13.2 (so-0/0/2.0) 4 pkts
  Explct route: 10.1.13.2 10.1.36.2
  Record route: <self> 10.1.13.2 10.1.36.2
Total 1 displayed, Up 1, Down 0

Egress RSVP: 1 sessions
10.0.0.1
  From: 10.0.0.6, LSPstate: Up, ActiveRoute: 0
  LSPname: R6-to-R1, LSPpath: Primary
  Suggested label received: -, Suggested label sent: -
  Recovery label received: -, Recovery label sent: -
  Resv style: 1 FF, Label in: 3, Label out: -
  Time left:  146, Since: Fri Nov  4 16:51:45 2005
  Tspec: rate 0bps size 0bps peak Infbps m 20 M 1500
  Port number: sender 1 receiver 51620 protocol 0
```

```
    PATH rcvfrom: 10.1.13.2 (so-0/0/2.0) 5 pkts
    Adspec: received MTU 1500
    PATH sentto: localclient
    RESV rcvfrom: localclient
    Record route: 10.1.36.2 10.1.13.2 <self>
Total 1 displayed, Up 1, Down 0

Transit RSVP: 0 sessions
Total 0 displayed, Up 0, Down 0
```

The configuration in this recipe creates 10 logfiles (the default) and uses the default trace file size of 10 MB, which is generally a useful size for logging events over a long period of time. If the router is the ingress or egress point for a large number of LSPs, you might want to increase the file size so that you have time to review or archive the logfiles before the files start overwriting each other:

```
[edit protocols rsvp]
aviva@RouterF# set traceoptions file size 100M
```

When debugging BGP, you can set one or more of the following trace flags to monitor BGP information:

```
[edit protocols rsvp]
aviva@R1# set traceoptions flag ?
Possible completions:
  all              Trace everything
  error            Trace error conditions
  event            Trace RSVP related events
  lmp              Trace RSVP-LMP related interactions
  packets          Trace all RSVP packets
  path             Trace RSVP path messages
  pathtear         Trace RSVP PathTear messages
  resv             Trace RSVP Resv messages
  resvtear         Trace RSVP ResvTear messages
  route            Trace routing information
  state            Trace state transitions
```

If you are receiving signaling errors when setting up or running RSVP, use the flag error flag to log erroneous conditions.

See Also

Recipe 5.10

CHAPTER 15
VPNs

15.0 Introduction

Customers want their internal networks to function as a single network so all employees can communicate and access corporate services regardless of location. Network service providers can create private networks that join all a customer's sites into a single network. These sites can be connected with point-to-point links, including leased lines, Frame Relay circuits, ATM circuits, and GRE tunnels that allow customer routers to peer with each other. This model of overlaying a private network on top of the public Internet leaves the network provider with the responsibility of designing and operating virtual backbones for all their customers. This solution presents several problems. Scaling issues will arise because a network provider must support more customers and more virtual backbones for an ever-increasing number of customers. When a customer adds a new site, the network provider will need to reconfigure all the existing sites and, as the number of sites grows, maintaining the private network will become more complex.

One solution to the scaling issues associated with private networks are BGP-MPLS VPNs, defined in RFC 2547bis and sometimes called *Layer 3 VPNs* because of the BGP component. Layer 3 VPNs can support thousands of VPNs with hundreds of sites per VPN and can support overlapping address space. BGP-MPLS VPNs set up private networks that run over the shared infrastructure of the Internet. As with private networks, VPNs interconnect geographically separate sites. They provide the same privacy and guarantees as private networks.

All Layer 3 VPN setup and maintenance is done by the network service provider on routers within its administrative domain. All that is required from the customer's point of view is to have normal connections to the service provider's routers from each customer site.

The discussion of Layer 3 VPNs involves three kinds of routers:

Provider edge (PE) routers
Are located in the service provider's network and connect the service provider to a customer. Within a VPN, pairs of PE routers are connected using a tunnel (created by MPLS, either with an RSVP-signaled LSP or an LDP tunnel). Each PE router maintains routes only for the VPNs it is connected to, storing routes for each VPN in separate routing tables to guarantee privacy within the VPN. All the VPN configuration is done on the PE routers connected to that VPN.

Customer edge (CE) routers
Are located in the customer's network and peer with PE routers, not with other CE routers. The CE routers just need a standard connection to the PE routers. They require no special configuration to participate in the VPN.

Provider (P) routers
Are within the core of the provider's network and are part of the tunnel between pairs of PE routers. They are not connected to any routers at a customer site. Provider routers run MPLS but know nothing about the VPNs.

Layer 3 VPNs use BGP extended community attributes to distribute routes within a VPN:

Target VPN (also called the route target or VRF target)
Identifies a set of sites within a VPN to which a PE router distributes routes. The target VPN determines the VPN to which a route belongs.

Site of origin
Uniquely identifies the set of routes that a PE router learns from a particular site. This attribute prevents looping, ensuring that a route is not distributed back to its origin through a different PE-CE connection.

VPN-IPv4 Addresses

Because VPNs connect private networks, addresses within the VPN might overlap. A common case is when two companies merge and then connect using a VPN. BGP-MPLS VPNs create unambiguous *VPN-IPv4 addresses* by prefixing a *route distinguisher*, which is a value that identifies the VPN to the private IPv4 address. As an example, for an IPv4 address of 10.0.31.0/24 and a route distinguisher of 65500:3, the VPN-IPv4 address is 65500:3:10.0.31.0/24. The VPN-IPv4 address is in the BGP VPN-IPv4 address family, which has been added as an extension to BGP (defined in RFC 2283). Only PE routers process VPN-IPv4 addresses, and these addresses are used only within the provider's network.

PE routers convert IPv4 routes received from devices in a VPN into VPN-IPv4 routes and then mark them with the VRF target, which is a BGP extended community attribute that identifies the VPN to which the route belongs. BGP running on the PE routers advertises the VPN-IPv4 routes to other PE routers. The receiving PE routers filter incoming VPN-IPv4 routes based on the extended community attribute to determine the VPN to which they belong. These routers then remove the route distinguisher and announce the IPv4 routes to their CE routers.

The route distinguisher is eight bytes and has three fields:

Type field (two bytes)
> Determines the length of the other two fields. If it is 0, the administrator (Adm) field is four bytes and the assigned number (AN) field is two bytes. If the Type field is 1, the Adm field is two bytes and the AN field is four bytes.

Adm field
> Identifies an assigned number authority. When the Type field is 0, the administrator field contains an IPv4 address, generally the router's IP address, which is a nonprivate address. When the Type file is 1, the Adm field contains an AS number, generally the IANA-assigned number.

AN field
> Number assigned by the service provider. For a Type field value of 0, the assigned number field is two bytes. For a Type field value of 1, the assigned number field is four bytes.

The VPN-IPv4 addresses are used by the routing protocols but do not appear in the IP packet headers, so they cannot be used for forwarding packets between PE routers. Layer 3 VPNs use MPLS as the forwarding mechanism. Each PE-CE interface is identified by a label, which is then distributed by BGP along with the VPN-IPv4 address. (Labels are assigned by interface, not by VPN, so if two CE routers in the same VPN are connected to same PE router, BGP will assign two different labels.) The result is that the VPN traffic carries two labels, the VPN label and the LSP label. The local PE router pops the VPN label and then uses the LSP label to forward traffic to the remote PE router, and the remote PE router uses the VPN label to determine the CE router to which it will forward the traffic.

Routing Tables for VPNs

JUNOS PE routers use some of the standard routing tables and create several routing tables just for VPNs.

Each PE router creates a bgp.l3vpn.0 routing table to resolve the VPN-IPv4 routes received from the MPLS tunnels that connect the PE routers. The PE router consults the inet.3 table of MPLS labels to resolve the route and converts it into an IPv4 prefix. The PE router filters the route against each VPN's import policy and distributes the prefix into the VPN's *VPN routing and forwarding* (VRF) table if the import filter passes.

Each PE router also creates a routing table for each VPN, called a VRF table and named *routing-instance*-inet.0 (you configure each VPN in a separate routing instance). The VRF contains the VPN's routes, which are the unicast IPv4 routes received from directly connected CE routers, any configured static routes in the

VPN, and routes announced by a remote PE router that match the VRF import policy for that VPN. Customer sites can access only the routes in their VPN's VRF. Maintaining the VRF separate from the standard inet.0 and inet.3 routing tables prevents a VPN's private routes from mixing with public (Internet) routes or with routes from other VPNs.

Each VPN has a policy that associates the VPN's VRF target or target community with each route before advertising the route and that filters which routes to advertise. A VPN label is distributed with each route, independently of the bgp.l3vpn.0 table. VPN routes are directly advertised to other PE routers; they are not distributed from the VRF table into the bgp.l3vpn.0 table.

The best routes from each VRF table are placed into a forwarding table in the router's Packet Forwarding Engine (PFE). This forwarding table is associated only with the VPN and is separate from the forwarding tables populated by the inet.0 and inet.3 routing tables.

The PE routers also maintain inet.0 and inet.3 routing tables for use with regular and VPN routing. inet.0 contains the usual intradomain routes (non-VPN routes only) and external (Internet) routes, including those learned by the IBGP sessions between PE routers. The inet.3 table stores the MPLS labels learned from the signaling protocol (either LDP or RSVP) that is used for VPN traffic.

Each VPN always has two policies associated with it. An import policy is applied to VPN-IPv4 routes learned from other PE routers to determine whether to add the route to the local bgp.l3vpn.0 table. Nonmatching routes are discarded. An export policy is applied to the VPN-IPv4 routes advertised by the local PE router to other PE routers. Nonmatching routes are not advertised.

15.1   Setting Up a Simple Layer 3 VPN

Problem

You want to set up a Layer 3 VPN for a customer who wants a private network for internal network communication and transactions.

Solution

Creating a Layer 3 VPN for the customer involves setting up your PE and P routers. The customer (or you) can set up the customer's routers (the CE routers). The PE and P routers must run an IGP, IBGP, MPLS, and a signaling protocol (RSVP or LDP). You establish an MPLS LSP between the PE routers and configure the VPN itself on the PE routers.

As a first step, set up the routing protocols necessary for the Layer 3 VPN. The PE and P routers must be running an IGP (this recipe uses OSPF). Following is the configuration for one of the PE routers, RouterG:

```
[edit protocols]
aviva@RouterG# set ospf area 0.0.0.0 interface t1-4/0/0
aviva@RouterG# set ospf area 0.0.0.0 interface lo0.0 passive
aviva@RouterG# set ospf area 0.0.0.0 interface fe-0/0/0 disable
aviva@RouterG# set ospf traffic-engineering
```

On the PE router, enable MPLS and RSVP on the interfaces that connect to the P router:

```
aviva@RouterG# set mpls interface t1-4/0/0
aviva@RouterG# set rsvp interface t1-4/0/0
```

Also, remember to configure family mpls on all interfaces between the PE and P router that carry MPLS and RSVP:

```
[edit interfaces]
aviva@RouterG# set t1-4/0/0 unit 0 family mpls
```

The IGP, MPLS, and RSVP configuration for the other PE router, RouterF, and for the P router, RouterJ, is the same, substituting the appropriate interface names.

On each PE router, set up an IBGP session to the other PE router. For PE RouterG, the following commands set up the session:

```
[edit protocols bgp group RouterG-PE-to-RouterF-PE]
aviva@RouterG# set type internal
aviva@RouterG# set local-address 192.168.19.1
aviva@RouterG# set neighbor 192.168.16.1
aviva@RouterG# set family inet-vpn unicast
```

Include the equivalent configuration on the other PE router, RouterF:

```
[edit protocols bgp group RouterF-PE-to-RouterG-PE]
aviva@RouterF# set type internal
aviva@RouterF# set local-address 192.168.16.1
aviva@RouterF# set neighbor 192.168.19.1
aviva@RouterF# set family inet-vpn unicast
```

The second step is to create an MPLS LSP between the two PE routers to carry the VPN traffic. On RouterG, configure the LSP to RouterF:

```
[edit protocols mpls]
aviva@RouterG# set label-switched-path RouterG-PE-to-RouterF-PE to 192.168.16.1
```

Remember that LSPs are unidirectional, so on RouterF, which is the far-end PE router, configure a return LSP to RouterG:

```
[edit protocols]
aviva@RouterF# set label-switched-path RouterF-PE-to-RouterG-PE to 192.168.19.1
```

The third and final step is to configure the VPN itself. You do this by creating a routing instance for the VPN. The following commands configure the routing instance on RouterG:

```
[edit routing-instances VPN2]
aviva@RouterG# set instance-type vrf
aviva@RouterG# set interface se-5/0/1
aviva@RouterG# set route-distinguisher 65500:2
aviva@RouterG# set vrf-target target:65520:100
aviva@RouterG# set routing-options static route 192.168.13.1/32 next-hop se-5/0/1
```

Discussion

This recipe shows how to configure a simple Layer 3 VPN for the network topology shown in Figure 15-1. In this network, a service provider connects two customer sites, Site A and Site B, with a VPN. The service provider network consists of two PE routers, RouterG and RouterF, and one internal router (the P router), RouterJ. At Site A, RouterG connects to the customer's CE router, RouterA. At Site B, RouterF connects to the customer's CE router, RouterD.

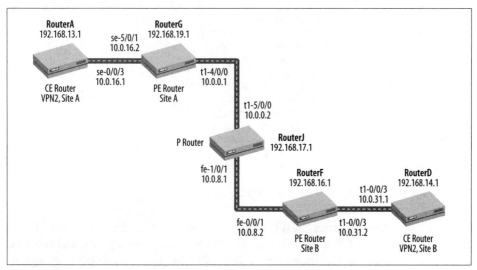

Figure 15-1. Simple Layer 3 VPN topology

Let's start by looking at what the service provider needs to do to support the customer's VPN. For the VPN to work, you first need to configure basic routing and signaling protocols within the service provider network. An IGP must be running on the network. This recipe uses OSPF, but you can also use IS-IS (see Recipe 11.1) or RIP (see Recipe 10.1). Use the show ospf interface, show ospf neighbor, and show route table inet.0 commands to make sure that the OSPF configuration in this recipe is working as expected.

For PE RouterG, these commands confirm that OSPF is operational and that the router is learning routes from OSPF:

```
aviva@RouterG> show ospf interface
Interface              State    Area            DR ID           BDR ID          Nbrs
lo0.0                  DRother  0.0.0.0         0.0.0.0         0.0.0.0            0
t1-4/0/0.0             PtToPt   0.0.0.0         0.0.0.0         0.0.0.0            1

aviva@RouterG> show ospf neighbor
  Address        Interface         State      ID              Pri  Dead
  10.0.0.2       t1-4/0/0.0        Full       192.168.17.1    128   39

aviva@RouterG> show route table inet.0
inet.0: 10 destinations, 11 routes (10 active, 0 holddown, 0 hidden)
+ = Active Route, - = Last Active, * = Both
0.0.0.0/0          *[Static/5] 1w1d 02:59:39
                    > to 172.19.121.1 via fe-0/0/0.0
10.0.0.0/24        *[Direct/0] 2d 08:29:31
                    > via t1-4/0/0.0
                    [OSPF/10] 00:48:34, metric 65
                    > via t1-4/0/0.0
10.0.0.1/32        *[Local/0] 2d 08:35:10
                    Local via t1-4/0/0.0
10.0.8.0/24        *[OSPF/10] 00:48:34, metric 66
                    > via t1-4/0/0.0
172.19.121.0/24    *[Direct/0] 1w1d 02:59:39
                    > via fe-0/0/0.0
172.19.121.119/32  *[Local/0] 5w1d 03:50:24
                    Local via fe-0/0/0.0
192.168.16.1/32    *[OSPF/10] 00:48:34, metric 66
                    > via t1-4/0/0.0
192.168.17.1/32    *[OSPF/10] 00:48:34, metric 65
                    > via t1-4/0/0.0
192.168.19.1/32    *[Direct/0] 2d 08:35:10
                    > via lo0.0
224.0.0.5/32       *[OSPF/10] 1d 02:40:52, metric 1
                    MultiRecv
```

The JUNOS software carries the VPN traffic across an MPLS LSP between the two PE routers. For the VPN to establish itself, MPLS and a signaling protocol must be running on all interfaces participating in the LSP. This recipe uses RSVP for signaling, but you can also use LDP (see Recipe 14.1). Check on each router to verify that MPLS and RSVP are running on the expected interfaces. The following commands confirm this on RouterG:

```
aviva@RouterG> show mpls interface
Interface       State      Administrative groups
t1-4/0/0.0      Up         <none>

aviva@RouterG> show rsvp interface
RSVP interface: 1 active
                    Active Subscr- Static   Available  Reserved  Highwater
Interface  State resv ption  BW       BW         BW        mark
t1-4/0/0.0 Up      1   100%  1.536Mbps 1.536Mbps 0bps      0bps
```

One last protocol that you need to set up on the PE routers is BGP. These routers need to be connected by an IBGP session that will exchange VPN routing information. Here's the IBGP configuration on PE RouterG:

```
[edit protocols bgp group RouterG-PE-to-RouterF-PE]
aviva@RouterG# set type internal
aviva@RouterG# set local-address 192.168.19.1
aviva@RouterG# set neighbor 192.168.16.1
aviva@RouterG# set family inet-vpn unicast
```

In the set neighbor command, use the loopback address of the other PE router, even though that router is not immediately adjacent. Here, 192.168.16.1 is the loopback address of RouterF. The set family inet-vpn unicast statement identifies that the session is for a VPN. Configure the other PE router, RouterF, in the same way.

Use the show bgp summary command to verify that the IBGP session is up:

```
aviva@RouterG> show bgp summary
Groups: 1 Peers: 1 Down peers: 0
Table          Tot Paths  Act Paths Suppressed   History Damp State    Pending
bgp.l3vpn.0            0          0          0         0         0            0
Peer             AS      InPkt    OutPkt    OutQ   Flaps Last Up/Dwn State|#A
ctive/Received/Damped...
192.168.16.1  65500       4627      4637       0       0 1d 14:33:01 Establ
  bgp.l3vpn.0: 0/0/0
```

The first line of the output shows that RouterG is in one BGP group and has one peer, and the State column in the Peer section tells you that the IBGP session is established. However, instead of the unicast routing table inet.0, the IBGP session is using the bgp.l3vpn.0 routing table, which stores the routes learned from other PE routers. Let's look at the contents of this table:

```
aviva@RouterG> show route table bgp.l3vpn.0
aviva@RouterG>
```

How come there aren't any entries in this table? It's because we haven't yet configured the VPN itself, so the PE routers are not exchanging VPN-related routes. We'll come back and look at this routing table in a little while.

The show bgp neighbor command also indicates that the IBGP session has been established:

```
aviva@RouterG> show bgp neighbor
Peer: 192.168.16.1+3136 AS 65500 Local: 192.168.19.1+179 AS 65500
  Type: Internal    State: Established    Flags: <Sync>
  Last State: OpenConfirm   Last Event: RecvKeepAlive
  Last Error: None
  Options: <Preference LocalAddress HoldTime AddressFamily Rib-group Refresh>
  Address families configured: inet-vpn-unicast
  Local Address: 192.168.19.1 Holdtime: 90 Preference: 170
  Number of flaps: 0
  Peer ID: 192.168.16.1     Local ID: 192.168.19.1     Active Holdtime: 90
  Keepalive Interval: 30        Peer index: 0
  NLRI advertised by peer: inet-vpn-unicast
```

```
NLRI for this session: inet-vpn-unicast
Peer supports Refresh capability (2)
Table bgp.l3vpn.0
  RIB State: BGP restart is complete
  RIB State: VPN restart is complete
  Send state: not advertising
  Active prefixes:              0
  Received prefixes:            0
  Suppressed due to damping:    0
Last traffic (seconds): Received 24    Sent 6    Checked 1
Input messages:  Total 4793    Updates 0     Refreshes 2    Octets 91101
Output messages: Total 4807    Updates 10    Refreshes 9    Octets 91913
Output Queue[0]: 0
```

The first two lines of the output show the peer's IP address, which is RouterF's address, and that the IBGP session is established. The `Address families configured` line shows that this interface can process VPN-IPv4 addresses (inet-vpn-unicast). Further down in the output, you see information about the bgp.l3vpn.0 routing table.

The VPN traffic between the two sites will be carried over an MPLS LSP. In the second part of the configuration, create this LSP on the two PE routers with the set `label-switched-path` commands. Use the show `mpls lsp` command to verify that the LSP is functional. Here, we check on RouterG:

```
aviva@RouterG> show mpls lsp
Ingress LSP: 1 sessions
To              From            State Rt ActivePath        P    LSPname
192.168.16.1    192.168.19.1    Up    0                    *    RouterG-PE-to-Ro
uterF-PE
Total 1 displayed, Up 1, Down 0

Egress LSP: 1 sessions
To              From            State    Rt Style Labelin Labelout LSPname
192.168.19.1    192.168.16.1    Up       0  1 FF      3        -    RouterF-PE-to-
RouterG-PE
Total 1 displayed, Up 1, Down 0

Transit LSP: 0 sessions
Total 0 displayed, Up 0, Down 0
```

The output shows what you expect. RouterG has one ingress LSP session, to RouterF, and one egress session, from RouterF.

At this point, you are ready to set up the VPN itself. Each VPN requires its own routing instance so that all information related to one VPN and its routing can be isolated from other routing and forwarding and from other VPNs that the router is managing. The set `instance-type vrf` command indicates the routing instance as being for a VPN and that its routes will be placed in the VRF routing table.

All routes that are part of the VPN are identified by a route distinguisher, which you define with the set route-distinguisher command:

```
[edit routing-instances VPN2]
aviva@RouterG# set route-distinguisher 65500:02
```

You can specify the route distinguisher in two ways. This recipe uses the AS number followed by a colon and an identifying value. You can also use an IP address followed by a colon and an identifying value. Neither format is better than the other. The format you choose depends entirely on your design and specific requirements. Using the *IP address:value* format allows you to identify the originating PE router when you are looking at a route and its communities, because you normally set the IP portion to the PE router's loo address. This format can assist with troubleshooting and operational monitoring. Using the *AS:value* format has the advantage of leaving more space for the Administrator variable (four bytes instead of two bytes). Service providers often choose this second format, using the value field to hold a numeric customer identifier. When looking at routes, this format makes it possible, on a network-wide basis, to identify the customer associated with a route.

For the VPN to know which routes belong to it, you define a VRF target using the set vrf-target command:

```
[edit routing-instances VPN2]
aviva@RouterG# set vrf-target target:65520:100
```

The command sets the route target (the target VPN), which is one of the BGP extended community attributes. The VRF target identifies which route belongs to which VPN and allows the VPN to accept routes into its VRF routing table and to advertise them.

The set vrf-target command also associates a default import and export policy with the VRF routing table to accept and advertise routes. The default policy uses the configured target, here 65520:100, as the match condition for routes received from remote PE routers. As the import policy states, any routes containing this target are placed into the VRF table. Similarly, when sending routes to local PE routers, the export policy is for the VPN to advertise any routes matching this target. The default routing policy is a simple policy that would look something like this if you configured it manually:

```
[edit policy-options]
aviva@RouterG# set community VPN2 members target:65500:2

[edit policy-options policy-statement VPN2-import-policy]
aviva@RouterG# set term 1 from protocol bgp
aviva@RouterG# set term 1 from community VPN2
aviva@RouterG# set term 1 then accept
aviva@RouterG# set term 2 then reject

[edit policy-options policy-statement VPN2-export-policy]
aviva@RouterG# set term 1 from protocol static
```

```
aviva@RouterG# set term 1 then community add VPN2
aviva@RouterG# set term 1 then accept
aviva@RouterG# set term 2 then reject
```

If you need more involved policies, configure them in the [edit policy-options] hierarchy and apply them to the VPN with the set vrf-import and set vrf-export commands, specifying the name of your policy. As an example, the following commands
apply the VPN2-import-policy and VPN2-export-policy policies to VPN2:

```
[edit routing-instances VPN2]
aviva@RouterG# set vrf-import VPN2-import-policy
aviva@RouterG# set vrf-export VPN2-export-policy
```

Finally, the VPN needs to know how to forward traffic to the CE router at the customer site. This recipe creates a static route to use for forwarding:

```
[edit routing-instances VPN2]
aviva@RouterG# set routing-options static route 192.168.13.1/32 next-hop se-5/0/1
```

You can also use BGP, OSPF, or RIP.

Now let's verify that the VPN is operational. First, check that you can ping the CE
router:

```
aviva@RouterG> ping 192.168.13.1 count 5
PING 192.168.13.1 (192.168.13.1): 56 data bytes
^C
--- 192.168.13.1 ping statistics ---
5 packets transmitted, 0 packets received, 100% packet loss
```

Why does the ping transmission fail if the static route is in the routing table? Let's
check the routing tables using a different command:

```
aviva@RouterG> show route 192.168.13.1 protocol static
inet.0: 12 destinations, 13 routes (12 active, 0 holddown, 0 hidden)
+ = Active Route, - = Last Active, * = Both
0.0.0.0/0          *[Static/5] 1w1d 20:56:23
                    > to 172.19.121.1 via fe-0/0/0.0

VPN2.inet.0: 5 destinations, 5 routes (5 active, 0 holddown, 0 hidden)
+ = Active Route, - = Last Active, * = Both
192.168.13.1/32    *[Static/5] 01:21:55
                    > via se-5/0/1.0
```

This command shows that the static route is present in the VPN2.inet.0 routing table
but not in the inet.0 routing table. To ping it, you need to specify the VPN routing
instance in the ping command:

```
aviva@RouterG> ping 192.168.13.1 count 5 routing-instance VPN2
PING 192.168.13.1 (192.168.13.1): 56 data bytes
64 bytes from 192.168.13.1: icmp_seq=0 ttl=255 time=18.399 ms
64 bytes from 192.168.13.1: icmp_seq=1 ttl=255 time=10.436 ms
64 bytes from 192.168.13.1: icmp_seq=2 ttl=255 time=25.565 ms
64 bytes from 192.168.13.1: icmp_seq=3 ttl=255 time=40.311 ms
64 bytes from 192.168.13.1: icmp_seq=4 ttl=255 time=10.346 ms
```

```
--- 192.168.13.1 ping statistics ---
5 packets transmitted, 5 packets received, 0% packet loss
round-trip min/avg/max/stddev = 10.346/21.011/40.311/11.186 ms
```

The ping operation now succeeds, and you have verified that static routing between PE RouterG and CE RouterA is working.

Let's take a moment and look back at the IBGP session between the two PE routers. When you first configured it, the session was up, but the router had not learned any routes from BGP because the VPN itself was not yet up. Now that the VPN is up, you expect to see BGP routes. Use the show bgp summary command on PE RouterG:

```
aviva@RouterG> show bgp summary
Groups: 1 Peers: 1 Down peers: 0
Table          Tot Paths  Act Paths Suppressed    History Damp State     Pending
bgp.l3vpn.0            2          2          0          0          0           0
Peer             AS       InPkt    OutPkt    OutQ    Flaps Last Up/Dwn State|#A
ctive/Received/Damped...
192.168.16.1   65500       5021      5034       0        0 1d 17:48:00 Establ
  bgp.l3vpn.0: 2/2/0
  VPN2.inet.0: 2/2/0
```

The last two lines show the two VPN-specific routing tables, bgp.l3vpn.0 and VPN2.inet.0 (the VRF table), both with BGP routes. Each table has two active routes and has received two routes. Recipe 15.2 explains how to view the contents of these routing tables.

See Also

Recipes 10.1, 11.1, 14.1, and 15.2

15.2   Viewing the VPN Routing Tables

Problem

You want to check the routing tables on the PE routers to determine that they contain all the expected routes.

Solution

The show route command displays the contents of all routing tables on the PE router:

```
aviva@RouterG> show route
inet.0: 12 destinations, 13 routes (12 active, 0 holddown, 0 hidden)
+ = Active Route, - = Last Active, * = Both
0.0.0.0/0          *[Static/5] 1w1d 21:04:56
                    > to 172.19.121.1 via fe-0/0/0.0
10.0.0.0/24        *[Direct/0] 3d 02:34:48
                    > via t1-4/0/0.0
                    [OSPF/10] 00:40:32, metric 65
                    > via t1-4/0/0.0
```

```
10.0.0.1/32          *[Local/0] 3d 02:40:27
                        Local via t1-4/0/0.0
10.0.1.0/24          *[Direct/0] 00:40:32
                        > via fe-1/0/1.0
10.0.1.2/32          *[Local/0] 00:40:32
                        Local via fe-1/0/1.0
10.0.8.0/24          *[OSPF/10] 00:40:32, metric 66
                        > via t1-4/0/0.0
172.19.121.0/24      *[Direct/0] 1w1d 21:04:56
                        > via fe-0/0/0.0
172.19.121.119/32    *[Local/0] 5w1d 21:55:41
                        Local via fe-0/0/0.0
192.168.16.1/32      *[OSPF/10] 00:40:32, metric 66
                        > via t1-4/0/0.0
192.168.17.1/32      *[OSPF/10] 00:40:32, metric 65
                        > via t1-4/0/0.0
192.168.19.1/32      *[Direct/0] 3d 02:40:27
                        > via lo0.0
224.0.0.5/32         *[OSPF/10] 1d 20:46:09, metric 1
                        MultiRecv


inet.3: 1 destinations, 1 routes (1 active, 0 holddown, 0 hidden)
+ = Active Route, - = Last Active, * = Both

192.168.16.1/32      *[RSVP/7] 1d 17:45:11, metric 66
                        > via t1-4/0/0.0, label-switched-path RouterG-PE-to-RouterF-PE


__juniper_private1__.inet.0: 2 destinations, 2 routes (2 active, 0 holddown, 0
hidden)
+ = Active Route, - = Last Active, * = Both
10.0.0.1/32          *[Direct/0] 5w1d 21:55:41
                        > via lo0.16385
10.0.0.16/32         *[Direct/0] 5w1d 21:55:41
                        > via lo0.16385


VPN2.inet.0: 5 destinations, 5 routes (5 active, 0 holddown, 0 hidden)
+ = Active Route, - = Last Active, * = Both
10.0.16.0/24         *[Direct/0] 01:30:28
                        > via se-5/0/1.0
10.0.16.2/32         *[Local/0] 01:30:30
                        Local via se-5/0/1.0
10.0.31.0/24         *[BGP/170] 00:40:32, localpref 100, from 192.168.16.1
                        AS path: I
                        > via t1-4/0/0.0, label-switched-path RouterG-PE-to-RouterF-PE
192.168.13.1/32      *[Static/5] 01:30:28
                        > via se-5/0/1.0
192.168.14.1/32      *[BGP/170] 00:40:32, localpref 100, from 192.168.16.1
                        AS path: I
                        > via t1-4/0/0.0, label-switched-path RouterG-PE-to-RouterF-PE


mpls.0: 5 destinations, 5 routes (5 active, 0 holddown, 0 hidden)
+ = Active Route, - = Last Active, * = Both
0                    *[MPLS/0] 1d 18:03:41, metric 1
                        Receive
```

```
1                      *[MPLS/0] 1d 18:03:41, metric 1
                          Receive
2                      *[MPLS/0] 1d 18:03:41, metric 1
                          Receive
100368                 *[VPN/170] 01:30:28
                        > via se-5/0/1.0, Pop
100384                 *[VPN/170] 01:30:28
                        > via se-5/0/1.0, Pop

bgp.l3vpn.0: 2 destinations, 2 routes (2 active, 0 holddown, 0 hidden)
+ = Active Route, - = Last Active, * = Both
65500:3:10.0.31.0/24
                       *[BGP/170] 00:43:17, localpref 100, from 192.168.16.1
                          AS path: I
                        > via t1-4/0/0.0, label-switched-path RouterG-PE-to-RouterF-PE
65500:3:192.168.14.1/32
                       *[BGP/170] 00:43:17, localpref 100, from 192.168.16.1
                          AS path: I
                        > via t1-4/0/0.0, label-switched-path RouterG-PE-to-RouterF-PE
```

Discussion

After Layer 3 VPNs are set up, you should check the routing tables on the PE router to make sure that the VPN is operating properly and to see which routes and MPLS labels the router has learned. The show route command in this recipe displays the contents of all the routing tables on the PE router. Let's examine the routing tables individually.

In the VPN configuration, you configured OSPF on the two PE routers and on the P router. The routes learned from OSPF are in the standard inet.0 routing table. To display just these routes on the PE router, use the show route table inet.0 command (see Recipe 8.1).

Because RSVP is running on the routers to support the MPLS LSP, the router creates the inet.3 table to store all MPLS routes learned from RSVP. Recipe 14.7 explains the routes in the inet.3 table.

Two of the routing tables are specific to the VPN. The first is the VRF table, which stores all the IPv4 routes received from the CE routers in the VPN. The JUNOS software names the VRF table using the name of the routing instance. In our recipe, the routing instance is named VPN2, so the routing table is named VPN2.inet.0:

```
aviva@RouterG> show route table VPN2.inet.0
VPN2.inet.0: 5 destinations, 5 routes (5 active, 0 holddown, 0 hidden)
+ = Active Route, - = Last Active, * = Both
10.0.16.0/24           *[Direct/0] 01:06:47
                        > via se-5/0/1.0
10.0.16.2/32           *[Local/0] 01:06:49
                          Local via se-5/0/1.0
10.0.31.0/24           *[BGP/170] 00:16:51, localpref 100, from 192.168.16.1
                          AS path: I
                        > via t1-4/0/0.0, label-switched-path RouterG-PE-to-RouterF-PE
```

```
192.168.13.1/32    *[Static/5] 01:06:47
                   > via se-5/0/1.0
192.168.14.1/32    *[BGP/170] 00:16:51, localpref 100, from 192.168.16.1
                    AS path: I
                   > via t1-4/0/0.0, label-switched-path RouterG-PE-to-RouterF-PE
```

The output shows five routes in the VRF table for VPN2. The 10.0.16.0/24 and 10.0.16.2/32 prefixes are the interface addresses between PE RouterG and its directly connected CE RouterA, and the prefix 192.168.13.1 is the loopback address of RouterA. The other two routes are received from the remote CE router, RouterF, at the other end of the LSP and have been learned from BGP as a result of the IBGP peering session between the two PE routers. The prefix 192.168.14.1 is the loopback address of the remote CE router in VPN2, RouterD, and 10.0.31.0/24 is the subnetwork between the remote PE and CE routers. Both these routes are reachable over the LSP:

```
> via t1-4/0/0.0, label-switched-path RouterG-PE-to-RouterF-PE
```

The VRF table shows that the route to the CE router 192.168.13.1 is a static route, which is what we configured in the recipe.

It's worth checking the VPN2.inet.0 routing table on the other PE router, RouterF, to make sure that it contains similar routing information:

```
aviva@RouterF> show route table VPN2.inet.0
VPN2.inet.0: 5 destinations, 5 routes (5 active, 0 holddown, 0 hidden)
+ = Active Route, - = Last Active, * = Both
10.0.16.0/24       *[BGP/170] 03:32:01, localpref 100, from 192.168.19.1
                    AS path: I
                   > to 10.0.8.1 via fe-0/0/1.0, label-switched-path RouterF-PE
-to-RouterG-PE
10.0.31.0/24       *[Direct/0] 02:44:50
                   > via t1-0/0/3.0
10.0.31.2/32       *[Local/0] 21:37:58
                    Local via t1-0/0/3.0
192.168.13.1/32    *[BGP/170] 03:32:01, localpref 100, from 192.168.19.1
                    AS path: I
                   > to 10.0.8.1 via fe-0/0/1.0, label-switched-path RouterF-PE
-to-RouterG-PE
192.168.14.1/32    *[Static/5] 02:44:50
                   > via t1-0/0/3.0
```

The two routes 10.0.16.0/24 and 192.168.13.1/32 use the LSP to reach the remote CE router. This is indicated in the third line of each entry, which shows to...via... label-switched-path RouterF-PR-to-RouterG-PE. The remaining three routes are for the local CE router (loopback address 192.168.14.1 and subnetwork 10.0.31.0/24).

The second VPN-specific routing table is bgp.l3vpn.0, which stores the VPN-IPv4 routes received from other PE routers. This table on PE RouterG contains the following routes:

```
aviva@RouterG> show route table bgp.l3vpn.0
bgp.l3vpn.0: 2 destinations, 2 routes (2 active, 0 holddown, 0 hidden)
+ = Active Route, - = Last Active, * = Both
```

```
65500:3:10.0.31.0/24
                    *[BGP/170] 00:03:40, localpref 100, from 192.168.16.1
                      AS path: I
                    > via t1-4/0/0.0, label-switched-path RouterG-PE-to-RouterF-PE
65500:3:192.168.14.1/32
                    *[BGP/170] 00:03:40, localpref 100, from 192.168.16.1
                      AS path: I
                    > via t1-4/0/0.0, label-switched-path RouterG-PE-to-RouterF-PE
```

The VPN-IPv4 routes in this table are for two routes in VPN2, which you configured with a route distinguisher of 65500:3. Looking at just the IPv4 portion of the address, 10.0.31.0/24 is the subnetwork between the remote PE and CE routers, and 192.168.14.1/32 is the loopback address of the remote CE router. To see the VRF target for the VPN-IPv4 routes, use the detail option of the show route command:

```
aviva@RouterG> show route table bgp.l3vpn.0 detail 10.0.31.0/24
bgp.l3vpn.0: 2 destinations, 2 routes (2 active, 0 holddown, 0 hidden)
65500:3:10.0.31.0/24 (1 entry, 0 announced)
        *BGP    Preference: 170/-101
                Route Distinguisher: 65500:3
                Next-hop reference count: 3
                Source: 192.168.16.1
                Next hop: via t1-4/0/0.0 weight 1, selected
                Label-switched-path RouterG-PE-to-RouterF-PE
                Label operation: Push 100032, Push 100048(top)
                Protocol next hop: 192.168.16.1
                Push 100032
                Indirect next hop: 85d5b00 262142
                State: <Active Int Ext>
                Local AS: 65500 Peer AS: 65500
                Age: 2:30       Metric2: 66
                Task: BGP_65500.192.168.16.1+179
                AS path: I
                Communities: target:65520:100
                VPN Label: 100032
                Localpref: 100
                Router ID: 192.168.16.1
                Secondary Tables: VPN2.inet.0
```

The second line shows the VPN-IPv4 address, and further down, along with other path attributes, you see the extended community VRF target in the Communities field. The PE routers filter based on the VRF target to determine which VPN the route belongs to and hence the VRF table into which to install the route.

The mpls.0 table also stores information used by the VPN. In this table, you see the distinct label that the VPN assigns to each PE-CE interface:

```
aviva@RouterG> show route table mpls protocol vpn
mpls.0: 5 destinations, 5 routes (5 active, 0 holddown, 0 hidden)
+ = Active Route, - = Last Active, * = Both
100048              *[VPN/170] 00:41:21
                    > via se-5/0/1.0, Pop
100064              *[VPN/170] 00:41:21
                    > via se-5/0/1.0, Pop
```

This output shows two labels to the CE router, not one. This is because of a detail in how VPN assigns labels. It actually assigns one for each next hop. The configuration is this recipe has two next hops to the CE router, one through the direct interface connection and one as a result of the static route configuration. You can see these two routes in the VPN2.inet.0 table:

```
aviva@RouterG> show route table VPN2.inet.0
VPN2.inet.0: 5 destinations, 5 routes (5 active, 0 holddown, 0 hidden)
+ = Active Route, - = Last Active, * = Both
10.0.16.0/24      *[Direct/0] 01:06:47
                   > via se-5/0/1.0
192.168.13.1/32   *[Static/5] 01:06:47
                   > via se-5/0/1.0
```

See Also

Recipes 8.1 and 14.7

15.3   Adding a VPN for a Second Customer

Problem

You want to configure a single PE router to keep the traffic for the two different VPNs separated.

Solution

Configure the VPN for the second customer on the PE router:

```
[edit routing-instances VPN1]
aviva@RouterG# set instance-type vrf
aviva@RouterG# set interface fe-1/0/1
aviva@RouterG# set route-distinguisher 65500:1
aviva@RouterG# set vrf-target target:65530:200
aviva@RouterG# set routing-options protocols bgp group VPN1-group type external
aviva@RouterG# set routing-options protocols bgp group VPN1-group peer-as 65530
aviva@RouterG# set routing-options protocols bgp group VPN1-group neighbor 10.0.1.1
```

Have the customer configure an EBGP session on her CE router that connects to your PE router:

```
[edit protocols bgp group to-ISP]
aviva@RouterH# set type external
aviva@RouterH# set peer-as 65500
aviva@RouterH# set neighbor 10.0.1.2
```

Discussion

From a service provider point of view, the whole point of Layer 3 VPNs is to allow a single edge router in your network to provide services to a number of different customers and to isolate each customer's network so that all information pertaining to it remains private. When configuring the PE router, you set up the router to keep each customer's routing information in separate routing tables and you establish unique route distinguishers so that the PE routers can identify which routes belong to which VPNs.

This recipe shows how to add a VPN called VPN1 for a second customer. Figure 15-2 shows the network topology with both customers' VPNs.

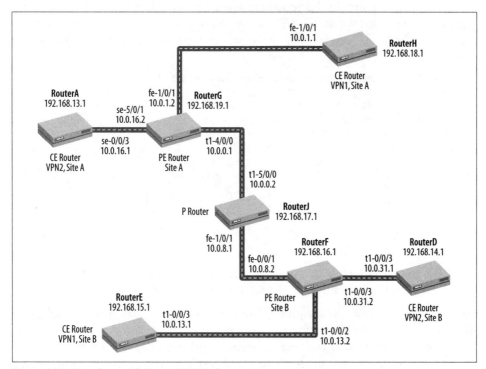

Figure 15-2. Topology with Layer 3 VPNs for two customers

Configuring the VPN for the second customer is somewhat simpler than for the first customer. An IGP, MPLS, and RSVP are already up and running on the PE and P routers, and the LSP between the two PE routers is already operational. What remains to be done is to configure the VPN itself. This VPN, named VPN1, connects to the CE routers using BGP rather than static routes. The following commands set the basic properties of VPN1:

```
[edit routing-instances VPN1]
aviva@RouterG# set instance-type vrf
aviva@RouterG# set interface fe-1/0/1
aviva@RouterG# set route-distinguisher 65500:1
aviva@RouterG# set vrf-target target:65530:200
```

The first command defines the routing instance type, which must be vrf for Layer 3 VPNs. The PE router connects to the CE router using interface fe-1/0/1. Each VPN must use a different route distinguisher and VRF target. VPN1 has a route distinguisher of 65500:1 and a VRF target of 65530:200. The VRF target attached to a route shows the VPN to which a route belongs.

Next, configure the EBGP session to the CE router. You do this within the VPN routing instance, not in the [edit protocols bgp] configuration hierarchy, because you are creating an *instance* of BGP that the JUNOS software associates with the VPN. The configuration commands in this recipe are also used to create a regular EBGP session, but they are included within the VPN at the [edit routing-instance VPN1 protocols bgp] hierarchy level. Here's what the completed configuration looks like on the router:

```
aviva@RouterG> show configuration routing-instances VPN1
instance-type vrf;
interface fe-1/0/1.0;
route-distinguisher 65500:1;
vrf-target target:65530:200;
protocols {
    bgp {
        group VPN1-group {
            type external;
            peer-as 65530;
            neighbor 10.0.1.1;
        }
    }
}
```

The BGP configuration establishes an external (EBGP) session with the neighbor 10.0.1.1 (the interface address of the CE router) that is in AS 65530.

For the VPN to work, the customer controlling the CE router, must establish an EBGP session with the PE router. On the CE router, the customer sets up a regular BGP session, configured at the [edit protocols bgp] hierarchy (see Recipe 13.1) and not part of a routing instance. Here's what the configuration on the CE router in this recipe looks like:

```
aviva@RouterH> show configuration interfaces fe-1/0/1
unit 0 {
    family inet {
        address 10.0.1.1/24;
    }
}

aviva@RouterH> show configuration routing-options
router-id 192.168.18.1;
autonomous-system 65530;

aviva@RouterH> show configuration protocols
bgp {
    group to-ISP {
        type external;
```

```
            peer-as 65500;
            neighbor 10.0.1.2;
        }
    }
```

As a first step in verifying the configuration, make sure that the EBGP session between the PE and CE routers is established. Check on the CE router:

```
aviva@RouterH> show bgp summary
Groups: 1 Peers: 1 Down peers: 0
Table          Tot Paths  Act Paths Suppressed   History Damp State    Pending
inet.0              1          1         0         0       0        0
Peer             AS     InPkt    OutPkt   OutQ  Flaps Last Up/Dwn State|#A
ctive/Received/Damped...
10.0.1.2         65500       69        69      0     1    33:25 1/1/0
                  0/0/0
```

The CE router has one BGP session to 10.0.1.2, the PE router. This is a regular EBGP session, and routes are placed in the inet.0 unicast routing table.

Checking on the PE router shows the BGP neighbors:

```
aviva@RouterG> show bgp summary
Groups: 2 Peers: 2 Down peers: 0
Table          Tot Paths  Act Paths Suppressed   History Damp State    Pending
bgp.l3vpn.0         3          3         0         0       0        0
Peer             AS     InPkt    OutPkt   OutQ  Flaps Last Up/Dwn State|#A
ctive/Received/Damped...
192.168.16.1     65500    23091     23102     0     0    1w1d0h Establ
  bgp.l3vpn.0: 3/3/0
  VPN1.inet.0: 1/1/0
  VPN2.inet.0: 2/2/0
10.0.1.1         65530       46        49      0     0    22:36 Establ
  VPN1.inet.0: 0/0/0
```

The last entry shows that the EBGP session to 10.0.1.1, the CE router, is established and that its routes are in the VPN1.inet.0 routing table.

VPN1 also has a CE router (RouterE) at the remote site that is connected to the remote PE router, RouterF. You configure these two routers the same way as the two routers shown in this recipe. Here's the VPN1 routing-instance configuration on the remote PE router, RouterF:

```
aviva@RouterF> show configuration routing-instances
VPN1 {
    instance-type vrf;
    interface t1-0/0/2.0;
    route-distinguisher 65500:4;
    vrf-target target:65530:200;
    routing-options {
        static {
            route 192.168.15.1/32 next-hop t1-0/0/2.0;
        }
    }
}
```

Now check the routing tables on the PE router. First, let's look at the VRF table for VPN1, which is VPN1.inet.0:

```
aviva@RouterG> show route table VPN1.inet.0
VPN1.inet.0: 4 destinations, 4 routes (4 active, 0 holddown, 0 hidden)
+ = Active Route, - = Last Active, * = Both
10.0.1.0/24        *[Direct/0] 00:42:02
                    > via fe-1/0/1.0
10.0.1.2/32        *[Local/0] 00:42:02
                     Local via fe-1/0/1.0
10.0.13.0/24       *[BGP/170] 00:07:11, localpref 100, from 192.168.16.1
                     AS path: I
                    > via t1-4/0/0.0, label-switched-path RouterG-PE-to-RouterF-PE
192.168.15.1/32    *[BGP/170] 00:07:11, localpref 100, from 192.168.16.1
                     AS path: I
                    > via t1-4/0/0.0, label-switched-path RouterG-PE-to-RouterF-PE
```

This table stores the routes for VPN1:

- 10.0.1.0/24 and 10.0.1.2/32 are the routes to the CE router, RouterH.

- 10.0.13.0/24 is the subnet to the remote VPN1 CE router (RouterE), which has a router address of 192.168.15.1/32.

If the VPN1.inet.0 table truly isolates the routes for VPN1 so they are not visible to other VPNs or routers on the network, you expect that these routes are not in any of the other routing tables. To verify this, look at the other routing tables on the PE router. Here is the inet.0 unicast routing table:

```
aviva@RouterG> show route table inet.0
inet.0: 8 destinations, 9 routes (8 active, 0 holddown, 0 hidden)
+ = Active Route, - = Last Active, * = Both
0.0.0.0/0          *[Static/5] 2w1d 04:49:05
                    > to 172.19.121.1 via fe-0/0/0.0
10.0.0.0/24        *[Direct/0] 1w2d 10:18:57
                    > via t1-4/0/0.0
                     [OSPF/10] 01:25:29, metric 65
                    > via t1-4/0/0.0
10.0.0.1/32        *[Local/0] 1w2d 10:24:36
                     Local via t1-4/0/0.0
10.0.8.0/24        *[OSPF/10] 01:25:29, metric 66
                    > via t1-4/0/0.0
192.168.16.1/32    *[OSPF/10] 01:25:29, metric 66
                    > via t1-4/0/0.0
192.168.17.1/32    *[OSPF/10] 01:25:29, metric 65
                    > via t1-4/0/0.0
192.168.19.1/32    *[Direct/0] 1w2d 10:24:36
                    > via lo0.0
224.0.0.5/32       *[OSPF/10] 1w1d 04:30:18, metric 1
                     MultiRecv
```

This table has no knowledge of the 10.0.1.1/24 or 10.0.13.1/24 subnets, nor does it know about the two VPN1 CE routers, 192.168.18.1 and 192.168.15.1.

The VPN2 routing table also knows nothing about these prefixes:

```
aviva@RouterG> show route table VPN2.inet.0
VPN2.inet.0: 5 destinations, 5 routes (5 active, 0 holddown, 0 hidden)
+ = Active Route, - = Last Active, * = Both
10.0.16.0/24       *[Direct/0] 6d 09:24:16
                    > via se-5/0/1.0
10.0.16.2/32       *[Local/0] 6d 09:24:18
                     Local via se-5/0/1.0
10.0.31.0/24       *[BGP/170] 01:35:08, localpref 100, from 192.168.16.1
                     AS path: I
                    > via t1-4/0/0.0, label-switched-path RouterG-PE-to-RouterF-PE
192.168.13.1/32    *[Static/5] 6d 09:24:16
                    > via se-5/0/1.0
192.168.14.1/32    *[BGP/170] 01:35:08, localpref 100, from 192.168.16.1
                     AS path: I
                    > via t1-4/0/0.0, label-switched-path RouterG-PE-to-RouterF-PE
```

A shortcut to verify that the VPN1 routes are only in the VPN1.inet.0 table is to look for routes to a prefix that you know is in this table:

```
aviva@RouterG> show route 10.0.1.1
inet.0: 10 destinations, 11 routes (10 active, 0 holddown, 0 hidden)
+ = Active Route, - = Last Active, * = Both
0.0.0.0/0          *[Static/5] 2w1d 04:58:17
                    > to 172.19.121.1 via fe-0/0/0.0

VPN1.inet.0: 3 destinations, 3 routes (3 active, 0 holddown, 0 hidden)
+ = Active Route, - = Last Active, * = Both
10.0.1.0/24        *[Direct/0] 01:36:31
                    > via fe-1/0/1.0
```

This output confirms that the route to the VPN1 subnet to the CE RouterH is present only in the VPN1.inet.0 table. The inet.0 table has no information about this route and uses the default route to try to reach it.

Next, check the bgp.l3vpn.0 routing table, which stores the routes received from other PE routers:

```
aviva@RouterG> show route table bgp.l3vpn.0
bgp.l3vpn.0: 4 destinations, 4 routes (4 active, 0 holddown, 0 hidden)
+ = Active Route, - = Last Active, * = Both
65500:3:10.0.31.0/24
                   *[BGP/170] 04:31:02, localpref 100, from 192.168.16.1
                    AS path: I
                   > via t1-4/0/0.0, label-switched-path RouterG-PE-to-RouterF-PE
65500:3:192.168.14.1/32
                   *[BGP/170] 04:31:02, localpref 100, from 192.168.16.1
                    AS path: I
                   > via t1-4/0/0.0, label-switched-path RouterG-PE-to-RouterF-PE
65500:4:10.0.13.0/24
                   *[BGP/170] 00:07:20, localpref 100, from 192.168.16.1
                    AS path: I
                   > via t1-4/0/0.0, label-switched-path RouterG-PE-to-RouterF-PE
65500:4:192.168.15.1/32
```

```
                    *[BGP/170] 00:07:20, localpref 100, from 192.168.16.1
                       AS path: I
                     > via t1-4/0/0.0, label-switched-path RouterG-PE-to-RouterF-PE
```

The PE router is now receiving routes from the remote PE router for both VPNs. The routes for VPN1 use the route distinguisher 65500:4, and the second two routes in the bgp.l3vpn.0 table are for VPN1. The first route, for IP prefix 10.0.13.0/24, is the subnet between the remote PE and CE routers, and the second route is to the CE router itself. These two prefixes match those contained in the VPN1.inet.0 table. The other two routes in the bgp.l3vpn.0 table use the route distinguisher 65500:3, which is for VPN2.

Let's also look at all the routing tables on the CE router to see what they contain:

```
aviva@RouterH> show route
inet.0: 5 destinations, 5 routes (5 active, 0 holddown, 0 hidden)
+ = Active Route, - = Last Active, * = Both
0.0.0.0/0          *[Static/5] 8w3d 04:25:38
                    > to 172.19.121.1 via fe-0/0/0.0
10.0.1.0/24        *[Direct/0] 1w0d 03:12:18
                    > via fe-1/0/1.0
10.0.1.1/32        *[Local/0] 1w0d 03:12:18
                      Local via fe-1/0/1.0
10.0.13.0/24       *[BGP/170] 01:39:35, localpref 100
                      AS path: 65500 I
                    > to 10.0.1.2 via fe-1/0/1.0
192.168.18.1/32    *[Direct/0] 1w0d 03:12:18
                    > via lo0.0

__juniper_private1__.inet.0: 2 destinations, 2 routes (2 active, 0 holddown, 0 h
idden)
+ = Active Route, - = Last Active, * = Both
10.0.0.1/32        *[Direct/0] 8w3d 04:26:16
                    > via lo0.16385
10.0.0.16/32       *[Direct/0] 8w3d 04:26:16
                    > via lo0.16385
```

What you see here is that the CE router is just a regular router. The only routing table it has is the inet.0 unicast routing table (and the private inet.0 table that is used internally by the JUNOS software). The CE router has no knowledge of the VPN. It has a route to the PE router using the prefix 10.0.1.0/24. [Direct/0], which indicates that the CE router is directly connected to the PE router. The CE router also has a route to the subnet between the remote PE router and the remote PE router, 10.0.13.0/24, which it learned from its EBGP session with PE RouterG. It's important to note that the CE router does not have any prefixes to reach any of the routers in VPN2. There is no prefix for CE RouterA (router address 192.168.13.1, on subnet 10.0.16.0/24), which is directly connected to PE RouterG, and there is no prefix to the remote VPN2 CE RouterD (address 192.168.14.1, subnet 10.0.31.0/24).

Just to make sure that prefixes are not leaking between VPNs, look at the routing tables on the VPN2 CE RouterA:

```
aviva@RouterA> show route
inet.0: 4 destinations, 4 routes (4 active, 0 holddown, 0 hidden)
+ = Active Route, - = Last Active, * = Both
0.0.0.0/0          *[Static/5] 2w1d 03:29:26
                    > to 172.19.121.1 via fe-0/0/0.0
10.0.16.0/24       *[Direct/0] 6d 10:05:34
                    > via se-0/0/3.0
10.0.16.1/32       *[Local/0] 2w1d 03:29:28
                      Local via se-0/0/3.0
192.168.13.1/32    *[Direct/0] 1w0d 08:31:19
                    > via lo0.0

__juniper_private1__.inet.0: 2 destinations, 2 routes (2 active, 0 holddown, 0 h
idden)
+ = Active Route, - = Last Active, * = Both
10.0.0.1/32        *[Direct/0] 2w1d 03:29:53
                    > via lo0.16385
10.0.0.16/32       *[Direct/0] 2w1d 03:29:53
                    > via lo0.16385
```

The router has prefixes to reach the PE router (over the subnet 10.0.16.0/24) but has no knowledge of the VPN1 CE router, RouterH.

See Also

Recipe 13.1

CHAPTER 16

IP Multicast

16.0 Introduction

The Internet was originally designed to carry two types of traffic, unicast and broadcast. Unicast traffic is sent from a single sender to a single host (or receiver), providing one-to-one delivery. Broadcast traffic goes from a single sender to all hosts, providing one-to-all delivery. Multicast traffic offers a third model, sending traffic from a single sender to many hosts (one-to-many delivery) and from many senders to many receivers (many-to-many delivery). Applications—such as streaming audio and video, collaborative groupware, teleconferencing, distributed online games, and "push" technology that sends periodic data delivery, such as stock quotes and sports scores—are well-suited for multicast because from a single source of data, they want to reach a specific, limited audience scattered across the Internet. If these applications use a unicast model, they must set up a session with each individual viewer. This places a heavy overhead burden on the source, which must replicate the video or audio stream for each customer. If these applications instead broadcast a single stream, the burden shifts to devices all across the network, which must replicate the stream regardless of whether there are downstream receivers interested in the video or audio stream. Multicast provides a way for these applications to deliver a single stream to all interested listeners.

Multicast networks consist of servers, which are the *sources* of a stream of multicast traffic, and clients, who are the *receivers* (or *listeners*) of the stream. A multicast stream is a flow of IP packets whose destination address is in the multicast address range of 224.0.0.0 through 239.255.255.255. (In classful routing, this is the Class D address space.) Each multicast address is the address of a *multicast group*. Routers use a combination of the source's unicast IP address and the multicast group to track multicast forwarding state. The notation used to represent this is (S,G), which is pronounced "ess comma gee." A common variant of this is (*,G), pronounced "star comma gee," where the asterisk is a wildcard that applies to any source sending to the group.

Multicast senders and receivers are generally PCs or hosts connected to a multicast-enabled router, which is the DR for the sender or receiver. Receivers use a group membership protocol to tell their DRs which multicast streams they want to receive and to dynamically join and leave multicast groups. Routers run a multicast routing protocol to direct the streams from the sources to the correct receiving networks. Using this protocol, the routers build a delivery tree, called a *distribution tree*, between the sender (or senders) and receivers of a multicast group. Multicast data follows the path of the distribution tree. Data flows *downstream* on an outgoing interface toward the receiver and *upstream* on an incoming interface toward the source.

Hosts use the Internet Group Membership Protocol (IGMP) to inform routers about which multicast groups they want to join, and routers use IGMP to verify that a host is still interested in listening to a group. There are three versions of IGMP, all supported by JUNOS software. Version 1 (RFC 1112) runs on Windows 95 computers, and Version 2 (RFC 2236) runs on most Unix hosts, including Mac OS X, and on Windows 98, Windows 2000, and Windows NT systems. IGMPv2 adds explicit leave functionality so hosts can report to the router when they are no longer interested in a group. (In IGMPv1, the host simply stops sending report messages, and after some time, the router assumes the host is no longer interested in the group and stops forwarding traffic for that group.) IGMPv3 (RFC 3376), supported by Windows XP systems, adds source filtering so the host can include and exclude specific sources when requesting multicast packets. Source filtering is required for SSM.

Perhaps the biggest difference between unicast and multicast is that unicast routing is concerned about where a packet is going and multicast routing is concerned about where a packet comes from. Unicast routing looks up a packet's destination address in the routing table to determine which interface leads toward the destination. The result is that unicast routing forwards packets from their source to (or toward) a destination. Multicast routing uses RPF to set up forwarding state from the receiver to the source (or root) of the distribution tree. RPF checks the routing table to determine the interface that is closest to the root of the tree, and this RPF interface becomes the incoming interface for the multicast group.

Multicast uses two methods to build distribution trees. With *shortest path tree* (SPT), the root of the tree is the multicast source. When a router learns that it has a directly connected listener for a group, it tries to join the tree for that group, building an SPT for that group. The router sends a Join message (specifically, an (S,G) Join message) out the upstream router for that group to let the upstream router know it wants to receive packets for the group. The upstream routers repeat this process until the Join message either reaches the DR for the multicast source or reaches a router that already has multicast forwarding state for the (S,G) pair. This process creates a branch from the receiver to the source.

The second way to build distribution tress is with a *shared tree*, in which the root of the distribution tree is not the source but rather is a router somewhere in the network. In Protocol-Independent Multicast Sparse Mode (PIM-SM), this router is called the *rendezvous point* (RP). With this model, the listener's DR router does not know the source's address but knows how to reach another router in the network (the RP) that does know the address.

There are two broad types of multicast routing protocols. *Dense protocols* use a push model, flooding traffic throughout a network and pruning back its distribution trees when the traffic is not wanted, a behavior called *flood and prune*. The Distance-Vector Multicast Routing Protocol (DVMRP) and Protocol-Independent Multicast-Dense Mode (PIM-DM) are examples of dense protocols. DVMRP was the first of the multicast routing protocols. It was developed in the early 1990s and was the first multicast protocol to run on the Internet Multicast Backbone (MBONE), starting in 1992. (The MBONE now uses PIM-SM.) DVMRP uses a simple distance-vector routing protocol similar to RIP to create its own routing table for forwarding and loop detection. PIM-DM also uses the flood-and-prune mechanism, but consults the unicast routing table populated to perform RPF checks, a property that gives PIM-DM (and PIM-SM) its protocol independence.

Dense protocols work well in domains that have a dense population of receivers, so most or all subnetworks are interested in receiving traffic from most or all active multicast groups. However, the flood-and-prune model does not scale for the Internet, where receivers are sparsely scattered throughout the network. For this reason, and because the flood-and-prune model uses a lot of network bandwidth and requires all routers to store all group state information, DVMRP and PIM-DM are rarely used. Also, DVMRP's underlying RIP-like distance-vector protocol does not scale across the Internet.

Sparse protocols use a pull model, waiting for explicit join requests from receivers and sending traffic only to where it is requested. Sparse protocols are a good choice when groups of multicast receivers are sparsely distributed across the network and network bandwidth is limited. Waiting to receive explicit join requests from receivers before forwarding multicast traffic is more scalable across the Internet and other large networks. PIM-SM is an example of a sparse protocol. PIM-SM was developed in the mid-1990s. As mentioned above, PIM uses the information in the standard unicast routing table, inet.0, when making RPF decisions. This routing-table information is learned from whatever unicast protocols are running on the router, and it is this property that makes PIM independent of any specific protocol.

In place of the DVMRP flood-and-prune model, PIM-SM uses RPs, which are routers that learn about all multicast sources and multicast receivers within their administrative domain. Multicast DRs send PIM Register messages to announce their existence, and they send PIM Join/Prune messages to announce their interest in a group. As the shared root, the RP is the matchmaker for the sources and the receivers.

You administratively configure the RPs in your domain, and one RP is active at a time. (Specifically, one RP per multicast group is active at one time in the case that some RPs do not service all groups.)

DVMRP and PIM are both multicast routing protocols, using RPF to forward multicast traffic. A number of other protocols support functions required by DVMRP and PIM, but they are not routing protocols because they do not handle forwarding state information. The Multicast Source Discover Protocol (MSDP) expands PIM-SM to allow RPs in different autonomous systems to learn about active multicast sources in other ASs. Effectively, MSDP makes it possible for multicast applications to run across the global Internet. Also, BGP has been extended with Multiprotocol BGP (MBGP; see RFC 2858) so that BGP carries NLRIs that can be used by other protocols, including multicast. MBGP allows a multicast router to create two separate routing tables, one that is used to make unicast routing decisions and a second to make RPF decisions.

For more information about multicast, see *Interdomain Multicast Routers: Practical Juniper Networks and Cisco Systems Solutions* (Addison-Wesley).

16.1 Configuring PIM-SM

Problem

You want to configure the router to support multicast within your AS.

Solution

Turn on PIM-SM on the router's interfaces:

```
[edit protocols pim]
aviva@RouterA# set interface all
```

Disable PIM on the router's out-of-band management interface. On J-series routers, disable PIM on the fe-0/0/0 interface:

```
[edit protocols pim]
aviva@RouterA# set interface fe-0/0/0.0 disable
```

On M-series and T-series routers, disable it on fxp0:

```
[edit protocols pim]
aviva@R1# set interface fxp0.0 disable
```

When you turn on PIM-SM, the JUNOS software automatically enables IGMP Version 2 on all LAN interfaces.

Discussion

Setting up PIM-SM on the router is very straightforward. In the PIM protocol configuration, specify the interfaces on which you want PIM to run. If you want the router to be a DR or RP, it must have a services PIC of some kind (Tunnel Services, Link Services, or AS PIC) to encapsulate and de-encapsulate PIM messages. The J-series and M7i routers, which are the routers used to create the recipes in this book, are the two exceptions. J-series routers can perform the encapsulation and de-encapsulation without a tunnel or services PIC, and the M7i routers have built-in AS PICs. Check for the PICs by looking at the router's hardware inventory:

```
aviva@R1> show chassis hardware
Hardware inventory:
Item            Version  Part number  Serial number   Description
Chassis                               29623           M7i
Midplane        REV 03   710-008761   CA6265          M7i Midplane
Power Supply 0  Rev 04   740-008537   PG10733         AC Power Supply
Routing Engine  REV 05   740-009459   1000431687      RE-5.0
CFEB            REV 05   750-010464   CF0420          Internet Processor II
FPC 0                                                 E-FPC
  PIC 0         REV 06   750-002971   CB0117          4x OC-3 SONET, MM
  PIC 3         REV 08   750-003845   HN4260          1x 800M Crypto
FPC 1                                                 E-FPC
  PIC 2         REV 07   750-009487   CF1068          ASP - Integrated
  PIC 3         REV 03   750-009099   CA6344          1x G/E, 1000 BASE
    SFP 0       REV 01   740-011782   P7J0Q0V         SFP-SX
```

This router has a built-in (integrated) AS PIC on FPC1 (also called AS Module [ASM]). The other M-series routers and T-series routers must have a services PIC installed on one of the FPCs. The following variant of the show chassis hardware command locates tunnel PICs in the router:

```
aviva@R3> show chassis hardware | match tunnel
  PIC 0         REV 01   750-004695   HD5980          1x Tunnel
```

The JUNOS software uses the services PIC to encapsulate and de-encapsulate PIM register messages, which the source's DR sends to the RP. Encapsulation and de-encapsulation requires a fair bit of router resources, so having a separate PIC that performs these functions is a good security feature. If a misconfigured or malicious DR starts sending a high rate of PIM register messages to the router, it is unlikely to bring the entire router's operations to a grinding halt. All PIM recipes in this chapter use the topology shown in Figure 16-1.

This recipe configures PIM to run on all the router's interfaces. To specify the PIM interfaces individually, list them in the configuration:

```
[edit protocols pim]
aviva@RouterA# set interface fe-0/0/1
aviva@RouterA# set interface se-0/0/3
aviva@RouterA# set interface fe-0/0/1
```

The default PIM mode is sparse, and the default version is Version 2. For a cleaner configuration, you should disable PIM on the router's out-of-band management interface, fxp0 on M-series and T-series routers and fe-0/0/0 on J-series routers.

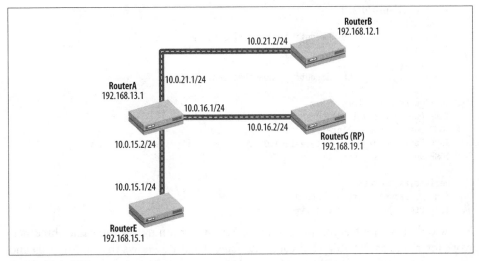

Figure 16-1. PIM network topology

PIM routers should also be running IGMP. Enabling JUNOS PIM automatically enables IGMP on the router, on all broadcast interfaces running PIM. This recipe turns on PIM on all interfaces, so IGMP is also running on them. IGMP allows the router's interfaces to handle group membership reports, so even if the interface is connected to a LAN on which none of the hosts or routers are running PIM, IGMP must be enabled on the interface so the hosts can join multicast groups.

To verify the configuration on the router, first make sure PIM is running on the expected interfaces:

```
aviva@RouterA> show pim interfaces
Instance: PIM.master
Name              Stat Mode       IP V State Count DR address
fe-0/0/1.0        Up   Sparse     4 2 DR        0 10.0.15.2
loo.0             Up   Sparse     4 2 DR        0 192.168.13.1
se-0/0/2.0        Up   Sparse     4 2 P2P       0
se-0/0/3.0        Up   Sparse     4 2 P2P       0
```

This output shows that PIM is running on the three network interfaces, fe-0/0/1, se-0/0/2, and se-0/0/3, and on the router's loopback interface. The Mode column verifies that PIM is in sparse mode, and the V column shows PIM Version 2. At this point, the router has no PIM neighbors, so the Count column shows 0 for all interfaces. The PIM.master in the first line indicates that you are looking at the main routing instance of PIM, because you are running only a single instance of PIM.

Next, check IGMP:

```
aviva@RouterA> show igmp interface
Interface: fe-0/0/1.0
    Querier: 10.0.15.2
    State:       Up Timeout:    None Version:  2 Groups:      0
```

```
Interface: se-0/0/3.0
   Querier: 10.0.16.1
   State:          Up Timeout:     None Version:  2 Groups:       0
Interface: se-0/0/2.0
   Querier: 10.0.21.1
   State:          Up Timeout:     None Version:  2 Groups:       0

Configured Parameters:
IGMP Query Interval: 125.0
IGMP Query Response Interval: 10.0
IGMP Last Member Query Interval: 1.0
IGMP Robustness Count: 2

Derived Parameters:
IGMP Membership Timeout: 260.0
IGMP Other Querier Present Timeout: 255.0
```

You see that without even configuring IGMP, it is running on the same three network interfaces as PIM-SM. For each interface, the State shows that IGMP is Up and operational and that the IGMP is Version 2. Because this recipe has not modified any of the default IGMP settings, the Configured Parameters section of the output shows the default JUNOS values of IGMP group membership parameters, which match the defaults specified in RFC 2236.

After configuring PIM on the other routers in the network, check again to see whether the router has located any PIM neighbors. You can check for PIM neighbors directly:

```
aviva@RouterA> show pim neighbors
Instance: PIM.master
Interface          IP V Mode     Option      Uptime Neighbor addr
fe-0/0/1.0           4 2          HPLG    5d 18:12:41 10.0.15.1
se-0/0/2.0           4 2          HPLG    5d 18:12:41 10.0.21.2
se-0/0/3.0           4 2          HPLG    4d 23:56:38 10.0.16.2
```

The three PIM-enabled interfaces each connect to one PIM neighbor. fe-0/0/1 connects to RouterE, se-0/0/2 to RouterB, and se-0/0/3 to RouterG.

Once you have configured PIM neighbors, the routers join IGMP groups:

```
aviva@RouterA> show igmp interface
Interface: fe-0/0/1.0
   Querier: 10.0.15.1
   State:          Up Timeout:      180 Version:  2 Groups:       4
Interface: se-0/0/3.0
   Querier: 10.0.16.1
   State:          Up Timeout:     None Version:  2 Groups:       4
Interface: se-0/0/2.0
   Querier: 10.0.21.1
   State:          Up Timeout:     None Version:  2 Groups:       4

Configured Parameters:
IGMP Query Interval: 125.0
IGMP Query Response Interval: 10.0
```

```
IGMP Last Member Query Interval: 1.0
IGMP Robustness Count: 2

Derived Parameters:
IGMP Membership Timeout: 260.0
IGMP Other Querier Present Timeout: 255.0
```

The output shows that each interface is in four IGMP groups. Use the show igmp group command to find out which groups the interfaces have joined:

```
aviva@RouterA> show igmp group
Interface: fe-0/0/1.0
    Group: 224.0.0.2
        Source: 0.0.0.0 Last reported by: 10.0.15.1
        Timeout:     64 Type: Dynamic
    Group: 224.0.0.5
        Source: 0.0.0.0 Last reported by: 10.0.15.1
        Timeout:     64 Type: Dynamic
    Group: 224.0.0.6
        Source: 0.0.0.0 Last reported by: 10.0.15.1
        Timeout:     63 Type: Dynamic
    Group: 224.0.0.22
        Source: 0.0.0.0 Last reported by: 10.0.15.1
        Timeout:     61 Type: Dynamic
    ...
```

This abridged output shows the IGMP groups for fe-0/0/1. The address 224.0.0.2 is the group for all routers on the local subnet, 224.0.0.5 and 224.0.0.6 are the groups for OSPF (OSPF is the IGP configured on these routers), and 224.0.0.22 is the IGMP group. (For a list of IP multicast groups, see *http://www.iana.org/assignments/multicast-addresses*.)

16.2 Manually Establishing a PIM-SM RP

Problem

For PIM-SM to function, the PIM domain needs to have an RP. You want to assign one of the PIM routers to be the RP.

Solution

Manually configure which router is to be the RP. Set the local router to be the RP:

```
[edit protocols pim]
aviva@RouterA# set rp local address 192.168.13.1
```

On the other routers, configure the address of the RP:

```
[edit protocols pim]
aviva@RouterB# set rp static address 192.168.13.1
```

Discussion

PIM-SM uses the RP as the shared root of a multicast distribution tree. Only a single RP is active for a group at any point in time. There are three mechanisms for creating RPs: static RP, auto-RP (see Recipe 16.3), and bootstrap router (BSR; see Recipe 16.4). Manually mapping RPs to groups is the simplest way to configure RPs in your network. A disadvantage of this method is that if an RP router becomes unavailable, no backup RP is immediately ready to take over, and multicast services will be unavailable until you manually configure another router to be the RP.

The first command in this recipe, set rp local, establishes the local router, RouterA, as the RP. For the address, use the router's loopback address. To verify the configuration, check the local router's loopback address and then list the PIM RPs:

```
aviva@RouterA> show interfaces terse lo0.0
Interface               Admin Link Proto Local                Remote
lo0.0                   up    up   inet  192.168.13.1         --> 0/0

aviva@RouterA> show pim rps
Instance: PIM.master
Address family INET
RP address       Type        Holdtime Timeout Active groups Group prefixes
192.168.13.1     static             0  None              0 224.0.0.0/4
Address family INET6
```

These commands show that the local loopback address is 192.168.13.1 and that this is the address of the RP. The Group prefixes column shows that the local RP is the RP for all groups in the range 224.0.0.0/4, which is the default for manually configured RPs.

The second command, set rp static, configures the non-RP routers to know the address of the RP so they know where to send PIM Join messages. Verify the configuration on the non-RP routers in the same way:

```
aviva@RouterB> show pim rps
Instance: PIM.master
Address family INET
RP address       Type        Holdtime Timeout Active groups Group prefixes
192.168.13.1     static             0  None              2 224.0.0.0/4
Address family INET6
```

The RP address column matches the RP's address.

To make the router be an RP for a more specific range than the default 224.0.0.0/4, include the range when configuring the RP:

```
[edit protocols pim]
aviva@RouterA# set rp local group-ranges 224.0.0.0/8
```

This command sets the local router to be an RP for 224.0.0.0/8 instead of the default 224.0.0.0/4. Different routers can be RPs for different ranges. The following command configures RouterG (192.168.19.1) is set to be the RP for the 234.0.0.0/8 range:

```
aviva@RouterA# set rp static address 192.168.19.1 group-ranges 234.0.0.0/8
```

Again, verify the configured group ranges:

```
aviva@RouterA> show pim rps inet detail
Instance: PIM.master
Address family INET
RP: 192.168.13.1
Learned via: static configuration
Time Active: 00:04:09
Holdtime: 0
Group Ranges:
        224.0.0.0/8

RP: 192.168.19.1
Learned via: static configuration
Time Active: 00:01:57
Holdtime: 0
Group Ranges:
        234.0.0.0/8
```

The detail version of the show pim rps command shows that both routers become RPs as a result of manual configuration.

See Also

Recipes 16.3 and 16.4

16.3   Using Auto-RP to Dynamically Map RPs

Problem

Instead of manually configuring the RP, you want the routers to decide among themselves which one should be the RP.

Solution

With auto-RP, the PIM routers determine which one should be the RP, thereby automating the distribution of the group-to-RP mappings. There are three steps for configuring auto-RP. First, configure PIM in sparse-dense mode on all routers in the PIM domain:

```
[edit protocols pim]
aviva@RouterA# set interface all mode sparse-dense
```

Then, configure the two multicast dense-mode groups 224.0.1.39/32 and 224.0.1.40/ 32 on all routers:

```
[edit protocols pim]
aviva@RouterA# set dense-groups 224.0.1.39/32
aviva@RouterA# set dense-groups 224.0.1.40/32
```

Finally, configure auto-RP on each router. One router in the PIM domain must announce auto-RP messages and another must map them. You can also configure the local router to perform both functions:

```
[edit protocols pim]
aviva@RouterA# set rp local address 192.168.13.1
aviva@RouterA# set rp auto-rp mapping
```

On the remaining routers in the PIM domain, configure sparse-dense mode and configure them to discover the RP:

```
[edit protocols pim]
aviva@RouterG# set interface all mode sparse-dense
aviva@RouterG# set rp auto-rp discovery
```

Discussion

Auto-RP dynamically maps groups to RPs, and PIM routers in the network automatically learn the addresses of the RPs. The auto-RP mechanism is not defined in an IETF RFC but is a proprietary mechanism developed by Cisco Systems for IOS routers and is supported by the JUNOS software so that JUNOS and IOS routers can interoperate within a PIM-SM domain.

Auto-RP provides a failover mechanism in case an RP router fails. You configure several routers as candidates to become the RP, and the routers elect the RP. If the elected RP becomes unavailable, the remaining candidate routers simply elect another RP. You do not need to intervene to modify any router configurations.

One of the first things to notice about this configuration is that auto-RP requires PIM be in sparse-dense mode rather than sparse mode. All routers in the PIM domain must be in this mode. Multicast groups can be in either sparse or dense mode, and PIM handles the groups appropriately. Auto-RP uses dense mode to flood messages throughout the network announcing RP candidates and to discover which routers have been elected as RPs.

If you commit the configuration after configuring just sparse-dense mode, use the show pim interface command to check the PIM mode:

```
aviva@RouterA> show pim interfaces
Instance: PIM.master
Name        Stat Mode       IP V State Count DR address
fe-0/0/1.0  Up   SparseDense 4 2 DR     1 10.0.15.2
loo.0       Up   SparseDense 4 2 DR     0 192.168.13.1
se-0/0/2.0  Up   SparseDense 4 2 P2P    1
se-0/0/3.0  Up   SparseDense 4 2 P2P    0
```

This output from RouterA shows that the three physical interfaces are all in sparse-dense mode.

In the second step in the configuration, configure the two multicast groups 224.0.1.39 and 224.0.1.40 as PIM dense-mode groups. The PIM routers use these two addresses, reserved by IANA for auto-RP, to elect the RP. All PIM routers that are willing to be an RP send RP Announcement messages to group 224.0.1.39. The PIM routers that are acting as RP-mapping agents join this group and select a single RP for each group address range. The group range and RP together are called an *RP mapping*. The RP-mapping agents then advertise the RP mappings to group 224.0.1.40. All PIM routers join this group to discover the RP for each group.

The final configuration step defines the auto-RP behavior for each PIM router. For auto-RP to work, at least one router in the PIM domain must announce its availability to serve as RP, and at least one router must map which multicast groups the RP wants to receive traffic from. This recipe configures a single router to perform both functions. The set rp local address 192.168.13.1 command establishes the local router as an RP candidate, and the set rp auto-rp mapping command configures the router to map RPs to multicast groups. All the remaining routers in this recipe are configured with the set rp auto-rp discovery command to discover the RP.

Check to see which router is the RP. Start on RouterA, which is the only router that has announced its willingness to be RP:

```
aviva@RouterA> show pim rps inet
Instance: PIM.master
Address family INET
RP address       Type        Holdtime Timeout Active groups Group prefixes
192.168.13.1     auto-rp          150     150             2 224.0.0.0/4
192.168.13.1     static             0    None             2 224.0.0.0/4
```

The output shows that this router is the RP both as a result of static configuration and of being elected by auto-RP. Check which RPs one of the other routers has learned about:

```
aviva@RouterG> show pim rps inet
Instance: PIM.master
Address family INET
RP address       Type        Holdtime Timeout Active groups Group prefixes
192.168.13.1     auto-rp          150     150             2 224.0.0.0/4
```

You see that RouterG has learned from auto-RP that RouterA (192.168.13.1) is the RP.

The net effect of this configuration in this recipe is that only one router in the domain, RouterA, is eligible to be the RP, so this router is still a single point of failure. To provide a backup RP candidate, configure another router to announce that it can be the RP:

```
[edit protocols pim]
aviva@RouterG# set rp local address 192.168.19.1
aviva@RouterG# set rp auto-rp announce
```

With this additional configuration, if RouterA goes down, RouterG automatically becomes RP. Checking on RouterG after the initial configuration, you see that RouterA is the elected RP:

```
aviva@RouterG> show pim rps inet
Instance: PIM.master
```

```
Address family INET
RP address      Type        Holdtime Timeout Active groups Group prefixes
192.168.13.1    auto-rp          150     150             2 224.0.0.0/4
192.168.19.1    static             0    None             0 224.0.0.0/4
```

When RouterA goes down, RouterG become the RP:

```
aviva@RouterG> show pim rps inet
Instance: PIM.master
Address family INET
RP address      Type        Holdtime Timeout Active groups Group prefixes
192.168.19.1    auto-rp          150     150             2 224.0.0.0/4
192.168.19.1    static             0    None             2 224.0.0.0/4
```

If you don't want the same PIM router to perform both the RP announcement and group mapping functions, configure one router to announce (as we did with RouterG above) and configure another one to map:

```
[edit protocols pim]
aviva@RouterE# set rp auto-rp mapping
```

After all routers are running auto-RP, look at the PIM interfaces on the routers. First, look at the RP router:

```
aviva@RouterA> show pim interfaces
Instance: PIM.master
Name             Stat Mode        IP V State Count DR address
fe-0/0/0.0       Up   SparseDense 4 2 NotDR     2 172.19.121.115
fe-0/0/1.0       Up   SparseDense 4 2 DR        1 10.0.15.2
lo0.0            Up   SparseDense 4 2 DR        0 192.168.13.1
pd-0/0/0.32769   Up   Sparse      4 2 P2P       0
se-0/0/2.0       Up   SparseDense 4 2 P2P       1
se-0/0/3.0       Up   SparseDense 4 2 P2P       0
```

Then, look at one of the non-RP routers:

```
aviva@RouterE> show pim interfaces
Instance: PIM.master
Name             Stat Mode        IP V State Count DR address
fe-0/0/0.0       Up   SparseDense 4 2 NotDR     3 172.19.121.119
fe-0/0/1.0       Up   SparseDense 4 2 NotDR     1 10.0.15.2
lo0.0            Up   SparseDense 4 2 DR        0 192.168.15.1
pe-0/0/0.32770   Up   Sparse      4 2 P2P       0
t1-0/0/3.0       Up   SparseDense 4 2 P2P       0
```

On both routers, you see that all the physical interfaces are running PIM in sparse-dense mode. You also see two new interfaces, pd-0/0/0 on the RP and pe-0/0/0 on the non-RP. pd stands for n and pe for PIM encapsulation, and they are interfaces on the tunnel, AS, or link services PICs that handle PIM Register messages. PIM Register messages use these two interfaces to encapsulate and de-encapsulate data packets. PIM-SM RPs create pd interfaces so they can remove multicast data from PIM Register messages, and PIM-SM routers that see a local multicast source on one of their interfaces use pe interfaces to send Register messages.

JUNOS routers perform the encapsulation and de-encapsulation in hardware, using the service PICs, not on the RE. This allows the routers to handle and forward PIM Register messages more quickly than if the RE were doing this. Also, the routing processes running on the Routing Engine do not have to be interrupted to handle PIM Register messages.

See Also

Recipes 16.2 and 16.4

16.4 Setting Up a PIM-SM Bootstrap Router

Problem

You want to use PIM in sparse mode, not in dense mode, and have it dynamically determine RPs, and you want to use a standard method, not auto-RP.

Solution

Configure a PIM bootstrap router to dynamically set up RPs for the PIM domain. First, configure the routers that are candidates to be bootstrap routers:

```
[edit protocols pim]
aviva@RouterB# set rp bootstrap-priority 50
aviva@RouterB# set interface all mode sparse

[edit protocols pim]
aviva@RouterA# set rp bootstrap-priority 50
aviva@RouterA# set interface all mode sparse
```

Then, configure which routers are candidates to be RPs:

```
[edit protocols pim]
aviva@RouterA# set rp local address 192.168.13.1

[edit protocols pim]
aviva@RouterG# set rp local address 192.168.19.1
aviva@RouterG# set interface all mode sparse
```

Discussion

PIM Version 2 supports a bootstrap protocol for dynamically learning the RPs in a PIM-SM domain and mapping multicast groups to RP addresses. A bootstrap router is responsible for constructing an RP set, which is a list of candidate RPs and the group prefixes that correspond to the RP set. The bootstrap router distributes this information in Bootstrap messages that are multicast to 224.0.0.13, which is the All-PIM-Routers group. Candidate RPs send Candidate RP Advertisement messages to announce their group prefixes to the elected bootstrap router. It is then the job of the elected bootstrap router to choose the RP for each group.

The PIM bootstrap protocol sets up a primary bootstrap router and a backup candidate bootstrap router, which is available in case the primary one goes down.

In this recipe, RouterA and RouterB act as the bootstrap routers, and RouterA and RouterG are the RPs. The set rp bootstrap-priority commands establish these two routers as the candidate bootstrap routers. The priority value ranks the likelihood for the router to actually become the bootstrap router. The value can be from 0 through 255, with a lower number representing a higher priority. However, setting the value to 0 makes the router ineligible to become the bootstrap router. The set rp local address commands on RouterA and RouterG configure these two routers as RPs. The commands in the recipe include the set mode sparse command to re-enforce the fact that the routers are running in sparse mode. If you are switching from auto-RP, which requires PIM to be in sparse-dense mode, make sure you change PIM back to sparse mode.

Verify that a bootstrap router has been elected. Both routers have the same priority for becoming bootstrap routers, so let's look on RouterA first:

```
aviva@RouterA> show pim bootstrap
Instance: PIM.master
BSR              Pri Local address   Pri State       Timeout
192.168.13.1      50 192.168.13.1     50 Elected         57
```

The BSR column shows that 192.168.13.1 (RouterA) is the bootstrap router. The State column confirms that this router has been elected as the bootstrap router. Now check RouterB:

```
aviva@RouterB> show pim bootstrap
Instance: PIM.master
BSR              Pri Local address   Pri State       Timeout
192.168.13.1      50 192.168.12.1     50 Candidate      124
```

The BSR column again shows that RouterA is the bootstrap router. The State column indicates that RouterB is the candidate bootstrap router. Why did RouterA win the bootstrap election? Because the bootstrap election priority is the same on both routers, the outcome is determined by choosing the router with the higher IP address.

Verify that the other routers know about the bootstrap router. We can look on RouterG:

```
aviva@RouterG> show pim bootstrap
Instance: PIM.master
BSR              Pri Local address   Pri State       Timeout
192.168.13.1      50 192.168.19.1      0 InEligible     121
```

Again, you see this router knows that RouterA (192.168.13.1) is the bootstrap router. The Pri column shows that RouterG's priority to become the bootstrap router is 0, which means it can never become the bootstrap router. The State column confirms this (Ineligible). The show pim bootstrap command output on the RouterE is similar to that on RouterG.

Now check the RP status on the routers. This recipe configured RouterA and RouterG as RPs. We check RouterA first:

```
aviva@RouterA> show pim rps inet
Instance: PIM.master
Address family INET
RP address      Type       Holdtime Timeout Active groups Group prefixes
192.168.13.1    bootstrap       150    None             3 224.0.0.0/4
192.168.13.1    static            0    None             3 224.0.0.0/4
```

The first line shows that this router (192.168.13.1) has been elected as the RP by the bootstrap router. The statically configured RP, shown in the second line of the output, is inactive because its hold time, which is how long the RP should remain active, is 0.

This recipe also configures RouterG as a candidate RP, so check its RP status:

```
aviva@RouterG> show pim rps inet
Instance: PIM.master
Address family INET
RP address      Type       Holdtime Timeout Active groups Group prefixes
192.168.13.1    bootstrap       150     150             3 224.0.0.0/4
192.168.19.1    static            0    None             0 224.0.0.0/4
```

The first line in the output confirms that RouterA (192.168.13.1) is the RP, as elected by the bootstrap router. The second line of the output confirms that we statically configured RouterG to be an RP, but the hold-time value of 0 shows you that this configuration is not active.

See Also

Recipes 16.2 and 16.3

16.5   Filtering PIM-SM Bootstrap Messages

Problem

Your PIM-SM domain uses bootstrap routers to elect RPs. Some of the routers have interfaces that connect to other PIM-SM domains. You need to ensure that Bootstrap messages do not cross the domain boundary.

Solution

On router interfaces that connect to other PIM-SM domains, create filters to prevent bootstrap router messages from crossing domain boundaries:

```
[edit policy-options]
aviva@RouterB# set policy-statement pim-bootstrap-import from interface se-0/0/3
aviva@RouterB# set policy-statement pim-bootstrap-import then reject
aviva@RouterB# set policy-statement pim-bootstrap-export from interface se-0/0/3
aviva@RouterB# set policy-statement pim-bootstrap-export then reject
```

```
[edit protocols pim]
aviva@RouterB# set rp bootstrap-import pim-bootstrap-import
aviva@RouterB# set rp bootstrap-export pim-bootstrap-export
```

Discussion

As a final part of the bootstrap router configuration, you need to make sure that Boot-strap messages from one PIM-SM domain don't accidentally cross into another PIM-SM domain. To prevent this from happening, configure bootstrap routing-policy filters that reject all incoming and outgoing traffic on interfaces that connect to other PIM-SM domains. The two policies you need to accomplish this are very simple:

```
aviva@RouterB> show configuration policy-options
policy-statement pim-bootstrap-import {
    from interface se-0/0/3.0;
    then reject;
}
policy-statement pim-bootstrap-export {
    from interface se-0/0/3.0;
    then reject;
}
```

Apply these policies directly in the PIM bootstrap configuration, with the set rp bootstrap-import and set rp bootstrap-export commands in the [edit protocols pim] hierarchy.

See Also

Recipes 9.1 and 16.4

16.6 Configuring Multiple RPs in a PIM-SM Domain with Anycast RP

Problem

Your PIM-SM domain has multiple RPs. When you use PIM bootstrap or auto-RP to establish RPs, PIM maps each group to a single RP, but you want to deploy more than one RP for a single group range.

Solution

Configure anycast RP on each RP router in the PIM-SM domain. First, configure the shared anycast address on the router's loopback interface:

```
[edit interfaces]
aviva@RouterA# set lo0 unit 0 family inet address 10.0.1.1/32
```

Also, make sure that the router's regular loopback address is the primary address for the interface:

```
[edit interfaces]
aviva@RouterA# set lo0 unit 0 family inet address 192.168.13.1/32 primary
```

When you configure the local RP address, use the shared address:

```
[edit protocols pim]
aviva@RouterA# set rp local address 10.0.1.1
```

Then, create MSDP sessions to the other RPs in the domain:

```
[edit protocols msdp]
aviva@RouterA# set local-address 192.168.13.1
aviva@RouterA# set peer 192.168.12.1
```

When you are configuring all the other non-RP PIM routers, configure a static RP using the shared address:

```
[edit protocols pim]
aviva@RouterG# set rp static address 10.0.1.1
```

Discussion

Anycast RP is probably the simplest and most redundant way to distribute RP-to-group mapping information among the PIM routers in a domain. Anycast lets you configure multiple routers to be RPs for the same group range, and traffic for all groups served by the RPs is load-balanced across the multiple RP routers. With other methods for setting up RPs, only a single RP is active at one time. If the active RP fails, the convergence time to elect another RP can be slow if you are using auto-RP or bootstrap, and it is even slower if you have to manually reconfigure the RP. Anycast RP significantly improves the convergence time over both auto-RP and bootstrap.

Anycast RP uses a shared anycast address across all the RP routers in the PIM-SM domain. This recipe uses 10.0.1.1/32 as the shared anycast address. To start the configuration of the RP routers, assign the shared address to the router's loopback address on each RP router. This address is not the primary lo0 address but is an additional address for lo0.

To make sure that BGP and OSPF use the main lo0 address as the router ID, include the primary keyword with that address in addition to explicitly configuring the router ID with the set routing-options router-id command. In this recipe, the primary address is 192.168.13.1, and the following command adds the primary keyword:

```
[edit interfaces]
aviva@RouterA# set lo0 unit 0 family inet address 192.168.13.1/32 primary
```

Check to make sure that both addresses are configured on the lo0 interface and that 192.168.13.1 is marked as the primary address:

```
[edit interfaces]
aviva@RouterA# show lo0
unit 0 {
```

```
        family inet {
            address 192.168.13.1/32 {
                primary;
            }
            address 10.0.1.1/32;
        }
    }
```

Also, check that the router ID is set:

```
[edit routing-options]
aviva@RouterA# show
router-id 192.168.13.1
```

As the next step in configuring the RP routers, use the shared anycast address as the local address when configuring the RP routers. Verify that all the RP routers have the same configuration:

```
[edit protocols pim]
aviva@RouterA# show rp
local {
    address 10.0.1.1;
}
```

The RPs in the PIM-SM domain use MSDP to discover each other and share information and to maintain a consistent view of the active sources. To set up MSDP on each RP, configure the address of the local router's loopback address and the addresses of the other RPs in the domain. This recipe shows the configuration on RouterA (local loopback address of 192.168.13.1) in a domain that has only one other RP, RouterB (loopback address of 192.168.12.1):

```
[edit protocols]
aviva@RouterA# show msdp
local-address 192.168.13.1;
peer 192.168.12.1;
```

Because anycast RP works in conjunction with an RP election method, you must also configure static, auto-RP, or bootstrap RPs on the appropriate PIM routers. This recipe uses static RP configuration, so you must configure the address of the RP on each of the non-RP routers. Here, you use the shared RP address, not the address of one of the router's primary loopback interfaces. Here's what the configuration looks like on the non-RP RouterG:

```
aviva@RouterG> show configuration protocols pim
rp {
    static {
        address 10.0.1.1;
    }
}
interface all;
interface fe-0/0/0.0 {
    disable;
}
```

Check to see which RPs the various routers have learned about. Let's start with one of the RPs, RouterA:

```
aviva@RouterA> show pim rps extensive inet
Instance: PIM.master
Address family INET
RP: 10.0.1.1
Learned via: static configuration
Time Active: 21:46:08
Holdtime: 0
Device Index: 130
Subunit: 32769
Interface: pd-0/0/0.32769
Group Ranges:
        224.0.0.0/4
Active groups using RP:
        224.2.127.254
        224.1.1.1
        224.0.1.40
        224.0.1.39
        total 4 groups active
```

The RP line shows that the shared address 10.0.1.1 is the RP for the group ranges 224.0.0.0/4. The output shows that four groups are actively using this RP. Looking on the other RP router, you see that it also lists the shared address as the RP for the group 224.0.0.0/4:

```
aviva@RouterB> show pim rps extensive inet
Instance: PIM.master
Address family INET
RP: 10.0.1.1
Learned via: static configuration
Time Active: 21:48:42
Holdtime: 0
Device Index: 130
Subunit: 32769
Interface: pd-0/0/0.32769
Group Ranges:
        224.0.0.0/4
```

Currently, no groups are using RouterB as the RP. As further verification, look at RouterG, one of the non-RP routers:

```
aviva@RouterG> show pim rps
Instance: PIM.master
Address family INET
RP address      Type      Holdtime Timeout Active groups Group prefixes
10.0.1.1        static           0    None              4 224.0.0.0/4
```

This router has also learned that the shared address 10.0.1.1 is the RP.

See Also

Recipes 16.2, 16.3, and 16.4

16.7 Configuring Multiple RPs in a PIM-SM Domain Anycast PIM

Problem

You want to configure multiple redundant RPs without the complexity of having to use MSDP.

Solution

Anycast PIM uses a mechanism similar to anycast RP but bypasses the need for MSDP. The configuration is similar to anycast RP. On each of the PIM-SM domain's RPs, configure the shared anycast address on the router's loopback interface:

```
[edit interfaces]
aviva@RouterA# set lo0 unit 0 family inet address 10.0.1.1/32
```

Set the router's regular loopback address as the primary address for the interface:

```
[edit interfaces]
aviva@RouterA# set lo0 unit 0 family inet address 192.168.13.1/32 primary
```

Then configure PIM. First, set the local RP to use the shared RP address:

```
[edit protocols pim]
aviva@RouterA# set rp local family inet address 10.0.1.1
```

Then, configure anycast PIM on the RP. First, configure the addresses of the other RPs in the PIM-SM domain:

```
[edit protocols pim]
aviva@RouterA# set rp local family inet anycast-pim rp-set 192.168.12.1
```

Second, configure the primary loopback address of the local router:

```
[edit protocols pim]
aviva@RouterA# set rp local family inet anycast-pim local-address 192.168.13.1
```

On the non-RP PIM routers, configure a static RP using the shared address:

```
[edit protocols pim]
aviva@RouterG# set rp static address 10.0.1.1
```

Discussion

Anycast RP provides the advantages of having redundant RPs, but the cost is that MSDP must run between all the anycast RP routers to synchronize the active source information. Anycast PIM, defined in IETF draft *draft-ietf-pim-anycast-rp.txt*, provides the same advantages but without the overhead of having to run MSDP to share active source information among the RPs. Anycast PIM extends the definition of PIM Register messages so that they carry active source information among all routers sharing the same unicast (anycast) address.

The anycast PIM configuration is quite similar to that for anycast RP. On the RP routers, configure the loopback interface with the shared RP address. This address tells other routers in the PIM-SM domain what IP address to use for the RP address. Mark the regular loopback address as the primary address so that address is used as the router ID by unicast routing protocols. Verify the loopback interface configuration:

```
aviva@RouterA> show configuration interfaces lo0
unit 0 {
    family inet {
        address 192.168.13.1/32 {
            primary;
        }
        address 10.0.1.1/32;
    }
}
```

On RouterA, 192.168.13.1 is the primary loopback address, to be used by BGP and OSPF as the router ID, and 10.0.1.1 is the shared RP address.

Instead of configuring the shared RP address at the [edit pim rp local] hierarchy as you did with anycast RP, you do this one level lower, at [edit pim rp local family inet]. You must configure three parameters: the shared RP address, a list of all the RP routers in the PIM-SM domain (called the RP set), and the primary loopback address of the local router. The RP set must be the same on all RP routers in the domain so that all the RPs have a consistent view of the active sources. If the lists are different, anycast PIM will not work. The configuration shown in this recipe looks like this:

```
[edit protocols]
aviva@RouterA# show
pim {
    rp {
        local {
            family inet {
                address 10.0.1.1; # <-- shared RP address
                anycast-pim {
                    rp-set {
                        address 192.168.12.1; # <-- primary lo0 of other RP
                    }
                    local-address 192.168.13.1; # <-- primary lo0 of this RP
                }
            }
        }
    }
    interface all {
        mode sparse;
    }
    interface fe-0/0/0 {
        disable;
    }
}
```

When you use the show pim rps command to verify that the anycast PIM RPs are configured and operating correctly, some additional information about the RP is displayed:

```
aviva@RouterA> show pim rps extensive inet
Instance: PIM.master
Address family INET
RP: 10.0.1.1
Learned via: static configuration
Time Active: 00:54:52
Holdtime: 0
Device Index: 130
Subunit: 32769
Interface: pd-0/0/0.32769
Group Ranges:
        224.0.0.0/4
Active groups using RP:
        224.1.1.1
        total 1 groups active
Anycast-PIM rpset:
        192.168.12.1
Anycast-PIM local address used: 192.168.13.1
Anycast-PIM Register State:
Group                           Source                          Origin
224.1.1.1                       192.168.15.1                    DIRECT
```

The first several lines show the shared RP address of 10.0.1.1 that was learned through static configuration, the group ranges this RP is servicing, and the active groups using the RP, all of which are displayed when you use anycast RP. For anycast PIM, you also see the set of RP routers in the PIM domain (in Anycast-PIM rpset) and the primary loopback address of the local router (in Anycast-PIM local address used). The last section of the output shows which groups the RPs have learned from the PIM Register messages that anycast PIM uses to share active source information among the RPs in the PIM-SM domain.

See Also

IETF draft, *draft-ietf-pim-anycast-rp.txt*, *Anycast-RP using PIM*

16.8   Limiting the Group Ranges an RP Services

Problem

When configuring the RPs for a PIM-SM domain, you want to limit the address range so the router acting as the RP does not need to handle traffic for so many multicast groups.

Solution

Specify the group address range when you configure the RP:

```
[edit protocols pim]
aviva@RouterA# set rp local address 192.168.13.1 group-ranges 224.0.0.0/8
```

Discussion

When you configure a PIM router to be an RP, by default it is eligible to be the RP for all groups. For IPv4 the default group range is 224.0.0.0/4, and for IPv6 it is FF70::/12 to FFF0::/12. If some multicast groups are sending a lot of traffic, a single RP might become overwhelmed with handling it all. To minimize router overload and congestion, configure several RPs and have each one of them act as RP only for a limited range of group addresses.

This recipe shows how to limit an RP to handle only groups in the 224.0.0.0/8 range. To verify that the configuration has taken effect, look at the RP routers:

```
aviva@RouterA> show pim rps
Instance: PIM.master
Address family INET
RP address      Type       Holdtime Timeout Active groups Group prefixes
192.168.13.1    bootstrap      150    None             4 224.0.0.0/8
192.168.13.1    static           0    None             4 224.0.0.0/8
Address family INET6
```

The Group prefixes column shows that this router is now RP only for the range 224.0.0.0/8. It is no longer RP for the default range of 224.0.0.0/4.

You can limit the group address range serviced by the RP regardless of the method you choose to establish the RP routers in your PIM-SM domain. The show pim rps output above tells you that the RP router was configured using a bootstrap router. You can also use the set rp local address group-ranges command if you configure the RP manually, with auto-RP, or with anycast.

16.9 Viewing Multicast Routes

Problem

You want to view the multicast routes that a router has learned.

Solution

The multicast protocols create a multicast forwarding cache, which the JUNOS software stores in the inet.1 routing table:

```
aviva@RouterA> show route table inet.1
inet.1: 1 destinations, 1 routes (1 active, 0 holddown, 0 hidden)
+ = Active Route, - = Last Active, * = Both
224.1.1.1,10.0.15.1/32*[PIM/105] 00:00:08
                        Multicast (IPv4)
```

Another way to get information about multicast routes is with the show multicast route command:

```
aviva@RouterA> show multicast route
Address family INET
Group: 224.1.1.1
    Source: 10.0.15.1/32
    Upstream interface: fe-0/0/1.0
    Downstream interface list:
        se-0/0/3.0
Address family INET6
```

Discussion

When a router receives multicast traffic, it places the (S,G) route information in the JUNOS multicast cache, inet.1. This recipe shows how to display the contents of this table with a variant of the show route command that displays just the inet.1 table. The output in this recipe shows one route, which is displayed as 224.1.1.1,10.0.15.1. The first part, 224.1.1.1, is the multicast group, and the second part is the source address of the route. Looking at the network topology, you see that 10.0.15.1 is the address of the fe-0/0/1 interface on RouterA, which connects to RouterE. This tells you that RouterA learned this route from a source connected to RouterE. The second column of the show route output reports that the route was learned from PIM, has a preference of 105 ([PIM/105]), and is a multicast route.

The format of the show route output is optimized for unicast routes, and really doesn't represent the details about multicast routes very well. A better command to use instead is show multicast route. The basic output is shown in this recipe. Use the extensive form to get more detailed information:

```
aviva@RouterA> show multicast route extensive
Address family INET
Group: 224.1.1.1
    Source: 10.0.15.1/32
    Upstream interface: fe-0/0/1.0
    Downstream interface list:
        se-0/0/3.0
    Session description: ST Multicast Groups
    Statistics: 0 kBps, 0 pps, 5 packets
    Next-hop ID: 359
    Upstream protocol: PIM
    Route state: Active
    Forwarding state: Forwarding
    Cache lifetime/timeout: 356 seconds
    Wrong incoming interface notifications: 0
```

The first several fields are common to the regular and detailed output. The Group field reports the multicast group that sent the route, which here is 224.1.1.1. The Source and Upstream interface lines tell that this route was learned from 10.0.15.1, which is the address of the fe-0/0/1 interface to RouterE. This interface is upstream, or toward the multicast source.

The interfaces toward the multicast receivers are listed next. Here, there is only one downstream interface, se-0/0/3, which connects to RouterG.

The extensive option displays additional information about the route. The Statistics line shows that this group has transmitted 5 packets, and Upstream protocol shows that PIM is the multicast protocol in use. Use the show multicast usage command to look at just the packet transmission statistics for each group and source:

```
aviva@RouterA> show multicast usage
Group               Sources Packets        Bytes
224.1.1.1           1       5              420

Prefix              /len Groups Packets     Bytes
10.0.15.1           /32  1      5          420
```

This output confirms that the router has received 5 packets from group 224.1.1.1, from the source 10.0.15.1 (RouterE).

If the router has not yet received any multicast traffic, the inet.1 table is empty because the routes have not learned any (S,G) state. For testing purposes, if you need to generate multicast traffic, you can issue ping commands. This is how the traffic in this recipe was generated because the test network being used is not connected to any multicast sources. To do this, first set up the Session Announcement Protocol (SAP) on a non-RP router to listen to a multicast address:

```
[edit]
aviva@RouterG# set protocols sap listen 224.1.1.1
```

Then from a non-RP router on the other side of the RP from the SAP-enabled router, ping the multicast address::

```
aviva@RouterE> ping 224.1.1.1 ttl 8 interface fe-0/0/1 count 5 bypass-routing
PING 224.1.1.1 (224.1.1.1): 56 data bytes
64 bytes from 10.0.16.2: icmp_seq=0 ttl=254 time=85.554 ms
64 bytes from 10.0.16.2: icmp_seq=1 ttl=254 time=10.612 ms
64 bytes from 10.0.16.2: icmp_seq=2 ttl=254 time=10.367 ms
64 bytes from 10.0.16.2: icmp_seq=3 ttl=254 time=10.365 ms
64 bytes from 10.0.16.2: icmp_seq=4 ttl=254 time=70.044 ms
--- 224.1.1.1 ping statistics ---
5 packets transmitted, 5 packets received, 0% packet loss
round-trip min/avg/max/stddev = 10.365/37.388/85.554/33.358 ms
```

16.10 Checking the Groups for Which a PIM-SM Router Maintains Join State

Problem

PIM-SM is enabled on all routers, and each router has discovered an RP. You want to check that the router has joined the desired multicast groups.

Solution

Look at the Join messages to see the groups for which the PIM router maintains join state:

```
aviva@RouterA> show pim join
Instance: PIM.master Family: INET
Group: 224.0.1.39
    Source: *
    RP: 192.168.13.1
    Flags: sparse,rptree,wildcard
    Upstream interface: local
Group: 224.0.1.40
    Source: *
    RP: 192.168.13.1
    Flags: sparse,rptree,wildcard
    Upstream interface: local
Group: 224.1.1.1
    Source: *
    RP: 192.168.13.1
    Flags: sparse,rptree,wildcard
    Upstream interface: local
Group: 224.1.1.1
    Source: 10.0.15.1
    Flags: sparse
    Upstream interface: fe-0/0/1.0
Group: 224.2.127.254
    Source: *
    RP: 192.168.13.1
    Flags: sparse,rptree,wildcard
    Upstream interface: local
Group: 230.0.1.1
    Source: *
    RP: 192.168.13.1
    Flags: sparse,rptree,wildcard
    Upstream interface: local
Instance: PIM.master Family: INET6
```

The extensive version of this command gives the details for each multicast group:

```
aviva@RouterA> show pim join extensive 224.1.1.1
Instance: PIM.master Family: INET
Group: 224.1.1.1
    Source: *
    RP: 192.168.13.1
    Flags: sparse,rptree,wildcard
    Upstream interface: local
    Upstream neighbor: Local
    Upstream State: Local RP
    Downstream Neighbors:
        Interface: se-0/0/3.0
            10.0.16.2 State: Join Flags: SRW Timeout: 165
Group: 224.1.1.1
    Source: 10.0.15.1
```

```
Flags: sparse
Upstream interface: fe-0/0/1.0
Upstream neighbor: 10.0.15.1
Upstream State: Local Source, Local RP
Keepalive timeout: 116
Downstream Neighbors:
    Interface: se-0/0/3.0
        10.0.16.2 State: Join Flags: S Timeout: 165
```

Discussion

When a host connected to a PIM router informs the router that it wants to receive traffic from a multicast group, the PIM router sends (S,G) Join messages out its RPF interfaces to inform the next upstream router that it wants to receive packets for that group. Each upstream router repeats this process until this branch of the multicast tree reaches the router directly connected to the multicast source or reaches a router that already has multicast forwarding state for the (S,G) pair.

The show pim join command lists all groups the router has sent Join messages to and has successfully joined. The output in this recipe indicates that RouterA has joined six multicast groups. For each group, you see the multicast source of the group. This is either the IP address of a source router or an asterisk (*) if the Join message is directed toward any source. The RP line shows the address of the rendezvous point for the group, and Upstream interface is the router's interface toward the group's source.

The extensive version of the command shows the upstream state, which is information about the upstream router, and downstream interfaces toward the multicast receiver.

The output of the show pim join extensive command for group 224.1.1.1 agrees with the route information displayed with the show multicast route extensive command (explained in Recipe 16.9):

```
aviva@RouterA> show multicast route extensive
Address family INET
Group: 224.1.1.1
    Source: 10.0.15.1/32
    Upstream interface: fe-0/0/1.0
    Downstream interface list:
        se-0/0/3.0
    Session description: ST Multicast Groups
    Statistics: 0 kBps, 0 pps, 5 packets
    Next-hop ID: 359
    Upstream protocol: PIM
    Route state: Active
    Forwarding state: Forwarding
    Cache lifetime/timeout: 356 seconds
    Wrong incoming interface notifications: 0
```

The information these two commands displays is subtly different. The show multicast route command describes forwarding plane information, while the show pim join command covers the control plane. The information in the two commands should agree, but each command shows some information that the other does not.

See Also

Recipe 16.9

16.11 Manually Configuring IGMP

Problem

The JUNOS software automatically turns on IGMP Version 2 when you configure PIM-SM. However, you want to use SSM, which requires IGMP Version 3.

Solution

Enable IGMPv3 on the desired router interfaces:

```
[edit protocols]
aviva@RouterA# set igmp interface all version 3
```

Discussion

For PIM-SM, you normally use IGMPv2, which is automatically enabled on all LAN interfaces when you configure PIM-SM. SSM requires that the router run IGMPv3, which supports source filtering so the host can include and exclude specific sources when requesting multicast packets.

To use IGMPv3, simply configure it on all the desired interfaces. This recipe configures IGMPv3 on all the router's interfaces. Use the show igmp interface command to verify that Version 3 is running:

```
aviva@RouterA> show igmp interface
Interface: fe-0/0/0.0
    Querier: 172.19.121.112
    State:         Up Timeout:     188 Version:  3 Groups:       4
Interface: fe-0/0/1.0
    Querier: 10.0.15.1
    State:         Up Timeout:     216 Version:  3 Groups:       0
Interface: se-0/0/3.0
    Querier: 10.0.16.1
    State:         Up Timeout:    None Version:  3 Groups:       0
Interface: se-0/0/2.0
    Querier: 10.0.21.1
    State:         Up Timeout:    None Version:  3 Groups:       2

Configured Parameters:
IGMP Query Interval: 125.0
```

```
IGMP Query Response Interval: 10.0
IGMP Last Member Query Interval: 1.0
IGMP Robustness Count: 2

Derived Parameters:
IGMP Membership Timeout: 260.0
IGMP Other Querier Present Timeout: 255.0
```

The output confirms that the three networking interfaces on this router are all running IGMPv3.

16.12 Using SSM

Problem

You want to directly join a multicast group without going through an RP.

Solution

Configure an SSM-only domain. First, enable PIM-SM on all interfaces on all routers in the domain:

```
[edit protocols pim]
aviva@RouterA# set interface all
```

Disable PIM on the router's out-of-band management interface. On J-series routers, this is the fe-0/0/0 interface:

```
aviva@RouterA# set interface fe-0/0/0.0 disable
```

On M-series and T-series routers, it is the fxp0 interface:

```
aviva@R1# set interface fxp0.0 disable
```

On the multicast receiver's DR, turn on IGMPv3 on the interface that faces the receiving host:

```
[edit protocols igmp]
aviva@RouterA# set interface fe-0/0/1 version 3
```

Discussion

SSM modifies the standard PIM-SM model, sometimes also called any-source multicast (ASM), by allowing routers to directly join a multicast group without using the RP as an intermediary. SSM can be used with multicast applications that are running IGMPv3.

SSM is really just a subset of ASM (plain-old PIM-SM). With SSM, the receiver is able to specify the source (using IGMPv3), so the receiver's DR sends an (S,G) message toward the source, and traffic flows down the SPT from the source to the receiver. SSM uses PIM-SM to get (S,G) state information. (PIM supports both (S,G) and (*,G) state.) So, just by turning on PIM-SM for an interface, it supports SSM and

ASM. This configuration mechanism is very easy, so if you are new to multicast, you should consider choosing SSM as the multicast protocol.

The steps for configuring SSM are very straightforward. First, configure PIM-SM on all interfaces and on all routers in your domain. Just by turning on PIM-SM and nothing else on these routers, they support SSM for all router roles except the receiver's DR. On the receiver's DR, you need to enable IGMPv3 on the interface that connects to the receiving host. Here's what the configuration looks like:

```
aviva@RouterA> show configuration protocols igmp
interface fe-0/0/0.0 {
    disable;
}
interface fe-0/0/1.0 {
    version 3;
}
```

The receiving host, typically a PC of some kind, must also be running IGMPv3.

Look at the IGMP interfaces to verify that the configuration has taken effect:

```
aviva@RouterA> show igmp interface
Interface: fe-0/0/1.0
    Querier: 10.0.15.1
    State:          Up Timeout:       185 Version:  3 Groups:        0
Interface: se-0/0/3.0
    Querier: 10.0.16.1
    State:          Up Timeout:      None Version:  2 Groups:        4
Interface: se-0/0/2.0
    Querier: 10.0.21.1
    State:          Up Timeout:      None Version:  2 Groups:        4

Configured Parameters:
IGMP Query Interval: 125.0
IGMP Query Response Interval: 10.0
IGMP Last Member Query Interval: 1.0
IGMP Robustness Count: 2

Derived Parameters:
IGMP Membership Timeout: 260.0
IGMP Other Querier Present Timeout: 255.0
```

You see that fe-0/0/1, the interface facing the receiver, is running IGMPv3, and all other router interfaces are running IGMPv2, which is enabled automatically when you turn on PIM-SM.

For the network to be an SSM-only domain, make sure it contains no RP routers. If the router receives a bootstrap routing message, it will automatically build an RP mapping and the network will no longer be SSM-only.

If you are not sure that the domain has no RPs, or if you want to ensure that the domain continues using SSM if an RP is later configured, block any Bootstrap messages from entering or leaving the router:

```
[edit policy-options]
aviva@RouterA# set policy-statement block-bootstrap then reject

[edit protocols pim]
aviva@RouterA# set rp bootstrap-import block-bootstrap
aviva@RouterA# set rp bootstrap-export block-bootstrap
```

See Also

RFC 3569, *An Overview of Source-Specific Multicast (SSM)*

16.13 Connecting PIM-SM Domains Using MSDP and MBGP

Problem

You want to configure the routers so that customers in your AS can receive multicast streams from sources that are managed and maintained by another ISP.

Solution

Use MSDP, along with Multiprotocol BGP (MBGP), to connect the two PIM-SM domains. The MSDP connection runs parallel to the MBGP connection. Start by setting up the BGP border routers. This recipe has redundant EBGP connections between the ASs, one that runs MSDP and carries the multicast traffic and one that carries only unicast traffic.

Let's start with the multicast-enabled border router. Create RIB groups for MSDP, PIM, and the router's interfaces to use:

```
[edit routing-options]
aviva@RouterG# set rib-group mcast-rib export-rib inet.2
aviva@RouterG# set rib-group mcast-rib import-rib inet.2
aviva@RouterG# set rib-group if-rib import-rib [inet.0 inet.2]
aviva@RouterG# set interface-routes rib-group inet if-rib
```

Configure MSDP, specifying the address of its peer and telling it to use the multicast RIB groups:

```
[edit protocols msdp]
aviva@RouterG# set local-address 192.168.19.1
aviva@RouterG# set peer 192.168.19.1
aviva@RouterG# set rib-group inet mcast-rib
```

Configure an EBGP session, enabling MBGP on it:

```
[edit routing-options]
aviva@RouterG# set router-id 192.168.19.1
aviva@RouterG# set autonomous-system 65500

[edit protocols bgp group external]
aviva@RouterG# set type external
aviva@RouterG# set peer-as 65520
aviva@RouterG# set neighbor 10.0.1.1
aviva@RouterG# set family inet any
```

The border router also needs to be the PIM-SM RP, and PIM needs to use the multicast RIB groups:

```
[edit protocols pim]
aviva@RouterG# set interface all
aviva@RouterG# set interface fe-0/0/0 disable
aviva@RouterG# set rp local address 192.168.19.1
aviva@RouterG# set rib-group inet mcast-rib
```

The configuration on the EBGP/MSDP peer router in the other AS should be the same, substituting the correct AS number and interface names and addresses.

Next, configure the border router that will handle the unicast traffic. Configure an EBGP session with the remote peer, configuring it to carry only unicast routes:

```
[edit routing-options]
aviva@RouterB# set router-id 192.168.12.1
aviva@RouterB# set autonomous-system 65500

[edit protocols bgp group external]
aviva@RouterB# set type external
aviva@RouterB# set peer-as 65520
aviva@RouterB# set neighbor 10.0.22.2
aviva@RouterB# set family inet unicast
```

Configure PIM-SM only on the interfaces facing the local AS:

```
[edit protocols pim]
aviva@RouterB# set interface se-0/0/2
aviva@RouterB# set rp static address 192.168.19.1
```

For all the other routers that are not on the AS border, just configure PIM-SM normally:

```
[edit protocols pim]
aviva@RouterE# set interface all
aviva@RouterE# set interface fe-0/0/0 disable
aviva@RouterE# set rp static address 192.168.19.1
```

All the routers must also be running an IGP. The routers in this example are running OSPF.

Discussion

With PIM-SM, the RP in each domain learns about active sources within its domain and the DRs learn the source information from the data that is received down the shared tree when they send a (*.G) toward the RP. MSDP enables RPs in different domains to share information about active sources. This allows customers in your AS to access multicast sources that are maintained somewhere else on the Internet. MSDP uses TCP to establish reliable sessions between PIM-SM domains and passes source active messages over the session so that the RPs can learn about external sources. Also, MSDP enables different RPs within a domain to exchange source information between the subdomains—with anycast, for example.

One way to set up MSDP to handle interdomain source information is to create redundant EBGP connections to the remote AS. One EBGP session carries the multi-cast traffic, and the other carries unicast traffic. On the multicast-enabled EBGP router, you enable MBGP and create a separate routing table that contains only the unicast routes whose next hop points to a multicast-enabled router. (It is still the case that most routers in the Internet don't support multicast.) PIM consults this table during RPF calculations instead of using the default inet.0 table to forward multicast traffic. Another way to set up the MSDP peering session is to do so between two RP routers that are in the core of the network instead of at the edge.

Figure 16-2 shows the topology used in this recipe. The following points summarize the overall configuration:

- There are two EBGP connections between the two ASs, one between RouterG and RouterH, the second between RouterB and RouterC.

- The EBGP connection between RouterG and RouterH is multicast-enabled. MSDP runs on both these routers, and each is the RP for its PIM-SM domain. PIM runs on interfaces, both the inward-facing ones and the one facing the remote AS.

- The EBGP connection between RouterB and RouterC carries the unicast traffic between the two ASs. These two routers run PIM only on internally facing inter-faces, and the PIM configuration points to their local RP.

- All routers within each AS have PIM enabled on all interfaces, and the PIM con-figuration points to their local RP.

- All routers within a domain are running OSPF as the IGP.

The bulk of the configuration is on the multicast-enabled border routers. First, cre-ate two JUNOS *RIB groups* (routing-table groups) that populate the multicast RPF table, inet.2, with the routes that PIM and MSDP will use.

PIM and MSDP normally consult inet.0 (the default unicast routing table) to make their RPF decisions. They never add multicast routes to inet.0. However, when mul-ticast and unicast topologies are not congruent, you can configure PIM and MSDP to

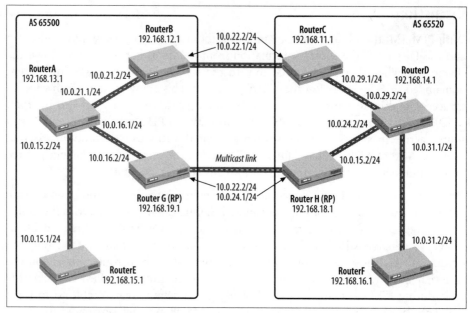

Figure 16-2. MSDP network topology

consult inet.2 as an alternative unicast routing table to use to base their RPF decisions on. (This network is not congruent because the RouterG–RouterH link carries only multicast traffic and the RouterB–RouterC link carries all unicast traffic.) The RIB groups populate inet.2 with unicast routes that are a subset of the unicast routes in inet.0. The routes placed in inet.2 are only those unicast routes that resolve to multicast-enabled routers. For PIM and MSDP to work, the inet.2 table needs to include all the source's prefixes, all the RP's prefixes, and all direct routes.

The first RIB group you create, called mcast-rib, imports routes into and exports routes from inet.2:

```
[edit routing-options]
aviva@RouterG# set rib-group mcast-rib export-rib inet.2
aviva@RouterG# set rib-group mcast-rib import-rib inet.2
```

When you associate this RIB group with MSDP and PIM, they consult it for their RPF decisions.

The second RIB group, called if-rib, is for interface (direct) routes:

```
[edit routing-options]
aviva@RouterG# set rib-group if-rib import-rib [inet.0 inet.2]
```

This RIB group populates inet.2 with the router's direct routes. Then associate the if-rib RIB group with the router's interfaces:

```
[edit routing-options]
aviva@RouterG# set interface-routes rib-group inet if-rib
```

The full RIB group configuration looks like this:

```
aviva@RouterG> show configuration routing-options
interface-routes {
    rib-group inet if-rib;
}
rib-groups {
    if-rib {
        import-rib [ inet.0 inet.2 ];
    }
    mcast-rib {
        export-rib inet.2;
        import-rib inet.2;
    }
}
```

Next, configure MSDP, PIM, and your IGP on the multicast-enabled border routers. For MSDP, specify the IP addresses of the local router and its remote peer, using the routers' loopback addresses. You also need to associate the mcast-rib RIB group, which populates the inet.2 routing table, with MSDP. Here's what the MSDP configuration looks like for RouterG:

```
aviva@RouterG> show configuration protocols
msdp {
    rib-group inet mcast-rib; # <-- RIB group to populate inet.2
    local-address 192.168.19.1; # <-- loopback address of RouterG
    peer 192.168.18.1; # <-- loopback address of RouterH
}
```

The multicast-enabled routers must be the PIM-SM RPs for their domains and must be running PIM both on the internally facing interfaces and on the interface facing the remote border router.

Although this recipe configures the EBGP and MSDP peering sessions between the same two routers (RouterG and RouterH), this is not necessary. The MSDP peering session can be configured between any two RPs.

You also need to associate the mcast-rib RIB group with PIM. Here's the PIM configuration on RouterG:

```
aviva@RouterG> show configuration protocols
pim {
    rib-group inet mcast-rib;
    rp {
        local {
            address 192.168.19.1;
        }
    }
    interface all;
    interface fe-0/0/0.0 {
        disable;
    }
}
```

For the EBGP connection, in addition to the standard configuration (see Recipe 13.1), enable MBGP on the connection so that the BGP connection can carry the NLRI for both unicast and multicast routes. Here is the EBGP configuration:

```
aviva@RouterG> show configuration protocols
bgp {
    group external {
        type external;
        family inet { # <-- turn on MBGP
            any; # <-- have BGP carry both unicast and multicast NLRIs
        }
        peer-as 65520;
        neighbor 10.0.1.1;
    }
}
```

This completes the configuration for the multicast-enabled border routers. For the border routers that will be carrying only unicast traffic, you must set up EBGP and can optionally set up PIM. For the EBGP session, turn on MBGP, specifying that it carry only the NLRIs for unicast routes. To do this, use the unicast option in the family inet statement:

```
aviva@RouterB> show configuration protocols bgp
group external {
    type external;
    family inet { # <-- turn on MBGP
        unicast; # <-- carry unicast NLRIs only
    }
    peer-as 65520;
    neighbor 10.0.22.2;
}
```

This border router does not need to be part of the PIM-SM domain. However, if it is, configure PIM only on the internally facing interface (on RouterB, this is se-0/0/2) and set the RP's address to be the address of the multicast-enabled border router, which in this recipe is RouterG (192.168.19.1). Here is RouterB's PIM configuration:

```
aviva@RouterB> show configuration protocols pim
rp {
    static {
        address 192.168.19.1; # <-- RP and EBGP/MSDP border router
    }
}
interface se-0/0/2.0;
```

For all the other PIM-SM routers within the AS, use a standard PIM-SM configuration, setting the RP to be the multicast-enabled border router. Here's an example, for RouterE:

```
aviva@RouterE> show configuration protocols
pim {
    rp {
        static {
```

```
            address 192.168.19.1; # <-- RP and EBGP/MSDP border router
        }
    }
    interface all;
    interface fe-0/0/0.0 {
        disable;
    }
}
```

You also need an IGP running within each AS. The router setup for this recipe uses OSFP.

When the configuration of the routers in both ASs is complete, the routers can handle a request from a multicast receiver in one of the ASs to a multicast source in the other. Let's follow a request from a receiver host connected to RouterF in AS 65200 to a source that is connected to RouterE in AS 65500. For this lab setup, the receiver is simulated by a ping command to multicast group 224.1.1.1. RouterE is configured with SAP to this group. Here is the ping command issued on RouterF:

```
aviva@RouterF> ping 224.1.1.1 interface t1-0/0/3 ttl 8 count 5 bypass-routing
PING 224.1.1.1 (224.1.1.1): 56 data bytes
64 bytes from 10.0.15.1: icmp_seq=0 ttl=251 time=27.881 ms
64 bytes from 10.0.15.1: icmp_seq=1 ttl=251 time=30.562 ms
64 bytes from 10.0.15.1: icmp_seq=2 ttl=251 time=30.341 ms
64 bytes from 10.0.15.1: icmp_seq=3 ttl=251 time=40.328 ms
64 bytes from 10.0.15.1: icmp_seq=4 ttl=251 time=30.336 ms
--- 224.1.1.1 ping statistics ---
5 packets transmitted, 5 packets received, 0% packet loss
round-trip min/avg/max/stddev = 27.881/31.890/40.328/4.332 ms
```

Let's follow the join request downstream to the multicast source. Look on the neighbor, RouterD, to see whether it has received the PIM Join/Prune messages for 224.1.1. 1:

```
aviva@RouterD> show pim join extensive 224.1.1.1
Instance: PIM.master Family: INET
Group: 224.1.1.1
    Source: 10.0.31.2
    Flags: sparse
    Upstream interface: t1-0/0/3.0
    Upstream neighbor: 10.0.31.2
    Upstream State: Local Source
    Keepalive timeout: 170
    Downstream Neighbors:
        Interface: t1-0/0/2.0
            10.0.24.1 State: Join Flags: S Timeout: 167
```

This output shows that the source of the PIM Join message is 10.0.31.2, which is the interface to RouterF. This is confirmed by the Upstream interface and Upstream neighbor fields, which show you the RPF interface and neighbor for the source address: t1-0/0/3 is the interface on RouterF that connects to RouterD. The Upstream State is Local Source, indicating that the source of the join request (here, RouterF) is directly connected to this router (RouterD). The `Downstream Neighbors` field shows where RouterD is forwarding the Join message. You see that the message has been forwarded out RouterD's interface `t1-0/0/2` to `10.0.24.1`, which is the `t1-5/0/0` interface on the border router, RouterH.

Moving to the next downstream router, which is the border router, check for PIM joins for group `224.1.1.1`:

```
aviva@RouterH> show pim join extensive 224.1.1.1
Instance: PIM.master Family: INET
Group: 224.1.1.1
    Source: 10.0.31.2
    Flags: sparse,spt-pending
    Upstream interface: t1-5/0/0.0
    Upstream neighbor: 10.0.24.2
    Upstream State: Local RP, Join to Source
    Keepalive timeout: 108
    Downstream Neighbors:
        Interface: fe-1/0/1.0
        10.0.1.2 State: Join Flags: S Timeout: 170
```

Again, you see that the source is RouterF (`10.0.31.2`) and that the upstream information points to RouterH's neighbor, RouterD. The `Upstream State` shows that this router is the RP and that it has sent a PIM Join/Prune message to the multicast source.

RouterH is the RP and is running MSDP. An MSDP-enabled RPs builds a cache of SA messages, which it then uses to notify the RPs in other domains about active sources. The RP creates the entries in this cache when it receives a PIM Register message from a DR advertising a new source. You already saw that RouterD sent a PIM register message, so look on RouterH to see the entries in the SA cache:

```
aviva@RouterH> show msdp source-active
Group address    Source address  Peer address    Originator     Flags
224.1.1.1        10.0.31.2       local           192.168.18.1   Accept
```

The output shows that the router has learned that `224.1.1.1` is an active source. RouterH should be advertising this source to its EBGP peer RouterG, so look at the MSDP SA cache there:

```
aviva@RouterG> show msdp source-active
Group address    Source address  Peer address    Originator     Flags
224.1.1.1        10.0.31.2       192.168.18.1    192.168.18.1   Accept
```

The group `224.1.1.1` is present, with the source `10.0.31.2` (RouterF in the remote AS), which confirms that the join request has crossed from AS 65200 into AS 65200.

```
aviva@RouterG> show pim join extensive 224.1.1.1
Instance: PIM.master Family: INET
Group: 224.1.1.1
    Source: *
    RP: 192.168.19.1
    Flags: sparse,rptree,wildcard
```

```
Upstream interface: local
Upstream neighbor: Local
Upstream State: Local RP
Downstream Neighbors:
     Interface: se-5/0/1.0
          10.0.16.1 State: Join Flags: SRW Timeout: 186
Group: 224.1.1.1
  Source: 10.0.31.2
  Flags: sparse,spt-pending
  Upstream interface: fe-1/0/1.0
  Upstream neighbor: 10.0.1.1
  Upstream State: Local RP, Join to Source
  Keepalive timeout: 194
  Downstream Neighbors:
     Interface: se-5/0/1.0
          10.0.16.1 State: Join Flags: S Timeout: 186
```

RouterG, the RP in the receiver's domain has two join entries for 224.1.1.1. The first is a (*,G) entry and the second is an (S,G) entry. The (*,G) join is from the receiver and propagates up to its domain RP and stops there. The Upstream interface and Upstream neighbor for this entry are both local, and the Upstream State field confirms that the upstream interface is the domain's RP router. The second entry, the (S,G) entry, is the one sending the Join message downstream to the multicast source. The MSDP-speaking RP sends the (S,G) entries to remote domains, so you see only (S,G) entries on the remote side.

To verify that RouterG learned this information from MBGP, use the show multicast rpf command:

```
aviva@RouterG> show multicast rpf 10.0.31.2
Multicast RPF table: inet.2 , 20 entries
10.0.31.0/24
     Protocol: BGP
     Interface: fe-1/0/1.0
     Neighbor: 10.0.1.1
```

The output shows that the inet.2 multicast RPF table has an entry for 10.0.31.2 (RouterF, the multicast receiver) and that this route was learned from BGP. The listed interface is the one that connects RouterH to RouterG, and the neighbor address is that of RouterH's interface to RouterG. You can also look at this route in the inet.2 table directly:

```
aviva@RouterG> show route table inet.2 10.0.31.2
inet.2: 20 destinations, 24 routes (20 active, 0 holddown, 0 hidden)
+ = Active Route, - = Last Active, * = Both
10.0.31.0/24      *[BGP/170] 16:46:35, MED 130, localpref 100
                    AS path: 65520 I
                  > to 10.0.1.1 via fe-1/0/1.0
```

Again, you see that this route was learned from EBGP and from AS 65520.

Continuing toward the multicast source, check the PIM joins on RouterA:

```
aviva@RouterA> show pim join extensive 224.1.1.1
Instance: PIM.master Family: INET
Group: 224.1.1.1
    Source: *
    RP: 192.168.19.1
    Flags: sparse,rptree,wildcard
    Upstream interface: se-0/0/3.0
    Upstream neighbor: 10.0.16.2
    Upstream State: Join to RP
    Downstream Neighbors:
        Interface: fe-0/0/1.0
            10.0.15.1 State: Join Flags: SRW Timeout: 187
```

The downstream neighbor is 10.0.15.1 (RouterE), which is the DR for the multicast receiver:

```
aviva@RouterE> show pim join extensive 224.1.1.1
Instance: PIM.master Family: INET
Group: 224.1.1.1
    Source: *
    RP: 192.168.19.1
    Flags: sparse,rptree,wildcard
    Upstream interface: fe-0/0/1.0
    Upstream neighbor: 10.0.15.2
    Upstream State: Join to RP
    Downstream Neighbors:
        Interface: local
Group: 224.1.1.1
    Source: 10.0.31.2
    Flags: sparse,spt
    Upstream interface: fe-0/0/1.0
    Upstream neighbor: 10.0.15.2
    Upstream State: Join to Source
    Keepalive timeout: 202
    Downstream Neighbors:
        Interface: local
```

The Downstream Neighbors field shows that the next interface is on the local router because this router is a SAP listener and so is acting as a receiver (sink) for the group. If the receiver was a host system, you would see the name of the interface toward the host here.

When both ASs have multicast sources and receivers, the MSDP-enabled routers have entries for all the groups in the SA cache. When a multicast receiver in AS 65500 joins group 225.2.2.2 in AS 65520, the SA cache on RouterG has two entries:

```
aviva@RouterG> show msdp source-active
Group address   Source address  Peer address   Originator     Flags
224.1.1.1       10.0.31.2       192.168.18.1   192.168.18.1   Accept
225.2.2.2       10.0.15.1       local          192.168.19.1   Accept
```

The first entry is for the source in the remote domain, and the second entry is for the source in the local domain. The Source address shows the IP address of the multicast source. For the first SA entry, the source is RouterF (10.0.31.2) in AS 65520, and for the second SA entry, the source is 10.0.15.1 (RouterE) in RouterG's AS. The Peer address field tells how MSDP learned the SA message. The first was learned from RouterG's MSDP peer, RouterH (192.168.18.1), and the second was learned in the local AS. This is confirmed by the Originator field, which is the address of the peer that originated the SA message.

Looking at the SA cache on the MSDP shows the same information, with the peer addresses being reversed:

```
aviva@RouterH> show msdp source-active
Group address   Source address  Peer address    Originator      Flags
224.1.1.1       10.0.31.2       local           192.168.18.1    Accept
225.2.2.2       10.0.15.1       192.168.19.1    192.168.19.1    Accept
```

Again, you can verify that RouterH has learned the route to RouterE from the multicast RPF table, inet.2:

```
aviva@RouterH> show multicast rpf 10.0.15.1
Multicast RPF table: inet.2, 20 entries
10.0.15.0/24
    Protocol: BGP
    Interface: fe-1/0/1.0
    Neighbor: 10.0.1.2

aviva@RouterH> show route table inet.2 10.0.15.1
inet.2: 20 destinations, 24 routes (20 active, 0 holddown, 0 hidden)
+ = Active Route, - = Last Active, * = Both
10.0.15.0/24       *[BGP/170] 17:19:46, MED 13, localpref 100
                      AS path: 65500 I
                    > to 10.0.1.2 via fe-1/0/1.0
```

The other two EBGP routers, RouterB and RouterC, which you configured to carry only unicast NLRIs, have only the standard inet.0 routing table for unicast routes. Issuing a show route table inet.2 command on these routers confirms that the multicast RPF table is empty.

See Also

Recipe 13.1

16.14 Configuring PIM-DM

Problem

You want to configure PIM-DM on the routers in your AS.

Solution

Set up PIM-DM on the domain's routers:

```
[edit protocols]
aviva@RouterA# set pim interface all mode dense
aviva@RouterA# set pim interface fe-0/0/0 disable
```

Discussion

For a small network that has a dense population of receivers and can tolerate the periodic flooding of multicast packets, using PIM-DM is an easier solution than using PIM-SM. With a dense population of receivers, PIM will not need to do much SPT pruning, so you don't need PIM-SM. Also, configuring PIM-DM is must simpler than configuring PIM-SM because you don't have to set up RPs.

As this recipe shows, to enable PIM-DM, just configure it on all the router's network interfaces. You should explicitly disable it on the router's management interface, either fe-0/0/0 (for J-series, as shown in this recipe) or fxp0 on M-series and T-series routers.

Look at the router interfaces to verify that PIM is running:

```
aviva@RouterA> show pim interfaces
Instance: PIM.master
Name            Stat Mode      IP V State Count DR address
fe-0/0/1.0      Up   Dense     4  2 DR      1 10.0.15.2
loo.0           Up   Dense     4  2 DR      0 192.168.13.1
se-0/0/2.0      Up   Dense     4  2 P2P     1
se-0/0/3.0      Up   Dense     4  2 P2P     1
```

The output confirms the configuration. All four router interfaces are listed as being up, and the Mode column shows they are all running dense mode. The V column indicates PIM Version 2. The three physical interfaces have each learned about one neighbor. You see that fe-0/0/1 is the DR for 10.0.15.2.

Enabling the JUNOS implementation of PIM automatically turns on IGMPv2, so check the IGMP interfaces:

```
aviva@RouterA> show igmp interface
Interface: fe-0/0/1.0
    Querier: 10.0.15.1
    State:         Up Timeout:    187 Version:  2 Groups:      0
Interface: se-0/0/3.0
    Querier: 10.0.16.1
    State:         Up Timeout:   None Version:  2 Groups:      4
Interface: se-0/0/2.0
    Querier: 10.0.21.1
    State:         Up Timeout:   None Version:  2 Groups:      4

Configured Parameters:
IGMP Query Interval: 125.0
IGMP Query Response Interval: 10.0
```

```
IGMP Last Member Query Interval: 1.0
IGMP Robustness Count: 2

Derived Parameters:
IGMP Membership Timeout: 260.0
IGMP Other Querier Present Timeout: 255.0
```

This output confirms that IGMPv2 is running on the three PIM interfaces.

In this network, a host on 10.0.15.2 is a source for group 225.1.1.1, and the receiver is on RouterB. To check PIM-DM forwarding, first check for multicast routes:

```
aviva@RouterA> show multicast route
Address family INET
Group: 225.1.1.1
    Source: 10.0.15.1/32
    Upstream interface: fe-0/0/1.0
    Downstream interface list:
        se-0/0/2.0
Address family INET6
```

RouterA has a multicast route for the group 225.1.1.1, and the source is 10.0.15.1, which is RouterE's subnet. The downstream interface toward the receiver is se-0/0/2, which you can confirm with the show multicast next-hops command:

```
aviva@RouterA> show multicast next-hops inet
Family: INET
ID       Refcount  KRefcount Downstream interface
348            2          1 se-0/0/2.0
```

Also, check the PIM join state on the router:

```
aviva@RouterA> show pim join extensive inet
Instance: PIM.master Family: INET
Group: 225.1.1.1
    Source: 10.0.15.1
    Flags: dense
    Upstream interface: fe-0/0/1.0
    Upstream neighbor: 10.0.15.1
    Downstream interfaces:
        se-0/0/3.0 (Pruned timeout 254)
        se-0/0/2.0
```

This output illustrates the PIM-DM flood-and-prune operation. Because there is only one receiver, on RouterB, PIM-DM maintains an SPT that includes se-0/0/2 (the interface to RouterB) but prunes the SPT from RouterG (interface se-0/0/3).

16.15 Tracing PIM Packets

Problem

As part of debugging the operation of PIM, you want to trace all PIM packets exchanged by your router.

Solution

Enable PIM packet tracing:

```
[edit protocols pim]
aviva@RouterA# set traceoptions file pim-trace world-readable
aviva@RouterA# set traceoptions flag packets
```

Discussion

As you are setting up and debugging a PIM domain, you can turn on tracing on PIM to keep a log of packet exchanges between routers. The option you choose depends on what you are interested in logging at any particular time. With JUNOS PIM, you can trace the following:

```
[edit protocols pim traceoptions]
aviva@RouterA# set flag ?
Possible completions:
  all                  Trace everything
  assert               Trace assert messages
  autorp               Trace bootstrap/RP/auto-RP messages
  bootstrap            Trace bootstrap/RP/auto-RP messages
  general              Trace general events
  graft                Trace join/prune/graft/graft-ack messages
  hello                Trace hello packets
  join                 Trace join/prune/graft/graft-ack messages
  mdt                  Trace messages related to multicast data tunnels
  normal               Trace normal events
  packets              Trace all PIM packets
  policy               Trace policy processing
  prune                Trace join/prune/graft/graft-ack messages
  register             Trace register/register-stop messages
  route                Trace routing information
  rp                   Trace bootstrap/RP/auto-RP messages
  state                Trace state transitions
  task                 Trace routing protocol task processing
  timer                Trace routing protocol timer processing
```

The trace options let you track all PIM operations and packets. More useful is being able to trace specific packet types, such as Join/Prune messages and auto-RP messages. You can also select additional options, to get either detailed traces or limit the traces only to packets sent or received by the router:

```
aviva@RouterA# set flag join ?
Possible completions:
  <[Enter]>            Execute this command
  detail               Trace detailed information
  disable              Disable this trace flag
  receive              Trace received packets
  send                 Trace transmitted packets
```

The command in this recipe is a simple example of tracing all PIM packets to a file named *pim-trace*. As soon as you commit the configuration, the file starts recording PIM messages:

```
aviva@RouterA> show log pim-trace
Nov 30 20:21:54 trace_on: Tracing to "/var/log/pim-trace" started
Nov 30 20:22:01 PIM se-0/0/3.0 RECV 10.0.16.2 -> 224.0.0.13 V2 JoinPrune to 10.0.16.1
holdtime 210 groups 1 sum 0xc0e6 len 34
Nov 30 20:22:03 PIM fe-0/0/1.0 RECV 10.0.15.1 -> 224.0.0.13 V2 Hello hold 105 T-bit
LAN prune 500 ms override 2000 ms pri 1 genid 300123470 sum 0xbe67 len 34
Nov 30 20:22:14 PIM fe-0/0/1.0 SENT 10.0.15.2 -> 224.0.0.13 V2 Bootstrap sum 0x46d4
len 36
Nov 30 20:22:14 PIM se-0/0/3.0 SENT 10.0.16.1 -> 224.0.0.13 V2 Bootstrap sum 0x46d4
len 36
Nov 30 20:22:14 PIM se-0/0/2.0 SENT 10.0.21.1 -> 224.0.0.13 V2 Bootstrap sum 0x46d4
len 36
Nov 30 20:22:14 PIM se-0/0/3.0 RECV 10.0.16.2 -> 224.0.0.13 V2 JoinPrune to 10.0.16.1
holdtime 210 groups 4 sum 0x4406 len 102
Nov 30 20:22:14 PIM fe-0/0/1.0 RECV 10.0.15.1 -> 224.0.0.13 V2 JoinPrune to 10.0.15.2
holdtime 210 groups 2 sum 0x5203 len 54
```

This output records PIM Join/Prune, Hello, and Bootstrap messages.

See Also

Recipe 5.10

Index

Symbols

" (quotation marks), 174, 445
(pound sign), 2, 11
+ (plus sign), 28
, (comma)
    S,G notation, 576
    username and, 82
. (dot), 29, 131
: (colon)
    IP addresses and, 561
    IPv6 addresses and, 249
    router identifier string, 174
    username and, 82
; (semicolon), 12
= (equals sign), 174
> (greater than sign), 2
? (question mark), 3, 7
{ } (curly braces), 5, 33
| (pipe), 8

A

ABRs (area border routers)
    defined, 383
    IS-IS and, 350
    multiarea OSPF networks and, 394
    stubby areas and, 397
    summarizing OSPF routes, 401
Abstract Syntax Notation 1 (ASN.1), 132
accept action
    description, 288
    firewall filters, 306
    routing policies, 298–300

access control
    allowing access to routers, 76–77
    customizing account privileges, 89–95
    firewall filters and, 138–140
    hiding encrypted passwords, 95
    logging access to routers, 147, 148
    logging in to console, 79
    restricting inbound router access, 98, 100
    root authentication, 77–79
    setting authentication methods, 80–81
    setting up login accounts, 81–84
    SNMP and, 129, 137, 138, 140, 141, 153
Access-Accept packets (RADIUS), 97
ACK bit, 329
active routes
    forwarding tables and, 515
    hidden routes and, 255
    LOCAL_PREF attribute and, 440
    prepending AS numbers to path, 443
    routing preference and, 440
    selecting, 250
Active state (BGP), 425, 477
active symmetric mode, 186
ad0 as flash drive, 44
ad1 as hard disk, 44
adaptive mode (bandwidth reservation), 527
Adaptive Services (AS) PIC, 107
add/drop multiplexer (ADM), 236–238
address family identifier (AFI), 350
address match term, 304
address spoofing, 266
adjacencies
    dead interval and, 387, 410

D

daemon facility, 163
DAEMON facility code, 163, 164
daemons (Unix), 57
damping action (BGP), 290
Data Encryption Standard (see DES)
Data Link Connection Identifier (DLCI), 231
data link layer, 349, 362
data terminal equipment (DCE), 64, 65
DCD process, 244
DCE (data terminal equipment), 64, 65
dd command, 53
DDoS (distributed denial of service), 72
deactivate command, 244, 378, 412
deactivate traceoptions command, 476
dead interval (OSPF), 387, 409, 414
debugging
    BGP, 477, 551
    failed commits, 24, 25
    IS-IS operations, 379, 380
    LDP operations, 500, 501
    OSPF operations, 413
    PIM, 619–621
    RIP, 346, 347
    show version detail command and, 56
    showing interface status, 195
    SONET interfaces, 234
    tracing and, 179
DEC (Digital Equipment Corporation), 349
default route (0.0.0.0/0), 246, 267
delete chassis redundancy command, 70
delete command, 5, 207
delete traceoptions command, 380, 475
deleting
    comments, 21
    crashfiles, 47
    deactivating instead of, 244
    logfile contents, 170
    logfiles, 47, 380, 415
    rescue configuration, 42
denial-of-service attacks (see DoS attacks)
dense protocols, 578
deny-commands attribute (TACACS+), 98
deny-configuration attribute (TACACS+), 98
DES (Data Encryption Standard)
    cipher block chaining, 107, 109, 133
    JUNOS support, 107
    overview, 75
    plain-text passwords and, 84–86
    SNMP and, 154
    3DES-CBC encryption, 107, 117
DES-CBC encryption, 107, 109, 133

designated intermediate system (DIS), 351,
    365–366
designated router (see DR)
destination addresses, 246, 335
destination-address match term, 304
destination-port match term, 305
destination-prefix-list match term, 304
detail option (show firewall log), 317
DF (don't fragment) bit, 437
dictionary attacks, 74
Diffie-Hellman scheme, 113, 117
DiffServ TE, 480
digital certificates, 121–127
Digital Equipment Corporation (DEC), 349
digital signature, 125
Dijkstra shortest-path first (SPF), 349, 382,
    387
directed broadcasts, 73
directories (see specific filesystems)
DIS (designated intermediate system), 351,
    365–366
disallowed keyword, 273
disaster recovery, 52, 53
discard action, 306
discretionary attributes (BGP), 420
display inheritance command, 63
display set command, 19
distance-vector algorithm, 332, 418
Distance-Vector Multicast Routing Protocol
    (DVMRP), 179, 285, 578, 579
distributed denial of service (DDoS), 72
distribution trees, 577
DLCI (Data Link Connection Identifier), 231
DNS name servers
    address spoofing, 266
    firewall filters, 99, 139, 321, 323
    IP addresses, 14, 16
    prefix lists, 292
documentation
    CLI, 9
    JUNOS software, 56
domains
    connecting, 607–617
    EGPs and, 418
    OSPF and, 382
don't fragment (DF) bit, 437
DoS (denial-of-service) attacks
    blackholing routes and, 265
    firewall filters and, 268, 319
    nonconfigurable interfaces and, 242
    RPF and, 266
dot (.), 29, 131

dotted quad notation, 248
down arrow, 9
DR (designated router)
    broadcast networks and, 351
    configuring IS-IS, 353
    configuring PIM-SM, 580
    controlling DIS election, 365, 366
    IP multicast and, 577
    Join messages and, 577
    OSPF and, 383, 386, 387, 394, 414
DRAM size (memory), 146
drive names, finding, 45
DSA (SSH Version 2), 75, 84
DVMRP (Distance-Vector Multicast Routing
        Protocol), 179, 285, 578, 579
dynamic SAs
    AS PICs and, 116–120
    configuring, 111–115
    digital certificates and, 121–127
    IKE and, 107
    IPSec and, 109

E

EBGP (external BGP)
    adding BGP community, 465–469
    advertising and, 419
    authenticating BGP peers, 450, 451
    BGP sessions, 423–424, 428
    BGP traffic problems, 478
    CE routers and, 570, 571
    configuring, 437
    connecting PIM-SM domains, 607–612
    defined, 419
    filtering long prefixes, 293
    filtering routes by AS paths, 448
    filtering traffic, 312
    load balancing traffic, 471, 473
    LOCAL_PREF attribute and, 440
    NEXT_HOP attribute and, 439
    prepending AS numbers to path, 443
    removing private AS numbers, 442
    restricting advertised routes, 449
    route flap damping, 459, 461
    routing policies, 288, 293
    setting up route reflectors, 453, 456
    unallocated prefix blocks, 296
EBGP multihop, 419
edit command
    configure command and, 3
    copying text from terminal windows, 33
    depicted, 11

exiting configuration mode, 25
functionality, 4, 6
edit filter command, 283
edit policy-statement command, 283
EGPs (exterior gateway protocols)
    AS and, 418
    IP routing and, 247
    IS-IS and, 349
    OSPF and, 382
egress routers
    configuring interfaces, 490
    defined, 480
    fast reroute and, 529
    FECs and, 491
    MD5 authentication, 498
    Path message, 484
    ping command and, 492
    protecting LSP paths, 521–528
    routing tables, 515
    turning on MPLS, 486
    verifying packet labels, 518
emergency boot disk, 52–53
encapsulation
    Ethernet interfaces, 197, 220
    Frame Relay, 231
    GRE, 217
    IP-IP, 217
    PIM de-encapsulation, 242, 588
    PIM encapsulation, 242, 588
    PIM pd- interfaces, 242, 588
    PIM pe- interfaces, 242, 588
    PIM Register messages, 580, 588
Encapsulation Security Payload (ESP), 106,
        107, 109
encryption
    authenticating BGP peers, 451
    FTP connections and, 50
    hiding passwords with, 95
    IPSec and, 106, 107
    IS-IS authentication, 367
    NTP authentication and, 188
    OSPF authentication and, 403
    passwords and, 74, 75, 84, 499
    plain-text passwords and, 85, 86
    private keys and, 123
    RIP and, 342
    show command and, 78
    SNMP and, 133
end systems, 349
enterprise-specific traps
    logging, 148, 149
    setting up, 136, 137

ISO/IEC 10589, 349
ISPs (Internet service providers)
    BGP and, 418, 419
    bogons and, 296
    chaining policies, 297
    JUNOS software and, xviii
    peering arrangements, 290
    restricting advertised routes, 448
    static routes to, 263

J

jbundle command, 44, 51
jinstall command, 44, 49, 50
jitter, 186, 189
jnxBoxAnatomy object, 144
jnxContentsTable object, 143, 144
jnxFanFailure chassis trap, 149
jnxFanOK chassis trap, 149
jnxFruInsertion chassis trap, 149
jnxFruPowerOff chassis trap, 149
jnxFruPowerOn chassis trap, 149
jnxFruRemoval chassis trap, 149
jnxOperatingTable table, 145, 146
jnxOverTemperature chassis trap, 149
jnxPowerSupplyFailure chassis trap, 149
jnxPowerSupplyOK chassis trap, 149
jnxRedundancySwitchOver chassis trap, 149
jnxTemperatureOK chassis trap, 149
Join messages, 577, 601–604, 613, 621
join state, 601–604
J-series routers
    alternate boot media, 48
    backing up filesystems, 46–48
    determining software versions, 54
    emergency boot disks, 53
    gathering hardware information, 59
    logging and, 162, 165
    management interfaces and, 13, 214
    PIC slots, 192
    upgrading software versions, 51, 52
    usage, 1
Juniper Networks
    overview, 1
    vendor ID, 97
    web site, xviii
Juniper-Allow-Commands attribute
        (RADIUS), 97
Juniper-Allow-Configuration attribute
        (RADIUS), 97
Juniper-Deny-Commands attribute
        (RADIUS), 97

Juniper-Deny-Configuration attribute
        (RADIUS), 97
Juniper-Local-User-Name attribute
        (RADIUS), 97
juniper-mibs-7.4R1.tgz file, 133
JUNOS Base OS Software Suite, 55
JUNOS Kernel Software Suite, 55
JUNOS operating system, 55
JUNOS Packet Forwarding Engine Support
        package, 55
JUNOS Routing Software Suite, 55
JUNOS Support Tools Package, 55
junos-jseries install package, 51, 52
J-Web browser, 13, 77

K

keepalive messages, 69, 490, 491, 501
kernel facility, 163, 174
KERNEL facility code, 163
keyboard sequences, 9, 289

L

Label Distribution Protocol (see LDP)
Label Request Object (LRO), 484
labels
    forwarding tables and, 516
    MPLS, 480–482
    PE routers and, 554
    signaling protocols and, 483–485
    switching tables and, 496
    verifying, 516–519
label-switched paths (see LSPs)
LACP (Link Aggregation Control
        Protocol), 224
LatNIC registry, 419
Layer 3 VPNs (see VPNs)
LDP (Label Distribution Protocol)
    authentication, 498–500
    configuration considerations, 485
    configuring label-switched
        paths, 485–493
    default routing policy actions, 286
    functionality, 479
    graceful restart, 278
    MPLS forwarding, 483
    overview, 483, 484
    routing tables and, 493–497
    tracing and, 179
    tracing operations, 500–502
    verifying traffic, 497, 498
    VPNs and, 558

O

Object Identifier (see OID)
OID (Object Identifier)
    overview, 130–133
    remote monitoring and, 151
    sysUpTime object, 154
online documentation
    CLI and, 9
    JUNOS software, 56
Open Shortest Path First (see OSPF)
OpenConfirm state (BGP), 425, 477
OpenSent state (BGP), 425, 477
operational mode
    commands in, 2, 3, 8
    displaying permissions needed, 93, 94
    functionality, 2
    logging out of routers, 103
operator privilege class
    operational mode and, 82, 87
    overview, 90
    permission bits for, 92
operators (regular expressions), 445, 446
optional attributes (BGP), 420
origin action (BGP), 291
ORIGIN attribute (BGP), 420, 430
ORIGINATOR_ID attribute (BGP), 422
orlonger keyword, 294
OSI Reference Model, 192, 349
OSPF (Open Shortest Path First)
    adjusting link costs, 406–408
    authentication, 402–405
    changing route preferences, 274–277
    configuring, 384–387
    configuring addresses, 206
    configuring for IPv6, 391–393
    configuring multiarea network, 393–396
    convergence times, 409–411
    CSPF and, 509
    default routing policy actions, 286
    disabling, 412, 413
    firewall filters, 99, 313, 320, 323
    graceful restart, 278–280
    IGPs and, 333
    IP routing, 246, 247, 258
    IPSec and, 107, 118
    IS-IS and, 350
    label-switched paths and, 544–545
    LDP and, 492
    link-state databases, 372, 383, 385, 390–391, 395
    loopback addresses, 205
    moving traffic off routers, 411
    MPLS and, 479, 486, 503
    NSSAs, 399–401
    overview, 382–384
    route convergence time, 333
    routing policy, 284–289
    static routes, 405, 406
    "sticky" DRs, 366, 383, 387
    stub areas, 397–399
    summarizing routes, 401, 402
    temporarily disabling, 378
    tracing traffic, 179, 413–417
    unicast routes, 546
    viewing routes, 387–389
    VPN routing tables, 565
    VPNs and, 558

P

P (provider) routers, 553, 555, 556
Packet Forwarding Engine (see PFE)
packet loss, fast reroute and, 528–534
packet-length match term, 305
packets
    tracing, 619–621
    verifying labels, 516–519
partial sequence number PDUs (PSNPs), 367
passwords
    authenticating, 80
    authenticating BGP peers, 451
    brute force attacks, 74, 99
    community strings and, 133, 138
    encrypting, 50, 74, 75, 84, 499
    hiding, 404
    IS-IS authentication, 367, 368
    login accounts and, 82, 83
    NTP authentication and, 188
    OSPF authentication, 403
    RIP and, 342
    root accounts and, 73
    root authentication, 77, 78
    root user and, 14
    router security, 72
    set archival command, 36
    show command and, 14
    SNMP and, 153
    strategies for choosing, 73, 74
    user accounts and, 73, 83
    (see also plain-text passwords)
Path message (RSVP), 484, 550
PathErr message (RSVP), 533, 550
pattern matching
    BERT tests, 229–231
    regular expressions and, 445

About the Author

Aviva Garrett has documented Juniper Networks technologies since joining the company as its first writer in 1997. She wrote the first JUNOS manuals and then oversaw the documentation as the company grew from a startup to an established network equipment provider. She recently stepped down as the Juniper Networks Director of Technical Publications to pursue other writing and business assignments, such as *JUNOS Cookbook*. Prior to Juniper Networks, Aviva worked at Cisco Systems for six years. She also worked for Excelan/Novell, Gavilan, and other technology companies and startups. She is the coauthor of *Juniper Networks Field Guide and Reference* (Addison-Wesley).

Colophon

The animal appearing on the cover of Junos Cookbook is the Angora goat (*Capra aegagrus hircus*), which is bred primarily for its fleece, called mohair. Angoras generally produce between 8 and 12 pounds of skirted (stains removed) fiber per year. Most Angoras are white since their mohair is easy to dye, but they also come in different shades. Black Angoras range in color from deep solid black to light gray or silver. Reds, often called "faded reds" because of the tendency of their coats to fade as the goat ages, range in color from apricot to copper.

Angora goats are browsers, meaning they thrive best where there is a good cover of brush, weeds, and grass. They like dry, mild climates but can do very well in the cold. Angora fleece grows about one inch per month, so within two or three months of shearing, these goats have fleece of sufficient length to withstand subzero temperatures. In the weeks after shearing, however, they must be protected from the elements, especially cold rain.

These goats are believed to have originated in the Himalaya Mountains before making their way to Ankara, Turkey, where they were first bred (and after which they were named). In 1848, seven female and two male Angoras were brought to the United States. Now the U.S. is the second largest mohair-producing nation in the world, with a Texas herd of 1,800,000 goats. The pure breed characteristics of the Angora goat, including its gently curved horns, loose-hanging ears, and short, high tail have been well preserved in the U.S. due to strict maintenance of breeding registries.

The cover image is from *Riverside Natural History*. The cover font is Adobe ITC Garamond. The text font is Linotype Birka; the heading font is Adobe Myriad Condensed; and the code font is LucasFont's TheSans Mono Condensed.

Better than e-books

Buy JUNOS Cookbook and access the
digital edition FREE on Safari for 45 days.

Go to www.oreilly.com/go/safarienabled
and type in coupon code 2WED-FLSD-WKPZ-NDDW-EDK2

Search
thousands of
top tech books

Download
whole chapters

Cut and Paste
code examples

Find
answers fast

Search Safari! The premier electronic reference
library for programmers and IT professionals.

Related Titles from O'Reilly

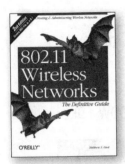

Networking

802.11 Wireless Networks: The Definitive Guide, *2nd Edition*

Asterisk: The Future of Telephony

Cisco Cookbook

Cisco IOS Access Lists

Cisco IOS in a Nutshell, *2nd Edition*

DNS & BIND Cookbook

DNS & BIND, 4th Edition

Essential SNMP, *2nd Edition*

Exchange Server Cookbook

IP Routing

IPv6 Essentials

IPv6 Network Administration

LDAP System Administration

Managing NFS and NIS, *2nd Edition*

Network Troubleshooting Tools

RADIUS

sendmail, *3rd Edition*

sendmail Cookbook

SpamAssassin

Switching to VoIP

TCP/IP Network Administration, *3rd Edition*

Unix Backup and Recovery

Using Samba, *2nd Edition*

Using SANs and NAS

VoIP Hacks

Time Management for System Administrators

Windows Server 2003 Network Administration

Wireless Hacks, *2nd Edition*

Zero Configuration Networking: The Definitive Guide

O'REILLY®

Our books are available at most retail and online bookstores.

To order direct: 1-800-998-9938 • *order@oreilly.com* • *www.oreilly.com*

Online editions of most O'Reilly titles are available by subscription at *safari.oreilly.com*

The O'Reilly Advantage

Stay Current and Save Money